WIN one of 10 Fa
with AA Lifestyl
association with T

See overleaf for terms

With our fantastic giveaway of 10 Fa
to rush home after a great day out! Follow up your day s
adventures with a good night's sleep at one of the conveniently
located 280 Travel Inns throughout the country.

**For more information on Travel Inn call 0870 242 8000 or visit
www.travelinn.co.uk**

HOW TO ENTER
Just complete (in capitals please) and send off this card or alternatively, send your name and
address on a stamped postcard to the address overleaf (no purchase required). Entries are
limited to one per household.
Closing date 28 November 2003.

MR/MRS/MISS/MS/OTHER, PLEASE STATE:

NAME:

ADDRESS:

POSTCODE:

TEL. NO: E-MAIL:

Are you an AA Member?   Yes/No
Have you bought this or any other AA Lifestyle Guide before?   Yes/No
If yes, please indicate the year of the last edition you bought:

AA Hotel Guide	____	AA Caravan & Camping (Europe)	____
AA Bed and Breakfast Guide	____	AA Britain Guide	____
AA Restaurant Guide	____	AA Days Out Guide	
AA Pub Guide	____	AA B&B France	
AA Caravan & Camping (Britain & Ireland)	____	Other, please state _____	____

CCBO

G000320383

Terms and Conditions

1. Two winners will be drawn from each of the five prize draws to take place on 03 March, 05 May, 01 September, 03 November and 01 December 2003.
2. Closing date for receipt of entries is midday on the relevant draw date. Final closing date for receipt of entries is **28 November 2003.**
3. Entries received after any draw date other than the final one will go forward into the next available draw. Each entry will only be entered in one draw. **Only one entry per household accepted.**
4. Winners will be notified by post within 14 days of the relevant draw date.
5. Prizes are not transferable and there is no cash alternative.
6. This prize cannot be used in conjunction with any other discount, promotion or special offer.
7. Each prize consists of 1 night's stay on a room only basis in a family room on any Friday, Saturday or Sunday night (for 2 adults and 2 children under 15). Any additional expenses will be charged as taken.
8. Travel Inn provides all hotel accommodation, services and facilities and AA Publishing is not party to your agreement with Travel Inn in this regard.
9. No purchase required.
10. The prize draw is open to UK residents over the age of 18, other than employees and agents of the Automobile Association or Travel Inn, members of their households or anyone else connected with the promotion.
11. For a list of winners, please send a stamped, self-addressed envelope to AA Lifestyle Guide Winners 2003, AA Publishing, Fanum House (14), Basingstoke, Hants, RG21 4EA.
12. This card must have an appropriate stamp.
13. Winners may be asked to participate in draw-related publicity.

AA Lifestyle Guide 2003 Prize Draw

AA PUBLISHING

FANUM HOUSE (14)

BASING VIEW

BASINGSTOKE

HANTS RG21 4EA

Fold along this line

Seal along this edge with sticky tape

Caravan&
Camping
Britain & Ireland 2003

Produced by AA Publishing

This edition published 2003

© The Automobile Association Developments Limited 2002

The directory is generated from the AA's establishment database, Information Research, AA Hotel Services.

Maps prepared by the Cartography Department of Automobile Association Developments Limited Maps © Automobile Association Developments Limited 2002

This product includes mapping data licensed from Ordnance Survey® with the permission of the Controller of Her Majesty's Stationery Office.
© Crown copyright 2002. All rights reserved. Licence number 399221

Northern Ireland mapping reproduced by permission of the Director and Chief Executive, Ordnance Survey of Northern Ireland, acting on behalf of the Controller of Her Majesty's Stationery Office © Crown copyright 2002. Permit No. 1674

Republic of Ireland mapping based on Ordnance Survey Ireland Permit No. MP008002
© Ordnance Survey Ireland and Government of Ireland

Advertisement Sales: advertisingsales@theAA.com

Editorial: lifestyleguides@theAA.com

Design by Kingswood Graphics, Theale Road, Burghfield, Reading RG30 3TP

Typeset and colour origination by Avonset, 11 Kelso Place, Bath

Printed by printer Trento srl, Italy

Editor: Denise Laing

The Automobile Association would like to thank the following organisation for their assistance in the use of pictures in this book.
Nova Development Corp 3rc, 3tr, 3cb, 3b, 7cb, 7br, 9c, 9b, 15c, 15b.
The remaining images are held in the Associations own library (AA PHOTO LIBRARY) with contributions from:
M Birkitt Back Cover ii; Ian Burgum Spine, Back Cover iv; Michael Busselle 315; Steve Day Front Cover l, r, 1, 4, 8; Jim Henderson 11, 16t, 18, 21; Tom Mackie 7, 27; Graeme Mathews 284; Peter Sharpe Back Cover i; Forbes Stephenson 2; Stephen Whitehorne 15t, 246; P Wilson Back Cover iii

A CIP catalogue record for this book is available from the British Library

ISBN 0 7495 35814

A01310

Published by AA Publishing, a trading name of Automobile Association Developments Limited, whose registered office is Millstream, Maidenhead Road, Windsor, Berkshire SL4 5GD

Registered number 1878835

Contents

How to Use This Guide

This guide aims to give you a great choice of over 1,000 quality caravan and camping parks across Great Britain and Ireland. To give you the most accurate information, the AA inspects and rates the parks in its scheme and updates the information in the guide annually. Please read the information on the Pennant Classification Scheme (page 7) so that you know what the classification symbols used in this guide mean.

Whether you are travelling around in a motorhome, camping at weekends or looking for somewhere to take your caravan for a two week holiday, this guide will help you find something to suit you. The AA pennant rating or holiday centre classification means that you can quickly find a park in the guide with the kind of facilities you are looking for. If you are looking for a park while you are on the road, the AA signs showing the pennants or holiday centre will point you in the right direction.

Sample Entry

Directory Entries
If the name of a park is printed in italics this indicates that we have not been able to get details or prices confirmed by the owners. A star (★) in front of the prices means that we only have information about the previous year's prices.

❶ Map Reference Each location in the directory has a map reference, starting with the map page number and followed by a number based on the National Grid and can be used in conjunction with the 16-page atlas at the back of the guide. To find a location, read the first figure horizontally and the second figure vertically within a lettered square. In order to find the precise location of a site, each entry in the directory has a 6-figure map reference also based on the National Grid. There is also a county map at the back of the guide to help you identify the counties within each country.

❷ AA Pennant Rating Sites are rated from 1-5 pennants. Parks are also awarded a Quality Score Percentage ranging from 50% to 80% according to how they compare with other parks within the same pennant rating. For a fuller explanation of the AA Scheme see page 7. **NEW** identifies parks new to the guide this year.

❸ David Bellamy Awards: Many AA recognised parks are also recipients of a David Bellamy Award for Conservation. The awards are graded Bronze, Silver and Gold. Beside each relevant park's entry we show a symbol to indicate the 2001/2 winners, the latest information at the time of going to press. For 2002/3 winners please contact: British Holiday & Homes Parks Association direct on: 01452 526911.

Best of British: A group of nearly 50 parks, both large and small, which focus on high quality facilities and amenities.

Countryside Discovery: A group of over 30 family-run parks with fewer than 150 pitches, each sharing a common theme of tranquillity.

❹ Website Addresses These are included where they have been supplied by the campsite and lead you to Web Sites that are not under the control of The Automobile Association Developments Ltd. The Automobile Association Developments Ltd has no control over and will not accept any responsibility or liability in respect of the material on any such Web Site. By including the addresses of third party Web Sites the AA does not intend to solicit business.

❺ Directions We give route directions as supplied by the site, but as space in the directory is limited we cannot go into great detail.

❻ Charges Charges given immediately after the appropriate symbol (caravan 🚐, tent ▲, motorvan 🚍) are the overnight cost for one tent or caravan, one car and two adults, or one motor caravan and two adults. The price may vary according to the number of people in your party, but some parks have a fixed fee per pitch regardless of the number of people. Please note that some parks may charge separately for some of the park's facilities, including the showers.

In the Republic of Ireland section of the guide the prices are given in Euros - €

Prices have been supplied to us in good faith by the park operators and are as accurate as possible. They are, however, only a guide and are subject to change at any time during the currency of this book. At the time of going to press electric charges were under review. Parks may charge an additional fee so it is advisable to check when booking.

❼ Booking Information (see also Useful Information p.11)

❽ No Dogs (see also Useful Information/Restrictions p.12)

❾ Pitches The brief description of the site includes the number of touring pitches and hardstandings. We give the number of static van pitches available in the entries in our guide in order to give a picture of the nature and size of the park. The AA pennant classification is based on an inspection of the touring pitches and facilities only. AA inspectors do not visit or report on static accommodation. The AA takes no responsibility for the

condition of rented caravans or chalets and can take no action whatsoever about complaints relating to them. We list static-only parks that have won Tourist Board awards for their accommodation. The awards are: Rose (England), Thistle (Scotland) and Dragon (Wales). Please see page 323.

❿ Additional Information We include in the entry any further or more specific information about facilities, supplied by the campsite, that is not represented by a symbol.

⓫ Symbols & Abbreviations See pages in the directory for explanation of symbols and abbreviations used in entries. Please note that any symbol appearing after the arrow symbol → represents facilities found within 3 miles of the site.

⅋ Disabled Facilities: It is advisable to phone the campsite for details of the actual facilities for disabled visitors.

⓬ Credit/Charge Cards Most of the larger parks now accept payment by credit or charge card. We use the following symbols at the end of the entry to show which cards are accepted

⬛	Access/Mastercard
⬛	Barclaycard/Visa
⬛	Connect
⑤	Switch
⬛	Delta

⓭ Notes These are the restrictions the park has told us about (see also Useful Information p.13)

⓮ A photograph or map extract may be included in the entry.

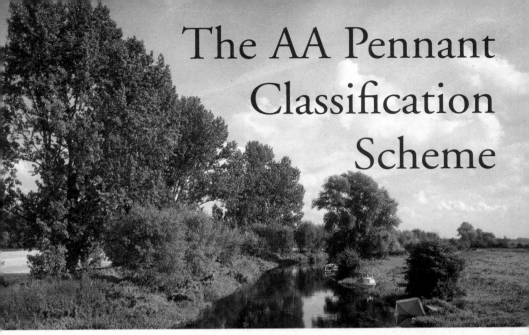

The AA Pennant Classification Scheme

AA Pennant Rating and Holiday Centres

AA parks are classified on a 5-point scale according to their style and the range of facilities they offer. As the number of pennants increases, so the quality and variety of facilities is greater. There is also a separate category for Holiday Centres which provide full day and night holiday entertainment as well as offering complete touring facilities for campers and caravanners.

New AA Quality % Score

AA Rated Parks and Holiday Centres are awarded a percentage alongside their pennant rating or holiday centre status. This is a qualitative assessment of various factors including customer care and hospitality, toilet facilities and park landscaping. The new % score runs from 50% to 80% and indicates the relative quality of parks with the same number of pennants. For example, one 3 pennant park may score 60%, while another 3 pennant park

may achieve 70%. Holiday Centres also receive a % score between 50% and 80% to differentiate between quality levels within this grading. Like the pennant rating, the percentage is reassessed annually. (Please note that the % quality score does not apply to the Republic of Ireland sites)

What can you expect at an AA-rated park?

All AA parks must meet a minimum standard: they should be clean, well maintained and welcoming. In addition they should have a local authority site licence (unless specially exempted), and satisfy local authority fire regulations.

About the AA inspection

Every year one of a team of highly-qualified inspectors pays an unannounced visit to each campsite in the guide to make a thorough check on its facilities, services and hospitality. Establishments pay an annual fee for the inspection, recognition and rating, and receive a basic text entry in the AA Caravan and Camping Guide. AA inspectors pay when they stay overnight on a park. The criteria used by AA inspectors in awarding the AA pennant rating are given on pages 8 and 9.

One Pennant Parks

These parks offer a fairly simple standard of facilities including:

- No more than 30 pitches per acre

- At least 6 pitches or 10% of total allocated to tourers

- An adequate drinking water supply and reasonable drainage

- Washroom with flush toilets and toilet paper provided, unless no sanitary facilities provided in which case this should be clearly stated

- Chemical disposal arrangements, ideally with running water, unless tents only

- Adequate refuse disposal arrangements, clearly signed

- Well-drained ground, and some level pitches

- Entrance and access roads of adequate width and surface

- Whereabouts of emergency telephone displayed

- Urgent telephone numbers signed

 Two Pennant Parks

Parks in this category should meet all of the above requirements, but offer a better level of facilities, services, customer care, security and ground maintenance. They should include the following:

- Separate washrooms, including at least 2 WCs and 2 washbasins per sex per 30 pitches

- Hot and cold water direct to each basin

- Externally-lit toilet blocks

- Warden to be available during day, times to be indicated

- Whereabouts of shop/chemist clearly signed

- Dish-washing facilities, covered and lit

- Reception area

Three Pennant Parks

Many parks come within this rating, and the range of facilities is quite wide. All parks will be of a very good standard meeting the following criteria:

- Facilities, services and park grounds very clean and well maintained, buildings in good repair, and attention paid to customer care and park security

- Evenly-surfaced roads and paths

- Decent modern or modernised toilet blocks, all-night lit, containing:

  Mirrors, shelves and hooks

  Shaver/hairdryer points

  Lidded waste bins in ladies toilets

  Uncracked toilet seats

  Soap and hand dryer/towels

- A reasonable number of modern shower cubicles with hot water, 1 per 35 pitches per sex

- Electric hook-ups

- Some hardstandings/wheel runs/firm, level ground

- Laundry with automatic washing and drying facilities, separate from toilets

- Children's playground with some equipment

- Public telephone on site or nearby, available 24 hours

- Warden's hours and 24-hour contact number clearly signed

 **Four Pennant Parks**

These parks have achieved an extremely high standard in all areas, including landscaping of grounds, natural screening and attractive park buildings, and also customer care and park security. Toilets are smartly modern and immaculately maintained, and offer the following:

- Spacious vanitory-style washbasins or similar, at least 2 per 25 pitches per sex

- Fully-tiled shower cubicles with doors, dry areas, shelves and hooks, at least 1 per 30 pitches per sex

- Some combined toilet/washing cubicles

Other requirements are:

- Shop on site, or within reasonable distance

- Warden available 24 hours

- Reception area open during the day, with tourist information available

- Internal roads, paths and toilet blocks lit at night

- Maximum 25 pitches per campable acre

- Toilet blocks heated October to Easter

- Minimum 50% electric hook-ups

- Minimum 10% hardstandings where necessary

- Late arrivals enclosure

 # AA Holiday Centres

In this category we distinguish parks which cater for all holiday needs. Anyone staying on one of these parks will have no need to go elsewhere for meals or entertainment. They provide:

- A wide range of on-site sports, leisure and recreational facilities.

- Supervision and security of a very high level

- A choice of eating outlets

- Touring facilities of equal importance to statics

- A maximum density of 30 pitches per acre

- Clubhouse with entertainment provided

- Automatic laundry

 Five Pennant Premier Parks

Premier parks are of an excellent standard, set in attractive surroundings with superb mature landscaping. Facilities, security and customer care are of an exceptional quality. As well as the above they will offer:

- Some fully-serviced 'super' pitches

- Electricity to most pitches

- First-class toilet facilities including several designated self-contained cubicles ideally with WC, washbasin and shower.

Many Premier Parks will also provide:

- Heated swimming pool

- Well-equipped shop

- Café or restaurant and bar

- Serious catering indoors and outdoors for young people

- A designated walking area for dogs (if accepted)

Useful Information

Booking Information

It is advisable to book in advance during peak holiday seasons and in school or public holidays. Where an individual park requires advance booking, 'advance bookings accepted' or 'booking advisable' (followed by dates) appears in the entry. It is also wise to check whether a reservation entitles you to a particular pitch. It does not necessarily follow that an early booking will get you the best pitch; you may just have the choice of what is available at the time you check in.

The words 'Advance bookings not accepted' indicate that a park does not accept reservations. Some parks may require a deposit on booking which may well be non-returnable if you have to cancel your holiday. If you have to cancel, notify the proprietor at once because you may be held legally responsible for partial or full payment unless the pitch can be re-let. Do consider taking out insurance such as AA Travel Insurance (telephone 0870 606 1612 or consult the AA website - www.theAA.com for details) to cover a lost deposit or compensation. Some parks will not accept overnight bookings unless payment for a full minimum period (e.g. two or three days) is made. If you are not sure whether your camping or caravanning equipment can be used at a park, check beforehand.

Please note: The AA does not undertake to find accommodation or to make reservations.

Last Arrival – Unless otherwise stated, parks will usually accept arrivals at any time of the day or night but some have a special 'late arrivals' enclosure where you have to make temporary camp so as not to disturb other people on park. Please note that on some parks access to the toilet block is by key or pass card only, so if you know you will be late, do check what arrangements can be made.

Last Departure – As with hotel rooms and self-catering accommodation, most parks will specify their overnight period – e.g. noon to noon. If you overstay the departure time you can be charged for an extra day. Do make sure you know what the regulations are.

Chemical Closet Disposal Point (CDP)

You will usually find one on every park, except those catering only for tents. It must be a specially constructed unit, or a WC permanently set aside for the purpose with adjacent rinsing and soak-away facilities. However, some local authorities are concerned about the effect of chemicals on bacteria in cesspools etc, and may prohibit or restrict provision of cdps in their areas.

Cold Storage

A fridge and/or freezer or icepacks for the use of holidaymakers.

Complaints

Speak to the park proprietor or supervisor immediately if you have any complaints, so that the matter can be sorted out on the spot. If this personal approach fails, you may decide, if the matter is serious, to approach the local authority or tourist board. AA guide users may write to:

The Editor, The AA Caravan & Camping Guide, AA Lifestyle Guides, Fanum House, Basing View, Basingstoke, Hants RG21 4EA

The AA will look into any reasonable complaints from guide users but will not in any circumstances act as negotiator or undertake to obtain compensation or enter into further correspondence. The AA will not guarantee to take any specific action.

Electric Hook-Up

This is becoming more generally available at parks with three or more pennants, but if it is important to you, you must check before booking. The voltage is generally 240v AC, 50 cycles, although variations between 200v and 250v may still be found. All parks in the AA scheme which provide electric hook-ups do so in accordance with International Electrotechnical Commission regulations. Outlets are coloured blue and take the form of a lidded plug with recessed contacts, making it impossible to touch a live point by accident. They are also waterproof. A similar plug, but with protruding contacts which hook into the recessed plug, is on the end of the cable which connects the caravan to the source of supply, and is dead.

These cables can usually be hired on site, or a plug supplied to fit your own cable. You should ask for the male plug; the female plug is the one already fixed to the power supply.

This supply is rated for either 5, 10 or 16 amps and this is usually displayed on a triangular yellow plate attached to source of supply. If it is not, be sure to ask at Reception. This is important because if you overload the circuit, the trip switch will operate to cut off the power supply. The trip switch can only be reset by a park official, who will first have to go round all the hook-ups on park to find the cause of the trip. This can take a long time and will make the culprit distinctly unpopular with all the other caravanners deprived of power, to say nothing of the park official. Tents and trailer tents are recommended to have a Residual Circuit Device (RCD) for safety reasons and to avoid overloading the circuit.

It is a relatively simple matter to calculate whether your appliances will overload the circuit. The amperage used by an appliance depends on its wattage and the total amperage used is the total of all the appliances in use at any one time. See the table below.

Portable black & white TV	
50 watts approx.	0.2 amp
Small colour TV	
90 watts approx.	0.4 amp
Small fan heater	
1000 watts (1kW) approx.	4.2 amp
One-bar electric fire	
NB each extra bar rates 1000 watts (1kW)	4.2 amp
60 watt table lamp	
approx.	0.25 amp
100 watt light bulb	
approx.	0.4 amp
Battery charger	
100 watts approx.	0.4 amp
Small refrigerator	
125 watts approx.	0.4 amp
Domestic microwave	
600 watts approx.	2.5 amp

Motor Caravans

At some parks motor caravans are only accepted if they remain static throughout the stay. Also check that there are suitable level pitches at the parks where you plan to stay.

Parking

Some park operators insist that cars be put in a parking area separate from the pitches; others will not allow more than one car for each caravan or tent.

Park Rules

Most parks display a set of rules which you should read on your arrival. Dogs may or may not be accepted on parks, and this is entirely at the owners' or wardens' discretion. Even when parks say they accept dogs, it is still discretionary and we most strongly advise that you check when you book. Dogs should always be kept on a lead and under control. Dogs sleeping in cars is not encouraged by most proprietors.

Most parks will not accept the following categories of people: single-sex groups, unsupervised youngsters and motorcyclists whether singly or in groups, even adults travelling on their own are sometimes barred. A handful will not accept children. See Child-Free Parks on page xx. If you are not a family group or a conventional couple, you would be well advised to make sure what rules apply before you try to book.

Pitches

Campsites are legally entitled to use an overflow field which is not a normal part of their camping area for up to 28 days in any one year as an emergency method of coping with additional numbers at busy periods.

When this 28 day rule is being invoked site owners should increase the numbers of sanitary facilities accordingly when the permanent facilities become insufficient to cope with extra

numbers. In these circumstances the extra facilities are sometimes no more than temporary portacabins.

Shops

The range of food and equipment in shops is usually in proportion to the size of the park. As far as our pennant requirements are concerned, a mobile shop calling several times a week, or a general store within easy walking distance of the park entrance is acceptable.

Telephone Numbers

The telephone authorities are liable to change some telephone numbers during the currency of this guide. If you have any difficulty please check with Directory Enquiries.

Importing Animals

The importation of animals into the UK is subject to strict controls. Penalties for trying to avoid these controls are severe. However, the Pet Travel Scheme (PETS) allows cats and dogs coming from the EU (and certain other countries and rabies free islands) to enter the UK without quarantine provided certain conditions are met. Visitors intending to bring a cat or dog into the UK from an EU country should consult a vet in their country of residence.

Details of other qualifying countries and further information are available on the Department for Environment, Food & Rural Affairs (DEFRA) website: www.defra.gov.uk/animalh/quarantine/index.htm PETS HELPLINE on 0870 241 1710 (08.30-17.00 Mon-Fri). E-mail to: pets.helpline@defra.gsi.gov.uk

Pets resident in the British Isles (UK, Republic of Ireland, Isle of Man and Channel Islands) are not subject to any quarantine or PETS rules when travelling within the British Isles.

Important Note on Restrictions
Many parks in our guide are selective about the categories of people they will accept on their parks. In the caravan and camping world there are many restrictions and some categories of visitor are banned altogether. Where a park has told us of a restriction/s this is included at the end of their entry.

On many parks in this guide, unaccompanied young people, single-sex groups, single adults, and motorcycle groups will not be accepted. The AA takes no stance in this matter, basing its pennant classification on facilities, quality and maintenance.

On the other hand, some parks cater well for teenagers and offer magnificent sporting and leisure facilities as well as discos; others have only very simple amenities.

Most parks accept dogs, but some have no suitable areas for exercise, and some will refuse to accept certain breeds, so you should always check with the park before you set out.

A small number of parks in our guide have decided to concentrate on the adults-only market, aiming to attract holiday makers who are in search of total peace and quiet.

Always telephone the park before you travel.

Useful Addresses

Camping and Caravanning Club
Greenfields House
Coventry
CV4 8JH
Tel: 02476 694995

British Holiday & Homes Parks Association Ltd
6 Pullman Court
Great Western Road
Gloucester
GL1 3ND
Tel: 01452 526911

Caravan Club
East Grinstead House
East Grinstead
West Sussex
RH19 1UA
Tel: 01342 326944

National Caravan Council Ltd
Catherine House
Victoria Road
Aldershot
Hampshire
GU11 1SS
Tel: 01252 318251

13

THE CARAVAN CLUB

You're welcome at our Sites!

Pandy Club Site, Abergavenny, Monmouthshire

We're pleased to welcome non-members* on many of our 200 Club Sites across the UK and Ireland.

Discover sites in outstanding locations...in National Parks, close to quiet beaches or more lively seaside resorts, in Country Parks, near heritage attractions and historic cities. Whichever you choose, you'll enjoy high standards, excellent facilities, a warm welcome and great value too!

✂ -

FOR YOUR **FREE** 2003 SITES BROCHURE

Call us free on
0800 521161
quoting ref AA9

www.caravanclub.co.uk

All Caravan Club members will automatically receive this brochure.
* Tourer and motor caravanners, trailer tenters and tent campers

Return coupon (or write) to: **The Caravan Club, Dept DC, FREEPOST WD3000, EAST GRINSTEAD, RH19 1BR**

Mr, Mrs, Miss, Ms	Initials	Surname
Address		
		Post Code
Tel. No.		AA9

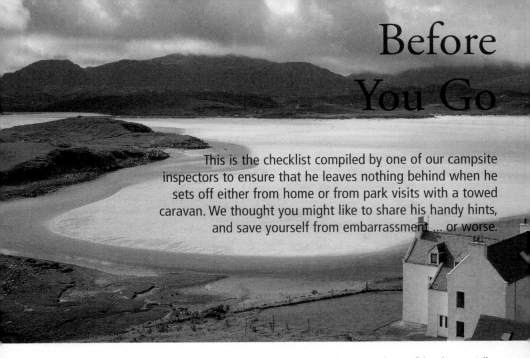

Before You Go

This is the checklist compiled by one of our campsite inspectors to ensure that he leaves nothing behind when he sets off either from home or from park visits with a towed caravan. We thought you might like to share his handy hints, and save yourself from embarrassment ... or worse.

- Check that all interior caravan items are safely stored, cupboards are closed, loos not full of moveable objects, all interior electrics set correctly.

  Remember that vase of flowers!

- Check roof lights are closed and windows secure.

- Corner steadies should be up tightly, blocks cleared away, steps stowed.

- Disconnect electric hook-ups to site and check that gas bottles are turned off.

- Make sure electrics to car are secure.

- Check that the tow-hook safety wire is clipped on, and, if used, that the anti-snake device is fitted correctly.

- Visually check that caravan number plate is secure - and that it reads the same as the one on the car.

- Using a second person to stand behind the caravan, check that all lights and indicators are working correctly.

- Move forward about 15 metres, then stop, get out and inspect your pitch for any items which have been left under the caravan.

- Check that the caravan door is locked and secure.

- Another useful and potentially life-saving tip is to always travel with a small fire extinguisher, fire blanket or both. Fires in caravans and tents are all too commonplace, and once started can take hold very quickly. By the time help has come, or you have gone to find the site's fire-fighting equipment, a tent in particular can already have burned down completely. Never treat fire lightly.

- If you use Calor Gas, they issue a free directory of stockists and dealers. Simply call free on 0800 626 626.

Campsite of the Year Awards 2003

All of our winning parks this year have won the title of Best Campsite within the past seven years. Although each year we aim to find new winners out of a terrific selection of excellent parks, sometimes we have to acknowledge that a park which we rewarded for scaling the heights some years ago still has the edge today. To maintain such consistently high standards takes a degree of commitment, vision and hard work which is in itself exceptional. All of our winning parks are family owned and run, with successive generations getting involved in the business, and bringing with them new ideas and ever greater ambition. It is a formula that has worked well for our three winners, still at their peak after many years.

Campsite of the Year for Wales, and Overall Winner of the Best Campsite of the Year 2003.

Home Farm Caravan Park, Marian-Glas, Isle of Anglesey

From the moment you leave the quiet roads of Anglesey and approach this caravan park, you realise it is going to be very special. Closely-mown grass borders the tarmac drive, and a profusion of flowers, shrubs, trees and palms fills the award-winning landscape. Within this beautiful space, the meticulously-maintained pitches are carefully divided by low walls, flower beds and hedges, giving everyone the feeling of shelter and privacy. Words like 'crisp', 'sharp' and 'spotless' describe the amazing attention to detail on this park, though there is nothing regimented about the friendly Jones family who have run their island paradise for many years. In the immaculate toilet facilities housed in two attractive blocks, various combinations of family rooms, bathrooms and disabled rooms cater for all needs and tastes. Children will love the outdoor adventure playground, and the well-equipped indoor playroom which comes into its own on wet days.

From arrival to departure, visitors can bask in the warm atmosphere radiated by the really welcoming and caring team, and enjoy their stay on a park that was designed with them in mind, and kept in tip-top condition for them to enjoy.

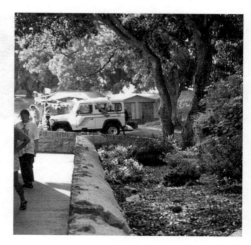

Campsite of the Year for Scotland 2003

Brighouse Bay Holiday Park, Brighouse Bay, Dumfries & Galloway

If a prize were offered to anyone finding fault with Brighouse Bay Holiday Park, it would never be won. The high standard set and achieved by the hard-working Gillespie family ensures that holidaymakers arrive full of expectations and leave with them all fulfilled. Given its location in glorious countryside beside the sea, it is not surprising that the park offers plenty of outdoor activities suitable for the active family. From golf at the 18-hole course to windsurfing, from pony-trekking to quad bikes, and from swimming in the fabulous indoor pool to fishing in the lakes, there need never be a dull moment here. Walkers can enjoy the 1200 acres of signposted trails over coastal paths, farmland and woodland in this Site of Special Scientific Interest, and the sandy beach offers a timeless appeal.

The touring park is attractively split into small fields screened with hedges, mature trees and stone walls, and served by two up-market toilet blocks offering versatile facilities for all needs. And after a hard day by the sea or trying to fit in all the leisure options, there are plenty of dining choices from the cafeteria, bistro, and bar to guarantee a relaxing evening.

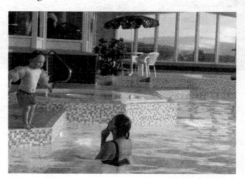

Campsite of the Year for England 2003

Holgate's Caravan Park, Silverdale, Lancashire

Set in a wooded Area of Outstanding Natural Beauty, this superb park continues to set standards of which other can only dream. On the one hand there is Morecambe Bay, sand-filled, ideal for lovers of watersports and boasting all the fun of the popular resort, while on the other hand the rugged fells offer an opportunity for escape into the wilds of the Lake District. In between these two extremes is a caravan park stamped throughout with quality, where visitors can give themselves over to pure pleasure. Top-class toilet facilities are housed in

attractive stone buildings, and every single pitch is fully serviced with TV, electricity, and fresh and waste water. Within a short walk is the stunning leisure complex housing a state-of-the-art swimming pool, licensed restaurant, bar and coffee shop, and the sensible menus of well-priced food offer just the right choice for most families. For the do-it-yourself cook, the shops offers a wide range of foods, and while mum and dad revel in their own private patch with all its own services, the kids can discover the two outdoor play areas and indoor games room.

Premier Parks & Holiday Centres

Premier Parks

ENGLAND

- **CORNWALL &
  ISLES OF SCILLY**
  BOSWINGER
  Sea View International
  Caravan & Camping Park

  BUDE
  Wooda Farm Park

  PENTEWAN
  Sun Valley Holiday Park

  ST IVES
  Polmanter Tourist Park

- **CUMBRIA**
  APPLEBY-IN-
  WESTMORLAND
  Wild Rose Park

  WINDERMERE
  Limefitt Park

  WINDERMERE
  Fallbarrow Park

- **DERBYSHIRE**
  MATLOCK
  Darwin Forest Country Park

- **DEVON**
  NEWTON ABBOT
  Dornafield

  NEWTON ABBOT
  Ross Park

- **DORSET**
  BRIDPORT
  Highlands End Farm
  Holiday Park

  WIMBORNE MINSTER
  Wilksworth Farm Caravan Park

  WIMBORNE MINSTER
  Merley Court Touring Park

- **LANCASHIRE**
  SILVERDALE
  Holgate's Caravan Park

- **LINCOLNSHIRE**
  WOODHALL SPA
  Bainland Country Park

- **NORTHUMBERLAND**
  BERWICK-UPON-TWEED
  Ord House Country Park

- **OXFORDSHIRE**
  STANDLAKE
  Lincoln Farm Park

- **SHROPSHIRE**
  SHREWSBURY
  Beaconsfield Farm Caravan Park

- **SOMERSET**
  CHEDDAR
  Broadway House Holiday
  Caravan & Camping Park

  GLASTONBURY
  The Old Oaks Touring Park

- **SUFFOLK**
  EAST BERGHOLT
  Grange Country Park

  WOODBRIDGE
  Moon & Sixpence

- **WIGHT, ISLE OF**
  NEWBRIDGE
  Orchards Holiday Caravan Park

  NEWCHURCH
  Southland Camping Park

  SANDOWN
  Camping & Caravanning
  Club Site

- **YORKSHIRE, NORTH**
  HARROGATE
  Rudding Holiday Park

  HARROGATE
  Ripley Caravan Park

CHANNEL ISLANDS

- **JERSEY**
  ST MARTIN
  Beuvelande Camp Site

SCOTLAND

- **DUMFRIES & GALLOWAY**
  BRIGHOUSE BAY
  Brighouse Bay Holiday Park

  CREETOWN
  Castle Cary Holiday Park

  ECCLEFECHAN
  Hoddom Castle Caravan Park

- **EAST LOTHIAN**
  DUNBAR
  Thurston Manor Holiday
  Home Park
- **FIFE**
  ST ANDREWS
  Craigtoun Meadows
  Holiday Park
- **HIGHLAND**
  CORPACH
  Linnhe Lochside Holidays
  INVERNESS
  Torvean Caravan Park
- **PERTH & KINROSS**
  BLAIR ATHOLL
  Blair Castle Caravan Park
  BLAIR ATHOLL
  River Tilt Caravan Park
- **STIRLING**
  ABERFOYLE
  Trossachs Holiday Park
  LUIB
  Glendochart Caravan Park

WALES

- **ANGLESEY, ISLE OF**
  DULAS
  Tyddyn Isaf Caravan Park
- **CARMARTHENSHIRE**
  NEWCASTLE EMLYN
  Cenarth Falls Holiday Park
- **WREXHAM**
  EYTON
  The Plassey Leisure Park

Holiday Centres

ENGLAND

- **CORNWALL &
  ISLES OF SCILLY**
  BUDE
  Sandymouth Bay Holiday Park
  HAYLE
  St Ives Bay Holiday Park
  HOLYWELL BAY
  Holywell Bay Holiday Park
  HOLYWELL BAY
  Trevornick Holiday Park
  LOOE
  Tencreek Holiday Park
  MULLION
  Mullion Holiday Park

NEWQUAY
Hendra Holiday Park
NEWQUAY
Newquay Holiday Park
PENTEWAN
Pentewan Sands Holiday Park
PERRANPORTH
Perran Sands Holiday Park
POLPERRO
Killigarth Manor
Holiday Centre
ST MINVER
St Minver Holiday Park
TORPOINT
Whitsand Bay Holiday Park
WHITECROSS
White Acres Holiday Park
WIDEMOUTH BAY
Widemouth Bay Caravan Parc

- **CUMBRIA**
  FLOOKBURGH
  Lakeland Leisure Park
  SILLOTH
  Stanwix Park Holiday Centre
- **DEVON**
  CHUDLEIGH
  Finlake Holiday Park
  CROYDE BAY
  Ruda Holiday Park
  DAWLISH
  Golden Sands Holiday Park
  DAWLISH
  Lady's Mile Touring &
  Caravan Park
  DAWLISH
  Peppermint Park
  EXMOUTH
  Devon Cliffs Holiday Park
  LADRAM BAY
  Ladram Bay Holiday Centre
  MORTEHOE
  Twitchen Parc
  PAIGNTON
  Beverley Parks Caravan &
  Camping Centre
  PAIGNTON
  Hoburne Torbay
  WOOLACOMBE
  Golden Coast Holiday Village
  WOOLACOMBE
  Woolacombe Bay
  Holiday Village

WOOLACOMBE
Woolacombe Sands
Holiday Park
- **DORSET**
  BRIDPORT
  Freshwater Beach Holiday Park
  BRIDPORT
  West Bay Holiday Park
  HOLTON HEATH
  Sandford Holiday Park
  ST LEONARDS
  Oakdene Forest Park
  WEYMOUTH
  Littlesea Holiday Park
  WEYMOUTH
  Seaview Holiday Park
  WEYMOUTH
  Waterside Holiday Park
  WEYMOUTH
  Weymouth Bay Holiday Park
- **ESSEX**
  MERSEA ISLAND
  Waldegraves Holiday Park
- **GLOUCESTERSHIRE**
  SOUTH CERNEY
  Hoburne Cotswold
- **HAMPSHIRE**
  FORDINGBRIDGE
  Sandy Balls Holiday Centre
  NEW MILTON
  Hoburne Bashley
- **LANCASHIRE**
  BLACKPOOL
  Marton Mere Holiday Village
  COCKERHAM
  Cockerham Sands Country Park
  HEYSHAM
  Ocean Edge Caravan Park
  MORECAMBE
  Regent Caravan Park
- **LINCOLNSHIRE**
  CLEETHORPES
  Thorpe Park Holiday Centre
  MABLETHORPE
  Golden Sands Holiday Park
- **NORFOLK**
  BELTON
  Wild Duck Holiday Park
  GREAT YARMOUTH
  Cherry Tree Holiday Park
  GREAT YARMOUTH
  Vauxhall Holiday Park

HUNSTANTON
Searles of Hunstanton

- **NORTHUMBERLAND**
BERWICK-UPON-TWEED
Haggerston Castle

- **SOMERSET**
BREAN
Warren Farm Holiday Park

BURNHAM-ON-SEA
Burnham-on-Sea
Holiday Centre

WATCHET
Doniford Bay Holiday Park

- **SUSSEX, WEST**
SELSEY
Warner Farm Touring Park

- **WIGHT, ISLE OF**
WHITECLIFF BAY
Whitecliff Bay Holiday Park

- **YORKSHIRE,
EAST RIDING OF**
SKIPSEA
Low Skirlington Leisure Park

- **YORKSHIRE, NORTH**
FILEY
Blue Dolphin Holiday Park

FILEY
Flower of May Holiday Park

FILEY
Reighton Sands Holiday Park

SCOTLAND

- **DUMFRIES & GALLOWAY**
GATEHOUSE-OF-FLEET
Auchenlarie Holiday Park

SOUTHERNESS
Southerness Holiday Village

- **EAST LOTHIAN**
LONGNIDDRY
Seton Sands Holiday Village

- **HIGHLAND**
DORNOCH
Grannie's Heilan Hame
Holiday Park

NAIRN
Nairn Lochloy Holiday Park

- **PERTH & KINROSS**
TUMMEL BRIDGE
Tummel Valley Holiday Park

- **SOUTH AYRSHIRE**
AYR
Craig Tara Holiday Park

COYLTON
Sandrum Castle Holiday Park

WALES

- **CONWY**
TOWYN
Ty Mawr Holiday Park

- **DENBIGHSHIRE**
PRESTATYN
Presthaven Sands

- **GWYNEDD**
PORTHMADOG
Greenacres

- **PEMBROKESHIRE**
TENBY
Kiln Park Holiday Centre

REPUBLIC OF IRELAND

- **CO KERRY**
KILLARNEY
Fossa Caravan Park

Island Camping

Scotland

The Shetland Islands
There are four official campsites on the Shetlands, but visitors can camp anywhere with prior permission. Caravans and motor caravans must stick to the main roads. Camping 'böds' offer budget accommodation in unisex dormitories for campers with their own bed rolls and sleeping bags. There is no camping or caravanning on Noss and Fair Isle, and the Tresta Links in Fetlar.

The Orkney Isles
There are no camping and caravanning restrictions, and plenty of beauty spots in which to pitch camp.

The Western Isles (Outer Hebrides)
There are official campsites on these islands, but 'wild' camping is allowed within reason, and with the landowner's prior permission.

The Inner Isles and other Scottish Islands
Skye is accessible to caravans and motor caravans, and has official camping sites, but its sister isles of Rhum and Eigg have no car ferries, and take only backpackers. Official camping only is allowed at Rothsay on the Isle of Bute. The islands of Mull, Islay, Coll and Arran have official campsites, and welcome caravans, motor caravans and tenters. Offsite camping is also allowed with the usual permission. Iona is car free, and a backpacker's paradise, while

Tiree does not accept caravans or motor caravans, and has no official sites. Colonsay and Cumbrae allow no caravanning or camping, although organized groups such as the Guides or Scouts may stay with official permission. Jura and Gigha allow neither camping nor caravanning, and Lismore bans caravans but permits camping, although there are no official sites and few suitable places.

The Channel Islands

Tight controls are operated because of the narrowness of the mainly rural roads. On all of the islands tents can be hired on recognized campsites.

Jersey
Only islanders may own and use towed caravans. Visitors cannot bring either caravans or motor caravans, but tents and trailer tents are allowed provided you stay on official campsites; booking is strongly recommended during July and August.

Guernsey
The same rules as on Jersey are applied, although motor caravans are allowed under strict conditions. A permit must be sought and received in advance, the vehicle must not be used for sleeping, and when not in use for transport the van must be left under cover at a camping park with prior permission

Herm and Sark
These two small islands are traffic free. Herm has a small campsite for tents, and these can also be hired. Sark has three campsites. New arrivals are met off the boat by a tractor which carries people and luggage up the steep hill from the harbour. All travel is by foot, on bicycle, or by horse and cart.

Alderney
Neither caravans nor motor caravans are allowed, and campers must have a confirmed booking on the one official camp site before they arrive.

Isle of Man
Motor caravans may enter without prior permission. Trailer caravans are only allowed in connection with trade shows and exhibitions, or for demonstration purposes, not for living accommodation. Written application for permission should be made to the Secretary, Planning Committee, Isle of Man Local Government Board, Murray House, Mount Havelock. The shipping line cannot accept caravans without this written permission..

Isles of Scilly
Caravans and motor caravans are not allowed, and campers must stay at official sites. Booking is advisable on all sites, especially during school holidays.

Please note that strict control is kept on the landing of animals on these islands.

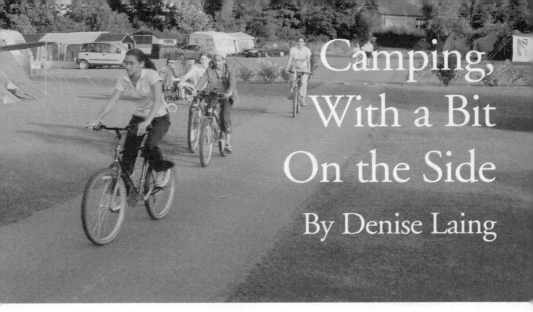

Camping, With a Bit On the Side

By Denise Laing

There was a time when hot showers, relatively level pitches, and a shop selling milk and bread spelt luxury on a caravan or camping holiday. If there was a beach nearby for kids and sun-worshippers, or hills for energetic walkers, then the icing had been positively shovelled onto the cake. We have gone way beyond such innocent pleasures now: fully-serviced 'super' pitches offering satellite TV connection, electricity, and fresh and waste water points are commonly found on all types of sites, along with de-luxe en-suite toilet facilities to rival those in good hotels. Even small sites often boast vast exotic indoor swimming pools with Caribbean temperatures and thrilling wave machines. Holiday centres have traditionally tapped into the search for the complete holiday experience, and they continue to develop to an impressive degree. Within their precincts guests might expect to find all the entertainment, organised activities, and sports and leisure facilities they want, and need

never set foot outside the gate for the duration of their break. These action-packed programmes do not suit everybody, though, and at the other end of the extreme, rural sites with clean toilets, some electric hook-ups, and little else on offer apart from bird song are as popular as ever. But something is changing down on the farm, and it is spreading like wildfire.

A new breed of site which caters for hobbies or other activities is emerging across all pennant ratings, and its popularity is rising. Many parks have created a niche market as a way of attracting a guaranteed following among enthusiasts, and this trend is escalating. Some owners have exploited the natural geographical features of their

parks, such as lakes, rivers and forests, and developed them as a way of attracting both new and returning visitors. Others offer activities as a natural extension of the owners' interests, and provide visitors with the chance to indulge their curiosity, or discover and share a passion. Still more sites provide an activity which runs separately from the caravan and camping side of the business, and which can offer an added bonus for unsuspecting visitors. A browse through the AA's database has come up with plenty of speciality parks to illustrate this growing trend.

Britain's fastest growing and currently most popular sport is **coarse fishing**, a phenomenon reflected by the sheer numbers of

AA-pennanted parks offering devotees a chance to combine their holiday with their chosen sport. Literally hundreds of parks offer fishing to their visitors, in some cases as a low-key sideline, but for others it is big business. Fly fishing or game fishing are popular too, but the search for the huge carp or perch which will be weighed, photographed and put back in the water leads the sport.

A charitable organisation has capitalised on the presence of large stretches of inland waters in the West Country by combining nature conservation with fishing and watersports and, in six of its twenty eight locations, camping as well. The South West Lakes Trust encourages people to discover and enjoy the countryside, and in particular the wildlife which can be found in and around the lakes. On its two AA-appointed sites, campers and caravanners can stay in peaceful countryside with good facilities on hand, and immerse themselves in their watery environment. At Tamar Lake near Kilkhampton is Cornwall's largest coarse fishery where you might expect to land anything up to a 28lb carp from the wild-flower filled banks of the lake. The excellent watersports centre here also offers dinghy sailing, windsurfing, surf skiing, kayaking and rowing in a safe environment. Wimbleball Lake is gloriously set just inside the Exmoor National Park near Dulverton in Somerset, and is nationally renowned for its trout fishing. Boats can be hired, including a Wheelie for disabled anglers (book 48 hours in advance), and rainbow trout weighting nearly 12lb have been caught in the lake. Sailing is also available here for those with their own boats.

Perhaps unsurprisingly, coarse fishing is male dominated, but at least one holiday park has taken pains to redress the balance, or minimise the exclusion experienced by (overwhelmingly) female partners of hooked anglers. At White Acres Holiday Centre in Whitecross, Cornwall a resident angling coach gives lessons to the uninitiated, with the result that many women become as addicted as men. Which is only fair, because the prize money can run into thousands of pounds. Some other AA parks which specialise in fishing include Springwater Lakes at Lampeter in Ceredigion, Thorney Lakes at Langport in Somerset, St Tinney Farm Holidays, Otterham in Cornwall, Cofton Country Holiday Park, Dawlish in Devon, and Oakbank Lakes Country Park in Longtown, Cumbria,

Watersports facilities are another frequently-found addition to caravan parks, and they too come in all shapes and sizes. The sub-aqua centre at Scoutscroft Holiday Centre in Coldingham on the Scottish Borders coast is a Mecca for divers of all levels. This part of the North Sea is a marine reserve filled with fascinating crustaceans, molluscs, corals and sponges, and marine biologists from all over the world join novices in underwater exploration. Scuba diving courses are arranged for beginners by professional instructors, and all the gear for an independent dive can also be hired at the centre. If it is the surface of the water

marvellous views of the Clwyd mountain range from their pitches, attractively set in a bend of the River Dee. Even better is the layout at Hexham Racecourse in Northumberland; here the campsite sits alongside the racecourse, so caravanners can enjoy the racing from their own units if they don't want to pay the concessionary rate to watch from the stands.

Many campsites have responded to the demand for active rather than passive land-based leisure activities. **Horse riding, cycling and golf** are all available on caravan parks, and taking the opportunity to improve or learn new skills is proving exceptionally popular. At Lakefield Caravan Park in Camelford, Cornwall there is a full equestrian centre where BHS-qualified instructors offer riding lessons in a smart indoor school. This park is in great demand from families with horse-mad children who want to continue their riding lessons while on holiday, and instructors can gear the lessons to all ability levels. It is a popular centre for the disabled who enjoy the freedom of being on a horse, and farm rides and off-road hacks are also conducted here. At Burrowhayes Farm Caravan Site in Porlock, Somerset the pony trekking is wildly popular, with rides tailored to suit experience, and from its lovely riverside location under Wenlock Edge, Mill Farm at Hughley in Shropshire also draws hordes of horse lovers.

For golfers, there are plenty of 9-hole courses to be tried, and at High Moor Farm Park in Harrogate visitors expecting to use the course might also be amazed to discover a full-size crown bowling green (bring your

rather than its depths that appeals, the choice is considerable. At Roydon Mill Leisure Park in Essex, a water-ski school is an attraction which has people queueing up for lessons. Formal training courses for those who want to impress with their verve and skill are run alongside the more casual banana rides for thrill-seekers. From March to October the 40-acre lake buzzes with the sound of speedboats tearing up and down the water, and this is a great spectator sport too: witness the steep learning curve of the hapless wannabee skier, or at the other end of the scale, the feats of the graceful pro. Drumaheglis Marina & Caravan Park near Ballymoney in Co Antrim is another magnet for the waterski enthusiast, and at Hatfield Waterpark near Doncaster in South Yorkshire, you can take your pick from canoeing, kayaking, sailing, windsurfing and power-boating, and either learn one (or more) of these sports from scratch or develop your skill up to a higher level. Equipment can be hired by those who do not need tuition,

and caravanners who prefer to keep their feet on dry land can sit and enjoy the immense activity taking place on the water. Loch Ken Holiday Park at Parton, Dumfries & Galloway is another AA site offering plenty of water sports.

Away from the water, campsites have a wealth of choices available for anyone looking for a challenge, or just the chance to spend more time on a hobby. For lovers of **horse racing**, the possibility of combining the sport with camping, and even getting reduced entry to the course on race days, must seem like manna from heaven. At Market Rasen in Lincolnshire, barely a few weeks go by without a race being held – the exception is the month of January – and the pleasant grass camping paddock is just a step away from the course. After an afternoon's racing, aficionados can avoid the large crowds exiting the ground and pop back to their unit in a trice. At the Camping & Caravanning Club Site at Bangor-on-Dee Racecourse in Wrexham, caravanners can enjoy

own bowls). Leisure Lakes at Mere Brow in Lancashire provide a resident professional golfer at its 9-hole golf course, with a driving range for anyone really determined to perfect their shots. Visitors to Suffolk can take their pick between Priory Park at Ipswich which boasts its own 9-hole course, and Cakes and Ale at Leiston where another driving range might prove a merciful distraction from family holidays.

As the explosion of cycle tracks, lanes and national routes must have made obvious to everyone by now, **cycling** is the new driving, and huge numbers of people have abandoned their cars – albeit temporarily – in favour

of two wheels. Campsites have been quick to maximise the potential here, and many now offer bicycles for hire, or advertise their proximity to good cycling country. As a result, they have been swamped with a new style of camper in lycra shorts and helmet, eager to spend their holidays healthily. At Cwmcarn Forest Drive Campsite in Caerphilly there is a 37km bike trail through this very scenic country park, and a bike wash at the site takes care of the accumulated dirt. Plenty of other parks offer bike hire because of their location near designated cycling areas – AA Welsh Campsite of the Year for 2002, Pencelli Castle Caravan & Camping Park in Brecon, Powys offers quality mountain bikes for

hire, as does 2001 Scottish winner Trossachs Holiday Park in Aberfoyle, Stirling, along with the Camping & Caravanning Club Site at Dunbar, East Lothian, the Isle of Avalon Touring Caravan Park at Glastonbury, Somerset, and many more. Dozens of sites are close to part of the 6,500-mile National Cycle Network run by the charity Sustrans, and their website (www.sustrans.co.uk) shows the routes. For example, many AA-listed sites between Lydford and Okehampton in Devon are on the 11-mile Granite Way, part of the national route which is mainly on a traffic-free former railway line.

At least two AA-listed parks offer **clay pigeon shooting**: at Wooda Farm which overlooks Bude Bay in Cornwall, visitors are taken to nearby farmland to have a go at this popular sport, and tuition is part of the package. According to the park, all you need is reasonable eyesight, and most beginners quickly get the hang of it. Clay Pigeon Caravan Park at Evershot in Dorset caters for serious competitors who take part in the clay pigeon championships there, as well as visitors to the site who fancy trying it. But the biggest draw at this park is the **go-karting** next door, where international competitions are often held at weekends. During the week it is possible to hire a kart, have a few lessons, and take to the racing track at high speeds.

Finally, a new venture is proving to be phenomenally successful at Waterow Touring Park in Wiveliscombe, Somerset, tucked well away from the crowds in a lovely wooded valley. Here visitors can **learn to paint** from a qualified instructor in a beautiful converted barn with fabulous views. From May to September would-be artists can try their hand at watercolour painting and drawing, or improve the skills they already have. All grades are catered for, including those hoping to increase their skills to an advanced level. Other courses held here include bridge and photography, and if a day behind the camera or easel is not enough to bring relaxation, there is fly fishing for wild brown trout on the River Tone; for more details see the park's website at www.waterrowpark.u-net.com.

The above is just a taste of what is available at today's multi-faceted caravan and camping parks. For more information, check out the entries given to each AA-classified park in the gazetteer, look at a park's website if the address is given, or contact them directly.

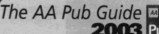

England

England

ENGLAND

ISLE OF   Places incorporating the words 'Isle of' or 'Isle' will be found under the actual name, eg Isle of Wight is listed under Wight, Isle of. Channel Islands and Isle of Man, however, are between England and Scotland and there is a section containing Scottish Islands at the end of the Scotland gazetteer.

BERKSHIRE

FINCHAMPSTEAD   Map 04 SU76

▶ ▶ ▶ *64% California Chalet & Touring Park (SU788651)*
Nine Mile Ride RG40 4HU ☎ 0118 973 3928
📄 0118 932 8720
Dir: From A321 S of Wokingham, turn right onto B3016 to Finchampstead, and follow Country Park signs along Nine Mile Ride to site
🚐 🚚 Å
Open Mar-Oct Booking advisable Last arrival 20.00hrs Last departure noon
A peaceful woodland site with secluded pitches among the trees, adjacent to the country park. Several pitches have a prime position beside the lake with their own fishing area. A 5.5-acre site with 30 touring pitches.

Facilities: 🅁 ⊙ ⅄ ℄ 🐾 🕭 **Services:** 🔌 🕥 → ∪ ▸ ⊚ 🥄

HURLEY   Map 04 SU88

▶ ▶ ▶ *61% Hurley Riverside Park (SU826839)*
Park Office SL6 5NE ☎ 01628 823501 &
824493 Bookings 📄 01628 825533
e-mail: info@hurleyriversidepark.co.uk
website: www.hurleyriversidepark.co.uk
Dir: Signed off A4130 Henley to Maidenhead road, just W of Hurley village
🚐 £8-£18 🚚 £8-£18 Å £8-£18

Open all year Booking advisable bank hols, school hols & Henley Regatta Last arrival 21.00hrs Last departure 12.00hrs
Large Thames-side site with good touring area close to river. Level grassy pitches in small, sectioned areas, and a generally peaceful setting. A 15-acre site with 200 touring pitches and 450 statics. Fishing in season
Facilities: 🅁 ⊙ 🤍 ✳ ⅄ ℄ 🐾 🕭 **Services:** 🔌 🕥 🛢 ⊘ 🕥 🕭
→ ∪ ▸ ⊚ ❄ 😀 🥄 **Notes:** No single sex groups, no unsupervised children 😀 💳 💳 🔧 🅖

Park Office, Hurley Riverside Park, Hurley, Maidenhead, Berks SL6 5NE
Tel: 01628 823501 Fax: 01628 825533
Website: www.hurleyriversidepark.co.uk
Email: info@hurleyriversidepark.co.uk

Our family run park is situated on the picturesque south bank of the River Thames. We are ideally located for visiting Windsor, (nearest park to Legoland), Oxford, London and the Thames Valley. Services include electric and multi-service hook-ups. Riverside walks – Fishing in Season – Slipway. We also have fully serviced Caravan Holiday Homes for hire, in individual gardens from £180 per week. Open 1 March – 31 October.

RISELEY   Map 04 SU76

▶ ▶ ▶ *63% Wellington Country Park (SU728628)*
RG7 1SP ☎ 0118 932 6445 📄 0118 932 6444
e-mail: info.wcp@btconnect.com
website: www.wellington-country-park.co.uk
Dir: Signed off A33 between Reading and Basingstoke, 4m S of M4 junct 11
★ 🚐 £8-£15 🚚 £8-£15 Å £8-£15

Open Mar-8 Nov Booking advisable peak periods Last departure 14.00hrs
A peaceful woodland site set within an extensive country park, which comes complete with lakes, nature trails, deer farm and boating. Ideal for M4 travellers. An 80-acre site with 70 touring pitches. Boating & fishing.
Leisure: 🌳 **Facilities:** 🅁 ⊙ 🤍 🐾
Services: 🔌 🕥 → ∪ ⊚ 🕭 ❄ 🥄 😀 💳 🔧 🅖

England

BRISTOL

BRISTOL See **Redhill (Somerset)**

BUCKINGHAMSHIRE

CHALFONT ST GILES Map 04 SU99

▶ ▶ ▶ **60% Highclere Farm Country Touring Park (SU977927)**
Highclere Farm, Newbarn Ln,
Seer Green HP9 2QZ
☎ 01494 874505 & 875665 ▤ 01494 875238
Dir: M40 junct 2, A355 towards Amersham, 1m right to Seer Green follow tourist signs.
★ ⊞ £10-£13 ⊞ £10-£13 ▲ £8-£12

Open Mar-Jan Booking advisable Last dep noon
A small chicken farm park surrounded by pasture and sheltered on one side by trees. Good hardstanding pitches and electrics cater for caravans in a separate hedged field. A 2.5-acre site with 60 touring pitches, 40 hardstandings.
Leisure: ⚠ **Facilities:** ⌂⊙⊠✳⌂⚰⚲⌂
Services: ⌨⛽⚱⊿⚙⊤→∪⌷⚲⊜⊜⚒⚒⚙

CAMBRIDGESHIRE

BURWELL Map 05 TL56

▶ ▶ ▶ **64% Stanford Park (TL578675)**
Weirs Drove CB5 0BP ☎ 01638 741547 & 07802 439997
website: www.stanfordcaravanpark.co.uk
Dir: Signed from B1102
★ ⊞ £10 ⊞ £10 ▲ £10

contd.

Highfield Farm Touring Park
Comberton, Cambridge CB3 7DG
Tel/Fax: 01223 262308

Please write or phone for colour brochure

A popular award-winning park with excellent facilities. Close to the historic university city of Cambridge, the Imperial War Museum, Duxford and ideally situated for touring East Anglia

email: enquiries@highfieldfarmtouringpark.co.uk
www.highfieldfarmtouringpark.co.uk

STANFORD PARK
Cambridge ▶▶▶ AA
Weirs Road, Burwell, Cambs
Tel: (01638) 741547 & (07802) 439997
www.stanfordcaravanpark.co.uk

We are ideally located for visiting Cambridge and the surrounding area. Several places of interest within easy reach, Wicken Fen National Trust, Newmarket Races, Ely Cathedral and Cambridge University. Camp site includes: modern toilet block with hot showers, hair dryer & iron, laundry room, electric hook-ups, fishing close by, disabled facilities. **Open all year.**

DISCOUNTED RATES FOR SEASONAL AND LONG TERM PITCHES

Open all year Booking advisable bank hols Last arrival 20.00hrs Last departure 11.00hrs
A secluded site on outskirts of Burwell with modern amenities including purpose-built disabled facilities. A 20-acre site with 100 touring pitches, 10 hardstandings and 3 statics.

Leisure: ⚠ **Facilities:** 🗟⊙🔍🕻🛁
Services: 🗟🛈🖉🔁🛈→ᑌ🝼🍴🗘🔘

See advertisement on page 29

CAMBRIDGE   See Burwell & Comberton

COMBERTON   Map 05 TL35

▶ ▶ ▶ ▶ **77% Highfield Farm Touring Park (TL389572)**
Long Rd CB3 7DG ☎ 01223 262308
🖨 01223 262308
e-mail: enquiries@highfieldfarmtouringpark.co.uk
website: www.highfieldfarmtouringpark.co.uk
Dir: From M11 junct 12, take A603 (Sandy) for 0.5m, then right onto B1046 to Comberton
★ 🚐 £8.25-£9.50 🚐 £8-£9.25 ▲ £8-£9.25

Open Apr-Oct Booking advisable bank hols wknds
Last arrival 22.00hrs Last departure 14.00hrs
Run by a very efficient and friendly family, the park is on a well-sheltered hilltop, with spacious pitches including a cosy backpacker's/cyclists area, and separate sections for couples and families. There is a 1.5 mile marked walk around the family farm, with stunning views. An 8-acre site with 120 touring pitches, 52 hardstandings.
Dishwashing facility, postbox.

Leisure: ⚠ **Facilities:** 🗟⊙🔍❄🛁🕻🛁🐾
Services: 🗟🖲🛈🖉🔁🛈→ᑌ🝼🗘

See advertisement on page 29

GRAFHAM   Map 04 TL16

▶ ▶ ▶ ▶ **71% Old Manor Caravan Park (TL160269)**
Church Rd PE28 0BB
☎ 01480 810264 🖨 01480 819099
e-mail: camping@old-manor.co.uk
website: www.old-manor.co.uk
Dir: Signed off A1, S of Huntingdon at Buckden and from A14, W of Huntingdon at Ellington
★ 🚐 £11-£13.50 🚐 £11-£13.50 ▲ £11-£13.50
Open all year (rs Nov-Feb on site shop closed)
Booking advisable weekends & peak times Last arrival 21.30hrs Last departure 18.00hrs
A secluded, well screened park in attractive gardens surrounding a 17th-century cottage. Pitches
contd.

have lovely views of the countryside and Grafham Water is only a mile away. A 6.5-acre site with 84 touring pitches, 7 hardstandings and 8 statics.*

Leisure: 🎣 ⚠ **Facilities:** 🗟⊙🔍❄🛁🕻🛁
Services: 🗟🛈🖉🔁🛈🖦→ᑌ🝼🗘🗙🗘
Notes: Dogs on leads 🔘🔳🔍

GREAT SHELFORD   Map 05 TL45

▶ ▶ ▶ **65% Camping & Caravanning Club Site (TL455539)**
19 Cabbage Moor CB2 5NB ☎ 01223 841185
website: www.campingandcaravanningclub.co.uk
Dir: M11 junct 11 onto B1309 signposted Cambridge. At 1st set of lights turn right. After 0.5m follow site sign on left, pointing down lane
★ 🚐 £12.30-£15.50 🚐 £12.30-£15.50 ▲ £12.30-£15.50
Open Mar-Oct Booking advisable bank hols & Jul-Aug Last arrival 21.00hrs Last departure noon
A popular, open site close to Cambridge and the M11, with well-maintained toilet facilities. Please see advertisement on page 10 for details of Club Members' benefits. An 11-acre site with 120 touring pitches.

Leisure: ⚠ **Facilities:** 🗟⊙🔍❄🛁🕻🛁🐾
Services: 🗟🖲🛈🖉🔁→ᑌ🝼🗘🐾🗘🝼🔘🔳🔍🗺🗘

HEMINGFORD ABBOTS   Map 04 TL27

▶ ▶ ▶ **67% Quiet Waters Caravan Park (TL283712)**
PE28 9AJ ☎ 01480 463405 🖨 01480 463405
website: www.quietwaterscaravanpark.co.uk
Dir: Follow village signs off A14, E of Huntingdon, site in village centre
★ 🚐 £9-£11 🚐 £9-£11 ▲ £9-£11
Open Apr-Oct Booking advisable high season Last arrival 20.00hrs Last departure noon
This attractive little riverside site is found in a most charming village just 1 mile off the A14 making an ideal centre to tour the Cambridgeshire area. A 1-acre site with 20 touring pitches, 18 hardstandings and 40 statics.
Fishing & boating.

Facilities: 🗟⊙🔍❄🕻
Services: 🗟🖲🛈🖉→ᑌ🝼🗘🐾🗘🝼🔘🔳🔍🗺🗘

HUNTINGDON   Map 04 TL27

▶ ▶ ▶ **72% Huntingdon Boathaven & Caravan Park (TL249706)**
The Avenue, Godmanchester PE29 8AF
☎ 01480 411977 🖨 01480 411977
e-mail: boathavenhunts@virgin.net
Dir: S of town off B1043 or leave A14 at Godmanchester junct, through Godmanchester on B1043 to site on left side by River Ouse
★ 🚐 £10-£12 🚐 £10-£12 ▲ £9-£11
Open Mar-Oct Booking advisable Last arrival 22.00hrs Last departure 10.00hrs
Small, well laid out site overlooking a boat marina and the River Ouse, set close to the A14 and within walking distance of Huntingdon town centre. Clean, well kept toilets. A 2-acre site with 24 touring pitches, 4 hardstandings.

Facilities: 🗟⊙🔍❄🛁🗗🐾
Services: 🗟🔁→🝼🗘🐾🗘🝼

▶ ▶ ▶ **68% The Willows Caravan Park (TL224708)**
Bromholme Ln, Brampton PE18 8NE
☎ 01480 437566
e-mail: willows@willows33.freeserve.co.uk
*Dir: Leave A14/A1 signed Brampton, follow signs for
Huntingdon. Site on right close to Brampton Mill pub*
★ ♥ £10 ♥ £10 ▲ £9-£10
Open all year (rs 31 Oct-1 Mar 10 pitches only plus 6
storage spaces) Booking advisable All bank hols &
school hols Last arrival 23.00hrs Last departure
13.00hrs
*A small, friendly site in a pleasant setting beside
the River Ouse, on the Ouse Valley Walk. New
bay areas have been added for caravans and
motorhomes, and more planting has been
completed to provide screening. There are
launching facilities beside the site, and free river
fishing. A 4-acre site with 50 touring pitches.*
Leisure: ⚖ Facilities: ♠ ⊙ ✳ & Services: ♥ ⊞ → ▸
✦ ☎ ✔ ⚖ Notes: Dogs must be kept on leads, ball
games on field provided, no generators, one-way
system strictly 5mph

ST NEOTS	Map 04 TL16

▶ ▶ ▶ **67% Camping & Caravanning Club Site
(TL182598)**
Hardwick Rd, Eynesbury PE19 2PR ☎ 01480 474404
website: www.campingandcaravanningclub.co.uk
*Dir: From A1 take A428 to Cambridge, 2nd rdbt left to
Tesco's, past Sports Centre. International Camping
signs to site*
★ ♥ £12.30-£17.50 ♥ £12.30-£17.50 ▲ £12.30-£17.50
Open 2 Mar-28 Oct Booking advisable bank hols &
peak periods Last arrival 21.00hrs Last departure
noon
*A level meadowland site adjacent to the River Ouse
on the outskirts of St Neots, with well maintained
and modern facilities, and helpful, attentive staff.
Please see the advertisement on page 10 for details
of Club Members' benefits. An 11-acre site with 180
touring pitches, 22 hardstandings.*
Coarse fishing.
Facilities: ♠ ⊙ ⚒ ✳ & ⚖ ♈
Services: ♥ ⊞ ▸ ⌀ ⊞ → ▸ ⌀ ✔ ⚖ ⊛ ▦ ▦ ▨ ⬚

CHESHIRE

CHESTER	Map 07 SJ46

▶ ▶ ▶ **63% Chester Southerly Caravan Park
(SJ385624)**
Balderton Ln, Marlston-Cum-Lache CH4 9LF
☎ 07976 743888 & 01244 671308 ▤ 01244 659804
website: www.chestersoutherlytouringpark.co.uk
Dir: Just off A55/A483 rdbt
★ ♥ £10 ♥ £10 ▲ £10
Open Mar-Nov Booking advisable bank hols
essential Last arrival 21.00hrs Last departure noon
*Set amidst very attractive and informal landscaping,
the park benefits from a number of recent
improvements under new management. Located on
the rural south side of the Roman city of Chester,
close to the bypass. An 8-acre site with 90 touring
pitches.* *contd.*

Duck pond & breeding cage.
Leisure: ⚖ Facilities: ♠ ⊙ ⚒ ✳ & ⚖ ⚖ 🀫 ⚖ ♈
Services: ♥ ⊞ ▸ ⌀ ⊞ ⊤ → ∪ ▸ ◉ ⚖ ✦ ☎ ✔ Notes: No
commercial vehicles, no dogs in tents

KNUTSFORD	Map 07 SJ77

▶ ▶ ▶ **66% Woodlands Park (SJ743710)**
Wash Ln, Allostock WA16 9LG ☎ 01565 723429 &
07976 702490 ▤ 01332 810818
*Dir: From Holmes Chapel take A50 N for 3m, turn into
Wash Lane by Boundary Water Park. Site 0.25m on left*
★ ♥ £8.50-£9 ♥ £8.50-£9 ▲ £8.50-£9
Open Mar-6 Jan Booking advisable bank hols Last
arrival 21.00hrs Last departure 11.00hrs
*A very attractive park in the heart of rural Cheshire,
and set in 16 acres of mature woodland. 3 miles
from Jodderel Bank. A 16-acre site with 50 touring
pitches and 100 statics.*
Facilities: ♠ ⊙ & Services: ♥ ⊞ ▸ → ▸ ✔ ⚖

MACCLESFIELD	Map 07 SJ97

▶ ▶ ▶ **66% Capesthorne Hall (SJ840727)**
Siddington SK11 9JY ☎ 01625 861779 & 861221
▤ 01625 861619
e-mail: info@capesthorne.com
Dir: On A34, 1m S of A537
★ ♥ fr £12 ♥
Open Mar-Oct Booking advisable public hols Last
arrival dusk Last departure noon
*Set in the magnificent grounds of the historic
Capesthorpe Hall, with access to the lakes, gardens
and woodland walks are free to site users. Pitches
in the open parkland are spacious and can easily
accommodate the larger motorhomes, and the
clean toilet facilities are housed in the old stable
block. The beautiful Cheshire countryside is easily
explored, and there is coarse fishing on site. A 5.5-
acre site with 30 touring pitches.*
Capesthorne Hall, gardens & fishing.
Facilities: ♠ ⊙ ✦ ♈ Services: ♥ → ✔ ⚖

WARRINGTON	Map 07 SU68

▶ ▶ ▶ **66% Holly Bank Caravan Park
(SJ693904)**
Warburton Bridge Rd WA3 6HU
☎ 0161 775 2842
*Dir: 2m E of M6 junct 21 on A57 (Irlam). Turn right
at 1st traffic lights, site 30yds on left*
★ ♥ £12-£14 ♥ £12-£14 ▲ £11-£13
Open all year Booking advisable bank hols &
wknds Apr-Oct Last arrival 20.00hrs Last
departure noon
*A well-run and attractive park in a rural setting
with mature trees. The spotless toilets are
located in the main block, with a good
portakabin facility on the touring field. A good
base for access to Warrington retail parks,
Manchester, and the Trafford Centre shopping
complex. A 9-acre site with 75 touring pitches,
2 hardstandings.*
Lending library.
Leisure: ♠ Facilities: ♠ ⊙ ⚒ ✳ ✦ ⚖ ♈
Services: ♥ ⊞ ▸ ⌀ ⊞ ⊤ ➡ → ∪ ▸ ⚖ ☎ ✔

CORNWALL & ISLES OF SCILLY

ASHTON   Map 02 SW62

► ► ► **64% Boscrege Caravan & Camping Park** (SW595305)
TR13 9TG ☎ 01736 762231 🖷 01736 762231
e-mail: enquiries@caravanparkcornwall.com
website: www.caravanparkcornwall.com
Dir: Follow signs from B3202, Hayle to Helston road, to Godolphin Cross. Turn right at pub to site
★ ⚲ £6.50-£13.50 ⚲ £6.50-£13.50 Å £6.50-£13.50

Open Mar-Nov Booking advisable Jul-Aug Last arrival 22.00hrs Last departure 11.00hrs
A quiet and bright little touring park divided into small paddocks with hedges, and offering plenty of open spaces for children to play in. The family-owned park offers clean, well-painted toilet facilities and neatly trimmed grass. In an Area of Outstanding Natural Beauty at the foot of Tregonning Hill. A 12-acre site with 50 touring pitches and 26 statics.
Recreation fields, microwave facility.

Leisure: ⚓ ⚠ ☐   **Facilities:** ⚲ ☉ ⚑ ⚹ ⚘ ⚲ ⚏ ⚓ ⚔
Services: ⚲ ⚏ ⚏ ⚏ ⚏ ⚏ → ∪ ▶ ◉ ⚒ ⚏ ⚏ ⚏ ⚏ ⚏ ⚏

BLACKWATER   Map 02 SW74

► ► ► **59% Chiverton Caravan & Touring Park** (SW743468)
East Hill TR4 8HS ☎ 01872 560667 🖷 01872 560667
Dir: Leave A30 at Three Burrows/Chiverton rdbt onto unclass rd signed Blackwater (3rd exit). Take 1st right and 300yds to site
★ ⚲ £5.25-£7.25 ⚲ £5.25-£8 Å £5.25-£7.25

Open 8 Feb-6 Jan (rs Feb-May & mid Sep-Jan limited stock kept in shop) Booking advisable mid

contd.

Jul-Aug Last arrival 22.00hrs Last departure noon
A small, well-maintained site with some mature hedges dividing pitches. Midway between Truro and St Agnes, and an ideal touring centre. A 4-acre site with 30 touring pitches and 40 statics.
Covered sink area, drying lines.

Leisure: ⚓ ⚠   **Facilities:** ⚲ ☉ ⚑ ⚹ ⚘ ⚲ ⚏ ⚏
Services: ⚲ ⚏ → ∪ ▶ ⚏ ⚒ ⚒

► ► ► **68% Trevarth Holiday Park** (SW744468)
TR4 8HR ☎ 01872 560266 🖷 01872 560379
e-mail: trevarth@lineone.net
Dir: Leave A30 at Chiverton rdbt onto unclass rd signed Blackwater. Site on right in 200mtrs
★ ⚲ £7.50-£10.50 ⚲ £7.50-£10.50 Å £7.50-£10.50

Open Etr or Apr-Oct Booking advisable Jul-Aug Last arrival 22.00hrs Last departure noon
A neat and compact park with touring pitches laid out on attractive, well-screened high ground

contd.

adjacent to A30/A39 junction. This pleasant little park is centrally located for touring, and is maintained to a very good standard. A 4-acre site with 30 touring pitches and 21 statics. Baby changing facilities

Leisure: ◕ ⚖ **Facilities:** ⬔ ⊙ ⬚ ✕ ⬚ ⬚
Services: ⬚ ⬚ ⬚ ⬚ ⬚ → ⬚ ⬚ ⬚ ⬚ ⬚ ⬚ ⬚

BODINNICK   Map 02 SX15

► ► ► **63% Penmarlam (SX134526)**
PL23 1LZ ☎ 01726 870088 📄 01726 870082
e-mail: fhc@foweyharbour.co.uk
Dir: From A390 at East Taphouse take B3359 signed Looe and Lanreath. Follow signs for Bodinnick and Fowey, via ferry
★ ⬚ £7-£10 ⬚ £7-£10 ⬚ £7-£10

Open Apr-Oct Booking advisable mid Jul-mid Aug Last arrival 21.30hrs Last departure 12.00hrs
A tranquil park set above the Fowey Estuary, with its own launching facility. Pitches are level and sheltered, and the toilet block is well maintained. Facilities are being gradually improved by the Fowey Harbour Commissioners who own the site. A 1-acre site with 33 touring pitches.
Private slipway/quay, storage for small boats.
Facilities: ⬔ ⊙ ⬚ ✕ ⬚
Services: ⬚ ⬚ ⬚ ⬚ ⬚ ⬚ → ⬚ ⬚ ⬚ ⬚ ⬚ ⬚ ⬚ ⬚ ⬚
See advertisement on page 40

BODMIN   Map 02 SX06

► ► ► **64% Camping & Caravanning Club Site (SX081676)**
Old Callywith Rd PL31 2DZ ☎ 01208 73834
website: www.campingandcaravanningclub.co.uk
Dir: A30 from N, at sign for Bodmin turn right crossing dual carriageway in front of industrial estate, turn left at international sign, site left
★ ⬚ £10.20-£12.90 ⬚ £10.20-£12.90 ⬚ £10.20-£12.90
Open Mar-Oct Booking advisable bank hols & Jul-Aug Last arrival 21.00hrs Last departure noon
Undulating grassy site with trees and bushes set in meadowland close to the town of Bodmin with all its attractions. The site is close to the A30 and makes a very good touring base. Please see the advertisement on page 10 for details of Club Members' benefits. An 11-acre site with 175 touring pitches.
Leisure: ⚖ **Facilities:** ⬔ ⊙ ⬚ ✕ ⬚ ⬚
Services: ⬚ ⬚ ⬚ ⬚ ⬚ → ⬚ ► ⬚ ⬚ ⬚ ⬚ ⬚ ⬚

BOLVENTOR   Map 02 SX17

► ► ► ► **66% Colliford Tavern Campsite (SX171740)**
Colliford Lake, St Neot PL14 6PZ ☎ 01208 821335
📄 01208 821335
e-mail: info@colliford.com
website: www.colliford.com
Dir: Leave A30 1.25m W of Bolventor onto unclass rd signed Colliford Lake. Site 0.25m on left
★ ⬚ £10 ⬚ £10 ⬚ £10
Open Etr-Sep Booking advisable bank hols & Jul-Aug Last arrival 22.30hrs Last departure 11.00hrs
An oasis on Bodmin Moor, a small site with spacious grassy pitches and very good quality facilities. The park is surrounded by mature trees and very sheltered. A 3.5-acre site with 40 touring pitches.
Leisure: ⚖ **Facilities:** ⬔ ⊙ ⬚ ✕ ⬚ ⬚ ⬚
Services: ⬚ ⬚ ⬚ ⬚ ✕ ⬚ → ⬚ **Notes:** Dogs must be kept on leads ⬚ ⬚ ⬚ ⬚ ⬚

BOSWINGER   Map 02 SW94

PREMIER PARK

► ► ► ► ► **80% Sea View International Caravan & Camping Park (SW990412)**
PL26 6LL ☎ 01726 843425
📄 01726 843358

e-mail: enquiries@seaviewinternational.com
website: www.seaviewinternational.com
Dir: From St Austell take B3273 signed Mevagissey. Turn right before village, follow signs to site
⬚ £5.50-£19.90 ⬚ £5.50-£19.90 ⬚ £5.50-£19.90

Open 23 Mar-Sep (rs opening-May Shop & takeaway closed) Booking advisable end Jul-Aug Last arrival 22.00hrs Last dep 11.00hrs
This award-winning park is set in a beautiful environment overlooking Veryan Bay, with colourful landscaping including attractive flowers and shrubs. Many times a winner of AA awards it continues to offer an outstanding holiday experience. A 28-acre site with 165 touring pitches,
12 hardstandings and 38 statics.
Crazy golf, volleyball, badminton, petanque, putting
See advertisement on page 34
contd.

Leisure: ⬚ Indoor swimming pool   ⬚ Outdoor swimming pool   ⬚ Tennis court   ⬚ Games room   ⚖ Children's playground   ⬚ Stables
► 9/18 hole golf course   ⬚ Boats for hire   ⬚ Cinema   ⬚ Fishing   ⊙ Mini golf   ⬚ Watersports   ⬚ Separate TV room

Leisure: Facilities: Services: Notes: No guard dogs

BRYHER   **Map 02**
See **Scilly, Isles of**

BUDE   **Map 02 SS20**
See also **Kilkhampton**

66% Sandymouth Bay Holiday Park (SS214104)
Sandymouth Bay EX23 9HW
☎ 01288 352563 ▤ 01288 354822
e-mail: sandymouthbay@aol.com
website: www.sandymouthbay.co.uk
Dir: Signed off A39 approx 0.5m S of Kilkhampton, 4m N of Bude
★ ⌖ £6.75-£13 ⌖ £6.75-£13 ▲ £6.75-£13
Open Apr-Oct Booking advisable Jul & Aug Last arrival 22.00hrs Last departure 10.00hrs
A friendly holiday park with glorious and extensive sea views. Many on-site facilities, and an extensive entertainment programme for all ages. A 4-acre site with 100 touring pitches and 125 statics.
Sauna, solarium, crazy golf.
Leisure: Facilities: Services:

▶ ▶ ▶ ▶ ▶ 74% **Wooda Farm Park (SS229080)**
Poughill EX23 9HJ ☎ 01288 352069
🖷 01288 355258
e-mail: enquiries@wooda.co.uk
website: www.wooda.co.uk
Dir: 2m E from A39 at edge of Stratton follow unclass Coombe Valley road
★ ⚲ £7.50-£12 ⚲ £7.50-£12 ▲ £7.50-£12

Open Apr-Oct (rs Apr-end May & mid Sep-end Oct shop & restaurant hours limited) Booking advisable Jul-Aug Last arrival 20.00hrs Last departure noon
Attractive park set on raised ground overlooking Bude Bay, with lovely sea views. The park is divided into paddocks by hedges and mature trees, and offers high quality facilities and a
contd.

variety of activities. The sandy surfing beaches are a short drive away. A 12-acre site with 200 touring pitches, 37 hardstandings and 55 statics. Coarse fishing, clay pigeon shooting, pets' corner.
Leisure: ⚲ ⚲ ⚲ Facilities: ⚲ ⚲ ⚲ ⚲ ⚲ ⚲ ⚲ ⚲ ⚲
⚲ Services: ⚲ ⚲ ⚲ ⚲ ⚲ ⚲ ⚲ ⚲ ⚲ ⚲ ⚲ ⚲ ⚲ ⚲ ⚲ ⚲ ⚲ ⚲
Notes: No single sex groups of 3 or more
⚲ ⚲ ⚲ ⚲ ⚲ ⚲

See advertisement on page 34

▶ ▶ ▶ ▶ 68% **Budemeadows Touring Holiday Park (SS215012)**
EX23 0NA ☎ 01288 361646 🖷 01288 361646
e-mail: wendyjo@globalnet.co.uk
website: www.budemeadows.com
Dir: 3m S of Bude on A39. Park entered via layby
★ ⚲ £6-£12 ⚲ £6-£12 ▲ £6-£12
Open all year (rs Oct-Spring BH shop, bar & pool closed) Booking advisable Jul-Aug Last arrival 21.00hrs Last departure 11.00hrs
A very well kept site of distinction, with good quality facilities. Budemeadows is set on a gentle sheltered slope in nine acres of naturally landscaped parkland, surrounded by mature hedges. Just one mile from the surf and sand of Widemouth Bay, and three miles from the unspoilt resort town of Bude. A 9-acre site with 146 touring pitches, 24 hardstandings.
contd.

Budemeadows Touring Holiday Park

Table tennis, giant chess, baby changing facilities

Leisure: ⚡ ⚓ ⚁ ⌂ ◻   **Facilities:** ➡ ⚲ ⊙ ⚑ ✳ ⚓ ☾ ⚑

⚒ ⚶ ⚹   **Services:** ⚿ ▣ ☒ ⚊ ⊘ ⊞ ⚐ → ∪ ▶ ⊙ ⚑ ✦ ⚧ ⚙

⚌ ⚍ ⚎ ▨ ⚏

See advertisement on page 35

▶ ▶ ▶ **66% Upper Lynstone Caravan Park**
(SS205053)

Lynstone EX23 0LP ☎ 01288 352017
🖺 01288 359034
e-mail: reception@upperlynstone.co.uk
website: www.upperlynstone.co.uk
Dir: 0.75m S of Bude on coastal road to Widemouth Bay
★ ⚑ £7-£11 ⚑ £7-£11 ⚑ £7-£11
Open Apr-Oct Booking advisable Last arrival
22.00hrs Last departure 10.00hrs

contd.

Penhalt Farm Holiday Park, Widemouth Bay,
Bude, Cornwall EX23 0DG
Tel: (01288) 361210

Breathtaking Panoramic sea views of the dramatic
Atlantic Coastline. Ideal for walking the Famous
Heritage coastal footpath, surfing the splendid
beaches, cycling and touring.

Shop: power showers: laundry: new toilets: new
disabled facilities: baby changing unit: games
room: play area.

3 pennants   3 ticks

There are extensive views over Bude to be enjoyed
from this quiet family-run park set on sheltered
ground. There is a small shop selling an extensive
range of camping spares, and a well-equipped
children's playground. A path leads directly to the
coastal footpath with its stunning sea views, and
the old Bude Canal is a pleasant stroll away.
A 6-acre site with 65 touring pitches and 41 statics.
Baby changing room

Leisure: ⚡   **Facilities:** ⚲ ⊙ ⚑ ✳ ☾ ☾ ⚑ ⚑

Services: ⚿ ▣ ☒ ⚊ ⊘ ⊞ ⊤ → ∪ ▶ ⊙ ⚑ ✦ ⚧ ⚙

Notes: No groups ⚌ ⚍ ▨

▶ ▶ ▶ **58% Willow Valley Holiday Park**
(SS236078)

Bush EX23 9LB ☎ 01288 353104 🖺 01288 353104
e-mail: willowvalley@talk21.com
website: www.caravansitecornwall.co.uk
Dir: On A39, 0.5m N of junct with A3072 at Stratton
⚑ £5.50-£9 ⚑ £5.50-£9 ⚑ £5.50-£9

Open Mar-Dec Booking advisable Jul & Aug
Last arrival 21.00hrs Last departure noon
*Small sheltered park in Strat Valley with a stream
running through and level grassy pitches. There is
direct access off A39. A 3-acre site with 41 touring
pitches and 4 statics.*

Leisure: ⚡   **Facilities:** ⚲ ⊙ ⚑ ✳ ☾ ☾ ⚓ ⚑ ⚑

Services: ⚿ ▣ ☒ ⚊ ⊘ ⊞ ⊤ → ∪ ▶ ⊙ ⚑ ✦ ⚙

⚌ ⚍ ⚎ ▨ ⚏

CAMELFORD   **Map 02 SX18**

▶ ▶ ▶ **64% NEW Juliot's Well Holiday Park**
(SX095829)

PL32 9RF ☎ 01840 213302 🖺 01840 212700
e-mail: juliotswell@travelsmith.co.uk
website: www.holidaysincornwall.net
*Dir: From A39 in Camelford turn right onto B3266, at
T-junct turn left and site 300yds on right*
Open Apr-Oct
*Set in the wooded grounds of an old manor house,
this quiet site enjoys lovely and extensive views
across the countryside. A rustic inn on site offers
occasional entertainment, and there is plenty to do
both on and in the vicinity of the park. 60 touring
pitches.*

Leisure: ⚡ ⚓ ⚁ ⌂   **Facilities:** ➡ ⚲ ☾

Services: ✕ ⚿ ▣ ⚹

▶ ▶ ▶ **64% Lakefield Caravan Park (SX095853)**
Lower Pendavey Farm PL32 9TX ☎ 01840 213279
▤ 01840 213279
e-mail: lakefield@pendavey.fsnet.co.uk
website: www.lakefieldcaravanpark.co.uk
*Dir: From A39 in Camelford turn right onto B3266, then
right at T-junct and site 1.5m on left*
★ ⊞ £6-£10 ⊞ £6-£10 ▲ £5-£10
Open Etr or Apr-Oct Booking advisable Jul-Aug Last
arrival 22.00hrs Last departure noon
*Set in a rural location, this friendly park is part of a
specialist equestrian centre, and offers good quality
services. Riding lessons and hacks always available,
with BHS qualified instructor. A 5-acre site with 40
touring pitches.*
Own lake & full equestrian centre.
Leisure: ⚠ Facilities: ♺⊙❑⚹⚫⛟ⴕ
Services: ⊞▯▯⊘⊞Ⓣ✕→∪▶△⌿

CARBIS BAY — Map 02 SW53

▶ ▶ ▶ **63% Little Trevarrack Tourist Park
(SW525379)** ✕
Laity Ln TR26 3HW ☎ 01736 797580 ▤ 01736 797580
e-mail: littletrevarrack@hotmail.com
website: www.littletrevarrack.com
*Dir: From A30 take A3074 signed 'Carbis Bay & St Ives',
and turn left opposite the turning to the beach. 150yds
along road, over x-rds, site on right*
★ ⊞ £8.50-£13 ⊞ £8.50-£13 ▲ £8.50-£13
Open May-mid Sep Booking advisable summer hols
Last arrival 21.30hrs Last departure 10.00hrs
*A pleasant grass park set in countryside but close to
lovely beaches and local amenities. Plenty of tree
planting will result in more shelter and privacy in
this well landscaped park, and there are superb
views out to sea and towards Godrevy lighthouse.
A 20-acre site with 254 touring pitches.*
Leisure: ⚠ Facilities: ♺⊙⚹⚫⛟ⴕ
Services: ⊞▯▯▯⊘Ⓣ→∪▶⊙△⚥⚫⌿⚇⚍⚏

CARLEEN — Map 02 SW63

▶ ▶ ▶ **65% *Lower Polladras Touring Park
(SW617308)***
TR13 9NX ☎ 01736 762220 ▤ 01736 762220
e-mail: polladras@hotmail.com
*Dir: From A394 turn onto B3302 Hayle road at Hilltop
Garage, take 2nd turning on left to Carleen, site 2m on
right*
⊞ ⊞ ▲

contd.

Open Apr-Oct Booking advisable Jul-Aug
arrival 22.00hrs Last departure noon
*A rural park with extensive views of the
surrounding fields, appealing to families w..
the quiet countryside. The recently-planted t..
and shrubs are now maturing, and divide the area
into paddocks with spacious grassy pitches. A 4-
acre site with 60 touring pitches.*
Leisure: ⚠ Facilities: ♺⊙⚹⚹⛟
Services: ⊞▯▯⊘⊞Ⓣ→∪▶⚥⚫⌿

▶ ▶ ▶ **63% Poldown Caravan Park (SW629298)**
Poldown TR13 9NN ☎ 01326 574560
▤ 01326 574560
e-mail: poldown@poldown.co.uk
website: www.poldown.co.uk
*Dir: From Helston follow Penzance signs for 1m then
right onto B3302 to Hayle, 2nd left to Carleen, continue
0.5m to site.*
★ ⊞ £7.50-£10.50 ⊞ £7.50-£10.50 ▲ £7.50-£10.50
Open Apr-Oct (rs Apr & Oct Statics only) Booking
advisable Jul-Aug Last arrival 22.00hrs Last
departure noon
*A small, quiet site set in attractive countryside with
bright, newly painted toilet facilities. All of the level
grass pitches have electricity, and the sunny park is
sheltered by mature trees and shrubs. A 2-acre site
with 13 touring pitches and 7 statics.*
Leisure: ⚠ Facilities: ♺⊙⚹⚹⛟⚫⛡ⴕ
Services: ⊞▯▯⊘⊞→∪▶△⚥⌿⚫

CARLYON BAY — Map 02 SX05

▶ ▶ ▶ ▶ **75% Carlyon Bay Caravan & Camping
Park (SX052526)**
Bethesda, Cypress Av PL25 3RE ☎ 01726 812735
▤ 01726 815496
e-mail: holidays@carlyonbay.net
website: www.carlyonbay.net
*Dir: Off A390 W of St Blazey, turn left on A3092 for Par,
and right again in 0.5m. On private road to Carlyon Bay*
★ ⊞ £8-£17 ⊞ £7-£16 ▲ £8-£17

Open Etr-3 Oct (rs Etr-mid May & mid Sep-3 Oct
swimming pool, take-away & shop closed) Booking
advisable mid Jul-mid Aug Last arrival anytime Last
departure 11.00hrs
*An attractive, secluded site set amongst a belt of
trees with background woodland. The spacious
grassy park offers plenty of on-site attractions, with
occasional family entertainment, and it's less than
0.5m from a sandy beach. The Eden Project is only 2
miles away. A 35-acre site with 180 touring pitches,
4 hardstandings.*
contd.

Leisure: 🏊 Indoor swimming pool 🏊 Outdoor swimming pool ⚹ Tennis court ⚫ Games room ⚠ Children's playground ∪ Stables
▶ 9/18 hole golf course ⚥ Boats for hire ⚏ Cinema ⌿ Fishing ◉ Mini golf △ Watersports ⎁ Separate TV room

AA CAMPSITE OF THE YEAR 1999 – SOUTH WEST

Carlyon Bay
CARAVAN & CAMPING PARK

- ◆ Award winning family park 2km from the Eden Project
- ◆ Set in over 30 acres of meadows and mature woodlands.
  - ◆ Up to 180 touring pitches (no statics)
    - ◆ Footpath to large sandy beach
    - ◆ Close to championship Golf Course.
    - ◆ Heated Swimming and paddling pool.
      - ◆ Ben's Play World for kids nearby.
  - ◆ Badminton, Pool, Table-tennis and crazy-golf..

For colour brochure ring:
01726 812735
www.carlyonbay.net
E-mail: holidays@carlyonbay.net

  RAC AA

CARLYON BAY CARAVAN & CAMPING PARK, ST. AUSTEL, CORNWALL

Crazy golf, children's entertainment in Jul & Aug.
Leisure: ⚞ ☌ ⚘ ⚠ ▢ **Facilities:** ⚞⚘⚑✳⚒⚞⚏⚡
Services: ⚑⚏⚒⚏⚟⚑⚟→ ⚌ ⚟⚘⚞⚘✦⚒⚐⚑
⚞⚞⚞⚞⚞

▶ ▶ ▶ **63% East Crinnis Camping & Caravan Park**
(SX062528)
Lantyan, East Crinnis PL24 2SQ ☎ 01726 813023
🖷 01726 813023
e-mail: judith.olford@virgin.net
*Dir: From A390, Lostwithiel to St Austell, take A3082
signed Fowey at rdbt by Brittania Inn, site on left*
★ ⚏ £6-£12 ⚊ £6-£12

Open Etr-Oct Booking advisable Jul & Aug Last
arrival 21.00hrs Last departure 11.00hrs
contd.

A small rural park with spacious pitches set in
individual bays about one mile from the beaches at
Carlyon Bay. The friendly owners keep the site very
clean. The Eden Project is just 2 miles away. A 2-
acre site with 25 touring pitches, 6 hardstandings.
Leisure: ⚠ **Facilities:** ⚞⚘✳⚒⚡
Services: ⚑→⚌⚟⚒⚞⚒⚑⚑
Notes: Dogs must be kept on leads at all times

COVERACK   Map 02 SW71

▶ ▶ ▶ **62% Little Trevothan Caravan Park**
(SW772179)
Trevothen TR12 6SD ☎ 01326 280260
🖷 01326 280260
e-mail: trevothan@connexions.co.uk
website: www.connexions.co.uk/
trevothan/index.htm
*Dir: From A3083 turn left onto B3293 signed Coverack,
approx 2m after Goonhilly Earth Satellite Station right
at Zoar Garage on unclass rd. Take 3rd on left, site 0.5m
on right*
★ ⚏ £5.50-£7.50 ⚏ £5.50-£7.50 ⚊ £5.50-£7.50
Open Apr-Sep (rs Mar tents & tourers only) Booking
advisable Aug Last arrival 21.00hrs Last departure
noon
A level grassy park with mature hedging for shelter,
in a peaceful rural location, close to the unspoilt
fishing village of Coverack. A 10.5-acre site with 65
touring pitches and 17 statics.
Leisure: ⚘⚠▢ **Facilities:** ⚞⚘⚑✳⚒⚞⚒⚞⚡
Services: ⚑⚒⚏⚟⚟→⚘⚒⚑⚒

CRACKINGTON HAVEN   Map 02 SX19

▶ ▶ **59% NEW** Hentervene Camping & Caravan
Park (SX155944)
EX23 0LF ☎ 01840 230365
e-mail: contact@hentervene.co.uk
website: www.hentervene.co.uk
*Dir: 10m SW of Bude off A39, Bude-Wadebridge road,
approach via Masrshgate*
★ ⚏ fr £9 ⚏ fr £9 ⚊ fr £9
Open Etr-Oct Booking advisable School Hols
Last departure 12.00hrs
Set in a rural location two miles from the sandy
beach of this North Cornwall village in an Area of
Outstanding Natural Beauty. Pitches are sited in
scenic meadowland bordered by hedges. An 8-acre
site with 44 touring pitches, 5 hardstandings and
24 statics.
Toddler's play area & trampoline
Leisure: ⚘⚠▢ **Facilities:** ⚞⚘⚑✳⚒⚞⚡ **Services:**
⚑⚏⚒⚏⚒→⚘⚒⚑⚒ **Notes:** Dogs must be kept on
lead at all times except in dog walk ⚞⚞⚞⚞⚞

CRANTOCK (NEAR NEWQUAY)   Map 02 SW76

▶ ▶ ▶ ▶ **68% Trevella Tourist**
Park (SW801599)
TR8 5EW ☎ 01637 830308
🖷 01637 830155
e-mail: trevellapark@aol.com
website: www.trevella.co.uk
Dir: Between Crantock and A3075

★ ⚏ £7.20-£12.30 ⚏ £6.50-£11.50 ⚊ £7.20-£12.30
contd.

Open Etr-Oct Booking advisable bank hols &
Jul-Aug
*A well established and very well run family site,
with outstanding floral displays. Set in a rural area
close to Newquay, this attractive park boasts three
teeming fishing lakes for the experienced and
novice angler, and a superb outdoor swimming
pool and paddling area. All areas are neat and
clean. A 15-acre site with 295 touring pitches and
50 statics.*
Crazy golf, fishing & badminton.
Leisure: ₹ ♦ ⋀ ☐ **Facilities:** ⋔ ☉ ♖ ☀ ✆ ⚡ ⋤ ⋔
Services: ⚑ ⛽ ⬚ ⌧ 🖉 ⊞ ⊤ ✕ ⤵ → ∪ ⌐ ◎ ♤ ✦ ⚎ ⟋
⬤ ▭ ▦ ▨ ⬚

See advertisement on page 53

**► ► ► 60% Crantock Plains Touring Park
(SW805589)**
TR8 5PH ☎ 01637 830955 & 831273
website: www.crantock-plains.co.uk
Dir: Leave Newquay on A3075 take 3rd turn on right
signed to park and Crantock. Park on left in 0.75m,
on narrow road
⌁ ⌁ ⚶
Open Etr/Apr-Sep Booking advisable Jul-Aug Last
arrival 22.00hrs Last departure noon
*A small rural park with pitches on either side of a
narrow lane, surrounded by mature trees for
shelter. The family-run park offers fairly simple but
clean facilities. A 6-acre site with 60 touring pitches.*
Leisure: ♦ ⋀ **Facilities:** ⋔ ☉ ♖ ☀ ✆ ⋤ ⋔ ⋔
Services: ⚑ ⛽ ⬚ 🖉 ⊞ → ∪ ⌐ ♤ ⚎ ⟋

**► ► ► 66% Treago Farm Caravan Site
(SW782601)**
TR8 5QS ☎ 01637 830277 & 830522 ⬚ 01637 830277
Dir: From A3075 W of Newquay turn right for Crantock.
Site signed beyond village
★ ⌁ £8-£11 ⌁ £8-£11 ⚶ £8-£11
Open mid May-mid Sep (rs Apr-mid May & Oct no
shop or bar) Booking advisable Jun-Aug Last arrival
23.00hrs Last departure 18.00hrs
*Grass site in open farmland in a south-facing
sheltered valley. This friendly family park has direct
access to Crantock and Polly Joke beaches, National
Trust Land and many natural beauty spots. A 5-acre
site with 90 touring pitches and 10 statics.*
Leisure: ♦ ☐ **Facilities:** ⋔ ☉ ♖ ☀ ✆ ⋤ ⋔ ⋔
Services: ⚑ ⛽ ⬚ ⌧ 🖉 ⊞ ⊤ → ∪ ⌐ ◎ ♤ ⟋
⬤ ▭ ◎ ▨ ⬚

► ► ► 70% Cottage Farm (SW786589)
Treworgans TR8 5HH ☎ 01637 831083
Dir: From A392 towards Newquay, left onto A3075
towards Redruth. In 2m turn right signed for Cubert,
right again in 1.5m signed Crantock and left in 0.5m
⌁ £8-£9.50 ⌁ £8-£9.50 ⚶ £8-£9.50
Open Apr-Sep Booking advisable Last arrival
22.30hrs Last departure noon ⚒

contd.

*A small grassy touring park nestling in the tiny
hamlet of Treworgans, in sheltered open
countryside close to a lovely beach at Holywell Bay.
This quiet family-run park boasts very good quality
facilities. A 2-acre site with 45 touring pitches and 1
static.*
Facilities: ⋔ ☉ ♖ ☀ ✆ ⋤
Services: ⚑ ⛽ ⬚ 🖉 ⊞ ⤵ → ∪ ⌐ ◎ ♤ ✦ ⚎ ⟋

► ► ► 59% Inny Vale Holiday Village (SX170870)
PL32 9XN ☎ 01840 261248 ⬚ 01840 261740
e-mail: jn.c@which.net
website: www.innyvale.com
Dir: Signed off A395 on single track road to Tremail,
approx 1m from junct with A39
★ ⌁ £10-£12 ⌁ £10-£12 ⚶ £10-£12

Open Etr-Oct Booking advisable Jul & Aug Last
arrival 16.00hrs Last departure 10.00hrs
*A level sheltered park with a stream running
through, adjacent to and enjoying benefit from a
small holiday bungalow village. A 2-acre site with
27 touring pitches, 2 hardstandings.*
Shop
Leisure: ₹ ♦ ⋀ **Facilities:** ⋔ ♖ ☀ ✆ ⋤ ⋤ ⋔ ⋔
Services: ⚑ ⛽ ⬚ ⌧ 🖉 ⊞ ✕ ⤵ → ∪ ⟋ **Notes:** No single
sex groups, no groups of under 21yrs ⬤ ▭ ▨ ⬚

**► ► ► 65% NEW Carbeil Caravan & Camping
Park (SX318544)**
Treliddon Ln PL11 3LS ☎ 01503 250636
e-mail: mark@picklesm.freeserve.co.uk
website: www.carbeilholidaypark.co.uk
Dir: Turn off A38 towards Torpoint, then follow signs for
Downderry, 500yds past Spar shop turn left up
Treliddon Lane. Site 500yds up lane
★ ⌁ £7.50-£13 ⌁ £7.50-£13 ⚶ £5-£13
Open Mar-Oct Booking advisable
*Set in a sheltered valley in an attractive coastal
village, this compact park has terraced, mainly level
grass pitches, and offers good quality facilities. New
owners have transformed the site, and the narrow
entrance road has been widened to accept large
units. A 1.25-acre site with 24 touring pitches,
2 hardstandings and 4 statics.*
Leisure: ⋀ **Facilities:** ⋔ ☉ ☀ ✆ ⋤ ⋔ ⋔
Services: ⚑ ⛽ ⬚ ⌧ ⊞ ✕ → ∪ ⟋

EDGCUMBE   Map 02 SW73

▶ ▶ ▶ 60% **Retanna Holiday Park (SW711327)**
TR13 OEJ ☎ 01326 340643 🖹 01326 340643
e-mail: retannaholpark@lineone.net
website: www.retanna.co.uk
Dir: 100mtrs off A394, signposted
🛱 🛱 ▲
Open Apr-Oct Booking advisable Jul & Aug Last
arrival 21.00hrs Last departure 11.00hrs
*A small family-owned and run park in a rural
location midway between Falmouth and Helston.
Its well-sheltered grassy pitches make this an ideal
location for visiting the lovely beaches and towns
nearby. An 8-acre site with 24 touring pitches, 2
hardstandings and 28 statics.*
Leisure: ✦ ⋀ ⬚ Facilities: ♛ ⊙ ⍺ ✳ ⚲ ♜ ✠ ⊁
Services: ⌷ ⚇ ⓘ ⌀ ⒣ ⑆ 🖦 → ∪ ▶ ⊚ ⚞ ⚘
💳 💳 💳 💳 🈺

FALMOUTH   Map 02 SW83
See also **Perranarworthal**

▶ ▶ ▶ 62% *Pennance Mill Farm Touring Park
(SW792307)*
Maenporth TR11 5HJ ☎ 01326 317431 & 312616
🖹 01326 317431
*Dir: From A39 Truro-Falmouth follow brown 'Camping'
signs towards Maenporth Beach*
🛱 🛱 ▲
Open Etr-Xmas (rs Jan-Etr) Booking advisable Jan-
Etr Last arrival 22.00hrs Last departure 10.00hrs
*Set approximately half a mile from the safe, sandy
Bay of Maenporth this is a mainly level farm park in
a rural location sheltered by mature trees and
shrubs and divided into three meadows. It has a
large dairy herd and there is a milking parlour with
viewing gallery. A 6-acre site with 75 touring
pitches and 4 statics.*
Leisure: ⚲ ✦ ⋀ Facilities: ♛ ⊙ ⍺ ✳ ⚲ ♜ ✠
Services: ⌷ ⚇ ⓘ ⌀ ⒣ 🖦 → ∪ ▶ ⊚ ⚞ ⚘ ⚞ ⚘

▶ ▶ 67% **NEW** Tregedna Farm Touring Caravan &
Tent Park (SW785305)
Maenporth TR11 5HL ☎ 01326 250529
*Dir: Take A39 from Truro to Falmouth. Turn off right at
Hill-Head rdbt. Campsite 2.5m on right*
★ 🛱 £7.50-£8 🛱 £7.50-£8 ▲ £7.50-£8
Open Jun-Sep Booking advisable Last arrival
23.00hrs Last departure 13.00hrs
*Set in the picturesque Maen Valley, this gently-
sloping, south-facing park is part of a 100-acre farm.
It is surrounded by beautiful wooded countryside
just minutes from the beach, with spacious pitches
and well-kept facilities. A 12-acre site with 40
touring pitches.*
Leisure: ⋀ Facilities: ♛ ⊙ ✳ ⚲ ✠ Services: ⌷ ⓘ ⌀
→ ▶ ⊚ ⚞ ⚘ ⚇ ⚞ Notes: One dog only per pitch

PENMARLAM
Caravan, Camping & Boat Park
Bodinnick by Fowey, Cornwall PL23 1LZ
Tel: 01726 870088
Email: FHC@foweyharbour.co.uk

A tranquil site set in an area of outstanding natural
beauty above the Fowey Estuary.
Excellent access for towing/larger vehicles
Spacious, sheltered, level pitches
Own private quay, slipway and boat storage
Low season discounts
Rallies welcome
30 mins. from Eden Project
Ideal touring base
Penmarlam Quay Cottage also available to let,
excellent accommodation for up to eight people.

FOWEY   Map 02 SX15

▶ ▶ ▶ 65% **Penhale Caravan & Camping Park
(SX104526)**
PL23 1JU ☎ 01726 833425 🖹 01726 833425
e-mail: info@penhale-fowey.co.uk
website: www.penhale-fowey.co.uk
Dir: Off A3082, 0.5m before junct with B3269
★ 🛱 £5.75-£9 🛱 £5.75-£9 ▲ £5.75-£9

Open Etr/Apr-Oct Booking advisable
*Set on a working farm 1.5m from a sandy beach
and the town of Fowey, this grassy park has
stunning coastal and country views. Pitches are well
spaced, and there is an indoor room for wet
weather. A 4.5-acre site with 56 touring pitches and
14 statics.*
Leisure: ✦ Facilities: ♛ ⊙ ⍺ ✳ ⚲ ⚲
Services: ⌷ ⚇ ⓘ ⌀ → ∪ ▶ ⚞ ⚘ ⚘

England

▶ ▶ 68% NEW **Polglaze Farm (SX108529)**
PL23 1JZ ☎ 01726 833642
e-mail: alanmartin@polglazefarm.freeserve.co.uk
website: www.polglazefarm.freeserve.co.uk
Dir: 1m from Fowey on B3269 towards Bodmin
🚐 £5-£7 🚐 £5-£7 ⚠ £5-£7
Open Jul-Aug Booking advisable Jul-Aug Last
arrival 20.30hrs Last departure 10.30hrs
*A countryside park set in the extensive gardens of
the farmhouse in a peaceful area only a mile from
the harbourside town of Fowey. The gently-sloping
grassland includes some level pitches, and sanitary
facilities are housed in a new toilet block. The Eden
Project is 8 miles away. A 2-acre site with 30 touring
pitches, 3 hardstandings and 1 static.*
Facilities: 🌀⊙☀ **Services:** 🖵⊞🔌→∪▶◎🔻⚡🧴🍴🗑
Notes: Under 18yrs must be accompanied
by an adult

GOONHAVERN   **Map 02 SW75**

▶ ▶ ▶ ▶ 69% **Penrose Farm Touring Park
(SW795534)**
TR4 9QF ☎ 01872 573185
*Dir: From Exeter, take A30, continue past Bodmin and
Indian Queens. Shortly after Wind Farm take B3285
towards Perranporth, Penrose on left on entering
Goonhavern*
🚐 £9-£13.50 🚐 £9-£13.50 ⚠ £9-£13.50

Open Apr-Oct Booking advisable Jul & Aug
Last arrival 21.30hrs
*A quiet sheltered park set in five paddocks divided
by hedges and shrubs, only a short walk from the
village. Lovely floral displays enhance the park's
appearance, and the grass and hedges are neatly
trimmed. Four en suite family rooms are very
popular, and there is a good laundry. A 9-acre site
with 100 touring pitches, 8 hardstandings.*
Leisure: 🅰 **Facilities:** 🌀⊙🔍☀⚷🦽🛒🏠🚾🔛
Services: 🖵⊞🔌→∪▶⚡🧴

▶ ▶ ▶ ▶ 72% **Silverbow Park (SW782531)**
Perranwell TR4 9NX ☎ 01872 572347
📠 01872 572347
Dir: Adjacent to A3075, 0.5m S of village
🚐 🚐 ⚠
Open mid May-mid Sep (rs mid Sep-Oct & Etr-mid
May swimming pool & shop closed) Booking
advisable Jul-Aug Last arrival 22.00hrs Last
departure noon

contd.

*This park has a quiet garden atmosphere, and
appeals to families with young children. The
landscaped grounds and good quality toilet
facilities are maintained to a very high standard
with attention paid to detail. A 14-acre site with
100 touring pitches and 15 statics.*
Badminton courts, short mat bowls rink.
Leisure: 🔍🅰⚷🅰 **Facilities:** ➡🌀⊙🔍☀⚷🦽🛒🚾🔛
Services: 🖵⊞🔌→∪▶⚡🧴
Notes: No unaccompanied teenagers
See advertisement on page 59

▶ ▶ ▶ 66% *Perran Springs Touring Park
(SW796535)*
TR4 9QG ☎ 01872 540568 📠 01872 540568
e-mail: perransprings@cwcom.net
website: www.perransprings.co.uk
*Dir: From A30 right onto B3285 to Perranporth. Follow
tourist signs Perran Springs for 1.5m, entrance clearly
marked*
🚐 🚐 ⚠
Open Apr-Oct Booking advisable Jul-Aug Last
arrival anytime Last departure 10.00hrs
*Set in over 20 acres within a valley in peaceful
countryside, a spacious park with good modern
facilities. The park has its own coarse fishing lake
with free fishing, and other facilities include a
licensed shop, take-away and children's play area.
A 21-acre site with 120 touring pitches and 3 statics.*
Coarse fishing lake
Leisure: 🅰 **Facilities:** 🌀⊙🔍☀⚷🦽🛒🚾🔛
Services: 🖵⊞🔌→∪▶⚡🧴

▶ ▶ ▶ 65% *Roseville Holiday Park (SW787540)*
TR4 9LA ☎ 01872 572448 📠 01872 572448
*Dir: From mini rdbt in Goonhavern follow B3285
towards Perranporth, site 0.5m on right*
🚐 🚐 ⚠
Open Whit-Oct (rs Etr-Whit shop) Booking advisable
Jul-Aug Last arrival 21.30hrs Last departure
11.00hrs
*Recently upgraded to a good standard, this family
park is set in a rural location with sheltered, gently
sloping and level pitches. There are distant views
across to St Agnes Head, and an attractive
swimming pool complex has been added, plus a
new shop. A 7-acre site with 95 touring pitches.
Off-licence in shop.*
Leisure: 🔍🅰🅰⎚ **Facilities:** 🌀⊙🔍☀⚷🦽🛒🚾🔛
Services: 🖵⊞🔌→∪▶◎⚡🧴

▶ ▶ ▶ 64% NEW **Sunny Meadows Tourist Park
(SW782542)**
Rosehill TR4 9JT ☎ 01872 572548 & 571333
📠 01872 571491
*Dir: Off A30 onto B3285 signed Perranporth. At
Goonhavern rdbt left to Perranporth. Sunny Meadows
on left*
★ 🚐 £7-£9 🚐 £7-£9 ⚠ £7-£9
Open Etr-Oct Booking advisable mid Jul-Aug

contd.

Leisure: 🔍 Indoor swimming pool 🔍 Outdoor swimming pool 🔍 Tennis court 🔍 Games room 🅰 Children's playground ∪ Stables
▶ 9/18 hole golf course 🔻 Boats for hire 🎬 Cinema 🔍 Fishing ◎ Mini golf 🔺 Watersports 🖵 Separate TV room

A gently-sloping park with mostly level pitches set into three small hedge-lined paddocks. Run in its peaceful rural location by a friendly family, the park is just 2 miles from the long sandy beach at Perranporth. A 14.5-acre site with 52 touring pitches, 1 hardstanding.
Pool table & TV family room

Leisure: ⚐ **Facilities:** ⬤☉❄♿⌕☂☇

Services: ⚑⊘☒☐→∪▶✦☒⚡

Notes: Dogs must be kept on leads ⬤☰

GORRAN   Map 02 SW94

▶ ▶ ▶ 69% **Tregarton Park (SW984437)**
PL26 6NF ☎ 01726 843666 ▤ 01726 844481
e-mail: holidays@tregarton.co.uk
website: www.tregarton.co.uk
Dir: From St Austell S on B3273, at top of Pentewan Hill turn right towards Gorran, follow tourist signs
★ ⚘ £4.99-£14.50 ⚘ £4.99-£14.50 ▲ £4.99-£14.50

Open Apr-Oct (rs mid May-mid Sep swimming pool & shop) Booking advisable Jun-Sep Last arrival 21.00hrs Last departure 11.00hrs
A sheltered park set in lovely countryside lying two miles from the sea and off a minor road to Gorran Haven. Many of the facilities have been upgraded and improved, and this friendly park attracts couples and families who want a quiet holiday. A 12-acre site with 130 touring pitches, 15 hardstandings.
Information centre, Off Licence, badminton, football.

Leisure: ⚒⚐ **Facilities:** ⬤☉⚭❄⌕☂⚡⊞☂☇

Services: ⚑☒▮⊘☒☐♨♦→∪▶△✦✦✦

⬤☰☰▦⑤

▶ ▶ ▶ 63% **Treveor Farm Caravan & Camping Site (SW988418)**
PL26 6LW ☎ 01726 842387 ▤ 01726 842387
Dir: From St Austell bypass left onto B3273 for Mevagissey. On hilltop before descent to village turn right on unclass road for Gorran. Right in 3.5m, site on right
★ ⚘ £5-£12 ⚘ £5-£12 ▲ £5-£12
Open Apr-Oct Booking advisable Last arrival 20.00hrs Last departure 11.00hrs
A small family run camping park with good facilities, situated on a working farm. There is a large coarse fishing pond, and this quiet park is close to the beaches. A 4-acre site with 50 touring pitches.

Leisure: ⚐ **Facilities:** ⬤☉⚭❄⌕

Services: ⚑☒→✦✦⚡

Ⓤ **Treveague Farm Campsite (SX002410)**
PL26 6NY ☎ 01726 842295
e-mail: treveague.farm@virgin.net
Dir: From St Austell take B3273 towards Mevagissey, past Pentewan, turn right signed Gorran. Past Heligan Gardens towards Gorran Churchtown, past pub. Right signed Penare. 500yds left at x-rds, site in 0.5m.
⚘ £8-£15 ⚘ £8-£15 ▲ £6-£12
Open Apr-Oct Booking advisable at all times Last arrival 20.00hrs Last departure 12.00hrs
At the time of going to press the pennant classification for this site was not confirmed.
A 4-acre site with 80 touring pitches.
Fridges & freezers available

Leisure: ⚐ **Facilities:** ⬤☉❄⌕☂☇

Services: ☐→✦✦⚡ **Notes:** No noise late at night & dogs must be kept under control

GORRAN HAVEN   Map 02 SX04

▶ ▶ 60% **Trelispen Caravan & Camping Park (SX008421)**
PL26 6HT ☎ 01726 843501 ▤ 01726 843501
e-mail: trelispen@care4free.net
Dir: From St Austell take B3273 for Mevagissey, on hilltop at x-roads before descent into Mevagissey turn right on unclass road to Gorran. Through village and 2nd right towards Gorran Haven, site signed on left.
⚘ ⚘ ▲
Open Etr & Apr-Oct Booking advisable Last arrival 22.00hrs Last departure noon
A very simple site in a beautiful quiet location within easy reach of beaches. The dated toilets have plenty of hot water, and there is a small laundry. A 2-acre site with 40 touring pitches.
A 30-acre nature reserve may be visited.

Leisure: ⚐ **Facilities:** ⬤☉❄ **Services:** ⚑☐→✦✦⚡

HAYLE   Map 02 SW53

66% **St Ives Bay Holiday Park (SW577398)**
73 Loggans Rd, Upton Towans
TR27 5BH ☎ 01736 752274 ▤ 01736 754523
e-mail: stivesbay@dialpipex.com
Dir: Exit A30 at Hayle. Immediate right at mini-rdbts. Park entrance 0.5m on left
⚘ ⚘ ▲

Open 3 May-27 Sep (rs Etr-3 May & 27 Sep-25 Oct no entertainment, food & bar service) Booking advisable Jan-Mar Last arrival 23.00hrs Last departure 09.00hrs ⊘
contd.

An extremely well maintained holiday park with a relaxed atmosphere, built on sand dunes adjacent to a 3-mile long beach. The touring section forms a number of separate locations in amongst the statics. The park is specially geared for families and couples, and as well as the large indoor swimming pool there are two pubs with seasonal entertainment. A 90-acre site with 240 touring pitches and 250 statics.
Crazy golf, video room.

Leisure: ⚹ ⚲ ⚱ ⚼ ▱ **Facilities:** ⚇⊙⚘☀⚏⚎

Services: ⚑⚙⚐⚁⚄⚏⚐✕⚱→∪▶⚒

⊜ ▭ ▦ ▩ ⚙

▶ ▶ ▶ **65% Higher Trevaskis Caravan Park (SW611381)**
Gwinear Rd, Conner Downs TR27 5JQ
☎ 01209 831736

SILVER

Dir: At Hayle rdbt on A30 take 1st exit signed Connor Downs, in 1m turn right signed Carnhell Green. Site 0.75m just past level crossing
★ ⚏ £6-£11 ⚏ £6-£11 ▲ £6-£11
Open mid Apr-Oct Booking advisable May-Sep Last arrival 20.00hrs Last departure 11.00hrs
A rural, grassy site divided into sheltered paddocks, and with views towards St Ives. This secluded park is personally run by owners who keep it quiet and welcoming. Fluent German spoken. A 6.5-acre site with 82 touring pitches, 3 hardstandings.

Leisure: ⚱ **Facilities:** ⚇⊙⚘☀⚎⚏⚑

Services: ⚑⚙⚁⚄⚏⚐→▶⊙⚏⚒

▶ ▶ ▶ **62% Parbola Holiday Park (SW612366)**
Wall, Gwinear TR27 5LE ☎ 01209 831503
🖷 01209 831503
e-mail: bookings@parbola.co.uk
website: www.parbola.co.uk
Dir: At Hayle rdbt on A30 take Connor Downs exit. In 1m turn right signed Carnhell Green. In village right to Wall and site in village on left
⚏⚑▲
Open Etr-Sep (rs Etr-spring bank hol & Sep shop & swimming pool closed) Booking advisable Jul-Aug Last arrival 22.00hrs Last departure noon ⚹
A level grassy site in Cornish downland, with pitches in both woodland and open areas. The spacious park is centrally located for touring the seaside resorts and towns in the area. A 13.5-acre site with 110 touring pitches and 28 statics.
Crazy golf & table tennis

Leisure: ⚹ ⚲ ⚱ ⚼ ▱ **Facilities:** ⚇⊙⚘☀⚎⚏⚑⚏

Services: ⚑⚙⚁⚄⚏⚐→∪▶⊙⚒⊜▭▦⚙

▶ ▶ ▶ **64% NEW Treglisson Camping & Caravan Park (SW581367)**
Wheal Alfred Rd TR27 5JT ☎ 01736 753141
Dir: 4th exit off rdbt on A30 at Hayle. Continue 100mtrs and at 1st mini rdbt turn left. Follow road 1.5km past golf course and Treglisson sign visible on left
Open Etr-Oct Booking advisable Jul-Aug Last arrival 20.00hrs Last departure 11.00hrs

contd.

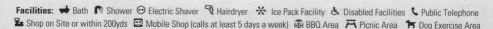

Facilities: 🛁 Bath 🚿 Shower ⊙ Electric Shaver 🪮 Hairdryer ❄ Ice Pack Facility ♿ Disabled Facilities ☎ Public Telephone
🏪 Shop on Site or within 200yds 🖬 Mobile Shop (calls at least 5 days a week) 🍖 BBQ Area 🌲 Picnic Area 🐕 Dog Exercise Area

...ecluded site in a peaceful wooded ... a former apple and pear orchard. This quiet rural site has a well-planned modern toilet block and level grass pitches, and is just 2 miles from the glorious beach at Hayle with its vast stretch of golden sand. A 3-acre site with 30 touring pitches.
Tourist infomation available

Leisure: ⚓ ⚏ **Facilities:** ╠⊙⚑✻ᕈ⚏⊞☃☂
Services: ⊟⬒⊟→▶◮⌇⛟ **Notes:** Max 6 people to a pitch, dogs must be on lead at all times

---

HELSTON   Map 02 SW62

▶ ▶ ▶ **64% Trelowarren Caravan & Camping Park (SW721238)**
Mawgan TR12 6AF ☎ 01326 221637 ▤ 01326 221427
Dir: From Helston on A3083 turn left past Culdrose Naval Air Station onto B3293. Site signed on left in 1.5m
★ ⛺ £7-£8 ⛟ £7-£8 ▲ £7-£8

contd.

Enjoy the real warmth of Cornwall

among our sheltered orchards and walled gardens, on a 1000 acre Cornish manor close to Frenchman's Creek on the Helford River.

Upgraded facilities for 2003. Electric hook-ups, Hard standings (electric), Rallies welcome, Gas, Take-away & Pub, Heated toilets & showers, SEASONAL PITCHES.

TRELOWARREN
Touring Caravan & Camping Park

Trelowarren, Mawgan, Helston, Cornwall TR12 6AF
Telephone: 01326 221637
www.trelowarren.co.uk

Open Apr-Sep Booking advisable bank hols & Jul-Aug Last departure noon
A very attractive setting in the extensive park of Trelowarren House. The superb location is over a mile from the nearest road, and visitors can explore the gardens and follow several woodland walks. A bar and bistro are popular attractions. A 20-acre site with 225 touring pitches, 14 hardstandings.

Leisure: ⚓ ⚏ ⊡ **Facilities:** ⇀╠⊙⚑✻ᕈ⚏⛟☃☂
Services: ⊟⬒⚑⌗⊘⊞⊟✕⬚⇀→∪▶

HOLYWELL BAY   Map 02 SW75

65% Holywell Bay Holiday Park (SW773582)
TR8 5PR ☎ 01637 871111
▤ 01637 850818
e-mail: enquiries@parkdean.com
website: www.parkdean.com
Dir: Leave A30 onto A392, take A3075 signed Redruth, then left in 2m signed Holywell/Cubert. Through Cubert past Trevornick to park on left
★ ⛺ £6-£18.50 ⛟ £6-£18.50 ▲ £6-£18.50
Open Mar-Oct Booking advisable Jun-Aug Last arrival 23.00hrs Last departure 10.00hrs ⌗
Close to lovely local beaches in a rural location, this level grassy park borders on National Trust land, and is only a short distance from the Cornish Coastal Path. The park provides a family entertainment programme. Some pitches are rather small and cramped. A 40-acre site with 75 touring pitches and 149 statics.

Leisure: ⚓ ⚏ **Facilities:** ╠⊙⛟⚑☃☂
Services: ⊟⬒⚑⌗⊘⊞⊟⬚→∪▶⊙◮⌇
Notes: No single sex groups under 25yrs
⬛⬛⬛

See advertisement on page 52

68% Trevornick Holiday Park (SW776586)
TR8 5PW ☎ 01637 830531
▤ 01637 831000
e-mail: info@trevornick.co.uk
website: www.trevornick.co.uk
Dir: 3m from Newquay off A3075, Newquay to Redruth road. Follow signs to Cubert & Holywell Bay
★ ⛺ £7.70-£13.30 ⛟ £7.70-£13.30 ▲ £7.70-£13.30
Open Etr & mid May-mid Sep Booking advisable Jul-Aug Last arrival 21.00hrs Last dep 10.00hrs
A large seaside holiday complex with excellent facilities and amenities. There is plenty of entertainment including a children's club and an evening cabaret, adding up to a full holiday experience for all the family. A sandy beach is a 15-minute footpath walk away. The park has 68 ready-erected tents for hire. A 20-acre site with 450 touring pitches, 6 hardstandings and 68 statics.
Fishing, golf course, entertainment.

Leisure: ⚓ ⚓ ⚏ **Facilities:** ⇀╠⊙⚑✻ᕈ⚏⛟☂
☃ **Services:** ⊟⬒⚑⌗⊘⊞⊟✕⬚→∪▶⊙◮⌇⬚
Notes: Families and couples only ⬛⬛⬛⬛ ⑤

See advertisement on page 54

INDIAN QUEENS — Map 02 SW95

▶ **58% *Gnome World Touring Park (SW890599)***
Moorland Rd TR9 6HN ☎ 01726 860812
*Dir: Signed from slip road at A30 & A39 rdbt in village
of Indian Queens - park on old A30, now unclass rd*
🚐🚐🛆

Open Etr-Oct (rs Nov-Mar) Booking advisable Jul-
Aug Last arrival 22.00hrs Last departure noon
*Set in extensive farmland, this park provides
touring pitches in the centre of a field, with statics
around the perimeter. It offers fairly basic but clean
facilities. A 4.5-acre site with 50 touring pitches.
Nature trail.*
Leisure: ⚶ **Facilities:** 🖟⊙🖥※🕭ୖ🞉🎗🖈🛏🏕
Services: 🖳⌀🖂→∪🖌⊡
Notes: Dogs must be kept on leads

JACOBSTOW — Map 02 SX19

▶ ▶ ▶ **64% *Edmore Tourist Park (SX184955)***
Edgar Rd, Wainhouse Corner EX23 0BJ
☎ 01840 230467 🖥 01840 230467
website: www.cornwallvisited.co.uk
Open 1 wk before Etr-Oct
*A quiet family-owned site in a rural location with
extensive views, set close to the sandy surfing
beaches of Bude, and the unspoilt sandy beach and
rock pools at Crackington Haven. Friendly owners
keep all facilities in a very good condition. A 3-acre
site with 28 touring pitches.*
Leisure: ⚶ **Facilities:** 🖟 **Services:** ⊡

KENNACK SANDS — Map 02 SW71

▶ ▶ ▶ **61% *Chy-Carne Holiday Park (SW725164)***
Kuggar, Ruan Minor TR12 7LX ☎ 01326 290200
e-mail: muxlow@ntlworld.com
website: www.caravancampingsites.co.uk/
cornwall/chycarne
*Dir: From A3083 turn left on B3293 after Culdrose Naval
Air Station. At Goonhilly ESS right onto unclass road
signed Kennack Sands. Left in 3m at junct*
★ 🚐 £10.50-£13.50 🚐 £10.50-£13.50 🛆 £6-£9
Open Etr-Oct Booking advisable Aug Last arrival
dusk
*Small but spacious park in a quiet, sheltered spot,
with extensive sea and coastal views from the
grassy touring area. A 6-acre site with 14 touring
pitches and 18 statics.*
Leisure: ⚭⚶ **Facilities:** 🖟⊙※🕭ୖ🞉🖈🛏
Services: 🖳⊡🖂⌀⊡⊡ **Notes:** No single
sex groups without permission

▶ ▶ ▶ **61% Gwendreath Farm Holiday Park
(SW738168)**
TR12 7LZ ☎ 01326 290666
e-mail: tom.gibson@virgin.net
website: www.tomandlinda.co.uk
*Dir: From A3083 turn left past Culdrose Naval Air
Station onto B3293. Right past Goonhilly ESS signed
Kennack Sands, left in 1m*
★ 🚐 £5.60-£7.20 🚐 £5.60-£7.20 🛆 £5.60-£7.20
Open Etr-Oct Booking advisable all times Last
departure 10.00hrs
*A grassy park in an elevated position with extensive
sea and coastal views. The beach is just a short
walk through the woods. Campers can use the
shop, bar, restaurant and takeaway at an adjoining
site. A 5-acre site with 10 touring pitches and 30
statics.*
Leisure: ⚶ **Facilities:** 🖟⊙※🕭ୖ🞉🖈🛏
Services: 🖳⊡🖂⌀⊡⊡→∪🖌🜄⌀🛆🖈🖳

▶ ▶ ▶ **63% Silver Sands Holiday
Park (SW727166)**
Gwendreath TR12 7LZ
☎ 01326 290631 🖥 01326 290631
e-mail: enquiries@silversandsholidaypark.co.uk
website: www.silversandsholidaypark.co.uk
*Dir: From Helston take A3083, then B3293, after 4m
right at x-roads signed Kennack Sands, continue 1.5m,
left at sign for Gwendreath, park 1m down lane*
★ 🚐 £7.30-£10.30 🚐 £7.30-£10.30 🛆 £5.70-£7.70
Open May-Sep Booking advisable Jul-Aug Last
arrival 21.00hrs Last departure 11.00hrs
*A small park in a remote location with individually
screened pitches providing sheltered sun-traps.
This family-owned park has access to the shop,
bar/restaurant and takeaway at an adjacent park. A
9-acre site with 34 touring pitches and 16 statics.*
Leisure: ⚶ **Facilities:** 🖟⊙※🕭ୖ🖈🛏
Services: 🖳⊡🖂⌀⊡→🜄🖌 **Notes:** No groups

KILKHAMPTON — Map 02 SS21

▶ ▶ ▶ ▶ **70% Penstowe Caravan &
Camping Park (SS230100)**
Penstowe Manor EX23 9QY ☎ 01288 321354
🖥 01288 321273
e-mail: info@penstoweleisure.co.uk
website: www.penstoweleisure.co.uk
*Dir: A39 4m N of Bude, turn left to Sandymouth site
200yds on right*
★ 🚐 £7-£12.50 🚐 £7-£12.50 🛆 £6-£12.50

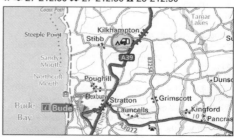

contd.

Open Apr-Oct Booking advisable August Last arrival 22.00hrs Last departure 10.00hrs
An all touring park with quality facilities located approximately two miles from Sandymouth Bay with its beaches and surf. This park has all level hardstanding and grassy pitches and visitors can take advantage of the adjoining Penstone Leisure Club which is just 0.25 mile away, on a private road through the estate. Some of the amenities require a small membership charge.
A 6-acre site with 80 touring pitches.
Sports facilities, 10pin bowling, green bowls
Leisure: ⚐ 🎾🏊⚓🎣 ⚅ **Facilities:** ⬤⊙⚋☼⚓♿⚹🕻♨ ⏏ ❟
Services: 🖭🗜🆚🅰🚿✕🧤➔∪🍴⬤ 🚽 ▦ ❊ 🔄 🔊

▶ ▶ **64% Tamar Lake (SS002818)**
Upper Tamar Lake ☎ 01288 321712
Dir: From A39 at Kilkhampton turn onto B3254, turn left in 0.5m onto unclass road and follow signs for approx 4m to site
★ 🚐 fr £7.40 🚐 fr £7.40 ▲

Open 31 Mar-Oct Booking advisable
A well-trimmed site overlooking the lake and surrounding countryside, with several signed walks. The site benefits from the excellent facilities provided for the watersports centre and coarse anglers, with a rescue launch on the lake when the flags are flying. A good family site, with Bude's beaches and surfing waves only 8m away. A 2-acre site with 36 touring pitches.
Watersports centre, canoeing, sailing & windsurfing
Leisure: ⚅ **Facilities:** ⬤♿🕻♨⏏❟ **Services:** ✕⏏
➔∪⚑➔ ✒ **Notes:** Dogs must be kept on a lead ⬤
▦ ❊ 🔄

LANDRAKE   Map 02 SX36

▶ ▶ ▶ **69% Dolbeare Caravan & Camping Park**
(SX363616)
St Ive Rd PL12 5AF ☎ 01752 851332 📠 01752 851332
e-mail: dolbeare@btopenworld.com
website: www.dolbeare.co.uk
Dir: A38 to Landrake, 4m W of Saltash. At footbridge over A38 turn N following signs to site (0.75m from A38)
🚐 £8.50-£9.50 🚐 £8.50-£9.50 ▲ £3.50-£8.50
Open all year Booking advisable peak periods only Last arrival 23.00hrs Last departure 12.00hrs
A mainly level grass site with trees and bushes set in meadowland. The keen and friendly owners set high standards, and the park is always neat and clean. A 4-acre site with 60 touring pitches.

contd.

Dolbeare Caravan and Camping Park
Volley ball pitch, boules pitch, information centre.
Leisure: ⚅ **Facilities:** ⬤⊙⚋☼♿🕻♨⏏❟
Services: 🖭🗜🅰🚿➔⚑⚑✒

LAUNCELLS   Map 02 SS20

▶ ▶ ▶ **61% Red Post Holiday Park (SS264052)**
EX23 9NW ☎ 01288 381305
e-mail: redpostinn@aol.com
Dir: At junct of A3072/B3254, 4m from Bude, entered by side of Red Post Inn
★ 🚐 £6.50-£8.50 🚐 £6.50-£8.50 ▲ £4-£6
Open 31 Mar-Oct Booking advisable Jul & Aug Last arrival 23.00hrs Last departure 11.00hrs
Set in rolling countryside just 4 miles from the seaside town of Bude, a fairly simple park at the rear of a country inn. Friendly owners keep the buildings looking fresh and clean. A 4-acre site with 50 touring pitches.
Leisure: ⚅ **Facilities:** ⬤⊙☼🕻♨❟
Services: 🖭🗜🅰✕⏏➔∪🍴⬤♨✒

LEEDSTOWN (NEAR HAYLE)   Map 02 SW63

▶ ▶ ▶ **65% Calloose Caravan &**
Camping Park (SW597352)
TR27 5ET ☎ 01736 850431 📠 01736 850431
e-mail: calloose@hotmail.com
website: www.calloose.co.uk
Dir: From Hayle take B3302 to Leedstown, turn left opp village hall, before entering village, park 0.5m on left at bottom of hill
🚐 🚐 ▲
Open Mar-Nov (rs Mar-mid May & late Sep-Nov swimming pool closed) Booking advisable Etr, May bank hols & Jun-Aug Last arrival 22.00hrs Last departure 11.00hrs
A comprehensively equipped leisure park in a remote rural setting in a small river valley. This very good park is busy and bustling, and offers bright and clean facilities. A 12.5-acre site with 120 touring pitches and 17 statics.
Crazy golf, skittle alley
Leisure: 🎾⚓⚅🏓 **Facilities:** ⬤⊙⚋☼♿🕻♨▦❟
Services: 🖭🗜🆚🅰🚿✕⏏➔✒ **Notes:** No single
sex groups ⬤ ▦ ❊ 🔄 🔊

See advertisement on page 43

LOOE   Map 02 SX25

63% Tencreek Holiday Park (SX233525)
Polpero Rd PL13 2JR ☎ 01503 262447
🖷 01503 262760
e-mail: reception@tencreek.co.uk
website: www.dolphinholidays.co.uk
Dir: Take A387 1.25m from Looe. Site on left
★ ⊞ £8-£15 ⊞ £8-£15 ▲ £8-£15
Open all year Booking advisable Jul & Aug
Last arrival 23.00hrs Last departure 10.00hrs
Occupying a lovely position with extensive countryside and sea views, this holiday centre is in a rural spot but close to Looe and Polperro. There is a full family entertainment programme, with indoor and outdoor swimming pools and an adventure playground. A 14-acre site with 254 touring pitches and 101 statics.
Nightly entertainment, solarium, 45m-flume in pool
Leisure: ᕽ ᕤ ৎ /ᕳ **Facilities:** ⌀⊙৭⋇ᕼৎ ⅀ᕝ
Services: ▣⊡ⵚℓ⌀⊟⚀⅋ⓧ╬→∪ᖴ⌂ᖵ⅋ᕵ⌇
Notes: Families & couples only ⬤ ▤ ▥ ▨ 🖃 🖾

► ► ► 65% **NEW** Camping Caradon Tourin
Park (SX218539)
Trelawne PL13 2NA ☎ 01503 272388
e-mail: moorings.9@virgin.net
website: www.campingcaradon.co.uk
Dir: Signed off B3359 near junct with A387, between Looe and Polperro
★ ⊞ £6.50-£9.50 ⊞ £6.50-£9.50 ▲ £6.50-£9.50
Open Etr-Oct Booking advisable Jul-Aug Last arrival 22.00hrs Last departure 12.00hrs
Set in a quiet rural location between the popular coastal resorts of Looe and Polperro, this family-run park is just 1.5 miles from the beach at Talland Bay. New owners have upgraded the bar and restaurant, and all facilities are very clean. A 3.5-acre site with 85 touring pitches.
Leisure: ᕽ /ᕳ **Facilities:** ⌀⊙৭⋇ᕼ⅀ᕝ
Services: ▣⊡ⵚℓ⌀⊟⚀ⓧ→⌂⅋⅋⌇ ⬤ ▤ ▥

► ► ► 67% Polborder House Caravan & Camping
Park (SX283557)
Bucklawren Rd, St Martins PL13 1QR
☎ 01503 240265 🖷 01503 240700
e-mail: rlf.polborder@virgin.net
website: www.peaceful-polborder.co.uk
Dir: On approaching Looe from E on A387, follow B3253 for 1m, then bear left at signpost to Polborder & Monkey Sanctuary. Site 0.5m on right
★ ⊞ £6.50-£9.50 ⊞ £6.50-£9.50 ▲ £6.50-£9.50
Open Etr or Apr-Oct Booking advisable Jul-Aug Last arrival 22.00hrs Last departure noon   *contd.*

All of the campsites in this guide
are inspected annually by an
experienced team of inspectors

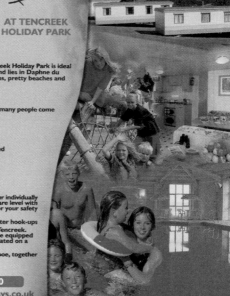

AT TENCREEK HOLIDAY PARK

The Setting

Lying close to the South Cornwall coast, in a rural but not isolated position Tencreek Holiday Park is ideal for exploring Cornwall and South Devon. Tencreek is the closest park to Looe and lies in Daphne du Maurier country: beyond are Bodmin Moor, Dartmoor, traditional Cornish towns, pretty beaches and picturesque ports such as Polperro and Fowey.

The Facilities

Tencreek is well known for its range of facilities, and that's one of the reasons so many people come back here again and again.

- Indoor and outdoor swimming pools
- 45-metre water flume
- Adventure playground
- Amusements
- Indoor sports (darts, pool)
- Live entertainment in the club
- Food shop and snack bar
- Modern toilet and laundry facilities
- Satellite TV in clubhouse
- FREE hot showers
- Public telephones
- Toilet facilities for the disabled
- Baby-changing room
- Children's Club
- Solarium

Accommodation

It's so easy when you bring your touring caravan or motor caravan to Tencreek. Our individually marked pitches are numbered ~ we can reserve a specific one on request. Most are level with good drainage, accessed by hard surfaced or tarmac roads, with street lighting for your safety and security.

It couldn't be simpler! Advance booking recommended, especially for electric/water hook-ups

A sea view guaranteed...that's just one of the pleasures of a caravan holiday at Tencreek. Whether you choose one which sleeps 6 or 8 people, our modern caravans come equipped with the items you need to make your holiday easy. Extra guests are accommodated on a double put-up-in the lounge.

The best of both worlds...your own holiday cottage in the pretty coastal town of Looe, together with FREE use of Tencreek Holiday Park's facilities!

LOOE • CORNWALL • PL13 2JR

TELEPHONE: **01503 262447**   FAX: **01503 262760**
E-MAIL: reception@tencreek.co.uk   www.dolphinholidays.co.uk

Facilities: ⬌ Bath   ⌀ Shower   ⊙ Electric Shaver   ৭ Hairdryer   ⋇ Ice Pack Facility   ᕼ Disabled Facilities   ৎ Public Telephone
⅀ Shop on Site or within 200yds   ⚀ Mobile Shop (calls at least 5 days a week)   ᕱ BBQ Area   ⌐ Picnic Area   ✕ Dog Exercise Area

A very neat and well-kept small grassy site on high ground above Looe in a peaceful rural setting. Friendly and enthusiastic owners. A 3-acre site with 31 touring pitches, 6 hardstandings.
Washing/food prep sinks, off-licence, info centre

Leisure: ⚲ **Facilities:** ╟⊙☖☀⛾⚓⛃☂
Services: ⚡☺⛽⚓⟶⛂⚑⟶♪△⅄⚵⚭⚋◨

▶ ▶ ▶ 65% **Talland Caravan Park** (SX230516)
Talland Bay PL13 2JA ☎ 01503 272715
🖷 01503 272224
website: www.tallandcaravanpark.co.uk
Dir: 1m from A387 on unclass road to Talland Bay
★ ⛺ £8-£15 ⛟ £7.50-£13

Open Apr-Oct Booking advisable School hols
Overlooking the sea just 300 yards from Talland Bay's two beaches, this quiet park has an elevated touring area with sea views. Surrounded by unspoilt countryside and with direct access to the coastal footpath, it is approximately halfway between Looe and Polperro. A 4-acre site with 80 touring pitches and 46 statics.
Leisure: ⚲ **Facilities:** ╟⊙☖☀⛾⚓⛃☂ ☂
Services: ⚡☺⛽⚑⚋⚓◨⟶✕⚱⟶♪△⅄⚵⚭⚋◨

▶ ▶ ▶ 66% **Tregoad Farm Camping & Caravanning Park** (SX272560)
St Martin's PL13 1PB ☎ 01503 262718
🖷 01503 264777
e-mail: tregoadfarmccp@aol.com
website: www.cornwall-online.co.uk/tregoad
Dir: Signed with direct access from B3253, or from E on A387 follow B3253 for 1.75m towards Looe and site on left
★ ⛺ £8.50-£12.50 ⛟ £8.50-£12.50 ▲ £5-£8.50
Open Apr-Oct Booking advisable Jul & Aug Last arrival 21.00hrs Last departure 12.00hrs
A terraced grassy site with fine sea and rural views, approx 1.5m from Looe. The upgraded facilities are well maintained and clean. A 10-acre site with 150 touring pitches and 3 statics.
Fishing lake.
Leisure: ⚓ ⚲ **Facilities:** ╟⊙☖☀⚓⛃☂☂
Services: ⚡☺⛽⚱⚓◨⟶✕⚱⟶⊍▶⊙△⅄⚇♪
⚭⚋◨◎◨

▶ ▶ ▶ 71% **Trelay Farmpark** (SX210544)
Pelynt PL13 2JX ☎ 01503 220900 🖷 01503 220900
Dir: Approaching from Looe on B3359 towards Pelynt, 1m on right
★ ⛟ £7-£9.50 ⛟ £7-£9.50 ▲ £7-£9.50
Open Apr-Oct Booking advisable Jul & Aug Last arrival 21.00hrs Last departure 12.00hrs
A small site with a friendly atmosphere set in a pretty rural area with extensive views. The good-size grass pitches are on slightly-sloping ground, and the toilets are immaculately kept. Looe and Polperro are just 3 miles away. A 4.5-acre site with 55 touring pitches and 20 statics.
Baby bath & mat, washing up sinks, fridge, freezer
Facilities: ╟⊙☖☀⛾⚓⛃☂ **Services:** ⚡☺⛽⚱◨◨
⚑⟶⊍△⅄♪⚋

LOSTWITHIEL Map 02 SX15

▶ ▶ ▶ 66% **Powderham Castle Tourist Park** (SX083593)
PL30 5BU ☎ 01208 872277 🖷 01208 872277
Dir: 1.5m SW of Lostwithiel on A390 turn right at brown/white signpost in 400mtrs
★ ⛟ £7.60-£12 ⛟ £7.60-£12 ▲ £7.60-£12
Open Etr or Apr-Oct Booking advisable peak periods Last arrival 22.00hrs Last departure 11.30hrs
A very quiet and well-run site in a good touring location, set in mature parkland and well screened. A 12-acre site with 75 touring pitches, 7 hardstandings and 38 statics.
Badminton & soft tennis
Leisure: ⚓ ⚲ ◻ **Facilities:** ╟⊙☖☀⚓☂
Services: ⚡☺⛽⚱◨◨⟶⊍▶△⅄⚇♪⚋ **Notes:** No unaccompanied groups of young adults

---

LUXULYAN Map 02 SX05

▶ ▶ ▶ 70% **Croft Farm Holiday Park** (SX044568)
PL30 5EQ ☎ 01726 850228 🖷 01726 850498
e-mail: lynpick@ukonline.co.uk
website: www.croftfarm.co.uk
Dir: Leave A30 at Bodmin for A391 towards St Austell. In 7m left at double rdbt onto unclass road towards Luxulyan/Eden Project, continue to T-junct, turn left signed Luxulyan. Croft Farm 1m on left. Do not approach any other way as roads are very narrow
⛟ £8-£11 ⛟ £8-£11 ▲ £6-£7.60
Open 21 Mar-21 Jan Booking advisable Jul & Aug Last departure noon
A peaceful, picturesque setting at the edge of a wooded valley, and only 1m from 'The Eden Project', Cornwall's new biodomes. A 5-acre site with 52 touring pitches, 10 hardstandings and 25 statics.
Mother & baby room, covered washing-up area.
Leisure: ⚓ ⚲ **Facilities:** ⚑╟⊙☖☀⚓☂☂
Services: ⚡☺⚱⚓◨◨⟶♪⚭⚋◨◎

MARAZION Map 02 SW53
See also **St Hilary**

▶ ▶ ▶ 65% **NEW** Wheal Rodney (SW525315)
Gwallon Ln TR17 0HL ☎ 01736 710605
e-mail: reception@whealrodney.co.uk
website: www.whealrodney.co.uk
*Dir: Turn off A30 at Crowlas, signed Rospeath. Site 1.5m
on right. From Marazion centre turn opposite Fire
Engine Inn, site 500mtrs on left.*
⊞ £6-£14 ⊞ £6-£14 ▲ £6-£12
Open all year Booking advisable Xmas & Etr-Oct
Last arrival 21.00hrs Last departure 11.00hrs
*Set in a quiet rural location surrounded by
farmland, with level grass pitches and well-kept
facilities. Just half a mile away are the beach at
Marazion and the causeway or ferry to St Michael's
Mount. A 2.5-acre site with 37 touring pitches.*
Sauna/spa room
Leisure: ♦ Facilities: ♦⊙♦※ Services: ⊞⊞⊞→
∪▶◎△♦⚓ Notes: No groups under 25yrs
⊞⊞⊞⊞

MAWGAN See **Helston**

MAWGAN PORTH Map 02 SW86

▶ ▶ ▶ ▶ 66% **Sun Haven Valley Holiday Park**
(SW861669)
TR8 4BQ ☎ 01637 860373 ▤ 01637 860373
e-mail: traceyhealey@hotmail.com
website: www.sunhavenvalley.co.uk
*Dir: From B3276 in Newquay take Padstow road, turn
right onto unclass rd just after petrol station complex &
park in 1.75m*
★ ⊞ £8-£13.50 ⊞ £8-£13.50 ▲ £8-£13.50
Open Apr-Oct (rs Oct-Mar Chalets only) Booking
advisable Jul-Aug Last arrival 22.00hrs Last
departure 11.00hrs
*An attractive site with level pitches on the side of a
river valley. The quality facilities include a TV
lounge and a games room in a Swedish-style
chalet, and a well-kept adventure playground. Trees
and hedges fringe the park, and the ground is well
drained. A 5-acre site with 118 touring pitches and
36 statics.*
Leisure: ♦ ⚠ ⊡ Facilities: ♦⊙♦※♦♦⚓⊞
Services: ⊞⊞♦⊡→∪▶◎♦ Notes: Families and
couples only ⊞⊞⊞⊞⊞
See advertisement on page 55

▶ ▶ ▶ 64% *Trevarrian Holiday Park (SW853661)*
TR8 4AQ ☎ 01637 860381 & 01637 860495
*Dir: From A39 at St Columb rdbt turn right onto A3059
towards Newquay. Fork right in approx 2m for St
Mawgan onto B3276. Turn right and site on left*
⊞⊞▲
Open Etr-Sep Booking advisable Jun-Aug Last
arrival 22.00hrs Last departure 11.00hrs
*A well-established and well-run holiday park
overlooking Mawgan Porth beach. This park has
a wide range of attractions including a free
entertainment programme in peak season.
A 7-acre site with 185 touring pitches.*
contd.

Sports field & pitch n putt.
Leisure: ♦♦♦⚠⊡ Facilities: ♦♦⊙♦※♦⚓
Services: ⊞⊞♦♦⊡⊡✕→∪▶◎♦♦♦⊞⊞

MEVAGISSEY
See **Gorran, Boswinger & Pentewan**

MULLION Map 02 SW61

 66% **Mullion Holiday Park (SW699182)**
Ruan Minor TR12 7LJ
☎ 01326 240000 & 240428
▤ 01326 241141
e-mail: bookings@weststarholidays.co.uk
website: www.weststarholidays.co.uk
*Dir: Follow road to the Lizard from Helston A3083
for about 7m, holiday park left opposite Mullion
turning.*
★ ⊞ £10-£19.50 ⊞ £10-£19.50 ▲ £10-£19.50

contd.

Leisure: ⛱ Indoor swimming pool ⛱ Outdoor swimming pool ♦ Tennis court ♦ Games room ⚠ Children's playground ∪ Stables
▶ 9/18 hole golf course ♦ Boats for hire ♦ Cinema ♦ Fishing ◎ Mini golf ♦ Watersports ⊡ Separate TV room

Caravan&CAMPING
MULLION
near Helston, Cornwall

Kynance Cove *near Mullion*

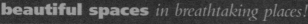

beautiful spaces *in breathtaking places!*

Award winning Park in an area of outstanding natural beauty and close to safe sandy beaches. With superb all-weather facilities for everyone you can choose between an all action holiday or a quieter relaxing break.

AA
Holiday Centre

What's included

☆ Spacious Level Serviced Pitches

☆ Modern Shower Blocks with Free Hot Water

☆ Indoor & Outdoor Heated Swimming Pools

☆ Great Evening Entertainment

☆ Children's Clubs & Play Areas

What's extra

☆ Launderette and Washing Up Area

☆ Well Stocked Shop

☆ Takeaway & Restaurant

☆ Crazy Golf, Multi Sports Court, Scuba Diving and More

HIGHLY
COMMENDED

Quote: AA

Corporate
MEMBER

☆ ☆ **book online**
www.weststarholidays.co.uk

☆ ☆ ☆ **booking line**
☎ **0870 444 5344**

WESTSTAR
Holiday★Parks

MEMBER

☆ ☆ ☆ **brochure hotline**
☎ **0870 444 5300**

Abbreviations: BH/bank hols-bank holidays   Etr-Easter   Whit-Whitsun   dep-departure   fr-from   hrs-hours   m-mile   mdnt-midnight   rdbt-roundabout   rs-restricted service   wk-week   wknd-weekend   ⊗-no dogs

Open 18 May-13 Sep Booking advisable Jul-Aug & bank holidays Last arrival 22.00hrs Last departure 10.00hrs
A comprehensively-equipped leisure park geared mainly for self-catering holidays, set in rugged moorland on the Lizard peninsula. There is plenty of on-site entertainment for all ages, with indoor and outdoor swimming pools. A 49-acre site with 150 touring pitches and 347 statics.
Adventure playgrounds, sandpit, amusement & arcade.
Leisure: ⚹ ⚲ ⚫ ⚠ ⬜ **Facilities:** �📶 ☉ ⚎ ⚹ 🕭 🗜 🚻 ⊞
🎍 🐕 **Services:** 🔌 🕒 🍴 🛁 🗑 ✕ 🛒 ➔ ∪ 🕐 ◎ 🔺 🧹
Notes: No unaccompanied groups under 25yrs or single sex groups 💳 💳 💳 💳 🔵

▶ ▶ ▶ 63% **'Franchis' Holiday Park** (SW698203)
Cury Cross Lanes TR12 7AZ ☎ 01326 240301
e-mail: franchis@lineone.net
website: www.franchis.co.uk
Dir: Off A3083 on left 0.5m past Wheel Inn PH, between Helston & The Lizard
★ 🚐 £8-£10 🚐 £8-£10 ▲ £8-£10
Open Apr-Oct Booking advisable end Jul-Aug Last arrival 22.00hrs Last departure noon
A level grassy site surrounded by hedges and coppices, and divided into two paddocks for tourers, in an ideal position for exploring the Lizard peninsula. A 4-acre site with 70 touring pitches and 12 statics.
Dishwashing, licensed shop
Facilities: 📶 ☉ ⚎ ⚹ 🕭 🗜 🐕 **Services:** 🔌 🛁 🗑 ⊞ 🕐 ➔ ∪
🕐 🔺 🧹 🗑 💳 💳 💳 💳 🔵

NANCEGOLLAN	Map 02 SW63

▶ ▶ 58% **Pengoon Farm Touring Caravan Park** (SW632309)
TR13 0BH ☎ 01326 561219
Dir: Direct access off B3302, 3m from Helston and 6m from Hayle. Do not follow any signs for Nancegollan
🚐 £6-£9 🚐 £6-£9 ▲ £6-£9
A grass park divided into two paddocks on a small working farm. In a very rural location, with friendly owners. A 3-acre site with 25 touring pitches.
Facilities: 📶 ⚹ **Services:** 🔌

NEWQUAY	Map 02 SW86

65% **Hendra Holiday Park** (SW833601)
TR8 4NY ☎ 01637 875778
📠 01637 879017
Dir: Leave A30 onto A392 signed Newquay. At Quintrell Downs over rdbt, signed Lane, park 0.5m on left
★ 🚐 £7.60-£12.80 🚐 £7.60-£12.80 ▲ £7.60-£12.80
Open Feb-Oct (rs Apr-Spring bank hol) Booking advisable Jul-Aug Last arrival dusk Last departure noon
A large complex with superb leisure facilities including an indoor fun pool with three slides, and an outdoor pool. There is a children's club for the over 6s, and evening entertainment during
contd.

high season. The touring pitches are set amongst mature trees and shrubs, and some have fully-serviced facilities. All of the amenities are open to the general public. A 46-acre site with 600 touring pitches and 188 statics.
Solarium, fish bar, sauna, kids club, train rides.
Leisure: ⚹ ⚲ ⚫ ⚠ ⬜ **Facilities:** 📶 ☉ ⚹ ⚎ 🗜 🚻 ⊞
🎍 🐕 **Services:** 🔌 🕒 🍴 🛁 🗑 ⊞ 🕐 ✕ 🛒 ➔ ∪ 🕐 ◎ 🔺 🧹
🧺 🧹 **Notes:** Families and couples only
💳 💳 💳 🔵
See advertisement on page 53

67% **Newquay Holiday Park** (SW853626)
TR8 4HS ☎ 01637 871111
📠 01637 850818
e-mail: enquiries@parkdean.com
website: www.parkdean.com
Dir: From Bodmin on A30 pass under low bridge and turn right towards RAF St Mawgan. Take A3059 towards Newquay, and site past Treloy Golf Club
★ 🚐 £6-£18.50 🚐 £6-£18.50 ▲ £6-£18.50
Open Mar-Oct Booking advisable Jun-Aug Last arrival 23.00hrs Last departure 10.00hrs ⊘
A well-managed and maintained holiday park with a wide range of indoor and outdoor activities. A children's playground and café/take-away have already enhanced the facilities here, and the club and bars have also been extended, offering quality entertainment for all ages. A 60-acre site with 259 touring pitches and 137 statics.
Snooker, pool table, 9-hole pitch & putt, crazy golf
Leisure: ⚲ ⚫ ⚠ ⬜ **Facilities:** 📶 ☉ ⚹ 🗜 🚻 ⊞ 🎍
Services: 🔌 🕒 🍴 🛁 🗑 ⊞ 🕐 ✕ 🛒 ➔ ∪ 🕐 🧹 **Notes:**
No single sex groups under 25yrs 💳 💳 🔵
See advertisement on page 52

▶ ▶ ▶ ▶ 65% **Trencreek Holiday Park** (SW828609)
Hillcrest, Higher Trencreek TR8 4NS
☎ 01637 874210 📠 01637 874210
e-mail: enquiries@trencreekholidaypark.co.uk
website: www.trencreekholidaypark.co.uk
Dir: A392 to Quintrell Downs, turn right in direction of Newquay, turn left at 2 mini rdbts into Trevenson Road to Trencreek
★ 🚐 £7.50-£12 🚐 £7.50-£12 ▲ £7.50-£12
Open Whit-mid Sep (rs Etr, Apr-May & late Sep swimming pool, cafe & bar closed) Booking advisable Jul-Aug Last arrival 22.00hrs Last departure noon ⊘
An attractively landscaped park in the village of Trencreek, with two well-stocked fishing lakes, and evening entertainment in the licensed clubhouse. Located about 2m from Newquay with its beaches and surfing. A 10-acre site with 194 touring pitches, 8 hardstandings and 6 statics.
Coarse fishing on site.
Leisure: ⚲ ⚫ ⚠ ⬜ **Facilities:** 📶 ☉ ⚹ ⚎ 🗜 🚻 ⊞ 🎍
Services: 🔌 🕒 🍴 🛁 🗑 ⊞ 🕐 ✕ 🛒 ➔ ∪ 🕐 ◎ 🔺 🧹

► ► ► **72%** *Porth Beach Tourist Park (SW834629)*
Porth TR7 3NH ☎ 01637 876531 🖹 01637 871227
e-mail: info@porthbeach.co.uk
website: www.porthbeach.co.uk
Dir: 1m NE off B3276 towards Padstow
🏕 🏕 ⅄

Open Mar-Oct Booking advisable Jul-Aug Last
arrival 21.00hrs Last departure 10.00hrs
*This attractive, popular park offers level, grassy
pitches in neat and tidy surroundings. A well-run
site set in meadowland adjacent to the sea and a
fine sandy beach. A 6-acre site with 201 touring
pitches and 18 statics.*
Leisure: 🅰 Facilities: 🍴⊙✳🛁🏪🎣 Services: 🔌🗄🛒
🍴🖼→∪📮⊙⚠⅄🥤🚰 💳🚮🏧🚮 🕹
See advertisement opposite

► ► ► **63% Riverside Holiday Park (SW829592)**
Ln TR8 4PE ☎ 01637 873617 🖹 01637 877051
e-mail: info@riversideholidaypark.co.uk
website: www.riversideholidaypark.co.uk
*Dir: From A30 take A392 signed Newquay, at Quintrell
Downs cross rdbt signed Lane. 2nd left in 0.5m onto
unclass rd signed Gwills. Park in 400yds.*
★ 🏕 £5.50-£10 🏕 £5.50-£10 ⅄ £5.50-£10

Open Mar-Dec Booking advisable Jul-Aug Last
departure 10.00hrs
*A lightly wooded park set alongside a river, with
level grass pitches. This family park offers a good
range of amenities. An 11-acre site with 100 touring
pitches and 65 statics.*
Fishing.
Leisure: 🎣⚓🅰🖵 Facilities: 🍴⊙🌂✳🛁🏪🐕
Services: 🔌🗄🛒⚙🖵🛁→∪📮⊙⚠⅄🥤
Notes: Families and couples only 💳🚮🚮 🕹

► ► ► **61% Trebellan Park (SW790571)**
Cubert TR8 5PY ☎ 01637 830522 🖹 01637 830277
e-mail: treago@aol.com
website: www.treagofarm.co.uk
*Dir: 4m S of Newquay, turn W off A3075 at Cubert
signpost and turn left in 0.75m onto unclass road*
★ 🏕 £8-£11 🏕 £8-£11 ⅄ £8-£11
Open May-Oct Booking advisable Jul-Aug Last
arrival 21.00hrs Last departure 23.00hrs
*A terraced rural park within a picturesque valley
with views of Cubert Common, and adjacent to the
Smuggler's Den, a 16th-century thatched inn. This
park has some excellent coarse fishing on site. An
8-acre site with 150 touring pitches and 6 statics.
Three well stocked coarse fishing lakes.*
contd.

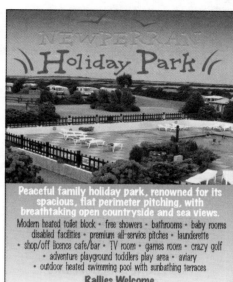

Leisure: ⟲🅰🖵 Facilities: 🍴⊙🌂✳🛁🏪🎣
Services: 🔌🗄🛒→∪📮⊙⚠⅄ Notes: Families &
couples only 💳🚮 🕹

► ► ► **68% Treloy Tourist Park
(SW858625)**
TR8 4JN ☎ 01637 872063 & 876279
🖹 01637 872063
e-mail: holidays@treloy.co.uk
website: www.treloy.co.uk
*Dir: From A30 turn right onto A3059 signed St Columb,
& after 3m at rdbt follow A3059 sign to Newquay. Site
signed in 4m*
★ 🏕 £6.40-£12 🏕 £6.40-£12 ⅄ £6.40-£12
Open Apr-Sep (rs Apr & Sep swimming pool & bar
closed) Booking advisable Jul-Aug Last arrival
23.00hrs Last departure 10.00hrs
*Attractive site with fine countryside views, within
easy reach of resorts and beaches. The pitches are
set in four paddocks with mainly level but some
slightly sloping grassy pitches. A children's club
and entertainment in the lounge bar during school
holidays make this a popular site with families.
A 12-acre site with 119 touring pitches, 22
hardstandings.*
Golf & entertainment
Leisure: ⟲⚓🅰🖵 Facilities: 🍴⊙🌂✳🛁🏪🐕
Services: 🔌🗄🛒⚙🖵✕🛁→∪🥤⅄🚰 💳🚮🚮 🕹
See advertisement opposite

CHALETS & CARAVANS FOR HIRE

TOURING PITCHES & HOOK-UPS

MINI-MARKET & OFF-LICENCE

TAKE-AWAY & RESTAURANT

LAUNDERETTE & GAMES ROOM

MODERN SHOWER BLOCK

ADJACENT 26 ACRE LEISURE PARK

**NEAREST PARK TO
TOWN CENTRE & BEACHES**

FAMILIES & COUPLES ONLY

Member B.H.H.P.A.
Graded 4 Ticks Tourist Board
**FREE PHONE BROCHURE LINE
0500-131243**

EDGCUMBE AVENUE, NEWQUAY

Telephone: 01637 873447
Fax: 01637 852677

▶ ▶ ▶ 61% **Trenance Caravan & Chalet Park**
(SW818612)
Edgcumbe Av TR7 2JY ☎ 01637 873447
🖹 01637 852677
e-mail: tony.hoyte@virgin.net
website: www.mywebpage.net/trenance
*Dir: Off A3075 near viaduct. Entrance by boating lake
rdbt*
★ ⊕ £8-£13.70 ⊕ £8-£13.70 ▲ £8-£13.70

Open 26 May-Oct (rs Apr-25 May no showers or
take-away restaurant) Booking advisable Jul-Aug
Last arrival 22.00hrs Last departure 10.00hrs ⊗
*A mainly static park popular with tenters and young
people, close to Newquay's vibrant nightlife, and
serving excellent breakfasts and takeaways. Set on
high ground in an urban area of town, with cheerful
owners and clean facilities. A 12-acre site with 50
touring pitches and 190 statics.*

contd.

Dishwashing facilities.
Leisure: ☚ Facilities: 🏠⊙🍴✳🔌 🛁 Services: 🔌🅱🛈
🚮⊞✗🚮→∪▮◎△↘🗲🍴🖸🛒🚮🎣🐟🖸

▶ ▶ ▶ 66% **Trethiggey Touring Park**
(SW846596)
Quintrell Downs TR8 4QR ☎ 01637 877672
🖹 01637 879706
e-mail: enquiries@trethiggey.co.uk
website: www.trethiggey.co.uk
*Dir: From A30 take A392 signed Newquay at Quintrell
Downs rdbt, turn left onto A3058 past pearl centre to
site 0.5m on left*
★ ⊕ £6.80-£10.50 ⊕ £6.80-£9.50 ▲ £6.80-£9.50

Open Mar-Dec Booking advisable Jul-Aug
*A family-owned park in a rural setting that is ideal
for touring this part of Cornwall. Pleasantly divided
into paddocks with maturing trees and shrubs, and
offering coarse fishing and tackle hire. A 15-acre
site with 145 touring pitches, 35 hardstandings and
12 statics.*
Off licence, dishwash sink, recreation field, fishing
Leisure: ☚ ⚠ 🗖 Facilities: 🏠⊙🍴✳🔌 🛁 🚿
🎣 🐟 Services: 🔌🅱🛈🚮⊞🛈🛒🚮→∪▮◎△↘🗲
🍴🖸🛒🚮🖸

See advertisement on pages 52 to 54

OTTERHAM   **Map 02 SX19**

▶ ▶ ▶ 66% **St Tinney Farm Holidays**
(SX169906)
PL32 9TA ☎ 01840 261274 🖹 01840 261575
e-mail: info@st-tinney.co.uk
website: www.st-tinney.co.uk
Dir: 1m off A39 via unclass road signed Otterham
★ ⊕ £6-£9.90 ⊕ £6-£9.90 ▲ £6-£9.90
Open Etr-Oct (rs Nov-Etr Self catering lodges/static
caravan only) Booking advisable Spring bank hol &
Jul-Aug Last arrival 21.00hrs Last departure
11.00hrs
*A family-run farm site in a rural area, with nature
trails, lakes, valleys and complete seclusion. Visitors
are free to walk around the 34-acre farmland lakes.
A 34-acre site with 20 touring pitches and 9 statics.*
Coarse fishing, horse/donkey rides, pony trekking
Leisure: ☚ ⚠ Facilities: 🏠⊙🍴✳🔌 🛁 🎣 🐟
Services: 🔌🅱🛈🚮⊞✗🚮→∪🍴🗲🍴🖸🛒🚮🖸

England

PADSTOW   Map 02 SW97

▶ ▶ ▶ **65% Dennis Cove Camping (SW920744)**
Dennis Cove PL28 8DR ☎ 01841 532349
Dir: Approach Padstow on A389, turn right into Sarah's Lane, 2nd right to Dennis Lane, follow lane to site at end
★ ⚓ £9.70-£13.50 ⚓ £9.70-£13.50 ▲ £9.70-£13.50
Open May-Sep Booking advisable Last arrival 23.00hrs Last departure 11.00hrs
Level and slightly sloping site with mature trees set in meadowland, overlooking Padstow Bay with access to River Camel estuary and Padstow Bay beach. A 3-acre site with 40 touring pitches.
Facilities: �📶⊙❋⊞ **Services:** 🛢⌀⊞→∪▶⊙♨✕☻
⌗🗑🛒 **Notes:** No single sex groups

▶ ▶ ▶ **67% Trerethern Touring Park (SW913738)**
PL28 8LE ☎ 01841 532061 📠 01841 532061
e-mail: camping.trerethern@btinternet.com
website: www.trerethern.co.uk
Dir: Situated 1m S of Padstow, on eastern side of A389, Padstow to Wadebridge road
★ ⚓ £8-£11 ⚓ £8-£11 ▲ £8-£11
Open Apr-mid Oct Booking advisable Jul-Aug Last arrival 19.00hrs Last departure 16.00hrs
Set in open countryside above the quaint fishing town of Padstow which can be approached by footpath directly from the park. This level grassy site is divided into paddocks by maturing bushes and hedges to create a peaceful and relaxing holiday atmosphere. A 13.5-acre site with 100 touring pitches.
Motorvan hardstanding, electric & pumpout.
Leisure: ⚠ **Facilities:** �📶⊙🎱❋&🛒🛎
Services: 🔌🛢⌀⊞⊞→∪▶♨✕☻⌗

▶ ▶ **62% Padstow Holiday Park (SW009073)**
Cliffdowne PL28 8LB ☎ 01841 532289
📠 01841 532289
e-mail: alex@cliffdowne.freeserve.co.uk
website: www.padstowholidaypark.co.uk
Dir: On B3274/A389 into Padstow. Signed 1.5m before Padstow
★ ⚓ £10 ▲ £10
Open Etr/Apr-Nov Booking advisable All times Last arrival 17.00hrs Last departure Noon ⚘
A mainly static park with some touring pitches in a small paddock and others in an open field. This quiet holiday site can be reached from Padstow (1m away) by a footpath. A 5.5-acre site with 27 touring pitches and 74 statics.
Leisure: ⚠ **Facilities:** ➡📶⊙🎱❋🍴 **Services:** 🔌
🛢⌀⊞→∪▶⊙♨✕☻⌗🛒 **Notes:** No dogs

PENTEWAN   Map 02 SX04

71% Pentewan Sands Holiday Park (SX018468)
PL26 6BT ☎ 01726 843485
📠 01726 844142
e-mail: info@pentewan.co.uk
website: www.pentewan.co.uk
Dir: On B3273 4m S of St Austell
★ ⚓ £6.45-£17.65 ⚓ £6.45-£17.65 ▲ £6.45-£17.65
contd.

Open Apr-Oct (rs Apr-14 May & 15 Sep-Oct shop, snacks, pool, clubhouse ltd closed)
Booking advisable Jul-Aug Last arrival 22.00hrs Last departure 10.30hrs ⚘
A large holiday park with a wide range of amenities, set on the dunes adjacent to a private beach where plenty of aquatic activities are available. A short stroll leads to the pretty village of Pentewan, and other attractions are a short drive away. A club on site offers evening entertainment. A 32-acre site with 500 touring pitches and 120 statics.
Cycle hire, boat launching, water sports.
Leisure: ⤢🎣🎱⚠ **Facilities:** ➡📶⊙🎱❋&🛒
Services: 🔌🛢⌀⊞⊞✕🖕→∪▶⊙♨✕ **Notes:** No dogs, no single sex groups, no jetskis
💳 ⚡ 📇 📶 🗒

▶ ▶ ▶ ▶ ▶ **75% Sun Valley Holiday Park (SX005486)**
Pentewan Rd PL26 6DJ
☎ 01726 843266 & 844393 📠 01726 843266
e-mail: reception@sunvalleyholidays.co.uk
website: www.sunvalleyholidays.co.uk
Dir: From St Austell take B3273 towards Mevagissey. Park is 2m on right
★ ⚓ £8.50-£22 ⚓ £8.50-£22 ▲ £8.50-£22
contd.

Discover River Valley

Located along the bank of a clear shallow stream, River Valley offers you a sense of utter peace and tranquillity.

- 150 Touring, Motorhome or Tent pitches
- Luxury Caravan Holiday Homes & Lodges Available
- 18 Acres of partly wooded countryside
- Shop & Launderette
- SEASONAL PITCHES FROM £520.00

River Valley Country Park, Relubbus, Penzance, Cornwall, TR20 9ER

Tel 0845 60 12516   Fax 01736 763398

www.rivervalley.co.uk   rivervalley@surfbay.dircon.co.uk

Open Apr (or Etr if earlier)-Oct Booking advisable May-Sep Last arrival 22.00hrs Last departure noon
In a picturesque valley and set amongst woodland, this neat park is presented to an exceptionally high standard throughout. The extensive amenities include tennis courts, indoor swimming pool, licensed clubhouse and restaurant. The sea is 1 mile away, and can be accessed via a footpath and cycle path along the river bank. A 4-acre site with 22 touring pitches and 75 statics.
Leisure: 🌊 🞈 🏐 🅐   Facilities: 🖻 ⊙ 🖃 ✳ 💧 🕰 🛒 🎠 🖍
Services: 🔌 🖺 🍸 🛢 🍴 🖭 ✕ 🚿 → ∪ ┡ 🗡 🛒 🖉
⊛ 🚆 🗺 🖿

▶ ▶ ▶ **65% Heligan Woods (SW998470)**
PL26 6BT ☎ 01726 842714 🖷 01726 844142
e-mail: info@pentewan.co.uk
website: www.pentewan.co.uk
Dir: From A390 take B3273 for Mevagissey at x-roads signed 'No caravans beyond this point'. Right onto unclass road towards Gorran, site 0.75m on left
★ 🚐 £6.25-£15.95 🚙 £6.25-£15.95 ▲ £6.25-£15.95
Open Apr-1 Nov Booking advisable Late July & Aug
A pleasant peaceful park adjacent to the Lost Gardens of Heligan, with views over St Austell Bay, and well-maintained facilities. Guests can also use the extensive amenities at the sister park, Pentewan Sands. A 12-acre site with 100 touring pitches and 25 statics.

contd.

Full use of Pentewan Sands facilities
Leisure: 🛝   Facilities: 🖻 🕰 🛒
Services: 🔌 🖺 ✕ 🛢 → ┡ 🛢 🗡 🚿 🖉 ⊛ 🚆 🗺 🖿 🖉

▶ ▶ ▶ **65% Penhaven Touring Park (SX008481)**
PL26 6DL ☎ 01726 843687 🖷 01726 843870
e-mail: enquiries@penhaventouring.co.uk
website: www.penhaventouring.co.uk
Dir: S from St Austell on B3273 towards Mevagissey. Site on left 1m after village of London Apprentice
★ 🚐 £7.80-£18.50 🚙 £7.80-£18.50 ▲ £7.80-£18.50
Open Apr-Oct Booking advisable public hols & end Jul-Aug Last arrival 21.00hrs Last departure 10.00hrs
A landscaped site in a wooded valley, with a river running by. Situated 1 mile from the sandy beach at Pentewan, which can be accessed by a footpath and cycle path along the river bank directly from the park. A 13-acre site with 105 touring pitches, 12 hardstandings.
Off-licence, motor van service point
Leisure: 🎣 🛝   Facilities: 🖻 ⊙ 🖃 ✳ 💧 🕰 🛒 🎠   Services:
🔌 🖺 🛢 🖉 🖃 🗠 🛢 → ┡ 🛢 🗡 🕳 🗡 ⊛ 🚆 🗺 🖿 🖉

PENZANCE   **Map 02 SW43**
See also **Relubbus & Rosudgeon**

▶ ▶ ▶ **63% Bone Valley Caravan & Camping Park (SW472316)**
Heamoor TR20 8UJ ☎ 01736 360313
🖷 01736 360313
Dir: A30 to Penzance then towards Land's End, at 2nd rdbt right into Heamoor, 300yds right into Josephs Lane, 1st left, Bone Valley site 50yds on left
★ 🚐 £9.50-£11 🚙 £9.50-£11 ▲ £9.50-£11

Open Mar-7 Jan statics open all year Booking advisable Jul-Aug Last arrival 22.00hrs Last departure 11.00hrs
A compact grassy park on the outskirts of Penzance, with well maintained facilities. It is divided into paddocks by mature hedges, and a small stream runs alongside. A 1-acre site with 17 touring pitches, 2 hardstandings and 1 static.
Baby changing facilities
Leisure: 🖵   Facilities: 🖻 ⊙ 🖃 ✳ 💧 🕰 🛒 🎴
Services: 🔌 🖺 🛢 🖉 🖃 🛢 → ∪ ⊙ 🛢 🗡 🕳 🗡

Remember sites which take dogs may not accept all breeds

PERRANARWORTHAL   Map 02 SW73

▶ ▶ ▶ **66% Cosawes Caravan Park (SW768376)**
TR3 7QS ☎ 01872 863724 & 863717 🖹 01872 870268
e-mail: info@cosawes.com
website: www.cosawesparkhomes.co.uk
*Dir: On A39 midway between Truro & Falmouth, with
direct access at park sign at Perranarworthal*
★ 🚐 fr £8.50 🚐 fr £7.50 ▲ fr £7
Open all year Booking advisable mid Jul-mid Aug
*A small touring park in a peaceful wooded valley,
midway between Truro and Falmouth. Its stunning
location is ideal for visiting the many nearby
hamlets and villages on the Carrick Roads, a stretch
of tidal water which is a centre for sailing and other
boats. A 2-acre site with 40 touring pitches and 100
statics.*
Squash court.
Facilities: ⋔ ⊙ ❄ ↻ ⊞ ⌨ ☂ ⍢ **Services:** 🖭 🖩 ⌂ ∅ ⊞ ⊤
→ ↻ ▶ ⊚ ⌂ ⅄ ↙ ⅀ **Notes:** Dogs must be kept on
leads at all times

PERRANPORTH   Map 02 SW75

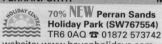

**70% NEW Perran Sands
Holiday Park (SW767554)**
TR6 0AQ ☎ 01872 573742
website: www.havenholidays.com
★ 🚐 £9-£38
Open Mar-Oct Booking advisable Last arrival
22.00hrs Last departure 12.00hrs
contd.

*Nestling amid 500 acres of protected dune
grassland, and with a footpath through to the
surf and 3 miles of golden sandy beach, this
lively park is set in a large village-style complex.
It offers a complete range of on-site facilities and
entertainment for all the family which make it an
extremely popular park. A 550-acre site with 359
touring pitches.*
Leisure: ᐓ ᐓ ❋ ⋒ ⊒ **Facilities:** 🛉
Services: 🖭 ⦿ ⌂ ✕ ⅏ ⦿ ═ ⑩ ▦ 🖩 ⑨

▶ ▶ ▶ **62% Perranporth Camping &
Touring Site (SW768542)**
Budnick Rd TR6 0DB ☎ 01872 572174
🖹 01872 572174
Dir: 0.5m E off B3285
★ 🚐 £10-£15 🚐 £10-£15 ▲ £10-£15
Open Whit-Sep (rs Etr-Whit & mid-end Sep shop &
club facilities closed) Booking advisable Jul-Aug
Last arrival 23.00hrs Last departure noon
*A mainly tenting site with few level pitches, located
high above a fine sandy beach which is much-
frequented by surfers. The park is attractive to
young people, and is set in a lively town on a
spectacular part of the coast. A 6-acre site with 120
touring pitches and 9 statics.*
Leisure: ᐓ ❋ ⋒ ⊒ **Facilities:** ⇥ ⋔ ⊙ ❋ ❄ ↻ 🛉
▦ ⍢ **Services:** 🖭 ⦿ ⌂ ⌂ ∅ ⊞ ⊤ ⅏ → ↻ ▶ ⊚ ⌂ ⅄ ↙
⅏ ═ ▥ ▦ ⑨

See advertisement on page 60

Leisure: ᐓ Indoor swimming pool   ᐓ Outdoor swimming pool   ❋ Tennis court   ❋ Games room   ⋒ Children's playground   ↻ Stables
▶ 9/18 hole golf course   ⅄ Boats for hire   ⛺ Cinema   ↙ Fishing   ⊚ Mini golf   ⌂ Watersports   ⊒ Separate TV room

▶ ▶ ▶ 65% **NEW** Tollgate Farm Caravan & Camping Park (SW768547)
Budnick Hill TR6 0AD ☎ 01872 572130
e-mail: tollgatefarm@aol.com
Dir: Off A30 onto B3285 to Perranporth. Site on right 1.5m after Goonhavern
★ ⊕ £8.50-£11 ⊕ £8.50-£11 Å £8.50-£11
Open Etr-Oct Booking advisable Jul-Aug Last arrival 21.00hrs Last departure 11.30hrs
A quiet site in a rural location with spectacular coastal views. Pitches are divided into four paddocks sheltered and screened by mature hedges. A new toilet block has enhanced the existing facilities, and children will enjoy the play equipment and pets corner. The three miles of sand at Perran Bay are just a walk away through the sand dunes, or a 0.75m drive. A 10-acre site with 140 touring pitches.
Breakfast bar & animal area
Leisure: 🅰 **Facilities:** 🅝☉🅠✳♨🅛🖿🌂
Services: 🅠🖃🅘⌀🅗🖼➔∪🍴☉🛆✕🥄
Notes: No large, young or single sex groups

POLPERRO	Map 02 SX25

65% *Killigarth Manor Holiday Centre (SX214519)*
PL13 2JQ ☎ 01503 272216 & 272409
🖷 01503 272065
e-mail: killigarthmanor@breathemail.net
website: www.killigarth.co.uk
Dir: Leave A38 at Trerulefoot rdbt onto A387, through Looe, over bridge signed Polperro. In 3.5m turn left past shelter/phone box. Park 400yds on left
⊕⊕Å

Open Etr-Oct Booking advisable 3rd wk Jul-Aug Last arrival 20.00hrs Last departure noon ⌧
Set on high ground at the approach to the historic fishing village, this large holiday centre offers a wide variety of leisure activities based around the indoor complex. In the evening the entertainment centres around the lively Harbour Lights Club. A 7-acre site with 202 touring pitches and 147 statics.
Amusement arcade, pool table & table tennis.
Leisure: 🐟 🥢 🎣 🅰 🖵 **Facilities:** 🅝☉🅠✳🅛🍼
🌂🌳 **Services:** 🅠🖃🅨🅘⌀🅗🅣✕🖼➔∪🛆🥤🦮🥄
🖭🎫🌀📶🖩

See advertisement on opposite page

POLRUAN
Map 02 SX15

► ► ► **70% Polruan Holidays-
Camping & Caravanning (SX133509)**
Polruan-by-Fowey PL23 1QH
☎ 01726 870263 📠 01726 870263
e-mail: polholiday@aol.com
Dir: A38 to Dobwalls, left onto A390 to East
Taphouse then left onto B3359. After 4.5m turn
right signposted Polruan

★ 🚐 £9-£12.75 🚐 £9-£12.75 ▲ £6.85-£12.75
Open Etr-Oct Booking advisable Jul, Aug & bank
hols Last arrival 21.00hrs Last departure noon
*A very rural and quiet site in a lovely elevated
position above the village, with good views. River
Fowey passenger ferry close by. A 3-acre site with
32 touring pitches, 7 hardstandings and 11 statics.
Tourist information.*
Leisure: ⚠ **Facilities:** 🏕⊙🔾☀🅲🖳🏛🎋
Services: 🖭🛈∅🖪🕱→∪◊🗘↯🗲

POLZEATH
Map 02 SW97

► ► ► **66% South Winds Caravan &
Camping Park (SW948790)**
Polzeath Rd PL27 6QU ☎ 01208 863267
📠 01208 862080
Dir: Leave B3314 on unclass road signed Polzeath, park
on right just past turn to New Polzeath
🚐🚐▲

Open Mar-Oct Booking advisable Jul & Aug &
school hols Last arrival 22.00hrs Last departure
11.00hrs
*A peaceful site with beautiful sea and panoramic
rural views, within walking distance of new golf
complex, and 0.75m from beach and village.
A 6-acre site with 50 touring pitches.*
Facilities: 🏕⊙🔾☀🅲🖳🏛🎋🐕 **Services:** 🖭🛈🖪∅🖪
🕱→∪🅟◊🗘↯🎎🍴🐾 **Notes:** No single sex groups,
no disposable barbecues, no noise 11pm-7am &
dogs must be on leads at all times 💳 🔲

► ► ► **67% Tristram Caravan & Camping Park
(SW936790)**
PL27 6UG ☎ 01208 862215 & 863267
📠 01208 862080
Dir: From B3314 take unclass road signed Polzeath.
Through village, up hill, site 2nd turn on right
🚐🚐▲
Open Mar-Nov Booking advisable Jul, Aug & school
hols Last arrival 23.00hrs Last departure 10.00hrs

contd.

Tristram Caravan & Camping Park
*An ideal family site, positioned on a gently-sloping
cliff with grassy pitches and glorious sea views.
There is direct gated access to the beach, where
surfing is very popular. The Wildfish seafood
restaurant is a new addition to this park. A 10-acre
site with 100 touring pitches.*
Private footpath onto beach
Facilities: 🏕⊙🔾☀🅲🖳🏛🎋🐕 **Services:** 🖭🖪🛈∅
🖪🕱✗👜→∪🅟◊🗘↯🎎🐾 **Notes:** No ball games, no
disposable BBQs, no noise between 11pm-7am,
dogs on leads at all times 💳 🔲 💳 💳 🔳 🔲

Facilities: 🚿 Bath 🏕 Shower ⊙ Electric Shaver 🔾 Hairdryer ✗ Ice Pack Facility ♿ Disabled Facilities 🕿 Public Telephone
🖳 Shop on Site or within 200yds 💳 Mobile Shop (calls at least 5 days a week) 🏛 BBQ Area 🎋 Picnic Area 🎋 Dog Exercise Area

PORTHTOWAN   Map 02 SW64

▶ ▶ ▶ ▶ **71% Rose Hill Touring Park** (SW693466)
TR4 8AR ☎ 01209 890802
e-mail: reception@rosehillcamping.co.uk
website: www.rosehillcamping.co.uk
*Dir: From A30 follow B3277 signposted St Agnes.
After 1m turn left signed Porthtowan. Site 100yds past
beach road*
★ 🚐 £9.80-£14.80 🚐 £9.80-£14.80 ▲ £9.80-£14.80
Open end Mar-end Oct Booking advisable Jun-Aug
Last arrival 21.30hrs Last departure 10.30hrs
*A small, well-kept park in an attractive position, set
into the hillside and terraced. The park is quiet and
sheltered, hidden away in a wooded valley, with
some hardstandings among many level pitches.
New toilet facilities are of a high standard. Only a
short way away is a popular sandy beach and surf
centre, plus village pubs and restaurants. A 2.5-acre
site with 50 touring pitches, 10 hardstandings.*
Tourist information, wet suit wash

Facilities: ⚓⊙🏧✳&⚑🛢🖻 **Services:** 🔌🖥🛢⊘🔲✕⚓
🛒→∪▶△✕💈🍴 🍺🚉 🖭 🍴 🗂

▶ ▶ ▶ **67% Porthtowan Tourist Park** (SW693473)
Mile Hill TR4 8TY ☎ 01209 890256 🖨 01209 890256
e-mail: admin@porthtowantouristpark.co.uk
website: www.porthtowantouristpark.co.uk
*Dir: Leave A30 at exit signed Redruth/Porthtowan. 3rd
exit from rdbt, follow road for 2m. Right at T-junct. Park
on left at top of hill*
★ 🚐 £6-£10 🚐 £6-£10 ▲ £6-£10

Open Etr-Oct Booking advisable Jul-Aug Last arrival
22.00hrs Last departure 11.00hrs
*A neat, level grassy site on high ground above
Porthtowan, with plenty of shelter from mature
trees and shrubs. This rural park in a peaceful
location offers good facilities, and is almost midway
between the small seaside resorts of Porthreath and
Porthtowan, with their beaches and surfing. A 5-
acre site with 50 touring pitches, 4 hardstandings.*
Leisure: ⚓♨ **Facilities:** ⚓⊙🏧✳&⚑🛢🖻🛒
Services: 🔌🖥🛢⊘🖻🔲→∪▶△✕💈🍴

▶ ▶ ▶ **63% Wheal Rose Caravan &
Camping Park** (SW717449)
Wheal Rose TR16 5DD ☎ 01209 891496
🖨 01209 891496
*Dir: Leave A30 at Scorrier sign and follow signs on
unclass road to Wheal Rose. Park 0.5m on left*
🚐🚐▲

Wheal Rose Caravan & Camping Park
Open Mar-Dec Booking advisable Aug Last arrival
23.00hrs Last departure 11.00hrs
*A quiet, peaceful park in a secluded valley setting,
central for beaches and countryside; 2 miles from
the surfing beaches of Porthtowan. The friendly
owners work hard to keep this park immaculate,
with a bright toilet block and well-trimmed pitches.
A 6-acre site with 50 touring pitches and 1 static.*
Leisure: ⚓♨ **Facilities:** ⚓⊙🏧✳&⚑🛢🖻🛒
Services: 🔌🖥🛢⊘🖻🔲🛒→∪▶🍴🍺🍴 **Notes:** 5mph
speed. Dogs on leads. Min noise after 11pm.
Gates locked 11pm.

PORTSCATHO   Map 02 SW83

▶ ▶ ▶ **68% NEW Trewince Manor** (SW868339)
TR2 5ET ☎ 01872 580289 🖨 01872 580694
e-mail: bookings@trewince.co.uk
website: www.trewince.co.uk
*Dir: Take A390 from St Austell to Truro. Bear left on
B3287 to Tregony, following signs to St Mawes. At
Trewithian, turn left to St Anthony. Trewince Manor
0.75m past church*
★ 🚐 £12-£19.50 🚐 £12-£19.50 ▲ £12-£19.50
Open May-Sep Booking advisable high season Last
arrival 23.00hrs Last departure 12.00hrs
*A newly-developed site in the grounds of a listed
Grade II Georgian manor house, with spectacular
sea views. The facilities of the house are open to
visitors to the touring park, including a bar and a
restaurant specialising in seafood. Dinghies can be
launched from a small slipway, and the new toilet
facilities are very good. A 3-acre site with 25 touring
pitches.*
Private quay & moorings
Leisure: ⚓⚓☐ **Facilities:** ⚓⊙🏧✳&⚑🛢🖻🍴
Services: 🔌🖥🍺🖻✕⚓→∪✕🍴🛢🍺🍴 🖭 🗂

▶ ▶ **63% Treloan Coastal Farm Holidays**
(SW876348)
Treloan Ln TR2 5EF ☎ 01872 580888 & 580899
🖨 01872 580989
e-mail: holidays@treloan.freeserve.co.uk
website: www.coastalfarmholidays.co.uk
*Dir: Take unclass road to Gerrans off A3078 Tregony to
St Mawes road. Immediately after Gerran's church road
divides - take Treloan Ln beside Royal Standard pub to
car park*
★ 🚐 £8.50-£13 🚐 £8.50-£13 ▲ £5.50-£13

contd.

contd.

Treloan Coastal Farm Holidays
Open all year Booking advisable High Season Last departure 11.00hrs
A quiet, well-screened coastal park with mature trees and bushes, and three nearby secluded beaches. All pitches offer sea views, and there is a camping barn for walkers on the South West Coastal Footpath. A 7-acre site with 49 touring pitches, 8 hardstandings and 8 statics.
Coastal Foot Path on site

Leisure: ⚠ Facilities: ⚿ ⊙ ⚙ ✻ & ⚲ ⚐ ⚑ ☆
Services: ⊟ ⓢ ⓘ ⓔ ⓣ → ∪ △ ↻ ⟊
Notes: Families only 💳 💳 💳 📶 ⓖ

See advertisement on page 75

REDRUTH	**Map 02 SW64**

▶ ▶ ▶ **64% Cambrose Touring Park (SW684453)**
Portreath Rd TR16 4HT ☎ 01209 890747
🖨 01209 891665
e-mail: cambrosetouringpark@supanet.com
website: www.cambrosetouringpark.co.uk
Dir: Leave A30 onto B3300 towards Portreath. Approx 0.75m at 1st rdbt right onto B3300. Take unclass rd on right signed Porthtowan. Site 200yds on left
☆ 🚐 £7.50-£11.50 🚐 £7.50-£11.50 ▲ £7.50-£11.50

Open Apr-Oct Booking advisable Jul-Aug Last arrival 22.00hrs Last departure 11.30hrs
Situated in a rural setting surrounded by trees and shrubs, this park is divided into grassy paddocks. About two miles from the harbour village of Portreath. A 6-acre site with 60 touring pitches.
Mini football pitch

Leisure: ᚾ ⚓ ⚠ Facilities: ⚿ ⊙ ⚙ ✻ & ⚲ ⚐ ☆
Services: ⊟ ⓢ ⓘ ⓐ ⓔ ⓣ ⓜ → ∪ ▶ ⊚ ⚎ ⟊

▶ ▶ ▶ **63% Lanyon Holiday Park (SW684387)**
Loscombe Ln, Four Lanes TR16 6LP ☎ 01209 313474 🖨 01209 313422
e-mail: jamierielly@supanet.com
website: www.lanyoncaravanandcampingpark.co.uk
Dir: Signed 0.5m off B2397 on Helston side of Four Lanes village
☆ 🚐 £7-£12 🚐 £7-£12 ▲ £5-£7
Open Mar-Oct Booking advisable Jul & Aug Last arrival 20.00hrs Last departure noon
Small, friendly rural park in an elevated position with fine views to distant St Ives Bay. This family owned and run park is being upgraded in all areas, and is close to a new cycling trail. Stithian's Reservoir for fishing, sailing and windsurfing is two miles away. A 14-acre site with 25 touring pitches and 49 statics.
Take away service, all day games room

Leisure: ᚾ ⚓ ⚠ ⚐ Facilities: ⚿ ⚿ ⊙ ⚙ ✻ & ⚲ ⚐ ☆
Services: ⊟ ⓢ ⓨ ⓘ ⓔ ⓧ ⓜ → ∪ ▶ ⊚ △ ⚎ ⟊ ⚒
💳 💳 Ⓓ 💳 📶 ⓖ

▶ ▶ ▶ **61% Tehidy Holiday Park (SW682432)**
Harris Mill, Illogan TR16 4JQ ☎ 01209 216489
🖨 01209 216489
e-mail: holiday@tehidy.co.uk
website: www.tehidy.co.uk
Dir: Leave A30 at Redruth/Portreath exit, continue on A3047 to 1st rdbt. Right onto B3300, approx 1m left onto unclass rd. Site 1m on left and signed
☆ 🚐 £6.50-£8 🚐 £6.50-£8 ▲ £6.50-£8
Open Apr-Oct Booking advisable Jul-Aug Last arrival 20.00hrs Last departure 10.00hrs
An attractive wooded location in a quiet rural area only 2.5 miles from popular beaches. Mostly level pitches on tiered ground. A 1-acre site with 18 touring pitches and 32 statics.
Badminton, trampoline, off-licence.

Leisure: ⚓ ⚠ ⚐ Facilities: ⚿ ⊙ ⚙ ✻ & ⚲ ⚐ ☆
Services: ⊟ ⓢ ⓘ ⓐ ⓔ ⓣ → ∪ ▶ △ ⚎ ⚒ ⟊ Notes: Dogs by arrangement - not Jul or Aug 💳 💳 📶 ⓖ

REJERRAH	**Map 02 SW75**

▶ ▶ ▶ **63% *Monkey Tree Touring Park* (SW803545)**
Scotland Rd TR8 5QR ☎ 01872 572032
🖨 01872 571602
Dir: Turn right off A30 onto B3285 to Perranporth, in 0.25m turn right into Scotland Rd, site on left in 1.5m
🚐 🚐 ▲

contd.

Newperran Holiday Park

Leisure: 〜❦⚓☐ Facilities: ⇥↾⊙♖✳&↳㊑⋔
Services: ▣♑♘❡⌀▦▥✕✦→∪♪◉◭✚♨♪
⊜⊟� 🌳 🔊

See advertisement on page 55

▶ ▶ ▶ **65%** *Perran-Quay Tourist Park (SW800554)*
Hendra Croft TR8 5QP ☎ 01872 572561
Dir: Direct access off A3075 behind Braefel Inn
🚐 🚐 🅰
Open Apr-Oct Booking advisable Jul-Aug Last
arrival anytime Last departure 10.00hrs
*A friendly family-run site set in paddocks with
mature trees and shrubs for shelter, midway
between Newquay and Perranporth, and just five
minutes' drive (a short footpath) from the sandy
beach at Holywell Bay. The site has its own pub
serving food and drink. A 5.5-acre site with 130
touring pitches and 15 statics.*
Washing up sinks.

Leisure: 〜❦⚓☐ Facilities: ↾⊙♖✳&↳㊑
Services: ▣♑♘❡⌀▦▥✕✦→∪♪◉◭✚♪
Notes: Families only , no single sex groups,
no motorcycles

RELUBBUS	**Map 02 SW53**

▶ ▶ ▶ ▶ **66%** River Valley Country
Park **(SW565326)**
TR20 9ER ☎ 01736 763398
🖳 01736 763398
e-mail: rivervalley@surfbay.dircon.co.uk
website: www.rivervalley.co.uk
*Dir: From A30 follow sign for Helston A394.
At next rbdt 1st left signed Relubbus*
★ 🚐 £6-£11 🚐 £6-£11 🅰 £6-£11

Open Mar-Dec (rs Nov-4 Jan hardstanding only)
Booking advisable Jul-Aug Last arrival 20.00hrs Last
departure 11.00hrs
contd.

Open Mar-Oct Booking advisable Jul & Aug Last
arrival 22.00hrs Last departure from 10.00hrs
*A rural park set in paddocks surrounded by mature
hedges, midway between Newquay and
Perranporth, with good access to local attractions.
A new restaurant and a larger clubhouse with
entertainment enhance the amenities. An 18-acre
site with 295 touring pitches and 22 statics.*
Sauna, solarium, mountain bike hire & football
pitch

Leisure: 〜❦⚓☐ Facilities: ↾⊙✳&↳㊑㊏⋔
Services: ▣♑♘❡⌀▦▥✕♨→∪♪◭✚♪
⊜⊟⊠ 🔊

▶ ▶ ▶ **67%** Newperran Holiday Park (SW801555)
TR8 5QJ ☎ 01872 572407 🖳 01872 571254
e-mail: holidays@newperran.co.uk
website: www.newperran.co.uk
Dir: 4m SE of Newquay & 1m S of Rejerrah on A3075
🚐 £8-£13.20 🚐 £8-£13.20 🅰 £8-£13.20
Open Etr-Oct Booking advisable Jul-Aug
*A family site in a lovely rural position near several
beaches and bays. This airy park offers screening to
some pitches, and there is plenty to occupy all the
family. Newquay and Perranporth are about 4 miles
away. A 25-acre site with 270 touring pitches.*
Crazy golf, adventure playground & pool
contd.

A quiet, attractive site of quality in a picturesque river valley with direct access to a shallow trout stream. This level park has a good mix of grass and hard pitches, and is partly wooded with pleasant walks. It is surrounded by farmland, and just a few miles from the sandy beaches of both the north and south coasts, as well as St Michael's Mount at Marazion. An 18-acre site with 150 touring pitches and 48 statics.
Washing up sinks, fishing, licensed shop.
Facilities: � ⊙ ⌐ ✻ ✆ ☎ ✝ **Services:** ⬚⊡ⓘ⌀⊞⊤
→ ∪ ⏏ ◎ ✔ **Notes:** No single sex groups, no pets in caravans ⬚ ▨ ☑

See advertisement on page 58

Ruthern Valley Holiday

Open Apr-Oct **Booking** advisable high season **Last arrival** 21.00hrs **Last departure** noon
An attractive woodland site peacefully located in a small river valley west of Bodmin Moor. This away-from-it-all park is ideal for those wanting a quiet holiday, and the informal pitches are spread in four natural areas, with plenty of sheltered space.
A 2-acre site with 29 touring pitches and 6 statics.
Off-licence.
Leisure: ⚴ **Facilities:** ♟ ⊙ ✻ ✆ ☎ ⊞
Services: ⬚⊡ⓘ⌀⊞→∪⏏✔ ⬚ ▨ ▤ ☑

ST AGNES	Map 02 SW75

► ► ► 65% **Beacon Cottage Farm Touring Park** (SW705502)
Beacon Dr TR5 0NU ☎ 01872 552347 & 553381
e-mail: beaconcottagefarm@lineone.net
Dir: From A30 at Threeburrows rdbt, take B3277 to St Agnes, left into Goonvrea Rd & right into Beacon Drive, follow signs to Dobles
★ ⊞ £6-£14 ⊞ £6-£14 ▲ £6-£14
Open Apr-Oct (rs Etr-Whitsun shop closed) **Booking** advisable Jul-Aug **Last arrival** 20.00hrs **Last departure** noon
A neat and compact site utilizing a cottage and outhouses, an old orchard and adjoining walled paddock. Unique location on a headland looking NE along the coast. A 4-acre site with 50 touring pitches.
Leisure: ⚴ **Facilities:** ♟ ⊙ ⌐ ✻ ✆ ☎ ✝
Services: ⬚⊡ⓘ⌀⊞→∪⏏◎△✕✔
Notes: No single sex youth groups ⬚ ▨ ▤ ☑

► ► ► 64% **Blue Hills Touring Park** (SW732521)
Cross Combe TR5 0XP ☎ 01872 552999
Dir: Leave A30 at Chiverton rdbt onto B3277, pass through St Agnes towards Perranporth, turn left at Trevallas with brown sign to site in 1m
⊞ ⊞ ▲
Open Etr-Oct
Set in a beautiful rural position close to a coastal footpath, a small site with good toilet facilities. A pleasant location for exploring nearby coves, beaches and villages. A 2-acre site with 30 touring pitches.
Facilities: ♟ ⌐ ✆ **Services:** ⬚⊡

ROSUDGEON	Map 02 SW52

► ► ► 65% **Kenneggy Cove Holiday Park** (SW562287)
Higher Kenneggy TR20 9AU ☎ 01736 763453
e-mail: enquiries@kenneggycove.co.uk
website: www.kenneggycove.co.uk
Dir: On A394 between Penzance & Helston, turn S into signed lane to site & Higher Kenneggy
★ ⊞ £6.50-£11 ⊞ £6.50-£11 ▲ £5-£11

Open Apr-Nov **Booking** advisable Jul-Aug **Last arrival** 21.00hrs **Last departure** 11.00hrs
Set in an Area of Outstanding Natural Beauty with spectacular sea views, this family-owned park is quiet and well kept. Most of the grass pitches are level, and a short walk along a country footpath leads to the Cornish Coastal Path, and on to the golden sandy beach at Kenneggy Cove. A 4-acre site with 60 touring pitches and 9 statics.
Leisure: ⚴ **Facilities:** ⌁ ♟ ⊙ ⌐ ✻ ✆ ☎ ⊞
Services: ⬚⊡ⓘ⌀⊞⊤⌀→∪⏏△✕✔
Notes: No unaccompanied teenagers, large or single sex groups

---

RUTHERNBRIDGE	Map 02 SX06

► ► ► 64% **Ruthern Valley Holidays** (SX014665)
PL30 5LU ☎ 01208 831395 ◰ 01208 831395
e-mail: ruthernvalley@hotmail.com
website: www.self-catering-ruthern.co.uk
Dir: From Bodmin take A391 to St Austell, 2nd right to Ruthernbridge. From W left off A30 just before rdbt at Innes Downs and follow signs to Ruthernbridge. From N (Wadebridge A389) turn right just past Borough Arms at Dunmere then follow signs to Ruthernbridge.
★ ⊞ £7.75-£9.75 ⊞ £7.75-£9.75 ▲ £7.75-£9.75

contd.

► ► ► **64% Presingoll Farm Caravan & Camping Park** (SW721494)
TR5 0PB ☎ 01872 552333
e-mail: pam@presingollfarm.fsbusiness.co.uk
website: www.presingollfarm.fsbusiness.co.uk
Dir: From A30 Chiverton rdbt (Little Chef) take B3277 towards St Agnes. Park 3m on right
★ ⬡ fr £7 ⬡ fr £7 ▲ fr £7
Open Etr/Apr-Oct Booking advisable Jul & Aug Last departure 10.00hrs
An attractive rural park adjoining farmland, with extensive views of the coast beyond. Family owned and run, with level grass pitches, and modernised toilet block in smart converted farm buildings. A 3-acre site with 90 touring pitches.
Microwave, coffee/tea making facilities, pony riding
Leisure: ⛰ Facilities: ⬡⊙⬡✳⬡⬡⬡⬡⬡
Services: ⬡⬡⬡→⬡⬡

ST AUSTELL	Map 02 SX05

See also **Carlyon Bay**

► ► ► ► **69% River Valley Holiday Park** (SX010503) ✂
London Apprentice PL26 7AP ☎ 01726 73533
🖹 01726 73533
e-mail: johnclemo@aol.com
website: www.cornwall-holidays.co.uk
Dir: Direct access to park signed on B3273 from St Austell at London Apprentice
★ ⬡ £7-£16 ⬡ £7-£16 ▲ £7-£16

Open end Mar-Sep Booking advisable Jul-Aug Last arrival 22.00hrs Last departure 11.00hrs
A neat, well-maintained family-run park set in a pleasant river valley. The quality new toilet block and attractively landscaped grounds make this a delightful base for a holiday. A 2-acre site with 45 touring pitches and 40 statics.
Cycle trail.
Leisure: ⬡⬡⛰ Facilities: ⬡⊙⬡✳⬡⬡⬡
Services: ⬡⬡⬡→▶⬡⬡⬡⬡⬡⬡

► ► ► **59% Trencreek Farm Holiday Park** (SW966485)
Hewas Water PL26 7JG ☎ 01726 882540
🖹 01726 883254
e-mail: trencreek@aol.com
Dir: Off B3287, 1m from junct with A390
⬡⬡▲

contd.

Holiday bungalows, caravans and a fully serviced touring park. All with country views and within easy reach of the sea. No gaming machines, but a heated swimming pool, tennis court and fishing lake etc. We provide a supervised Kids Club in the main season and the park is safely situated a quarter of a mile off the main road, down our own private lane. **Special Offers:** Easter to mid July. Touring: **£45.00** per pitch, per week, including electric and the family.

**Trencreek Farm Holiday Park,
Hewaswater, St Austell,
Cornwall PL26 7JG
Telephone: 01726 882540
www.trencreek.co.uk**

Open Spring bank hol-13 Sep (rs Etr-Spring bank hol & 14 Sep-Oct restricted shop hours & pool closed) Booking advisable Jul-Aug Last arrival 21.00hrs Last departure noon
A working farm site with mature trees and bushes, close to river and lake. Animals roam around this friendly family park, and there are organised activities for children indoors and out. An 8-acre site with 184 touring pitches and 37 statics.
Fishing, fitness & agility course & mini golf.
Leisure: ⬡⬡⬡⛰⬡ Facilities: ⬡⬡⊙⬡⬡⬡⬡⬡
Services: ⬡⬡⬡⬡⬡⬡⬡→⬡▶⬡⬡⬡⬡⬡⬡⬡

► ► ► **61% Trewhiddle Holiday Estate** (SX010508)
Pentewan Rd PL26 7AD ☎ 01726 879420
🖹 01726 879421
e-mail: mcclelland@btinternet.com
website: www.trewhiddle.co.uk
Dir: Take B3273 from St Austell towards Mevagissey. Trewhiddle 0.75m from rdbt on right
★ ⬡ £6-£12 ⬡ £6-£12 ▲ £6-£12
Open all year Booking advisable Jul & Aug
Secluded wooded site with well-kept gardens, lawns and flower beds, set in the grounds of a mature estate, and with country club facilities. A 16.5-acre site with 105 touring pitches and 74 statics.
Leisure: ⬡⬡⛰ Facilities: ⬡⬡✳⬡⬡⬡
Services: ⬡⬡⬡⬡⬡⬡✕⬡→⬡▶⬡⬡⬡⬡
⬡⬡⬡⬡⬡⬡⬡

ST BLAZEY GATE   Map 02 SX05

▶ ▶ 68% **Doubletrees Farm** (SX060540)
Luxulyan Rd PL24 2EH ☎ 01726 812266
e-mail: doubletrees@eids.co.uk
website: www.eids.co.uk/doubletrees
*Dir: On A390 at Blazey Gate turn by Leek Seed Chapel,
after approx 300yds right by public seat into site*
★ ⊞ £7-£11 ⊞ £7-£11 ▲ £7-£9
Open all year Booking advisable Last arrival
22.30hrs Last departure 11.30hrs
*A popular park with terraced pitches offering
superb sea and coastal views. Close to beaches,
and the nearest park to the Eden Project, it is very
well maintained by friendly owners. A 1.75-acre site
with 30 touring pitches.*

Facilities: ⋔ ⊙ ⋒ ⊁ **Services:** ⊟ ⊞ → ∪ ⊳ ⊚ ⊡ ⊑

ST BURYAN   Map 02 SW42

▶ ▶ ▶ 65% **Camping & Caravanning
Club Site** (SW378276)
Higher Tregiffian Farm TR19 6JB ☎ 01736 871588
⊟ 024 7669 4886
website: www.campingandcaravanningclub.co.uk
*Dir: Follow A30 towards Lands End. Turn right onto
A3306 St Just/Pendeen Rd. Site 50yds on left*
★ ⊞ £11.10-£14.50 ⊞ £11.10-£14.50 ▲ £11.10-£14.50
Open May-Sep Booking advisable bank hols & Jul-
Aug Last arrival 21.00hrs Last departure noon
*Set in a rural area with distant views of Carn Brae
and the coast just 2m from Land's End, this very
good club site is well run with modern, clean
facilities. Recent development has resulted in a
children's playfield, late arrivals area and a dog-
exercising paddock. Please see the advertisement
on page 10 for details of Club Members' benefits. A
4-acre site with 75 touring pitches, 6 hardstandings.
Ball game area*

Leisure: ⚙ **Facilities:** ⋔ ⊙ ⚑ ⚒ ⚭ ⊹ ⊑ ⊁
Services: ⊟ ⊞ ⓘ ⌀ ⊞ → ∪ ⊳ ⚠ ⌨ ⊕ ▦ ▨ ⑨

▶ ▶ ▶ 64% **Lower Treave Caravan & Camping
Park** (SW388272)
Crows-an-Wra TR19 6HZ ☎ 01736 810559
⊟ 0870 0553647
e-mail: camping@lowertreave.demon.co.uk
website: www.lowertreave.demon.co.uk
*Dir: Direct access off A30 approx 0.25m after Crows-an-
Wra & just after unclass rd to St Buryan*
★ ⊞ £7-£9 ⊞ £7-£9 ▲ £7-£9
Open Apr-Oct Booking advisable Jul-Aug Last
arrival 22.30hrs Last departure 11.00hrs
*A terraced grass site sheltered by mature trees and
bushes, but still enjoying extensive rural views. The
popular blue-flag beaches at Whitesand Bay and
Sennen Cove are just 2.5m away, and ideal for
families and surfers. A 5-acre site with 80 touring
pitches and 5 statics.*

Facilities: ⋔ ⊙ ⚑ ⊹ ⊑ **Services:** ⊟ ⊞ ⓘ ⌀ ⊞ Ⓣ
→ ∪ ⊳ ⌨ ⊕ ▦ ▨ ⑨

▶ ▶ ▶ 63% **Tower Park Caravans &
Camping** (SW406263)
TR19 6BZ ☎ 01736 810286 ⊟ 01736 810954
e-mail: enquiries@towerparkcamping.co.uk
website: www.towerparkcamping.co.uk
*Dir: 4m from Sennen Cove & Porthcurno. Situated off
A30 & B3283*
⊞ £6-£8.50 ⊞ £6-£8.50 ▲ £6-£8.50
Open 8 Mar-Oct (rs Mar-Whit shop & cafe closed)
Booking advisable Jul-Aug Last arrival 22.00hrs
Last departure noon
*A rural site sheltered by mature trees, and divided
into four paddocks with all grass pitches. The
friendly owners keep the toilet facilities in a very
clean condition, and there are plenty of fishing
villages and unspoilt sandy coves to discover in this
remote area of Cornwall. A 6-acre site with 102
touring pitches and 5 statics.*

Leisure: ⚓ ⚙ ⊡ **Facilities:** ⋔ ⊙ ⚑ ⊹ ⚭ ⊹ ⊑ ⊞ ⋒ ⊁
Services: ⊟ ⊞ ⓘ ⌀ ⊞ ⊠ ⚒ → ∪ ⌨ ⊕ ▦ ▨ ⑨

▶ ▶ ▶ 66% **Treverven Touring Caravan &
Camping Site** (SW410237)
Treverven Farm TR19 6DL
☎ 01736 810200 & 871221 ⊟ 01736 871977
website: www.chycor.co.uk/camping/treverven
*Dir: Leave A30 onto B3283 1.5m after St Buryan, left
onto B3315. Site on right in 1m*
★ ⊞ £6.50-£10 ⊞ £6.50-£10 ▲ £6.50-£10
Open Etr-Oct Booking advisable Jul-Aug Last
departure noon
*Situated in a quiet Area of Outstanding Natural
Beauty with panoramic views, this family-owned
site is off a traffic-free lane leading directly to the
coastal path. Ideal for touring West Cornwall. Toilet
facilities have been refurbished and are very good.
A 6-acre site with 115 touring pitches.*

Treverven Touring Caravan & Camping Site

Leisure: ⚙ **Facilities:** ⋔ ⊙ ⚑ ⊹ ⚭ ⊑ ⊞ ⋒ ⊁
Services: ⊟ ⊞ ⓘ ⌀ ⚒ → ∪ ⌨ ⊕ ▦ ⑨

> **Campsites in popular areas get
> very crowded at busy times – it is
> advisable to book well in advance**

Leisure: 🏊 Indoor swimming pool   🏊 Outdoor swimming pool   ⚙ Tennis court   ⚫ Games room   ⚙ Children's playground   ∪ Stables
▶ 9/18 hole golf course   ⚓ Boats for hire   🎬 Cinema   ⚒ Fishing   ⊚ Mini golf   ⚠ Watersports   ⊡ Separate TV room

England

ST COLUMB MAJOR   Map 02 SW96

► ► ► 65% **Southleigh Manor Tourist Park (SW918623)**
TR9 6HY ☎ 01637 880938 🖷 01637 881108
e-mail: enquiries@southleigh-manor.com
Dir: Leave A30 at sign to RAF St Mawgan and St Columb onto A3059. Park 3m on left
★ �caravan £13.50-£15 �caravan £13.50-£15 ▲ £13.50-£15
Open Etr-Oct Shop open peak times only Booking advisable Jun-Aug Last arrival 20.00hrs Last departure noon
*A very well maintained **naturist park** in the heart of the Cornish countryside, catering for families and couples only. Seclusion and security are very well planned, and the lovely gardens provide a calm setting. A 2.5-acre site with 50 touring pitches. Sauna, Spa bath & croquet lawn.*
Leisure: ﹨⚲⊡ Facilities: ⚲⊙🢅⚲⟍ﾊ⚑⊼
Services: ⚙🗑🛢🖉⊞🎱→∪▶🝳

ST DAY   Map 02 SW74

► ► ► 63% **Tresaddern Holiday Park (SW733422)**
TR16 5JR ☎ 01209 820459
e-mail: holidays@tresaddern.co.uk
website: www.tresaddern.co.uk
Dir: From A30 at Scorrier onto B3298 towards Falmouth. St Day 2m, site signed, access on right
�caravan�caravan▲
Open Etr & Apr-Oct Booking advisable Jul-Aug
A tidy grass park, with friendly owners who keep it well maintained. Situated in a quiet spot in a rural area between Falmouth & Newquay, and within close walking distance of the attractive village of St Day. A 2-acre site with 15 touring pitches and 17 statics.
Facilities: ⚲⊙⚹ﾊﾊ Services: ⚙🗑🛢🖉⊞
→∪▶🝳🝳⚑

ST GENNYS   Map 02 SX19

► ► ► 65% **Camping & Caravanning Club Site (SX176943)**
Gillards Moor EX23 0BG ☎ 01840 230650
website: www.campingandcaravanningclub.co.uk
Dir: From S on A39 site on right in lay-by, 9m from Bude. From N on A39 site on left in lay-by 9m from Camelford. Approx 3m from B3262 junct.
★ �caravan £12.30-£15.50 �caravan £12.30-£15.50 ▲ £12.30-£15.50
Open May-Sep Booking advisable bank hols & Jul-Aug Last arrival 21.00hrs Last departure noon
A well-kept, level grass site with good quality facilities. Located midway between Bude and Camelford in an area full of sandy coves and beaches with good surfing. Please see the advertisement on page 10 for details of Club Members' benefits. A 6-acre site with 100 touring pitches, 12 hardstandings.
Recreation hall
Leisure: ⚲⊡ Facilities: ⚲⊙🢅⚹⚲ﾊﾊ
Services: ⚙🗑🛢🖉⊞🢅→∪▶🝳⚑🚌🖷🚐🝳

ST HILARY   Map 02 SW53

► ► ► 74% **Wayfarers Caravan & Camping Park (SW558314)**
Relubbus Ln TR20 9EF ☎ 01736 763326
e-mail: wayfarers@eurobell.co.uk
Dir: Turn left off A30 onto A394 towards Helston. Turn left at rdbt onto B3280 after 2m. Site 1.5m on left of main road
★ �caravan £7-£9.50 �caravan £7-£9.50 ▲ £7-£9.50
Open 5 Mar-Nov Booking advisable Jul & Aug Last arrival 21.00hrs Last departure 11.00hrs
A quiet sheltered park in a peaceful rural setting within 2.5m of St Michael's Mount. It offers spacious, well-drained pitches and very well cared for facilities. A 4.75-acre site with 54 touring pitches, 14 hardstandings and 4 statics.
Tourist information room, dish-washing room
Facilities: ⚲⊙🢅⚹ﾊ⚲ﾊ⊼ Services: ⚙🗑🛢🖉⊞🎱
→∪▶◎⚑🝳🝳⚑ Notes: Adults only

ST ISSEY   Map 02 SW97

► ► ► ► 66% **Trewince Farm Holiday Park (SW937715)**
PL27 7RL ☎ 01208 812830 🖷 01208 812835
Dir: From Wadebridge on A39 take A389 signed Padstow. Site 2m on left
�caravan�caravan▲
Open Etr-Oct Booking advisable anytime Last departure 11.00hrs
A family-owned park run to high standards amongst rolling farmland close to the coast. Part of a working farm, Trewince has been beautifully landscaped and offers good facilities. This comfortable and friendly park has a relaxed feel, and is only three miles from Padstow. A 6-acre site with 120 touring pitches and 35 statics.
Crazy golf, farm rides in summer, near Camel trail
Leisure: ﹨◖⚲ Facilities: 🢅⚲⊙🢅⚹⚲ﾊﾊ⚑🖷⊼ﾊ
Services: ⚙🗑🛢🖉⊞🢅→∪▶⚑🝳⚑🚌🖷🚐🝳🝳

See advertisement on page 57

Abbreviations: BH/bank hols-bank holidays   Etr-Easter   Whit-Whitsun   dep-departure   fr-from   hrs-hours   m-mile   mdnt-midnight   rdbt-roundabout   rs-restricted service   wk-week   wknd-weekend   ✂-no dogs

ST IVES   Map 02 SW54

▶ ▶ ▶ ▶ ▶ 72% **Polmanter Tourist Park (SW510388)**
Halsetown TR26 3LX ☎ 01736 795640
🖹 01736 795640
e-mail: reception@polmanter.com
website: www.polmanter.com
Dir: Signed off B3311 at Halsetown
★ 🚐 £10-£15 🚙 £10-£15 ▲ £10-£15
Open Whit-10 Sep (rs Mar-Whit & 12 Sep-Oct
shop, pool, bar & takeaway food closed)
Booking advisable Jul-Aug Last arrival 21.00hrs
Last departure 10.00hrs
*A well-developed touring park on high ground,
Polmanter offers high quality in all areas, from
the immaculate modern toilet blocks to the
outdoor swimming pool and hard tennis courts.
Pitches are individually marked and sited in
meadows, and the park has been tastefully
landscaped. The fishing port and beaches of
St Ives are just 1.5m away, and there is a bus
service in high season. A 20-acre site with 240
touring pitches.*
Putting, sports field, two family shower rooms.
Leisure: ⊰ ⊶ ◖ ⚠ **Facilities:** ⋒ ⊙ ⦑ ☀ ⦉ ⓩ ㅏ
Services: 🔌 🎱 ⓨ 🖹 ⌀ 🖃 Ⓣ ✕ 🛒 ➔ ∪ ⋏ ⊙ ⛟ ⛄ 🐾 ⅃
🍴 💳 VISA 📳 📶 ⑨

▶ ▶ ▶ 66% **Ayr Holiday Park (SW509408)**
TR26 1EJ ☎ 01736 795855 🖹 01736 798797
e-mail: recept@ayrholidaypark.co.uk
website: www.ayrholidaypark.co.uk   GOLD
*Dir: From A30 follow St Ives 'large vehicles' route via
B3311 through Halestown onto B3306. Park signed
towards St Ives town centre*   ⊀
★ 🚐 £10.75-£17 🚙 £10-£15.90 ▲ £10.75-£17

Open all year Booking advisable Jun-Aug Last
arrival 22.00hrs Last departure 10.00hrs
*A well-established park on a cliffside overlooking
St Ives Bay. There are stunning views from most
pitches, and the town centre, harbour and beach are
only 0.5m away. A 4-acre site with 40 touring
pitches, 20 hardstandings and 51 statics.*
Leisure: ◖ ⚠ **Facilities:** ⋒ ⊙ ⦑ ☀ ⦉ ⓩ 🖃 ㅠ ㅏ
Services: 🔌 🎱 ⅃ ⌀ 🖃 Ⓣ ➔ ∪ ⋏ ⛟ ⛄ 🐾 ⅃
🍴 💳 📳 📶 ⑨

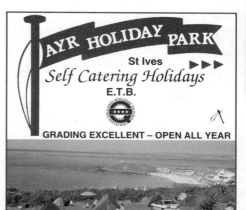

The only holiday park in St Ives itself, less than ½ mile
from the harbour, town centre and beaches. Beautiful
views over St Ives Bay. Holiday caravans and chalets, also
touring van and tent pitches. Electric hook-ups, free
showers, modern clean amenities. Signposted from
B3306, ½ mile west of town centre.

www.ayrholidaypark.co.uk
For brochure, write to:
**AA Baragwanath, Ayr Holiday Park, Ayr, St Ives,
Cornwall TR26 1EJ. Telephone: (01736) 795855**

▶ ▶ ▶ 65% **NEW Penderleath Caravan &
Camping Park (SW496375)**
Towednack TR26 3AF ☎ 01736 798403
website: www.penderleath.co.uk   GOLD
*Dir: From A30 take A3074 towards St Ives. At 2nd mini
rdbt, turn left and follow road to T-junct, approx 3m.
Turn left and then immediatley right, turn left at
next fork*
★ 🚐 £8-£12.50 🚙 £8-£12.50 ▲ £8-£12.50

Open Spring BH-Sep Booking advisable Jul-Aug
Last arrival 21.00hrs Last departure 10.30hrs
*Set in a rugged rural location, this tranquil park has
extensive views towards St Ives Bay and the north
coast. Facilities are all housed in modernised
granite barns, and include a quiet licensed bar with
beer garden, breakfast room and bar meals. The
owners are welcoming and helpful. A 10-acre site
with 75 touring pitches.*

contd.

Leisure: ◣ ⚐ **Facilities:** ⌐⊙◨❋◶ᴌ▯

Services: ⬜◨ᴥ⋆◐◨◨✕→∪▸◉◭✦♨◣

Notes: Dogs must be well behaved & kept on a lead

▶ ▶ ▶ **65% Trevalgan Holiday Farm Park (SW490402)**
Trevalgan TR26 3BJ ☎ 01736 796433
🖨 01736 799798
e-mail: trevalgan@aol.com
website: www.trevalganholidayfarm.co.uk ✗
Dir: From A30 follow St Ives 'large vehicles' route via B3311 through Halsetown. Turn left at junct with B3306 and site 0.5m on the right
🚐 £8-£14 🚐 £8-£14 ▲ £8-£14
Open Etr-Sep shop & takeaway open mid Jun-end Aug Booking advisable mid Jul-mid Aug Last arrival 23.30hrs Last departure noon
An open park next to a working farm in a rural area on the coastal road from St Ives to Zennor. The park is surrounded by mature hedges, but there are extensive views out over the sea. There is a good range of facilities. A 4.75-acre site with 120 touring pitches.
Farm trail, pets corner, mini golf

Leisure: ◣ ⚐ ▱ **Facilities:** ⌐⊙◨❋◶ᴌ▯⊞⊓⚡

Services: ⬜◨ᴥ⊙◨⊓✕⊞→∪▸♨◣⚫▦▣◨⚡

ST JUST (NEAR LAND'S END)   Map 02 SW33

▶ ▶ ▶ **63% Kelynack Caravan & Camping Park (SW374301)**
Kelynack TR19 7RE ☎ 01736 787633 🖨 01736 787633
e-mail: steve@kelynackholidays.co.uk
website: www.ukparks.co.uk/kelynack ✗
Dir: 1m S of St Just 5m N of Land's End on B3306
★ 🚐 £7 🚐 £7 ▲ £7
Open Apr-Oct Booking advisable Jul-Aug Last arrival 22.00hrs Last departure noon
A small secluded park nestling alongside a stream in an unspoilt rural location. The level grass pitches are in two areas, and the park is close to many coves, beaches, and ancient villages. A 2-acre site with 20 touring pitches, 5 hardstandings and 13 statics.
Wash-up room, dining & cooking shelter

Leisure: ◣ ⚐ **Facilities:** ⌐⊙◨❋◶ᴌ▯⊞⊓⚡

Services: ⬜ᴥ⊙◨⊓→▸♨◨

▶ ▶ ▶ **64% Roselands Caravan Park (SW387305)**
Dowran TR19 7RS ☎ 01736 788571 🖨 01736 788571
e-mail: camping@roseland84.freeserve.co.uk
website: www.roselands.co.uk
Dir: From A30 Penzance bypass turn right for St Just on A3071. Continue for 5m, turn left after Tin Mine Chimney at sign, follow signs to park
★ 🚐 £5-£8 🚐 £5-£8 ▲ £5-£8
Open Jan-Oct Booking advisable Jun-Sep Last arrival 21.00hrs Last departure 11.00hrs
A small, friendly park in a sheltered rural setting, an ideal location for a quiet family holiday. The owners are continuing to upgrade the park, and in addition to the attractive little bar there is an indoor games room, new children's playground, and good toilet facilities. A 3-acre site with 12 touring pitches and 15 statics.   *contd.*

Roselands Caravan Park

Cycle hire

Leisure: ◣ ⚐ **Facilities:** ⌐⊙◨❋ᴌ▯⊞⊓⚡

Services: ⬜◨ᴥ⊙◨✕⊞→∪▸♨

Notes: No single sex groups

▶ ▶ ▶ 65% **NEW** Trevaylor Caravan & Camping Park (SW368222)
Botallack TR19 7PU ☎ 01736 787016 ✗
e-mail: bookings@trevaylor.com
website: www.trevaylor.com
Dir: On B3306 St Just to St Ives road, campsite on right 0.75m from St Just
★ 🚐 £7-£8.50 🚐 £7-£8.50 ▲ £7-£8.50
Open Etr or 1 Apr-Oct Booking advisable Jul & Aug Last departure 12.00hrs
A sheltered grassy site located off the beaten track in a peaceful location at the western tip of Cornwall. The dramatic coastline and the pretty villages nearby are truly unspoilt. Clean, well-maintained facilities and a good shop are offered along with a bar serving tasty bar meals. A 6-acre site with 50 touring pitches.

Leisure: ◣ ⚐ **Facilities:** ⌐⊙◨❋ᴌ▯

Services: ⬜◨ᴥ⊙◨◨⊓✕→▸♨

▶ ▶ ▶ **65% Secret Garden Park, Bosavern House (SW370305)**
Bosavern House TR19 7RD ☎ 01736 788301
🖨 01736 788301
e-mail: marcol@bosavern.u-net.com
website: www.bosavern.u-net.com
Dir: Turn off A3071 near St Just onto B3306 Land's End road. Park 0.5m on left
★ 🚐 fr £8.50 🚐 fr £8.50 ▲ fr £8.50
Open Mar-Oct Booking advisable Jul-Aug Last arrival 22.00hrs Last departure 14.00hrs
A neat little site in a walled garden behind a guest house, where visitors can enjoy breakfast, and snacks in the bar in the evening. This site is in a fairly sheltered location with all grassy pitches. A 1.5-acre site with 12 touring pitches.

Leisure: ▱ **Facilities:** ⌐⊙❋ᴌ⊞

Services: ⬜◨⊞ᴥ→∪▸◭♨◨ᴌ⚫▦▣◨▦⚡

Remember sites which
take dogs may not accept
all breeds

ST JUST-IN-ROSELAND   Map 02 SW83

► ► ► **72% Trethem Mill Touring Park**
(SW860365)
TR2 5JF ☎ 01872 580504 📠 01872 580968
e-mail: reception@trethem-mill.co.uk
website: www.trethem-mill.co.uk
*Dir: From Tregony follow A3078 to St Mawes. 2m after
passing through Trewithian, follow signs to park*
★ 🚐 £8-£12 🚐 £8-£12 ▲ £8-£12

Open Apr-Oct Booking advisable Jul-Aug Last
arrival 21.00hrs Last departure 11.00hrs
*A carefully-tended and sheltered park in a rural
setting, with spacious pitches separated by young
trees and shrubs. This quiet park is personally run
by a very keen family. An 11-acre site with 84
touring pitches, 15 hardstandings.
Information centre*
Leisure: ⚓ ⚠ Facilities: 📵 ⊙ ❄ ✻ ↖ ⚑ ♂
Services: 🔌 🔋 ⚟ ⊿ 🗑 🛒 ➔ ∪ ⚊ ↘ ✒ 💳 💳 🏧

ST KEW HIGHWAY   Map 02 SX07

► ► **62% *Lanarth* (SX033751)**
PL30 3EE ☎ 01208 841215
*Dir: 3m NE of Wadebridge off A39, just before
entering village*
🚐
Open Etr/Apr-Oct Booking advisable
Last departure noon
*A sheltered site with level pitches, in the grounds of
a country hotel whose amenities are available to
those staying on site. Situated 3m from
Wadebridge, the centre of the famous Camel trail,
and only 4m from Port Isaac and the nearest beach.
A 9-acre site with 86 touring pitches.*
Facilities: 📵 ❄ ✻ ↖ 🚿 ♂
Services: 🔌 ⚟ 🔋 ⚟ ✗ ➔ ∪ ⚊ ⚞ ✒ 🗑

ST MABYN   Map 02 SX07

► ► ► **63% Glenmorris Park (SX055733)**
Longstone Rd PL30 3BY ☎ 01208 841677
📠 01208 841677
e-mail: glenmorrissw@aol.com
website: www.glenmorris.cornwall.eu.org
*Dir: S of Camelford on A39, left after BP garage to
B3266 to Bodmin, 6m to Longstone, right at x-rds to St
Mabyn, site approx 400mtrs right.*
★ 🚐 £6.50-£9.50 🚐 £6.50-£9.50 ▲ £6.50-£9.50
Open Etr-Oct Booking advisable Jul-Aug, all year for
statics Last departure 10.30hrs

Glenmorris Park
*A very good, mainly level park in a peaceful rural
location offering clean and well-maintained facilities
- a small games room, heated outdoor swimming
pool and sunbathing area, and shop. An ideal
location for visiting this unspoilt area. An 11-acre
site with 80 touring pitches and 6 statics.*
Leisure: ⚓ ⚓ ⚠ Facilities: 📵 ⊙ ❄ ✻ ↖ ⚑ ♂ ♒
Services: 🔌 🔋 ⚟ 🗑 ➔ ∪ ⚊ ✒ Notes: Quiet after 10pm

ST MARY'S   Map 02
See **Scilly, Isles**

ST MERRYN (NEAR PADSTOW)   Map 02 SW87

► ► ► **65% Carnevas Farm Holiday Park**
(SW862728)
Carnevas Farm PL28 8PN
☎ 01841 520230 & 521209 📠 01841 520230
*Dir: Leave St Merryn village on B3276 towards
Porthcothan Bay, in approx 2m turn right at site sign
into unclass road opposite Tredrea Inn, site in 0.25m on
right*
★ 🚐 £6.50-£11.75 🚐 £6.50-£11.75 ▲ £6.50-£11.75

Open Apr-Oct (rs Apr-Whit & mid Sep-Oct shop, bar
& restaurant closed) Booking advisable Jul-Aug
*A family-run park on a working farm, divided into
four paddocks on slightly sloping grass. The toilets
are central to all areas, and there is now a small
licensed bar serving bar meals. An 8-acre site with
195 touring pitches and 14 statics.*
Leisure: ⚓ ⚠ Facilities: 📵 ⊙ ❄ ✻ ↖ ⚑ ♂
Services: 🔌 🔋 ⚟ ⚟ ⊿ 🗑 ✗ ➔ ∪ ⚊ ❄ ⚞ ✒

contd.

For full details of the AA pennant
ratings scheme see page 7

► 62% Point Curlew Chalet & Touring Park
(...90717)
St Merryn PL28 8PY ☎ 01841 520855
🖹 01841 521413
e-mail: pointcurlew@lineone.net
website: www.pointcurlew.co.uk
Dir: Leave A39 Wadebridge to St Columb Road at
Winnards Perch rdbt onto B3274 towards Padstow. In
3m turn left onto unclass road to St Merryn follow
brown signs to park
★ 🚐 £7-£12 🚐 £7-£12 ▲ £5-£9

Open Etr-Oct No pets Booking advisable end Jun-
early Sep Last arrival 24.00hrs Last departure
12.00hrs ⚛
*A newly developed touring area, part of a larger
chalet park set in a quiet rural spot yet only 2 miles
from seven popular bays. Free entertainment is
available in high season and there are children's fun
nights, but there is also a quiet bar. A 4.5-acre site
with 70 touring pitches.*
Leisure: ♦ ⚠ 🎱 **Facilities:** 🛈 ⊙ ⚑ ※ ⚿ ℃ 🟤 🖬 🎋
Services: 🔌 🏪 ⚡✕ → ∪ ▶ ◉ ⚠ ⤴ ☕ ✈
💳 📧 🔷 📶 🚿

► ► 60% Tregavone Touring Park (SW898732)
Tregavone Farm PL28 8JZ ☎ 01841 520148
Dir: Leave A39 Wadebridge to St Columb Rd onto A389
towards Padstow, turn right after Little Petherick, in 1m
just beyond Padstow Holiday Park turn left into unclass
road signed St Merryn. Site on left in approx 1m
★ 🚐 £6.50-£8 🚐 £6.50-£8 ▲ £6.50-£8
Open Mar-Oct Booking advisable end Jul-beg Aug
*This rather open grassy park on a working farm has
good facilities in well-converted farm buildings. Run
by friendly owners, and handy for the beaches and
surfing areas on the North Cornish coast.
A 3-acre site with 40 touring pitches.*
Facilities: 🛈 ⊙ ※ 🎋
Services: 🔌 🏪 🖬 → ∪ ▶ ◉ ⚠ ⤴ ☕ ✈ 🟤

**► ► 66% Trevean Caravan & Camping Park
(SW875724)**
Trevean Ln PL28 8PR ☎ 01841 520772
🖹 01841 520772
Dir: From St Merryn take B3276 to Newquay for 1m.
Turn left for Rumford. Site 0.25m on right
🚐 £7-£8 🚐 £7-£8 ▲ £7-£8
Open Apr-Oct shop open Whit-Sep Booking
advisable mid Jul-Aug Last arrival 22.00hrs Last
departure 11.00hrs

Trevean Caravan & Camping Park
*A small working farm site with level grassy pitches
in open countryside. The toilet facilities are clean
and well kept, and there is a laundry and good
children's playground. A 1.5-acre site with 36
touring pitches and 3 statics.*
Leisure: ⚠ **Facilities:** 🛈 ⊙ ⚑ ※ ℃ ⚿ 🖬 🎋 **Services:** 🔌
🔋 🛢 ∅ 🖬 → ∪ ▶ ⤴ ☕ ✈ **Notes:** No teenage groups

ST MINVER   **Map 02 SW97**

**62% St Minver Holiday Park
(SW965772)**
PL27 6RR ☎ 01208 862305
🖹 01208 862265
website: www.parkdeanholidays.com
Dir: From A39 N of Wadebridge take B3314 Port
Isaac road. Site signed on left in 3m
★ 🚐 £6-£25 🚐 £6-£25 ▲ £6-£25
Open Etr-27 Oct Booking advisable Jul-Sep
Last arrival mdnt Last departure 10.00hrs
*A large holiday park set around St Minver House
in sylvan surroundings. The park offers a wide
range of holiday activities, including crazy golf,
table tennis and large indoor fun pool and
waterslide. A programme of family
entertainment is offered during evenings in the
high season, and there is an adult-only bar.
A 40-acre site with 120 touring pitches and 300
statics.*
Crazy golf, free evening entertainment,
amusements.
Leisure: ⚑ ♦ ⚠ **Facilities:** 🛈 ⊙ ⚑ ※ ℃ 🟤 🎋
Services: 🔌 🔋 ⚡ 🛢 ∅ 🖬 🖬 ✕ ⚓ → ▶ ⚠ ☕
💳 📧 🔷 📶 🚿

**► ► ► 67% Gunvenna Touring
Caravan & Camping Park (SW969782)**
PL27 6QN ☎ 01208 862405 🖹 01208 862405
Dir: From A39 N of Wadebridge take Port Isaac
road B3314, park 4m on right
🚐 🚐 ▲
Open Etr-Oct Booking advisable Jul-Aug Last arrival
mdnt Last departure 11.00hrs
*Attractive park with extensive rural views in a quiet
country location, yet within three miles of Polzeath.
This popular park is family owned and run, and
provides good facilities in an ideal position for
touring north Cornwall. A 10-acre site with 75
touring pitches and 25 statics.*

contd.

contd.

Abbreviations: BH/bank hols-bank holidays   Etr-Easter   Whit-Whitsun   dep-departure   fr-from   hrs-hours   m-mile   mdnt-midnight
rdbt-roundabout   rs-restricted service   wk-week   wknd-weekend   ⚛-no dogs

Gunvenna Touring Caravan and Camping Park

Leisure: ॰ ◆ ⚠ Facilities: ➡ ₨ ⊙ ⍰ ✳ ◟ ☎ ⊞ ⿴ ⼊

Services: ▣ ⊡ ▤ ▨ ⌀ → ∪ ▶ △ ⅄ ☲ ⤏

SCILLY, ISLES

BRYHER   Map 02

▶ ▶ ▶ 69% **Bryher Camp Site (SV880155)**
TR23 0PR ☎ 01720 422886 ▤ 01720 423092   ✗
★ **▲** £4.25-£5.75
Open Apr-Oct Booking advisable summer months
⚘

*Set on the smallest Scilly Isle with spectacular
scenery and white beaches, this tent-only site is in a
sheltered valley surrounded by hedges. Pitches are
located in paddocks at the northern end of the
island, and easily reached from the quay. There is a
good newly-built toilet block, and plenty of peace
and quiet. A 2.25-acre site with 38 touring pitches.*

Facilities: ₨ ⊙ ⍰ ✳ ☎ **Services:** ▤ ⌀ → ∪ ▶ ⊙ △ ⅄ ⤏
▣ **Notes:** No pets

ST MARY'S   Map 02

▶ ▶ ▶ 68% **Garrison Campsite (SV897104)**
Tower Cottage, The Garrison TR21 0LS
☎ 01720 422670 ▤ 01720 422625
e-mail: tedmoulson@aol.com
website: www.isles-of-scilly.co.uk
Dir: 10 mins walk from the Quay to the Garrison
★ **▲** £9.30-£13.10
Open Etr-Oct Booking advisable Jul & Aug Last
arrival 20.00hrs Last departure 19.00hrs ⚘
*Set on the top of an old fort with superb views, this
park offers tent-only pitches in a choice of well-
sheltered paddocks. There are modern toilet
facilities and a good shop at this attractive site,
which is only 10 mins from the town, the quay and
the nearest beaches. A 9.5-acre site with 120 touring
pitches.*

Facilities: ₨ ⊙ ⍰ ✳ ◟ ☎ **Services:** ▣ ▤ ⌀ ⊞ → ∪ ▶ △ ⅄
⤏ **Notes:** No pets, no open fires, no cars by tents

SENNEN   Map 02 SW32

▶ ▶ ▶ 65% **NEW** Trevedra Farm Caravan &
Camping Site (SW368276)
TR19 7BE ☎ 01736 871818 & 871835   ✗
▤ 01736 871835
e-mail: nicholastrevedra@ farming.co.uk
website: www.sennen-cove.com/trevedra
*Dir: Take A30 to Land's End. After B3306 junct turn right
off A30 into farm lane*
🚐 £9.50-£12 🚐 £9.50-£12 **▲** £7-£10
Open Good Fri or 1 Apr-Oct Booking advisable peak
seasons Last arrival 24.00hrs Last departure
12.00hrs
*A working farm with dramatic sea views over the
Scilly Isles, just a mile from Land's End. The
popular campsite offers refurbished toilets, a well-
stocked shop, and a cooked breakfast or evening
meal in the food bar. There is direct access to the
coastal footpath, and two beautiful beaches are a
short walk away. An 8-acre site with 100 touring
pitches.*

Facilities: ₨ ⊙ ⍰ ✳ ◟ ☎ ⼊ **Services:** ▣ ▣ ▤ ⌀ ⊞ ⊡ ⤴
➡ → ∪ ▶ △ ⤏ **Notes:** Dogs must be kept on leads at
all times

Facilities: ➡ Bath   ₨ Shower   ⊙ Electric Shaver   ⍰ Hairdryer   ✳ Ice Pack Facility   ◟ Disabled Facilities   ☎ Public Telephone
☎ Shop on Site or within 200yds   ▣ Mobile Shop (calls at least 5 days a week)   ⊞ BBQ Area   ⿴ Picnic Area   ⼊ Dog Exercise Area

TINTAGEL
Map 02 SX08

See also **Camelford**

▶ ▶ ▶ 65% **Headland Caravan & Camping Park (SX056887)**

Atlantic Rd PL34 0DE ☎ 01840 770239
🖺 01840 770925

e-mail: headland.cp@virgin.net
website: www.headlandcp-tintagel.co.uk
Dir: From B3263 follow brown tourist signs through village to Headland
🚐 🚙 ⅄

Open Etr-Oct Booking advisable Jul-Aug Last arrival 21.00hrs

A peaceful family-run site in the mystical village of Tintagel, close to the ruins of King Arthur's Castle. The Cornish coastal path and the spectacular scenery are just two of the attractions here, and there are safe bathing beaches nearby. A 5-acre site with 62 touring pitches and 28 statics.

Leisure: ⚠ Facilities: 🍳⊙🔧✳🕿🌢🛁⅄ Services: 🚱🔋🛢∅🔲🔳→∪🛆↯ ⅃ Notes: Dogs must be kept on short leads & exercised off park 💳 ⬛ ⬛ ⬛ 🔟

TORPOINT
Map 02 SX45

61% **Whitsand Bay Holiday Park (SX410515)**

Millbrook PL10 1JZ ☎ 01752 822597
🖺 01752 823444

e-mail: enquiries@whitsandbayholidays.co.uk
website: www.whitsandbayholidays.co.uk
Dir: From Torpoint take A374, turn left at Anthony onto B3247 for 1.25m to T-junct. Turn left, 0.25m then right onto Cliff Rd. Site 2m on left
★ 🚐 £4-£19 🚙 £4-£19 ⅄ £4-£19

Open all year Booking advisable Last arrival 24.00hrs Last departure 10.00hrs

contd.

A very well equipped park with panoramic views from its terraced pitches, and plenty of on-site entertainment including discos and children's club in high season in the lively clubhouse. A 27-acre site with 100 touring pitches and 100 statics.

Sauna, sunbed, entertainment, putting, chapel, library

Leisure: 🏊 ⚓ ⚠ 🖵 Facilities: 🍳⊙🔧✳🕿🌢🛁⅄🏪 🎪 🕿 Services: 🚱🔋🍴🛢∅🔲🔳✗🛒→∪🛈◉🛆↯ ⅃

Notes: Families & couples only 💳 ⬛ ⬛ ⬛ 🔟
See advertisement on page 73

TREGURRIAN
Map 02 SW86

▶ ▶ ▶ 69% **Camping & Caravanning Club Site (SW853654)**

TR8 4AE ☎ 01637 860448
website: www.campingandcaravanningclub.co.uk
Dir: From A3059 to Newquay. 1.5m on, after service station, right to Newquay Airport. Continue to junct then left to Tregurrian. Follow Watergate Bay signs
★ 🚐 £12.30-£15.50 🚙 £12.30-£15.50 ⅄ £12.30-£15.50
Open May-Sep Booking advisable bank hols & Jul-Aug Last arrival 21.00hrs Last departure noon

A level grassy site close to the famous beaches of Watergate Bay, with a modern amenity block. This upgraded club site is an excellent touring centre for the Padstow-Newquay coast. Please see the advertisement on page 10 for details of club membership. A 4.25-acre site with 90 touring pitches, 8 hardstandings.

Parent & child room, motor caravan service area.

Facilities: 🍳⊙🔧✳🕿🌢🛁 Services: 🚱🔋🛢∅🔲🔳→∪🛈◉🛆↯🛒💳⬛⬛⬛🔟

TRURO
Map 02 SW84

▶ ▶ ▶ ▶ 69% **Ringwell Valley Holiday Park (SW805408)**

Bissoe Rd, Carnon Downs TR3 6LQ
☎ 01872 862194 & 865409 🖺 01872 864343
e-mail: keith@ringwell.co.uk
Dir: Signed off A39 at 3rd rdbt from Truro into Carnon Downs. Bissoe Rd 3rd on right
★ 🚐 £9-£15 🚙 £9-£15 ⅄ £9-£15
Open Etr-Sep Booking advisable Jul & Aug Last arrival 21.30hrs Last departure noon

A well-run park nestling in a tranquil valley with open countryside views. Four separate touring areas are allocated for caravans, tents and motor vans, with the freedom to pitch on a favoured spot. The park is set in 12 acres of lush parkland, and at the bottom of the valley in a sheltered sun-trap is the swimming pool, next to the pub. A 12-acre site with 34 touring pitches and 44 statics.

Leisure: 🏊 ⚓ ⚠ Facilities: 🛁🍳⊙🔧✳🕿🛁🏪 🎪 🕿 Services: 🚱🔋🍴🛢∅🔲✗🛒→🛆↯🛢🛒 ⅃

Notes: No single sex groups 💳 ⬛ ⬛ ⬛ 🔟

► ► ► **71% Carnon Downs Caravan & Camping Park (SW805406)**
Carnon Downs TR3 6JJ
☎ 01872 862283
e-mail: info@carnon-downs-caravanpark.co.uk
website: www.carnon-downs-caravanpark.co.uk
Dir: Take A39 from Truro towards Falmouth. Site just off the main Carnon Downs rdbt, on left
★ ⊞ £7.50-£13.50 ⊞ £7.50-£13.50 ▲ £7.50-£13.50

OPEN ALL YEAR

Open all year Booking advisable Jul-Aug Last arrival 22.00hrs Last departure 11.00hrs
A mature park with a high standard of landscaping, set in meadowland and woodland close to the village amenities of Carnon Downs. The toilet facilities have been upgraded to provide quality and comfort in an en suite environment. An 11-acre site with 110 touring pitches and 1 static.
Baby & child bathroom, 3 family bathrooms.
Leisure: ⚠ ⬜ **Facilities:** ⇥ ⍨⊙⛱☀♿⌲☎
Services: ⊞⊟⍮⊿⊞⊤→∪▶⚠⅄⚿⊿⚡
⚫ ⚞ ⚞ ⚞ ⚞

► ► ► **68% Summer Valley (SW800479)**
Shortlanesend TR4 9DW ☎ 01872 277878
e-mail: res@summervalley.co.uk
website: www.summervalley.co.uk
Dir: 3m NW off B3284
★ ⊞ £8.50-£10.50 ⊞ £8.50-£10.50 ▲ £8.50-£10.50

Open Apr-Oct Booking advisable Jul-Aug Last arrival 22.00hrs Last departure noon
A very attractive and secluded site in a rural setting midway between the A30 and the cathedral city of Truro. Keen owners maintain the facilities to a good standard. A 3-acre site with 60 touring pitches.
Campers' lounge.
Leisure: ⚠ **Facilities:** ⍨⊙⛱☀⚿⚡☎
Services: ⊞⊟⍮⊿⊞⊤→∪▶⚿⊿⚫⚞⚞

Treloan Coastal Farm

Treloan Lane, Portscatho, The Roseland,
Truro, Cornwall TR2 5EF
Tel:/Fax: (01872) 580989
Tel:/Answerphone: (01872) 580899
E-mail: holidays@treloan.freeserve.co.uk
Website: www.coastalfarmholidays.com

CORNWALL

AA ▪▶   APPROVED

Idyllic site with uninterrupted views on coastal footpath, private access to three beautiful, clean and safe coves. Traditional organic working farm of the 1930s with Shire horses. Facilities: Mobile homes with telephone/modem points, touring and camping pitches with electric hook-ups, also super pitches, hot showers, laundry, sea fishing, river moorings. Three minutes walk from Portscatho with shops, pubs and churches. Half hour drive from Truro and the Eden Project, St Austell. Pets welcome.

► ► **67% Killiwerris Touring Park (SW752455)**
Penstraze, Chacewater TR4 8PF ☎ 01872 561356
Dir: At Chiverton Cross rdbt on A30, 3rd exit signed Blackwater, after 200yds 1st left to unclassified rd. Site 1m right.
⊞ fr £7 ⊞ fr £7 ▲ fr £7
Open Apr-Oct Booking advisable Jul-Sep Last arrival 21.00hrs Last departure 14.00hrs
A very comfortable park for adults, run by friendly owners in a rural location within easy reach of Truro and St Agnes. The purpose-built toilet block is kept very neat and clean, and the grass is well trimmed. A 1-acre site with 20 touring pitches.
Facilities: ⍨⊙☀⚲ **Services:** ⊞⊟→∪▶⊿⊞⚡
Notes: Adults only

VERYAN   **Map 02 SW93**

► ► ► **65% Camping & Caravanning Club Site (SW934414)**
Tretheake Manor TR2 5PP ☎ 01872 501658
website: www.campingandcaravanningclub.co.uk
Dir: Left off A3078 at filling station signed Veryan/Portloe on unclass road. Site signed on left
★ ⊞ £12.30-£15.50 ⊞ £12.30-£15.50 ▲ £12.30-£15.50
Open Mar-Nov Booking advisable Jul-Aug & BH's
Last arrival 21.00hrs Last departure noon

contd.

A level grassy site close to the famous beaches of Watergate Bay, with a modern amenity block. This upgraded club site is an excellent touring centre for the Padstow-Newquay coast. Please see the advertisement on page 10 for details of Club Member's benefits. A 9-acre site with 150 touring pitches, 7 hardstandings.
Fishing
Leisure: ◄ /Å/ Facilities: ⌐⊙╣☀⚹◄ ⌂ ⍏
Services: ⊟⬚🅱🔒⌐⊞→↘↗⌦⏚☎☰☰☰ 🗺 ⑤

WADEBRIDGE
Map 02 SW97

▶ ▶ ▶ 66% **The Laurels Holiday Park (SW957715)**
Padstow Rd, Whitecross PL27 7JQ
☎ 01208 813341 & 07799 777715 🖹 01208 816590
e-mail: anicholson@thelaurels-park.freeserve.co.uk
website: www.thelaurels-park.freeserve.co.uk
Dir: Off A389 Padstow road nr junct with A39, W of Wadebridge
★ ⊞ £5-£12 ⊞ £5-£12 ▲ £5-£12
Open Apr/Etr-Oct Booking advisable Jul-Sep Last arrival 20.00hrs Last departure 12.00hrs
Much recent upgrading has resulted in a very smart, well-equipped park with new laundry, reception, dish-wash area, and dog walk. Individual pitches are screened by hedges and young shrubs, and the keen, friendly owners keep the park in very good condition. The Camel cycle trail and Padstow are not far away. A 2.25-acre site with 30 touring pitches.
Leisure: /Å/ Facilities: ⌐⊙╣☀⚹⌦☎☰⍏
Services: ⊟🅱⊞→⌦↘↗⌦
Notes: Dogs must be kept on leads

▶ ▶ ▶ 63% **Little Bodieve Holiday Park (SW995734)**
Bodieve Rd PL27 6EG ☎ 01208 812323
e-mail: berry@littlebodieveholidaypark.fsnet.co.uk
website: www.littlebodieve.co.uk
Dir: From A39 rdbt on Wadebridge by-pass take B3314 signed Rock/Port Isaac, site 0.25m on right
★ ⊞ £7.70-£10.70 ⊞ £7.70-£10.70 ▲ £7.70-£10.70

Open Apr-Oct (rs early & late season pool & shop closed) Booking advisable Jul-Aug Last arrival 20.00hrs Last departure 11.00hrs
Set in a rural area with pitches located in three large paddocks of mostly level grass, this family park is close to the Camel Estuary. The licensed clubhouse provides bar meals, with an entertainment

contd.

programme in high season, and there is a swimming pool with sun terrace, and a separate waterslide and splash pool. A 20-acre site with 195 touring pitches and 75 statics.
Crazy golf, water shute/splash pool.
Leisure: ⌐ ◄ /Å/ Facilities: ⍖⌐⊙╣☀⚹◄⌦☎⍏
Services: ⊟🅱🔒🔒⌐⊞①✕⏚→⌦⌦☎⌦☰☰☰☰🗺⑤

WATERGATE BAY
Map 02 SW86

▶ ▶ ▶ 71% **Watergate Bay Tourist Park (SW850653)**
Watergate Bay TR8 4AD ☎ 01637 860387
🖹 01637 860387 ✕
e-mail: watergatebay@email.com
website: www.watergatebaytouringpark.co.uk
Dir: 4m N of Newquay on B3276 coast road at Watergate Bay
★ ⊞ £7.50-£12.80 ⊞ £7.50-£12.80 ▲ £7.50-£12.80
Open 22 May-12 Sep (rs Mar-21 May & 13 Sep-Nov restricted bar, cafe, shop & swimming pool)
Booking advisable Jul-Aug Last arrival 22.00hrs Last departure noon
A well-established park set on high ground above Watergate Bay, with its acres of golden sands and many rock pools. The toilet facilities have been refurbished to a superb standard in two out of three blocks, and there is a regular entertainment programme in the clubhouse. A 32-acre site with 171 touring pitches, 14 hardstandings.
Entertainment, free minibus to beach.
Leisure: ⌐ ◄ /Å/ ⊡ Facilities: ⍖⌐⊙╣☀⚹◄⌦☎⍏
Services: ⊟🅱🔒🔒⌐⊞①✕⏚→⌦⊙▲⌦
☰☰☰☰🗺⑤

WHITECROSS
Map 02 SW85

70% **White Acres Holiday Park (SW890599)**
TR8 4LW ☎ 01726 860220 &
0845 4580065 🖹 01726 860777
e-mail: reception@whiteacres.co.uk
website: www.whiteacres.co.uk
Dir: From A30 at Indian Queens take A392 signed Newquay. Site 2m on right
⊞ £9-£27 ⊞ £9-£27 ▲ £9-£27
Open end Mar-end Oct Booking advisable Etr-Whit & Jul-Aug Last arrival midnight Last departure 10.00hrs
A large holiday complex, partially terraced, in a rural setting, with one of the best coarse fishing centres in the South West on site. The centre covers 100 acres of woodland, water and grass, and there is a wide range of leisure activities. A 140-acre site with 40 touring pitches and 245 statics.
Entertainment, sauna, solarium, fishing, gym, bowling
Leisure: ⌐ ◄ /Å/ Facilities: ⌐⊙╣☀⚹◄⌦☎⍏
Services: ⊟🅱🔒🔒⌐⊞①✕⏚→⌦⌦
☰☰☰☰🗺⑤

England

▶ ▶ ▶ **65%** *Summer Lodge Holiday Park*
(SW890597)
TR8 4LW ☎ 01726 860415 🗎 01726 861490
e-mail: reservations@summerlodge.co.uk
*Dir: From Indian Queens on A30 take A392 to Newquay.
Site on left at Whitecross in 2.5m*
🚐 🚐 ⚠
Open Whit-Oct (rs Etr-Whit & Sep-Oct shop cafe
closed) Booking advisable Jul-Aug Last arrival
20.00hrs Last departure noon ⚘
*Small holiday complex offering use of good
facilities. This park has a nightly cabaret in the
licensed pub, plus other on-site entertainment. A
26-acre site with 75 touring pitches and 114 statics.*
Leisure: ⚓ ⚓ ⚠ **Facilities:** ↖⊙⚘✻⚃⚓⚓⚓⚓
Services: ⚓⚓⚓⚓⚓⚓⚓✕⚓→∪⚓ ⚓ ⚓⚓⚓ ⚓

WIDEMOUTH BAY   **Map 02 SS20**

65% **Widemouth Bay Caravan Park**
(SS199008)
EX23 0DF ☎ 01288 361208 &
01271 866766 🗎 01271 866791
e-mail: bookings@jfhols.co.uk
website: www.johnfowlerholidays.com
*Dir: take Widemouth Bay coastal road off A39,
turn left. Park on left*
★ 🚐 £9-£25 🚐 £9-£25 ⚠ £9-£25
Open Mar-Oct Booking advisable Last arrival
23.00hrs Last departure 10.00hrs
*A partly sloping rural site set in countryside
overlooking the sea and one of Cornwall's finest
beaches. Nightly entertainment in high season
with emphasis on children's and family club
programmes. This park is located less than half
a mile from the sandy beaches of Widemouth
Bay. A 10-acre site with 100 touring pitches and
150 statics.*
Leisure: ⚓ ⚓ ⚠ **Facilities:** ↖⊙⚘✻⚃⚓⚓⚓⚓⚓
Services: ⚓⚓⚓⚓⚓⚓✕⚓→∪⚓⊙⚓⚓⚓
⚓⚓⚓⚓
See advertisement on page 34

▶ ▶ ▶ **61%** *Cornish Coast Caravan & Camping*
(SS202981)
Middle Penlean, Poundstock EX23 0EE
☎ 01288 361380
e-mail: enquiries@cornishcoasts.co.uk
website: www.cornishcoasts.co.uk
*Dir: 5m S of Bude, access from layby on coastal
side of A39*
★ 🚐 £5.50-£7.50 🚐 £5.50-£7.50 ⚠ £4.50-£7.50
Open Etr-Oct Booking advisable School summer
holidays Last departure 10.30hrs
*A quiet family-run park, with terraced pitches
making the most of the stunning views over the
countryside to the sea at Widemouth Bay.
Reception is in a 13th-century cottage, and the park
is well equipped and tidy. A 3.5-acre site with 45
touring pitches and 4 statics.*
Leisure: ⚠ **Facilities:** ↖⊙⚘✻⚃⚓⚓⚓
Services: ⚓⚓⚓⚓⚓⚓→⚓⚓⚓
Notes: Single sex groups by application only

▶ ▶ ▶ **62%** Penhalt Farm Holiday Park (SS194003)
EX23 0DG ☎ 01288 361210 🗎 01288 361210
e-mail: denandjennie@penhaltfarm.fsnet.co.uk ✗
*Dir: From Bude take Widemouth Bay road off A39, left
at end of road signed Millook onto Cornish coastal road.
Site 0.75m on left*
★ 🚐 £6-£12 🚐 £6-£12 ⚠ £5.50-£10

Open Etr-Oct Booking advisable Jul & Aug
*Splendid views of the sea and coast can be enjoyed
from all pitches on this sloping but partly level site,
set in a rural area on a working farm. An 8-acre site
with 100 touring pitches.*
Pool table.
Leisure: ⚓ ⚠ **Facilities:** ↖⊙⚘✻⚃⚓⚓⚓
Services: ⚓⚓⚓⚓⚓→∪⚓⚓⚓⚓⚓ ⚓ ⚓⚓⚓⚓
See advertisement on page 36

CUMBRIA

AMBLESIDE   **Map 07 NY30**

▶ ▶ ▶ ▶ **68%** *Skelwith Fold Caravan*
Park (NY355029)
LA22 0HX ☎ 015394 32277 🗎 015394 32327
*Dir: Leave Ambleside on A593 towards
Coniston, turn left at Clappersgate on 1m
onto B5286 Hawkshead road. Park 1m on right*
🚐 🚐
Open Mar-15 Nov Booking advisable public hols &
Jul-Aug Last departure noon
*In the grounds of a former mansion, this park is in a
beautiful setting close to Lake Windermere. Touring
areas are dotted in paddocks around the extensively
wooded grounds, and the all-weather pitches are
set close to the many facility buildings. There is a
5-acre family recreation area which has spectacular
views of Loughrigg Fell. A 10-acre site with 150
touring pitches and 300 statics.*
Family recreation area.
Leisure: ⚠ **Facilities:** ↖⊙⚘✻⚃⚓⚓⚓⚓⚓
Services: ⚓⚓⚓⚓⚓⚓→∪⚓⊙⚓⚓⚓

▶ ▶ ▶ **65%** Low Wray National Trust Campsite
(NY372013)
Low Wray LA22 0JA ☎ 015394 32810
🗎 015394 32810
*Dir: 3m SW via A583 to Clappersgate, then B5286 and
unclass road*
★ ⚠ fr £10
contd.

Open wk before Etr-Oct Last arrival 21.00hrs no cars by caravans no cars by tents

Picturesquely-set on the wooded shores of Lake Windermere, this site is a favourite with tenters and watersports enthusiasts. The well-maintained facilities are housed in wooden cabins, and tents can be pitched in wooded glades with lake views or open grassland. Off-road biking, walks and pub food are all nearby. A 10-acre site with 200 touring pitches.

Launching for sailing.

Leisure: ⚲ **Facilities:** ⬧⊙⬧⬧⬧→⬧⬧⬧⬧
⬧⬧⬧⬧⬧

APPLEBY-IN-WESTMORLAND   Map 12 NY62

PREMIER PARK

▶ ▶ ▶ ▶ ▶ 75% **Wild Rose Park**
(NY698165)
Ormside CA16 6EJ
☎ 017683 51077 ▤ 017683 52551
e-mail: hs@wildrose.co.uk
website: www.wildrose.co.uk
Dir: *Signed on unclass road to Great Ormside, off B6260*
★ ⬧ £10.20-£16.90 ⬧ £10.20-£16.90
⚠ £10.20-£16.90

Open all year (rs Nov-Mar shop, swimming pool & restaurant closed) Booking advisable bank & school hols Last arrival 22.00hrs Last departure noon

Situated in the Eden Valley, this large family-run park has been carefully landscaped and offers superb facilities maintained to an extremely high standard. There are several individual pitches, and extensive views from most areas of the park. Traditional stone walls and the planting of lots of indigenous trees help it to blend into the environment, and wildlife is actively encouraged. A 40-acre site with 240 touring pitches, 140 hardstandings and 240 statics.

Tourist Information, pitch and putt.

Leisure: ⬧⬧⚲⬧ **Facilities:** ⬧⊙⬧⬧⬧⬧⬧⬧
Services: ⬧⬧⬧⬧⬧⬧⬧×⬧→▶⬧ **Notes:** No unaccompanied teenagers, no dangerous dogs
⬧⬧⬧⬧⬧

Friendly park in beautiful Eden Valley, twixt Lakes and Dales. Excellent facilities include – Heated outdoor pools, play areas, indoor TV and games rooms, mini-market and licensed restaurant. Luxury holiday homes for sale, but no letting, no bar, no club. Brochure with pleasure.

Ormside, Appleby-in-Westmorland, Cumbria CA16 6EJ
Tel: Appleby (017683) 51077
E-Mail: broch@wildrose.co.uk
or visit our Website www.wildrose.co.uk

AYSIDE   Map 07 SD38

▶ ▶ ▶ 60% **Oak Head Caravan Park** (SD389839)
LA11 6JA ☎ 015395 31475
website: www.oakheadcaravanpark.co.uk
Dir: *From M6 junct 36, follow A590 towards Newby Bridge, 14m. Park sign on L, 1.25m past High Newton*
★ ⬧ £10-£12 ⬧ £10 ⚠ £8.50-£10
Open Mar-Oct Booking advisable bank hols Last arrival anytime Last departure noon

A pleasant terraced site with two separate areas - grass for tents and all gravel pitches for motorhomes and caravans. The site is enclosed within mature woodland and surrounded by hills. A 3-acre site with 60 touring pitches, 30 hardstandings and 71 statics.

Facilities: ⬧⊙⬧⬧⬧⬧⬧⬧ **Services:** ⬧⬧⬧⬧⬧
→⬧⬧⬧⬧⬧ **Notes:** No singles groups unless supervised

BARROW-IN-FURNESS   Map 07 SD26

▶ ▶ ▶ 68% **South End Caravan Park** (SD208628)
Walney Island LA14 3YQ ☎ 01229 472823 & 471556
e-mail: enquiries@walney-island-caravan-park.com
website: www.walney-island-caravan-park.co.uk
Dir: *In Barrow follow signs for Walney Island. Turn left after crossing bridge. 4m S*
★ ⬧ £9-£13 ⬧ £9-£13 ⚠ £8-£13

contd.

South End Caravan Park

Open Mar-Oct Booking advisable Jul-Aug Last arrival 22.00hrs Last departure noon
Mainly level grass site adjacent to the sea, and close to a nature reserve, on the southern end of Walney Island. This friendly family run park offers an extensive range of good quality amenities and high standards of cleanliness and maintenance. A 7-acre site with 60 touring pitches and 100 statics. Bowling green

Leisure: ♀ ♠ ⚓ ☐ Facilities: ☂ ⊙ ☀ ₺ ℂ ℥ ⅂
Services: ▢ ▥ ⅁ ₷ ⌀ ⊟ ⅏ → ∪ ⌲ ⅍ ⅃ ▩ ⊠ ▨ ⅁

BASSENTHWAITE LAKE
See map for locations of sites in the vicinity

BECKFOOT
⛺ **Rowanbank Caravan Park (NY193497)**
CA7 4LA ☎ 016973 31653 ▤ 016973 31653
Dir: On B5300 coast road, 3m S of Silloth. Park on left, 0.25m past Beckfoot village sign
⊞ £8-£10 ⊕ £8-£10 ▲ £6-£10
Open Mar-14 Nov Booking advisable BH's Last arrival 21.00hrs Last departure 12.00hrs
At the time of going to press, the pennant rating for this site was not confirmed.
A 3.5-acre site with 30 touring pitches, 11 hardstandings and 30 statics.
Leisure: ⚓ Facilities: ☂ ⊙ ☀ ℂ Services: ▢ ▥ ₷ ⊟ ⊞
→ ⌲ ◎ ⌀ ⅃ ℥ Notes: No groups of unaccompanied young people or large non-family groups

BOOT   Map 07 NY10
▶ ▶ ▶ **68% Hollins Farm Campsite (NY178011)**
Hollins Farm CA19 1TH ☎ 019467 23253
e-mail: james.bogg@tesco.net
website: www.hollinsfarmcampsite.co.uk
Dir: Leave A595 at Gosforth or Holmbrook to Eskdale Green and on to Boot. Site on left towards Hardknott Pass after railway
★ ▲ fr £8
Open all year Booking advisable BH's Last departure 18.30hrs
A very pleasant farm site that is an ideal touring base with excellent hill walking, and a popular site with backpackers/tenters. Only 0.25m from Boot station on the Ravenglas/Eskdale railway, 'The Ratty'. There are no electric hook-ups or chemical disposal points. A 2-acre site with 35 touring pitches, 4 hardstandings.

contd.

Facilities: ☂ ⊙ ℥ → ▤ Notes: No under 18s unless accompanied by mature adult, no groups of 4+ without notice, no open fires

BOWNESS-ON-WINDERMERE
Sites are listed under **Windermere**

BRAITHWAITE   Map 11 NY22
▶ ▶ ▶ 59% Scotgate Holiday Park (NY235235)
CA12 5TF ☎ 017687 78343 ▤ 017687 78099
website: www.scotgateholidaypark.co.uk
Dir: At junct of A66 and B5292, 2m from Keswick
⊞ £13-£16 ⊕ £7-£9.50 ▲ £7.50-£9

Open Mar-Oct Last arrival 22.00hrs Last departure 11.00hrs
Dramatic views of Skiddaw and the northern Fells dominate this pleasant rural site, which is frequented by with tenters and close to the starting point of several walking routes. A popular café serves breakfast and other meals, and there is easy access to Whinlatter Forest, Keswick, and Bassenthwaite Lake. An 8-acre site with 165 touring pitches and 35 statics.
Leisure: ⚓ Facilities: ☂ ⊙ ℥ ☀ ℂ ℥ ⅂
Services: ▢ ▥ ₷ ⌀ ⊟ ✗ ⅏ → ◎ ⌀ ⅄ ⅍ ⅃ ▩ ⊠ ▨ ⅁

BRAMPTON   Map 12 NY56
▶ ▶ ▶ 58% Irthing Vale Holiday Park (NY522613)
Old Church Ln CA8 2AA ☎ 016977 3600
e-mail: glen@irthingvale.freeserve.co.uk
website: www.ukparks.co.uk/irthingvale
Dir: From A69 take A6071 to site, 0.5m outside town. Turn opposite entrance to leisure centre by the school & take care in narrow lane
★ ⊞ £9-£11 ⊕ £9-£11 ▲ £9-£11

contd.

England

Orton Grange Caravan Park
Wigton Road, Carlisle
Tel: 01228 710252

Orton Grange is set in the beautiful Cumbrian countryside yet within 4 miles of the great border city of Carlisle. Facilities of a high standard include, children's play area, camping accessory shop and in the summer season an outdoor swimming pool, a café and take away food. This pleasantly wooded park makes an ideal touring base for exploring the historic city of Carlisle, the northern lake district, the border country, Hadrians Wall and the beautiful Eden Valley. We welcome tent and tourers and have fully equipped holiday caravans for hire on site.

Open Mar-Oct Booking advisable public hols & Jul-Aug Last arrival 23.30hrs Last departure noon
A grassy site on the outskirts of the market town on the A6071. A 4.5-acre site with 20 touring pitches and 25 statics.
Leisure: ⚙ Facilities: ⬔⊙✳⚲⬛
Services: ⬛⬛⬛⬛→∪▶⬱⬗

CARLISLE	Map 11 NY35

▶ ▶ ▶ **65% Dandy Dinmont Caravan & Camping Park (NY399620)**
Blackford CA6 4EA ☎ 01228 674611 ▤ 01228 674611
e-mail: dandydinmont@btopenworld.com
website: www.caravan-camping-carlisle.itgo.com
Dir: From M6 junct 44 take A7 & continue N. Site 1.5m on right, follow sign after Blackford sign
★ ⛺ £8.25-£8.50 ⛺ £8.25-£8.50 ▲ £6.25-£7.50

Open Etr-Oct (rs Mar showers not available) Booking advisable Last arrival anytime Last departure 15.00hrs   *contd.*

A level sheltered site, screened on two sides by hedgerows. The grass pitches are immaculately kept, and there are some larger hardstandings for motor homes. Keen owners maintain good standards in all areas, and this rural park is only one mile from the M6 and Carlisle. A 4-acre site with 47 touring pitches, 20 hardstandings and 15 statics.
Facilities: ⬔⊙✳⬛ Services: ⬛⬛⬛⬛→∪▶⊚⬱⬛
Notes: Dogs must be kept on leads at all times & exercised off site

▶ ▶ ▶ **72% Green Acres Caravan Park (NY416614)**
High Knells, Houghton CA6 4JW ☎ 01228 675418
e-mail: info@caravanpark-cumbria.com
website: www.caravanpark-cumbria.com
Dir: Leave M6/A74(M) at junct 44, take A689 towards Brampton for 1m. Left at Scaleby sign and site 1m on left
⛺ £7.50-£8.50 ⛺ £7.50-£8.50 ▲ £7.50-£8.50
Open Etr-Oct Booking advisable bank hols Last arrival 21.00hrs Last departure 14.00hrs
A small family touring park in rural surroundings with distant views of the fells. This pretty park is run by keen, friendly owners who maintain high standards throughout. A 1.5-acre site with 30 touring pitches, 11 hardstandings.
Leisure: ⚙ Facilities: ⬔⊙✳⬔
Services: ⬛→▶⬛

▶ ▶ ▶ **61% Orton Grange Caravan & Camping Park (NY355519)**
Orton Grange, Wigton Rd CA5 6LA ☎ 01228 710252
▤ 01228 712225
e-mail: chris@ortongrange.flyer.co.uk
Dir: From A595 4m SW of Carlisle turn for Dalston Stn & site signed 50yds on left
★ ⛺ £7.60-£9 ⛺ £7.60-£9 ▲ £7.60-£9

Open all year Cafe & restaurant only open in summer Booking advisable bank hols & Jul-Aug Last arrival 22.00hrs Last departure noon
Pleasant owners keep this rural site in very good condition. The park offers an extensive camping shop selling good spares, a heated outdoor swimming pool, and hardstandings for motorvans. A 6-acre site with 50 touring pitches and 22 statics. Cafe & fast food facilities in Apr-Sep only.
Leisure: ⚡⬔⚙⬛ Facilities: ⬔⊙⬛✳⬛⬛⬛⬛⬛
Services: ⬛⬛⬛⬛⬛⬛✗⬛→∪▶⬛⬱
⬛⬛⬛⬛⬛⬛

CARTMEL Map 07 SD37

► ► **66% Greave Farm Caravan Park** (SD391823)
Prospect House, Barber Green LA11 6HU
☎ 015395 36329 & 36587
Dir: From M6 junct 36 onto A590 signed Barrow. Approx 1m before Newby Bridge, turn left at x-roads signed Cartmel/Staveley. Site 2m on left just before church
★ ⊞ £8-£10 ⊞ £8-£10 ▲ £8-£10

Open Mar-Oct Booking advisable
Last arrival 21.00hrs Last departure Midday
A small family-owned park close to a working farm in a peaceful rural area. The well-tended grass and flower gardens distinguish this carefully nurtured park, and there is always a sparkle to the toilet facilities. A 3-acre site with 3 touring pitches and 20 statics.
Facilities: ⋒⊙☜⚒✆⊞ Services: ⊟▮→∪►⚘⤚⚲⚡

COCKERMOUTH Map 11 NY13

► ► ► **55% Violet Bank Holiday Home Park Ltd** (NY126295)
Simonscales Ln, Lorton Rd CA13 9TG
☎ 01900 822169 ▤ 01900 822169
website: www.violetbank.co.uk
Dir: Approach on B5292 Lorton Road via town centre
★ ⊞ £7.20-£8.20 ⊞ £7.20-£8.20 ▲ £7.20-£8.20
Open Mar-15 Nov Booking advisable Spring bank hol & Jul-Aug Last arrival 24.00hrs Last dep 12.00hrs
Well-maintained site, with a slightly sloping touring area, in a pleasant rural setting affording excellent views of Buttermere Hills. 1m from the town centre. An 8.5-acre site with 30 touring pitches, 15 hardstandings and 92 statics.
Leisure: ⚑ Facilities: ⋒⊙✳✆⚞⚲ⵆ
Services: ⊟▤⌀⊞→∪►⚲

CROOKLANDS Map 07 SD58

► ► ► **71% Waters Edge Caravan Park** (SD533838)
LA7 7NN ☎ 015395 67708 & 67414 ▤ 015395 67610
Dir: From M6 follow signs for Kirkby Lonsdale A65, at 2nd rdbt follow signs for Crooklands/Endmoor. Site 1m on right at Crooklands garage.
★ ⊞ £10.50-£14.50 ⊞ £10.50-£14.50 ▲ £5-£13.50
Open Mar-14 Nov Booking advisable bank hols Last arrival 22.00hrs Last departure 12.00hrs
A peaceful, well-run park close to the M6, pleasantly bordered by streams and woodland. A Lakeland-style building houses a shop and bar, and the attractive toilet block is clean and modern.

contd.

Ideal either as a stopover or for longer stays. A 3-acre site with 30 touring pitches and 14 statics.
Leisure: ⚘⏷ Facilities: ⋒⊙☜✳⚹⚲⚞⚒⚑
Services: ⊟⚲▮⌀⊞→∪⚲⤚⚡

CROSTHWAITE Map 07 SD49

► ► ► **52% Lambhowe Caravan Park** (SD422914)
LA8 8JE ☎ 015395 68483 ▤ 015395 723339
Dir: On A5074 between Lancaster and Windermere, opposite Damson Dene Hotel.
★ ⊞ £11-£13 ⊞ £11-£15
Open Mar-mid Nov Booking advisable Etr, Spring bank hol & Jul-Aug Last arrival 21.00hrs Last departure noon
A secluded mainly static site in a former quarry, with touring pitches laid out in one large tarmac area. The toilets are housed up steep roads. Centrally placed for touring the Lake District National Park. A 1-acre site with 14 touring pitches and 112 statics.
Facilities: ⋒⊙✆ Services: ⊟▤⚲▮→►⚲

DALSTON Map 11 NY35

► ► ► **69% Dalston Hall Caravan Park** (NY378519)
Dalston Hall Estate CA5 7JX ☎ 01228 710165
Dir: 2.5m SW of Carlisle, just off B5299 & signed
⊞ ⊞ ▲
Open Mar-Oct Booking advisable Jul-Aug Last arrival 21.00hrs Last departure 13.00hrs
A neat, well-maintained site on level grass in the grounds of an estate located between Carlisle and Dalston. All facilities are to a very high standard, and amenities include a 9-hole golf course, a bar and clubhouse serving breakfast and bar meals, and salmon and trout fly fishing. A 3-acre site with 60 touring pitches and 17 statics.
9-hole golf course & fly fishing.
Leisure: ⚑ Facilities: ⋒⊙☜✳✆⚲⚞⚑ⵢ
Services: ⊟▤⚲▮⌀⊞⊞✕⤶→►⚲⚲⚲

ESKDALE Map 07 SD19

► ► ► **57% Fisherground Farm Campsite** (NY152002)
Fisherground CA19 1TF ☎ 01946 723349
e-mail: camping@fisherground.co.uk
website: www.fisherground.co.uk
Dir: Leave A595 at Gosforth or Holmrook, follow signs on unclass road to Eskdale Green, on towards Boot. Site signed on left
⊞ £10 ▲ £10

contd.

Old Park Wood Caravan Park

Holker, Cark-in-Cartmel, Cumbria LA11 7PP

Tel: 015395 58266

Exceptional views of the hills. The park is ideal for those who wish to enjoy the beauty of the area. Touring & motor caravans welcomed by resident manager. Facilities include toilets, showers, a covered swimming pool, launderette and shop.

Open 8 Mar-14 Nov
A mainly level grassy site on farmland amidst beautiful scenery, in Eskdale Valley below Hardknott Pass, between Eskdale and Boot. Own railway halt on the Eskdale-Ravenglass railway, 'The Ratty'. A 3-acre site with 30 touring pitches and 5 statics.
Adventure playground and miniature railway.
Leisure: ⚠ Facilities: ↿⊙♉⚹ᴕ♨ ⋔
Services: ⬚⬚⬚⬚ → ✈ ⤮ Notes: No caravans

FLOOKBURGH   Map 07 SD37

68% *Lakeland Leisure Park (SD372743)*
Moor Ln LA11 7LT
☎ 015395 58556 ◧ 015395 58559
Dir: Approach on B5277 through Grange-over-Sands to Flookburgh, turn left at village square and park 1m
⬚⬚⬚ Å

contd.

Open late Mar-early Nov Booking advisable May-Oct Last arrival 21.00hrs Last departure 11.00hrs
A complete leisure park with full range of activities and entertainments, making this flat, grassy site ideal for families. The touring area is quietly situated away from the main amenities, but the swimming pools, all-weather bowling green and evening entertainment are just a short stroll away. A 105-acre site with 125 touring pitches and 740 statics.
Horse riding.
Leisure: ⤞ ⤞ ⤞ ⚹ ⚠ Facilities: ↿⊙⚹⚹ᴕ♨ ⚹ ⚹
⚹ ⋔ Services: ⬚⬚⬚⬚⬚⬚⬚⬚⬚ → ∪ ► ⦿ ✈
⬚⬚ ⬚⬚ ⬚⬚ ⬚⬚ ⬚

GRANGE-OVER-SANDS   See **Cartmel & Holker**

GREAT LANGDALE   Map 07 NY20

► ► ► 66% **NEW** Great Langdale National Trust Campsite (NY286059)
LA22 9JU ☎ 015394 37668 ◧ 015394 37668
e-mail: rlcamp@smtp.ntrust.org.uk
website: www.nationaltrust.org.uk/main/holidays
Dir: Take A593 to Skelwith Bridge, turn right onto B5343 for approx 5m to the New Dungeon Ghyll Hotel, and site entrance on left in 1m just before Old Dungeon Ghyll Hotel
★ ⬚ £9-£10 Å £9-£10
Open all year
Nestling in a green valley, sheltered by mature trees and surrounded by stunning fell views, this site is an ideal base for campers, climbers and fell walkers. The large grass tent area has some gravel parking for cars and camper vans, and there is a separate area for groups and one for families with a children's play area. Attractive wooden cabins house the toilets, a shop, and drying rooms. A 9-acre site with 300 touring pitches.
Facilities: ⚹ ⚹ Services: ⬚ ⬚⬚ ⬚⬚

GREYSTOKE   Map 12 NY43

► ► ► 63% Hopkinsons Whitbarrow Hall Caravan Park (NY405289)
Berrier CA11 0XB ☎ 01768 483456
Dir: From M6 junct 40 take A66 to Keswick, after 8m turn right, follow tourist signs to Hopkinsons
★ ⬚ fr £9 ⬚ fr £9 Å fr £9
Open Mar-Oct Booking advisable bank hols & for electric hook up Last arrival 22.00hrs Last departure 23.00hrs
A rural park in a peaceful location surrounded by trees and shrubs, on the fringe of the Lake District National Park. This family-run park offers plenty of amenities including a small bar and clubhouse, a games room and a tennis court. There is a good mix of grass pitches and hardstandings, and very clean toilet facilities. An 8-acre site with 81 touring pitches and 167 statics.
Table tennis, pool table & video games.
Leisure: ⚹ ⚹ ⚠ Facilities: ↿⊙⚹⚹ᴕ♨⚹⚹⋔
Services: ⬚⬚⬚⬚⬚ → ∪ ► ⬚⬚ ⬚⬚ ⬚

Services: ⊤ Toilet Fluid ✗ Café/ Restaurant ⬚ Fast Food/Takeaway ➥ Baby Care ⬚ Electric Hook Up
⬚ Launderette ⚲ Licensed Bar ⬚ Calor Gaz ⊘ Camping Gaz ⬚ Battery Charging

HAVERTHWAITE   Map 07 SD38

► ► ► **61% Bigland Hall Caravan Park (SD344833)**
LA12 8PJ ☎ 01539 531702 & 723339
📄 01539 531702
*Dir: From A590 in Haverthwaite turn left opposite steam
railway, left at T-junct signed B5278, park on left,1.5m*
★ 🚐 £11-£13 🚐 £11-£15
Open Mar-16 Nov Booking advisable bank hols Last
arrival 22.30hrs Last departure 13.00hrs
*A wooded site in lovely countryside 3m from the
southern end of Lake Windermere and near the
Haverthwaite Steam Railway. The various touring
areas are dotted around this large park, and the
three toilet blocks are strategically placed. A 30-acre
site with 36 touring pitches and 29 statics.
Off-licence on site.*
Facilities: �🅡⊙☀❌ 🌡 **Services:** 🔌📶→∪🍴

HOLKER   Map 07 SD37

► ► ► **66% Old Park Wood Caravan Park
(SD335784)**
Holker Estates Co Ltd LA11 7PP
☎ 015395 58266 📄 015395 58101
*Dir: 2m W of Cark in Cartmel. Off B5278, follow signs for
Holker Hall*
🚐 🚐

Open Mar-Oct Booking advisable bank hols Last
departure 17.30hrs
*Terraced park gently sloping towards the River
Leven estuary, surrounded on three sides by
woodland; very well maintained and with good
facilities. The park is adjacent to Holker Hall house
and gardens which are open to the public. A 4-acre
site with 50 touring pitches and 360 statics.*
Leisure: 🏊 🅐 **Facilities:** ๏⊙🅡 🌡
Services: 🔌📶→∪🍴
See advertisement opposite

KENDAL   Map 07 SD59

► ► ► **61% Camping & Caravanning Club Site
(SD526948)**
Millcrest, Shap Rd LA9 6NY ☎ 01539 741363
website: www.campingandcaravanningclub.co.uk
*Dir: On A6 1.5m N of Kendal. Site entrance is 100yds N
of nameplate 'Skelsmergh'*
★ 🚐 £12.30-£15.50 🚐 £12.30-£15.50 ▲ £12.30-£15.50
Open Mar-Oct Booking advisable bank hols & high
season Last arrival 21.00hrs Last departure noon
*Sloping grass site, set in hilly wood and
meadowland, with some level all-weather*
contd.

*pitches. Please see advertisement on page 10 for
details of Club Members' benefits. A 3.5-acre site
with 50 touring pitches, 4 hardstandings.*
Leisure: 🅐 **Facilities:** ๏⊙🅡☀❌🌡🐾
Services: 🔌📶📶→∪🍴

► ► ► **64% Camping & Caravanning Club Site
(SD478962)**
Ashes Ln LA8 9JS ☎ 01539 821119 📄 01539 821282
website: www.campingandcaravanningclub.co.uk
*Dir: Signed off A591, 0.75m from rdbt with B5284
towards Windermere*
★ 🚐 £14.60-£18 🚐 £14.60-£18 ▲ £14.60-£18
Open Mar-Jan Booking advisable bank hols Last
arrival 21.00hrs Last departure noon
*A newly acquired Club site in an attractive location
with good security. Facilities were due to be
refurbished during the winter 2002/3. Please see
advertisement on page 10 for details of Club
Members' benefits. A 22-acre site with 150 touring
pitches, 95 hardstandings and 71 statics.*
Leisure: ❈ 🅐 **Facilities:** ๏⊙🅡☀❌🌡🐾
Services: 🔌📶📶→∪🍴

KESWICK   Map 11 NY22

► ► ► **73% Camping & Caravanning Club Site
(NY258234)**
Crow Park Rd CA12 5EP ☎ 01768 772392
website: www.campingandcaravanningclub.co.uk
*Dir: A5271 from Penrith into Keswick, right past bus stn,
past rugby club, right to site*
★ 🚐 £14.50-£17.50 🚐 £14.50-£17.50 ▲ £14.50-£17.50
Open Feb-Dec Booking advisable Jul-Aug & BH's
Last arrival 21.00hrs Last departure noon
*A well-situated lakeside site within walking distance
of the town centre. Boat launching is available from
the site onto Derwentwater, and this level grassy
park also offers a number of all-weather pitches.
Please see advertisement on page 10 for details of
Club Members' benefits. A 14-acre site with 250
touring pitches, 96 hardstandings.
Boat launching*
Leisure: 🅐 **Facilities:** ๏⊙🅡☀❌🌡🐾
Services: 🔌📶📶→∪🍴

► ► ► **70% Camping & Caravanning Club Site
(NY257234)**
Crow Park Rd CA12 5EN ☎ 017687 72579
📄 017687 80443
website: www.campingandcaravanningclub.co.uk
Dir: Signed off B5289 in town centre
★ 🚐 £11.10-£15.50 🚐 £11.10-£15.50
Open Mar-14 Nov Booking advisable at all times
*Last arrival 21.00hrs Last departure noon
A peaceful location close to Derwentwater for this
well-managed park which is divided into two areas
for tourers. Please see advertisement on page 10
for details of Club Members' benefits. A 16-acre site
with 44 touring pitches and 160 statics.*
Leisure: 🅐 **Facilities:** ๏⊙☀❌🅡
Services: 🔌📶📶→🌡
Notes: No tents or awnings 📶

Leisure: ❈ Indoor swimming pool ❈ Outdoor swimming pool ❊ Tennis court ♣ Games room 🅐 Children's playground ∪ Stables
🍴 9/18 hole golf course ❊ Boats for hire ❊ Cinema 🎣 Fishing ◉ Mini golf ⚠ Watersports ▭ Separate TV room

GILL HEAD CARAVAN AND CAMPING PARK
Troutbeck, Penrith, Cumbria CA11 0ST

With panoramic views of the surrounding fells we have a level, sheltered site in well cared for grounds run to a high standard. There are modern, spacious and well maintained shower, toilet and laundry facilities on site. Central for touring the Lake District.
Brochures on request.
www.gillheadfarm.co.uk
Tel/Fax: 017687 79652

▶ ▶ ▶ 63% **Gill Head Farm Caravan & Camping Park (NY380269)**
Troutbeck CA11 0ST ☎ 017687 79652
📠 017687 79130
e-mail: gillhead@talk21.com
Dir: From M6 J40 avoiding Kirkstone Pass. Site 200yds from A66/A5091
★ 🚐 £9-£11 🚙 £9-£11 ▲ £3.50-£5

Open Apr-Oct Booking advisable bank hols Last arrival 22.30hrs Last departure noon
This level family-run park is part of a hill farming business. An attractive and well-maintained site, with spacious and comfortable facilities, set against a backdrop of Blencathra and the northern fells. A 5.5-acre site with 42 touring pitches and 17 statics.
Facilities: ↖⊙ℝ☼✿ⓈⅢ⌅ⲏ
Services: 🖸🖥🛢🇦→Ⴎ▶△✛⅃ **Notes:** No fires

▶ ▶ ▶ ▶ 70% **Woodclose Caravan Park (SD618786)**
Casterton LA6 2SE ☎ 01524 271597 📠 01524 272301
e-mail: michaelhodgkins@ woodclosecaravanpark.fsnet.co.uk
website: www.woodclosepark.com
Dir: On A65, 0.25m beyond Kirkby Lonsdale, towards Skipton
★ 🚐 £12-£13.50 🚙 £12-£13.50 ▲ £5-£10

Open Mar-Oct (rs Nov-Dec) Booking advisable bank hols, Jul-Aug & Sep Last arrival 21.00hrs Last departure 13.00hrs
A peaceful park with excellent toilet facilities set in idyllic countryside in the beautiful Lune Valley. Ideal for those seeking quiet relaxation, and for visiting the Lakes and Dales. Devil's Bridge with its riverside walks, and historic Kirkby Lonsdale with shops, pubs and restaurants are an easy walk from the park. A 9-acre site with 50 touring pitches and 52 statics.
Dog area off site
Leisure: ♠⊙∧ **Facilities:** ↖⊙ℝ☼✿ⓈⅢ⅃ⲏ
Services: 🖸🖥🛢🇦→Ⴎ⅃

▶ ▶ ▶ 69% **New House Caravan Park (SD628774)**
LA6 2HR ☎ 015242 71590
e-mail: colinpreece9@aol.com
Dir: 1m SE of Kirkby Lonsdale on A65, turn right into site entrance 300yds past Whoop-Hall Inn
★ 🚐 £7.50 🚙 £7.50
Open Mar-Oct Booking advisable Bank hols Last arrival 22.00hrs
A very pleasant base in which to relax or tour the surrounding area, developed around a former farm. The excellent toilet facilities are purpose built, and there are new roads and hardstandings, all in a lovely rural setting. A 3-acre site with 50 touring pitches, 50 hardstandings.
Facilities: ↖⊙ℝ☼✿ⓈⅢⲏ
Services: 🖸🖥🛢🇦🖽🇹→Ⴎ▶⅃🖢

▶ ▶ ▶ 66% **Inglenook Caravan Park (NY084206)**
Fitzbridge CA14 4SH ☎ 01946 861240
📠 01946 861240
Dir: On left of A5086 in the direction of Egremont
★ 🚐 £8-£9 🚙 £8-£9 ▲ £7-£9
Open all year (rs Oct-Etr shop closed) Booking advisable bank hols Last arrival 20.00hrs Last departure noon *contd.*

An ideal touring site, well-maintained and situated in beautiful surroundings. The picturesque village of Lamplugh is close to the western lakes of Ennerdale, Buttermere and Loweswater, and a short drive from sandy beaches. A 3.5-acre site with 28 touring pitches and 29 statics.

Leisure: 🅰 **Facilities:** 🝖⊙🔆🕭❄😊 **Services:** 🔌🚰🛢↘🅹😊🔋🎦🔀🔇

LONGTOWN   Map 11 NY36

▶ ▶ **63% Camelot Caravan Park (NY391666)**
CA6 5SZ ☎ 01228 791248 🖨 01228 791248
Dir: Leave M6 junct 44. Site 5m N on A7, 1m S of Longtown
★ 🚐 fr £8 🚐 fr £8 ▲ fr £6
Open Mar-Oct Booking advisable Jul-Aug Last arrival 22.00hrs Last departure noon
Very pleasant level grassy site in a wooded setting near the M6, with direct access from the A7. This park is an ideal stopover site. A 1.5-acre site with 20 touring pitches and 2 statics.

Facilities: 🝖⊙🔆🕭 **Services:** 🔌🚰🛢↘🅹∪🅹❄

▶ ▶ **62% Oakbank Lakes (NY369700)**
CA6 5NA ☎ 01228 791108 🖨 01228 791108
e-mail: oakbank@nlaq.globalnet.co.uk
Dir: From Longtown take A7 towards Langholm/Galashiels. Turn left after 1m signed Corries Mill Chapelknowe, site in 200yds
★ 🚐 £6-£8 🚐 £6-£8 ▲ £5-£7
Booking advisable Last arrival 20.00hrs Last departure 14.00hrs no cars by tents
A wooded park in a peaceful setting with three fishing lakes and a nature reserve, making a relaxing haven for anglers and nature lovers. A shop and self-service kitchen add to facilities here, and the toilets are well kept and clean. A 60-acre site with 22 touring pitches and 4 statics. Coarse fishing.

Leisure: 🔲 **Facilities:** 🝖⊙🔆🕭❄🎍🕭
Services: 🔌🛢↘🅹❄ **Notes:** No fires 😊🔋🔇

MEALSGATE   Map 11 NY24

▶ ▶ ▶ ▶ **65% Larches Caravan Park (NY205415)**
CA7 1LQ ☎ 016973 71379 & 71803 🖨 016973 71782
Dir: On A595, Carlisle to Cockermouth road
🚐 £10-£12.50 🚐 ▲

Open Mar-Oct (rs early & late season) Booking advisable Etr Spring bank hol & Jul-Aug Last arrival 21.30hrs Last departure noon

contd.

This over 18s-only park is set in wooded rural surroundings on the fringe of the Lake District National Park. Touring units are spread out over two sections with well-maintained en suite facilities. The friendly family-run park offers well cared for facilities, and a small indoor swimming pool. A 20-acre site with 73 touring pitches and 100 statics.

Leisure: 🟆 🔲 **Facilities:** 🝖⊙🔆🔆🕭❄🎍🕭
Services: 🔌🛢🚰🛢🅴🖵↘▶🅹 **Notes:** Adults only

MELMERBY   Map 12 NY63

▶ ▶ ▶ **68% *Melmerby Caravan Park (NY614374)***
CA10 1HE ☎ 01768 881311
Dir: Approximately 9m from Penrith, on the edge of village A686 Penrith/Alston Road
🚐 🚐 ▲
Open mid Mar-Nov
A pleasant park on the edge of a small, traditional village with a good pub/eating house and a locally famous organic bakery. The tiny touring area has its own good toilet block, and all pitches are hardstanding with electricity. A 2-acre site with 6 touring pitches and 41 statics.

Facilities: 🝖 **Services:** 🔌

MILNTHORPE   Map 07 SD48

▶ ▶ **61% Hall More Caravan Park (SD502771)**
Hale LA7 7BP ☎ 01524 781695 🖨 01524 781673
e-mail: slcar@freenetname.co.uk
Dir: Leave M6 junct 35 onto A6 towards Milnthorpe for 3.5m. Take 1st left after crossing Cumbrian border, site is signed after 0.75m
🚐 🚐 ▲
Open Mar-Oct Booking advisable bank hols & wknds Last arrival 22.00hrs
A mainly level grassy site in meadowland, adjacent to main road, with all hardstanding pitches and unsophisticated facilities. Close to farm and stables offering pony trekking, and there is trout fishing nearby. A 6-acre site with 50 touring pitches and 65 statics.

Leisure: 🅰 **Facilities:** 🝖⊙🔆🔆🕭❄🎍
Services: 🔌🛢🚰🛢🅴↘∪▶⊙🅹❄😊🔋🔇

PATTERDALE   Map 11 NY31

▶ ▶ ▶ **58% *Sykeside Camping Park (NY403119)***
Brotherswater CA11 0NZ ☎ 017684 82239
🖨 017684 82558
website: www.sykeside.co.uk
Dir: Direct access off A592 Windermere to Ullswater road at the foot of Kirkstone Pass. Not suitable for caravans
🚐 ▲
Open all year Booking advisable bank hols & Jul-Aug Last arrival 22.30hrs Last departure 14.00hrs
A camper's delight, this family-run park is sited at the foot of Kirkstone Pass, under the 2000ft Hartsop Dodd in a spectacular area with breathtaking views. The park has mainly grass pitches with a few hardstandings, and for those campers without a tent there is bunkhouse accommodation. A small camper's kitchen and bar serves breakfast and bar meals. A 5-acre site with 86 touring pitches.

Facilities: 🝖⊙🔆🔆🕭❄🎍🕭
Services: 🔌🛢🟡🚰🛢🅴🖵✕↘⚠❄🅹😊🔋🎦🔀🔇

PENRITH   Map 12 NY53

See also **Greystoke**

▶ ▶ ▶ ▶ 73% **Lowther Holiday Park** (NY527265)

Eamont Bridge CA10 2JB ☎ 01768 863631

🖹 01768 868126

e-mail: holiday.park@lowther.co.uk

website: www.lowther-holidaypark.co.uk

Dir: 3m S of Penrith on A6

★ 🏕 £12-£15 🚐 £12-£15 ▲ £12-£15

GOLD

Open mid Mar-mid Nov Booking advisable bank hols Last arrival 23.00hrs

A secluded natural woodland site with lovely riverside walks and glorious surrounding countryside. The park is home to a rare colony of red squirrels, and trout fishing is available on the 2-mile stretch of the River Lowther which runs through it. A 50-acre site with 269 touring pitches and 403 statics.

Leisure: 🅐 **Facilities:** ➡🏕⊙🔍❋⟵🛒🛁 **Services:** 🔌🖥♨🅻🅳🅱🆃✖🔥→∪🅿◉♨🥄 **Notes:** No single sex groups (families only), no cats, no rollerblades, no skateboards 💳 💳 💳 💳

See advertisement in Preliminary Section

PENRUDDOCK   Map 12 NY42

▶ ▶ 52% **Beckses Caravan Park** (NY419278)

CA11 0RX ☎ 01768 483224 🖹 01768 483006

Dir: Leave M6 junct 40 onto A66 towards Keswick. Approx 6m at caravan park sign turn right onto B5288, site on right in 0.25m

🚐 £7.50 🚐 £7.50 ▲ £5

Open Etr-Oct Booking advisable public hols Last arrival 20.00hrs Last departure 11.00hrs

A small, pleasant site on sloping ground with level pitches and views of distant fells, on edge of National Park. This sheltered park is in a good location for touring the North Lakes. A 4-acre site with 23 touring pitches and 18 statics.

Leisure: 🅐 **Facilities:** 🏕⊙🔍❋⟵🛒

Services: 🔌🅱🅳🆃→∪🥄

POOLEY BRIDGE   Map 12 NY42

▶ ▶ ▶ 70% **Park Foot Caravan & Camping Park** (NY469235)

Howtown Rd CA10 2NA ☎ 017684 86309

🖹 017684 86041

Dir: M6 junct 40 onto A66 towards Keswick, then A592 to Ullswater. Turn left for Pooley Bridge, right at church, right at x-roads signed Howtown

🚐 🚐 ▲

Open Mar-Oct Booking advisable bank hols Last arrival 22.00hrs Last departure noon

A lively park, popular with campers and families seeking good outdoor sports facilities, and with direct access to Lake Ullswater and its own boat-launching facility. The Country Club bar and restaurant provides family meals, discos, live music and entertainment. This attractive, mainly tenting park has many mature trees and lovely views across the lake. An 18-acre site with 323 touring pitches and 131 statics.

Lake access/boat launch, pony trekking.

Leisure: 🔍🍴🎱🏓 **Facilities:** 🏕⊙🔍❋⟵🛒🛁🎣🛒

Services: 🔌🖥♨🅻🅳🅱🆃✖🔥→∪🅿▲🥄🥄

💳 💳 💳 💳 💳

▶ ▶ 66% **Hillcroft Caravan & Camping Site** (NY478241)

Roe Head Ln CA10 2LT ☎ 017684 86363

🖹 017684 86010

Dir: From A592 bear left into Pooley Bridge. Turn right at church, straight across x-rds to Roe Head. Park is on left

★ 🚐 fr £13 🚐 fr £13 ▲ fr £10

Open 7 Mar-14 Nov Booking advisable bank hols

A pleasant rural site close to the village and Ullswater, with good fell views. There are spacious grassy pitches for tents, and hardstandings with electricity for motor homes and caravans. A 10-acre site with 125 touring pitches, 6 hardstandings and 200 statics.

Leisure: 🅐 **Facilities:** 🏕⊙🔍❋⟵🛒🛁🛒

Services: 🔌🖥🅱🅳🅱→∪▲🥄🥄

Notes: No groups, family camping only

RAVENGLASS — Map 06 SD09

▶ ▶ ▶ 68% **Walls Caravan & Camping Park (SD087964)**
CA18 1SR ☎ 01229 717250 🖨 01229 717250
e-mail: wallscaravanpark@
ravenglass98.freeserve.co.uk
website: www.ravenglass98.freeserve.co.uk
Dir: On coast, midway between Millom & Whitehaven.
Leave A595 to Ravenglass. Left at 30mph sign. Site on left
★ 🚐 £9.25 🚐 £9.25 ▲ £4-£9
Open Mar-Oct Booking advisable bank hols &
summer Last arrival 22.00hrs Last departure noon
*A pleasant wooded park with open farmland views,
a short stroll from the charming fishing village of
Ravenglass. Friendly owners maintain the park to a
high standard, and some pitches are suitable for
very large motorhomes. There is easy access to
Muncaster Castle, the Ravenglass-Eskdale narrow-
gauge railway, and the coast. A 5-acre site with 50
touring pitches, 50 hardstandings.*
Washing up sinks with free hot water.
Facilities: ⓘⓔⓠ✳✕🛒🌢 **Services:** ⊕ⓘⓣ⌀ⓔ→△⌀

SILECROFT — Map 06 SD18

▶ ▶ ▶ 66% **Silecroft Caravan Site (SD124811)**
LA18 4NX ☎ 01229 772659 🖨 01229 772659
e-mail: silcroftpark@aol.com
website: www.caravanholidayhomes.com
Dir: Turn off A595 at Silecroft onto A5039 towards
Millom, right onto unclass road, continue through
Silecroft village and park is on left just before beach
🚐 🚐 ▲
contd.

Open Mar-15 Nov Booking advisable
*Quietly situated close to the shore in a beautiful but
little-known area of the Lake District. Access to
lovely beach for fishing, windsurfing and canoeing,
with waterskiing and village pub food nearby. A
5-acre site with 60 touring pitches and 124 statics.*
Sauna, gym & Jacuzzi.
Leisure: ₹ ◖ ⚠ **Facilities:** ⓘ❄✳✕☾🌢
Services: ⊕ⓘⓣ→∪▶△⌀

SILLOTH — Map 11 NY15

74% **Stanwix Park Holiday Centre (NY108527)**
Green Row CA7 4HH ☎ 016973 32666
🖨 016973 32666
e-mail: enquiries@stanwix.com
website: www.stanwix.com
Dir: 1m SW on B5300. From Wigton bypass (A596),
follow signs to Silloth on B5302. In Silloth follow
signs to Stanwix Park Holiday Centre, approx 1m
on B5300.
★ 🚐 £13.80-£16.90 🚐 £13.80-£16.90
▲ £13.80-£16.90
Open Mar-Oct (rs Nov-Feb no mid week
entertainment) Booking advisable Etr, Spring
bank hol & Jul-Aug Last arrival 22.00hrs
Last departure 11.00hrs
*A large well-run family park within easy reach of
the Lake District. Attractively laid-out, with lots
of amenities to ensure a lively holiday, including
a 4-lane, automatic, 10-pin bowling alley. A 4-acre
site with 121 touring pitches and 212 statics.*
contd.

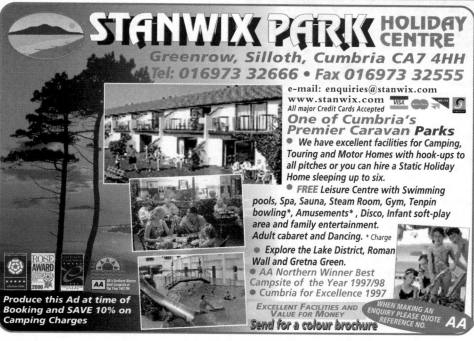
Leisure: ₹ Indoor swimming pool ₹ Outdoor swimming pool ◖ Tennis court ◖ Games room ⚠ Children's playground ∪ Stables
▶ 9/18 hole golf course ⅃ Boats for hire ☷ Cinema ⌀ Fishing ◎ Mini golf △ Watersports ⎕ Separate TV room

Stanwix Park Holiday Centre
Ten pin Bowling, amusement arcade, gym, kitchen
Leisure: ⚽ ⛳ ♋ ⚓ ⚙ ⊡ **Facilities:** ➡ ⬆ ⊙ ⚬ ※ ♿ ☎ ⓩ **Services:** ⚑ ⚑ ⚑ ⚑ ⓘ ∅ ⊤ ✕ ⬛ → ▶ ◎ ✈
💳 💳 💳 💳 🅿

▶ ▶ ▶ ▶ **70% Hylton Caravan Park (NY113533)**
Eden St CA7 4AY ☎ 016973 31707 🖷 016973 32555
e-mail: enquiries@stanwix.com
website: www.stanwix.com
Dir: On entering Silloth on B5302 follow signs Hylton Caravan Park, approx 0.5m on left, (end of Eden St)
★ ⚑ £13.40-£14.82 ⚑ £13.40-£14.82 ⚑ £13.40-£14.82

Open Mar-15 Nov Booking advisable School holidays Last arrival 21.00hrs Last departure 11.00hrs
A completely redeveloped touring park with excellent toilet facilities including several bathrooms. This very high quality park is a sister site to Stanwix Park, which is just a mile away and offers all the amenities of a holiday centre. An 18-acre site with 90 touring pitches and 213 statics. Use of facilities at Stanwix Park Holiday Centre
Leisure: ⚙ **Facilities:** ➡ ⬆ ⊙ ⚬ ♿ ☎ ⓩ **Services:** ⚑ ⓘ ∅ → ▶ ◎ ✈ **Notes:** Families only, no single sex groups 💳 💳 💳 💳 🅿

▶ ▶ ▶ **59% Tanglewood Caravan Park (NY131534)**
Causewayhead CA7 4PE ☎ 016973 31253
Dir: Adjacent to B5302 (Wigton-Silloth), 4m from Abbeytown, on left
★ ⚑ £10 ⚑ £10 ⚑ £8
Open Mar-Oct Booking advisable Etr, Whit & Jul-Aug Last arrival 23.00hrs Last departure 10.00hrs

contd.

A pleasant park sheltered by mature trees and shrubs, set in meadowland close to the town. There is a clubhouse and bar, and two small toilet blocks for tourers. A 7-acre site with 31 touring pitches, 21 hardstandings and 58 statics.
Leisure: ♋ ⚓ ⊡ **Facilities:** ⬆ ⊙ ⚬ ※ ♿ **Services:** ⚑ ⚑ ⓩ ⓘ ⊞ → U ▶ ◎ ✈ ⓩ **Notes:** Minimum age 2yrs

TEBAY   **Map 07 NY60**
▶ ▶ ▶ **65% Tebay Caravan Site (NY609060)**
Orton CA10 3SB ☎ 015396 24511 🖷 015396 24511
Dir: Leave M6, 1m N of junct 38 at Tebay service area. Site is accessed through service area from either north or southbound carriageways. Follow caravan park signs
★ ⚑ £8.40-£10.50 ⚑ £8.50-£10.50

Open Mar-Oct Booking advisable Jul-Aug & wknds Last arrival anytime Last departure noon no cars by tents
An ideal stopover site adjacent to the Tebay service station on the M6, and handy for touring the Lake District. The park is screened by high grass banks, bushes and trees, and is within walking distance of a shop and restaurant. A 4-acre site with 70 touring pitches, 70 hardstandings and 39 statics.
Facilities: ⬆ ⊙ ⚬ ※ ♿ ☎ ⓩ 🖹 ⓐ **Services:** ⚑ ⓩ ⓘ ⊞ ✕ ⬛ → U ✈

ULVERSTON   **Map 07 SD27**
▶ ▶ ▶ ▶ **70% Bardsea Leisure Park (SD292765)**
Priory Rd LA12 9QE ☎ 01229 584712
🖷 01229 580413
e-mail: reception@bardsealeisure.co.uk
website: www.bardsealeisure.co.uk
Dir: Off A5087
★ ⚑ £10.50-£17 ⚑ £10.50-£17 ⚑ £10

Open all year Booking advisable bank hols & Jul-Aug Last arrival 21.00hrs Last departure 18.00hrs
Attractively landscaped former quarry making a

contd.

quiet and very sheltered site. Many of the generously-sized pitches offer all-weather full facilities, and a luxury new toilet block provides plenty of privacy. Set on the southern edge of the town, convenient for both the coast and the Lake District. A 5-acre site with 83 touring pitches and 83 statics.

Leisure: ⚒ **Facilities:** ⬤⊙✳✆☕⚄⚘↑ **Services:** ⚙
⬛▮⬭▣Ⓣ✕⬛→⋃▶⚏♒╱⬤▦▦⬛⬛

WASDALE HEAD — Map 11 NY10

► ► ► 65% NEW **Wasdale Head National Trust Campsite** (NY183076)
CA20 1EX ☎ 019467 26220
e-mail: rwascp@smtp.ntrust.org.uk
website: www.nationaltrust.org.uk/main/holidays
Dir: From A595(N) turn L at Gosforth/ from A595(S) turn R at Holmrook for Santon Bridge & follow signs to Wasdale Head
★ ⊞ ▲ £9.50
Open all year
Set in a remote and beautiful spot at Wasdale Head, under the stunning Scafell peaks at the head of the deepest lake in England. Clean, well-kept facilities are set centrally amongst open grass pitches and trees. The renowned Wasdale Head Inn is close by. 120 touring pitches.
Facilities: ⚘ **Services:** ▮⬤▦◉

WATERMILLOCK — Map 12 NY42

► ► ► 67% *Cove Caravan & Camping Park* (NY431236)
Ullswater CA11 0LS ☎ 017684 86549
▤ 017684 86549
Dir: From M6 junct 40 follow signs for Ullswater (A592). Turn right at lake junct, then right at Brackenrigg Hotel. Site 1.5m on right
⊞ ⊞ ▲

Open Etr-Oct Booking advisable bank & school hols Last arrival 21.00hrs Last departure noon
A peaceful family site in an attractive and elevated position with extensive fell views and glimpses of Ullswater Lake. The ground is gently sloping grass, but there are also hardstandings for motorhomes and caravans. A 3-acre site with 50 touring pitches and 38 statics.
Dishwashing area, drinks machine.
Leisure: ⚒ **Facilities:** ⬤⊙❄✳✆☕⚄⚘↑
Services: ⚙▮▣✿⬭▣Ⓣ→⋃✕╱

► ► ► 63% **The Quiet Site** (NY431236)
Ullswater CA11 0LS ☎ 01768 486337
▤ 017684 486610
e-mail: info@thequietsite.co.uk
website: www.thequietsite.co.uk
Dir: Leave M6 at junct 40, turn W following signs to Ullswater (A592). Turn right at lake junct, then right at Brackenrigg Hotel. Site is 1.5m on right
★ ⊞ £10-£12 ⊞ £8-£10 ▲ £8-£10
Open Mar-Oct Booking advisable bank hols & Jul-Aug Last arrival 22.00hrs Last departure noon
A well-maintained site in a lovely, peaceful location, with very good facilities, including a charming olde-worlde bar. A 6-acre site with 60 touring pitches and 23 statics.
Pets corner, pool/darts(for adults), caravan storage
Leisure: ⚓⚒❐ **Facilities:** ⬤⊙❄✳✆☕⚘
Services: ⚙▮▣☷✿⬭▣Ⓣ⬆→⋃✕╱

► ► ► 68% **Ullswater Caravan Camping Site & Marine Park** (NY438232)
High Longthwaite CA11 0LR ☎ 017684 86666
▤ 017684 86095
e-mail: info@uccmp.co.uk
website: www.uccmp.co.uk
Dir: M6 junct 40, turn W for Ullswater (A592) for 5m. Right alongside Ullswater for 2m, then right at telephone box. Site 0.5m on right
★ ⊞ fr £10 ⊞ fr £9 ▲ fr £9

contd.

England

Ullswater Caravan & Camping & Marine Park
Open Mar-Nov bar open weekends only in low
season Booking advisable public hols Last arrival
21.00hrs Last departure noon
*A pleasant rural site with own nearby boat
launching and marine storage facility making it
ideal for sailors. The family-owned and run park
enjoys fell and lake views, and there is a bar and
café on site. A 12-acre site with 155 touring pitches,
34 hardstandings and 55 statics.*
Boat launching & moorings.
Leisure: ♦ ⚑ ⬛ **Facilities:** ⬤⊙☜✳⬤⬛⬤☀
Services: ⬤⬛⬤⬤⬤⬛⬛→∪⬤☀⬤ **Notes:** No open
fires, no single sex groups ⬤ ⬛ ⬛ ⬛ ⬛

WINDERMERE   **Map 07 SD49**

PREMIER PARK

▶ ▶ ▶ ▶ ▶ 77% **Fallbarrow Park**
(SD401973)
Rayrigg Rd LA23 3DL ☎ 015394 44422
🖨 015394 88736
website: www.fallbarrow.co.uk
*Dir: 0.5m N of Windermere on A591. At mini rdbt
take road to Bowness Bay & The Lake. Fallbarrow
1.3m on the right*
★ ⬤ £15.55-£21.95 ⬤ £15.55-£21.95

Open 7 Mar-8 Nov Booking advisable bank hols
& Jul-Aug Last arrival 23.00hrs Last departure
13.00hrs
*A very high quality park with excellent facilities,
a few minutes' walk from Bowness on the shore
of Lake Windermere. There is direct access to
the lake through the wooded park. A restaurant
with a specialist chef is a popular feature, and
there is a pets' corner. A 32-acre site with 38
touring pitches and 263 statics.*

contd.

Boat launching, lakeside picnic area, pets corner
Leisure: ♦ ⚑ ⬛ **Facilities:** ⬤⊙☜✳⬤⬛⬤☀
Services: ⬤⬛⬤⬤⬛⬛✖⬤➡→∪⬤⊙⬤☀⬤⬤
Notes: No tents ⬤ ⬛ ⬛ ⬛ ⬛

See advertisement opposite

PREMIER PARK

▶ ▶ ▶ ▶ ▶ 77% **Limefitt Park (NY416032)**
LA23 1PA ☎ 015394 32300
website: www.camping-windermere.co.uk
*Dir: From Windermere take A592 to Ullswater.
Limefitt is 2.5m on right*
⬤ £10.50-£14 ⬤ £8.50-£13 ▲ £9.50-£14

Open 28 Mar-1 Nov Booking advisable bank hols
& Jul-Aug Last arrival 22.00hrs Last departure
noon ⬤
*An attractive family site with superb facilities in
a lovely location in the Lake District National
Park. Buildings are well-integrated into the
landscape, and the River Troutbeck runs through
the grounds. From its valley setting there are
spectacular views of the surrounding hills, with
direct access to the fells and plenty of walks.
This is a family park and does not accept single
sex groups. A 12-acre site with 165 touring
pitches and 45 statics.*
River pool for paddling & swimming (with beach)
Leisure: ♦ ⚑ ⬛ **Facilities:** ⬤⊙☜✳⬤⬛⬤
Services: ⬤⬛⬤⬤⬤⬛✖⬤➡→∪⬤⬤☀⬤
Notes: No single sex pairs or groups, no dogs
⬤ ⬛ ⬛ ⬛ ⬛

See advertisement on inside front cover

▶ ▶ ▶ ▶ 70% **Park Cliffe Camping & Caravan
Estate (SD391912)**
Birks Rd, Tower Wood LA23 3PG
☎ 01539 531344 🖨 01539 531971
e-mail: info@parkcliffe.co.uk
website: www.parkcliffe.co.uk
*Dir: Leave M6 at junct 36 onto A590. Turn right at
Newby Bridge onto A592. After 4m turn right into site.
(Due to difficult access from main road this is the only
advised direction for approaching the site)*
★ ⬤ £13-£17 ⬤ £13-£17 ▲ £10-£14
Open Mar-15 Nov Booking advisable bank hols &
Aug Last arrival 22.00hrs Last departure noon
*A lovely hillside park set in 25 secluded acres of fell
land. The camping areas are well drained and
sheltered; some pitches have spectacular views of*

contd.

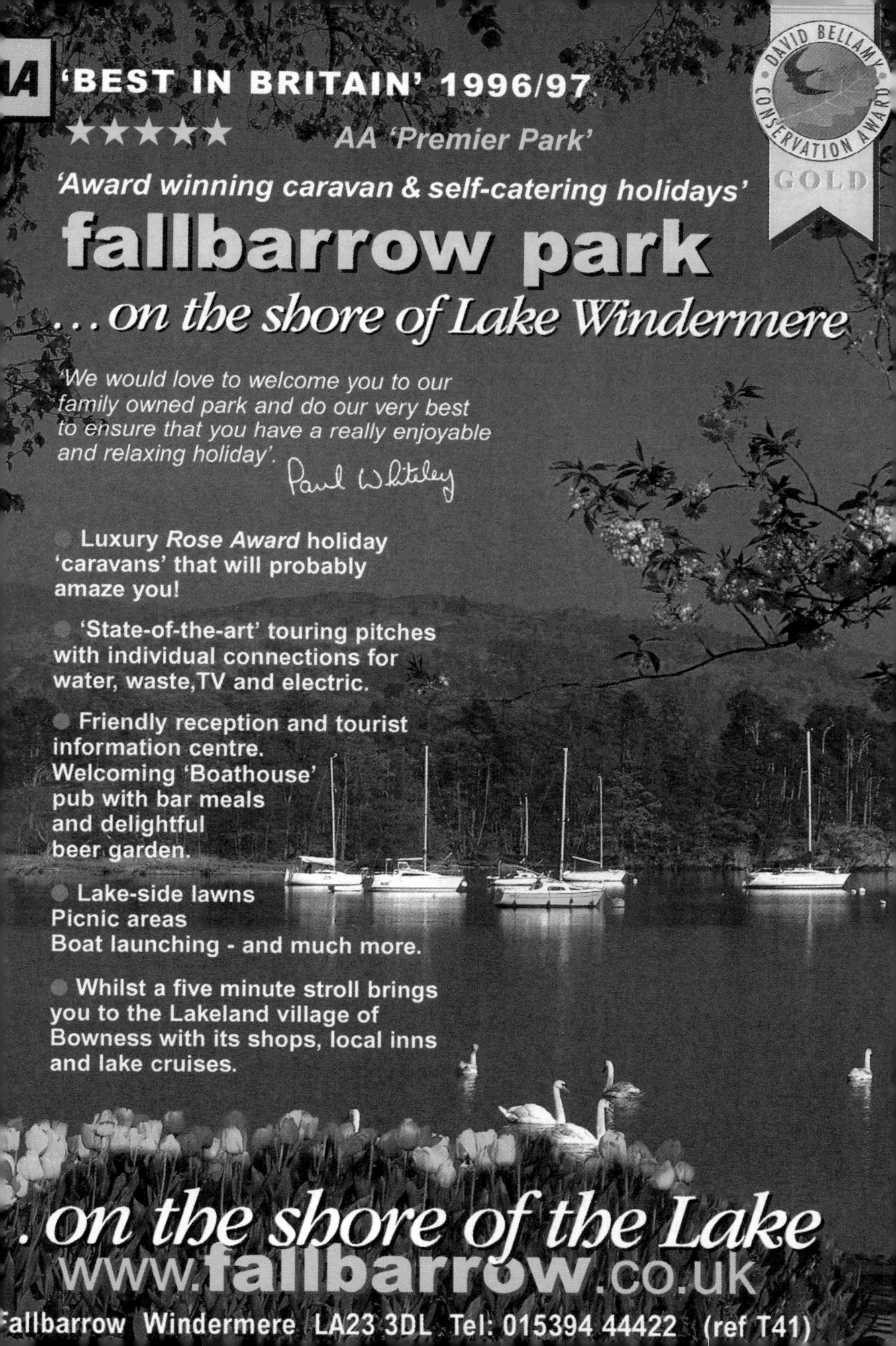

'BEST IN BRITAIN' 1996/97
★★★★★ AA 'Premier Park'
'Award winning caravan & self-catering holidays'
DAVID BELLAMY CONSERVATION AWARD GOLD
fallbarrow park
...on the shore of Lake Windermere
'We would love to welcome you to our family owned park and do our very best to ensure that you have a really enjoyable and relaxing holiday'. Paul Whiteley
Luxury Rose Award holiday 'caravans' that will probably amaze you!
'State-of-the-art' touring pitches with individual connections for water, waste,TV and electric.
Friendly reception and tourist information centre. Welcoming 'Boathouse' pub with bar meals and delightful beer garden.
Lake-side lawns Picnic areas Boat launching - and much more.
Whilst a five minute stroll brings you to the Lakeland village of Bowness with its shops, local inns and lake cruises.
...on the shore of the Lake
www.fallbarrow.co.uk
Fallbarrow Windermere LA23 3DL Tel: 015394 44422 (ref T41)

England

PARK CLIFFE
CAMPING AND CARAVAN ESTATE
BIRKS ROAD, WINDERMERE
CUMBRIA LA23 3PG
Tel: 015395 31344   Fax: 015395 31971
E-mail: parkcliffe@btinternet.com
Internet: www.parkcliffe.co.uk
FAMILY CAMPING AND CARAVANNING
GRADED EXCELLENT BY THE CUMBRIA TOURIST BOARD

Situated within 25 acres of peaceful natural Lakeland beauty with magnificent views of Lake Windermere and surrounding hills, yet within minutes of all the attractions that the Lake District has to offer. Ideal Centre for hill walking with direct access to the fells.
Facilities include:- Squirrel's Bar and Licensed Restaurant, Luxury Heated Shower Block with private Bathrooms, Children's Play Area.

Static Caravans
For Sale
AA ANWB

Lake Windermere and the Langdales. The park is very well equipped for families, and there is no loud entertainment to spoil the peace and tranquillity. A 25-acre site with 250 touring pitches and 50 statics. Off-licence.

Park Cliffe Camping & Caravan Estate

Leisure: ✦ ⚠ **Facilities:** ➤ 🌂 ⊙ ❅ ⅏ ☪ ♿ ⚮ ✓ 🏕 ★
Services: 🕭 ⊡ ♀ ﹟ ⌀ ⊞ T ✕ ♨ → ∪ ┣ ⊙ ♨ ✿ ❆ 🍴 ┛
Notes: No single sex groups, no noise 10.30pm -7.30am ⊜ 🚮 ▦ ❖ 🐟

NEW - AA Quality % Score for each pennant category. See page 7 for a full explanation

---

DERBYSHIRE

ASHBOURNE   Map 07 SK14
See also **Fenny Bentley & Osmaston**

▶ ▶ ▶ **70% Rivendale Touring Caravan & Leisure Park (SK162566)**
Buxton Rd, Alsop en le Dale DE6 1QU
☎ 01335 310311 & 01332 843000
🖹 01335 310311
e-mail: rivendale@fsmail.net
website: rivendalecaravanpark.co.uk
Dir: Off A515 (Ashbourne-Buxton) opposite turn for Biggin
★ 🚐 £7.60-£9.80 🚃 £7.60-£9.80 ▲ £6.80-£9.80
Open Mar-Jan (rs low & mid season Bar & cafe opening hours restricted) Booking advisable Jul & Aug Last arrival 21.00hrs Last departure 11.00hrs
A sheltered site built in a long-closed quarry, with all hardstandings. The site is well equipped with excellent facilities, and run by enthusiastic staff. A 37-acre site with 105 touring pitches, 60 hardstandings and 20 statics. Nature walk, dog walking field
Leisure: ✦ ⚠ ⊡ **Facilities:** 🌂 ⊙ ❅ ⅏ ♿ ⚮ ⅏ ⊞ ♿ ★
Services: 🕭 ⊡ ♀ ﹟ ⌀ ⊞ T ✕ → ∪ ♨ 🚮 ▦ ❖ 🐟

BAKEWELL   Map 08 SK26
See also **Youlgreave**

▶ ▶ ▶ **68% Greenhills Caravan & Camping Park (SK202693)**
Crow Hill Ln DE45 1PX ☎ 01629 813052 & 813467
🖹 01629 815131
e-mail: info@greenhillsleisure.com
website: www.greenhillsleisure.com
Dir: 1m NW of Bakewell on A6. Signed before Ashford in the Water, 50yds along unclass rd on right
🚐 🚃 ▲
Open May-Sep (rs Oct, Mar & Apr bar & shop closed) Booking advisable Etr-Sep Last arrival 21.00hrs Last departure noon
A well-established family-run park with a separate tenting field, and easy access to all facilities. The tenting field is well cut and there is a path of shorter grass to the toilet block. An 8-acre site with 130 touring pitches and 60 statics.
Leisure: ⚠ **Facilities:** 🌂 ⊙ ❅ ⅏ ♿ ⚮ ⅏ ⊞ ★
Services: 🕭 ⊡ ♀ ﹟ ⌀ ⊞ T → ∪ ┣ ⊙ 🍴 ⊜ 🚮 ▦ ❖ 🐟

BUXTON   Map 07 SK07
See **also Longnor (Staffordshire)**

▶ ▶ ▶ ▶ **71% Lime Tree Park (SK070725)**
Dukes Dr SK17 9RP ☎ 01298 22988
Dir: 1m S, between A515 & A6
🚐 🚃 ▲
Open Mar-Oct Booking advisable bank hols & Jul-Aug Last arrival 21.00hrs Last departure noon
A most attractive and well-designed site, set on the side of a narrow valley in an elevated situation of gently sloping land with views. A 10.5-acre site with 99 touring pitches and 43 statics.

contd.

Lime Tree Park

Leisure: ♠ 瓜 ♫ **Facilities:** ⬚⊙♋✳⚹⚹⛵㊀♈⛄

Services: 🔲⊞🛢⬚⊞Ⓣ→U▸⊙♨⅏⬚⫿⫿⬚⬚⬚

► ► **66% Cottage Farm Caravan Park (SK122720)**
Blackwell in the Peak SK17 9TQ ☎ 01298 85330
e-mail: mail@cottagefarmsite.co.uk
website: www.cottagefarmsite.co.uk
*Dir: 6m E of Buxton off A6 and B6049, signed Blackwell
in the Peak*
★ ⊞ fr £7 ⊞ fr £7 ▲ fr £7
Open mid Mar-Oct (rs Nov-Mar hook up and water
tap only) Booking advisable Last arrival 21.30hrs
*A small terraced site in an attractive farm setting
with lovely views. Hardstandings are provided for
caravans, and there is a separate field for tents. An
ideal site for those touring or walking in the Peak
District. A 3-acre site with 30 touring pitches, 25
hardstandings.*
Facilities: ⬚⊙✳⚹⚹⛵ **Services:** 🔲🛢⬚Ⓣ

► ► **63% Thornheyes Farm Campsite (SK084761)**
Thornheyes Farm, Longridge Ln, Peak Dale
SK17 8AD ☎ 01298 26421
*Dir: 1.5m from Buxton on A6 turn E for Peak Dale.
After 0.5m S at x-rds to site on right*
★ ⊞ fr £6 ⊞ fr £5.50 ▲ fr £5
Open Etr-Oct Booking advisable bank hols & high
season Last arrival 21.30hrs Last departure
evenings
*A pleasant farm site run by a friendly family team in
the central Peak District. Facilities are very basic but
extremely clean. A 2-acre site with 10 touring
pitches.*
Facilities: ⬚✳ **Services:** 🔲🛢⬚→U▸⊡⛋
Notes: Site not suitable for children,
no ball games, no bicycles, unisex showers

► ► **68% Camping & Caravanning Club Site
(SK072992)**
SK13 1HZ ☎ 01457 866057
website: www.campingandcaravanningclub.co.uk
*Dir: A628 Manchester to Barnsley rd. At Crowden follow
sign for car park Youth Hostel and Camp site. Site
approx 300yds from main road*
★ ▲ £6.90-£10.40
Open 21 Mar-23 Sep Booking advisable bank hols &
Jun-Aug Last arrival 21.00hrs Last departure noon

contd.

*A beautifully located moorland site, overlooking the
reservoirs and surrounded by hills. Tents only, with
backpackers' drying room. Please see
advertisement on page 10 for details of Club
Members' benefits. A 2.5-acre site with 45 touring
pitches.*
Drying room for wet items
Facilities: ⬚⊙♋✳⛵
Services: →🛢⅃⅃⬚⫿⫿⬚⬚⬚

► ► **62% Coopers Caravan Site (SK121859)**
Newfold Farm, Edale Village S30 2ZD
☎ 01433 670372
*Dir: From A625 at Hope take minor road for 4m to
Edale. Turn right onto unclass road, and site on left in
800yds opposite school*
⊞⊞▲

Open all year Booking advisable bank hols Last
arrival 23.30hrs Last departure 15.00hrs
*Rising grassland behind a working farm, divided by
a wall into two fields, culminating in the 2062ft
Edale Moor. Facilities have been converted from
original farm buildings, and include a new café for
backpackers, serving all-day meals. A 6-acre site
with 135 touring pitches and 11 statics.*
Facilities: ⬚⊙♋✳⛵⚹⛵ **Services:** 🔲🛢⬚⊡⊞✖→U

► ► ► **66% Bank Top Farm (SK181498)**
DE6 1LF ☎ 01335 350250
*Dir: Leave Ashbourne on A515, take B5056,
200yds on right*
★ ⊞ £8.50-£10.50 ⊞ £8.50-£10.50 ▲ £6-£12
Open Mar/Etr-Sep Booking advisable peak periods
Last arrival 20.00hrs Last departure 14.00hrs
*A dairy farm with good toilet facilities including a
laundry. The gently sloping grass site has some
level pitches. A 3-acre site with 36 touring pitches
and 15 statics.*
Facilities: ⬚⊙♋✳⛵ **Services:** 🔲→▸⅃

► ► **66% Camping & Caravanning Club Site
(SK048868)**
Kinder Rd SK22 2LE ☎ 01663 745394
website: www.campingandcaravanningclub.co.uk
*Dir: Off A624, Glossop to Chapel-en-le-Frith (Hayfield
by-pass). Well signed into the village, follow wooden
carved signs to site*
★ ⊞ £7.80-£12 ▲ £7.80-£12   *contd.*

Open Mar-Oct Booking advisable bank hols & peak periods Last arrival 21.00hrs Last departure noon
On level ground along the River Sett valley, a peaceful location overlooked on three sides by mature woodland, with the hills of the North Derbyshire moors on the fourth side. The camping area is in two fields with central amenities. Please see the advertisement on page 10 for details of Club Members' benefits. A 6-acre site with 90 touring pitches.
Facilities: ⚹☉🕾⚹☀🥤🛒 **Services:** 🔌🚽🗑→🚰▶🔧🔋
Notes: No towed caravans 📞 💳 💳 💳 📷

HOPE   Map 07 SK18

▶ **65% Pindale Farm Outdoor Centre (SK163825)**
Pindale Rd S33 6RN ☎ 01433 620111
📠 01433 620729
e-mail: bookings@pindale.fsbusiness.co.uk
website: www.pindale.fsbusiness.co.uk
Dir: From A625 in Hope turn into Pindale Lane between church and Woodroffe Arms. Pass cement works over bridge, site in 400yds, well signed
★ 🚐 ⛺ £6-£7
Open Mar-Oct Booking advisable Last departure 11.00hrs no cars by caravans
An ideal base for walking, climbing and various outdoor pursuits, offering good facilities for campers and with a self-contained bunkhouse for up to 60 people. A 1-acre site with 10 touring pitches.
Facilities: ⚹☉☀🍴🅿 **Services:** 🚽→🚰▶🔧🛒
Notes: Dogs must be kept on leads

MATLOCK   Map 08 SK35

PREMIER PARK

▶▶▶▶▶ **74% Darwin Forest Country Park (SK302649)**
Darley Moor, Two Dales DE4 5LN
☎ 01629 732428 📠 01629 735015
e-mail: admin@darwinforest.co.uk
website: www.darwinforest.co.uk
Dir: From M1 Chesterfield take A632 to Matlock. Turn onto B5057 towards Darley Dale. Park is on right. Caravans must not approach from A6 due to a very steep hill
★ 🚐 £10-£12 ⛺ £10-£12

Open Mar-Oct Booking advisable bank hols & Jul-Aug Last arrival 20.00hrs Last departure 10.00hrs

contd.

A mostly level woodland site set amongst tall pines in the heart of the Derbyshire Dales. The park has an excellent indoor swimming pool complex, and good facilities for children both indoors and out. There is also a licensed bar and restaurant, and the area is ideal for touring and walking. A 44-acre site with 48 touring pitches, 48 hardstandings and 90 statics.
Orienteering, woodland walks, mini golf
Leisure: ⚹ ⚹ ⚹ ⚹ **Facilities:** ⚹☉🕾⚹🥤
⚹🍴🥤 **Services:** 🔌🚽🔋🔌🗑✕💧→🚰▶☉✚🔧
📞 💳 💳 📷

▶▶▶ **72% NEW Lickpenny Caravan Site (SK339597)**
Lickpenny Ln, Tansley DE4 5GF ☎ 01629 583040
📠 01629 583040
e-mail: lickpenny@btinternet.com
Dir: From A615 between Alfreton and Matlock, approx 1m N of Tansley. Turn into Lickpenny lane at x-rds
★ 🚐 £10-£14 ⛺ £10-£14
Open all year Booking advisable Last departure 12.00hrs
A new site developed in an old plant nursery, with small, well-screened areas surrounded mainly by rhododendrons. With its good standard of facilities this is an excellent base for touring the Peak District. A 7-acre site with 45 touring pitches, 45 hardstandings.
Leisure: ⚹ **Facilities:** ⚹☉🕾🥤🍴🅿 **Services:** 🔌🚽🔋
🛒→🚰▶☉✚🔧🛒 📞 💳 💳 💳 📷

▶▶▶ **63% Sycamore Caravan & Camping Park (SK329615)**
Lant Ln, Tansley DE4 5LF ☎ 01629 55760
Dir: 2.5m NE of Matlock off A632
🚐 🚐 ⛺
Open 15 Mar-Oct Booking advisable bank hols & summer hols Last arrival 21.00hrs Last departure noon
An open grassland site with mainly level touring pitches housed in a separate field from the statics. The park is well maintained, and the facilities are very clean. A 6.5-acre site with 55 touring pitches and 52 statics.
Leisure: ⚹ **Facilities:** ⚹☉🕾⚹🥤
Services: 🔌🚽🗑🔋→🚰▶🔧✚🔋🛒🔌📞 💳 💳 📷

▶▶▶ **64% Wayside Farm Caravan Park (SK361620)**
Chesterfield Rd, Matlock Moor DE4 5LF
☎ 01629 582967 📠 01629 582967
Dir: From Matlock on Chesterfield road, site on right in 2m opposite golf course
🚐 🚐 ⛺
Open all year Booking advisable all year Last arrival 22.00hrs Last departure flexible
A small hilltop farm overlooking Matlock with two camping fields and good facilities. A 1.5-acre site with 30 touring pitches.
Leisure: ⚹ **Facilities:** ⚹☉🕾⚹⚹🥤🍴🅿
Services: 🔌🚽🗑🔋✕🥤→🚰▶☉✚🔧🚽

NEWHAVEN   Map 07 SK16

▶ ▶ ▶ **69% Newhaven Holiday Camping & Caravan Park** (SK167602)
SK17 0DT ☎ 01298 84300 ◻ 01332 726027
Dir: Halfway between Ashbourne & Buxton at junct with A515 & A5012
★ ⊞ £7.50-£8.75 ⊞ £7.50-£8.75 ▲ £7.50-£8.75

Open Mar-Oct Booking advisable public hols Last arrival 23.00hrs Last departure anytime
Pleasantly situated within the Peak District National Park, with three areas well screened by mature trees. Very good toilet facilities catering for touring vans and large tent field. A 30-acre site with 125 touring pitches, 4 hardstandings and 73 statics.
Leisure: ✦ ⚕ **Facilities:** ⋒⊙⚖✳⛌⚲⊞⊼⋔
Services: ⊞⊡⊠⊘⊞⊞→∪⚐⚒⤳⟊⊞⊟⊞⊞⊞

OSMASTON   Map 07 SK14

▶ ▶ **67% Gateway Caravan Park** (SK194449)
DE6 1NA ☎ 01335 344643 ◻ 01335 344643
e-mail: admin@gatewaycaravanpark.co.uk
website: www.gatewaycaravanpark.co.uk
Dir: 1m S of Ashbourne turn off A52 signed Osmaston, site 400yds on right
★ ⊞ £8.50 ⊞ £8.50 ▲ £8.50
Open all year (rs Nov-Feb Bar closures) Booking advisable All bank hols & school hols Last arrival 21.00hrs Last departure 17.00hrs
A well-established site with mature trees and shrubs and a mixture of grass and hard pitches. The toilet facilities are continually being improved, and there are plans to develop the site further in the near future. A 13-acre site with 200 touring pitches, 20 hardstandings.
Function room with entertainment, squash court
Leisure: ✦⊡ **Facilities:** ⋒⊙✳⚲⛌⚲⊼⋔
Services: ⊞⊡⊠⊘→∪▶⚐⤳⟊
Notes: Family park, no large groups

ROWSLEY   Map 08 SK26

▶ ▶ ▶ **63% Grouse & Claret** (SK258660)
Station Rd DE4 2EL ☎ 01629 733233
⊞⊞
Open all year Booking advisable wknds, bank hols & peak periods Last arrival 20.00hrs Last dep noon
A well-designed, purpose-built park at the rear of an eating house on A6 between Bakewell and Chatsworth, and adjacent to the New Peak Shopping Village. The park comprises a

contd.

level grassy area running down to the river, and all pitches have hardstandings and electric hook-ups. A 2.5-acre site with 29 touring pitches.
Leisure: ✦⚕ **Facilities:** ⋒⊙✳⛌⚲⊼ **Services:** ⊞
⊠✗⛯→∪▶⟊⚒ **Notes:** No tents ⊞⊞⊞⊞⊞

SHARDLOW   Map 08 SK43

▶ ▶ ▶ **65% Shardlow Marina Caravan Park** (SK444303)
London Rd DE72 2GL ☎ 01332 792832
◻ 01332 792832
Dir: M1 junct 24, take A6, then A50 Derby southern bypass. Take exit for Shardlow junct 1 off bypass, do not take exit Shardlow (Cavendish bridge). Site 0.5m on right.
★ ⊞ £8-£10.75 ⊞ £8-£10.75 ▲ £8-£9.75
Open Mar-Jan Booking advisable bank hols Last arrival 20.00hrs Last departure 14.00hrs
A large marina site with restaurant facilities, situated on the Trent/Mersey canal. The spacious pitches are on grass surrounded by mature trees, and there are good toilet facilities. A 25-acre site with 70 touring pitches and 36 statics.
Leisure: ⚕ **Facilities:** ⋒⊙✳⚲
Services: ⊞⊠⊘⊞⊞⊞✗→▶⤳⟊⊞

YOULGREAVE   Map 07 SK26

▶ **66% Camping & Caravanning Club Site** (SK206632)
c/o Hopping Farm DE45 1NA ☎ 01629 636555
website: www.campingandcaravanningclub.co.uk
Dir: A6/B5056, after 0.5m turn right to Youlgreave. Turn sharp left after church down Bradford Lane, opposite George Hotel. 0.5m to sign turn right
★ ⊞ £9-£10 ⊞ £9-£10 ▲ £9-£10
Open Mar-Sep Booking advisable bank hols & peak periods Last arrival 21.00hrs Last departure noon
Ideal for touring and walking in the Peak District National Park, this gently sloping grass site is accessed through narrow streets and along unadopted hardcore. Own sanitary facilities essential. Please see the advertisement on page 10 for details of Club Members' benefits. A 14-acre site with 100 touring pitches, 6 hardstandings.
Leisure: ⚕ **Facilities:** ✳⚲⚐⋔ **Services:** ⊞⊘⊘⊞
→∪▶⊙⚐⟊⊞⊞⊞⊞⊞

> Remember that prices and opening times are liable to change within the currency of this guide. It is always best to telephone in advance

Leisure: ⚆ Indoor swimming pool ⚆ Outdoor swimming pool ⚬ Tennis court ✦ Games room ⚕ Children's playground ∪ Stables
▶ 9/18 hole golf course ⤳ Boats for hire ⚏ Cinema ⟊ Fishing ⊙ Mini golf ⚐ Watersports ⊡ Separate TV room

England

DEVON

ASHBURTON Map 03 SX77

►►►► 65% **Ashburton Caravan Park (SX753723)**
Waterleat TQ13 7HU ☎ 01364 652552
01364 652552
e-mail: info@ashburtoncaravanpark.co.uk
website: www.ashburtoncaravanpark.co.uk
Dir: *Leave A38 into centre of Ashburton, turn into North St, bear right before bridge. Follow brown camping sign for Waterleat Park in 1.5m*
★ £7.50-£10 ▲ £7.50-£10
Open Etr-Sep Booking advisable bank hols & Jul-Aug Last arrival 22.30hrs Last departure noon
This well-maintained and attractive park is in a sheltered south-facing valley alongside the River Ashburn, and bordered by mature trees and shrubs. Catering only for tents and motorhomes, it is set in a very rural location within the Dartmoor National Park. An ideal location from which to explore the moors and coast. A 2-acre site with 35 touring pitches and 40 statics.
Facilities: **Services:**

►►►► 69% **Parkers Farm Holidays (SX779713)**
Higher Mead Farm TQ13 7LJ
☎ 01364 652598 01364 654004
e-mail: parkersfarm@btconnect.com
website: www.parkersfarm.co.uk
Dir: *From Exeter on A38, take 2nd left after Plymouth 26m sign, at Alston, signed Woodland-Denbury. From Plymouth on A38 take A383 Newton Abbot exit, turn right across bridge and rejoin A38, then as above.*
★ £5.50-£10.50 £5.50-£10.50 ▲ £5.50-£10.50

SILVER

Open Etr-end Oct Booking advisable Whitsun & school hols Last departure 10.00hrs
A well-developed site terraced into rising ground. Part of a working farm, this park offers beautifully maintained, quality facilities. Large family rooms with two shower cubicles, a large sink and a toilet are especially appreciated by families with small children. There are regular farm walks when all the family can meet and feed the various animals. An 8-acre site with 60 touring pitches and 25 statics.
Leisure: **Facilities:**
Services:

►►►► 73% ***River Dart Country Park (SX734700)***
Holne Park TQ13 7NP ☎ 01364 652511
01364 652020
Dir: *From M5 take A38 towards Plymouth, turn off at Peartree Cross junct (between Ashburton & Buckfastleigh) onto unclass road towards Holne*
▲

Open May-Aug (rs Etr-Sep no evening facilities ie bar) Booking advisable Spring bank hol & Jul-Aug Last arrival 21.00hrs Last departure 11.00hrs
Set in 90 acres of magnificent parkland that was once part of a Victorian estate, with many specimen and exotic trees, and in spring, a blaze of colour from the many azaleas and rhododendrons. There are numerous outdoor activities for all ages including abseiling, caving and canoeing, plus high

contd.

quality, well-maintained facilities. The open moorland of Dartmoor is only a few minutes away. A 7-acre site with 170 touring pitches.

Leisure: ᐩ ᐸ ᐸ ⚏ ▢ Facilities: ⬸ ⋒ ☉ ◥ ☀ ᕯ ᖷ ☖ ⊞
⊟ ᖷ Services: ⊠ ⊡ ♈ ◪ ⊞ ⊤ ✕ ⬛ ⬸ → ∪ ▶ ⏌
⊜ ▥ ▥ ⊠ ▨

► ► ► ► 68% **Andrewshayes Caravan Park (SY248088)**
Dalwood EX13 7DY ☎ 01404 831225
🖺 01404 831893
e-mail: enquiries@andrewshayes.co.uk
website: www.andrewshayes.co.uk
Dir: On A35 3m from Axminster. Turn N at Taunton Cross signed Stockland/Dalwood. Site 150mtrs on right
⊞ £8.50-£10 ⊞ £8.50-£10 ⚊ £8.50-£10
Open Mar-Jan (rs Apr-21 May & Oct-Jan shop hours limited, pool closed Sep-mid May) Booking advisable Spring bank hol & Jul-Aug Last arrival 22.00hrs
Last departure noon
A lively park within easy reach of Lyme Regis, Seaton, Branscombe and Sidmouth in an ideal touring location. This popular park boasts an attractive bistro beside the swimming pool, a bar,

contd.

laundry and shop. A 4-acre site with 90 touring pitches, 60 hardstandings and 80 statics. Licensed bistro May-Sep.

Leisure: ᐩ ᐸ ⚏ ▢ Facilities: ⋒ ☉ ◥ ☀ ᕯ ☖ ᖷ
Services: ⊠ ⊡ ♈ ◪ ⊞ ✕ ⬛ → ∪ ⏌ ᕯ Notes: Dogs must be kept on leads, no teenage groups
⊜ ▥ ▥ ⊠ ▨

► ► ► 63% **Midland Holiday Park (SS533346)**
Braunton Rd, Ashford EX31 4AU ☎ 01271 343691
🖺 01271 326355
website: www.midlandpark.co.uk
Dir: 2m from Barnstaple on A361 towards Chivenor. (This is a fast dual-carriageway & care should be taken)
⊞ ⊞ ⚊
Open Mar-Nov Booking advisable all year Last arrival 22.00hrs Last departure noon
A gently-sloping grass park divided into paddocks, and close to the Tarka cycle trail. The park has been extensively improved recently, and now offers a licensed bar with occasional entertainment, a pitch and putt, a bouncy castle and children's playground. The site is about 5m from sandy beaches. A 10-acre site with 35 touring pitches, 10 hardstandings and 61 statics.
Bouncy castle

contd.

Midlands Holiday Park

Leisure: ◣ ⋀ **Facilities:** ♄⊙☜※✶⛁⠀ **Services:**
🔌🔲🍽❓∅→∪▶◎⚡⁑⚒✂🍴🔳🔳🔳🔳

BERRYNARBOR   Map 02 SS54
See also **Combe Martin & Ilfracombe**

▶ ▶ ▶ 66% **NEW** **Mill Park (SS559471)**
Mill Ln EX34 9SH ☎ 01271 882647 📠 01271 882667
e-mail: millpark@globalnet.co.uk
website: www.millpark.co.uk
*Dir: M5 junct 27 for A361 to Barnstaple. Take A399 coast
road towards Combe Martin & turn opposite Sawmills
Restaurant to Berrynarbor*
★ 🚐 £7-£11.50 🚐 £6.50-£10 ▲ £6-£10
Open mid Mar-mid Nov Last departure noon
*An attractive wooded valley with a stream running
through into a lake and a waterfall, where coarse
fishing is available. There is a quiet bar with a
family room, and the friendly, cheerful owners keep
the facilities and ground in good condition. A 30-
acre site with 160 touring pitches.*
Leisure: ◣ **Facilities:** ☜⛁ **Services:** 🔌🔳

▶ ▶ ▶ 71% **Napps Camping Site (SS561477)**
Old Coast Rd EX34 9SW ☎ 01271 882557
📠 01271 882557
e-mail: bookings@napps.fsnet.co.uk
website: www.napps.co.uk
*Dir: From A361 South Molton take A399 to Combe
Martin. Through village, site 1.5m past beach on right*
★ 🚐 £5-£13 🚐 £5-£13 ▲ £5-£11

Open Etr-Oct (rs Etr-Whit & Sep-Nov shop, pool, bar
& takeaway closed) Booking advisable always for
caravans & BH's in Jul & Aug Last arrival 22.00hrs
Last departure noon

contd.

---

*A family-owned and run cliff-top site close to
Combe Martin. Spectacular views of the bay below
can be enjoyed through the perimeter trees from its
lofty position, and the coastal path is popular with
walkers. An 11-acre site with 250 touring pitches,
12 hardstandings and 2 statics.*
Children's paddling pool & slide.
Leisure: ⌇◣◣⋀⎙ **Facilities:** ♄⊙☜※✶⛁⠀♄
Services: 🔌🔲❓▯∅🔳▯✖🚾→∪▶◎△⚡⁑✂
Notes: Dogs must be kept on leads 🔳 🔳 🔳 🔳 🔳

BICKINGTON (NR. ASHBURTON)   Map 03 SX87

▶ ▶ ▶ ▶ 72% **The Dartmoor Halfway Caravan
Park (SX804719)**
TQ12 6JW ☎ 01626 821270 📠 01626 821820
e-mail: BHUGG22430@aol.com
*Dir: Direct access from A383, 1m from A38 Exeter-
Plymouth road*
🚐🚐
Open all year Booking advisable high season &
bank hols Last departure 10.00hrs
*A well-developed park tucked away on the edge of
Dartmoor, beside the River Lemon and adjacent to
the Halfway Inn. The neat and compact park has a
small toilet block with immaculate facilities, and
pitches separated by mature shrubs. An extensive
menu at the inn offers reasonably-priced food all
day and evening. A 2-acre site with 22 touring
pitches.*
Leisure: ⋀ **Facilities:** ♄⊙※✶⛁☜⚲♄ **Services:** 🔌
❓▯✖→∪▶⁑✂▯⛁🔳🔳🔳🔳🔳

▶ ▶ ▶ ▶ 72% **Lemonford Caravan Park
(SX793723)**
TQ12 6JR ☎ 01626 821242 & 821263
📠 01626 821242
e-mail: mark@lemonford.co.uk
website: www.lemonford.co.uk
*Dir: From Exeter A38 take A382 turn, then 3rd exit on
rdbt and follow Bickington signs.*
★ 🚐 £6-£9.50 🚐 £6-£9.50 ▲ £6-£9.50
Open mid Mar-Oct Booking advisable School
Holidays Last arrival 22.00hrs Last departure
11.00hrs
*Small, secluded and well-maintained park with a
good mixture of attractively laid out pitches. The
friendly owners pay a great deal of attention to
detail, and the toilets in particular are kept
spotlessly clean. This good touring base is only
1m from Dartmoor and 10m from the seaside at
Torbay. A 7-acre site with 85 touring pitches, 48
hardstandings and 22 statics.*
Clothes drying area.
Leisure: ⋀ **Facilities:** ⚲♄⊙☜※✶⛁⚲♄
Services: 🔌🔲❓∅▯▯→∪▶⁑✂

BRATTON FLEMING   Map 03 SS63

▶ ▶ ▶ **66% Greenacres Farm Touring Caravan Park (SS658414)**
EX31 4SG ☎ 01598 763334
Dir: From M5 junct 27 onto A361 towards Barnstaple. At 2nd rdbt near South Molton turn right onto A399 signed Blackmoor Gate & Combe Martin. In approx 10m turn left at Stowford Cross & site signed on left. Do not take signs to Bratton Fleming
★ ♣ £4-£7.50 ♣ £4-£7.50
Open Apr-Oct Booking advisable all times Last arrival 23.00hrs Last departure 11.00hrs
Located on the edge of Exmoor National Park, this small park is sheltered behind mature hedges, and well landscaped with a mix of grass and hard pitches. There are extensive views, and very well maintained facilities. A 4-acre site with 30 touring pitches, 6 hardstandings.
Leisure: ⋒ **Facilities:** ℝ⊙ℚ⚹⚿Ꮭ☐Ⓜ
Services: ⊡❶⊞→ᑌᵭ🏋

BRAUNTON   Map 02 SS43

▶ ▶ ▶ **62% Lobb Fields Caravan & Camping Park (SS475378)**
Saunton Rd EX33 1EB ☎ 01271 812090
▤ 01271 812090
e-mail: info@lobbfields.com
website: www.lobbfields.com
Dir: At x-rds in Braunton take B3231 to Croyde. Site signed on right leaving Braunton
♣ £6.50-£16.50 ♣ £5-£16.50 ▲ £5-£16.50

Open 28 Mar-Oct Booking advisable Jul-Aug Last arrival 21.00hrs Last departure 10.30hrs
Gently-sloping grass park divided into two areas, each rather open but bright and tree lined. Braunton is an easy walk away, and the golden beaches of Saunton Sand and Croyde are within close reach. A 14-acre site with 180 touring pitches, 7 hardstandings.
Baby changing facilities.
Leisure: ⋒ **Facilities:** ℝ⊙ℚ⚹Ꮭ☐Ⓜ **Services:** ⊡❶❶
⊘⊞→ᑌ▶⚹ᵭ🏋 **Notes:** No under 18s unless accompanied by an adult ⊞▨▨🄌

BRIDESTOWE   Map 02 SX58

▶ ▶ ▶ **61% Bridestowe Caravan Park (SX519893)**
EX20 4ER ☎ 01837 861261
Dir: Leave A30 at Sourton Down junct with A386, follow B3278 signed Bridestowe, and turn left in 3m. In village centre, left down unclass road for 0.5m
★ ♣ £6.80-£8.60 ♣ £6.80-£8.60 ▲ £6.80-£8.60
Open Mar-Dec Booking advisable summer Last arrival 22.30hrs Last departure noon
A small, well-established park in a rural setting close to Dartmoor National Park. This mainly static park has a small, peaceful touring area, and there are many activities to enjoy in the area including fishing and riding. A 1-acre site with 13 touring pitches and 40 statics.
Leisure: ◣ ⋒ **Facilities:** ℝ⊙ℚ⚹🏋☐
Services: ⊡▨❶⊘⊞→ᑌᵭ

BRIDGERULE   Map 02 SS20

▶ ▶ ▶ **62% Hedleywood Caravan & Camping Park (SS262013)**
EX22 7ED ☎ 01288 381404 ▤ 01288 381644
e-mail: alan@hedleywood.co.uk
website: www.hedleywood.co.uk
Dir: From B3254 take Widemouth road (unclass) at the Devon/Cornwall border
★ ♣ £6-£8.50 ♣ £6-£8.50 ▲ £6-£8.50

contd.

Open all year Booking advisable public hols & Jul-Aug Last arrival anytime Last departure anytime
Set in a very rural location about 4 miles from Bude, this relaxed family-owned site has a peaceful, easy-going atmosphere. Pitches are in separate paddocks, some with extensive views, and this wooded park is quite sheltered in the lower areas. A 16.5-acre site with 120 touring pitches, 6 hardstandings and 16 statics.
Dog kennels, nature trail.

Hedleywood Caravan & Camping Park

Leisure: ♦ ⚙ ☐ **Facilities:** ⋒ ⊙ ⬚ ✳ ⚹ ⚘ ⛿ 冊 戸 ★
Services: ☷ 圓 ⚲ ⅃ ⌷ ⊞ ⏇ ✕ ⬥ → ∪ ⊩ ⛺ ⌡
See advertisement on page 99

See advertisement on page 99

BRIXHAM   Map 03 SX95

▶ ▶ ▶ 67% **Galmpton Touring Park**
(SX885558)
Greenway Rd TQ5 0EP ☎ 01803 842066
e-mail: galmptontouringpark@hotmail.com
website: www.galmptontouringpark.co.uk
Dir: Signed from A3022 Torbay-Brixham road at Churston
★ ⊞ £7-£11 ⊞ £7-£11 ▲ £7-£11

Open Etr-Sep Booking advisable Jul-Aug & bank hols Last arrival 22.00hrs Last departure 11.00hrs
An excellent location on high ground overlooking the River Dart, with outstanding views of the creek and anchorage. Pitches are set on level terraces, and facilities are bright and clean. A 10-acre site with 120 touring pitches.
Under 5's bathroom (charged)
Leisure: ⚙ **Facilities:** ⋒ ⊙ ⬚ ✳ ⚹ ⚘ ⚲ ⛿ ★
Services: ☷ 圓 ⚲ ⅃ ⊞ → ⊩ ⊚ ⬥ ⛺ ⌡
Notes: Families and couples only, no dogs during peak season ⬤ ▭ ▭ ▩ ⑨

BRIXTON   Map 02 SX55

▶ ▶ 61% **Brixton Caravan & Camping Park**
(SX550520)
Venn Farm PL8 2AX ☎ 01752 880378
🖩 01752 880378
⛿ ⛿ ▲
Open 15 Mar-14 Oct (rs 15 Mar-Jun & Sep-14 Oct no warden) Booking advisable Jul-Aug Last arrival 23.00hrs Last departure noon
A small park adjacent to a farm in the village, in a quiet rural area. The park is divided into two paddocks, and is just 100yds from the village services. A 2-acre site with 43 touring pitches.
Facilities: ⇥ ⋒ ⊙ ✳ ⚘ ⊞ **Services:** ☷ → ∪ ⊩ ⚴ ⛺ ⌡

BUCKFASTLEIGH   Map 03 SX76

▶ 69% **Beara Farm Caravan & Camping Site**
(SX751645)
Colston Rd TQ11 0LW ☎ 01364 642234
Dir: From Exeter take Buckfastleigh exit at Dart Bridge, follow signs to South Devon Steam Railway & Butterfly Farm. 1st left after 200mtrs to Old Totnes Rd, after 0.5m right at brick cottages signed to Beara Farm
★ ⊞ £6.50-£7.50 ⊞ £6.50 ▲ £6.50
Open all year Booking advisable peak periods Jul-Aug Last arrival anytime Last departure anytime
A very good farm park with clean unisex facilities and very keen and friendly owners. A well-trimmed camping field offers peace and quiet. Close to the River Dart and the Dart Valley steam railway line, within easy reach of sea and moors. Approach is narrow with passing places and needs care. A 3.75-acre site with 30 touring pitches.
River Dart adjoining site
Facilities: ⋒ ⊙ ✳ ⚘ 戸 ★ **Services:** ⊞ → ⌡ ⚴

▶ 72% **Churchill Farm Campsite (SX743664)**
TQ11 0EZ ☎ 01364 642844
Dir: A38 Dart Bridge exit for Buckfastleigh/Totnes towards Buckfast Abbey. Left at mini-rdbt, left at x-roads to site opposite Holy Trinity church
★ ⊞ £7 ⊞ £7 ▲ £7
Open May-Oct Booking advisable Jul & Aug Last arrival 22.30hrs
A working family farm in a relaxed and peaceful setting, with keen, friendly owners. Set on the hills above Buckfast Abbey, this attractive park is maintained to a good standard. A 3-acre site with 25 touring pitches.
Facilities: ⋒ ⊙ ✳ **Services:** ☷ ⊞ → ⚴ **Notes:** Dogs must be kept on leads (working farm)

BUDLEIGH SALTERTON   See **Ladram Bay**

CHIVENOR   Map 02 SS53

▶ ▶ ▶ 64% **Chivenor Caravan Park (SS501351)**
EX31 4BN ☎ 01271 812217 & 07071 228478
🖩 01271 812644
Dir: On rdbt at Chivenor Cross. Adjacent to RMB Chivenor
★ ⊞ £6.50-£9 ⊞ £6.50-£9 ▲ £6-£8

contd.

Open mid Mar-mid Nov (rs Nov-Jan Static caravans only) Booking advisable Jun-Aug
A nicely-maintained grassy park with some hard pitches, set in a good location for touring North Devon, and handy for the bus stop into Barnstaple. The site is about 5 miles from sandy beaches. A 3-acre site with 32 touring pitches, 2 hardstandings and 10 statics.
Leisure: ⚠ **Facilities:** ↑⊕✻ᴸ🛒
Services: 🐕🚰🛢🥄🍴→∪▶🍽🍴🍺🚐🗄🛒📋

CHUDLEIGH Map 03 SX87

65% Finlake Holiday Park (SX855786)
TQ13 0EJ ☎ 01626 853833
🖪 01626 854031
e-mail: info@finlake.co.uk
website: www.finlake.co.uk
Dir: Signposted off A38 at Chudleigh exit
★ 🚐 £10-£18.50 🚐 £10-£18.50 ▲ £8-£18.50

Open all year limited facilities during winter months Booking advisable bank hols & Jul-Aug Last arrival 21.30hrs Last departure 11.00hrs
A very well-appointed holiday centre set in a wooded valley surrounded by 130 acres of parkland. A wide range of leisure facilities and entertainment for adults and children is available, and the park has its own golf course and fishing lake. A 130-acre site with 410 touring pitches, 320 hardstandings and 30 statics. Fishing, horseriding, golf & fitness suite.
Leisure: ₹ ৭ ⚠ **Facilities:** ➡↑⊕✻க
ᴸ🛒📺🍴 **Services:** 🐕🚰🛢🖥🛢✕🧹→∪▶🍴
🍺🗄🛒📋

CLIFFORD BRIDGE Map 03 SX78

▶ ▶ ▶ **66% Clifford Bridge Park** (SX782897)
EX6 6QE ☎ 01647 24226 🖪 01647 24116
e-mail: info@clifford-bridge.co.uk
website: www.ukparks.co.uk/cliffordbridge
Dir: From Cheriton Bishop turn by Old Thatch Inn & follow signs for 2m. Turn right at x-rds signed Clifford Bridge, continue over junct & bridge
★ 🚐 £8.75-£11.95 🚐 £7.65-£11.95 ▲ £7.65-£11.95
Open May-Sep Booking advisable school & bank hols Last arrival 22.00hrs Last departure 11.00hrs

contd.

A very attractive location in a deep wooded valley in the Dartmoor National Park, with pitches laid out alongside a lovely river bank. The approach roads are narrow and steep in places, and care is needed in towing large units. A 6-acre site with 65 touring pitches and 8 statics.
Fly fishing on site.
Leisure: ₹ ▲ ⚠ **Facilities:** ↑⊕৭✻ᴸ🛒🐕
Services: 🐕🚰🛢🥄🖥🍴→∪▶🍴

COLYTON Map 03 SY29

▶ ▶ ▶ ▶ **70% Leacroft Touring Park** (SY217925)
Colyton Hill EX24 6HY ☎ 01297 552823
Dir: 1m from Stafford Cross on A3052 towards Colyton

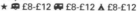
SILVER

★ 🚐 £8-£12 🚐 £8-£12 ▲ £8-£12
Open Etr-Oct Booking advisable Jul-Aug & Spring bank hol Last arrival 21.00hrs Last departure 11.00hrs
Set outside the little village of Colyton, this park stands on a hill in a rural area with open views over the countryside to the south, and backed by woods. The park slopes slightly, and pitches are well spaced. A 10-acre site with 138 touring pitches. Off-licence.
Leisure: ▲ ⚠ **Facilities:** ↑⊕৭✻க ᴸ🛒🏓🍴🐕
Services: 🐕🚰🛢🥄🖥🍴→∪▶🍴🍴🥄🍴

▶ ▶ **64% Ashdown Caravan Park** (SY216922)
Colyton Hill EX24 6HY ☎ 01297 21587 & 20292
Dir: From W take A3052 through Sidmouth towards Seaton, turn left at Stafford Cross, site 0.5m on left. From the E turn off A35 onto A358 signed Seaton, turn right onto A3052 signed Sidmouth, in 4m at Stafford Cross turn right for site
★ 🚐 £7-£8 🚐 £7-£8
Open Apr-Oct Booking advisable public hols Last departure noon
Sheltered by mature trees and shrubs in quiet, unspoilt surroundings, this grassy park is divided into two spacious areas around the perimeter. Most pitches have electricity, and Seaton with its famous tramway is only 3 miles away. 90 touring pitches and 3 statics.
Facilities: ↑✻ᴸ🐕🐕 **Services:** 🛢🖥→▶🥄🍴🥄🚰
Notes: Dogs must be kept on leads

COMBE MARTIN Map 02 SS54

▶ ▶ ▶ ▶ **69% Stowford Farm Meadows** (SS560427)
Berry Down EX34 0PW ☎ 01271 882476
🖪 01271 883053
e-mail: enquiries@stowford.co.uk
website: www.stowford.co.uk
Dir: Leave M5 junct 27 onto A361 to Barnstaple. Take A39 for Lynton through Barnstaple town centre & in 1m turn left onto B3230. Turn right at garage at Lynton Cross onto A3123 & site is 1.5m on right
★ 🚐 £4.30-£11.40 🚐 £4.30-£11.40 ▲ £4.30-£11.40

contd.

Open Apr-Oct (rs Etr-Spring bank hol & Oct some amenities may be available ltd hrs) Booking advisable bank hols & Jul-Aug Last arrival 20.00hrs Last departure 10.00hrs

Stowford Farm Meadows

Very gently sloping, grassy, sheltered and south-facing site approached down a wide, well-kept driveway. This large farm park is set in 500 acres, and offers many quality amenities, including a large swimming pool, horse riding and crazy golf. A 60-acre wooded nature trail is an added attraction, as is the mini zoo with its stock of friendly animals. A 100-acre site with 700 touring pitches.

Horse rides, fun golf, mini zoo, snooker & cycle hire

Leisure: 🏊 🐎 🎿 🎡 ☐   **Facilities:** 🚿 🖙 ⊙ 🎯 ✳ 🕭 🛒 🛎 ⌕
Services: 🖳 🖩 🛢 🛎 🚽 🖶 🗊 ✗ ⚓ → ∪ ▶ ⊙ 🗲 🚌 ▦ 🎇 🎮

CROCKERNWELL   **Map 03 SX79**

► ► ► **64% Barley Meadow Caravan & Camping Park** (SX757925)
EX6 6NR ☎ 01647 281629 🖷 01647 281629
e-mail: info@barleymeadow.co.uk
website: www.barleymeadow.co.uk
Dir: From M5 junct 31 take A30 to 3rd exit signed Woodleigh. Through Cheriton Bishop and park signed just beyond Crockernwell. From Cornwall take A30 to Merrymead rdbt, then 1st exit to Cheriton Bishop, park 2m on right
★ 🚐 £7.50-£8.50 🚐 £7.50-£8.50 🛖 £5-£8.50
Open 15 Mar-15 Nov Booking advisable bank hols & Jul-Aug Last arrival 23.00hrs Last departure noon
A small, very well maintained park set on high ground in the Dartmoor National Park in a quiet location. The grassy pitches are mostly level, and the park is well placed to explore Dartmoor. A 4-acre site with 40 touring pitches, 5 hardstandings. Picnic tables.

Leisure: 🏊 🐎 ☐   **Facilities:** 🖙 ⊙ 🎯 ✳ 🕭 🛒 🛎 🎯 ⌕
Services: 🖳 🖩 🛢 🛎 🖶 🗊 → ∪ ▶ 🗲

CROYDE   **Map 02 SS43**

► ► ► **66% NEW Bay View Farm Caravan & Camping Park** (SS443388)
EX33 1PN ☎ 01271 890501
website: www.bayviewfarm.co.uk
Dir: M5 junct 27 onto A361, through Barnstaple to Braunton, left onto B3231. Site at entry to Croyde
★ 🚐 £11-£13.50 🚐 £11-£13.50 🛖 £11-£12.50

contd.

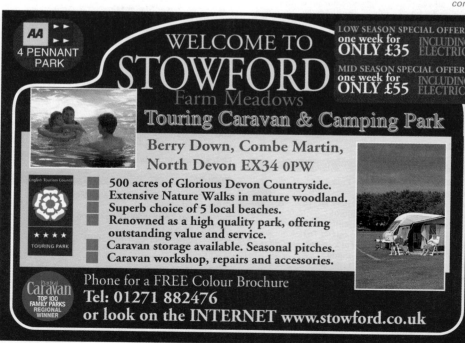
Services: 🗊 Toilet Fluid ✗ Café/ Restaurant 🍴 Fast Food/Takeaway 🚼 Baby Care 🔌 Electric Hook Up
🖳 Launderette 🍺 Licensed Bar 🛢 Calor Gaz 🖋 Camping Gaz 🗲 Battery Charging

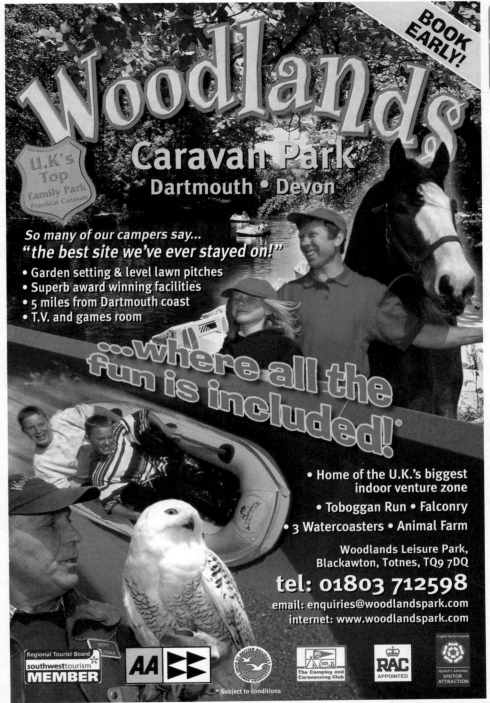

England

Open Mar-Nov
Set in a stunning location with views out over the Atlantic to Lundy Island, this family-run park offers clean, well-maintained facilities and tidy pitches. The village is just a stroll away, with its old world charm and choice of thatched pubs and eating places. A footpath from the park leads directly to a lovely beach with rock pools. A 10-acre site with 70 touring pitches, 30 hardstandings and 3 statics.

Facilities: 🍴 🎱   **Services:** 🚽 🗑

CROYDE BAY   Map 02 SS43

68% **NEW** Ruda Holiday Park
(SS438397)
EX33 1NY ☎ 01271 890671 & 890656
e-mail: enquiries@ruda.co.uk
website: www.ruda.co.uk
Dir: M5 junct 27, follow A361 to Braunton. Left at main traffic lights and follow signs for Croyde
★ 🚐 £9-£32 🚐 £6-£24 ▲ £6-£24
Open mid Mar-Oct Booking advisable all times Last arrival 22.00hrs Last departure 10.00hrs ⌦
A spacious, well-managed park with its own glorious Blue Flag sandy beach, a surfer's paradise. Set in well-landscaped grounds, and with a full leisure programme plus daytime and evening entertainment for all the family. Cascades tropical adventure pool, and a nightclub are very popular features. A 220-acre site with 328 touring pitches and 322 statics. Nightly entertainment

Leisure: 🏊 🎱 🎣 🎮 🖵 **Facilities:** 🛒 🔥 🕤 🍴 ✻ 🚿 ♿ 🕻
🎱 🎋 **Services:** 🚽 🗑 🖵 🍴 ⓘ ∅ 🗙 🛒 → ∪ ▶ ▲ 🗲
Notes: Family groups preferred, no dogs
💳 ▭▭ ▭▭ 🔲 🖲

DARTMOUTH   Map 03 SX85

▶ ▶ ▶ ▶ 72% **Little Cotton Caravan Park**
(SX858508)
Little Cotton TQ6 0LB ☎ 01803 832558
▤ 01803 834887
e-mail: enquiries@littlecotton.co.uk
website: www.littlecotton.co.uk
Dir: Exit A38 at Buckfastleigh, A384 to Totnes, A381 to Halwell, then A3122 Dartmouth Rd, park on right at entrance to town
★ 🚐 £6-£10 🚐 £6-£10 ▲ £6-£10
Open 15 Mar-Oct Booking advisable Jul & Aug Last arrival 22.00hrs Last departure noon
A very good grassy touring park set on high ground above Dartmouth, with quality facilities, and park and ride to the town from the gate. The toilet blocks are heated, and superbly maintained. The friendly owners are happy to offer advice on touring in this pretty area. A 7.5-acre site with 95 touring pitches, 20 hardstandings.

Facilities: 🔥 🕤 🍴 ✻ ♿ 🕻 🎱 🎋 🛒
Services: 🚽 🗑 🖵 ∅ 🕤 ⓘ → ▶ ◎ ▲ ✷ 🗲 💳 ▭▭ ▭▭ 🔲 🖲

▶ ▶ ▶ ▶ 72% **Woodlands Leisure Park**
(SX813522)
Blackawton TQ9 7DQ ☎ 01803 712598
▤ 01803 712680
e-mail: fun@woodlandspark.com
website: www.woodlandspark.com
Dir: 4m from Dartmouth on A3122. From A38 take turn for Totnes & follow brown tourist signs
★ 🚐 £7.50-£14.50 🚐 £7.50-£14.50 ▲ £7.50-£14.50

Open Easter-5 Nov Booking advisable anytime Last departure 11.00hrs ⌦
An extensive woodland park with a terraced grass camping area, and quality facilities which are maintained to a very high standard. The park caters for all the family in a relaxed atmosphere under the supervision of the owner's family. There is a large games room, and a wildlife park is attached, with entry free to campers who stay two nights. A 16-acre site with 225 touring pitches, 16 hardstandings. Watercoasters, toboggan run, gliders, falconry centre

Leisure: 🎣 🎮 🖵 **Facilities:** 🛒 🔥 🕤 🍴 ✻ ♿ 🕻 🎱
🎋 🎋 **Services:** 🚽 🗑 ⓘ ∅ 🕤 🖵 🗙 🛒 → ∪ ▶ ✷ 🗲
💳 ▭▭ ▭▭ 🔲 🖲

See advertisement on page 103

▶ ▶ ▶ 65% **Deer Park Holiday Estate**
(SX864493)
Dartmouth Rd, Stoke Fleming TQ6 0RF
☎ 01803 770253
website: www.deerparkinn.co.uk
Dir: Direct access from A379 from Dartmouth before Stoke Fleming
★ 🚐 £8.50-£11.50 🚐 £8.50-£11.50 ▲ £8.25-£11
Open 15 Mar-Nov Booking advisable Jul-Aug Last arrival anytime Last departure 11.00hrs
Set on high ground with extensive sea views over Start Bay, this park is divided into three lawned paddocks. Good food is served next door at the Deer Park Inn, and there is a bus service to local beaches and Dartmouth. A 6-acre site with 160 touring pitches.

Leisure: 🎣 🎣 🎮 **Facilities:** 🔥 🕤 ✻ ♿ 🕻 🎱
Services: 🚽 🗑 🖵 ∅ 🕤 🗙 🛒 → ∪ ▶ ▲ ✷ 🗲
Notes: Dogs must be kept on leads
💳 ▭▭ ▭▭ 🔲 🖲

DAWLISH — Map 03 SX97

66% Golden Sands Holiday Park (SX968784)
Week Ln EX7 0LZ ☎ 01626 863099
🖨 01626 867149
e-mail: info@goldensands.co.uk
website: www.goldensands.co.uk
Dir: Signed off A379 Exeter/Dawlish road. 1m from Dawlish
★ 🚐 £6-£13 🚐 £6-£13

Open Etr-Oct Booking advisable May-Sep Last arrival 22.00hrs Last departure 10.00hrs
A holiday centre for all the family, offering a wide range of entertainment. The small touring area is surrounded by mature trees and hedges in a pleasant area, and visitors enjoy free use of the licensed club, and heated swimming pools. Organised children's activities are a popular feature. A 2.5-acre site with 60 touring pitches and 188 statics.
Leisure: ⚓ 🎣 ◆ ⚏ **Facilities:** 🌂⊙♿☎🛒
Services: 🔌🔲🅿💧🚰📶🔥→🏪⊙🎵
Notes: No dogs in high season 💳 🎫 🔳

65% *Lady's Mile Holiday Park* (SX968784)
EX7 0LX ☎ 01626 863411
🖨 01626 888689
Dir: 1m N of Dawlish on A379
🚐 £8.50-£15 🚐 £8.50-£15 ▲ £8.50-£15

Open 17 Mar-27 Oct Booking advisable bank hols & Jul-Aug Last arrival 20.00hrs Last departure 11.00hrs
contd.

A beautifully-run holiday site with all grass touring pitches, and plenty of activities for everyone. Two swimming pools with waterslides, a large adventure playground, 9-hole golf course, and a bar with entertainment in high season all add to the enjoyment of a stay here. Facilities are kept very clean, and the surrounding beaches are easily accessed. A 16-acre site with 243 touring pitches and 43 statics.
Leisure: ⚓ 🎣 ◆ ⚏🖥 **Facilities:** ➡🌂⊙❄♿☎ 🛒🐴 **Services:** 🔌🔲🅿💧📶🔥🅿✖🔥→U🏪⊙△🚰☎ 🎵 💳🎫🔳🔳

See advertisement on page 106

69% Peppermint Park (SX978788)
Warren Rd EX7 0PQ
☎ 01626 863436 🖨 01626 866482
e-mail: info@peppermintpark.co.uk
website: www.peppermintpark.co.uk
Dir: From A379 at Dawlish follow signs for Dawlish Warren. Site 1m on left
★ 🚐 £6-£11.50 🚐 £6-£11.50 ▲ £6-£11.50
contd.

THE NEAREST TOURING & CAMPING PARK TO THE BEACH AT DAWLISH WARREN

Peppermint Park

Open Etr-Oct Booking advisable Spring bank hol & Jul-Aug Last arrival 20.00hrs Last departure 11.00hrs

Well-managed attractive park close to the coast, with excellent facilities including club and bar which are well away from pitches. Nestling close to sandy beaches, the park offers individually marked pitches on level terraces in pleasant, sheltered grassland. The many amenities include a heated swimming pool and water chute, coarse fishing and launderette. A 26-acre site with 250 touring pitches and 34 statics. Licensed club, entertainment, coarse fishing lake

Leisure: ༀ ✦ ⚙ **Facilities:** ℕ ⊕ ❄ & ↻ 🛒 ✈
Services: 📺 🎦 🍽 🛢 ⬛ 🅃 → ▶ ✚ ⚓ 💳 ▦ 🎌 ⑨

▶ ▶ ▶ ▶ 69% **Cofton Country Holiday Park** (SX967801)
Starcross EX6 8RP ☎ 01626 890111
🖨 01626 891572
e-mail: info@coftonholidays.co.uk
website: www.coftonholidays.co.uk
Dir: On A379 Exeter/Dawlish road 3m from Dawlish
★ 🚐 £7-£12 🚙 £7-£12 ▲ £7-£12

Open Etr-Oct (rs Etr-Spring bank hol & mid Sep-Oct swimming pool closed) Booking advisable bank hols & Jul-Aug Last arrival 20.00hrs Last dep 11.00hrs

Set in a rural location surrounded by spacious open grassland, with plenty of well-kept flower beds throughout the park. Most pitches overlook either the swimming pool complex or the fishing lakes and woodlands. An on-site pub, and a mini-market
contd.

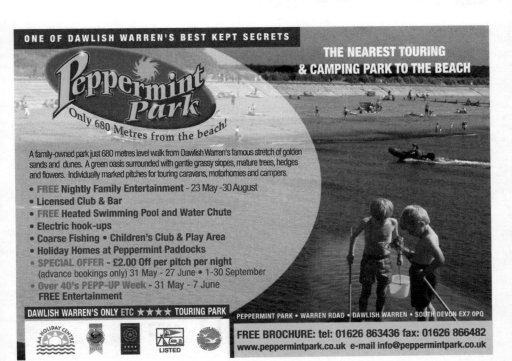
Leisure: ༀ Indoor swimming pool ༀ Outdoor swimming pool ⚘ Tennis court ✦ Games room ⚙ Children's playground ⋃ Stables
▶ 9/18 hole golf course ✚ Boats for hire 🎬 Cinema ⚓ Fishing ◎ Mini golf ⚐ Watersports ⬚ Separate TV room

caters for most shopping needs. A 16-acre site with 450 touring pitches and 62 statics.
Coarse fishing, pub with family room.
Leisure: ⟡ ⚑ ⚐ **Facilities:** ⌂ ⊙ ⚐ ✻ ⚙ ⚷ ⚑ ⚓
Services: ⚡ ⚅ ⚑ ⚓ ⚐ ⚑ ⊞ ✕ ⚑ → ⛏ ◖ ⚓ ✦ ⚒
Notes: No pets in accommodation, mainly non-smoking 💳 VISA CONNECT ⛔ ⊘

▶ ▶ ▶ **67% Leadstone Camping (SX974782)**
Warren Rd EX7 0NG ☎ 01626 864411
🖺 01626 873833
e-mail: info@leadstonecamping.co.uk
website: www.leadstonecamping.co.uk
Dir: From M5 junct 30 take A379 to Dawlish. Before village turn left on brow of hill, signed Dawlish Warren. Site 0.5m on right
★ ⊞ £11.90-£13.15 ⊞ £8.90-£9.90 ▲ £8.90-£9.90
Open 20 Jun-8 Sep Booking advisable 19 Jul-31 Aug Last departure noon

contd.

A traditional, mainly level grassy camping park approx 0.5m walk from sands and dunes at Dawlish Warren, an Area of Outstanding Natural Beauty. This mainly tented park has been run by the same friendly family for many years, and is an ideal base for touring south Devon. A regular bus service from outside the gate takes in a wide area. An 8-acre site with 137 touring pitches.
Leisure: ⚑ **Facilities:** ⌂ ⊙ ⚐ ✻ ⚷ ⚑
Services: ⚡ ⚅ ⚑ ⚐ ⊞ → ⛏ ◖ ⊙ ⚒
Notes: No noise after 11pm 💳 VISA CONNECT ⛔ ⊘

See advertisement on opposite page

DOLTON   **Map 02 SS51**

▶ ▶ ▶ **61% Dolton Caravan Park (SS573122)**
Acorn Farm House, The Square EX19 8QF
☎ 01805 804536
Dir: Dolton is on B3217 approx 1m S of junct with A3124
⊞ ⊞ ▲
Open Etr-15 Nov Booking advisable Jul-Aug Last arrival 22.00hrs Last departure noon
A well-maintained landscaped paddock with wide countryside views, at the rear of the Royal Oak Inn in the centre of Dolton. The village boasts three pubs, a good post office store, and a selection of craft and gift shops. A 2-acre site with 25 touring pitches.
Leisure: ⚑ **Facilities:** ⌂ ⊙ ✻ ⚑
Services: ⚡ ⚅ ⚑ ⚐ ⊞ → ⛏ ◖ ⚒

England

DREWSTEIGNTON　　　　Map 03 SX79

► ► **65% Woodland Springs Adult Touring Park** (SX695912)
Venton EX6 6PG ☎ 01647 231695 🖺 01647 231695
e-mail: enquiries@woodlandsprings.co.uk
website: www.woodlandsprings.co.uk
Dir: Leave A30 at Merrymeet rdbt, turn left onto A382 towards Moretonhampstead. Site 2m on left
★ 🚐 £7.50-£9.50 🚐 £7.50-£9.50 ▲ £5-£9.50
Open 15 Mar-15 Nov Booking advisable Last arrival 22.30hrs Last departure 11.00hrs
An attractive park in a rural area within Dartmoor National Park. This site is surrounded by woodland and neighbouring farmland, and is very peaceful. Children are not admitted. A 4-acre site with 60 touring pitches, 20 hardstandings.
Facilities: ᚠ ⊙ ✳ ৬ ♨ 🎋 ⋔ **Services:** ⊕ 🛢 🖉
➝ ∪ ▶ ♪ 🛒 **Notes:** Adults only, no fires, no bikes, no noise 11pm-8am

EAST ANSTEY　　　　Map 03 SS82

► ► ► **70% Zeacombe House Caravan Park** (SS860240)
Blackerton Cross EX16 9JU ☎ 01398 341279
Dir: M5 junct 27 onto A361 signed Barnstaple, turn right at next rdbt onto A396 signed Dulverton/Minehead. In 5m at Exeter Inn turn left onto B3227 towards S Molton, site in 7m on left
🚐 £11-£15 🚐 £11-£15 ▲ £9-£13

Open 7 Mar-Oct Booking advisable BHs & Jul-Aug Last arrival 21.00hrs Last departure noon
Set on the southern fringes of Exmoor National Park, this 'garden' park is nicely landscaped in a tranquil location, and enjoys panoramic views towards Exmoor. This adult-only park offers a choice of grass or hardstanding pitches, and a unique restaurant-style delivery service allows you to eat an evening meal in the comfort of your own unit. A 5-acre site with 50 touring pitches, 12 hardstandings.
Off licence
Facilities: ᚠ ⊙ ৭ ✳ ৬ 🛒 ⋔ **Services:** ⊕ 🛢 🖉 🖃 🇹 🍴
➝ ∪ ♪ **Notes:** Adults only 💳 ▤ ▦ 🏴 🉐

The new Quality % Score ranges from 50-80%. For full details of how the score works see page 7

EAST WORLINGTON　　　　Map 03 SS71

► ► ► ► **65% Yeatheridge Farm Caravan Park** (SS768110)
EX17 4TN ☎ 01884 860330
e-mail: yeatheridge@talk21.com
website: www.yeatheridge.co.uk
Dir: On B3042 1.5m W of Thelbridge Cross Inn. (Site is NOT in East Worlington village which is unsuitable for caravans)
★ 🚐 £6.50-£9 🚐 £6.50-£9 ▲ £6.50-£9

Open Etr-Sep Booking advisable Etr, Spring bank hol & school hols Last arrival 22.00hrs Last departure 22.00hrs
Gently sloping grass site with mature trees, set in meadowland in rural Devon. There are good views of distant Dartmoor, and the site is of great appeal to families with its farm animals, horse riding, and two indoor swimming pools, one with flume. There are many attractive villages in this area.

contd.

Facilities: 🛁 Bath 🕅 Shower ⊙ Electric Shaver 🗲 Hairdryer ✳ Ice Pack Facility ৬ Disabled Facilities 📞 Public Telephone 🛒 Shop on Site or within 200yds 🖃 Mobile Shop (calls at least 5 days a week) 🍖 BBQ Area 🎋 Picnic Area ⋔ Dog Exercise Area

A 9-acre site with 85 touring pitches and 4 statics.
Horse riding, fishing & pool table.

Leisure: 🏄 🎣 🅰 ▢ **Facilities:** 🚿 📶 ⊙ 🕽 ⚒ ❄ ⌖ 🎣 ⛲

🏖 **Services:** 🔌 🐟 ⚗ 🔗 ⚿ 🅣 🛒 🚐 → ∪ ⚓ 💳 💳 📶

See advertisement on page 125

EXETER   See **Kennford**

EXMOUTH   Map 03 SY08

See also **Woodbury Salterton**

**69% NEW Devon Cliffs Holiday Park
(SY036807)**
Sandy Bay EX8 5BT ☎ 01395 226226
website: www.havenholidays.com
★ 🚐 £10-£38 🚐 £10-£38 ▲ £10-£38
Open Mar-Oct Booking advisable Last arrival
22.00hrs Last departure 12.00hrs
*A very large holiday centre on a hillside setting
close to Exmouth, with spectacular views across
Sandy Bay. The all-action park offers plenty of
entertainment, sports and leisure facilities, but
those who just want to sit and relax will find lots
to watch. A 163-acre site with 144 touring
pitches.*

Leisure: 🏄 ✨ 🎣 🅰 ▢ **Facilities:** ⌖ ⛲
Services: 🔌 🐟 🅣 ⚗ ✕ 💳 💳 ⓞ 💳 📶 📶

► ► ► ► **76% Webbers Farm Caravan &
Camping Park (SY018874)**
Castle Ln, Woodbury EX5 1EA
☎ 01395 232276 📠 01395 233389
e-mail: reception@webbersfarm.co.uk
website: www.webbersfarm.co.uk
*Dir: 4m from M5 junct 30. Take A376, then B3179 to
Woodbury. Site is 500yds E of village*
🚐 £8-£12 🚐 £8-£12 ▲ £8-£12

Open Etr-Sep Booking advisable Peak season &
BH's Last arrival 20.00hrs Last departure 11.00hrs
*An unspoilt family park set in three areas, offering a
quiet and relaxing touring location. A new toilet
block has been built to the highest design, and now
provides en suite family rooms and plenty of quality
private facilities. The park has good views towards
the hills, and plenty to explore including 3,000 acres
of Woodbury Common and nearby beaches.
An 8-acre site with 115 touring pitches.*
Pets corner, caravan storage facilities

Leisure: 🅰 **Facilities:** 🚿 📶 ⊙ 🕽 ⚒ ❄ ⌖ 🎣 ⛲
Services: 🔌 🐟 ⚗ ⚗ 🅣 🛒 → ∪ ⚓ ⚿ 💳 💳 📶 📶

► ► **64% NEW St Johns Caravan & Camping
Park (SY027834)**
St Johns Rd EX8 5EG ☎ 01395 263170
e-mail: st.johns.farm@amserve.net
*Dir: Exit M5 at junct 30, left to Exmouth A376 left
through Woodbury to Budleigh Salterton on B3180, St
Johns Rd 0.5m on right*
★ 🚐 £8-£9 🚐 £8-£9 ▲ £7-£9
Open mid Feb-Dec Booking advisable School
Summer Hols Last arrival 22.00hrs Last departure
noon
*A quiet rural site with attractive country views, only
2 miles from Exmouth's sandy beaches, and half a
mile from Woodbury Common. Owners are
committed to upgrading the facilities over the next
few years, and offer a warm welcome to visitors.
A 6-acre site with 45 touring pitches.*

Leisure: 🅰 **Facilities:** 📶 ⊙ 🕽 ❄ ⌖ 🎣 🎣 🛒 **Services:**
🔌 🐟 ⚗ → ∪ ▶ ⊚ ▲ 🛒 ⚿ 🐟 🅣 **Notes:** Minimum age 18,
no single sex groups 💳 💳 📶 📶

HONITON   Map 03 ST10

See also **Kentisbeare**

► ► **63% Camping & Caravanning Club Site
(ST176015)**
Otter Valley Park EX14 8ST ☎ 01404 44546
📠 024 7669 4886
website: www.campingandcaravanningclub.co.uk
*Dir: Leave at 1st exit to Honiton from A30. Keep left off
slip road, road skirts perimeter of site*
★ 🚐 £11.10-£14.50 🚐 £11.10-£14.50 ▲ £11.10-£14.50
Open May-Sep Booking advisable bank hols & Jul-
Aug Last arrival 21.00hrs Last departure noon
*Set within walking distance of the market town of
Honiton, this grassy site makes an ideal stopover
point when visiting the West Country. The cathedral
city of Exeter is not far away, and there are plenty
of beaches within driving distance. Please see the
advertisement on page 10 for details of Club
Members' benefits. A 5-acre site with 90 touring
pitches.*
Dish washing sinks & area for ball games

Facilities: 📶 ⊙ 🕽 ❄ 🕽 🎣
Services: 🔌 🐟 ⚗ ⚗ → ▶ ▲ 🛒 💳 💳 💳 📶 📶

ILFRACOMBE   Map 02 SS54

► ► ► **65% Mullacott Cross Caravan Park
(SS511446)**
Mullacott Cross EX34 8NB ☎ 01271 862212
📠 01271 862979
Dir: Adjacent to A361 Braunton-Ilfracombe road
🚐 🚐 ▲
Open Etr-Sep (rs Etr-Whit & Oct) Booking advisable
Whit & Jul-Aug Last arrival 21.00hrs Last dep noon
*A meadowland site on high ground with views over
the Atlantic coastline. The park is an ideal touring
base, and just 2m from Ilfracombe and 3m from the
golden sands of Woolacombe. An 8-acre site with
115 touring pitches and 160 statics.*
Caravan accessory shop.

Leisure: 🅰 **Facilities:** 📶 ⊙ 🕽 ❄ ⌖ 🎣 🛒 **Services:** 🔌 🐟
🅣 ⚗ ⚗ 🅣 ✕ → ∪ ▶ ⚓ 🛒 🐟 💳 💳 💳 📶 📶

► ► ► **66% Watermouth Cove Holiday Park (SS558477)**
Berrynarbor EX34 9SJ ☎ 01271 862504
e-mail: info@watermouthcoveholidays.co.uk
website: www.watermouthcoveholidays.co.uk
Dir: M5 junct 27, A361 to 2nd rdbt at South Molton. A399 through Combe Martin. Left at seafront. Site 2m on right
★ 🚐 £7.50-£19.80 🚐 £7.50-£19.80 ▲ £7.50-£19.80
Open Etr-Oct (rs Etr-Whit & Sep-Nov pool, takeaway, club shop limited) Booking advisable Whit & Jul-Aug Last departure 11.00hrs
A popular site in very attractive surroundings, with access to sea and beach. This beautiful cove has a private sandy beach, and offers launching for boats and other water craft, as well as swimming. The site is two miles from both Combe Martin and Ilfracombe. A 6-acre site with 90 touring pitches, 10 hardstandings.
Leisure: ⚲ ♠ ⚠ ▢ **Facilities:** ⋔ ⊙ ⚑ ✳ ⛊ ▨ 🏪 ⊓
⋔ **Services:** 🖵 🗔 ⌖ ▨ ✎ 🖳 ⊞ Ⓣ ✕ 🖕 → ∪ ⏵ ◎ ♦ ✛ 🎱 ⤴
Notes: No motorcycles, no single sex groups
🍴 ▦ 📶 🌀

KENNFORD   Map 03 SX98

► ► ► **69% Kennford International Caravan Park (SX912857)**
EX6 7YN ☎ 01392 833046 🖷 01392 833046
e-mail: ian@kennfordint.fsbusiness.co.uk
website: www.kennfordint.co.uk
Dir: From M5, take A38, site signed at Kennford road
★ 🚐 £7.50-£10.50 🚐 £7.50-£10.50 ▲ £7.50-£10.50
Open all year Booking advisable
contd.

Screened by trees and shrubs from the A38, this park offers many pitches divided by hedging for privacy. A good, centrally located base for touring the coast and countryside of Devon, and Exeter is easily accessible via a nearby bus stop. A 15-acre site with 113 touring pitches and 3 statics.
Leisure: ♠ ⚠ **Facilities:** ➔ ⋔ ⊙ ⚑ ✳ ⛊ ⚲ 🖳 🏪 ⊓ ⋔
Services: 🖵 ⌖ ▨ ✕ → ∪ ⏵ ✛ 🎱 ⤴ 🖳 🍴 ▦ 🌀

Ⓤ **Haldon Lodge Farm Caravan & Camping Park (SX894868)**
EX6 7YG ☎ 01392 832312
Dir: Leave A38 at Kennford Services. Follow signs to Haldon Lodge, L through village. L at bridge to Dunchideock for 1m, L signed Underdown. Site 200yds on R.
🚐 £7-£9 🚐 £7-£9 ▲ £7-£9
Open all year At the time of going to press the pennant classification for this site was not confirmed.
Leisure: ∪ ⚠ **Facilities:** ⋔ ⚑ ✳ ⋔ ⛊
Services: 🖵 🗔 ⌖ ✎

KENTISBEARE   Map 03 ST00

► ► ► ► **65% Forest Glade Holiday Park (ST100075)**
Cullompton EX15 2DT
☎ 01404 841381 🖷 01404 841593
e-mail: enquiries@forest-glade.co.uk
website: www.forest-glade.co.uk
Dir: Tent traffic from A373, signed at Keepers Cottage Inn, 2.5m E of M5 junct 28. Touring caravans via Honiton/Dunkeswell road, phone for details of access
contd.

Leisure: 🏊 Indoor swimming pool 🏊 Outdoor swimming pool ⚲ Tennis court ♠ Games room ⚠ Children's playground ∪ Stables
▶ 9/18 hole golf course ⚓ Boats for hire 🎦 Cinema ⤴ Fishing ◎ Mini golf ♦ Watersports ⊡ Separate TV room

England

FOREST GLADE HOLIDAY PARK
CULLOMPTON, DEVON EX15 2DT
Tel: (01404) 841381 (Evgs to 8pm)

A small country estate surrounded by forest in which deer roam. Situated in an area of outstanding natural beauty.
Large, flat, sheltered camping/touring pitches.
Modern facilities building, luxury 2/6 berth full service holiday homes, also self contained flat for 2 persons.

COLOUR BROCHURE ON REQUEST

Fax: (01404) 841593 • www.forest-glade.co.uk
email: enquiries@forest-glade.co.uk

Forest Glade Holiday Park

★ ⊞ £10.60-£13.95 ⊞ £10.60-£13.95 ▲ £8.75-£11.75
Open 2 wks before Etr-end Oct (rs low season limit shop hours) Booking advisable school hols Last arrival 21.00hrs
A quiet, attractive park in a forest clearing with well-kept gardens and beech hedge screening. One of the main attractions is the immediate proximity of the forest, which offers magnificent hillside walks with surprising views over the valleys. Please telephone for route details. A 15-acre site with 80 touring pitches, 40 hardstandings and 57 statics. Adventure play area & children's paddling pool.
Leisure: ⚑ ⚒ ⚔ ⚁ Facilities: ⬤⊙⚑⚒
⚓⚒⚏⚎⚔ Services: ⚏⚏⚏⚎⚎⚏⚏⚎⚎⚏
Notes: Couples & families only ⚎ ⚎ ⚎ ⚎ ⚎

LADRAM BAY — Map 03 SY08

71% Ladram Bay Holiday Centre (SY096853)
EX9 7BX ☎ 01395 568398
🖷 01395 568338
e-mail: welcome@ladrambay.co.uk
website: www.ladrambay.co.uk
Dir: Leave M5 junct 30 onto A3052 signed Sidmouth. At Newton Poppleford take B3178 to Budleigh Salterton, through Colaton Raleigh, after 1m left at brick monument, signed Otterton/Ladram Bay. Fork right at Otterton, follow signs to Ladram Bay
⚑ ⚑ ▲
Open Spring bank hol-Sep (rs Etr-Spring bank hol no boat hire & entertainment) Booking advisable for caravans, school & spring bank hols Last arrival 18.00hrs
A country holiday centre beside the sea, offering a variety of free family entertainment, and with its own private beach with sand and rock pools at low tide. Most pitches are set on tiered grassy banks to take advantage of the views. The park also boasts a superb indoor swimming pool, and there is a good shop and café. A 50-acre site with 305 touring pitches and 469 statics.
Boat/canoe hire, crazy golf, doctor's surgery (in season)
Leisure: ⚑ ⚔ ⚁ Facilities: ⬤⊙⚒⚁⚔⚒⚏⚎
Services: ⚏⚏⚒⚁⚎⚏✕⚎→⚏▶⚒⚎⚎
Notes: No under 25s ⚎ ⚎ ⚎ ⚎

LYDFORD — Map 02 SX58

▶ ▶ ▶ **64% Camping & Caravanning Club Site (SX512853)**
EX20 4BE ☎ 01822 820275
website: www.campingandcaravanningclub.co.uk
Dir: From A30 take A386 to Tavistock. Continue to a filling station on right. Turn right to Lydford. At War Memorial turn right. Site signed 200yds
★ ⊞ £11.10-£14.50 ⊞ £11.10-£14.50 ▲ £11.10-£14.50
Open Mar-Oct Booking advisable bank hols & peak periods Last arrival 21.00hrs Last departure noon
Site on mainly level ground looking towards the western slopes of Dartmoor at the edge of the village, near the spectacular gorge. This popular park is close to the Devon coast-to-coast cycle route. Please see advertisement on page 10 for details of Club Members' benefits. A 7.75-acre site with 70 touring pitches.
Facilities: ⬤⊙⚒⚔⚁⚒⚏
Services: ⚏⚏⚒⚁⚎→⚏▶⚁⚔⚎ ⚎ ⚎ ⚎ ⚎

LYNTON — Map 03 SS74

▶ ▶ ▶ ▶ **64% Channel View Caravan and Camping Park (SS724482)**
Manor Farm EX35 6LD ☎ 01598 753349
🖷 01598 752777
e-mail: relax@channel-view.co.uk
website: www.channel-view.co.uk
Dir: From Lynton take A39 E for 0.5m. Site signed on left
★ ⊞ £8.50-£12 ⊞ £8-£11.50 ▲ £8-£11.50

contd.

Channel View Caravan Park

Open Etr-mid Oct Booking advisable Jul-Aug Last
arrival 22.00hrs Last departure noon
*On the top of the cliffs overlooking the Bristol
Channel, a well-maintained park on the edge of
Exmoor, and close to both Lynton and Lynmouth.
Pitches can be selected from a hidden hedged area,
or with panoramic views over the coast. A 6-acre
site with 76 touring pitches, 15 hardstandings and
36 statics.*
Parent & baby room
Leisure: ⚠ Facilities: ↖⊙ℚ✳&ℂ♈
Services: 🔌▣🔋⊘▣▣→∪◎♨♨🔦🍴⬛⬛⬛⬛⬛⬛

▶ ▶ ▶ 66% **Camping & Caravanning Club Site
(SS700484)**
Caffyns Cross EX35 6JS ☎ 01598 752379
website: www.campingandcaravanningclub.co.uk
*Dir: From M5 junct 27 onto A361 to 2nd South Molton
rdbt. Right onto A399 to Blackmoor Gate. Right onto
A39 towards Lynmouth/Lynton, left after 3m signed
Caffyns, immediately right to site in 1m*
★ 🚐 £11.10-£14.50 🚐 £11.10-£14.50 ▲ £11.10-£14.50
Open Mar-Sep Booking advisable bank hols & peak
periods Last arrival 21.00hrs Last departure noon
*Set on high ground with excellent views over the
Bristol Channel, and close to the twin resorts of
Lynton & Lynmouth. This area is known as Little
Switzerland because of its wooded hills, and the
park is ideal for walking, and cycling on the nearby
National Cycle Network. Please see the
advertisement on page 10 for details of Club
Members' benefits. A 5.5-acre site with 105 touring
pitches, 6 hardstandings.*
Ball game area
Leisure: ⚠ Facilities: ↖⊙ℚ✳ℂ♈
Services: 🔌▣🔋⊘▣→∪♭✄♨🍴🔦⬛⬛⬛⬛⬛⬛

▶ ▶ ▶ 66% **Sunny Lyn Holiday Park (SS719486)**
Lynbridge EX35 6NS ☎ 01598 753384
e-mail: info@caravandevon.co.uk
website: www.caravandevon.co.uk
*Dir: Leave M5 junct 27 onto A361 to S Molton, turn right
onto A399 to Blackmoor Gate, right onto A39 and right
onto B3234 towards Lynmouth. Site on right in 1m*
🚐 £11.50-£13 🚐 £11.50-£13 ▲ £8.50-£11
Open Mar-Nov Booking advisable Etr, spring bank
hol & mid Jul-Aug Last arrival 20.00hrs Last
departure 11.00hrs
*Set in a sheltered riverside location in a wooded
combe within 1m of the sea. This family-run park
offers good facilities including a café. A 4.5-acre site
with 37 touring pitches and 31 statics.* *contd.*

Sunny Lyn Holiday Park

Table tennis, trout fishing on site.
Facilities: ↖⊙ℚ✳ℂ🦺 Services: 🔌▣🔋⊘▣✕🚿
→∪◎✄♨🍴⬛⬛⬛⬛⬛⬛

| MODBURY | Map 03 SX65 |

▶ ▶ ▶ 70% **Camping & Caravanning Club Site
(SX705530)**
PL21 0SG ☎ 01548 821297
website: www.campingandcaravanningclub.co.uk
*Dir: Leave A38 at Wrangaton Cross onto A3121,
continue to x-rds. Cross over onto B3196, left after
California Cross sign before petrol station, site on right*
★ 🚐 £11.10-£14.50 🚐 £11.10-£14.50 ▲ £11.10-£14.50
Open Mar-Oct Booking advisable Spring bank hol &
Jul-Aug Last arrival 21.00hrs Last departure noon
contd.

Moor View Touring Park

Rural family run park, backing onto woodland, with panoramic views towards Dartmoor, close to coastal walks and beaches. This is a superb base for touring and walking. 68 individual level pitches all with electric hook-up. Hardstanding fully serviced pitches. Seasonal Pitches. Centrally heated luxury showers, shop and laundry, play area, 2 acre recreational field. TV, games and information room. Brochure available, with excellent Special Offers.

Moor View Touring Park
Telephone : 01548 821 485
California Cross, Modbury,
South Devon, PL21 0SG
www.moorviewtouringpark.co.uk
Email: info@moorviewtouringpark.co.uk

A gently-sloping site with some terracing, set in a rural location midway between Ivybridge and Kingsbridge. This well-ordered site is protected by high hedging, and is an ideal base for exploring the lovely South Devon countryside. Please see advertisement on page 10 for details of Club Members' benefits. A 3.75-acre site with 80 touring pitches, 7 hardstandings.

Leisure: /A **Facilities:** ⋒⊙ℚ✳⛄& ℭ
Services: 🔌🔋🅰⌀🔲➡→∪▶🔺♨🔧🔌〓📶🐕🔅

▶ ▶ ▶ **71% Moor View Touring Park** (SX705533)
California Cross PL21 0SG
☎ 01548 821485 📠 01548 821485
e-mail: info@moorviewtouringpark.co.uk
website: www.moorviewtouringpark.co.uk
Dir: A38 onto B3121. Over x-rds onto B3196, 4m past petrol station, park 1m
★ 🚐 £7.50-£11 🚐 £7.50-£11 🛆 £7.50-£11

contd.

Open 15 Mar-15 Nov Booking advisable bank hols & mid Jul-Aug Last arrival 19.00hrs Last dep noon
A compact terraced park in picturesque South Hams, with wide views of Dartmoor. Many pitches are divided by low mature hedging, and there is a good mix of hardstandings and grass. The excellent facilities include a bright, modern toilet block, and a games room/TV lounge. A 3.5-acre site with 68 touring pitches, 13 hardstandings.
Leisure: ⚓ /A **Facilities:** ⋒⊙ℚ✳⛄& ℭ🔌
Services: 🔌🔋🅰⌀🔲⊤🛀➡→∪▶🔧🔌〓📶📶🔅

▶ ▶ ▶ **66% Pennymoor Camping & Caravan Park** (SX685516)
PL21 0SB ☎ 01548 830542 & 830020
📠 01548 830542
website: www.pennymoor-camping.co.uk
Dir: Leave A38 at Wrangaton Cross. Turn left & straight over x-roads. Continue for 4m, pass petrol station & take 2nd left. Site 1.5m on right
🚐 £5.50-£10 🚐 £4.50-£9 🛆 £5.50-£10

Open 15 Mar-15 Nov (rs 15 Mar-mid May 1 toilet & shower block only open) Booking advisable Jul-Aug Last arrival 20.00hrs Last departure noon
A well-established rural park on gently sloping grass with good views over distant Dartmoor. The park is very carefully tended, and has a relaxing atmosphere. A 12.5-acre site with 154 touring pitches and 70 statics. Dishwashing facilities.
Leisure: /A **Facilities:** ⋒⊙ℚ✳&ℭ🔌🐕 **Services:**
🔌🔋🅰⌀🔲⊤→∪🔧 **Notes:** No single sex groups
See advertisement on page 115

MOLLAND   **Map 03 SS82**

▶ ▶ ▶ **63% NEW Yeo Valley Holiday Park** (SS788265)
EX36 3NW ☎ 01769 550297 📠 01769 550101
e-mail: info@yeovalleyholidays.com
website: www.yeovalleyholidays.com
Dir: off A361 onto B3227 towards Bampton. Follow brown signs for Blackcock Inn. Site is opposite
★ 🚐 £7-£10 🚐 £7-£10 🛆 £7-£10
Open all year (rs Sep-Mar swimming pool closed) Booking advisable Jul-Aug Last arrival 22.30hrs Last departure 10.00hrs
Set in a beautiful secluded valley on the edge of Exmoor National Park, this family-run park has easy access to both the moors and the North Devon

contd.

coastline. The recently-upgraded park is adjacent to the Blackcock Inn (under the same ownership), and has a very good heated indoor pool. A 7-acre site with 65 touring pitches, 5 hardstandings and 12 statics.
Fishing lake & bike hire

Leisure: 🔾 ♦ 🎢 🖵 Facilities: 🏮⊙🏴※🌣🐾🎠
Services: 🖵🖳🍴🛒🅿️∅✕→∪🧺 💳 🚾 ⦿

MORTEHOE Map 02 SS44
See also **Woolacombe**

68% Twitchen Parc
(SS465447)
EX34 7ES ☎ 01271 870343
🖨 01271 870089
e-mail: goodtimes@woolacombe.com
website: www.woolacombe.com
Dir: From Mullacott Cross rdbt take B3343 Woolacombe Rd to Turnpike Cross junct. Take the right fork & site is 1.5m on the left
★ 🚐 £11-£34 🚐 £11-£34 ⛺ £8-£22
Open Mar-Oct Booking advisable Etr/Whit & Jul-Aug Last arrival 23.30hrs Last departure 10.00hrs
A very attractive park with good leisure facilities. Visitors can use the facilities at all three of Woolacombe Bay holiday parks, and a bus service connects them all with the beach. The touring area has been redeveloped, with pitches offering either sea views or a country and woodland outlook. A 45-acre site with 220 touring pitches, 110 hardstandings and 274 statics.
Table tennis, snooker, sauna, bus to beach, kids' club

Leisure: 🔾 🥢 ♦ 🎢 🖵 Facilities: 🏮⊙🏴※🌣🐾🎠
🎬 🎠 Services: 🖵🖳🍴🛒∅🎛️🔄✕♨→∪🅿️⊙🔺⚡🎪
🍴 💳 🚾 ⦿

▶ ▶ ▶ **66% Easewell Farm Holiday Park & Golf Club (SS465455)**
EX34 7EH ☎ 01271 870225 🖨 01271 870225
Dir: From Mullacott Cross take B3343 to Mortehoe. Turn right at unclass road & site is 2m on right
🚐 🚐 ⛺

Open Etr-Sep (rs Etr no shop) Booking advisable Jul-Aug Last arrival 22.00hrs Last dep 10.00hrs
A clifftop park with full-facility pitches for caravans and motorhomes, and an undulating area of grassy pitches for tents, most with superb views. The park offers a range of activities including indoor bowling,
contd.

and a golf course. A 17-acre site with 250 touring pitches.
9-hole golf on site.

Leisure: 🔾 ♦ 🎢 Facilities: 🏮⊙🏴※🌣🐾🎠
Services: 🖵🖳🍴🛒∅🎛️🔄✕♨→∪🅿️⊙🔺⚡🎪🍴
💳 🚾 ⦿

See advertisement on page 128

▶ ▶ ▶ **69% NEW North Morte Farm Caravan & Camping Park (SS462455)**
North Morte Rd EX34 7EG ☎ 01271 870381
🖨 01271 870115
e-mail: info@northmortefarm.co.uk
website: www.northmortefarm.co.uk
Dir: Turn off B3343 into Mortehoe Village, then right at post office. Park 500yds on left
★ 🚐 £8-£13.50 🚐 £8-£12 ⛺ £8-£10
Open Etr-Sep (rs Oct Caravan owners only)
Booking advisable Last arrival 23.30hrs
Last departure 12.00hrs
Set in spectacular coastal countryside close to National Trust land and 500yds from Rockham Beach. This attractive park is very well run and maintained by friendly family owners, and the quaint village of Mortehoe with its cafes, shops and pubs is just a five minutes' walk away. A 22-acre site with 180 touring pitches, 5 hardstandings and 24 statics.

Leisure: 🎢 Facilities: 🏮⊙🏴※🌣🐾🎠
Services: 🖵🖳🍴🛒∅🎛️→∪🅿️🍴 Notes: No large groups, no single sex groups & dogs must be on lead at all times 💳 🚾 ⦿

Leisure: 🔾 Indoor swimming pool 🥢 Outdoor swimming pool 🏴 Tennis court ♦ Games room 🎢 Children's playground ∪ Stables
🅿️ 9/18 hole golf course 🔄 Boats for hire 🎬 Cinema 🍴 Fishing ⊙ Mini golf 🔺 Watersports 🖵 Separate TV room

► ► ► 63% **Warcombe Farm Camping Park**
(SS478445)
Station Rd EX34 7EJ ☎ 01271 870690 07774 428770
▤ 01271 871070
*Dir: N towards Mortehoe from Mullacot Cross rdbt at
A361 junct with B3343. Site 2m on right*
★ ⚑ £7.50-£11 ⚑ £7.50-£11 ▲ £6.50-£10
Open 15 Mar-Sep Booking advisable Jul & Aug Last
departure noon
*An open site extending to the cliffs, with views over
the Bristol Channel. The superb sandy beach at
Woolacombe with its Blue Flag award is only 1.5m
away, and there is an attractive fishing lake on site.
A 19-acre site with 100 touring pitches.*
Private fishing.

Leisure: ⚑ **Facilities:** ⚑⊙⚑✳⚑⚑⚑⚑⚑
Services: ⚑⚑⚑⚑⚑⚑→∪▶◎⚑⚑

Notes: No groups unless booked in advance

NEWTON ABBOT   **Map 03 SX87**
See also **Bickington**

PREMIER PARK

► ► ► ► ► 74% **Dornafield**
(SX838683)
Dornafield Farm, Two Mile Oak
TQ12 6DD
☎ 01803 812732 ▤ 01803 812032
e-mail: enquiries@dornafield.com
website: www.dornafield.com
*Dir: Take A381 (Newton Abbot-Totnes) for 2m.
At Two Mile Oak Inn turn right, then left at x-roads
in 0.5m to site on right*
★ ⚑ £8.50-£13 ⚑ £8.50-£13 ▲ £8.50-£13

Open Mar-Oct Booking advisable bank hols &
Jul-Aug Last arrival 22.00hrs Last dep 11.00hrs
*An excellent park in a secluded wooded valley
setting, with well laid out pitches and a peaceful
atmosphere. A lovely 15th-century farmhouse
sits at the entrance, and reception and the shop
are housed in converted barns around a
courtyard. The park is divided into three
separate areas, served by two modern, heated
toilet blocks, and the friendly family owners are
always available. A 30-acre site with 135 touring
pitches, 60 hardstandings.*
Leisure: ⚑⚑⚑⚑ **Facilities:** ⚑⊙⚑✳⚑⚑⚑⚑⚑
Services: ⚑⚑⚑⚑⚑⚑⚑→∪▶⚑⚑
Notes: Commercial vehicles by prior
arrangement only ⚑⚑⚑⚑⚑

PREMIER PARK

► ► ► ► ► 80% **Ross Park**
(SX845671)
Park Hill Farm, Ipplepen TQ12 5TT
☎ 01803 812983 ▤ 01803 812983
e-mail: enquiries@rossparkcaravan.co.uk
*Dir: Off A381, 3m from Newton Abbot towards
Totnes, signed opposite Jet garage towards
'Woodland'*
★ ⚑ £7.70-£13 ⚑ £7.70-£13 ▲ £7.70-£13

Open mid Feb-4 Jan (rs Nov-Feb & 1st 3wks of
Mar Restaurant/bar closed (ex Xmas/New Year))
Booking advisable Jul, Aug & BH's Last arrival
21.00hrs Last departure 10.00hrs
*A top-class park in every way, with large
secluded pitches, high quality toilet facilities and
lovely floral displays throughout the 26 acres.*
contd.

The beautiful tropical conservatory also offers a breathtaking show of colour. This very rural park enjoys superb views of Dartmoor, and good quality meals to suit all tastes and pockets are served in the restaurant. A 26-acre site with 110 touring pitches.
Snooker, table tennis, badminton, croquet.
Leisure: ♦ ⋀ ☐ Facilities: ⋔ ⊙ � ⚡ ⅍ & ⅃ ⊑ ⋒ ⁔
Services: ⊞ ⊚ ⅃ ⌀ ⌀ ⊞ ⏽ ✕ ⬥ ➜ ↻ ⊦ ⚎ ⅃

► ► ► 71% **Twelve Oaks Farm Caravan Park (SX852737)**
Teigngrace TQ12 6QT ☎ 01626 352769
▤ 01626 352769
website: www.twelveoaksfarm.co.uk
Dir: From Exeter on A38 turn left signed Teigngrace (only), 0.25m before Drumbridges rdbt. Continue 1.5m through village, site on left. From Plymouth pass Drumbridges rdbt , take slip road for Chudleigh Knighton. Right over bridge, rejoin A38 towards Plymouth. Left for Teigngrace (only), then as above
★ ⚘ £6.50-£10.50 ⚘ £6.50-£10.50 ⚑ £8.50-£9.50
Open all year Booking advisable Last arrival 21.00hrs Last departure 11.00hrs
An attractive small park on a working farm close to Dartmoor National Park, and bordered by the River Teign. The tidy pitches are located amongst trees and shrubs, and the modern facilities are very well maintained. Children will enjoy all the farm animals, and nearby is the Templar Way walking route. A 2-acre site with 35 touring pitches, 17 hardstandings.
Leisure: ⅃ Facilities: ⋔ ⊙ ঀ ✳ & ⅃ ⊑
Services: ⊞ ⅃ ➜ ↻ ⊦ ⚎ ⅃ ⊚

OKEHAMPTON — Map 02 SX59
See also **Whiddon Down**

► ► ► 64% **Yertiz Caravan & Camping Park (SX602954)**
Exeter Rd EX20 1QF ☎ 01837 52281
e-mail: yertiz@dial.pipex.com
website: www.dialspace.dial.pipex.com/yertiz
Dir: Leave A30 at Belstone Services onto B3260 towards Okehampton, site on left in 1m
★ ⚘ £6.50-£7.50 ⚘ £6.50-£7.50 ⚑ £5.50-£7.50
Open all year Booking advisable bank holidays & Aug Last arrival 23.59hrs
Small friendly park with lovely views of Dartmoor, and pleasant local walks. Close to the popular town of Okehampton which now boasts a train service onto Dartmoor, and the Granite Way cycle trail from Okehampton to Lydford. A 3.5-acre site with 30 touring pitches, 2 hardstandings and 5 statics.
Leisure: ⋀ Facilities: ⋔ ⊙ ঀ ✳ & ⅃ ⊑ ⊞ ⅃ ⋒
Services: ⊞ ⊚ ⅃ ⌀ ⊞ ➜ ↻ ⊦ ⚎ ⅃

For full details of the AA pennant ratings scheme see page 7

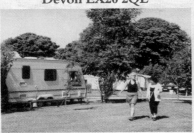

Dartmoor View Holiday Park
Whiddon Down Okehampton Devon EX20 2QL

★ Superb 5 star family run park ★ Ideally located for exploring Dartmoor and the West Country ★ Heated Pool, Bar and Childrens Park ★ Luxury Static Holiday Homes for Hire ★ Spacious Touring Caravan and Tent Pitches ★ Pets Welcome ★ Supersavers and other great offers available
For colour brochure and information
**Tel: 01647 231545   Fax: 01647 231654
E-mail: info@dartmoorview.co.uk
Website: www.dartmoorview.co.uk**

PAIGNTON — Map 03 SX86

 72% **Beverley Parks Caravan & Camping Park (SX886582)**
Goodrington Rd TQ4 7JE
☎ 01803 843887 ▤ 01803 845427
e-mail: info@beverley-holidays.co.uk
website: www.beverley-holidays.co.uk
Dir: Along A380/A3022, 2m S of Paignton turn left into Goodrington Road
★ ⚘ £9.50-£23 ⚘ £9.50-£23 ⚑ £7.50-£21

Open Feb-Nov Booking advisable Jun-Sep Last arrival 22.00hrs Last departure 10.00hrs ⌀
A high quality family-run park with extensive views of the bay, and plenty of on-site amenities. The park boasts indoor and outdoor heated swimming pools, and the toilet facilities are very modern and clean. The park complex is
contd.

Facilities: ⋔ Bath ⋔ Shower ⊙ Electric Shaver ঀ Hairdryer ✳ Ice Pack Facility & Disabled Facilities ⅃ Public Telephone
⊑ Shop on Site or within 200yds ⊞ Mobile Shop (calls at least 5 days a week) ⊞ BBQ Area ⊓ Picnic Area ⋒ Dog Exercise Area

attractively laid out. A 12-acre site with 189 touring pitches, 30 hardstandings and 195 statics.

Table tennis, pool, spa bath, crazy golf, sauna

Leisure: ⚄ ⚄ ⚄ ⚄ ⚄ **Facilities:** ⚄ ⚄ ⚄ ⚄ ⚄ ⚄ ⚄ ⚄
Services: ⚄ ⚄ ⚄ ⚄ ⚄ ⚄ ⚄ ⚄ → ∪ ⚄ ⚄ ⚄ ⚄ ⚄ ⚄
⚄ ⚄ ⚄ ⚄ ⚄

66% Hoburne Torbay
(SX888588)
Grange Rd TQ4 7JP
☎ 01803 558010 🖷 01803 696286
e-mail: enquiries@hoburne.com
website: www.hoburne.com
Dir: S on A380 past junct A385, left at traffic lights into Goodrington Road, 0.75m turn left into Grange Road, site in 500yds
★ ⚄ £10-£23 ⚄ £10-£23
Open Mar-Oct Booking advisable public hols & Jul-Aug Last arrival 22.00hrs Last departure 10.00hrs ⚄
A large grass park set amongst woodland with spectacular views across Torbay town to the sea about 0.5m away. The leisure and entertainment complex has been refurbished, and offers something for all ages. The touring pitches are divided into two areas, and three separate toilet blocks are kept in very good condition. A 65-acre site with 146 touring pitches and 492 statics.

Crazy golf, sauna, steam room, snooker, bowling

Leisure: ⚄ ⚄ ⚄ ⚄ **Facilities:** ⚄ ⚄ ⚄ ⚄ ⚄ ⚄
Services: ⚄ ⚄ ⚄ ⚄ ⚄ ⚄ ⚄ → ∪ ⚄ ⚄ ⚄ ⚄ ⚄
Notes: No commercial vehicles allowed on touring fields ⚄ ⚄ ⚄ ⚄ ⚄

▶ ▶ ▶ ▶ **68% Widend Touring Park**
(SX852619)
Berry Pomeroy Rd, Marldon TQ3 1RT
☎ 01803 550116 🖷 01803 550116
SILVER
Dir: Signed off the Torbay ring road
★ ⚄ £5.50-£11.50 ⚄ £5.50-£11.50 ▲ £5.50-£11.50
Open Apr-end Sep (rs Apr-mid May & mid Sep swimming pool & club house closed) Booking advisable Jul-Aug & Whit Last arrival 21.00hrs Last departure 10.00hrs
A terraced grass park paddocked and screened on high ground overlooking Torbay with views of Dartmoor. This attractive park is well laid out, divided up by mature trees and bushes but with plenty of open grassy areas. Facilities are of a high standard and offer a heated outdoor swimming pool with sunbathing area, a small lounge bar and a well-stocked shop. A 22-acre site with 207 touring pitches.

Leisure: ⚄ ⚄ ⚄ **Facilities:** ⚄ ⚄ ⚄ ⚄ ⚄ ⚄ ⚄
Services: ⚄ ⚄ ⚄ ⚄ ⚄ ⚄ ⚄ ⚄ → ∪ ⚄ ⚄ ⚄ ⚄ ⚄
⚄ ⚄ ⚄ ⚄ ⚄

RIVERSIDE
CARAVAN PARK
Longbridge Road, Marsh Mills, Plymouth
Telephone: Plymouth (01752) 344122

"The award-winning touring park that'll stop you touring!"

"Riverside" the conveniently situated, secluded, countryside park has all the amenities, scenery, and relaxed atmosphere that will make you want to stay for the rest of your holiday. Surrounded by woodlands, and bordered by the River Plym, this pleasant site has the luxury of permanent facilities without losing the country charm.

Within a short distance you can also reach the freedom of Dartmoor, the shops and history of Plymouth, and the fun of many beaches and coves. The numerous sports, activities and attractions of the whole area mean "Riverside" can be the centre of a complete holiday experience. Ring or write for details.

★ Bar, Restaurant and Takeaway ★ Heated swimming pool ★ Games room ★ TV room and play areas ★ Shop and Telephone ★ Coffee bar ★ Off licence ★ Level pitches ★ Electricity ★ Tarmac roads ★ Street lights ★ Toilet and shower blocks ★ Laundry and dishwashing facilities ★ Special over 50's rates.

▶ ▶ ▶ **70% Byslades International Touring & Camping Park (SX853603)**
Totnes Rd TQ4 7PY ☎ 01803 555072
🖷 01803 555072
e-mail: byslasesitp@lineone.net
website: www.byslaadestouringpark.co.uk
Dir: 2m W on A385. Signposted at entry to town
⚄ ⚄ ▲
Open Jun-mid Sep (rs Mar-May & Oct bar & swimming pool closed) Booking advisable Jul-Aug Last arrival 22.00hrs Last departure 10.00hrs
A well-kept terraced park in beautiful countryside, only 2m from Paignton. It offers a good mix of amenities, and a licensed club with high season entertainment, plus a children's playground, and large heated outdoor swimming pool with special area for toddlers. A 23-acre site with 170 touring pitches.

Crazy golf.

Leisure: ⚄ ⚄ ⚄ ⚄ **Facilities:** ⚄ ⚄ ⚄ ⚄ ⚄ ⚄ ⚄ ⚄
Services: ⚄ ⚄ ⚄ ⚄ ⚄ ⚄ ⚄ ⚄ → ∪ ⚄ ⚄ ⚄ ⚄
Notes: No single sex groups, no commercial vehicles ⚄ ⚄ ⚄ ⚄ ⚄

Not all campsites accept pets.
Check when booking

► ► ► **67% Marine Park Holiday Centre**
(SX886587)
Grange Rd TQ4 7JR ☎ 01803 843887
🖹 01803 845427
e-mail: info@beverley-holidays.co.uk
website: www.beverley-holidays.co.uk
*Dir: S on A380/A3022 past junct with A385, turn left at
traffic lights into Goodrington Rd, in 0.75m turn left into
Grange Rd, follow brown signs left at public house*
🚐 £9.50-£19 🚐 £9.50-£19
Open Etr-Oct Booking advisable Jul-Aug Last arrival
22.00hrs Last departure 10.00hrs ⚘
*A mainly static site catering for those who prefer
peace and quiet. Next door to sister site Beverley
Park whose amenities are available. A 2-acre site
with 23 touring pitches and 61 statics.*
Leisure: ⚠ Facilities: ➟ 🏠 ⊙ ⚋ 🌡 ᕴ Services: 🗩 🖬 ▮
🗑 🖵 → ∪ �┠ ◎ ⚠ ⚒ 🎒 ᴊ ⚋ 🗨 🔜 🔲 🔳 🔜 🗐

PLYMOUTH   **Map 02 SX45**

► ► ► ► **72% *Riverside Caravan Park* (SX515575)**
Longbridge Rd, Marsh Mills, Plympton PL6 8LD
☎ 01752 344122 🖹 01752 344122
e-mail: info@riversidecaravanpark.com
website: www.riversidecaravanpark.com
Dir: Access via Longbridge Road, E of Marsh Mills rdbt
🚐 🚐 ▲

Open all year (rs Oct-Etr Bar, Restaurant & Take-
away closed) Booking advisable Jun-Aug Last
arrival 22.00hrs Last departure 10.00hrs
*A well-groomed site on the outskirts of Plymouth
on the banks of the River Plym, in a quiet location
surrounded by woodland. The upgraded facilities
are of a very good standard and include private
cubicles. An 11-acre site with 293 touring pitches.*
Leisure: ⚞ ⚓ ⚠ 🖵 Facilities: 🏠 ⊙ ⚋ 🌡 ⚊ ᕴ
Services: 🗩 🖬 🍽 ▮ 🗑 🖵 🗑 ✕ ⬛ → ∪ ⎾ ◎ ⚠ ⚒ ⚋ ᴊ
🗨 🔜 🗐

See advertisement on page 119

SALCOMBE   **Map 03 SX73**

► ► ► **63% Bolberry House Farm Caravan &
Camping Park (SX687395)**
Bolberry TQ7 3DY ☎ 01548 561251
e-mail: bolberry.house@virgin.net
website: www.bolberryparks.co.uk
*Dir: At Malborough on A381 turn right signed Hope
Cove & Bolberry. Take left fork after village signed Soar
& Bolberry. Site signed in 0.5m*

contd.

★ 🚐 £7.50-£10.50 🚐 £7.50-£10.50 ▲ £7-£10
Open Etr-Oct Booking advisable Jul & Aug Last
arrival 20.00hrs Last departure 11.00hrs

Bolberry House Farm Camping & Caravan Park
*A level, well maintained, family run park in peaceful
setting on coastal farm with sea views, fine cliff
walks and nearby beaches. Discount in low season
for senior citizens. A 6-acre site with 70 touring
pitches and 10 statics.*
Children's play area & play barn.
Leisure: ⚠ Facilities: 🏠 ⊙ ⚋ 🌡 ⚊ ⚒ ᕴ
Services: 🗩 🖬 ▮ 🗑 🖵 → ∪ ⎾ ◎ ⚠ ⚒ ⚋ ᴊ

► ► ► **64% Higher Rew Caravan &
Camping Park (SX714383)**
Higher Rew, Malborough TQ7 3DW
☎ 01548 842681 & 843681 🖹 01548 843681
e-mail: enquiries@higherrew.co.uk
website: www.higherrew.co.uk
*Dir: Follow A381 to Salcombe. Turn right at Townsend
Cross & follow signs to Soar for 1m. Left at Rew Cross*
★ 🚐 £7-£9 🚐 £7-£9 ▲ £7-£9
Open Etr-Oct Booking advisable Spring bank hol &
mid Jul-Aug Last arrival 22.00hrs Last dep noon
*A long-established park in a remote location in sight
of the sea. The spacious, open touring field has
some tiered pitches in the sloping grass, and there
are lovely countryside or sea views from every pitch.
Friendly family owners are continually improving
the facilities. A 5-acre site with 85 touring pitches.*
Play Barn
Leisure: ⚓ Facilities: 🏠 ⊙ ⚋ 🌡 ⚊ ⚒ ᕴ
Services: 🗩 🖬 ▮ 🗑 🖵 → ⚠ ⚒ ᴊ Notes: No groups
of young people in peak season.

► ► ► **68% Karrageen Caravan & Camping Park
(SX686395)**
Malborough TQ7 3EN ☎ 01548 561230
🖹 01548 560192 e-mail: phil@karrageen.co.uk
website: www.karrageen.co.uk
*Dir: At Malborough on A381, turn sharp right through
village, after 0.6m right again, after 0.9m site on right.*
★ 🚐 £7.50-£12 🚐 £7.50-£12 ▲ £7.50-£12
Open 15 Mar-15 Nov Booking advisable bank &
school hols Last arrival 21.00hrs Last dep 11.30hrs
*A small friendly, family-run park with terraced grass
pitches giving extensive sea and country views.
There is a varied takeaway menu available every
evening, and a well-stocked shop. Friendly owners
keep all facilities spotless. A 7.5-acre site with 75
touring pitches and 20 statics.*

contd.

Karrageen Caravan & Camping Park
Baby room, licensed shop, 2 play areas, family shower
Facilities: ♠☉❄✻♿☎⚑⌖
Services: ☎◻🛈🗑🗑🚻→∪◬✕⚙

▶ ▶ ▶ **64% Sun Park Caravan & Camping Site (SX707379)**
Soar Mill Cove TQ7 3DS ☎ 01548 561378
🗎 01548 561378
website: www.sun-park.co.uk
Dir: On entering village of Malborough on A381, turn sharp right signed Soar. Follow signs on this road to Soar Mill Cove. Site situated 1.5m on right
★ ♥ £6.50-£10 ▲ £6.50-£10

Open Etr-Oct Booking advisable Jul-Aug Last arrival 20.00hrs Last departure 11.00hrs
An open park in a peaceful rural location, with extensive country views and glimpses of the sea. The safe sandy beach at Soar Cove is approx 0.75m from this well-managed park run by keen and friendly owners. A 4.5-acre site with 65 touring pitches and 34 statics.
Leisure: ♠ ⋔ ▢ **Facilities:** ♠☉❄✻ **Services:** ☎
🛈✎🗑→◬✕⚙⚑ **Notes:** No single sex groups

SAMPFORD PEVERELL   **Map 03 ST01**

▶ ▶ ▶ ▶ **73% Minnows Caravan Park (SS042148)**
Holbrook Ln EX16 7EN ☎ 01884 821770
🗎 01884 829199
website: www.ukparks.co.uk/minnows
Dir: From M5 junct 27 take A361 signed Tiverton and Barnstaple, after 600yds take 1st slip rd, then turn right over bridge, site ahead
★ ♥ £6.50-£12.50 ♥ £6.50-£12.50 ▲ £6.50-£9.50
Open 8 Mar-11 Nov Booking advisable bank hols & Jun-Sep Last arrival 20.00hrs Last departure 11.30hrs

contd.

Attractive park bounded by the Grand Western Canal, with plenty of screening from mature hedges and a newly-created woodland. The neatly set out pitches are mostly hardstandings amongst grassy areas, all immaculately maintained. Good toilet facilities are kept sparklingly clean, and both owner and wardens are friendly and helpful. A 5.5-acre site with 45 touring pitches, 36 hardstandings.
Tourist information centre, full service pitches
Leisure: ⋔ **Facilities:** ♠☉❄✻♿☎⌖🛏
Services: ☎🛈✎🗑🚻→▶✕⚙◻⚑
Notes: No cycling 💳 ▨▨ ▨▨ ▨▨ 🖉

SEATON   See **Colyton**

SIDMOUTH   **Map 03 SY18**

▶ ▶ ▶ ▶ **75% Oakdown Touring & Holiday Home Park (SY167902)**
Weston EX10 0PH ☎ 01297 680387
🗎 01297 680541
e-mail: oakdown@btinternet.com
website: www.bestcaravanpark.co.uk
Dir: Off A3052, 2.5m E of junct with A375
★ ♥ £8.10-£12.15 ♥ £8.10-£12.15 ▲ £8.10-£12.15
Open Apr-Oct Booking advisable Spring bank hol & Jul-Aug Last arrival 22.00hrs Last departure 10.30hrs
Friendly, well-maintained park with good landscaping and plenty of maturing trees. Pitches are grouped in paddocks surrounded by shrubs, and the park is well screened from the A3502.

contd.

Welcome to Oakdown. Regency Sidmouth's first 5 star, multi award winning Park. Set within the beautiful East Devon Heritage Coast, Oakdown is level, sheltered and landscaped into groves to give privacy, with floral displays to delight you. Our award winning heated amenities include aids for the disabled. Enjoy our Field Trial to the world famous Donkey Sanctuary. Free colour brochure with pleasure.

**Oakdown Touring & Holiday Home Park,
Weston, Sidmouth, Devon EX10 0PH
Tel: 01297 680387 Fax: 01297 680541
E-mail: oakdown@btinternet.com
Web: www.bestcaravanpark.co.uk**

Oakdown Touring & Holiday Home Park
*The park's conservation areas with their natural flora and fauna offer attractive walks, and there is a hide by the lagoon for both casual and dedicated bird watchers. A 13-acre site with 120 touring pitches, 90 hardstandings and 63 statics.
6 dishwashing sinks, free use of microwave.*

Leisure: ⚏ ▭ Facilities: ➡ ♠ ⊙ ℛ ✕ ♿ ⚰ ⚓ ⊺
Services: ▣ ▤ ♦ ⊿ ⊞ ⊤ ➡ → ∪ ▶ ⊙ △ ✕ ⚒ ✦ ⚲ ⚍

Notes: Dogs must be kept on leads & exercised off park, no bikes, no skateboards ● ▩ ▩ ▩ ⊙

▶ ▶ ▶ **62% Kings Down Tail Caravan & Camping Park (SY173907)**
Salcombe Regis EX10 0PD ☎ 01297 680313
🖹 01297 680313
e-mail: info@kingsdowntail.co.uk
website: www.kingsdowntail.co.uk
Dir: Off A3052 3m E of junct with A375
⊞ ⊞ ▲

contd.

Kings Down Tail Caravan & Camping Park
Open 15 Mar-15 Nov Booking advisable Whit, bank hols & mid Jul-Sep Last arrival 22.00hrs Last departure noon
*A well-kept site on level ground in a tree-sheltered spot on the side of the Sid Valley. This neat family-run park makes a good base for exploring the east Devon coast. A 5-acre site with 100 touring pitches, 31 hardstandings and 2 statics.
Off licence.*
Leisure: ⚏ ⚏ Facilities: ♠ ⊙ ℛ ✕ ♿ ⚰ ⚓ ⊺
Services: ▣ ♦ ⊿ ⊞ ⊤ → ∪ ▶ ✕ ⚒ ⚲ ⊙ ● ▩ ▩ ▩ ⊙

See advertisement on page 121

▶ ▶ ▶ **70% Salcombe Regis Caravan & Camping Park (SY153892)**
Salcombe Regis EX10 0JH ☎ 01395 514303
🖹 01395 514303
e-mail: info@salcombe-regis.co.uk
website: www.salcombe-regis.co.uk
Dir: Off A3052 1m E of junct with A375. From other direction take left past Donkey Sanctuary
★ ⊞ £7.25-£11.75 ⊞ £7.25-£11.75 ▲ £7.25-£11.75
Open Etr-Oct Booking advisable bank hols & Jul-Aug Last arrival 20.00hrs Last departure 10.00hrs
*Set on the coastal path with glorious views, this spacious park has well-maintained facilities, and a good mix of grass and hardstanding pitches. A footpath runs from the park to the coastal path and the beach. A 16-acre site with 100 touring pitches, 40 hardstandings and 10 statics.
Off licence, bike hire, putting & barbecue hire.*
Leisure: ⚏ Facilities: ➡ ♠ ⊙ ✕ ♿ ⚰ ⚓ ⊺ Services: ▣ ▤ ♦ ⊿ ⊞ ⊤ → ∪ ▶ ⊙ △ ✕ ⚒ ⚲ ● ▩ ▩ ▩ ⊙

SLAPTON   **Map 03 SX84**

▶ ▶ ▶ **69% Camping & Caravanning Club Site (SX825450)**
Middle Grounds TQ7 2QW ☎ 01548 580538
website: www.campingandcaravanningclub.co.uk
Dir: On A379 from Kingsbridge, site entrance is 0.25m from A379, beyond brow of hill approaching Slapton
★ ⊞ £12.30-£17.50 ▲ £12.30-£17.50
Open Mar-Oct Booking advisable bank hols & Jul-Aug Last arrival 21.00hrs Last departure noon
A very attractive location and well-run site open to non-members. The site overlooks Start Bay within a few minutes' walk of the beach. Please see the advertisement on page 10 for details of Club Members' benefits. A 5.5-acre site with 125 touring pitches, 10 hardstandings.
Leisure: ⚏ Facilities: ♠ ⊙ ℛ ✕ ♿ ⚓ ⊺
Services: ▣ ♦ ⊿ ⊞ → ∪ ▶ △ ⚲ ⚲
Notes: Members touring caravans only ● ▩

England

SOURTON CROSS — Map 02 SX59

▶ ▶ ▶ **62% Bundu Camping & Caravan Park (SX546916)**
EX20 4HT ☎ 01837 861611
e-mail: bundusargent@aol.com
website: www.bundu.co.uk
Dir: W on A30, past Okehampton. Take A386 to
Tavistock. Take 1st left & left again
★ ⊞ £7-£10 ⊞ £7-£10 ▲ £5-£7
Open 15 Mar-15 Nov Booking advisable Jul & Aug
Last arrival 23.30hrs Last departure 14.00hrs
*A level grassy site in an ideal location, on the
border of the Dartmoor National Park and offering
fine views. A 4.5-acre site with 38 touring pitches,
8 hardstandings.*
Leisure: /Λ Facilities: ℕ⊙℞✻▨➔♒
Services: ☷◉🔥⌀🖫➔∪▶☺

SOUTH BRENT — Map 03 SX66

▶ ▶ **59% Webland Farm Holiday Park (SX715594)**
Avonwick TQ10 9EX ☎ 01364 73273
Dir: Leave A38 at junct with A385 signed Marley Head.
Site in 1m on unclass single track road
⊞ ⊞ ▲
Open Etr-15 Nov Booking advisable school hols Last
arrival 22.00hrs Last departure noon
*A very rural park with extensive views, surrounded
by farmland, with sloping pitches mainly for tents.
For towed caravans, access can be awkward. A 5-
acre site with 35 touring pitches and 50 statics.*
Leisure: /Λ Facilities: ℕ⊙✻⌜♒
Services: ☷◉🖫➔∪▶⌁▨

STARCROSS — See Dawlish

STICKLEPATH — Map 03 SX69

▶ ▶ ▶ **58% Olditch Holiday Park (SX645935)**
EX20 2NT ☎ 01837 840734 ▤ 01837 840877
e-mail: stay@olditch.co.uk
website: www.olditch.co.uk
Dir: Leave A30 at Merrymeet rdbt onto unclass road
signed Sticklepath. Park on left at entry to village
★ ⊞ £8-£10 ⊞ £8-£10 ▲ £8-£10

Open 14 Mar-14 Nov Booking advisable bank hols &
Jul-Aug Last arrival 22.00hrs Last departure
16.00hrs
*A mainly sloping grassy park with some tiered level
pitches, on the outskirts of this now by-passed
village. A 3-acre site with 32 touring pitches, 12
hardstandings and 20 statics.* *contd.*

Small tourist information area
Leisure: ◈ /Λ ⊡ Facilities: ℕ⊙℞✻⌂♒⛭
Services: ☷◉🔥⌀🖫➔∪▶☺⌁▨🖫⊟● ▦ ▨

STOKENHAM — Map 03 SX84

▶ ▶ ▶ **66% Old Cotmore Farm (SX804417)**
TQ7 2LR ☎ 01548 580240 581252 ▤ 01548 580875
e-mail: graham.bowsher@btinternet.com
Dir: Leave Kingsbridge on A379 Dartmouth rd, passing
through Frogmore & Chillington to mini rdbt at
Stokenham. Right towards Beesands, site 1m on right
★ ⊞ £8-£11.50 ⊞ £8-£11.50 ▲ £8-£11.50

Open 15 Mar-Oct Booking advisable Jul & Aug Last
arrival 20.00hrs Last departure 11.00hrs
*A quiet park with some gentle slopes and mainly
flat pitches set in an Area of Outstanding Natural
Beauty. The family-run park enjoys fine views of the
picturesque countryside of the South Hams.
Facilities are modern and well maintained, and
pebble and sandy beaches with cliff walks through
woods and fields are within walking distance. A 3-
acre site with 30 touring pitches, 3 hardstandings.*
Leisure: ◈ /Λ Facilities: ℕ⊙℞✻⌂♒⛭▨➔♒
Services: ☷◉🔥⌀🖫➔∪⌁⌁ Notes: Dogs must
be kept on leads ●▦▨▨ ▨

TAVISTOCK — Map 02 SX47

▶ ▶ ▶ ▶ **70% Higher Longford Caravan &
Camping Park (SX520747)**
Moorshop PL19 9LQ ☎ 01822 613360
▤ 01822 618722
e-mail: stay@higherlongford.co.uk
website: www.higherlongford.co.uk
Dir: From A30 to Tavistock take B3357 towards
Princetown. 2.5m on right before hill onto moors
★ ⊞ £8-£10 ⊞ £8-£10 ▲ £8-£10

Open all year Bar & restaurant only open Apr-Oct
Booking advisable Jun-Aug Last arrival 22.30hrs
Last departure noon *contd.*

Leisure: 🏊 Indoor swimming pool 🏊 Outdoor swimming pool ℴ⃝ Tennis court ◈ Games room /Λ Children's playground ∪ Stables
▶ 9/18 hole golf course ⌁ Boats for hire ☺ Cinema ⌁ Fishing ◎ Mini golf ⊿ Watersports ⊡ Separate TV room

A very pleasant small park in Dartmoor National Park, with panoramic views of the moors. The mainly grassy pitches are sheltered, and some are secluded for extra peace and quiet. Higher Longford is surrounded by moorland parks, lanes and pretty rivers, yet Tavistock is only 2.5m away. The park is open all year round, and is well served with a bar, restaurant and shop. A 7-acre site with 82 touring pitches, 10 hardstandings and 24 statics.
Pool table

Leisure: ⚙ Facilities: 📶⊙🏪✳⚓🛒🏪🎄🏕
Services: 🔌🚐🗲🖦⊟🖫✕🖳→∪🏴🍴🚌🎿 Notes: Dogs must be kept on leads 💳 📇 ▣ 📇 📇

► ► ► ► 68% **Woodovis Park** (SX432744)
Gulworthy PL19 8NY ☎ 01822 832968
🖨 01822 832948
e-mail: info@woodovis.com
website: www.woodovis.com
Dir: From Tavistock take A390 signposted to Liskeard. At top of hill turn right at x-roads signed Lamerton & Chipshop. Park 1m on left.
★ 🚐 £12-£14 🚎 £12-£14 ▲ £12-£14
Open Apr-Oct Booking advisable Jun-Aug Last arrival 22.00hrs Last departure noon
A well-kept park in a remote woodland setting on the edge of the Tamar Valley. This peacefully-located park is set at the end of a half-mile private tree-lined road, and has lots of on-site facilities. The toilets are excellent, and there is a new indoor swimming pool, all in a friendly, purposeful atmosphere. A 14.5-acre site with 50 touring pitches, 2 hardstandings and 34 statics.
Mini-golf, sauna, jacuzzi.

Leisure: ❅ ⚓⚙ Facilities: ➡📶⊙🏪✳⚓🛒🏪🎄🏕
Services: 🔌🚐🗲🖦⊟🖫→∪🏴🍴🎿
Notes: Dogs must be kept on leads 💳 📇 ▣ 📇 📇

► ► ► 65% **Harford Bridge Holiday Park** (SX504767)
Peter Tavy PL19 9LS ☎ 01822 810349
🖨 01822 810028
e-mail: enquiry@harfordbridge.co.uk
website: www.harfordbridge.co.uk
Dir: 2m N of Tavistock, off A386 Okehampton Rd, take Peter Tavy turn, entrance 200yds on right.
★ 🚐 £6.50-£11 🚎 £6.50-£11 ▲ £6.50-£11

Open end Mar-mid Nov contact for other times of year Booking advisable Aug Last arrival 21.00hrs Last departure noon   *contd.*

This beautiful spacious park is set beside the River Tavy in the Dartmoor National Park. Pitches are located beside the river and around the copses, and the park is very well equipped for the holidaymaker. An adventure playground and games room entertain children, and there is fly-fishing and a free tennis court. A 16-acre site with 120 touring pitches, 3 hardstandings and 80 statics.
Fly fishing.

Leisure: ❅⚓⚙🏓 Facilities: 📶⊙🏪✳⚓🛒🏪🎄🏕
Services: 🔌🖦🗲🖫⊟→∪🏴🍴⊙⚓🚌🎿🛒🖳 💳 🖦 📇 📇

► ► ► 68% **Langstone Manor Camping & Caravan Park** (SX524738)
Moortown PL19 9JZ ☎ 01822 613371
🖨 01822 613371
e-mail: jane@langstone-manor.co.uk
website: www.langstone-manor.co.uk
Dir: Take B3357 from Tavistock to Princetown, after approx 3m turn right at x-rds, follow signs
★ 🚐 £7-£9 🚎 £7-£9 ▲ £7-£9

Open 15 Mar-15 Nov Booking advisable bank hols & Jul-Aug Last arrival 23.00hrs Last departure 11.00hrs
A secluded site set in the well-maintained grounds of a manor house in Dartmoor National Park. Many attractive mature trees provide a screen within the park, and there are plenty of activities and places of interest within the surrounding moorland. A 5.5-acre site with 40 touring pitches, 5 hardstandings and 25 statics.

Leisure: ⚓⚙ Facilities: 📶⊙🏪✳⚓🛒🏪🎄🏕
Services: 🔌🚐🗲🖦⊟🖫✕→∪🏴⊙⚓🎿

TEDBURN ST MARY   **Map 03 SX89**

► ► ► 64% **Springfield Holiday Park** (SX788935)
Tedburn Rd EX6 6EW ☎ 01647 24242
🖨 01647 24131
e-mail: springhol@aol.com
website: www.springfieldholidaypark.co.uk
Dir: From M5 junct 31 onto A30. 3rd exit signed Woodleigh, up slip road to rdbt. Right and follow signs
★ 🚐 £8-£10 🚎 £8-£10 ▲ £7.50-£9
Open 15 Mar-15 Nov Booking advisable Jul-Aug Last arrival 22.00hrs Last departure 14.00hrs
A terraced park with a tranquil atmosphere and panoramic views of the surrounding countryside. The park is particularly well equipped, with a heated outdoor swimming pool, good shop, licensed family bar and restaurant, and a games room with skittle alley. A 9-acre site with 76 touring pitches and 20 statics.

                                                    contd.

Leisure: ⚲ ◀ ⋀ **Facilities:** ➡ ↰ ⊙ ⚲ ✳ ♿ ⛽ ⏢ 🏕 ⋔
Services: ⊟ ⊞ ⊞ ⚲ ⊘ ⊟ ⊡ ✕ 🖪 → ∪ ▸ ✈ ⊛ ⬛ ⬛ 🐾 ⬛

TIVERTON See **East Worlington**

TORQUAY Map 03 SX96
See also **Newton Abbot**

▶ ▶ ▶ ▶ 70% **Widdicombe Farm Tourist Park**
(SX880650)
Marldon TQ3 1ST ☎ 01803 558325 🖷 01803 559526
e-mail: chrisglynn@farmersweekly.net
website: www.torquaytouring.co.uk
Dir: On A380 dual carriageway.
★ ⊞ £6-£11.50 ⊞ £6-£11.50 ⋀ £6-£11.50
Open mid Mar-mid Nov Booking advisable Whit &
Jul-Aug Last arrival 21.30hrs Last dep 11.00hrs
*A friendly family-owned and run park on a working
farm, with good quality facilities and extensive
views. The level pitches are terraced to take
advantage of the views towards the coast and
Dartmoor. A happy but quiet atmosphere pervades
this park, encouraged by a large children's play area.
Other amenities include a well-stocked shop,
a restaurant, and a lounge bar. An 8-acre site with
200 touring pitches, 140 hardstandings and 3 statics.*
Baby and family bathrooms, BBQ patio
Leisure: ◀ ⋀ **Facilities:** ➡ ↰ ⊙ ⚲ ✳ ♿ ⛽ ⏢ 🏕 ⋔
Services: ⊟ ⊞ ⊞ ⚲ ⊘ ⊟ ⊡ ✕ 🖪 → ∪ ▸ ⊙ ⬛ ⇗
Notes: Families & couples only. ⊛ ⬛ ⬛ 🐾 ⬛

▶ ▶ 60% **Manor Farm Campsite** (SX903678)
Daccombe TQ12 4ST ☎ 01803 328294
🖷 01803 328294
*Dir: From A380 Newton Abbot to Torquay road, up hill
to Kingskerswell Rd, follow camp site signs*
★ ⊞ ⋀ fr £10
Open Etr-1 Oct Booking advisable peak times
*A spacious grassy campsite enjoying unbelievable
panoramic views of Devon's countryside and
Dartmoor. This peaceful park is on a working farm,
with flat pitches in a lovely sloping field. Facilities
are simple but adequate and clean. A 3-acre site
with 75 touring pitches.*
Facilities: ↰ ⊙ ✳ 🖪 ⋔ **Services:** 🖪 ⊘ → ▸ ⊙ ⚲ ✚ ⬛ ⇗ ⊟
Notes: Families and couples only

TOTNES Map 03 SX86

▶ ▶ ▶ 64% **Edeswell Farm** (SX731606)
Edeswell Farm TQ10 9LN ☎ 01364 72177
🖷 01364 72619
e-mail: welcome@edeswellfarm.co.uk
website: www.edeswellfarm.co.uk
*Dir: Leave A38 at Marley Head onto A385 to Paignton.
Park 0.5m on right*
★ ⊞ £7-£14 ⊞ £7-£14 ⋀ £7-£14
Open all year (rs Nov-Mar Static hire only) Booking
advisable school & bank hols Last arrival 21.00hrs
Last departure 11.00hrs
*A terraced site in rolling countryside, with the
individual pitches making the most of the superb
scenery. Natural woodland and the attractive
River Harbourne are delightful features of the park,*
contd.

Yeatheridge Farm
Caravan & Camping Park
E. WORLINGTON, CREDITON, DEVON EX17 4TN
Telephone Tiverton (01884) 860 330
www.yeatheridge.co.uk
OFF THE A377 AND B3137 ON THE B3042

WHY ARE WE DIFFERENT? We are a small Central Park with panoramic
views on a genuine working farm with plenty of animals to see! We also offer
peace and space with freedom to roam the farm with its 2½ miles of woodland
and river bank walks, coarse fishing lakes, 2 indoor heated swimming pools with
200 ft water flume, TV lounge, children's play area, hot and cold showers, wash
cubicles – ALL FREE. Other amenities include horse riding from the park,
electric hook-up points, campers' dish washing, laundry room, shop with frozen
foods, fresh dairy products, ice pack service, a welcome for dogs ★ Summer
parking in our storage area to save towing ★ Ideally situated for touring coast,
Exmoor and Dartmoor. Golf and Tennis locally.
ALSO 4 CARAVANS TO LET –
PROPRIETORS/OWNERS – GEOFFREY & ELIZABETH HOSEGOOD
WRITE OR PHONE FOR FREE COLOUR BROCHURE

*and there is an animal and wildlife discovery centre,
where visitors can take part in environmental
projects. A 22-acre site with 46 touring pitches and
22 statics.*

Edeswell Farm

Table tennis, adventure playground, animal centre.
Leisure: ⚲ ◀ ⋀ **Facilities:** ↰ ⊙ ⚲ ✳ ♿ ⛽ ⏢ 🏕 ⋔
Services: 🖪 ⊞ ⊞ ⚲ ⊘ ⊟ ⊡ ✕ 🖪 ➡ → ∪ ▸ ⇗
⊛ ⬛ ⬛ 🐾 ⬛

UMBERLEIGH Map 02 SS62

▶ ▶ ▶ 62% **Camping & Caravanning Club Site**
(SS606242)
Over Weir EX37 9DU ☎ 01769 560009
website: www.campingandcaravanningclub.co.uk
*Dir: On A377 from Barnstaple turn right into B3227 at
Umberleigh sign, site on right in 0.25m*
★ ⊞ £11.10-£14.50 ⊞ £11.10-£14.50 ⋀ £11.10-£14.50
contd.

Open Mar-Oct Booking advisable bank hols & Jul-Aug Last arrival 21.00hrs Last departure noon
There are fine country views from this compact site set on high ground. The site has the advantage of a games room with table tennis and skittle alley, an adjacent wooded area for walks, and a nearby fishing pond. Please see advertisement on page 10 for details of Club Members' benefits. A 3-acre site with 60 touring pitches, 8 hardstandings.
Fishing, pool table, table tennis & skittles
Leisure: ⚲ ⚓ ⚑ ▭ **Facilities:** 🅁 ⊙ ⚑ ✳ ⚲ 🜚 ★
Services: 🕮 🅔 🛈 🖉 🕮 → ▶ ⚠ 🔧 🥄 🔋 ⚙ 🚐 🔤 🐾 🛢

WEST DOWN — Map 02 SS54

▶ ▶ ▶ ▶ **73% Hidden Valley Park**
(SS499408)
EX34 8NU ☎ 01271 813837 🗎 01271 814041
e-mail: relax@hiddenvalleypark.com
website: www.hiddenvalleypark.com
Dir: Direct access off A361, 8m from Barnstaple & 2m from Mullacott Cross
★ 🚐 £4.50-£14 🚐 £4.50-£14 ▲ £4.50-£14

Open all year (rs 15 Nov-15 Mar All weather pitches only) Booking advisable high season Last arrival 21.30hrs Last departure 11.00hrs
A delightful, well-appointed family site set in a wooded valley, with superb facilities and a restaurant. The park is set in a very rural, natural position not far from the beautiful coastline around Ilfracombe. A 25-acre site with 135 touring pitches, 74 hardstandings.
Gardens, woodland walks & lake
Leisure: ⚓ ⚑ **Facilities:** 🅁 ⊙ ⚑ ✳ ⚲ 🜚 🐾 🛢 🔤 ★
Services: 🕮 🅔 🛈 🖉 🕮 🅣 ✕ ⚒ → ∪ ▶ ↯ 🐾 🥄
🔋 🚐 🔤 🄳 🔤 🛢

See advertisement on page 111

WHIDDON DOWN — Map 03 SX69

▶ ▶ ▶ ▶ **70% Dartmoor View Holiday Park**
(SX685928)
EX20 2QL ☎ 01647 231545 🗎 01647 231654
e-mail: jo@dartmoorview.co.uk
website: www.dartmoorview.co.uk
Dir: From M5 junct 31, take A30 towards Okehampton. Turn left at 1st rdbt towards Whiddon. Site is 1m on right
★ 🚐 £7.50-£10.50 🚐 £7.50-£10.50 ▲ £6.50-£10.50
Open Mar-Oct Booking advisable Etr, Whitsun & Jul-Aug Last arrival 22.30hrs Last dep 12.00hrs
Located on high ground on the northern edge of Dartmoor National Park, this family-run park is well presented throughout. A pleasant, informal site
contd.

Dartmoor View Holiday Park
with all facilities maintained to a high standard.
A 5-acre site with 52 touring pitches and 34 statics.
Off licence, cycle/hire service, games room, putting.
Leisure: ⚲ ⚓ ⚑ ▭ **Facilities:** 🅁 ⊙ ⚑ ✳ ⚲ 🐾 ★
Services: 🕮 🅔 🛈 🖉 🕮 🅣 → ∪ 🥄 ⚙ 🚐 🔤 🐾 🛢

See advertisement on page 117

WOODBURY SALTERTON — Map 03 SY08

▶ ▶ ▶ **69% Browns Farm Caravan Park (SY016885)**
Browns Farm EX5 1PS ☎ 01395 232895
Dir: From M5 junct 30 take A3052 for 3.7m. Right at White Horse Inn follow sign to Woodbury, at village road junct turn right, site on left
★ 🚐 £4-£7 🚐 £4-£7 ▲ £4-£7
Open all year Booking advisable All times
A small farm park adjoining a 14th-century thatched farmhouse, and located in a quiet village. Pitches back onto hedgerows, and there are plenty of attractive trees. Friendly owners keep the facilities spotlessly clean. A 2.5-acre site with 20 touring pitches, 12 hardstandings.
Hard standings for winter period, caravan storage
Leisure: ⚓ **Facilities:** 🅁 ⊙ ⚑ ✳ 🜚 ⚲
Services: 🕮 🅔 → ∪ ▶ 🥄 🐾
Notes: No ground sheets in awnings, no music

WOOLACOMBE — Map 02 SS44
See also **Mortehoe**

68% Golden Coast Holiday Village (SS482436)
Station Rd EX34 7HW
☎ 01271 870343 🗎 01271 870089
e-mail: goodtimes@woolacombe.com
website: www.woolacombe.com
Dir: Follow road to Woolacombe Bay from Mullacott & site is 1.5m on left
★ 🚐 £11-£34 🚐 £11-£34 ▲ £8-£22
Open Feb-Dec Booking advisable Bank Holidays & mid Jul-end Aug Last arrival 23.30hrs Last departure 10.00hrs ⚠
A holiday village with a small touring park, offering excellent leisure facilities as well as the amenities of the other Woolacombe Bay holiday parks. It is maintained to a high standard, and staff are endlessly cheerful and friendly. A 10-acre site with 70 touring pitches and 80 statics.
Sauna, solarium, jacuzzi, tennis, entertainment
Leisure: ⚡ ⚲ ⚓ ⚑ ▭ **Facilities:** 🅁 ⊙ ⚑ ✳ ⚲ 🐾 🛢
🔤 **Services:** 🕮 🅔 🅈 🛈 🖉 🕮 🅣 ✕ ⚒ → ∪ ▶ ◎ ⚠ 🐾 🥄
🥄 ⚙ 🚐 🔤 🔤 🐾 🛢

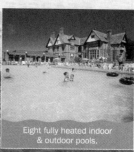

Leisure: 🐟 Indoor swimming pool 🐟 Outdoor swimming pool 🎾 Tennis court 🎱 Games room ⛰ Children's playground U Stables
▶ 9/18 hole golf course ⛵ Boats for hire 🎬 Cinema 🎣 Fishing ◎ Mini golf ⚠ Watersports ⬜ Separate TV room

England

70% **Woolacombe Bay Holiday Village** (SS465442)
Sandy Ln EX34 7AH
☎ 01271 870343 ▯ 01271 870089
e-mail: goodtimes@woolacombe.com
website: www.woolacombe.com
Dir: From Mullacott Cross rdbt take B3343 Woolacombe rd to Turnpike Cross junct. Turn right to Morthoe, site approx 1m left
★ ▲ £8-£22

Open May-Sep Booking advisable Whitsun & summer holidays Last arrival 24.00hrs Last departure 10.00hrs
A well-developed touring section in a holiday complex with a full entertainment and leisure programme. This tents-only park offers excellent facilities including a steam room and sauna. For a small charge a bus takes holidaymakers to the other two Woolacombe Bay holiday centres where they can take part in any of the activities offered, and there is also a bus to the beach. An 8.5-acre site with 150 touring pitches and 236 statics.
Entertainment, children's club, health suite, bowls

Leisure: ⚲ ⚛ ⚘ △ ◪ Facilities: ➊⊙▢✳⚲⛾⚑⊞
◫ ♜ Services: ▦▢⚲▯⌂⊞✕⬆→∪▸⊚△⚐⚇⚋
⊜ ▭ ▩ ◪ ▨

See advertisement on page 127

66% **Woolacombe Sands Holiday Park** (SS471434)
Beach Rd EX34 7AF ☎ 01271 870569
▯ 01271 870606
e-mail: lifesabeach@woolacombe-sands.co.uk
website: www.woolacombe-sands.co.uk
Dir: From M5 junct 27 take A361 to Barnstaple. Follow signs to Ilfracombe, until Mullacott Cross. Turn left onto B3343 to Woolacombe. Site on left
⛺ £10-£27.50 ⛺ £10-£27.50 ▲ £10-£27.50
Open Apr-Oct Booking advisable 24-31 May & 19 Jul-30 Aug Last arrival 22.00hrs Last departure 10.00hrs
Set in rolling countryside with grassy terraced pitches, most with spectacular views overlooking the sea at Woolacombe. The lovely blue flag beach can be accessed directly by footpath in 10-15 minutes, and there is a full entertainment programme for all the family in high season. A 20-acre site with 200 touring pitches and 80 statics.

contd.

Leisure: ⚲ ⚛ ⚘ △ Facilities: ➊⊙▢✳⚲⛾⚑♜
Services: ▦▢⚲▯⌂⊞▢⬆→∪▸⊚⚇
⊜ ▭ ▩ ◪ ▨

See advertisement opposite

GOLD

DORSET

BERE REGIS   **Map 03 SY89**

▶ ▶ ▶ 69% **Rowlands Wait Touring Park** (SY842933)
Rye Hill BH20 7LP ☎ 01929 472727
▯ 01929 472727

GOLD

e-mail: aa@rowlandswait.co.uk
website: www.rowlandswait.co.uk
Dir: Approaching Bere Regis follow signs to Bovington Tank Museum. At top of Rye Hill, 0.75m from village turn right for 200yds to site
★ ⛺ £7-£10 ⛺ £7-£10 ▲ £7-£10

Open Mar-Oct (winter by arrangement) Booking advisable bank hols & Jul-Aug Last arrival 21.30hrs Last departure noon
This park lies in a really attractive setting overlooking Bere and the Dorset countryside, set amongst undulating areas of trees and shrubs. Within a few miles of the Tank Musuem, and the mock tank battles are an attraction of the area. An 8-acre site with 71 touring pitches.

Leisure: ⚘ △ Facilities: ➊⊙▢✳⚲⛾⚑◫♜
Services: ▦▢▯⌂⊞▢→∪▸⊚⚇⊜▭▩◪▨

BLANDFORD FORUM   **Map 03 ST80**

▶ ▶ ▶ ▶ 64% **The Inside Park** (ST869046)
Down House Estate DT11 9AD ☎ 01258 453719
▯ 01258 459921
e-mail: inspark@aol.com
website: http://members.aol.com/inspark/inspark
Dir: From town cross River Stour and follow signs for Winterbourne Stickland. Site in 1.5m
★ ⛺ £9-£13.75 ⛺ £9-£13.75 ▲ £9-£13.75
Open Etr-Oct Booking advisable bank hols & Jul-Aug Last arrival 22.00hrs Last departure noon
An attractive, well-sheltered and quiet park, 0.5m off a country lane in a wooded valley. Spacious pitches are divided by mature trees and shrubs, and amenities are housed in an 18th-century coach house and stables. There are some lovely woodland walks within the park. A 12-acre site with 125 touring pitches.

contd.

Farm trips (main season), kennels for hire.
Leisure: ✎ ⚲ **Facilities:** ⬤⊖⬤✳⬤⬤⬤⬤
Services: ⬤⬤⬤⬤⬤⬤⬤➔⬤⬤⬤⬤⬤⬤⬤⬤

BRIDPORT   **Map 03 SY49**

**66% Freshwater Beach
Holiday Park (SY493892)**
Burton Bradstock DT6 4PT
☎ 01308 897317 📠 01308 897336
e-mail: enquiries@freshwaterbeach.co.uk
website: www.freshwaterbeach.co.uk
Dir: Take B3157 from Bridport towards Burton
Bradstock. Located 1.5m on right from Crown rdbt
★ ⊞ £10-£26 ⊞ £10-£26 ⚑ £10-£26

Open 15 Mar-10 Nov Booking advisable Jul-Aug
Last arrival 23.30hrs Last departure 10.00hrs
*A family holiday centre sheltered by a sandbank
and enjoying its own private beach. The park*
contd.

*offers a wide variety of leisure and
entertainment programmes for all the family.
It is well placed at one end of the
Weymouth/Bridport coast with spectacular
views of Chesil Beach. A 40-acre site with
400 touring pitches and 250 statics.*
Entertainment, amusement arcade, horse riding
Leisure: ⇘✎ ⚲ **Facilities:** ⬤⊖⬤✳⬤⬤⬤⬤⬤
Services: ⬤⬤⬤⬤⬤⬤⬤✖⬤➔⬤⬤⬤⬤⬤
Notes: No single sex groups or unaccompanied
teenagers ⬤⬤⬤⬤

**66% *West Bay Holiday Park
(SY461906)***
West Bay DT6 4HB
☎ 01308 422424 & 459491 📠 01308 421371
e-mail: office-west-bay@lineone.net
website: www.parkdeanholidays.com
Dir: From A35 Dorchester road, W towards Bridport,
take 1st exit at 1st rdbt, 2nd exit at 2nd rdbt into
West Bay, park on right
⊞ ⊞ ⚑
Open 23 Mar-2 Nov (rs 6 Apr-25 May & 14-19
Sep Entertainment restricted) Booking advisable
Last arrival 21.00hrs Last departure 10.00hrs
*Overlooking the pretty little harbour at West
Bay, and close to the shingle beach, this park
offers a full entertainment programme for all
ages. There are children's clubs and sports
activities for all the family, and plenty of evening*
contd.

fun with talent shows and cabaret etc. The grassy touring area is terraced to enjoy the seaward views. A large new adventure playground is proving popular. A 6-acre site with 150 touring pitches and 29 statics. Entertainment & childrens clubs

Leisure: ♜ ♣ ♨ ⚖ **Facilities:** 🅿⊙🖎✳🕭🛁🎯🍴

Services: 🚐🗑🍽🔋💧🖭✕🛒🚮➔∪🏳◎⚡🔥🌀

💳 ◻ ◧ 🗲 ⑨

▶ ▶ ▶ ▶ ▶ **75% Highlands End Farm Holiday Park (SY454913)**
Eype DT6 6AR ☎ 01308 422139
🖷 01308 425672
e-mail: holidays@wdlh.co.uk
website: www.wdlh.co.uk
Dir: 1m W of Bridport turn south for Eype. Park signed
★ 🚐 £8.25-£13 🚐 £8.25-£13 ▲ £8.25-£13

Open mid Mar-mid Nov Booking advisable public hols & Jul-Aug Last arrival 22.00hrs Last departure 11.00hrs
A well-screened site with magnificent clifftop views over the Channel and Dorset coast, adjacent to National Trust land and overlooking Lyme Bay. Pitches are mostly sheltered by hedging and well spaced on hardstandings. There is a mixture of statics and tourers, but the tourers enjoy the best clifftop positions. A 9-acre site with 195 touring pitches, 45 hardstandings and 160 statics.
Gym, steam room, sauna & pitch & putt

Leisure: ♜ ♣ ♣ ♨ ⚖ **Facilities:** 🅿⊙🖎✳🕭🛁🎯🍴

Services: 🚐🗑🍽🔋💧🖭✕🛒🚮➔∪🏳◎⚡🔥

💳 ◻ ⑨

▶ ▶ ▶ ▶ **68% Binghams Farm Touring Caravan Park (SY478963)**
Melplash DT6 3TT ☎ 01308 488234
e-mail: binghamsfarm@hotmail.com
website: www.binghamsfarm.co.uk
Dir: From Bridport take A3066 signposted Beaminster. After 3-4m turn left into private road to farm
★ 🚐 £9-£15 🚐 ▲
Open Mar-Nov Booking advisable bank hols Last arrival 21.00hrs Last departure 11.00hrs
A very good adults-only site with quality buildings, fittings and services, in a lovely rural setting. The park is secluded down a steep drive, and offers
contd.

great views over the hilly, unspoilt countryside. The terrain is slightly sloping, with shrub beds and ornamental trees, and pitches tastefully arranged around the park. A 5-acre site with 60 touring pitches.

Leisure: ♣ **Facilities:** 🅿⊙🖎✳🕭🛁🍴🐕

Services: 🚐🗑🍽🔋🅿➔∪🏳✚🍴🌀🛁

Notes: Adults only 💳 ◻ ◧ 🗲 ⑨

▶ ▶ **57% Giant's Head Caravan & Camping Park (ST675029)**
Giants Head Farm, Old Sherborne Rd DT2 7TR
☎ 01300 341242
e-mail: giantshead@westcountry.net
Dir: From Dorchester into town avoiding the by-pass, at Top O'Town rdbt take Sherborne road, after 500yds right fork at Esso (Loder's garage) site is signposted from here.
🚐 £7.50-£9.50 🚐 £7-£9.50 ▲ £7.50-£9.50
Open Etr-Oct (rs Etr shop & bar closed) Booking advisable Aug Last arrival anytime Last departure 13.00hrs
A pleasant park set in Dorset downland near Cerne Giant (a figure cut into the chalk) with stunning views. A good stopover site ideal for tenters and back-packers on the Ridgeway route. A 4-acre site with 50 touring pitches.

Facilities: 🅿⊙🖎✳🕭🛁🍴🐕

Services: 🚐🗑🔋💧🖭➔∪🏳🌀🛁

England

CHARMOUTH Map 03 SY39

▶ ▶ ▶ ▶ **72% Monkton Wyld Farm Caravan Park (SY336964)**
DT6 6DB ☎ 01297 34525 & 631131 (May-Sep)
🖺 01297 33594
e-mail: holidays@monktonwyld.co.uk
website: www.monktonwyld.co.uk
Dir: Leave A35 3m NW of Charmouth and take B3165 signed Marshwood. Site 0.25m on left
★ 🛱 £7-£12 🛱 £7-£12 ▲ £7-£12

Open Etr-Oct Booking advisable Last arrival 22.00hrs Last departure 11.00hrs
A pleasant family park in a secluded location yet central for Charmouth, Lyme and the coast. Owned and run by working farmers, it has been tastefully designed with maturing landscaping. The slightly sloping pitches face south, and trees bordering the perimeter shield them from the lane. Opposite the entrance is the mainly sheep farm which children enjoy visiting. A 6-acre site with 60 touring pitches. Family shower room.
Leisure: ⚠ Facilities: ↟☉☜☀↻ℂ☲☶☝
Services: ♨☷⬛⬤☷☐→↻►☉△↯☷↲ ⬤ ☲ ☷ ☷

▶ ▶ ▶ ▶ **67% Wood Farm Caravan & Camping Park (SY356940)**
Axminster Rd DT6 6BT
☎ 01297 560697 🖺 01297 561243
e-mail: holidays@woodfarm.co.uk
website: www.woodfarm.co.uk
Dir: Accessed directly off A35 rdbt on Axminster side of Charmouth. (Not necessary to go through village)
★ 🛱 £8.50-£16 🛱 £8.50-£16 ▲ £8.50-£16
Open Etr-Oct Booking advisable school hols Last arrival 19.00hrs Last departure noon
A pleasant, well-established and mature park overlooking Charmouth, the sea and the Dorset hills and valleys. It stands on a high spot, and the four camping fields are terraced, each with its own toilet block. Convenient for Lyme Regis, Axminster, and this famous fossil coastline. A 13-acre site with 216 touring pitches, 175 hardstandings and 83 statics. Coarse fishing lake.
Leisure: ₹ ☜ ☜ ⚠ ☐ Facilities: ↟☉☜☀↻ℂ☲☝
Services: ♨☷⬛☐☐☝→↻►☉△↯☷↲
Notes: No skate boards, scooters or roller skates
⬤ ☲ ☷ ☷ ☷

▶ ▶ ▶ **66% Newlands Caravan & Camping Park (SY374935)**
DT6 6RB ☎ 01297 560259 🖺 01297 560787
e-mail: enq@newlandsholidays.co.uk
website: www.newlandsholidays.co.uk
Dir: 4m W of Bridport on A35
🛱 🛱 ▲
Open all year (rs Nov-Mar Rest, bar & shop closed)
Booking advisable school hols Last arrival 22.30hrs Last departure 10.00hrs
A very smart site with excellent touring facilities, including five 'millennium' pitches complete with water, electricity, chemical disposal point, washing machine and tumble dryer. The park offers a full cabaret and entertainment programme for all ages, and boasts an indoor swimming pool with spa and an outdoor pool with water slide. Set on gently sloping ground in hilly countryside near the sea. A 23-acre site with 240 touring pitches and 86 statics.
Leisure: ₹ ☜ ☜ ⚠ ☐ Facilities: ↟☉☜☀☝
Services: ℂ☲☝ Services: ♨☷⬛☐☐☝→↻►☉☲↲
Notes: No single sex groups ⬤ ☲ ☷ ☷ ☷

CHIDEOCK Map 03 SY49

▶ ▶ ▶ ▶ **76% Golden Cap Caravan Park (SY422919)**
Seatown DT6 6JX ☎ 01297 489341 & 01308 422139 🖺 01297 489788
e-mail: holidays@wdlh.co.uk
website: www.wdlh.co.uk
Dir: On A35, in Chideock turn S for Seatown
★ 🛱 £8.25-£13 🛱 £8.25-£13 ▲ £8.25-£13
Open mid Mar-early Nov Booking advisable public hols & Jul-Aug Last arrival 22.00hrs Last departure 11.00hrs
A grassy site, overlooking sea and beach and surrounded by National Trust parkland. This uniquely placed park slopes down to the sea, although pitches are generally level. A slight dip hides the beach view from the back of the park, but this area benefits from having trees, scrub and meadows, unlike the barer areas closer to the sea. Ideal base for touring Dorset and Devon. An 11-acre site with 108 touring pitches, 29 hardstandings and 234 statics.
Leisure: ⚠ Facilities: ↟☉☜☀☝℄ℂ☲☶☝
Services: ♨☷⬛☐☐☝⬛→↻►↯☷↲ ⬤ ☲ ☷

CHRISTCHURCH Map 04 SZ19

▶ ▶ ▶ ▶ **74% Grove Farm Meadow Holiday Caravan Park (SZ136946)**
Stour Way BH23 2PQ ☎ 01202 483597
🖺 01202 483878
e-mail: enquiries@meadowbank-holidays.co.uk
website: www.meadowbank-holidays.co.uk
Dir: Take Christchurch/Airport exit off A338, turn left for Christchurch and follow signs
★ 🛱 £6-£21 🛱 £6-£21
Open Mar-Oct Booking advisable at all times Last arrival 21.00hrs Last departure noon ✇
A very smart park on the banks of the River Stour, with a colourful display of hanging baskets and flower-filled tubs around the superb reception area.

contd.

Toilet facilities are modern and spotless, and there is excellent play equipment for children. Visitors can choose between pitch sizes, including some luxury fully-serviced ones. A 2-acre site with 41 touring pitches, 22 hardstandings and 180 statics. Fishing on site, 21 fully serviced pitches

Leisure: ◕ ⚏ **Facilities:** ⌁ ╭ ⊙ ⍾ ⌂ ⌯ ☲ 冊 **Services:**
⊟ ⊡ ⬟ ⌀ ⊞ ⊤ ⌁ → ∪ ┣ △ ☇ ⚐ ⌑ ⊜ ▦ 囲 ▧ ▨

DORCHESTER   See **Cerne Abbas**

EVERSHOT   **Map 03 ST50**

▶ ▶ ▶ 63% **NEW** Clay Pigeon Caravan Park **(ST610077)**
Wardon Hill DT2 9PW ☎ 01935 83492
Dir: Turn off A37 onto unclassified road signed Batcombe, site on right 150yds
⊕ £8-£10 ⊕ £8-£10 Å £8-£10

contd.

Open all year Booking advisable Last arrival 21.00hrs
A level, close-mown park with mature trees in a rural area. The refurbished toilet block is well equipped, and adjacent to the site is a go-kart track and clay pigeon shooting range. A 3-acre site with 60 touring pitches, 12 hardstandings.
Leisure: ⚼ Facilities: ⬚⊙⬚⬚⬚⬚⬚ Services: ⬚⬚
⬚⬚⬚✕⬚ Notes: Dogs must be kept on leads

HOLTON HEATH   Map 03 SY99

66% Sandford Holiday Park (SY939916)
BH16 6JZ ☎ 01202 631600 & 622513 ▤ 01202 625678
e-mail: bookings@weststarholidays.co.uk
website: www.weststarholidays.co.uk
Dir: From Poole take A35 towards Dorchester, at lights turn onto A351 towards Wareham. Turn right at Holton Heath. Park 100yds on left on Organford road
⬚⬚⬚

Open Apr-Dec & Feb half term Booking advisable Jul-Aug & bank hols Last arrival 22.00hrs Last departure 10.00hrs
With touring pitches set individually in 20 acres surrounded by woodland, this park offers a full range of leisure activities and entertainment for the whole family. The touring area is neat and well maintained, and there are children's clubs in the daytime and nightly entertainment. A 64-acre site with 500 touring pitches and 284 statics. Fun factory, bowling, entertainment, crazy golf.
Leisure: ⬚ ⬚⬚⬚⬚⬚ Facilities: ⬚⬚⊙⬚⬚⬚
⬚⬚⬚⬚ Services: ⬚⬚⬚⬚⬚✕⬚→⬚⬚⬚
Notes: No single sex groups or unaccompanied teenagers ⬚⬚⬚⬚⬚
See advertisement on page 136

HORTON   Map 04 SU00

▶ ▶ ▶ **65% Meadow View Touring Caravan Park (SU045070)**
Wigbeth BH21 7JH ☎ 01258 840040
Dir: Follow unclass road from Horton to site, 0.5m from Druscilla pub
★ ⬚ fr £7.60 ⬚ fr £7.60
Open all year Booking advisable Jul-Aug Last arrival 21.00hrs Last departure 11.00hrs
A small family-owned park, part of a specialised commercial turf farm, and set in a very rural area
contd.

---

with its own lake and nature reserve. This very good park is always neatly trimmed and clean. A 1.5-acre site with 15 touring pitches.
Coarse fishing, pitch & putt
Leisure: ⚼ Facilities: ⬚⊙⬚✳⬚⬚⬚ Services: ⬚
⬚⬚→ ∪ ▶ Notes: Dogs must be kept on leads

HURN   Map 04 SZ19

▶ ▶ ▶ ▶ 72% **Mount Pleasant Touring Park (SZ129987)**
Matchams Ln BH23 6AW ☎ 01202 475474
▤ 01202 475428
e-mail: enq@mount-pleasant-cc.co.uk
website: www.mount-pleasant-cc.co.uk
Dir: A338 from Ringwood to Bournemouth, 1st exit towards Hurn at T-junct, after 1m right at mini rdbt, then 1st left into Matcham's Lane, site 1m on right
★ ⬚ £9-£13 ⬚ £9-£13 ⬚ £8-£13

Open Mar-Oct Booking advisable High season Last arrival 21.30hrs Last departure 11.00hrs
Sheltered by the mature trees of the surrounding forest, this well-maintained park offers a high level of security. Ideal for visiting the Dorset coast and the traditional villages of the New Forest, it has two very well-appointed toilet blocks. Close to Bournemouth International Airport. A 7.5-acre site with 174 touring pitches.
Leisure: ⚼ Facilities: ⬚⬚✳⬚⬚⬚⬚
Services: ⬚⬚⬚⬚⬚✕⬚→▶⬚⬚⬚⬚⬚

LYME REGIS   Map 03 SY39
See also **Charmouth**

▶ ▶ ▶ 65% **NEW** Shrubbery Touring Park **(SY300914)**
Rousdon DT7 3XW ☎ 01297 442227 ▤ 01297 442227
website: www.ukparks.co.uk/shrubbery
Dir: 3m W of Lyme Regis on A3052 coast road
⬚ £6.50-£10.25 ⬚ £6-£9.25 ⬚ £6-£9.25

contd.

Open Mar-Oct Booking advisable BH's & Jul-Aug Last arrival 23.00hrs Last departure 11.00hrs
Mature trees enclose this peaceful park which has distant views of the lovely surrounding countryside. The modern facilities are well kept, and there is plenty of space for children to play in the grounds. Located on the Devon/Dorset borders, just 3 miles from Lyme Regis. A 10-acre site with 120 touring pitches.

Leisure: ⚠ **Facilities:** ⬡⋇🅰🏧 **Services:** 🔌🅾🛒🏧
🍴➔⏵◉♨♨🛒💳🚐🚗🏧🔲

LYTCHETT MINSTER   Map 03 SY99

► ► ► **64% South Lytchett Manor Caravan Park (SY954926)**
The Lodge, Dorchester Rd BH16 6JB
☎ 01202 622577 🖹 01202 622620
e-mail: slmcp@talk21.com
website: www.eluk.co.uk/camping/dorset/slytchett
Dir: On B3067, off A35, 1m E of Lytchett Minster
★ 🚐 £8.50-£10.50 🚗 £8.50-£10.50 ▲ £8.50-£10.50

Open Mar-Oct Booking advisable bank hols & mid Jul-Aug Last arrival 22.00hrs Last departure 11.00hrs
A pleasant family-owned park set along the tree-lined driveway of the old manor house, with pitches enjoying open views of pastureland. Facilities are basic but clean and well cared for, and the park is only 3m from Poole. An 11-acre site with 150 touring pitches, 5 hardstandings.
Washing up sinks, pool table & table tennis

Leisure: ⚠🔲 **Facilities:** ⬡⊙♨⋇🅰💧🏧
Services: 🔌🅾🛒🏧➔⏵◉♨💳🚐🚗
Notes: Dogs must be kept on leads 💳🚐🚗🏧🔲
See advertisement on page 138

MORETON   Map 03 SY88

► ► ► **67% Camping & Caravanning Club Site (SY782892)**
Station Rd DT2 8BB ☎ 01305 853801
website: www.campingandcaravanningclub.co.uk
Dir: From Poole on A35, continue past Bere Regis, turn left onto B3390 signposted Alfpuddle. After approx 2m site on left before Moreton Station
★ 🚐 £12.30-£15.50 🚗 £12.30-£15.50 ▲ £12.30-£15.50
Open Mar-Nov Booking advisable bank hols & peak periods Last arrival 21.00hrs Last departure noon
Modern purpose-built site on level ground with good amenities. This tidy, well-maintained park offers electric hook-ups to most pitches, and there
contd.

is a first class play area for children. Please see the advertisement on page 10 for details of Club Members' benefits. A 7-acre site with 130 touring pitches, 3 hardstandings.
Leisure: ⚠ **Facilities:** ⬡⊙♨⋇🅰💧🏧🏇
Services: 🔌🅾🛒🏧➔⏵◉♨💳🚐🚗🏧🔲

ORGANFORD   Map 03 SY99

► ► ► **68% Organford Manor (SY943926)**
BH16 6ES ☎ 01202 622202 & 623278
🖹 01202 623278
e-mail: organford@lds.co.uk
Dir: On A35, 1st on left after Lytchett rdbt at junct with A351. Site entrance on right
★ 🚐 £8.50-£10 🚗 £7.50-£9 ▲ £8.50-£10

Open 15 Mar-Oct Booking advisable peak periods Last arrival 22.00hrs Last departure noon
A quiet, secluded site in the grounds of the manor house with level grassy areas amongst trees and shrubs. The toilet facilities are newly refurbished and smart, and the laundry boasts efficient new equipment. An 8-acre site with 75 touring pitches, 2 hardstandings and 45 statics.
Facilities: ⬡⊙♨⋇🅰💧🏧 **Services:** 🔌🅾🛒🏧➔⏵◉♨➔⏵♨

► ► ► **75% Pear Tree Touring Park (SY938915)**
Organford Rd, Holton Heath BH16 6LA
☎ 01202 622434 🖹 01202 631985
e-mail: info@visitpeartree.co.uk
website: www.visitpeartree.co.uk
Dir: From Poole take A35 towards Dorchester, turn onto A351 towards Wareham at traffic lights. Turn right at Holton Heath for 300yds. Park on left on Organford Rd
🚐 £8-£12 🚗 £8-£12 ▲ £8-£12

Open Etr & Apr-Oct Booking advisable Etr, Spring bank hol & end Jul-Aug Last arrival 21.00hrs Last departure 11.00hrs
contd.

Leisure: 🐟 Indoor swimming pool   🦆 Outdoor swimming pool   ⚹ Tennis court   🎱 Games room   ⚠ Children's playground   ∪ Stables
⏵ 9/18 hole golf course   🦆 Boats for hire   🎦 Cinema   🎣 Fishing   ◉ Mini golf   💧 Watersports   🔲 Separate TV room

England

Caravan & CAMPING
near Poole, Dorset

SANDFORD

Durdle Door near Sandford
Courtesy of Lulworth Estate

beautiful spaces *in breathtaking places!*

Award winning Park in an area of outstanding natural beauty and close to safe sandy beaches. With superb all-weather facilities for everyone you can choose between an all action holiday or a quieter relaxing break.

What's included

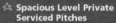

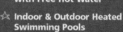

- ☆ Spacious Level Private Serviced Pitches
- ☆ Modern Shower Blocks with Free Hot Water
- ☆ Indoor & Outdoor Heated Swimming Pools
- ☆ Great Evening Entertainment
- ☆ Children's Clubs & Play Areas

What's extra

- ☆ Launderette and Washing Up Area
- ☆ Well Stocked Shop
- ☆ Takeaway & Restaurant
- ☆ Crazy Golf, Go Karting, Tennis Courts, Horseriding, Bike Hire and More

Quote: AA

☆ ☆ **book online**
www.weststarholidays.co.uk

☆ ☆ ☆ **booking line**
☎ **0870 066 7793**

☆ ☆ ☆ ☆ **brochure hotline**
☎ **0870 444 5300**

WESTSTAR
Holiday Parks

Abbreviations: BH/bank hols-bank holidays   Etr-Easter   Whit-Whitsun   dep-departure   fr-from   hrs-hours   m-mile   mdnt-midnight   rdbt-roundabout   rs-restricted service   wk-week   wknd-weekend   ✗-no dogs

A quiet, sheltered country park surrounded by woodland, with a bridle path leading from the park into Wareham Forest. Despite the trees the park is bright and spacious, and facilities and grounds are well maintained. A 7.5-acre site with 125 touring pitches, 10 hardstandings.

Leisure: ⚠ Facilities: 🏠⊙🔾❊✤👇🐾🐕🗮
Services: 🔧🔌🛢🗑🎛🚽➔∪►🅿⚡🐶💷🅹 ⊜ 🔲 🔩🛒🅶

OSMINGTON MILLS Map 03 SY78

► ► ► 62% **NEW** **Osmington Mills Holidays**
(SY736820)
DT3 6NB ☎ 01305 832311 📄 01305 835251
e-mail: holidays@osmingtonmills.fsnet.co.uk
website: www.osmington-mills-holidays.co.uk
Dir: Take A353 towards Weymouth & at Osmington Mills sign opposite garage, turn L to site
★ 🚐 £8-£15 🚍 £8-£15 ▲ £8-£16
Open mid Mar-mid Dec
A large sloping field with hedging and natural screening in a peaceful setting close to the Dorset coastline and footpaths. There is a small, secluded area for caravans and a separate tent area, with seasonal entertainment in a ranch-style bar, and a heated outdoor swimming pool with paddling pools. A 14-acre site with 245 touring pitches and 83 statics.

Facilities: 🔾🐾 Services: 🔧🗑

OWERMOIGNE Map 03 SY78

► ► ► 72% **Sandyholme Caravan Park**
(SY768863)
Moreton Rd DT2 8HZ ☎ 01305 852677
📄 01305 854677 *SILVER*
e-mail: smeatons@sandyholme.co.uk
website: www.sandyholme.co.uk
Dir: From A352 (Wareham to Dorchester road) turn right to Owermoigne for 1m. Site on left.
★ 🚐 £7.50-£12.50 🚍 £7.50-£12.50 ▲ £7-£12.50
Open Apr-Oct Booking advisable peak periods Last arrival 21.30hrs Last departure 10.30hrs
A quiet family-run site in a tree-lined rural setting within easy reach of the coast at Lulworth Cove, and handy for several seaside resorts. The facilities are very good, including a superb new toilet block, and food is available in the lounge/bar. A 6-acre site with 53 touring pitches and 52 statics.
Restaurant/takeaway in peak season, table tennis

Leisure: ◆⚠ Facilities: 🏠⊙🔾❊✤👇🐾🗮 Services:
🔧🗑🍺🛢🎛🚽✕🚿➔🅹 Notes: Dogs must be kept on leads, no single sex groups ⊜ 🔲 🔩🛒🅶

POOLE Map 03 SZ09

See also **Lytchett Minster, Organford & Wimborne Minster**

► ► ► 66% **Beacon Hill Touring Park**
(SY977945)
Blandford Rd North BH16 6AB
☎ 01202 631631 📄 01202 625749
e-mail: bookings@beaconhilltouringpark.co.uk
website: www.beaconhilltouringpark.co.uk
Dir: On A350, 0.25m N of junct with A35, 4m N of Poole *GOLD*
contd.

BEACON HILL TOURING PARK
POOLE • DORSET

Set in 30 acres of lovely English woodland with open grassy spaces and nature rambles, but only minutes from the South's most beautiful beaches; Beacon Hill offers some of the best facilities available at Touring Parks today plus the delights of Poole, Bournemouth and Dorset's endless tourist attractions.
Overnight stops for Poole-Cherbourg, Poole-St. Malo, Poole-Channel Islands. Only 3 miles from ferry terminal.
Heated Swimming Pool ★ Games Rooms ★ Children's Adventure Playgrounds ★ Tennis Court ★ Fishing ★ Seasonal Take-away food/coffee shop and bar (with entertainment high season) ★ Well stocked shop ★ Best beaches for windsurfing ★ Riding nearby ★ Free showers – disabled facilities (accessibility grading 2) ★ Laundry Rooms ★ Hair Driers and Razor Points ★ Dishwashing facilities with free hot water ★ Calor Gas ★ Public Telephone ★ Caravan Rallies welcome ★ Electric Hook-ups ★ Some hard standings. Beacon Hill Touring Park, Blandford Road North, near Poole, Dorset.
Tel. (01202) 631631   www.beaconhilltouringpark.co.uk
bookings@beaconhilltouringpark.co.uk
DIRECTIONS: Situated a ¼ of a mile north from the junction of the A35 and A350 towards Blandford, approximately 3 miles north of Poole.

Beacon Hill Touring Park
★ 🚐 £9-£17 🚍 £8.50-£17 ▲ £8.50-£17
Open Etr-Sep (rs low & mid season some services closed/restricted opening) Booking advisable Etr, Whit & Jul-Aug Last arrival 23.00hrs Last departure 11.00hrs
Set in attractive, wooded area with conservation very much in mind. Two large ponds are within the grounds and the terraced pitches offer some fine views. A 30-acre site with 170 touring pitches, 10 hardstandings.
Fishing & view point.

Leisure: 🛶🎣◆⚠🖵 Facilities: 🏠⊙🔾❊✤👇🐾🗮
Services: 🔧🗑🍺🛢🗑🎛🚽✕🚿➔∪►🅿⚡🐶🅹

For full details of the AA pennant ratings scheme see page 7

POOLE   DORSET

SOUTH LYTCHETT MANOR
CARAVAN PARK ▶▶▶

Camping & Touring Caravan Park
LYTCHETT MINSTER ▪ POOLE
DORSET ▪ BH16 6JB

TEL: (01202) 622577 FAX: (01202) 622620

Popular rural site situated in lovely parkland surroundings, just west of Poole. Ideal base for sandy beaches, sailing and windsurfing and for touring the Purbeck area, Poole, Bournemouth etc, Well stocked shop, take-away in high season, modern washing facilities, free hot showers, facilities for people with disabilities. Useful overnight stop for the cross channel ferries.

FREE BROCHURE
ON REQUEST

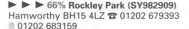

▶ ▶ ▶ 66% **Rockley Park** (SY982909)
Hamworthy BH15 4LZ ☎ 01202 679393
▤ 01202 683159
website: www.british-holidays.co.uk
Dir: Take A31 off M27 to Poole town centre, then follow signs to park
🚐 🚑 Å

Open Mar-Oct Booking advisable Jul-Aug & bank hols Last arrival 20.00hrs Last departure noon
A complete holiday experience including a wide range of day and night entertainment, and plenty of sports and leisure activities. Water sports are comprehensively covered, and there is also mooring and launching from the park. The touring area has been upgraded to provide good quality facilities. A 4.25-acre site with 71 touring pitches and 1077 statics.

Leisure: 🐟 🎣 ⚴ ◗ ⚒ **Facilities:** 🏳️☉🎱⚒☆⚹⚿🛉🛍
Services: 🔌🍴🗜🧴✗⛟→🍴◎⌂⚓♨🍴🛒🔪 ▨ ▤ ▩ 🅟 ⬛ 🍴 🅂

ST LEONARDS
Map 04 SU10

68% Oakdene Forest Park (SZ095023)
BH24 2RZ ☎ 01590 648331
🖷 01590 645610
e-mail: holidays@shorefield.co.uk
website: www.shorefield.co.uk
Dir: 3m W of Ringwood off A31, turn left after foot bridge over A31
🚐 £7.50-£28 🚘 £7.50-£28
Open Feb-2 Jan Booking advisable all times
Last arrival 22.00hrs Last departure 10.00hrs
Set in 55 acres of parkland beside the beautiful Avon Forest, this full-entertainment park offers premier pitches for tourers complete with electricity and fresh and waste water points. 'Fun and games' are promised here, and there are both indoor and outdoor pools, and a riding stable on site. A special children's programme is offered during high season, and there is plenty to occupy the whole family. A 55-acre site with 68 touring pitches and 105 statics.
Woodland walks, mini bowling & crazy golf
Leisure: ✎ ⚲ ◗ ⚑ **Facilities:** ⬤⊙❄⚷⚿⛾
Services: ⬤▤⚲⬤⬤⊡✕⬤→ ➤ ♫ **Notes:** No single sex groups, no under 25s unless in a family group ⬤ 🚗 ⬤ 🔧 🄵

▶ ▶ ▶ **60% Shamba Holiday Park (SU105029)**
230 Ringwood Rd BH24 2SB ☎ 01202 873302
🖷 01202 873302
e-mail: holidays@shamba.co.uk
website: www.shamba.co.uk
Dir: 3m W of Ringwood off A31
★ 🚐 £9-£13.50 🚘 £9-£13.50 ▲ £9-£13.50
Open Mar-Oct Booking advisable bank hols & Jul-Aug Last arrival 23.30hrs Last departure 11.00hrs
A relaxed touring park in pleasant countryside between the New Forest and Bournemouth. The park is very well equipped for holidaymakers, with outdoor swimming pool, good playground, and bar, shop and takeaway. A 7-acre site with 150 touring pitches.
Leisure: ⚲ ◗ ⚑ **Facilities:** ⬤⊙◗❄⚷⚿⛾ **Services:**
⬤▤⚲⚲⊡⬤✕⬤→∪➤♫⬤🚗⬤🔧🄵

SHAFTESBURY
Map 03 ST82

▶ ▶ **58% Blackmore Vale Caravan & Camping Park (ST835233)**
Sherborne Causeway SP7 9PX
☎ 01747 851523 & 852573 🖷 01747 851671
website: www.caravancampingsites.co.uk/dorset/blackmorevale.htm
Dir: From Shaftesbury's Ivy Cross rdbt take A30 signed Sherborne. Site 2m on right
★ 🚐 £7.50-£8 🚘 £6.50-£7 ▲ £6-£6.50
Open all year Booking advisable bank hols
A comfortable touring park with spacious pitches and well-maintained facilities. Set behind a caravan sales showground and dealership, and about 2m from Shaftesbury. A 3-acre site with 26 touring pitches and 12 statics.
Cycle hire, caravan sales & accessories
Facilities: ⬤⊙❄⚷⛾⚿
Services: ⬤⚲⚲⊡⊡→∪➤♫⬤🄶⬤🚗🔧🄵

SIXPENNY HANDLEY
Map 03 ST91

▶ ▶ **60% Church Farm Caravan & Camping Park (ST994173)**
The Bungalow, Church Farm High St SP5 5ND
☎ 01725 552563 🖷 01725 552563
Dir: Between Salisbury and Blandford, turn off towards Sixpenny Handley, and site at top of village
★ 🚐 £7-£9 🚘 £7-£9 ▲ £7
Open all year Booking advisable BHs May & Aug Last arrival 23.00hrs Last departure anytime
A spacious, open park located within the Cranborne Chase in an Area of Outstanding Natural Beauty. A new toilet block offers good quality facilities, and the pretty village of Sixpenny Handley with all its amenities is 200yds away. A 5-acre site with 20 touring pitches, 2 hardstandings and 2 statics.
Leisure: ⚑ **Facilities:** ⬤⊙❄⚷⚿⛾⛾
Services: ⬤⚲⬤→➤

SWANAGE
Map 03 SZ07

▶ ▶ ▶ **70% Ulwell Cottage Caravan Park (SZ019809)**
Ulwell Cottage, Ulwell BH19 3DG
☎ 01929 422823 🖷 01929 421500
e-mail: enq@ulwellcottagepark.co.uk
website: www.ulwellcottagepark.co.uk
Dir: From Swanage N for 2m on unclass road towards Studland
★ 🚐 £11-£25 🚘 £11-£25 ▲ £11-£25

Open Mar-7 Jan (rs Mar-spring bank hol & mid Sep-early Jan takeaway closed, shop open variable hours) Booking advisable bank hols & Jul-Aug Last arrival 23.00hrs Last departure 11.00hrs
Nestling under the Purbeck Hills surrounded by scenic walks and only 2 miles from the beach. This family-run park caters well for families and couples, offering high quality facilities including an indoor heated swimming pool and village inn. A 13-acre site with 77 touring pitches, 12 hardstandings and 140 statics.
Leisure: ✎ ⚑ **Facilities:** ⬤⊙❄⚷⚿⛾⛾ **Services:**
⬤▤⚲⚲⊡✕⬤→∪➤⊚⚲♫⬤🚗⬤🔧🄵

See advertisement on page 140

Fewer than 50 parks have been awarded the coveted 5-pennant rating. For a full list see page 18

Leisure: ✎ Indoor swimming pool ⚲ Outdoor swimming pool ⚲ Tennis court ◗ Games room ⚑ Children's playground ∪ Stables ➤ 9/18 hole golf course ⚲ Boats for hire ⚲ Cinema ♫ Fishing ⊚ Mini golf ⚲ Watersports ⬜ Separate TV room

Ulwell Cottage
Caravan Park, Swanage, Dorset

For Brochure
Tel: 01929 422823 Fax 01929 421500
www.ulwellcottagepark.co.uk

Nestling under the beautiful **"Purbeck Hills"**, 1 mile from the beach. Ideal for families, walkers, golfers and all watersport enthusiasts.
Open Winter months.

Indoor heated pool • Village Inn & Restaurant • Shop

Birchwood Tourist Park
North Trigon, Wareham, Dorset BH20 7PA

Tel: 01929 554763 Fax: 01929 556635
www.birchwoodtouristpark.co.uk

Family-run park, ideally situated for exploring Dorset.
Well-stocked Shop, Off-licence, Take-Away, Free Hot Showers, Children's Paddling Pool, Bike Hire, Fully Serviced Pitches, Pitch and Putt, Large games field.
Hard-standings.
We accept 🔳 🔲 and 💳

VERWOOD   Map 04 SU00

▶ ▶ ▶ 66% **Camping & Caravanning Club Site** (SU069098)
Sutton Hill, Woodlands BH21 8NQ ☎ 01202 822763
website: www.campingandcaravanningclub.co.uk
Dir: *Turn left on A354 13m from Salisbury onto B3081, site is 1.5m W of Verwood*
★ 🚐 £12.30-£15.50 🚐 £12.30-£15.50 ▲ £12.30-£15.50
Open Mar-Oct Booking advisable Jul-Aug & BH's
Last arrival 21.00hrs Last departure noon
Set on rising ground between the woodland of the New Forest and the rolling downs of Cranborne Chase and Salisbury Plains. This comfortable site is well kept by very keen wardens. Please see the advertisement on page 10 for details of Club Members' benefits. A 12.75-acre site with 150 touring pitches, 16 hardstandings.
Recreation room, pool table, table tennis.
Leisure: ◆ 🔥 **Facilities:** 🏠⊙🍴✻🔥🛠💺 **Services:**
🍴🚽🛢🚿⊞📞⇾∪🕨⚡✕🔧🏪💳 🔳 🔲 🐕 🗑

WAREHAM   Map 03 SY98

▶ ▶ ▶ 72% **Birchwood Tourist Park** (SY896905)
Bere Rd, North Trigon BH20 7PA ☎ 01929 554763
📠 01929 556635
website: www.birchwoodtouristpark.co.uk
Dir: *From Poole (A351) or Dorchester (A352) on N side of railway line at Wareham, follow road signed Bere Regis (unclassified). 2nd tourist park after 2.25m*
★ 🚐 £6.50-£11.50 🚐 £6.50-£11.50 ▲ £6.50-£11.50

Open Mar-Oct (rs Nov-Feb Some restrictions)
Booking advisable bank hols & Jul-Aug Last arrival 22.00hrs Last departure 11.30hrs
Set in 50 acres of parkland located within Wareham Forest, this site offers direct access into ideal areas for walking, mountain biking, and horse and pony riding. The modern facilities are centrally located and well-organised. A 25-acre site with 175 touring pitches, 8 hardstandings.
Games field, bike hire, pitch & putt, paddling pool
Leisure: ◆ 🔥 **Facilities:** 🏠⊙🍴✻🔥💺🛠🐕
Services: 🍴🚽🛢🚿⊞🅃🛠⇾∪🕨✕🎣🔧 **Notes:** No generators, no groups at Bank Hols 💳 🔳 🔲 🐕 🗑

▶ ▶ ▶ 67% **Lookout Holiday Park** (SY927858)
Stoborough BH20 5AZ ☎ 01929 552546
📠 01929 556662
e-mail: enquiries@caravan-sites.co.uk
website: www.caravan-sites.co.uk
Dir: *On B3075 1m S*
🚐🚐▲
contd.

Lookout Holiday Park
Open Feb-Nov (rs Feb & Nov Static holidays only)
Booking advisable bank hols & Jul-Aug Last arrival
22.00hrs Last departure noon ✍
*Divided into two paddocks and set well back from
the Swanage road, this touring park is separated
from the static part of the operation. A superb
children's playground and plenty of other
attractions make this an ideal centre for families.
150 touring pitches and 90 statics.*

Leisure: ♣ 瓜 **Facilities:** 🏵⊙🔍✳🌡 **Services:** 🅾
🅾🛢🖉🖃🔢🏧⇨∪▶🎱🥄🍴🥢 🍷 🚾 CONNECT 🐕 🗑

▶ ▶ ▶ **62% Manor Farm Caravan Park (SY872866)**
1 Manor Farm Cottage, East Stoke BH20 6AW
☎ 01929 462870 🗎 01929 462870
e-mail: info@manorfarmcp.co.uk
website: www.manorfarmcp.co.uk
*Dir: From Wareham follow A352 for 2m towards
Dorchester, then left onto B3070. At 1st x-roads turn
right, at next x-rds right, site 400yds on left*
Open Etr-Sep Booking advisable school hols Last
arrival 22.00hrs Last departure 11.30hrs
*An attractive, mainly touring park in a quiet rural
setting. Most pitches have electricity, and the site is
bordered by mature trees. A 2.5-acre site with 50
touring pitches, 3 hardstandings.*

Leisure: 瓜 **Facilities:** 🏵⊙🔍✳♿🌡🏧🐕
Services: 🅾🛢🖉🖃⇨∪▶🎱🥄🗑
Notes: Dogs must be kept on leads

▶ ▶ ▶ **60% Ridge Farm Camping & Caravan
Park (SY936868)**
Barnhill Rd, Ridge BH20 5BG ☎ 01929 556444
e-mail: info@ridgefarm.co.uk
website: www.ridgefarm.co.uk
*Dir: From Wareham take A351 towards Corfe Castle,
cross river to Stoborough, then left to Ridge and follow
site signs for 1.5m*
★ 🚐 £7.50-£9.50 🚐 £7.50-£9.50 ▲ £7.50-£9.50
Open Etr-Oct Booking advisable Jul & Aug Last
arrival 21.00hrs Last departure noon
*A quiet rural park, adjacent to a working farm and
surrounded by trees and bushes. This away-from-it-
all park is ideally located for touring this part of
Dorset, and especially for bird watchers, or those
who enjoy walking and cycling. A 3.5-acre site with
60 touring pitches.*

Facilities: 🏵⊙🔍✳🌡 **Services:** 🅾🛢🖉🖃⇨∪▶
🥄🍴 **Notes:** No dogs Jul-Aug

▶ ▶ **60% Woodlands Camping Park Ltd (SY867861)**
Bindon Ln, East Stoke BH20 6AS ☎ 01929 462327
🗎 01929 462327
e-mail: woodlandscamping@zoom.co.uk
website: www.woodlandscampingpark.co.uk
*Dir: At Wool rail crossing turn off A352 onto B3071, at
right bend turn left into Bindon Lane. Park 1.5m on
right.*
★ ▲ £7-£8
Open all year (rs 30 Sep-Apr shop not open)
Booking advisable May-Aug Last arrival 21.00hrs
Last departure noon
*A tent-only park in an Area of Outstanding Natural
Beauty surrounded by woodland. The park is
divided into three areas by trees, and is appreciated
by people looking for peace and quiet. Facilities are
well kept, and security is good. A 2.25-acre site with
50 touring pitches.*
Tumble dryer

Facilities: 🏵⊙🔍✳♿🌡 **Services:** 🖉⇨∪▶🗑
Notes: No single sex groups, camp fires,
loud radios, dogs to be kept on leads.

WARMWELL **Map 03 SY78**

▶ ▶ ▶ **63% Warmwell Country Touring Park
(SY764878)**
DT2 8JD ☎ 01305 852313 🗎 01305 852313
e-mail: warmwell@btopenworld.com
website: www.warmwell.touring.20m.com
Dir: Take B3390 1m N of Warmwell
★ 🚐 £8.70-£10.85 🚐 £8.70-£10.85 ▲ £8.70-£10.85
Open all year Booking advisable Etr-Sep & Xmas
Last arrival 22.00hrs Last departure 11.00hrs
*A lovely setting in an old quarry, with small open
areas or sheltered pitches amongst evergreen trees.
The site is visited by plenty of wildlife including
deer, badgers and foxes, and is in an Area of
Outstanding Natural Beauty around the Purbeck
Peninsula. A 15-acre site with 190 touring pitches.*

Leisure: 瓜 **Facilities:** 🏵⊙🔍✳♿🌡🐕 **Services:**
🅾🛢🍷🖉🖃🔢⇨∪▶⊙△🥄🍴🥢 🍷 🚾 CONNECT 🐕 🗑

WEYMOUTH **Map 03 SY67**

67% NEW Littlesea (SY654783)
Lynch Ln DT4 9DT ☎ 01305 774414
website: www.havenholidays.com
★ 🚐 £9-£30 🚐 £9-£30 ▲ £9-£30
Open Mar-Oct Booking advisable Last arrival
22.00hrs Last departure 12.00hrs
*Just 3 miles from Weymouth with its lovely
beaches and many attractions, Littlesea has a
cheerful family atmosphere and fantastic
facilities. Indoor and outdoor entertainment and
activities are on offer for all the family, and the
toilet facilities on the touring park are of a good
quality. A 75-acre site with 220 touring pitches.*

Leisure: 🎯 ⟲ ♣ 瓜 ▢ **Facilities:** 🌡
Services: 🅾🍷✕🍴 🍷 🚾 📀 🚾 CONNECT 🐕 🗑

67% NEW Seaview Holiday Park (SY707830)
Preston DT3 6DZ ☎ 01305 833037
website: www.havenholidays.com
🚐 £9-£30 🚐 £9-£30 ▲ £9-£30
Open Mar-Oct Booking advisable Last arrival
22.00hrs Last departure 12.00hrs
*A fun-packed holiday centre for all the family,
with plenty of activities and entertainment
during the day and evening. Terraced pitches
are provided for caravans, and there is a
separate field for tents. The park is close to
Weymouth and other coastal attractions.
A 20-acre site with 79 touring pitches.*
Leisure: 🏊 🎯 🎱 🏊 🎠 🖥 Facilities: 🛁
Services: 🔌🍴📶✕🦽 ⊙ 🎱 📷 🎰 🎲

70% Waterside Holiday Park (SY702822)
Bowleaze Cove DT3 6PP
☎ 01305 833103 📄 01305 832830
e-mail: info@watersideholidays.co.uk
website: www.watersideholidays.co.uk
*Dir: From Weymouth take A353 E for 2m, then right
fork to park in 0.5m*
★ 🚐 £11-£22 🚐 £11-£22 ▲ £11-£22
Open Mar-Oct Booking advisable
Last departure 10.00hrs ✂
*A complete leisure park with a full range of
activities and entertainment. The touring area
of this large complex is ideal for families of all
ages, offering individual grass pitches divided
by hedging. The beach is a short distance away,
and a frequent bus service connects this holiday
centre with Weymouth. A 35-acre site with 120
touring pitches and 475 statics.*
Leisure: 🏊 🎯 🎱 🏊 Facilities: 🎠⊙🎱✕🦽🍴🛁🎰
🎎 Services: 🔌🍴🍽🦽✕🦽➝∪🏊⊙🍴✕🎲🍴
Notes: No commercial vehicles 🎱 🎰 🎲 🎰 🎲

**65% NEW Weymouth Bay
Holiday Park (SY701829)**
Preston DT3 6BQ
☎ 01305 832271
website: www.havenholidays.com
★ 🚐 £7-£30 🚐 £7-£30 ▲ £7-£30
Open Mar-Oct Booking advisable Last arrival
22.00hrs Last departure 12.00hrs
*A large holiday complex on the coast at
Weymouth, offering a full programme of
activities and entertainment to keep the whole
family amused without leaving the park. Close
to other attractions such as Brownsea Island
and Poole, this popular park offers level grassy
pitches for tourers. A 58-acre site with 250
touring pitches.*
Leisure: 🏊 🎯 🎱 🏊 🎠 🖥 Facilities: 🛁
Services: 🔌🍴📶✕🦽 🎱 🎰 ⊙ 🎱 📷 🎰 🎲

BRONZE

▶ ▶ ▶ **65% Bagwell Farm Touring Park
(SY627816)**
Chickerell DT3 4EA ☎ 01305 782575 📄 01305 780554
e-mail: enquiries@bagwellfarm.co.uk
website: www.bagwellfarm.co.uk
*Dir: 4m W of Weymouth on B3157 (Abbotsbury-
Bridport), 500yds past Victoria Inn pub*
★ 🚐 £6-£11.50 🚐 £6-£11.50 ▲ £6-£11.50

Open all year Booking advisable Jul-Aug Last
arrival 21.30hrs Last departure 11.00hrs
*An idyllically-placed terraced site on a hillside and a
valley overlooking Chesil Beach. The park is well
equipped with mini-supermarket, children's play
area and pets corner, and a bar and grill serving
food in high season. A 14-acre site with 320 touring
pitches, 10 hardstandings.*
Wet suit shower, campers' shelter.
Leisure: 🎱 🎠 Facilities: 🚽🎠⊙🎱✕🦽🛁📷🎎🐾
Services: 🔌🍴🍽🦽✕🎱🦽➝∪🏊⊙🍴🎲🎱🎰🎲

▶ ▶ ▶ **62% Pebble Bank Caravan Park (SY659775)**
Camp Rd, Wyke Regis DT4 9HF ☎ 01305 774844
*Dir: From Weymouth take the Portland road. At last rdbt
turn right, then 1st left to Army Tent Camp. Site
opposite*
🚐 🚐 ▲

Open Etr-mid Oct bar open high season & wknds
only Booking advisable peak times Last arrival
21.00hrs Last departure 11.00hrs
*Overlooking Lyme Bay and Chesil Beach, this gently
sloping grass site is only 1.5m from Weymouth
town centre. A 4-acre site with 40 touring pitches
and 80 statics.*
Leisure: 🎠 Facilities: 🎠⊙🎱✕🦽🛁
Services: 🔌🍴🍽🦽⊙🎱➝∪🏊⊙🦽✕🎲🍴

► ► **61% NEW Sea Barn Farm** (SY625807)
Fleet DT3 4ED ☎ 01305 782218 ▤ 01305 775396
e-mail: fleetcamp@lineone.net
website: www.seabarnfarm.co.uk
*Dir: From Weymouth take B3157 towards Bridport for
3m. Turn left at mini rdbt towards Fleet, site 1m on left*
★ ▲ £8-£11
Open Etr-Oct (rs Etr-Apr & Oct Pool closed) Booking
advisable Spring & Aug BH & school hols Last
arrival 22.30hrs Last departure 12.00hrs
*A quiet site bordering the Fleet nature reserve, and
close to the Dorset coastal path. Optional use of the
clubhouse and swimming pool at West Fleet
Holiday Farm is available. Pitches are sheltered by
hedging, and there is plenty of space for games. A
12-acre site with 250 touring pitches and 1 static.
Cafe & fast food available from next door site*
Leisure: ⚞ ⋀ Facilities: ⬤⊙☀⬤⬤⬤ Services:
⬤⬤⬤⬤⬤⬤⬤ Notes: Non family groups by
arrangement, dogs must be kept on lead at all times

► ► **61% NEW West Fleet Holiday Farm**
(SY625811)
Fleet DT3 4EF ☎ 01305 782218 ▤ 01305 775396
e-mail: fleetcamp@lineone.net
website: www.seabarnfarm.co.uk
*Dir: From Weymouth take B3157 towards Bridport for
3m. Turn left at mini rdbt to Fleet, 1m on right*
★ ▲ £9-£12.50
Open Etr-Oct (rs Etr-Apr & Oct Pool closed) Booking
advisable BH's & school hols Last arrival 22.30hrs
Last departure 12.00hrs
*A spacious farm site with both level and sloping
pitches divided into paddocks, and screened with
hedging. Good views of the Dorset countryside, and
a relaxing site for a family holiday with its heated
outdoor pool and club house. A 12-acre site with
250 touring pitches.*
Leisure: ⚞⬤⋀⬤ Facilities: ⬤⊙☀⬤⬤⬤⬤⬤
Services: ⬤⬤⬤⬤⬤⬤⬤⬤⬤ Notes: Non-family
groups by arrangement, dogs must be kept on
leads at all times & have restricted camping areas

WIMBORNE MINSTER   Map 03 SZ09

PREMIER PARK

► ► ► ► ► **67% Merley Court
Touring Park** (SZ008984)
Merley BH21 3AA ☎ 01202 881488
▤ 01202 881484
e-mail: holidays@merley-court.co.uk
website: www.merley-court.co.uk
*Dir: Merley Court is clearly signed on A31
Wimborne by-pass & Poole junct rdbt*
★ ⬤ £8-£13 ⬤ £8-£13 ▲ £8-£13
Open Mar-7 Jan (rs low season pool closed &
bar, shop open limited hrs) Booking advisable
bank hols & Jun-Sep Last arrival 21.00hrs
Last departure 11.00hrs
contd.

WOOLSBRIDGE MANOR FARM CARAVAN PARK

THREE LEGGED CROSS WIMBORNE, DORSET BH21 6RA

Tel: (01202) 826369

Situated approx. 3½ miles from the New Forest
Market town of Ringwood – easy access to the
South Coast. 7 acres of level, semi sheltered, well
drained spacious pitches. Quiet country location
on a working farm – ideal and safe for families.
Childrens play area on site. Fishing, Moors Valley
Country Park, Golf Course, Pub/Restaurant all
close by. AA 3 pennant grading

Merley Court Touring Park
*A superb site in a quiet rural position on the
edge of Wimborne, with woodland on two sides
and good access roads. The park is well
landscaped, and offers generous individual
pitches in sheltered grassland. There are plenty
of amenities for all the family, including heated
outdoor pool, tennis court and adventure
playground. A 20-acre site with 160 touring
pitches, 42 hardstandings.*
Badminton, mini football, table tennis, crazy golf
Leisure: ⚞⬤⬤⋀⬤ Facilities: ⬤⬤⊙⬤☀⬤⬤
⬤⬤ Services: ⬤⬤⬤⬤⬤⬤⬤⬤⬤→∪⬤⬤⬤⬤⬤
Notes: No dogs 19 Jul-29 Aug ⬤⬤⬤⬤⬤

WILKSWORTH FARM CARAVAN PARK

Cranborne Road,
Wimborne BH21 4HW
Telephone: (01202) 885467 ▶▶▶▶▶
www.wilksworthfarmcaravanpark.co.uk

AA Best Campsite for South of England 1994

A family run park for families. A high standard awaits you at our peaceful secluded park, close to Kingston Lacy, Poole and Bournemouth. An attractively laid out touring and camping park, with heated outdoor swimming pool and tennis court. No statics to hire.
Completely re-furbished toilet block with family bathroom and disabled shower room.
New coffee shop and takeaway.

PREMIER PARK

▶ ▶ ▶ ▶ ▶ 71% **Wilksworth Farm Caravan Park (SU004018)**
Cranborne Rd BH21 4HW ☎ 01202 885467
🖹 01202 885467
e-mail: royandwendy@
wilksworthfarmcaravanpark.co.uk
website: www.wilksworthfarmcaravanpark.co.uk
Dir: 1m N of Wimborne on B3078
★ 🚐 £6-£14 🚍 £6-£14 ▲ £6-£14

Open Mar-Oct (rs Mar & Oct no shop or coffee shop) Booking advisable Spring bank hol & Jul-Aug Last arrival 21.00hrs Last departure 11.00hrs
A popular and attractive park set in the grounds of a listed house, peacefully placed in the heart of rural Dorset. The spacious site has much to offer visitors, including a heated swimming

contd.

pool, take-away and café, and games room.
An 11-acre site with 85 touring pitches, 20 hardstandings and 77 statics.
Paddling pool, volley ball, mini football pitch.
Leisure: ☀🏊⛱🝆 Facilities: 🏦⊙🥤✳🏧⛴🛢🚃🎏
🍴 Services: 🔌🚽🅱🔧🗑🚮🆃✗🚶→🅿◎🐾💈🎣

▶ ▶ ▶ 70% **Springfield Touring Park (SY987989)**
Candys Ln, Corfe Mullen BH21 3EF ☎ 01202 881719
Dir: Turn left off Wimborne by-pass (A31) western end, after Caravan Sales follow brown sign.
★ 🚐 £10-£11 🚍 £10-£11 ▲ £6-£11
Open mid Mar-Oct Booking advisable bank hols & Jul-Aug Last arrival 22.00hrs Last departure 11.00hrs
A small touring park with extensive views over the Stour Valley, with a quiet and friendly atmosphere. The park is maintained immaculately, and has a well-stocked shop. A 3.5-acre site with 45 touring pitches, 18 hardstandings.
Leisure: 🝆 Facilities: 🏦⊙🥤✳🏧🚶🛢
Services: 🔌🚽🅱🔧🗑🚮→🅿🐾💈🎣

WOOL
Map 03 SY88

▶ ▶ ▶ 66% **Whitemead Caravan Park (SY841869)**
East Burton Rd BH20 6HG ☎ 01929 462241
🖹 01929 462241
e-mail: whitemeadcp@aol.com
website: www.whitemeadcaravanpark.co.uk
Dir: Signed from A352 at level crossing on Wareham side of Wool
★ 🚐 £6.50-£10.70 🚍 £6.50-£10.70 ▲ £6.50-£10.70

Open mid Mar-Oct Booking advisable bank hols & mid Jul-Aug Last arrival 22.00hrs Last departure noon
A well laid-out site in the valley of the River Frome, close to the village and surrounded by woodland. A new reception, shop and games room have enhanced the facilities here, and the toilet block, though dated, is very clean and well maintained. A 5-acre site with 95 touring pitches.
Leisure: 🝆 Facilities: 🏦⊙🥤✳🚶🛢🚃🍴
Services: 🔌🚽🅱🔧🗑🚮🆃💈→🅿🐾🎣

DURHAM, COUNTY

BARNARD CASTLE   Map 12 NZ01

▶ ▶ ▶ ▶ **70% Camping & Caravanning Club Site**
(NZ025168)
Dockenflatts Ln, Lartington DL12 9DG
☎ 01833 630228 📠 024 7669 4886
website: www.campingandcaravanningclub.co.uk
*Dir: B6277 to Middleton-in-Teesdale. After 1m left turn
signed Raygill Riding Stables. Site 500mtrs on left*
★ 🚐 £12.30-£15.50 🚐 £12.30-£15.50 ▲ £12.30-£15.50
Open Mar-Oct Booking advisable Jan-Mar Last
arrival 21.00hrs Last departure noon
*A peaceful site surrounded by mature woodland
and meadowland, with first class facilities. This
immaculately-maintained park is set in the heart of
the countryside. Pitches are well laid out and
generous, on mainly level grass with some
hardstandings. Please see the advertisement on
page 10 for details of Club Members' benefits.
A 10-acre site with 90 touring pitches.*

Leisure: 🅐 **Facilities:** ฿⊙🎇⚬ᵭᵭᶜ⊓
Services: 🖪📧⊘→∪▶⚊&⊠ 💳📠 ▩📡 𝟃

▶ ▶ ▶ **67% Pecknell Farm Caravan Park**
(NZ028178)
Lartington DL12 9DF ☎ 01833 638357
*Dir: 1.5m from Barnard Castle. From A66 take B6277.
Site on right 1.5m from junction with A67*
★ 🚐 £6.50-£7.50 🚐 £6.50-£7.50 ▲ £6-£7
Open Mar-Oct Booking advisable Jul, Aug & Bank
hols Last arrival 21.00hrs Last departure flexible
*A small well laid out site on a working farm in
beautiful rural meadowland, with spacious marked
pitches on level ground. A 1.5-acre site with 10
touring pitches, 5 hardstandings.*
Facilities: ฿⊙🎇⚬ᶜ **Services:** 🖪⊟⊟→∪▶⊚◢⚊
Notes: No young groups in tents.
Showers are unisex.

BEAMISH   Map 12 NZ25

▶ ▶ ▶ **65% Bobby Shafto Caravan Park**
(NZ232545)
Cranberry Plantation DH9 0RY ☎ 0191 370 1776
*Dir: From A1693 signed Beamish to sign for Beamish
Museum. Take approach road, turn right immediately
before museum, left at pub. Site 1m on right*
★ 🚐 £10.50 🚐 £10.50 ▲ £7-£10.50
Open Mar-Oct Booking advisable school hols Last
arrival 23.00hrs Last departure 11.00hrs
*A tranquil rural park surrounded by trees, with very
clean and well-organised facilities. The suntrap
touring area has plenty of attractive hanging
baskets, and there is a clubhouse with bar, TV and
pool. A convenient location for visiting Beamish
Open Air Museum, Gateshead Metro shopping
complex, and the cities of Durham and Newcastle.
A 9-acre site with 20 touring pitches, 4
hardstandings and 35 statics.*

Leisure: ⚈🅐⊡ **Facilities:** ฿⊙🎇⚬ᶜ⊟ **Services:**
🖪🍺⊟⊟⊞→∪▶⚊⚊◢🖪 💳📠 ▩📡 𝟃

CASTLESIDE   Map 12 NZ04

▶ ▶ ▶ **54% Allensford Caravan & Camping Park**
(NZ083505)
DH8 9BA ☎ 01207 505572
*Dir: 2m SW of Consett, N on A68 for 1m, then right at
Allensford Bridge*
🚐 🚐 ▲
Open Mar-Oct Booking advisable Wknds & peak
periods Last arrival 22.00hrs Last departure noon
*Level parkland with mature trees, in hilly moor and
woodland country near the urban area adjacent to
River Derwent and A68. A 2-acre site with 40
touring pitches and 50 statics.*
Tourist information centre.

Leisure: 🅐 **Facilities:** ฿⊙🎇⚬ᵭᶜ⚊⊓
Services: 🖪📧⊟⊘→▶⚊◢ **Notes:** Dogs must be
kept on leads, no motorcycles 💳 📠 ▩📡 𝟃

DURHAM   Map 12 NZ24

▶ ▶ ▶ **66% NEW Strawberry Hill Farm**
(NZ337399)
Old Cassop DH6 4QA ☎ 0191 372 3457 & 372 2512
📠 0191 372 2512
e-mail: howarddunkerley@
strawberryhillfarm.freeserve.co.uk
*Dir: 2.5m from junct 6 A1M on eastbound carriageway
of A181*
★ 🚐 £10-£13.50 🚐 £10-£13.50 ▲ £8-£13.50

Open Apr-Sep Booking advisable Jun-Aug & bank
holidays Last arrival 22.00hrs Last departure
21.00hrs
*An attractive new park, planted with many young
trees and shrubs and well screened from the road.
The terraced pitches have superb panoramic views
across lovely wooded countryside. Good new toilet
and laundry facilities, and a useful base for visiting
Durham Castle and Cathedral, Beamish Museum
and the coast. A 6.5-acre site with 30 touring pitches
and 1 static.*
Facilities: ฿⊙🎇⚬ᶜᵭ⚊⚊⊓
Services: 🖪📧🍺⊘⊞→▶ 💳 📠 ▩📡 𝟃

The new Quality % Score ranges
from 50-80%. For full details of how
the score works see page 7

Facilities: 🛁 Bath ฿ Shower ⊙ Electric Shaver 🎇 Hairdryer ❋ Ice Pack Facility ᵭ Disabled Facilities ᶜ Public Telephone
⚊ Shop on Site or within 200yds 📧 Mobile Shop (calls at least 5 days a week) ⚊ BBQ Area ⊓ Picnic Area ⚊ Dog Exercise Area

ESSEX

BRENTWOOD   Map 05 TQ59

▶ ▶ ▶ **64% Camping & Caravanning Club Site (TQ577976)**
Warren Ln, Doddington, Kelvedon Hatch CM15 0JG
☎ 01277 372773
website: www.campingandcaravanningclub.co.uk
Dir: M25 junct 28. Brentwood 2m left on A128 signed Ongar. After 3m turn right
★ 🚐 £11.10-£14.50 🚐 £11.10-£14.50 ▲ £11.10-£14.50
Open Mar-Oct Booking advisable bank hols & Jul-Aug Last arrival 21.00hrs Last departure noon
A very pretty rural site with many separate areas amongst the trees, and a secluded field for campers. This peaceful site has older-style toilet facilities which are kept very clean, and smart laundry equipment. Please see the advertisement on page 10 for details of Club Members' benefits A 12-acre site with 90 touring pitches, 18 hardstandings.
Leisure: ⚠ Facilities: 🏪⊙🏴※🔥♿🐕🛝
Services: 🚱🗑🅿🖎🎛→🍴🧴🧺 🌐 🚾 🏧 🌉 🟢

COLCHESTER   Map 05 TL92

▶ ▶ ▶ ▶ **70% Colchester Camping Caravan Park (TL971252)**
Cymbeline Way, Lexden CO3 4AG ☎ 01206 545551
🖨 01206 710443
e-mail: enquiries@colchestercamping.co.uk
website: www.colchestercamping.co.uk
Dir: Follow tourist signs from A12, then A133 Colchester Central slip road
★ 🚐 £8-£13.50 🚐 £8-£13.50 ▲ £8-£13.50
Open all year Booking advisable public hols Last arrival 20.00hrs Last departure noon
A well-designed campsite on level grassland, on the west side of Colchester near the town centre. There is good provision for hardstandings, and the owner's attention to detail is reflected in the neatly trimmed grass and well-cut hedges. Toilet facilities are housed in a smart main block and in two older buildings. A 12-acre site with 168 touring pitches, 38 hardstandings.
Badminton court & putting green on site.
Leisure: ⚠ Facilities: 🏪⊙🏴※🔥♿🛝🎣🐕 Services: 🚱🗑🅿🖎🎛→∪🍴🔺🧺🧴 Notes: No commercial vehicles, no single sex groups 🌐 🚾 🏧 🌉 🟢

MERSEA ISLAND   Map 05 TM01

65% Waldegraves Holiday Park (TM033133)
West Mersea, Mersea Island
CO5 8SE ☎ 01206 382898 🖨 01206 385359
e-mail: holidays@waldegraves.co.uk
website: www.waldegraves.co.uk
Dir: B1025 to Mersea Island across the Strood. Left to East Mersea, 2nd turn on right, follow tourist signs to park
contd.

★ 🚐 £10-£20 🚐 £10-£20 ▲ £10-£20
Open Mar-Nov Booking advisable all times Last arrival 22.00hrs Last departure noon
A spacious and pleasant site, located between farmland and its own private beach on the Blackwater Estuary. Facilities include two freshwater fishing lakes, heated swimming pool, club, amusements, café and golf, and there is generally good provision for families. A 25-acre site with 60 touring pitches and 205 statics. Boating and fishing on site.
Leisure: 🏊🎣⚠🖵 Facilities: 🏪⊙🏴※🔥♿🛝🎣🐕
🏇 Services: 🚱🗑🅿🖎🎛🍴×🔺→🍴⊙🔺🧴
🌐 🚾 🏧 🌉 🟢

ROYDON   Map 05 TL41

▶ ▶ ▶ **62% Roydon Mill Leisure Park (TL403104)**
CM19 5EJ ☎ 01279 792777 🖨 01279 792695
e-mail: info@roydonpark.com
website: www.roydonpark.com
Dir: From A414 between Harlow & A10. Follow tourist signs to park. Situated at N end of High Street by railway station
🚐 🚐 ▲
Open all year Booking advisable bank hols & school holidays Last arrival 22.00hrs Last departure 22.00hrs 🚭
A busy complex with caravan sales and water sports. The attractive camping field is behind an old mill in a hedged meadow, and the caravan pitches have hardstandings. An 11-acre site with 120 touring pitches and 149 statics.
Large lake, waterski school
Leisure: ⚠ Facilities: 🏪⊙※🔥♿🛝🎣🐕
Services: 🚱🗑🅿🖎🎛×🔺→∪🍴🔺🧺🧴
Notes: No unaccompanied children, no single sex groups 🌐 🚾 🏧 🌉 🟢

GLOUCESTERSHIRE

CHELTENHAM   Map 03 SO92

▶ ▶ ▶ **65% Briarfields (SO899215)**
Gloucester Rd GL51 0SX ☎ 01242 235324 & 274440
Dir: From Cheltenham take A40 to Golden Valley rdbt, then 3rd turning left and follow signs
🚐 🚐 ▲
Open all year Booking advisable Last arrival 22.00hrs Last departure Noon
A well-designed level park with motel facilities adjacent. The park is well-positioned between Cheltenham and Gloucester, with easy access to the Cotswolds. A 6-acre site with 87 touring pitches.
Facilities: 🏪⊙🔥🐕🛝
Services: 🚱🗑🅿🖎→∪🍴🔺🧺🧴🔺🌐 🚾 🏧 🌉 🟢

England

CIRENCESTER — Map 04 SP00

▶ ▶ ▶ **66% Mayfield Touring Park (SP020055)**
Cheltenham Rd, Perrott's Brook GL7 7BH
☎ 01285 831301 ▤ 01285 831301
e-mail: jhutson@btclick.com
*Dir: From Cirencester bypass take Burford rd/A429 junct
exit, then via A417 to A435, direct access onto site on
left in 0.5m*
★ ⊞ £8.10-£10.60 ⊞ £7.30-£10.60 ▲ £7.30-£10.60

Open all year Booking advisable public hols & Jun-
Aug Last arrival 22.30hrs Last departure noon ⌘
*A gently sloping grassy park set in hilly
meadowland in the Cotswolds. Popular with
couples, and an ideal base for exploring Cirencester
and touring the surrounding Area of Outstanding
Natural Beauty. A 4-acre site with 72 touring pitches.
Dishwashing area.*

Facilities: ↖⊙♨☀↖🚽🎋

Services: ⊞🗑🛢🧹⊞Ⓣ→▶♨🔌💳💳💳🔋

Leisure: ⌇ Indoor swimming pool ⌇ Outdoor swimming pool ⦿ Tennis court ♠ Games room ⌂ Children's playground ∪ Stables
▶ 9/18 hole golf course ↳ Boats for hire ♟ Cinema ✦ Fishing ◉ Mini golf ⬙ Watersports ⬚ Separate TV room

GLOUCESTER   Map 03 SO81

► ► ► 66% Red Lion Camping & Caravan Park
(SO849258)
Wainlode Hill, Norton GL2 9LW ☎ 01452 730251
📠 01452 730251
website: www.redlioninn-
caravancampingpark.co.uk
Dir: Turn off A38 at Norton and follow road to river
🚐 £9-£11.50 🚐 £9-£11.50 ▲ £8-£11

Open all year Booking advisable Spring Bank
Holiday Last arrival 22.00hrs Last departure
11.00hrs
An attractive meadowland park, adjacent to a
traditional pub, with the River Severn just across a
country lane. This is an ideal touring and fishing
base. A 13-acre site with 60 touring pitches and 20
statics.
Freshwater fishing & private lake
Leisure: 🏊 **Facilities:** 🏪⊙🥪⚡🛁🛒🏧🚻
Services: 🔌🍴🏪🛒🚽🅿✕🛒➜♨▶🗑🍺💳📶🔲

SLIMBRIDGE   Map 03 SO70

► ► ► 64% Tudor Caravan & Camping
(SO728040)
Shepherds Patch GL2 7BP ☎ 01453 890483
& 07702 989940 📠 01453 890483
e-mail: info@tudorcaravanpark.co.uk
website: www.tudorcaravanpark.co.uk
Dir: From M5 junct 13 follow signs for WWT Wetlands
Wildlife Centre-Slimbridge. Site at rear of Tudor Arms
pub
★ 🚐 £8-£8.50 🚐 £8-£8.50 ▲ £5-£8.50

Open all year Booking advisable bank & school hols
Last arrival 21.00hrs Last departure 18.00hrs
An orchard-style park sheltered by mature trees and
shrubs, set in an attractive meadow beside a canal.
contd.

This tidy site offers both level grass and gravel
pitches complete with new electric hook-ups, and
there is a separate area for adults only. Slimbridge
Wetlands Centre is close by, and there is much
scope locally for bird-watching. An 8-acre site with
75 touring pitches, 30 hardstandings.
Facilities: 🏪⊙🥪⚡🛁🏧🚻🐕
Services: 🔌🍴🏪🛒🚽🅿✕➜♨🗑

SOUTH CERNEY   Map 04 SU09

72% Hoburne Cotswold
(SU055958)
Broadway Ln GL7 5UQ
☎ 01285 860216 📠 01285 868010
e-mail: enquiries@hoburne.com
website: www.hoburne.com
Dir: From Cirencester take A419 for 3m. Turn right at
sign for Cotswold Water Park and right again in 1m.
Site on left
★ 🚐 £10.50-£24.50 🚐 £10.50-£24.50
▲ £10.50-£24.50
Open Mar-Oct Booking advisable public hols &
high season Last arrival 21.00hrs Last departure
10.00hrs 🐕
A large holiday centre set out on level grassy
ground adjoining the Cotswold Water Park. This
well-equipped park is located close to several
lakes, each one adapted for either sailing, water
skiing, fishing or a nature reserve. There is also
a lake on site with a good stock of tench for
anglers to enjoy. Excellent menu and bar
facilities at the newly-opened Prickly Pike
pub/restaurant. A 70-acre site with 294 touring
pitches and 285 statics.
Crazy golf, fishing, pedal-boat hire, mini bowling
Leisure: 🎣 🏊🏌️🏊🏊 **Facilities:** 🏪⊙🥪🛁🛒
Services: 🔌🍴🏪🛒🚽🅿✕🛒➜♨▶🛒🗑🍺💳
🍺💳📶🔲

WINCHCOMBE   Map 04 SP02

► ► ► 70% Camping & Caravanning Club Site
(SP007324)
Brooklands Farm, Alderton GL20 8NX
☎ 01242 620259
website: www.campingandcaravanningclub.co.uk
Dir: Leave M5 junct 9 onto A46, keep straight on at rdbt
and onto B4077 signed Stow-on-the-Wold. Site 3m on
right
★ 🚐 £12.30-£15.50 🚐 £12.30-£15.50 ▲ £12.30-£15.50
Open 16 Mar-15 Jan Booking advisable Last arrival
21.00hrs Last departure 12.00hrs
A pleasant rural park with pitches spaced around
two attractive lakes offering good fishing, and the
benefit of a long season. This flower-filled park is in
an area of historic buildings and picturesque
villages between Cheltenham and Tewkesbury.
Please see advertisement on page 10 for details of
Club Members' benefit. A 20-acre site with 90
touring pitches, 42 hardstandings.
Fishing, pool table, table tennis
Leisure: 🎣🏊 **Facilities:** 🏪⊙🥪⚡🛁🛒🚻
Services: 🔌🛢🛒🚽➜▶🗑🛒🍺💳📶🔲

GREATER MANCHESTER

LITTLEBOROUGH — Map 07 SD91

► ► ► 66% **Hollingworth Lake Caravan Park** (SD943146)
Round House Farm, Rakewood Rd, Rakewood OL15 0AT ☎ 01706 378661 & 373919
Dir: From Littleborough or Milnrow (M62 junct 21), follow 'Hollingworth Lake Country Park' signs to Fishermans Inn. Take 'No Through Road' to Rakewood
★ ⊞ £8-£12 ⊞ £6-£12 ▲ £6-£12

Open all year Booking advisable bank hols Last arrival 20.00hrs Last departure 14.00hrs
A popular park adjacent to Hollingworth Lake, at the foot of the Pennines, within easy reach of many local attractions. Backpackers walking the Pennine Way are welcome at this family-run park, and there are also large rally fields. A 5-acre site with 50 touring pitches, 25 hardstandings and 53 statics. Pony Treking.
Facilities: ⋔⊙⚡☆₲⅃ঌ₼ **Services:** 🖵🖩🅰🔘🎛🎵
→ ∪ ▶ ♨ ↴ ✦ **Notes:** Dogs must be kept on leads

ROCHDALE — Map 07 SD81

► ► ► 68% **Gelder Wood Country Park** (SD852127)
Ashworth Rd, Heywood OL11 5UP
☎ 01706 364858 & 620300 ▤ 01706 364858
e-mail: gelderwood@aol.com
website: www.ukparks.co.uk/gelderwood
Dir: Signed midway off B6222 Bury/ Rochdale Road. Turn into Ashworth Rd, continue past the mill and uphill for 800yds, sight on right
⊞ ⊞ ▲
Open Mar-Oct Booking advisable Etr Last departure 11.00hrs
A very rural site in a peaceful private country park with excellent facilities. All pitches have extensive views of the moor, and this is a popular base for walkers and birdwatchers. The park is for adults only, and children are not allowed to visit. A 10-acre site with 34 touring pitches.
Facilities: ⋔⊙₲ঌ🐾 **Services:** 🖵🅰🎛→∪✦🔘🅱
Notes: Adults only

HAMPSHIRE

BRANSGORE — Map 04 SZ19

► ► ► 67% **Harrow Wood Farm Caravan Park** (SZ194978)
Harrow Wood Farm, Poplar Ln BH23 8JE
☎ 01425 672487 ▤ 01425 672487
e-mail: harrowwood@caravan-sites.co.uk
website: www.caravan-sites.co.uk
Dir: Leave village from S and take last turning on left past shops. Site at top of lane
★ ⊞ £9.75-£14 ⊞ £9.75-£14

Open Mar-6 Jan Booking advisable bank & school hols Last departure noon ⚘
A well laid out site in a pleasant rural position adjoining onto woodland and fields. Free on-site coarse fishing is available at this peaceful park. A 6-acre site with 60 touring pitches.
Washing up facilities.
Facilities: ⋔⊙⚡☆ঌ
Services: 🖵🖩🅰🎛→✦🅱🔘🚽🚿🎵
See advertisement on page 150

CRAWLEY — Map 04 SU43

► ► 65% **NEW Folly Farm Camping Park** (SU415337)
SO21 2PH ☎ 01962 776486
Dir: Midway between Winchester and Stockbridge on B3049. Site 0.75m past Rack & Manger Pub
⊞ £10 ⊞ £10 ▲ £10
Open all year Booking advisable Last arrival 22.30hrs
A small farm site set in rural mid-Hampshire between Stockbridge and Winchester, ideal for visiting the ancient capital of Wessex and the New Forest, and a short drive from the South coast. The clean facilities are located in farm outbuildings, and there is a small campers' kitchen. A 2.5-acre site with 30 touring pitches.
Leisure: ⚠ **Facilities:** ⋔⊙⚡☆ঌ₼🎪🐾
Services: 🖵→∪✦🅱 **Notes:** No children on farm area & dogs must be on a lead

England

HARROW WOOD FARM

Caravan Park

AA ▶▶▶ ETB ★★★★ BH&HPA Member

Open 1 March – 6 January

Bransgore, nr. Christchurch, Dorset BH23 8JE

Telephone: 01425 672487

Email: harrowwood@caravan–sites.co.uk

http://www.caravan–sites.co.uk

Situated in a pleasant village right on the edge of the New Forest, our six acre site offers the perfect centre from which to explore the surrounding area. Christchurch, Highcliffe and the market town of Ringwood are but a short drive away. In the village at Bransgore, there are a variety of shops to suit your everyday needs, all within walking distance.

FORDINGBRIDGE   **Map 04 SU11**

72% Sandy Balls Holiday Centre (SU167148)
Sandy Balls Estate Ltd, Godshill SP6 2JY ☎ 01425 653042 ▤ 01425 653067
e-mail: post@sandy-balls.co.uk
website: www.sandy-balls.co.uk
Dir: Leave M27 at junct 1 & take B3078/B3079, W 8m to Godshill. Park 0.25m after cattle grid
★ ⊞ £12.75-£24 ⊞ £12.75-£24 ▲ £11.25-£21

Open all year (rs Nov-Feb Activities & pitches reduced or closed) Booking advisable BH's, school hols & wknds Last arrival 21.00hrs Last departure 11.00hrs
A large, mostly wooded New Forest holiday complex with good provision of touring facilities on terraced, well laid-out fields. Pitches are fully serviced with shingle bases, and groups can be
contd.

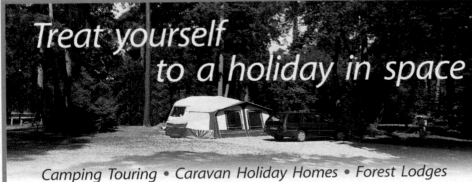

Treat yourself to a holiday in space

Camping Touring • Caravan Holiday Homes • Forest Lodges

Set within 120 spacious acres of idyllic New Forest woods and parkland, Sandy Balls Holiday Centre offers a unique blend of luxury accommodation, top class facilities, and sheer natural beauty.

For a FREE colour brochure call

01425 653 042

e.mail: post@sandy-balls.co.uk
www.sandy-balls.co.uk

OPEN ALL YEAR ROUND

Sandy Balls Holiday Centre, Godshill, Fordingbridge, Hants SP6 2JZ Fax: (01425) 653067

Services: Ⓣ Toilet Fluid ✕ Café/ Restaurant 🏛 Fast Food/Takeaway ➹ Baby Care ⊞ Electric Hook Up
🔳 Launderette ⊻ Licensed Bar ▆ Calor Gaz ⊘ Camping Gaz ⊞ Battery Charging

sited beside the river and away from the main site. Excellent sport, leisure and entertainment facilities for the whole family. A 120-acre site with 256 touring pitches, 256 hardstandings and 294 statics.

Jacuzzi, steam room, sauna, sunbeds, gym, orienteering

Leisure: ☜ ☝ ♠ ⚠ **Facilities:** ⊨ ⋒☉☜☼⚷♨☎☎⊞
☶ ☈ **Services:** ⚌⊡♈▯⬚⊞▯✕♁➡→∪⚏⚐

Notes: Groups by prior arrangement only
⬤ ☰☰☰ 〰 ⎙

FRITHAM   See **Landford (Wiltshire)**

HAMBLE   **Map 04 SU40**

▶ ▶ ▶ 61% **Riverside Park (SU481081)**
Satchell Ln SO31 4HR ☎ 023 80453220
▤ 023 80453611
e-mail: enquiries@riversideholidays.co.uk
website: www.riversideholidays.co.uk
Dir: M27 junct 8, follow signs to Hamble B3397. Turn left into Satchell Lane, 1m down lane on left
★ ⚏ £8.50-£11.50 ⚏ £8.50-£11.50 ▲ £8.50-£11.50

Open Mar-Oct (rs Nov-Feb open wknds & bank hols for statics only) Booking advisable BH's, peak season & boat show wk Last arrival 22.00hrs Last departure 11.00hrs
A small pleasant and peaceful site adjacent to the marina, and close to the pretty village of Hamble. The well-maintained toilet facilities are housed in portacabins. A 6-acre site with 60 touring pitches and 57 statics.
Bike hire, baby changing facilities
Facilities: ⋒☉☜☼⚷ **Services:** ⚌⊡▯⊞→∪▸⚏
⚒⚐⚏ **Notes:** No single sex groups ⬤ ☰☰☰ 〰 ⎙

MILFORD ON SEA   **Map 04 SZ29**

▶ ▶ ▶ ▶ 69% **Lytton Lawn Touring Park (SZ293937)**
Lymore Ln SO41 0TX ☎ 01590 648331
▤ 01590 645610
e-mail: holidays@shorefield.co.uk
website: www.shorefield.co.uk
Dir: From Lymington A337 to Christchurch for 2.5m to Everton. Left onto B3058 to Milford-on-Sea. After 0.25m left onto Lymore Lane
⚏ £7.50-£28 ⚏ £7.50-£28 ▲ £7.50-£28

contd.

Beautiful views over the marina and River Hamble
Serviced touring pitches
Free showers
Excellent sailing, walking, fishing and horse riding nearby
Luxurious self catering accommodation
Launderette
Lodges available all year including Xmas breaks

Satchell Lane, Hamble, Hants SO31 4HR
Ring now for your free colour brochure
023 80453220
enquiries@riversideholidays.co.uk

Lytton Lawn Touring Park
Open Feb-2 Jan Booking advisable at all times Last arrival 22.00hrs Last departure 10.00hrs
A pleasant, well-run park with good facilities, located near the coast. Premier pitches on hardstanding come with water, electricity and good screening, and standard pitches are on gently-sloping grass. Good toilet facilities, and continual improvement is being made to the park. A 5-acre site with 136 touring pitches, 48 hardstandings. Dishwashing & free use of local leisure club
Leisure: ♠ ⚠ **Facilities:** ⋒☉☜☼⚷♨⚏☈
Services: ⚌⊡▯⬚⊞→∪▸⚐⚏ **Notes:** Family park only, no single sex groups, no under 25s unless in family group ⬤ ☰☰☰ 〰 ⎙

See advertisement on page 152

Leisure: ☜ Indoor swimming pool ☝ Outdoor swimming pool ☜ Tennis court ♠ Games room ⚠ Children's playground ∪ Stables
▸ 9/18 hole golf course ⚒ Boats for hire ☷ Cinema ⚐ Fishing ◎ Mini golf ⚏ Watersports ▱ Separate TV room

England

South Coast
and New Forest

With three high quality destinations to choose from, Shorefield Holidays offers you the best of both worlds in touring locations.

All three of our touring parks are set in parkland in the beautiful New Forest / South Coast area. Both Oakdene Forest Park and Forest Edge Touring Park at St Leonards near Ringwood offer easy access to the Avon Forest, while Lytton Lawn Touring Park at Milford on Sea is just over a mile from the beach. There are comprehensive facilities including entertainment and Free Leisure Club membership. For full details ask for our brochure or browse on-line.

For further details telephone:

01590 648331

e-mail: holidays@shorefield.co.uk

RALLIES WELCOME AT ALL SITES

SHOREFIELD
HOLIDAYS LIMITED

Lytton Lawn Touring Park
Lymore Lane, Milford on Sea, Hants SO41 0TX
Oakdene Forest Park
St. Leonards, Ringwood, Hants BH24 2RZ
Forest Edge Touring Park
St. Leonards, Ringwood, Hants BH24 2SD

www.shorefield.co.uk   Ref. AA

NEW MILTON — Map 04 SZ29

71% Hoburne Bashley (SZ245972)
Sway Rd BH25 5QR
☎ 01425 612340 & 632732
e-mail: enquiries@hoburne.com
website: www.hoburne.com
Dir: 1m N of New Milton on B3055
★ 🚐 £10-£30 🚐 £10-£30
Open Mar-Oct Booking advisable Last arrival
22.00hrs Last departure 10.00hrs
A large, well-organised park bordered by woodland and a shrubbery and set in 100 acres with indoor and outdoor swimming pools, clubhouse and entertainment. There is plenty to occupy the whole family. The new multi-service pitches are an excellent addition to the touring area, and these are well screened by discreet planting. A 100-acre site with 307 touring pitches and 425 statics.
Crazy golf, 9 hole par 3, petanque, indoor play area

Leisure: ⚑ ⚑ ⚑ ⚑ ⚑ **Facilities:** ℝ ⊙ ⚑ & ℂ 🐕
Services: 🚐 ▤ ⚑ ▤ ⌀ ▥ → ∪ ▶ ⊙ ✱ ⚑ 🗘 ▤ ▥ ▤

OWER — Map 04 SU31

▶ ▶ ▶ **65% Green Pastures Farm (SU321158)**
SO51 6AJ ☎ 023 80814444
e-mail: enquiries@greenpasturesfarm.com
website: www.greenpasturesfarm.com
Dir: M27 junct 2. Follow Salisbury signs for 0.5m. Then follow brown tourist signs for Green Pastures. Also signed from A36 & A3090 at Ower
🚐 £12 🚐 £12 ⚑ £12
Open 15 Mar-Oct Booking advisable BH's & peak periods Last departure noon
A pleasant site on a working farm, with good screening of trees and shrubs around the perimeter. The touring area is divided by a border of shrubs and colourful foxgloves, and this peaceful location is close to the M27 and New Forest. A 5-acre site with 45 touring pitches, 2 hardstandings.

Facilities: ℝ ⊙ ✱ & ℂ 🐕 **Services:** 🚐 ⚑ ⌀ ▤ → ▶ ⚑

RINGWOOD — Map 04 SU10

▶ ▶ ▶ **64%** *Woolsbridge Manor Farm Caravan Park (SZ103050)*
Three Legged Cross BH21 6RA ☎ 01202 826369
▤ 01202 813172
Dir: 2m off A31, 3m W of Ringwood. From Three Legged Cross continue S to Woolsbridge. Site 1.75m on left
🚐 🚐 ⚑
Open Etr-Oct Booking advisable bank hols & Aug Last arrival 22.00hrs Last departure 13.00hrs
A small farm site with spacious pitches on a level field. This quiet site is an excellent central base for touring the New Forest, Salisbury and the South coast, and is close to Moors Valley Country Park for outdoor family activities. A 6.75-acre site with 60 touring pitches.

contd.

Woolsbridge Manor Farm Caravan Park

Leisure: ⚑ **Facilities:** ℝ ⊙ ⚑ ✱ & ℂ ℒ 🎋 🐕
Services: 🚐 ⚑ ⌀ ▤ ▤ → ∪ ▶ ⚑ ▤

See advertisement on page 145

ROMSEY — Map 04 SU32

▶ ▶ ▶ **67% Hill Farm Caravan Park (SU287238)**
Branches Ln, Sherfield English SO51 6FH
☎ 01794 340402 ▤ 01794 342358
e-mail: gjb@hillfarmpark.com
website: www.hillfarmpark.com
Dir: Signed off A27 Salisbury to Romsey road in Sherfield English, 4m NW of Romsey and M27 junct 2
★ 🚐 £9-£14 🚐 £9-£14 ⚑ £8-£11
Open Mar-Oct Booking advisable Last arrival
20.00hrs Last departure 11.30hrs

A small, well sheltered site, peacefully located amidst mature trees and fields. A new toilet block has provided quality unisex shower facilities, and the far-sighted owners have further plans to refurbish the second toilet block, and build a new shop.
A 10.5-acre site with 70 touring pitches, 10 hardstandings and 6 statics.
9 hole par 3 pitch 'n' putt.

Leisure: ⚑ **Facilities:** ℝ ⊙ ✱ & ℂ ℒ 🎋 🐕
Services: 🚐 ▤ ⚑ ⌀ ▤ ▤ → ▶ ⚑ ⚑ ⚑ **Notes:** Minimal noise after 11pm, one unit per pitch.

WARSASH — Map 04 SU40

▶ ▶ ▶ **64% Dibles Park (SU505060)**
Dibles Rd SO31 9SA ☎ 01489 575232
Dir: From M27 junct 8, turn left onto A27 to Fareham. At 1st rdbt 3rd exit, at next rdbt 2nd exit. Straight to bottom of road, turn left at Warwash Motors, after 1m turn right and take 2nd right
★ 🚐 £7-£10 🚐 £7-£10 ⚑ fr £6

contd.

Open all year Booking advisable bank hols & Jul-Aug Last arrival 20.30hrs Last departure 13.00hrs
A small grassy touring area with hardstandings, adjacent to a private residential park. This site continues to improve, and there is always a warm welcome for visitors. Within easy reach of the River Hamble and the Solent. A 0.75-acre site with 14 touring pitches and 46 statics.

Facilities: ➤⊙➤✱ ✆ 🅗 **Services:** ☎🛢🅔🅣→∪⤳🛢⚡

HEREFORDSHIRE

LITTLE TARRINGTON   Map 03 SO64

▶ ▶ ▶ **69% The Millpond (SO625410)**
HR1 4JA ☎ 01432 890243 🖹 01432 890243
e-mail: enquiries@millpond.co.uk
website: www.millpond.co.uk
Dir: 300yds off A438 on Ledbury side of Tarrington
★ 🚐 £8-£9 🚐 £8-£9 ▲ £8-£9
Open Mar-Oct Booking advisable peak periods Last arrival 20.30hrs Last departure 11.00hrs
A spacious grassy park set beside a fishing lake in a peaceful location. Recently-planted trees and shrubs will help to divide and screen the park, and the modern toilet block provides good facilities. A 2-acre site with 30 touring pitches.
3 acre coarse fishing lake.

Facilities: ➤⊙➤✱✆✆🐾 **Services:** ☎🅔→⤳

Notes: Dogs must be kept on lead at all times

MUCH COWARNE   Map 03 SO64

▶ **72% NEW Starcroft (SO627482)**
HR7 4JB ☎ 01432 820277
Dir: From Hereford to Bromyard on A465. At Burly Gate rdbt straight over towards Burly Gate Post Office. Branch to right at post office towards Bishops Frome. Camp site approx 1.5m
★ 🚐 £5-£7 🚐 £5-£7 ▲ fr £5

Open all year Booking advisable Last arrival 22.00hrs Last departure 12.00hrs
A peaceful site in attractive countryside offering superb views. All facilities are well cared for and, as the site is limited to five caravans and 15 tents, advance booking is advised. A 0.75-acre site with 5 touring pitches.
Facilities: ➤✱ **Services:** ☎→⚡ **Notes:** Toilets & showers are unisex. Dogs must be kept on a lead at all times

PETERCHURCH   Map 03 SO33

▶ ▶ ▶ ▶ **77% Poston Mill Caravan & Camping Park (SO355373)**
HR2 0SF ☎ 01981 550225 🖹 01981 550885
e-mail: enquiries@poston-mill.co.uk
website: www.ukparks.co.uk/postonmill
Dir: 11m W of Hereford on B4348
★ 🚐 £8-£12 🚐 £8-£12 ▲ £5-£12
Open all year (rs Nov-Mar Limited toilet facilities) Booking advisable bank & summer hols Last departure noon
Delightfully set in the Golden Valley and surrounded by hills, with beautiful views. This quality park has excellent facilities including sporting amenities which are to one side of the site. There is also an adjoining restaurant, The Mill, and there is a pleasant walk alongside the River Dore. A 33-acre site with 93 touring pitches, 63 hardstandings and 83 statics.

Leisure: ⚲ ♠ ⚏ 🎱 **Facilities:** ➤⊙➤✱♿✆⚡🅔
🅗 ⛱ 🐾 **Services:** ☎🛢🍴🛢∅🅔🅣✖🖨⤳→▶⤳
💳 ▦ ▦ ▦ 🖐

STANFORD BISHOP   Map 03 SO65

▶ ▶ ▶ **69% Boyce Caravan Park (SO692528)**
WR6 5UB ☎ 01886 884248
Dir: From B4220 Malvern road take sharp turn opposite Herefordshire House pub, then right after 0.25m
★ 🚐 £7.50-£10.50 🚐 £7.50-£10.50 ▲ £7.50-£10.50

Open Feb-Dec (rs Feb-Mar & Oct-Dec) Booking advisable bank hols & Jun-Aug Last arrival 18.00hrs Last departure noon
A friendly and peaceful park with access allowed onto the 100 acres of farmland. Coarse fishing is also available in the grounds, and there are extensive views over the Malvern and Suckley Hills. A 10-acre site with 25 touring pitches and 80 statics.
Course fishing available

Leisure: ⚏ **Facilities:** ➤⊙➤✱♿✆🐾
Services: ☎🛢🛢∅🅔→⤳⚡

Notes: Certain dog breeds not accepted

SYMONDS YAT (WEST)   Map 03 SO51

▶ ▶ **71% Doward Park Camp Site (SO539167)**
Great Doward HR9 6BP ☎ 01600 890438
website: www.doward-park.co.uk
Dir: 2m from A40 between Ross-on-Wye & Monmouth. Take Symonds Yat (West) turn, then Crockers Ash, follow signs to site
★ 🚐 £9-£11.50 ▲ £9-£9.50

contd.

Open Etr-mid Oct (rs wk before Etr Bookings only)
Booking advisable wknds, Jul & Aug Last arrival
21.00hrs Last departure noon
*A very attractive site in woodland on the hillside
above the River Wye, run by friendly owners. The
timber-built toilet block is well appointed. Light
refreshments are available on site. A 1.5-acre site
with 40 touring pitches.*

Facilities: ♪⊙✳ & ⛄ 🏕   **Services:** 🔌→🍴🍼♨🚽🛒

Notes: No bike riding, no fires, quiet after 10pm,
dogs must be kept on leads

HERTFORDSHIRE

HERTFORD   Map 04 TL31

▶ ▶ ▶ ▶ **71% Camping & Caravanning Club Site**
(TL334113)
Mangrove Rd SG13 8QF ☎ 01992 586696
website: www.campingandcaravanningclub.co.uk
Dir: Follow A414 Hertford signs. Straight over rdbt.
After 200yds left signed Balls Park. Left at T-junct into
Mangrove Rd. Site on left
★ 🚐 £12.30-£15.50 🚙 £12.30-£15.50 ▲ £12.30-£15.50
Open Mar-Oct Booking advisable Jul-Aug & BH's *A
spacious, well-landscaped club site in a rural setting
one mile south of Hertford, with immaculate
modern toilet facilities. There are several hedged
areas with good provision of hardstandings, and a
cosy camping section in an old orchard. All kinds of
wildlife flourish around the lake. Please see
advertisement on page 10 for details of Club
Members' benefits. A 32-acre site with 250 touring
pitches, 34 hardstandings.*
Area for ball games

Leisure: 🛝 **Facilities:** ♪⊙🍴✳& ⛄🏕
Services: 🔌📧💧🍽→🍴🍼🛒♨🚽🔆💳🚾 🔅

HODDESDON   Map 05 TL30

▶ ▶ ▶ **66% Lee Valley Caravan Park (TL383082)**
Dobbs Weir, Essex Rd EN11 0AS ☎ 01992 462090
📠 01992 462090
website: www.leevalleypark.org.uk
Dir: Leave A10 at Hoddesdon junct, follow signs for
Dobbs Weir. Park 1m on right
★ 🚐 fr £10.88 🚙 fr £10.88 ▲ fr £10.88
Open Etr-Oct Booking advisable public hols Last
arrival 21.30hrs Last departure noon
*Neat, well kept site in a peaceful field surrounded
by hedges and tall trees, with a good play area and
local walks. An 8-acre site with 100 touring pitches
and 100 statics.*

Leisure: 🛝 **Facilities:** ♪⊙🍴✳& ⛄🏕
Services: 🔌📧💧🍽→🍼♨🍴🛒♨🚾 🔅

WALTHAM CROSS   Map 05 TL30

▶ ▶ **60% Camping & Caravanning Club Site**
(TL344005)
Theobalds Park, Bulls Cross Ride EN7 5HS
☎ 01992 620604
website: www.campingandcaravanningclub.co.uk
Dir: M25 junct 25. A10 towards London keep in right
lane. Right at 1st lights. Right at T-junct, right behind
dog kennels. Site towards top of lane on right   *contd.*

★ 🚐 £10.20-£12.90 🚙 £10.20-£12.90 ▲ £10.20-£12.90
Open Mar-Oct Booking advisable Jul-Aug & BH's
Last arrival 21.00hrs Last departure noon
*Lovely open site surrounded by mature trees, and
set in parkland at Theobalds Hall. Please see the
advertisement on page 10 for details of Club
Members' benefits. A 14-acre site with 90 touring
pitches.*

Leisure: 🎱 🛝 **Facilities:** ♪⊙🍴✳⛄🏕
Services: 🔌📧💧🍽→🍼🍴♨🛒♨🔆💳🚾 🔅

KENT

ASHFORD   Map 05 TR04

▶ ▶ ▶ **76% Broad Hembury Holiday**
Park (TR009387)
Steeds Ln, Kingsnorth TN26 1NQ
☎ 01233 620859 📠 01233 620918
e-mail: holidays@broadhembury.co.uk
website: www.broadhembury.co.uk
Dir: From M20 junct 10 take A2070 for 3m. Left at 2nd
rdbt signed Kingsnorth, then left at 2nd x-roads in
village
★ 🚐 £10-£14 🚙 £10-£14 ▲ £10-£14
Open all year Booking advisable Jul-Aug Last
arrival 23.00hrs Last departure noon
*Well-run and maintained small family park
surrounded by open pasture and neatly landscaped,
with pitches sheltered by mature hedges. Some
super pitches have proved a popular addition, and
there is a well-equipped campers' kitchen. A 7-acre
site with 60 touring pitches and 25 statics.*
Football, volleyball & kitchen appliances

Leisure: 🎱 🛝 🛝 **Facilities:** ♪⊙🍴✳⛄& ⛄🏕
Services: 🔌📧💧🍽→🍼🍴🍽♨🛒♨🔆💳 🔅

▶ ▶ **62% Dunn Street Farm (TR992480)**
Westwell TN25 4NJ ☎ 01233 712537
Dir: From M20 junct 9 follow A20 W towards Hothfield,
at junct 1m after end of dual c/way turn right. Site 0.5m
N of village on North Downs Way
🚐 £7-£10 🚙 £7-£10 ▲ £7-£10
Open Apr-Oct Booking advisable BH's, Jul & Aug
Last arrival anytime Last departure anytime
*Peaceful, partly-sloping grassy site situated behind
the farm and beside the Pilgrims Way on top of the
North Downs, just north of Westwell. Simple, clean
sanitary facilities housed in a converted farm
building. Well placed for visiting Canterbury and the
Weald of Kent. A 3-acre site with 30 touring pitches.*

Facilities: ♪⊙✳🖫🎣 **Services:** 🔌💧🚽🚾→🍼🛒

Notes: Dogs must be kept on leads

BIDDENDEN   Map 05 TQ83

▶ ▶ ▶ **60% Woodlands Park (TQ867372)**
Tenterden Rd TN27 8BT ☎ 01580 291216
📠 01580 291216
e-mail: woodlandsp@aol.com
Dir: Turn off A28 onto A262. Site 1.5m on right
🚐 🚙 ▲
Open Mar-Oct (rs Mar-Apr weather permitting)
Booking advisable bank hols & Jul-Aug Last arrival
anytime Last departure anytime   *contd.*

Leisure: 🎣 Indoor swimming pool 🎣 Outdoor swimming pool 🎾 Tennis court 🎱 Games room 🛝 Children's playground ♨ Stables
▶ 9/18 hole golf course 🚣 Boats for hire 🎬 Cinema 🎣 Fishing ◎ Mini golf 💧 Watersports 🖵 Separate TV room

Woodlands Park

A site of level grassland bordered by hedges and trees, with two ponds and a smart and well-maintained modern toilet block. Ideal centre for Kent, Sussex and Channel ports. A 9-acre site with 200 touring pitches and 205 statics.
Camping accessory sales & small site shop.

Leisure: ⚑ **Facilities:** ⊓⊙ॡ✳&८ॾ⌗

Services: ◪◫ॢ╕◿ⒽⓉ→∪⌐◉◞

BIRCHINGTON   Map 05 TR36

▶ ▶ ▶ 69% **Quex Caravan Park**
(TR321685)
Park Rd CT7 0BL ☎ 01843 841273
e-mail: info@keatfarm.co.uk
website: www.keatfarm.co.uk
Dir: From Birchington (A28) turn SE into Park Road to site in 1m
★ ◪ £10-£12 ◪ £10-£12
Open Mar-Nov Booking advisable BH's Last arrival anytime Last departure noon
A small parkland site in a quiet and secluded spot, with a very clean toilet block housed in a log cabin. This picturesque site is just one mile from the village of Birchington, and Ramsgate, Margate and Broadstairs are all within easy reach. An 11-acre site with 48 touring pitches and 145 statics.

Leisure: ⚑ **Facilities:** ⊓⊙ॡ✳८ॾ⌗

Services: ◪◫◱◿ⒽⓉ→∪⌐✛ॾ◞ ⊕ ▨ ▩ 瑣

▶ ▶ ▶ 63% **Two Chimneys Caravan Park**
(TR320684)
Shottendane Rd CT7 0HD ☎ 01843 841068 & 843157
🖨 01843 848099 & 843157
e-mail: info@twochimneys.co.uk
website: www.twochimneys.co.uk
Dir: From A28 at Birchington turn SE into Park Road. In 1m turn right at T junct, and site in 100yds on left
★ ◪ £10.50-£17.50 ◪ £10.50-£17.50 ▲ £10.50-£17.50

contd.

Open Mar-Oct (rs Mar-May & Sep-Oct shop, bar, pool & takeaway restricted) Booking advisable bank & school hols Last arrival 23.00hrs Last departure noon
A good, well-managed site with two swimming pools and a fully-licensed clubhouse. Other facilities include a sauna, solarium and spa bath, and there is a tennis court and children's play areas. A 9-acre site with 75 touring pitches and 65 statics.
Sauna, spa bath, amusement arcade.

Leisure: ⌇ ॡ ⚑ **Facilities:** ⊓⊙ॡ✳&८ॾ **Services:**
◪◫ॢ◱◿ⒽⓉ♨→∪⌐◉♨✛✿◞ ⊕ ▨ ▩ 瑣

CANTERBURY   Map 05 TR15

▶ ▶ ▶ 72% **Camping & Caravanning Club Site**
(TR172577)
Bekesbourne Ln CT3 4AB ☎ 01227 463216
🖨 024 7669 4886
website: www.campingandcaravanningclub.co.uk
Dir: From Canterbury follow A257 signs (Sandwich), turn right opposite golf course
★ ◪ £12.30-£15.50 ◪ £12.30-£15.50 ▲ £12.30-£15.50
Open all year Booking advisable bank hols & peak periods Last arrival 21.00hrs Last departure noon
An attractive tree-screened site in pleasant rural surroundings yet within walking distance of the city centre. The park is well landscaped, and offers very smart toilet facilities in one block, with another older but well-kept building housing further facilities. Please see the advertisement on page 10 for details of Club Members' benefits. A 20-acre site with 200 touring pitches.

Leisure: ⚑ **Facilities:** ⊓⊙ॡ✳&८ॾ⌗

Services: ◪◫◿ⒽⓉ→⌐✿⊕ ▨ ▩ 瑣

▶ ▶ ▶ 65% **Yew Tree Park (TR137507)**
Stone St, Petham CT4 5PL ☎ 01227 700306
🖨 01227 700306
e-mail: info@yewtreepark.com
website: www.yewtreepark.com
Dir: 5m S of Canterbury on B2068
★ ◪ £8.50-£13 ◪ £8-£12.50 ▲ £8-£12.50
Open Mar-Oct Booking advisable Jul, Aug & Bank Hols Last arrival 21.00hrs Last departure noon 🐕
A very attractive park set in rolling countryside with views across Chatham Downs. An excellent base for visiting Canterbury, with well-refurbished toilet facilities, a new family/disabled room, and cosy tent pitches that make the most of the view. A 4.5-acre site with 45 touring pitches and 13 statics.

Leisure: ⚑ **Facilities:** ⊓⊙ॡ✳&८ॾ

Services: ◪◫◱◿✛→∪⊕ ▨ ▩ 瑣

▶ ▶ 62% **Ashfield Farm (TR138508)**
Waddenhall, Petham CT4 5PX ☎ 01227 700624
e-mail: mpatterson@ashfieldfarm.freeserve.co.uk
Dir: 7m S of Canterbury on B2068
★ ◪ £9-£12 ◪ £9-£12 ▲ fr £9
Open Apr-Oct Booking advisable Jul & Aug Last arrival anytime Last departure noon
Small rural site with simple facilities and well-drained pitches, set in beautiful countryside and enjoying lovely open views. Located south of

contd.

Canterbury, and with very security-conscious owners. A 4.5-acre site with 20 touring pitches and 1 static.

Ashfield Farm

Mini golf, short term kennelling.

Facilities: ⚡ ☉ ✳ ⚒ ☎ 🅃 **Services:** ⚡ 🛢 ⌀ ⊞ 🅃 → ∪ ▶ 🛒

CHATHAM　　　　　　　　Map 05 TQ76

▶ ▶ **64% Woolmans Wood Caravan Park (TQ746638)**
Bridgewood ME5 9SB ☎ 01634 867685 & 07957 765839 ▤ 01634 867685
e-mail: woolmans.wood@currantbun.com
website: www.woolmans-wood.co.uk
Dir: From M2 junct 3 take A229 & B2097 for 0.75m, 3.25m S of Rochester
★ 🚐 £10-£13 🚐 £10-£13 Å £9-£10
Open all year Booking advisable Last arrival 22.00hrs Last departure 14.00hrs
Small site alongside the city airport and close to the London-Dover road with clean and well maintained facilities, and a refurbished toilet block. A 5-acre site with 60 touring pitches, 10 hardstandings.
Caravan servicing, washing & valeting.

Facilities: ⚡ ☉ 🍳 ✳ ⚒ 🛒 🅰 ☎
Services: ⚡ 🗄 🛢 ⌀ ⊞ 🅃 → ∪ ▶ ✚ 🛒 ⌁

DOVER　　　　　　　　　　See **Martin Mill**

FAVERSHAM　　　　　　　　Map 05 TR06

▶ ▶ **69% Painters Farm Caravan & Camping Site (TQ990591)**
Painters Forstal ME13 0EG ☎ 01795 532995
Dir: Leave A2 at Faversham, signs to Painters Forstal & Eastling. 1.5 m down 'No through road' at Forstal
★ 🚐 £7-£9 🚐 £7-£9 Å £7-£9
Open Mar-Oct Booking advisable bank hols Last arrival 23.59hrs
Delightful simple farm site in immaculately kept cherry orchard, with spotless toilets in converted farm buildings. A 3-acre site with 50 touring pitches.
Facilities: ⚡ ☉ ✳ 🛢 ☎
Services: ⚡ 🛢 ⌀ ⊞ 🅃 → ∪ ▶ ✚ 🛒

> Not all campsites accept pets.
> Check when booking

FOLKESTONE　　　　　　　Map 05 TR23

▶ ▶ ▶ **73% Camping & Caravanning Club Site (TR246376)**
The Warren CT19 6PT ☎ 01303 255093
website: www.campingandcaravanningclub.co.uk
Dir: From A2 or A20 join A260 & follow signs to Country Park. At rdbt E into Hill Rd (dual carriageway), at x-rds ahead into Wear Bay Rd (signed Martello Tower) and 2nd left to site
★ 🚐 £11.10-£14.50 Å £11.10-£14.50
Open Mar-Oct Booking advisable bank hols & peak periods Last arrival 21.00hrs Last departure noon
This site commands marvellous views across the Strait of Dover and is well located for the Channel ports. It nestles on the side of the cliff and is tiered in some areas. Please see the advertisement on page 10 for details of Club Members' benefits. A 4-acre site with 80 touring pitches.
Facilities: ⚡ ☉ ✳ ⚒ 🛒
Services: ⚡ 🛢 ⌀ ⊞ → ▶ ✚ 🍴 🎪 🚮 🔲 ▦ ⌁

▶ ▶ ▶ **68% Little Satmar Holiday Park (TR260390)**
Winehouse Ln, Capel Le Ferne CT18 7JF
☎ 01303 251188 ▤ 01303 251188
e-mail: info@keatfarm.co.uk
website: www.keatfarm.co.uk/touringparks/littlesatmar.htm
Dir: Signposted off B2011
★ 🚐 £10-£12 🚐 £10-£12 Å £10-£12
Open Mar-Oct Booking advisable bank hols & Jul-Aug Last arrival 23.00hrs Last departure 14.00hrs
A quiet, well-screened site well away from the road and statics, with clean and tidy facilities. A useful base for visiting Dover and Folkestone, and just a short walk from cliff paths with their views of the Channel, and sandy beaches below. A 5-acre site with 60 touring pitches and 80 statics.
Leisure: ⚓ ⚠ **Facilities:** ⚡ ☉ 🍳 ✳ ⚒ 🛒
Services: ⚡ 🗄 🛢 ⌀ ⊞ 🅃 → ∪ ▶ ✚ 🍴 ⌀ 🔲 ▦ ⌁

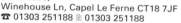

▶ ▶ **61% Little Switzerland Camping & Caravan Site (TR248380)**
Wear Bay Rd CT19 6PS ☎ 01303 252168
e-mail: littleswitzerland@lineone.net
website: www.caravancampingsites.co.uk/kentlittleswitzerland
Dir: Signposted from A20 E of Folkestone. Approaching from A259 or B2011 on E outskirts of Folkestone, follow signs for Wear Bay and Martello Tower, then tourist sign to site
★ 🚐 £8-£14 🚐 £8-£14 Å £2.25-£4.50
Open Mar-Oct Booking advisable from Mar Last arrival mdnt Last departure noon
Set on a narrow plateau below the 'white cliffs', this unusual site enjoys fine views across Wear Bay and the Strait of Dover. A licensed café with an alfresco area is popular. The toilet facilities are unsuitable for the disabled. A 3-acre site with 32 touring pitches and 13 statics.
Facilities: ⚡ ☉ ✳ ⚒ 🛒 🔲 🛢 ☎
Services: ⚡ 🗄 🍳 🛢 ⌀ ⊞ ✖ ⬆ → ∪ ▶ ⌀ △ ✚ 🛒

Facilities: 🛁 Bath　⚡ Shower　☉ Electric Shaver　🍳 Hairdryer　✳ Ice Pack Facility　⚒ Disabled Facilities　☎ Public Telephone
🛒 Shop on Site or within 200yds　🔲 Mobile Shop (calls at least 5 days a week)　🛢 BBQ Area　🎋 Picnic Area　☎ Dog Exercise Area

England

HARRIETSHAM   Map 05 TQ85

▶ ▶ ▶ ▶ **67% Hogbarn Caravan Park (TQ885550)**
Hogbarn Ln, Stede Hill ME17 1NZ ☎ 01622 859648
🖷 01622 859912
e-mail: mail@hogbarn.fsnet.co.uk
*Dir: From A20 at Harrietsham follow tourist caravan
sign along minor road & site 1.5m N of village*
🚐 🚛 Å
Open Apr-Oct (rs Oct-Mar rallies only) Booking
advisable bank hols & Jul-Aug Last arrival 22.00hrs
Last departure noon
*A peaceful rural park tucked away along lanes on
top of the North Downs, with improving super
pitches, first-class toilets, and a secluded touring
area well screened from the static site. Attractive
low walls and much planting enhance the bar and
swimming pool area. A 23-acre site with 36 touring
pitches and 134 statics.*
Coffee bar & Sauna.
Leisure: 🎣 🎱 ⚒ 🎪 🏛 **Facilities:** 🎯☉🥤🌲💧♿🍴🏪🎋🐾
Services: 🔌🅿️🍽💧🧴🚽🅃🔻→🏴🚱🍴♨️💳💳💳💳 🔃

LEYSDOWN-ON-SEA   Map 05 TR07

▶ ▶ ▶ **67% Priory Hill (TR038704)**
Wing Rd ME12 4QT ☎ 01795 510267
🖷 01795 511503
e-mail: philip@prioryhill.co.uk
website: www.prioryhill.co.uk
*Dir: Take A249 signed to Sheerness then B2231 to
Leysdown*
★ 🚐 £6-£18 🚛 £6-£18 Å £6-£18
Open Mar-Oct Booking advisable bank hols, wknds
& Jul-Aug Last arrival 20.00hrs Last departure noon
*A small well-maintained touring area on an
established family-run holiday park close to the sea,
with views of the North Kent coast. Amenities
include a clubhouse and a swimming pool.
A 1.5-acre site with 50 touring pitches.*
Leisure: 🎣 🎱 ⚒ □ **Facilities:** 🎯☉🥤🌲💧❆♿🐾🎋
Services: 🔌🅿️🍽💧🧴✖️🏪→🍴♨️💳💳💳 🔃 🔃

MAIDSTONE   Map 05 TQ75

▶ ▶ ▶ **67% Pine Lodge Touring Park (TQ815549)**
Ashford Rd, Bearsted, Hollingbourne ME17 1XH
☎ 01622 730018 🖷 01622 734498
e-mail: booking@pinelodgetouringpark.co.uk
website: www.pinelodgetouringpark.co.uk
*Dir: M20 junct 8, keep to right. Right at next rdbt. 0.5m
on A20 towards Maidstone East on left hand side of road*
★ 🚐 £10-£12 🚛 £10-£12 Å £8-£10
Open all year Booking advisable bank hols Last
arrival 22.00hrs Last departure 12.00hrs ♨
*A well-run park suitable for all touring units from
large motorhomes to small tents. The modern
facilities are maintained to a high standard by the
owners, and the site is handy for the M20 and
visiting Leeds Castle. A 7-acre site with 100 touring
pitches.*
Waste disposal points.
Leisure: 🏛 **Facilities:** 🎯☉🥤🌲❆♿🍴🏪
Services: 🔌🅿️💧🧴🅃→🍴🍽♨️
Notes: No commercial vehicles 💳 💳 💳 🔃 🔃

Pine Lodge Touring Park

MANSTON   Map 05 TR36

▶ ▶ ▶ **67% Manston Caravan & Camping Park
(TR348662)**
Manston Court Rd CT12 5AU ☎ 01843 823442
e-mail: enquiries@manston-park.co.uk
website: www.manston-park.co.uk
*Dir: From B2050, N of Manston Airport, take minor road
(Manston Court Rd) to site in 0.24m on right*
🚐 🚛 Å
Open Apr/Etr-Oct (rs Apr shop open weekends only
(off-peak)) Booking advisable bank hols & Jul-Aug
Last arrival 23.55hrs Last departure 11.00hrs
*A neatly-kept grassy park broken up by mature
trees, handy for Manston Airport and the seaside
resorts on the Isle of Thanet. The older-style toilet
facilities are well maintained, and there is an
excellent children's play area. A 5-acre site with
100 touring pitches and 46 statics.*
Leisure: 🏛 **Facilities:** 🎯☉❆💧🍴🏛🐾🎋
Services: 🔌💧🧴🅃→🍴♨️♨️♨️💳💳🍴♨️
Notes: Camp rules on display 💳 💳 🔃 🔃

MARTIN MILL   Map 05 TR34

▶ ▶ ▶ ▶ **66% Hawthorn Farm
Caravan Park (TR342464)**
Station Rd CT15 5LA
☎ 01304 852658 & 852914
🖷 01304 853417
e-mail: info@keatfarm.co.uk
website: www.keatfarm.co.uk/
touringparks/hawthorn.htm
Dir: Signed from A258
🚐 £10-£12 🚛 £10-£12 Å £10-£12
Open Mar-mid Dec (rs winter water off if weather
cold) Booking advisable bank hols & Jul-Aug Last
arrival anytime Last departure noon
*This pleasant rural park set in 28 acres of
beautifully-landscaped gardens is screened by
young trees and hedgerows, in grounds which
include woods and a rose garden. The decent
facilities include a shop and laundry. A 15-acre site
with 250 touring pitches and 176 statics.*
Facilities: 🎯☉🥤❆💧🍴🐾🎋 **Services:** 🔌🅿️💧🧴🅃✖️
→🍴♨️♨️♨️🍴♨️💳💳💳💳 🔃 🔃

See advertisement on opposite page

SANDWICH — Map 05 TR35

▶ ▶ ▶ 69% *Sandwich Leisure Park*
(TR326581)
Woodnesborough Rd CT13 0AA
☎ 01304 612681 & 01227 771777
📄 01304 612681
e-mail: info@coastandcountryleisure.com
website: www.coastandcountryleisure.com
Dir: From Sandwich town centre, then follow tourist signs

🚐 🚐 ▲
Open Mar-Oct Booking advisable Etr, Spring bank hol & Jul-Aug Last arrival 20.00hrs Last departure 11.00hrs
A large site with impressive new toilet facilities, and fully-serviced pitches being installed for 2003. There is a choice of pitches with hook-ups or those in a separate field with a more natural ambience. The park backs onto open farmland on the edge of Sandwich. A 19-acre site with 140 touring pitches and 103 statics.
Washing-up area.

Leisure: 🎢 Facilities: 🅿️⊙🍴✲🕭🗪🏇
Services: 🔌🗑️🛁🚮→∪🅿️◎🛆🚿🚽🍽️🎪🍺 🍽️ 🔄

SEVENOAKS — Map 05 TQ55

▶ ▶ ▶ 62% *Camping & Caravanning Club Site*
(TQ577564)
Styants Bottom, Seal TN15 0ET ☎ 01732 762728
website: www.campingandcaravanningclub.co.uk
Dir: Take A25 from Sevenoaks towards Borough Green. Left just after Crown Point Inn, on right, down narrow lane to Styants Bottom. Site on left

★ 🚐 £11.10-£14.50 🚐 £11.10-£14.50 ▲ £11.10-£14.50
Open Mar-Oct Booking advisable bank hols & peak periods Last arrival 21.00hrs Last departure noon
A quiet park in the centre of National Trust woodlands, with buildings blending well into the surroundings. Please see the advertisement on page 10 for details of Club Members' benefits. A 6-acre site with 60 touring pitches.
Leisure: 🎢 Facilities: 🅿️⊙🍴✲🕭🗪
Services: 🔌🗑️🛁🚮🖵→∪🍽️🍺 🔄

ST NICHOLAS AT WADE — Map 05 TR26

▶ 57% St Nicholas Camping Site *(TR254672)*
Court Rd CT7 0NH ☎ 01843 847245
Dir: Signed off A299 and A28, at W end of village near church

★ 🚐 £8.50-£13.50 🚐 £8.50-£11 ▲ £8.50-£11
Open Etr-Oct Booking advisable Jul-Aug Last arrival 22.00hrs Last departure 14.00hrs
A gently-sloping field with mature hedging, on the edge of the village close to the shop. This rustic site offers simple facilities, and is conveniently located close to primary routes. A 3-acre site with 75 touring pitches.
Leisure: 🎢 Facilities: 🅿️⊙✲🏇
Services: 🔌🛁🖵→∪🍽️🗑️🍺

THREE *beautiful parks in Kent*
HAWTHORN FARM
LITTLE SATMAR
QUEX CARAVAN PARK
CALL FREEPHONE
0800 30 50 70
for further details and colour brochure
www.keatfarm.co.uk

WHITSTABLE — Map 05 TR16

▶ ▶ ▶ 65% Seaview Holiday Village *(TR145675)*
St John's Rd CT5 2RY ☎ 01227 792246
📄 01227 792247
e-mail: seaviewpark@fsnet.co.uk
Dir: From A299 take A2990 then B2205 to Swalecliffe, site between Herne Bay & Whitstable

★ 🚐 fr £9.50 🚐 fr £9.50 ▲ fr £9.50
Open Mar-Oct (rs Feb & Nov limited facilities)
Booking advisable all times Last arrival 21.30hrs Last departure noon
A pleasant open site on the edge of Whitstable, set well away from the static area, with a smart, modern toilet block and new super and hardstanding pitches. A 12-acre site with 20 touring pitches and 452 statics.
Amusements in games room & adventure trail.
Leisure: ◣🎢🖵 Facilities: 🅿️⊙🍴✲🕭🗪🏇
Services: 🔌🗑️🛁🖵✗🛗→∪🅿️◎🛆🚿🍽️
🍽️ 🍺 🔄

WROTHAM HEATH — Map 05 TQ65

▶ ▶ ▶ 73% Gate House Wood Touring Park
(TQ635585)
Ford Ln TN15 7SD ☎ 01732 843062
Dir: From A20 near junct with A25 turn into Ford Lane, site 200yds on left
★ 🚐 £8-£10 🚐 £8-£10 ▲ £8-£10

contd.

Open Apr-Oct Booking advisable Last arrival 22.00hrs Last departure noon ⌖
A maturing site in a disused sand quarry, well sheltered by tall trees and banks, and with smart new facilities. A 3.5-acre site with 55 touring pitches.
Leisure: ⚑ **Facilities:** ↖⊙❂☆⅃↗Ⅎ⊞
Services: ⊟⊞⬛◍⊡→∪▶

LANCASHIRE

See also sites under **Greater Manchester & Merseyside**

BLACKPOOL   Map 07 SD33
See also **Lytham St Annes & Thornton Cleveleys**

65% *Marton Mere Holiday Village (SD347349)*
Mythop Rd FY4 4XN
☎ 01253 760771 ▤ 01253 767544
Dir: From M55 junct 4 onto A583 towards Blackpool. Turn right past windmill at 1st traffic lights into Mythop Rd. Park 150yds on left
⚏ ⚏
Open Mar-Oct Booking advisable Last arrival 22.00hrs Last departure noon
A large holiday centre with plenty of on-site entertainment directed at all ages, and a regular bus service into Blackpool. The separate touring area on this extensive park has all hardstanding and electric pitches. This area is on the edge of the mere, where plenty of birdlife is to be spotted. A 30-acre site with 431 touring pitches and 921 statics.
Leisure: ⚐ ◔ ◔ ⚑ ⬛ **Facilities:** ↖⊙❂☆↖⅃↗⊞
❅ **Services:** ⊟⊞⬛◍⊞⊡✕⬚→∪▶⊙⚘♨✦
⬤ ⊟ ⊟ ⊟ ⊡

▶ ▶ ▶ **67% Mariclough Hampsfield Camping Site (SD356329)**
Preston New Rd, Peel Corner FY4 5JR
☎ 01253 761034
website: www.maricloughhampsfieldcamping.com
Dir: On A583 0.5m S of M55 junct 4
★ ⚏ £7-£8 ⚏ £7-£8 ⚑ £7-£8
Open Etr-Oct Booking advisable high season bank hols (for caravans) Last arrival 22.00hrs Last departure noon
A small, tidy site set in peaceful open countryside on the outskirts of Blackpool. The family-run park has an attractive layout, and is for adults only. A 2-acre site with 50 touring pitches, 10 hardstandings and 2 statics.
Facilities: ↖⊙❂↖ **Services:** ⊟⬛◍⊡→∪▶♨
♨ ✦ ⊟ **Notes:** Adults only, no single sex groups

> NEW - AA Quality % Score for each pennant category. See page 7 for a full explanation

BOLTON-LE-SANDS   Map 07 SD46
▶ ▶ ▶ **61% Sandside Caravan & Camping Park (SD472681)**
The Shore LA5 8JS ☎ 01524 822311
▤ 01524 822311
website: www.sandside.co.uk
Dir: From M6 junct 35 follow A6 through Carnforth, turn right at Little Chef in Bolton-le-Sands, and over level crossing to site
⚏ ⚏ ⚑
Open Mar-Oct Booking advisable bank hols & Jul-Aug Last arrival 22.00hrs Last departure 13.00hrs
Located in a pleasant spot overlooking Morecambe Bay with distant views of the Lake District, this sloping site is next to a busy main West Coast railway line with a level crossing. A 9-acre site with 92 touring pitches and 35 statics.
Facilities: ↖⊙❂☆↖⅃↗❅
Services: ⊟⊞⬛→∪▶⊙⚘♨✦✦

▶ ▶ **60% Bolton Holmes Farm (SD481693)**
Mill Ln LA5 8ES ☎ 01524 732854
Dir: On W side of A6 in Bolton-Le-Sands turn into Mill Ln. Over railway bridge onto Shore Front. Road to left of White House
★ ⚏ fr £7 ⚏ fr £7 ⚑ fr £7
Open Apr-Sep Booking advisable peak periods
A gently sloping site forming part of a farm complex, offering good views across Morecambe Bay and to the hills of the Lake District. The friendly owners keep the field well trimmed and neat, and the toilet facilities are very clean. Site is signed off A6 between Morecambe and Carnforth. A 5-acre site with 30 touring pitches and 45 statics.
Facilities: ↖⊙❂↖ **Services:** ⊟⊞⊡→♨✦⊟⊟
Notes: Dogs must be kept on leads

▶ ▶ **65% Detron Gate Farm (SD478683)**
LA5 9TN ☎ 01524 732842 & 733617 (night)
Dir: W of A6, 1m N of Bolton-le-Sands
⚏ ⚏ ⚑
Open Mar-Oct (rs Mar-May shop hours restricted) Booking advisable bank hols Last arrival 22.00hrs Last departure 18.00hrs
A rural grassy site with lovely views out over Morecambe Bay to the Lakeland hills, on slightly sloping ground close to a small farm. An attractive barn houses the shop, paperback library and table tennis. A 10-acre site with 100 touring pitches and 42 statics.
Leisure: ◔ ⚑ ⬛ **Facilities:** ↖⊙❂↖⅃
Services: ⊟⊞⬛◍⊞⊡→∪▶♨♨✦✦

CAPERNWRAY   Map 07 SD57
▶ ▶ ▶ **73% Old Hall Caravan Park (SD533716)**
LA6 1AD ☎ 01524 733276 ▤ 01524 734488
e-mail: oldhall@charis.co.uk
website: www.oldhall.uk.com
Dir: M6 junct 35 follow signs to Over Kellet, left onto B6254, left at village green signed Capernwray. Site 1.5m on right
★ ⚏ £15-£17 ⚏ £15-£17
contd.

Open Mar-10 Jan Booking advisable bank hols & Jul-Aug
A lovely secluded park set in a clearing amongst trees at the end of a half-mile long drive. This peaceful park is home to a wide variety of wild life, and there are marked walks in the woods. Facilities are well maintained by friendly owners. A 3-acre site with 38 touring pitches, 38 hardstandings and 160 statics.

Leisure: ⚲ **Facilities:** 🖳⊙🚿&⚡🚽🖘
Services: 🖵🗑🎱🖉🗑→∪⬦⅄🪣⚱

CLITHEROE
Map 07 SD74

▶ ▶ ▶ 63% **Camping & Caravanning Club Site (SD727413)**
Edisford Rd BB7 3LA ☎ 01200 425294
website: www.campingandcaravanningclub.co.uk
Dir: A671 to Clitheroe. Left at Longridge sign. Turn into Greenacre Rd. Left at Edisford Rd T-junct. Sports Centre on right, site 50mtrs on left
★ 🚐 £10.20-£12.90 🚐 £10.20-£12.90 ▲ £10.20-£12.90
Open Mar-Oct Booking advisable bank hols & peak periods Last arrival 21.00hrs Last departure noon
Set on the banks of the River Ribble, this park is attractively landscaped with mature trees and shrubs. An ideal spot for walking and fishing, and the site is also adjacent to a park with a café, pitch and putt, leisure centre, swimming pool and miniature steam railway. The Ribble Country Way is nearby. Please see the advertisement on page 10 for details of Club Members' benefits. A 6-acre site with 80 touring pitches.

Facilities: 🖳⊙🚿✳⚡🚽
Services: 🖵🗑🎱🖉🗑→∪⬦⊙🎱🪣🖘🔲🔲🔲🔲

COCKERHAM
Map 07 SD45

65% *Cockerham Sands Country Park (SD435529)*
LA2 0BB ☎ 01524 751387
🖨 01524 752275
Dir: 2m N of Cockerham take unclass rd off A588 signed Cocker Sands & follow signs to shore
🚐🚐
Open Mar-11 Dec Booking advisable
Last departure 10.00hrs
A small touring area close to all the amenities of a large holiday complex on the estuary of the River Lune. The emphasis is on entertainment for all the family on site. A 7-acre site with 9 touring pitches and 260 statics.

Leisure: ⚱🛶⚲ **Facilities:** 🖳⊙🚿⚡🚽
Services: 🖵🗑🎱⚱🖉🗑🛒→∪🪣🖘🔲🔲🔲🔲

▶ ▶ ▶ 73% **Mosswood Caravan Park (SD456497)**
Crimbles Ln LA2 0ES ☎ 01524 791041
🖨 01524 792444
e-mail: info@mosswood.co.uk
website: www.mosswood.co.uk
Dir: Approx 4m from A6/M6 junct 33, 1m W of Cockerham on A588
★ 🚐 £10-£11 🚐 £10-£11 ▲ £10-£11

contd.

Open Mar-Oct Booking advisable bank hols & Jul-Sep Last arrival 20.00hrs Last departure 16.00hrs
A tree-lined grassy park with sheltered, level pitches, located on peaceful Cockerham Moss. The modern toilet block is attractively clad in stained wood, and the facilities include cubicled washing facilities and a launderette. A 25-acre site with 25 touring pitches and 143 statics.

Leisure: ⚲ **Facilities:** 🖳⊙🚿✳⚡🚽🖘
Services: 🖵🗑🎱🖉🗑→∪⬦🪣🖘🔲🔲🔲🔲

CROSTON
Map 07 SD41

▶ ▶ ▶ ▶ 71% **Royal Umpire Caravan Park (SD504190)**
Southport Rd PR26 9JB ☎ 01772 600257
🖨 01772 600662
website: www.royalumpire.co.uk
Dir: From Chorley take A581, 3.5m & on approach to Croston, park on right
★ 🚐 £9-£17.80 🚐 £9-£17.80 ▲ £9-£13.50
Open all year only serviced pitches available
Booking advisable bank hols & peak season Last arrival 22.00hrs Last departure noon
A pleasant level site set in open countryside, with an attractive sunken garden and seating area. Plenty of leisure opportunities include a large games room, an interesting children's playground, and a large playing field. The toilets, laundry and dishwashing area are of a very good quality. A 60-acre site with 200 touring pitches, 130 hardstandings.
Assault course, five a side football pitch.

Leisure: 🎱⚲ **Facilities:** 🖳⊙🚿✳&⚡🚽🖘
Services: 🖵🗑🎱🖉🗑🛒→∪⬦🪣 **Notes:** No large groups of young people 🔲🔲🔲🔲

GARSTANG
Map 07 SD44

▶ ▶ ▶ ▶ 75% **Claylands Caravan Park (SD496485)**
Cabus PR3 1AJ ☎ 01524 791242 🖨 01524 792406
e-mail: alan@claylands-park.co.uk
website: www.claylands-caravan-park.co.uk
Dir: Turn off M6 junct 33 S to Garstang, approx 6m pass Little Chef, signed off A6 into private road on Lancaster side of Garstang
★ 🚐 £8-£10 🚐 £8-£10 ▲ £8-£10
Open Mar-4 Jan (rs Jan & Feb Holiday park only) Booking advisable bank hols & Jul-Aug Last arrival 23.00hrs Last departure 14.00hrs
A well-maintained site with lovely river and woodland walks and good views over the River Wyre towards the village of Scorton. This friendly park is set in delightful countryside. Guests can enjoy fishing, and the atmosphere is very relaxed. The quality facilities and amenities are of a high standard, and everything is immaculately maintained. A 14-acre site with 30 touring pitches, 30 hardstandings and 68 statics.
Fishing.

Leisure: ⚲ **Facilities:** 🖳⊙✳&⚡🚽🖘
Services: 🖵🗑🎱🖉🗑🗑✕🛒🛒→∪⬦⅄🖉
Notes: No single sex groups 🔲🔲🔲🔲

▶ ▶ ▶ 66% **Bridge House Marina & Caravan Park** (SD483457)
Nateby Crossing Ln, Nateby PR3 0JJ
☎ 01995 603207 ▤ 01995 601612
Dir: Off A6 at pub and sign for Knott End, immediately right into Nateby Crossing Lane, over canal bridge to site on left
★ 🚐 £10 🚐 £10
Open Mar-4 Jan Booking advisable bank hols Last arrival 22.00hrs Last departure 13.00hrs
A well-maintained site in attractive countryside by the Lancaster Canal, with good views towards the Trough of Bowland. A 4-acre site with 50 touring pitches and 20 statics.
Leisure: Ⓐ **Facilities:** ⏢⊙🥄✳💧🛒🛅
Services: 🔌🗓🍴🧴🖽Ⓣ→▶🔥🍴🚵🕹💳💳📶🚉

GISBURN　　　　　　　　　　Map 07 SD84

▶ ▶ ▶ 75% **Rimington Caravan Park** (SD825469)
Hardacre Ln, Rimington BB7 4EE
☎ 01200 445355 & 447235 ▤ 01200 445355
e-mail: rg@classicfm.net
Dir: Off A682 1m S of Gisburn
★ 🚐 £12-£14 🚐 £12-£14 ▲ £10-£12
Open 15 Mar-Oct (rs Mar hardstanding available only) Booking advisable bank hols & Jul-3 Sep Last arrival 20.00hrs Last departure noon no cars by caravans no cars by tents
A well-cared for site set in an attractive rural valley close to the Pendle Hills. The sanitary facilities have been refurbished recently, and the family owners pay great attention to the details of design and maintenance. An 11-acre site with 30 touring pitches and 150 statics.
Facilities: ⏢⊙🥄✳💧🛒🛅
Services: 🔌🗓🍴🧴🖽Ⓣ→🔥🍴

HEYSHAM　　　　　　　　　　Map 07 SD46

61% *Ocean Edge Caravan Park* (SD407591)
Moneyclose Ln LA3 2XA
☎ 01524 855657
Dir: From M6 junct 34 follow A683 to Heysham. In Heysham site signed before ferry point
🚐🚐▲
Open Mar-Oct
A newly-developed touring area of a large holiday complex adjacent to the sea, and with good sea views. Facilities include a large bar, fish and chips and bar meals, and children's entertainment. A 10-acre site with 100 touring pitches and 629 statics.
Leisure: 🏊 Ⓐ **Facilities:** 🥄🛅 **Services:** 🗓🍴✖💧

LANCASTER　　　　　　　　　Map 07 SD46

▶ ▶ ▶ 68% **New Parkside Farm Caravan Park** (SD507633)
Denny Beck, Caton Rd LA2 9HH
☎ 01524 770723 & 770337
website: www.ukparks.co.uk/newparkside
Dir: From M6 junct 34 onto A683 E towards Kirkby Lonsdale. Park 0.75m on right
🚐 £7-£8 🚐 £7-£8 ▲ £7-£8
contd.

Open Mar-Oct Booking advisable bank hols & Jul-Aug Last arrival 22.00hrs Last departure 16.00hrs
Peaceful, friendly grassy park on a working farm with extensive views of Lune Valley and Ingleborough. A 3-acre site with 40 touring pitches and 10 statics.
Facilities: ⏢⊙🥄✳💧🐕🛒 **Services:** 🔌🧴🔥→▶
📶🍴🖽🛅 **Notes:** Dogs must be kept on leads

LONGRIDGE　　　　　　　　　Map 07 SD63

▶ ▶ ▶ 64% **Beacon Fell View Caravan Park** (SD618382)
110 Higher Rd PR3 2TF ☎ 01772 785434 & 783233
▤ 01772 784204
Dir: Leave A6 at Broughton on B5269 into Longridge & follow B6243 out of town centre. Take left fork signed Jeffrey Hill. Site 0.75m on right
🚐🚐▲
Open 2 Mar-16 Nov (rs after Etr-end May entertainment weekends only) Booking advisable Bank hols, school hols & wknds Last arrival 21.00hrs Last departure 12.00hrs
An elevated park with views over Beacon Fell. This tiered park with level pitches has an indoor swimming pool, and an extensive free evening entertainment programme in the clubhouse. A 7-acre site with 90 touring pitches and 397 statics. Free evening entertainment, pool tables, darts.
Leisure: 🏊 🎯 🌀 Ⓐ **Facilities:** ⏢⊙🥄💧🛅🛒
Services: 🔌🗓🍴🧴→🔄🍴🕹💳💳📶🚉

LYTHAM ST ANNES　　　　　　Map 07 SD32

▶ ▶ ▶ 63% **Bank Lane Caravan Park** (SD403277)
Warton PR4 1TB ☎ 01772 633513 ▤ 01772 633513
Dir: On unclass road, off A584 at Warton, 3m from Lytham
★ 🚐 £9-£11.50
Open Mar-Oct Booking advisable
A grassy touring area with open aspect at edge of a mainly static park, situated close to British Aerospace aerodrome, and handy for beaches. A 13.5-acre site with 50 touring pitches and 180 statics.
Leisure: Ⓐ **Facilities:** ⏢⊙🥄🛒🖽🛅
Services: 🔌🗓🧴→🔄🍴🗑💧🔀🕹🍴

▶ ▶ ▶ 69% **Eastham Hall Caravan Site** (SD379291)
Saltcotes Rd FY8 4LS ☎ 01253 737907
Dir: Leave M55 junct 3. Straight over 3 rdbts onto B5259. Through Wrea Green & Moss Side, park 1m after level crossing
★ 🚐 £10-£13 🚐 £10-£13
Open Mar-Oct Booking advisable bank hols & Jul Last arrival 21.00hrs Last departure 16.00hrs
Secluded park with trees and hedgerows in a rural setting. Helpful owners ensure that facilities are maintained to a high standard. A 15-acre site with 200 touring pitches, 30 hardstandings and 200 statics.
Leisure: Ⓐ **Facilities:** ⏢⊙🥄✳💧🔄🛅🛒
Services: 🔌🗓🧴🖽Ⓣ→🔄▶🧴🔥🍴 **Notes:** No tents, no groundsheets in awnings 💳📶🚉

MERE BROW   Map 07 SD41

▶ ▶ ▶ 56% **Leisure Lakes (SD408176)**
PR4 6JX ☎ 01772 813446 & 814502 📠 01772 816250
e-mail: gab@leisurelakes.co.uk
*Dir: From Southport, take A565 for 3.5m, right turn on
B5246 to site*
★ 🚐 £9-£12 🚐 £9-£12
Open all year Booking advisable bank hols, Jun-Aug
& wknds Last arrival 21.00hrs Last departure 16.30hrs
*A level grassy site in spacious parkland with ample
amenities including watersports, fishing and
walking. A 30-acre site with 90 touring pitches.*
Golf range & course fishing
Leisure: ♦ 🏕 Facilities: 🐾⊙❋🕹🔌🛍🚿🐾
Services: 🔌🔋🍴🚿🍴✕🛒→∪▶🍴🚂🎠🚌📷

MIDDLETON (NEAR MORECAMBE) Map 07 SD45

▶ ▶ ▶ 61% **Melbreak Caravan Park (SD415584)**
Carr Ln LA3 3LH ☎ 01524 852430
*Dir: M6 junct 34 onto A683. After 6m turn left at rdbt,
pass Middleton & turn right into village. Site in 0.5m*
★ 🚐 fr £10.50 🚐 fr £10.50 ▲ fr £7.25
Open Mar-Oct Booking advisable Jul-Aug Last
arrival 22.00hrs Last departure noon
*Small, well run, tidy site in open countryside south
of Morecambe. A 2-acre site with 20 touring pitches
and 30 statics.*
Facilities: 🐾⊙🕹❋🚿
Services: 🔌🔋🍴🚿🛒→∪▶🍴

MORECAMBE   Map 07 SD46

65% *Regent Caravan Park (SD431629)*
Westgate LA3 7DB
☎ 01524 413940
*Dir: From A589 turn left towards town centre at 3rd
large rdbt. Park 1.5m on left*
🚐🚐
Open Mar-1 Jan Booking advisable Last arrival
21.00hrs Last departure noon
*A full entertainment complex for all ages, close
to the town and promenade. Amenities include
extensive bars with snooker tables, pool tables,
darts and wide-screen television. A 2-acre site
with 24 touring pitches and 330 statics.*
Leisure: 🎣 🏕 Facilities: 🐾🛍🔌🐾
Services: 🔋🍴✕🛒→∪▶📷🚌🍴

▶ ▶ ▶ 62% **Riverside Caravan Park
(SD448615)**
Lancaster Rd, Snatchems LA3 3ER
☎ 01524 844193
e-mail: info@riverside-morecambe.co.uk
website: www.riverside-morecambe.co.uk
Dir: On unclass road off B5273 near Heaton
★ 🚐 £7-£8 🚐 £7-£8 ▲ £7-£8
Open Mar-Oct Booking advisable public hols & high
season Last arrival 22.00hrs Last departure noon
*A grassy site with views over the River Lune and
Morecambe Bay. The sanitary facilities in a modern
toilet block are clean and fresh. Road access is
subject to tidal river flooding, and it is advisable to
check tide times before crossing. A 2-acre site with
50 touring pitches and 20 statics.* *contd.*

Riverside Caravan Park

Leisure: 🏕 Facilities: 🐾⊙🕹❋🔌🛍🐾
Services: 🔌🔋🖥→∪▶🔼🚌🍴📷🚿

▶ ▶ ▶ 66% **Venture Caravan Park (SD436633)**
Langridge Way, Westgate LA4 4TQ
☎ 01524 412986 📠 01524 422029
e-mail: mark@venturecaravanpark.co.uk
website: www.venturecaravanpark.co.uk
*Dir: From M6 junct 34 take A683 to Lancaster. Follow
signs to Morecambe. Straight over 2 rdbts, then left at
3rd. 0.75m right into Langridge Way*
★ 🚐 £9-£11 🚐 £9-£11 ▲ £9-£11
Open all year (rs 6 Jan-22 Feb touring vans only,
one toilet block open) Booking advisable bank hols
& peak periods Last arrival 22.00hrs Last departure
noon
*A large park with good modern facilities, including
a small indoor heated pool, a licensed clubhouse
and a family room with children's entertainment.
The site has many statics, and is close to the town
centre. A 17.5-acre site with 56 touring pitches and
304 statics.*
Amusement arcade & off licence.
Leisure: 🎣 ♦ 🏕 🖥 Facilities: 🔌🐾⊙🕹❋🔌🛍🐾
Services: 🔌🔋🍴🚿🖥🍴→▶🎠🍴

ORMSKIRK   Map 07 SD40

▶ ▶ ▶ ▶ 76% **Abbey Farm Caravan
Park (SD434098)**
Dark Ln L40 5TX
☎ 01695 572686 📠 01695 572686
e-mail: abbeyfarm@yahoo.com
website: www.abbeyfarmcaravanpark.co.uk
*Dir: M6 junct 27 onto A5209 to Burscough. 4m left onto
B5240. Immediate right into Hobcross Ln. Park 1.5m on
right*
★ 🚐 £8.50-£13.75 🚐 £8.50-£13.75 ▲ £4.50-£10.50

contd.

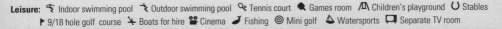

England

Open all year Booking advisable public hols & Jul-Aug Last arrival 22.00hrs Last departure 13.00hrs
Delightful hanging baskets and flower beds brighten this garden-like rural park which is sheltered by hedging and mature trees. Modern, very clean facilities include a family bathroom, and there are special pitches for the disabled near the toilets. A superb recreation field caters for children of all ages, and there is an indoor games room, large library, fishing lake and dog walk. Tents have their own area with BBQ and picnic tables. A 6-acre site with 56 touring pitches and 44 statics.
Undercover washing up area, off-licence, farm walk

Leisure: ◆ ⚅ **Facilities:** ⇥ ⍀⊙⍣✻⩔⛱⬚⛽⊞ **ᚁ**
Services: ▣🖾🛢⌨⊞⊡ → ∪ ▶ **Notes:** No single sex groups 🍴 🖙 🛒 🐎 🖵

▶ ▶ ▶ **64% Shaw Hall Caravan Park (SD397119)**
Smithy Ln, Scarisbrick L40 8HJ ☎ 01704 840298
🖥 01704 840539
e-mail: shawhall@btconnect.com
website: www.shawhall.co.uk
Dir: 200yds S of canal bridge at Scarisbrick, 0.25m off A570 at Smithy Lane
★ ⊞ £13-£21 ⊞ £13-£21 ▲ £13-£21
Open Mar-7 Jan Booking advisable bank hols & peak periods Last arrival 20.30hrs
A large, pleasant park with 20 super pitches and good toilets. The clubhouse and bar offer cabaret and discos which are popular with families. The park also boasts canal walks from its direct access to the Leeds-Liverpool Canal, a football field, and putting and bowling greens. A 26-acre site with 65 touring pitches and 300 statics.
bowling green, putting green

Leisure: ⚅ ▱ **Facilities:** ⍀⍉✻⩔⛱⬚⊞ **ᚁ**
Services: ▣🖾🛢⌨⊞▣ → ∪ ▶ **J** 🍴 🖙 🛒 🐎 🖵

PREMIER PARK

▶ ▶ ▶ ▶ ▶ **78% Holgate's Caravan Park (SD455762)**
Middlebarrow Plain, Cove Rd LA5 0SH
☎ 01524 701508 🖥 01524 701580
e-mail: caravan@holgates.co.uk
website: www.holgates.co.uk
Dir: M6 junct 35. 5m NW of Carnforth. From Carnforth centre take unclass Silverdale road & follow tourist signs after Warton
★ ⊞ £20.50-£21.75 ⊞ £20.50-£21.75
▲ £20.50-£21.75
Open mid Feb-2 Nov Booking advisable school & public hols & wknds Last arrival 22.00hrs Last departure 14.00hrs
A superb family holiday park set in wooded countryside next to the sea. This park demonstrates high quality in all areas, and offers a wide range of leisure amenities. Its relaxing position overlooking Morecambe Bay combined with excellent touring facilities mark this park out as special. Winner of the AA Best English Campsite of the Year for 2003. A 10-acre site with 70 touring pitches, 70 hardstandings and 350 statics.
contd.

Holgate's Caravan Park
Sauna, spa bath, steam room & mini-golf.

Leisure: 🏊 ◆ ⚅ **Facilities:** ⍀⊙⍣✻⩔⛱⬚ **ᚁ**
Services: ▣🖾🛢🍷⌨⊞▣✕🛒→ ▶ **J** **Notes:** No single sex groups or unaccompanied children
🍴 🖙 🛒 🐎 🖵

▶ ▶ ▶ ▶ **70% Kneps Farm Holiday Park (SD353429)**
River Rd, Stanah FY5 5LR ☎ 01253 823632
🖥 01253 863967
e-mail: enquiries@knepsfarm.co.uk
website: www.knepsfarm.co.uk
Dir: Leave A585 at rdbt onto B5412 to Little Thornton. Turn right at mini rdbt after school onto Stanah Rd, over 2nd mini rdbt, leading to River Rd
★ ⊞ £11-£12.50 ⊞ £11-£12.50 ▲ £11-£12.50
Open Mar-mid Nov Booking advisable at all times Last arrival 20.00hrs Last departure noon
A quality park adjacent to the River Wyre and the Wyre Estuary Country Park, handily placed for the attractions of Blackpool and the Fylde coast. This family-run park offers an excellent toilet block with immaculate facilities, and a mixture of hard and grass pitches. The park is quietly located, but there is some noise from a nearby plastics plant. A 10-acre site with 70 touring pitches, 40 hardstandings and 80 statics.

Leisure: ⚅ **Facilities:** ⇥ ⍀⊙⍣✻⩔⛱⬚⛽
Services: ▣🖾🛢⌨⊞⊡→▶⊙⟁**J** 🍴 🖙 ◉ 🐎 🖵

LEICESTERSHIRE

▶ ▶ ▶ **64% Donington Park Farmhouse Hotel (SK414254)**
Melbourne Rd, Isley Walton DE74 2RN
☎ 01332 862409 🖥 01332 862364
e-mail: info@parkfarmhouse.co.uk
website: www.parkfarmhouse.co.uk
Dir: M1 junct 24, pass airport to Isley Walton, right towards Melbourne. Park 0.5m on right
★ ⊞ £10-£12 ⊞ £10-£12 ▲ £6-£12
Open Jan-23 Dec (rs winter months hardstanding only) Booking advisable summer season Last arrival 21.00hrs Last departure noon
contd.

A developing site at the rear of a hotel beside Donington Park motor racing circuit. Booking is essential on race days but this is quiet rural site at other times. A 7-acre site with 60 touring pitches, 10 hardstandings.

Leisure: ⚙ **Facilities:** ₨⊙♿℄ **Services:** ⊞♀🛈✗ ➔♻▶♨🍴🛒💷 ⊡◎ ▣ ▦🔧 ⓢ

ULLESTHORPE   Map 04 SP58

▶ 57% **Ullesthorpe Garden Centre (SP515872)**
Lutterworth Rd LE17 5DR ☎ 01455 202144
📄 01455 202585
e-mail: enquiries@ullesthorpegardencentre.com
website: www.ullesthorpegardencentre.com
Dir: From M1 junct 20 take A4303 through Lutterworth, then B577 for 2m. Site just SE of Ullesthorpe
★ 🚐 £4-£5.50 🚎 £4-£5.50
Open Mar-Oct Booking advisable at all times Last arrival 18.00hrs Last departure sunset
A pleasant site next to the garden centre, ideal for the self-contained caravanner, with nature walk and fishing site. A 7-acre site with 16 touring pitches.

Facilities: ✳🐾 **Services:** ⊞✗🛒➔♻▶🔧🛒

Notes: Tents only allowed with a caravan
💳 💳 💳 ▦ ⓢ

LINCOLNSHIRE

ANCASTER   Map 08 SK94

▶ ▶ ▶ 69% **Woodland Waters (SK979435)**
Willoughby Rd NG32 3RT ☎ 01400 230888
📄 01400 230888
e-mail: info@woodlandwaters.co.uk
website: www.woodlandwaters.co.uk
Dir: On A153 W of x-roads with B6403
★ 🚐 £7-£9 🚎 £7-£9 ▲ £5.50-£7
Open all year Booking advisable BH's
A developing park peacefully set around impressive fishing lakes, with a few log cabins in a separate area. The pleasant access road is through mature woodland, and there is a very good heated toilet block, and a pub/club house with restaurant. A 5-acre site with 62 touring pitches and 8 statics.

Leisure: ♦ ⚙ **Facilities:** ₨⊙🧺♿℄🛒▦🐾
Services: ⊞◎♀▣✗🛒➔♻▶🔧

Notes: Dogs must be kept on leads at all times

ANDERBY   Map 09 TF57

▶ ▶ ▶ 64% *Manor Farm Caravan Park (TF533761)*
Sea Rd PE24 5YB ☎ 01507 490372
Dir: On unclass road off A52 Skegness-Mablethorpe
🚐 🚎 ▲
Open Mar-Nov Booking advisable bank hols
A well-laid out site on a working farm in a peaceful rural location well away from roads. The central toilet facilities include a family bathroom and disabled room, and there is a modern laundry. A 3-acre site with 30 touring pitches.

Leisure: ⚙ **Facilities:** ➔₨⊙🧺✳♿℄🅵🐾
Services: ⊞◎▣➔▶ 💳 💳 ▦ ⓢ

BARTON-UPON-HUMBER   Map 08 TA02

▶ ▶ ▶ 69% **Silver Birches Tourist Park (TA028232)**
Waterside Rd DN18 5BA ☎ 01652 632509
Dir: Follow Bridge Viewing Point signs to Waterside road, site just past Sloop pub
★ 🚐 fr £7 🚎 fr £7 ▲ fr £7
Open Apr-Oct Booking advisable bank hols Last arrival 23.00hrs Last departure 20.00hrs
A very pleasant, well-screened site, convenient for Humber Bridge as well as East Riding of Yorkshire and Lincolnshire. A 2-acre site with 24 touring pitches. Putting green.

Leisure: ⚙ **Facilities:** ₨⊙✳♿℄🛒▦
Services: ⊞🛈⊘▣➔♻🔧

BOSTON   Map 08 TF34

▶ ▶ ▶ ▶ 78% **Pilgrims Way (TF358434)**
Church Green Rd, Fishtoft PE21 0QY
☎ 01205 366646 📄 01205 366646
e-mail: maria@pilgrims-way.co.uk
website: www.pilgrims-way.co.uk
Dir: From Boston travel N on A16 (T), turn right onto A52 and right again at Ball House pub to Fishtoft 1m on left
★ 🚐 £10 🚎 £10 ▲ £8
Open Etr & Apr-Sep Booking advisable bank hols Last arrival 20.00hrs Last departure noon
A very attractive site in the gardens of the Grange, with individually screened pitches and purpose-built toilet facilities. This park is ideal for those seeking peace and tranquillity, and is well placed for touring around the Boston area, and visiting the Pilgrim Fathers Memorial. A 1-acre site with 22 touring pitches.

Facilities: ₨⊙🧺✳♿℄🛒▦
Services: ⊞◎🛈⊘▣➔♻▶♨❄🍴🔧

▶ ▶ ▶ 63% **Midville Caravan Park (TF386578)**
Stickney PE22 8HW ☎ 01205 270316
📄 01205 270316
Dir: From A16 at Stickney take unclass rd to Midville. Turn left at bridge (Hobhole Drain), site clearly signed
🚐 🚎 ▲
Open Mar-Nov Booking advisable bank & school hols Last arrival 22.00hrs
Set in the heart of flat fenland country in a very rural, quiet position. The rather old-style portaloo facilities are generally well maintained. A 3-acre site with 24 touring pitches and 40 statics.

Leisure: ⚙ **Facilities:** ₨⊙℄🅵
Services: ⊞◎🛈➔♻🔧🛒

CLEETHORPES   Map 08 TA30

69% *Thorpe Park Holiday Centre (TA321035)*
DN35 0PW ☎ 01472 813395
📄 01472 813395
Dir: Take unclass road off A180 at Cleethorpes, signed Humberstone and Holiday Park
🚐 🚎 ▲
Open Mar-Oct Booking advisable bank hols & school hols Last departure noon

contd.

A large static site with new touring facilities, including fully-serviced pitches, adjacent to the beach. This holiday centre offers excellent recreational and leisure activities, including an indoor pool with bar, bowling greens, crazy golf, tennis courts, and a games area. Parts of the site overlook the sea. A 100-acre site with 95 touring pitches and 2500 statics.
Crazy golf & pets corner.

Leisure: ᐅ ᐳ ◀ ⋔ **Facilities:** ⋒ ✕ �& ⋐ ⌺ ⊡ 큐
Services: ⊞ ⓔ ⓠ ᵢ ⌀ ⊡ ✕ ⬛ → ∪ ▶ ⊚ ᵥ ⚏ ✔
⬤ ▭ ▭ 🐾 🔒

FLEET HARGATE
Map 09 TF32

▶ ▶ ▶ 74% **Delph Bank Touring Caravan & Camping Park** (TF388248)
Old Main Rd PE12 8LL ☎ 01406 422910
e-mail: enquiries@delphbank.fsnet.co.uk
website: www.delphbank.co.uk
Dir: Turn off A17, King's Lynn to Sleaford road, into Fleet Hargate and follow signs
★ ⊞ £6.50-£10.50 ⊞ £6.50-£10.50 ▲ £6.50-£10.50
Open Mar-Nov Booking advisable 1-10 May & BH's Last arrival 22.30hrs Last departure noon
A quiet, well-screened park, neatly laid out in two fields with trimmed grass and colourful flower beds. The older-style toilet facilities have been upgraded and are immaculately maintained. This adult-only park which is being improved constantly, is set well away from the village and the A17, and there is no traffic noise. A 3-acre site with 45 touring pitches, 13 hardstandings.

Facilities: ⋒ ⊙ ⍾ ✕ ⋐ ⒉ ☆
Services: ⊞ ⓔ ᵢ ⌀ ⊡ ⊡ → ✔ **Notes:** Adults only

LOUTH
Map 08 TF38

▶ ▶ 60% **Manby Caravan Park** (TF392876)
Manby Leisure Ltd, Middlegate, Manby LN11 8SY
☎ 01507 328232 ⍾ 01507 327867
Dir: Approx 3m E of Louth off the B1200
★ ⊞ £7.50-£11.50 ⊞ £7.50-£11.50 ▲ £7.50-£11.50

Open Apr-Oct Booking advisable All Bank Hols Last arrival 20.00hrs Last departure noon
A simple touring park behind a health and leisure club, with level, well-drained pitches. A 5-acre site with 80 touring pitches and 7 statics.
Temporary membership to Health Club
Leisure: ᐅ ⋔ **Facilities:** ⋒ ⊙ ⍾ ✕ �& ⒉ 큐 ☆
Services: ⊞ → ∪ ▶ ⚏ ✔ ⓔ **Notes:** No all male groups

MABLETHORPE
Map 09 TF58

63% **Golden Sands Holiday Park** (TF501861)
Quebec Rd LN12 1QJ ☎ 01507 477871
⍾ 01507 472066
Dir: 1m W of town off A1031, Cleethorpes road
⊞ ⊞ ▲
Open Apr-Oct Booking advisable May/spring bank hol & Jul-Sep Last arrival 20.00hrs Last departure 10.00hrs
A large, well-equipped seaside holiday park with separate touring facilities on two sites, including fully modernised toilets. The first floor entertainment rooms are only accessible via stairs (no lifts). A 127-acre site with 350 touring pitches and 1300 statics.
Mini bowling alley, snooker/pool, indoor fun palace.
Leisure: ᐅ ᐳ ◀ ⋔ **Facilities:** ⋒ ✕ �& ⋐ ⒉ 큤 큐
Services: ⊞ ⓔ ⓠ ᵢ ⌀ ⊡ ✕ ⬛ → ▶ ⚏ ✔ **Notes:** No single sex groups, some dog breeds not accepted ⬤ ▭ ▭ 🐾 🔒

▶ ▶ ▶ 68% **Camping & Caravanning Club Site** (TF499839)
Highfield, 120 Church Ln LN12 2NU
☎ 01507 472374
website: www.campingandcaravanningclub.co.uk
Dir: On outskirts of Mablethorpe, on A1104, just after the 'Welcome to Mablethorpe' sign turn right into Church Ln. Continue 800yds to end of lane. Site on right
★ ⊞ £11.10-£14.50 ⊞ £11.10-£14.50 ▲ £11.10-£14.50
Open Mar-Oct Booking advisable bank hol & peak periods Last arrival 21.00hrs Last departure noon
Located next to flat agricultural land 1m from the sea, and well away from the road. The camping area is in two hedged fields with rural views, and the modern toilet facilities and laundry are centrally sited. Please see advertisement on page 10 for details of Club Members' benefits. A 6-acre site with 105 touring pitches.
Leisure: ⋔ **Facilities:** ⋒ ⊙ ⍾ ✕ �& ⋐ ⒉
Services: ⊞ ⓔ ᵢ ⌀ ⊡ ⊡ → ∪ ▶ ⚏ ✔ ⬤ ▭ ▭ 🐾 🔒

▶ ▶ ▶ 69% **Kirkstead Holiday Park** (TF509835)
North Rd, Trusthorpe LN12 2QD ☎ 01507 441483
⍾ 01507 443447
e-mail: mark@kirkstead.force9.co.uk
website: www.kirkstead.force9.co.uk
Dir: From Mablethorpe town centre take A52 S towards Sutton on Sea, after 1m turn sharp right at 2 telephone boxes into North Rd, site signed in 300yds
★ ⊞ £10-£14.50 ⊞ £10-£14.50 ▲ £9-£15.50
Open Mar-Nov Booking advisable bank hols & Jul-Aug Last arrival mdnt Last departure 15.00hrs
Controlled entry is a welcome security feature of this pleasant family-run site. The touring area and good quality toilets are centrally located, and the grounds are particularly well maintained. A 6-acre site with 50 touring pitches and 75 statics.
Snooker room, childrens room, evening bar meals.

contd.

Kirkstead Holiday Park

Leisure: ♦ ⚠ 🏳 **Facilities:** 🅿️ ⊙ 🖳 ✳ ⅃ ⌖ ℒ ⛗ 🎁 ➶
Services: 🐟 ⊡ 🍺 🗑 ⌷ 🖫 ♒ → ∪ ▸ ⊙ 🍴 🥄
🐟 ═══ ⊙ 🏧 🔌 🥄

MARKET RASEN   Map 08 TF18

▶ ▶ ▶ **66% Racecourse Caravan Park (TF123883)**
Legsby Rd LN8 3EA ☎ 01673 842307 & 843434
🖳 01673 844532
e-mail: marketrasen@rht.net
website: www.marketrasenraces.co.uk
*Dir: E of Market Rasen on A631, turn right 300yds after
lights into Legsby Rd, site racecourse entrance is 0.75m
on left*
★ 🚐 £13-£16 🚐 £13-£16 🛆 £13.50-£16.50

Open 29 Mar-7 Oct Shared toilet & shower on race
days Booking advisable bank hols & race days Last
arrival 20.00hrs Last departure 14.00hrs
*Set in a grass paddock adjacent to but separate
from the racecourse, and screened by a hedge. The
site has a golf course with a discount for campers,
and there is a large children's playground. A 3-acre
site with 55 touring pitches.*
Reduced rate for racing & golf
Leisure: ♦ ⚠ **Facilities:** 🅿️ ⊙ ✳ ⅃ ℒ ⛗ ➶ **Services:**
🐟 🗑 ⌷ 🖫 ♒ → ∪ ▸ ⊙ **Notes:** Family park 🐟 ═══ 🔌

▶ ▶ ▶ **69% Walesby Woodlands Caravan Park
(TF117906)**
Walesby Rd LN8 3UN ☎ 01673 843285
*Dir: B1203 from Market Rasen to Tealby. After 0.75m,
turn left onto the road to Walesby. After 0.25m take lane
on left. Site is 150yds on right*
🚐 🚐 🛆
Open Mar-Oct Booking advisable public hols Last
arrival 22.00hrs Last departure 17.00hrs
*Set in a quiet rural location and surrounded by
mature woodland, with a parkland atmosphere.*

contd.

---

*The immaculate facilities and the site shop are
housed in low-level, modern buildings to one side
of the owner's house. A 3-acre site with 60 touring
pitches.*
Leisure: ⚠ **Facilities:** 🅿️ ⊙ ✳ ⅃ ℒ ⛗
Services: 🐟 ⊡ 🗑 ⌷ 🖫 ♒ → ∪ ▸ 🥄 🐟 ═══

OLD LEAKE   Map 09 TF45

▶ ▶ ▶ **64% White Cat Park (TF415498)**
Shaw Ln PE22 9LQ ☎ 01205 870121
e-mail: mkibby@whitecat.freeserve.co.uk
website: www.whitecatpark.com
Dir: Just off A52, 7m NE of Boston
★ 🚐 £6.50-£7.50 🚐 £6.50-£7.50 🛆 £6.50-£7.50
Open mid Mar-Oct Booking advisable bank hols
Last arrival 22.00hrs Last departure 14.00hrs
*A pleasant, well-maintained small touring park set
down a rural lane just off the A52, with very little
traffic noise. It makes a peaceful base for exploring
Boston and the Lincolnshire coast. A 2.5-acre site
with 40 touring pitches and 4 statics.*
Leisure: ⚠ **Facilities:** 🅿️ ⊙ ✳ ℒ ⛗
Services: 🐟 🗑 ⌷ 🖫 ♒ → 🥄

ORBY   Map 09 TF46

▶ ▶ ▶ **61% Heron's Mead Fishing Lake &
Touring Park (TF508673)**
Marsh Ln PE24 5JA ☎ 01754 873357
e-mail: watercolours@freeuk.com
website: www.ukparks.co.uk/herons
*Dir: From A158 Lincoln to Skegness road turn left at
rdbt, through Orby for 0.5m*
★ 🚐 £7-£9 🛆 £7-£9
Open Etr-Oct Booking advisable bank hols & school
hols Last arrival 21.00hrs Last departure noon
*A pleasant fishing and touring park with coarse
fishing and an 8-acre woodland walk. Quiet couples
and elderly visitors are particularly welcome. A 4-
acre site with 30 touring pitches.*
Fishing on site, 2 disabled pegs
Facilities: 🅿️ ⊙ ✳ ⅃ ℒ ⛗ ➶ **Services:** 🐟 ♒
→ ▸ ⊙ ⚠ 🥄 ⊡ ℒ **Notes:** No ball games

SALTFLEETBY ST PETER   Map 09 TF48

▶ ▶ ▶ **73% The Fisheries (TF425892)**
Main Rd LN11 7SS ☎ 01507 338272
*Dir: On B1200 6m E from junct of A16 and 3m W of the
A1031*
★ 🚐 fr £8 🚐 fr £8 🛆 fr £8

contd.

Leisure: 🐟 Indoor swimming pool 🐟 Outdoor swimming pool ⚿ Tennis court ♦ Games room ⚠ Children's playground ∪ Stables
▸ 9/18 hole golf course ⅃ Boats for hire 🎦 Cinema 🥄 Fishing ⊙ Mini golf ⚠ Watersports 🏳 Separate TV room

England

Horncastle Road, Woodhall Spa, Lincolnshire, LN10 6UX
Tel: Woodhall Spa (01526) 352903

Classified as one of the top parks in Lincolnshire, Bainland is situated on the edge of the Wolds, surrounded by woodland, 1½ miles from the centre of Woodhall Spa. The Park of over 40 acres, caters for caravans, motorhomes and campers alike with Super and Standard pitches, electric hook-ups and satellite T.V. points.

18 hole Par 3 – Golf Course – Practice Putting Green – All weather Bowling Green – Indoor/Outdoor Tennis – Crazy Golf – Trampoline – Table Tennis – Indoor Swimming Pool – Childrens Adventure Playground – Sauna – Jacuzzi – Sunbed – Childrens 'Poachers Den' soft playroom – Bar – Restaurant – Rallies Welcome

Open Apr-Nov Booking advisable All Bank Hols Last arrival 18.00hrs Last departure noon
A pretty little site beside a well-stocked fishing lake behind the owner's house. There are electric hook-ups, spacious hardstandings, and an excellent new toilet block with quality facilities. A 12-acre site with 18 touring pitches and 1 static.
2 acre coarse fishing pond & 2 fishing lakes

Facilities: ₨⊹↺⅍⊞⊓π
Services: ♨⊡╏→∪►⅏⎳ **Notes:** Adult park only

SUTTON ST EDMUND   Map 08 TF31

► ► ► 58% *Orchard View Caravan & Camping Park* (TF365108)
Broadgate PE12 0LT ☎ 01945 700482
e-mail: raymariaorchardview@btinternet.com
Dir: *A47 Peterborough to Wisbech at Guyhirn. Turn towards Wisbech St Mary & Murrow. Through Murrow, over double bridge, then 2nd right. Site 0.5m on right*
⊞⊡Å
Open 31 Mar-Oct Booking advisable bank hols & Spalding Flower Festival Last arrival anytime Last departure anytime
A neat meadowland site with good planting for shelter and screening, located in remote and unspoilt fenland. The park has its own clubhouse, and is being continually upgraded. A 6-acre site with 35 touring pitches and 2 statics.
Pot wash, pets corner & rally field.
Leisure: ⚑⊡ **Facilities:** ₨⊙⅍⊹↺⅏⊞π⊓π
Services: ♨⊡⅌╏⊞→∪►⅏

SUTTON ST JAMES   Map 09 TF31

► ► ► 74% Foremans Bridge Caravan Park (TF409197)
Sutton Rd PE12 0HU ☎ 01945 440346
e-mail: foremans.bridge@btinternet.com
website: www.foremans-bridge.co.uk
Dir: *2m from A17 on B1390*
★ ⊞ £6.50-£8.50 ⊞ £6.50-£8.50 Å £5-£6.50
Open Mar-Nov Booking advisable Bank hols Last arrival 21.00hrs
A lovely, well-maintained little site set beside the South Holland Main Drain which flows past, and offers good fishing. The enthusiastic hands-on owners keep the facilities in immaculate condition, and their quiet park is mainly used by adults. A 2.5-acre site with 40 touring pitches and 7 statics.
Cycle hire centre, fishing on site.
Facilities: ₨⊙⅍⊹↺⅏⊞π⊓π **Services:** ♨⊡╏⌀⊞
⊡→►⅏ **Notes:** No cycling or ball games in park

WADDINGHAM   Map 08 SK99

► 63% NEW Brandy Wharf Leisure Park (TF014968)
Brandy Wharf DN21 4RT ☎ 01673 818010
▤ 01673 818010
e-mail: brandywharflp@freenetname.co.uk
website: www.brandywharfleisurepark.co.uk
Dir: *Turn off A15 onto B1205, through Waddingham. Campsite 3m from Waddingham*
★ ⊞ fr £7 ⊞ fr £7 Å fr £6
Open all year Booking advisable Etr-Sep
A simple, quiet site in a very rural area on the banks of the River Ancholme, where fishing is available. The basic unisex facilities are clean, and there are level grassy pitches, all with electricity, and a playing/picnic area. A 5-acre site with 10 touring pitches.
Fishing & boat mooring
Leisure: ⚑ **Facilities:** ₨⊹↺⊞π
Services: ♨⅏⌀⊞→⅏

WOODHALL SPA   Map 08 TF16

► ► ► ► ► 72% Bainland Country Park (TF215640)
Horncastle Rd LN10 6UX
☎ 01526 352903 & 353572 ▤ 01526 353730
e-mail: bainland@bainland.com
website: www.bainland.com
Dir: *1.5m from town, on B1191*
★ ⊞ £9.50-£30 ⊞ £9.50-£30 Å £7.50-£13

contd.

Open all year Booking advisable all year Last arrival 21.30hrs Last departure 11.30hrs
More a country club than a purely touring park, this is one of the best equipped parks in the country with an impressive array of leisure facilities, combined with high standards of maintenance. The touring pitches are all screened by shrubs and trees, and many are fully serviced. Children are well catered for, and there is an indoor swimming pool. A 12-acre site with 170 touring pitches, 51 hardstandings and 10 statics.
Jacuzzi, solarium, sauna, par 3 golf, putting, boules.

Leisure: ⚡ ⚲ ⚫ ⌂ ▢ Facilities: ➡ ⋔ ☉ ☜ ✱ ⚒ ☜
⚒ ⚏ ♫ ⋔ Services: ☎ Ⓨ ⋔ ⌂ ▣ ⟙ ✕ ⟐ ➡ → ∪ ▶ ◎
△ ⚌ ⚊ ⚌ ▦ ☰ ❋ ▨

▶ ▶ ▶ **68% Camping & Caravanning Club Site** (TF225633)
Wellsyke Ln, Kirkby-on-Bain LN10 6YU
☎ 01526 352911
website: www.campingandcaravanningclub.co.uk
Dir: From Sleaford or Horncastle take A153 to Haltham. At garage turn onto side road. Over bridge, left towards Kirkby-on-Bain. 1st turn right, signed
★ ⚐ £12.30-£15.50 ⚐ £12.30-£15.50 ▲ £12.30-£15.50
Open Mar-Oct Booking advisable bank hols & Jul-Aug Last arrival 21.00hrs Last departure noon
A pleasant site in silver birch wood and moorland, with pitches laid out around a central lake (no fishing). Facilities include a family room and a unisex room with en suite facilities. Please see the advertisement on page 10 for details of Club Members' benefits. A 6-acre site with 99 touring pitches.

Facilities: ⋔ ☉ ⚒ ✱ ⚒ ⟙ ⋔ Services: ☎ ▣ ⌂ ⟙ ▣ ➡
→ ∪ ▶ △ ⚌ ⚊ ⚌ ⚏ ☰ ❋ ▨ ▨

LONDON

E4 CHINGFORD Map 05 TQ39

▶ ▶ ▶ **68% Lee Valley Campsite** (TQ381970)
Sewardstone Rd E4 7RA ☎ 020 8529 5689
🖳 020 8559 4070
e-mail: scs@leevalleypark.org.uk
Dir: From M25 junct 26 to A112 and signed
★ ⚐ £11.20 ⚐ £11.20 ▲ £11.20

contd.

Perfectly Placed for the
City of London
and the countryside of Hertfordshire and Essex
Lee Valley Regional Park is a perfect place to stay. All sites have modern facilities, offer value for money and are located in pleasant surroundings with their own leisure attractions.

Lee Valley Caravan Park, Dobbs Weir, Hoddesdon, Herts
Enjoy the peace and tranquillity of this riverside site with good fishing, walking and boating nearby. Get to the West End by train and tube in under an hour.
Tel/Fax: 01992 462090
caravanpark@leevalleypark.org.uk

Lee Valley Campsite, Chingford, London
Situated on the edge of Epping Forest and close to the historic town of Waltham Abbey, this site is easily accessible from the M25 and

just 42 minutes from the West End by public transport.
Tel: 020 8529 5689
Fax: 020 8559 4070
scs@leevalleypark.org.uk

Lee Valley Camping and Caravan Park, Edmonton, London
Not only is this peaceful site within easy reach of central London, the site boasts an 18-hole golf course and a 12 screen UCI cinema.
Tel: 020 8803 6900
leisurecentre@leevalleypark.org.uk

For more information, call the Lee Valley Park Information Centre on 01992 702200 or find us on the web at: www.leevalleypark.com **Lee Valley Park**

Open Apr-Oct Booking advisable bank hols & Jul-Aug Last arrival 22.00hrs Last departure noon
Well-run useful North London site with excellent modern facilities and a peaceful atmosphere, with easy access to town. Overlooking King George's reservoir and close to Epping Forest. A 12-acre site with 200 touring pitches.

Leisure: ⌂ Facilities: ⋔ ☉ ☜ ✱ ⚒ ⚏ ⚒ ⋔
Services: ☎ ▣ ⌂ ⟙ ▣ ⟙ → ∪ ▶ ◎ ⚌ ⚊
Notes: No single sex groups ☰ ❋ ▨

N9 EDMONTON Map 05 TQ39

▶ ▶ ▶ **77% Lee Valley Camping & Caravan Park** (TQ360945)
Meridian Way N9 0AS ☎ 020 8803 6900 & 8345 6666 🖳 020 8884 4975
e-mail: leisurecentre@leevalleypark.org.uk
website: www.leevalleypark.org.uk
Dir: from M25 junct 25, A10 S,1st left, approx 5m to Leisure Centre. From A406 (North Circular), N on A1010, left after 0.25m, right (Pickets Lock Ln)
⚐ ⚐ ▲
Booking advisable Jul-Aug Last arrival 22.00hrs Last departure noon
A pleasant, open site within easy reach of London yet peacefully located close to two large reservoirs. The very good toilet facilities are beautifully kept by dedicated wardens, and the site has the advantage of being adjacent to a restaurant and bar, and a multi-screen cinema. A 4.5-acre site with 160 touring pitches, 32 hardstandings.

contd.

Facilities: ⋔ Bath ⋔ Shower ☉ Electric Shaver ⚒ Hairdryer ✱ Ice Pack Facility ⚒ Disabled Facilities ⟙ Public Telephone
⚏ Shop on Site or within 200yds ▣ Mobile Shop (calls at least 5 days a week) ▦ BBQ Area ⚊ Picnic Area ⋔ Dog Exercise Area

England

Leisure: ⚠ **Facilities:** ⬚⊙⬚⬚⬚⬚⬚⬚⬚
Services: ⬚⬚⬚⬚⬚⬚⬚✕⬚⬚→⬚⬚⬚⬚⬚
Notes: No commercial vehicles, max length of units 26 feet ⬚⬚⬚⬚⬚

MERSEYSIDE

SOUTHPORT   Map 07 SD31

► ► ► 68% **Hurlston Hall Country Caravan Park**
(SD398107)
Southport Rd L40 8HB ☎ 01704 841064
📠 01704 841700
Dir: On A570, 3m from Ormskirk towards Southport
★ 🏕 £10-£15 🚐 £10-£15
Open Etr-Oct Booking advisable bank hols Last
arrival 21.00hrs Last departure 17.00hrs ⌖
*A peaceful tree-lined touring park next to a static
site in attractive countryside about 10 minutes'
drive from Southport. The park is maturing well,
with growing trees and a coarse fishing lake. No
dogs permitted. A 5-acre site with 60 touring
pitches and 68 statics.*
Coarse fishing, golf facilities
Leisure: ⚠ **Facilities:** ⬚⬚⬚⬚⬚
Services: ⬚⬚⬚⬚✕→⬚⬚⬚ **Notes:** No tents

► ► ► 73% **Willowbank Holiday
Home & Touring Park (SD305110)**
Coastal Rd, Ainsdale PR8 3ST
☎ 01704 571566 📠 01704 571566
e-mail: mail@willowbankcp.co.uk
website: www.willowbankcp.co.uk
*Dir: From A565 between Formby and Ainsdale turn at the
Woodvale lights onto coastal road, site 150mtrs on left*
★ 🏕 £8.50-£12.50 🚐 £9.50-£12.50 ⛺ £7-£10
Open Mar-10 Jan Booking advisable bank hols &
special events Last arrival 22.00hrs Last departure
16.00hrs
*Set in a wooded clearing on a nature reserve next
to the beautiful sand dunes, this attractive park is
just off the coastal road to Southport. The
immaculate toilet facilities are well equipped. A 6-
acre site with 64 touring pitches, 30 hardstandings
and 102 statics.*
Baby changing facility
Leisure: ⚠ **Facilities:** ⬚⬚⬚⬚⬚⬚⬚
Services: ⬚⬚⬚⬚→⬚⬚⬚⬚⬚ ⬚⬚⬚⬚⬚⬚

NORFOLK

BARNEY   Map 09 TF93

► ► ► ► 77% **The Old Brick Kilns**
(TG007328)
Little Barney Ln, Barney NR21 0NL
☎ 01328 878305 📠 01328 878948
e-mail: enquire@old-brick-kilns.co.uk
website: www.old-brick-kilns.co.uk
*Dir: Follow brown tourist signs from A148
(Fakenham-Cromer) to Barney, then Little Barney*
★ 🏕 £8.25-£12.25 🚐 £8.25-£12.25 ⛺ £8.25-£12.25

contd.

Open 20 Feb-6 Jan (rs low season bar
food/takeaway selected nights only) Booking
advisable bank hols & Jul-Aug Last arrival 22.00hrs
Last departure noon
*A secluded and peaceful park approached via a
quiet leafy country lane. The park is on two levels
with its own boating and fishing pool and many
mature trees. Excellent, well-planned toilet facilities
can be found in two blocks, and there is a short dog
walk. A 12.75-acre site with 65 touring pitches, 65
hardstandings.*
Boules, outdoor draughts, chess, family games
area.
Leisure: ⬚⚠⬚ **Facilities:** ⬚⊙⬚⬚⬚⬚⬚⬚⬚
Services: ⬚⬚⬚⬚⬚⬚⬚✕→⬚⬚⬚⬚⬚⬚⬚

BELTON   Map 05 TG40

61% *Wild Duck Holiday Park
(TG475028)*
Howards Common NR31 9NE
☎ 01493 780268 📠 01493 782308
Dir: Signed from A143
Open Mar-Oct (rs Off peak Restricted times of
certain venues) Booking advisable Jun-Aug &
school holidays Last arrival 23.00hrs
Last departure noon
*This a large holiday complex with facilities for
all ages indoors and out. Level grassy site in
forest with small cleared areas for tourers and
well laid out facilities. A 97-acre site with 240
touring pitches and 370 statics.*
Sauna & jacuzzi
Leisure: ⬚⬚⬚⬚⚠ **Facilities:** ⬚⊙⬚⬚⬚⬚⬚⬚⬚
Services: ⬚⬚⬚⬚⬚⬚⬚⬚→⬚⬚⬚⬚⬚
Notes: No single sex groups ⬚⬚⬚⬚⬚

► ► ► 72% **Rose Farm Touring &
Camping Park (TG488033)**
Stepshort NR31 9JS ☎ 01493 780896
📠 01493 780896
*Dir: Follow signs to Belton off A143, right at lane called
Stepshort, site 1st on right*
★ 🏕 £7-£8 🚐 £7-£8 ⛺ £7-£8
Open all year Booking advisable Jul-Aug
*A former railway line is the setting for this very
peaceful site which enjoys rural views. The ever-
improving facilities are spotlessly clean, and the
park is brightened with many flower and herb beds.
A 6-acre site with 80 touring pitches.*
Leisure: ⬚⚠⬚ **Facilities:** ⬚⊙⬚⬚⬚
Services: ⬚⬚⬚⬚⬚→⬚⬚⬚⬚⬚

CAISTER-ON-SEA   Map 09 TG51

► 65% **Grasmere Caravan Park (TG521115)**
9 Bultitude's Loke, Yarmouth Rd NR30 5DH
☎ 01493 720382
*Dir: From A149 at Stadium rdbt after 0.5m sharp left
turn just before bus stop*
★ 🏕 £7.15-£9.40 🚐 £7.15-£9.40
Open Apr-Oct Booking advisable school & bank
hols Last arrival 22.00hrs Last departure 11.00hrs ⌖
Mainly level grass and gravel site with mature trees.
contd.

Set in meadowland in an urban area with access to A149. A 2-acre site with 46 touring pitches and 62 statics.

Leisure: � **Facilities:** ⊕⊕❄❄&& **Services:** 🔌📷🍴
📷📺→ひ🍴🧹 **Notes:** Non-family groups at owner's discretion 💳 💳 🔳 🔳

CLIPPESBY   Map 09 TG41

▶ ▶ ▶ **70% Clippesby Hall** (TG423147)
Clippesby Hall NR29 3BL ☎ 01493 367800
📠 01493 367809
e-mail: holidays@clippesby.com
website: www.clippesby.com
Dir: From A47 follow tourist signs for The Broads. At Acle rdbt take A1064, after 2m left onto B1152, 0.5m turn left opposite village sign, 400yds on right
★ 🚐 £10-£18 🚐 £10-£18 ▲ £10-£18

Open Etr wk, May-23 Sep (rs Etr-23 May No swimming or tennis) Booking advisable school hols Last arrival 17.30hrs Last departure 11.00hrs
A lovely country house estate with secluded pitches hidden among the trees or in sheltered sunny glades. There are good toilet facilities, and amenities include a café, clubhouse and family crazy-golf. A 30-acre site with 100 touring pitches, 16 hardstandings and 16 statics.
bicycle hire & mini golf
Leisure: 🏊❄🎱⚱️ **Facilities:** ⊕⊕🍴❄&&
🔳🐕 **Services:** 🔌📷🍴🍴📷📺Ⓣ🧹→🍴
Notes: Dogs must be kept on leads 💳 💳 🔳 🔳

CROMER   Map 09 TG24

▶ ▶ ▶ ▶ **71% Seacroft Camping Park** (TG206424)
Runton Rd NR27 9NJ ☎ 01263 511722
📠 01263 511512
Dir: 1m W of Cromer on A149 coast road
★ 🚐 £10.50-£16.70 🚐 £10.50-£16.70 ▲ £10.50-£16.70

contd.

Open Mar-Oct Booking advisable school hols, 22-31 May & 4 Sep Last arrival 23.00hrs Last departure noon
A very good touring site, well laid out and landscaped. Touring pitches are well screened for privacy, and there is a separate large playing field with children's play equipment. Toilets and showers in the sanitary buildings are tiled and spotless. There is a heated swimming pool and bar/restaurant. A 5-acre site with 120 touring pitches.
Baby change.
Leisure: 🏊❄⚱️🖥️ **Facilities:** ⊕⊕🍴❄&&🔳🍴
🏕️🐕 **Services:** 🔌📷🍴📷📺Ⓣ🧹⬆️→ひ🍴◎🧹🍴
💳 💳 🔳 🔳

▶ ▶ ▶ **65% Forest Park Caravan Site**
(TG233405)
Northrepps Rd NR27 OJR ☎ 01263 513290
📠 01263 511992
e-mail: forestpark@netcom.co.uk
website: www.forest-park.co.uk
Dir: A140 from Norwich, left at T-junct signed Cromer, right signed Northrepps, right then immediate left, left at T-junct, park on right
★ 🚐 £8.50-£12.50 🚐 £8.50-£12.50 ▲ £8.50-£12.50
Open Mar-Jan Booking advisable Etr, Spring bank hol & Jul-Aug Last arrival 22.00hrs Last departure 14.00hrs

contd.

FAKENHAM RACECOURSE

Caravan & Camping Site
The ideal choice for your Norfolk holiday
A country site. Near the sea.

Set in beautiful countryside and sheltered by tall conifers, the grounds and modern facilities are excellently maintained. Pitches accommodating touring caravans, motorvans and tents. Ideally located for visiting Norfolk's coastal resorts, stately homes, wildlife and bird sanctuaries and many other attractions.
★★★ TOURING PARK English Tourism Council
Fakenham Racecourse Caravan and Camping Site
The Racecourse, Fakenham, Norfolk NR21 7NY
Tel: 01328 862388 Fax: 01328 855908
info@fakenhamracecourse.co.uk
www.fakenhamracecourse.co.uk

Forest Park Caravan Site

Surrounded by forest, this gently sloping park offers a wide choice of pitches. Visitors have the use of a heated indoor swimming pool, and a large clubhouse with entertainment. An 85-acre site with 344 touring pitches and 372 statics.
BMX track.

Leisure: **Facilities:**
Services:

▶ ▶ ▶ 62% Manor Farm Caravan & Campsite (TG198416)
East Runton NR27 9PR ☎ 01263 512858
e-mail: caravansite@manor-farm.sagehost.co.uk
website: www.manor-farm.sageweb.co.uk
Dir: *1m W of Cromer, turn off A148 or A149 at sign Manor Farm*
★ £7.90-£9.40 £7.90-£9.40 ▲ £7.90-£9.40

contd.

Open Etr-Oct Booking advisable bank hols & all season for EHU points Last arrival 20.30hrs Last departure noon
A well-established family-run site on a working farm with panoramic sea views. There are good modern toilet facilities on the recently-developed caravan-only area, and adequate facilities for tenters. A 17-acre site with 250 touring pitches.
3 dog free fields

Leisure: **Facilities:**
Services:

DISS See Scole

ERPINGHAM Map 09 TG13

▶ ▶ ▶ 61% Little Haven Caravan & Camping Park (TG204323)
The Street NR11 7QD ☎ 01263 768959
01263 768959
e-mail: patl@haven30.fsnet.co.uk
website: www.thegoodguides.co.uk/littlehaven
Dir: *From A140 6m S of Cromer turn by Horseshoes pub signed Erpingham. Site 200yds on right*
£10-£12 £10-£12 ▲ £8-£10
Open Mar-Oct Booking advisable bank holidays Last arrival 21.00hrs Last departure 14.00hrs
A delightful small family-run park surrounded by hawthorn hedges and trees, with good facilities. The large pitches are arranged around a central grass area with flower beds and pergola with seating. An ideal park for relaxing, and for this reason children are not accepted. A 3-acre site with 25 touring pitches, 5 hardstandings.

Facilities: **Services:**
Notes: Adults only

FAKENHAM Map 09 TF92

▶ ▶ ▶ 67% Caravan Club M.V.C. Site (TF926288)
Fakenham Racecourse NR21 7NY ☎ 01328 862388
01328 855908
e-mail: info@fakenhamracecourse.co.uk
website: www.fakenhamracecourse.co.uk
Dir: *0.75m SW of Fakenham off A1065 Swaffham road*
★ £8-£12 £8-£12 ▲ £8-£10

Open all year (rs race days all caravans moved to centre of course) Booking advisable Jun-Sep Last arrival 17.00hrs Last departure 14.00hrs
A level site set around the racecourse, with a new grandstand offering smart modern toilet facilities. Tourers move to the centre of the course on race

contd.

days, and enjoy free racing. An 11.5-acre site with 120 touring pitches.
TV aerial hook-ups
Facilities: 🛖⊙🔌❄️🅰️🔥🔌🚿🔥🐕 **Services:** 🔌🔲🍴🛢️💧🚹
✕🚬➡️⊙▶️🚮🔨💳🏧🔲🔲🔲

GREAT YARMOUTH   Map 05 TG50
See also **Caister-on-Sea**

64% NEW **Cherry Tree Holiday Park**
(TG491055)
     Mill Rd, Burgh Castle NR31 9QR
☎ 01493 780024
website: www.havenholidays.com
★ 🏕️ £8-£25 🚐 £8-£25
Open Mar-Nov Booking advisable Last arrival 22.00hrs Last departure 12.00hrs
A small touring area within a large holiday park with good on-site family entertainment and leisure facilities. The coast and the bustling resort of Great Yarmouth are three miles away. A 31-acre site with 21 touring pitches.
Leisure: 🌊🎿♠️🎢🎱 **Facilities:** 🛒
Services: 🔲🍴🛢️✕🛒💳🔲 ⓓ 🔲🔲🔲

68% Vauxhall Holiday Park
(TG520083)
     4 Acle New Rd NR30 1TB
☎ 01493 857231 📠 01493 331122
e-mail: vauxhall.holidays@virgin.net
website: www.vauxhall-holiday-park.co.uk
Dir: On A47 approaching Great Yarmouth
★ 🏕️ £13-£26 🚐 £13-£26 ▲ £13-£26
        contd.

Vauxhall Holiday Park
Open Etr, mid May-Sep & Oct half term Booking advisable mid Jul-Aug Last arrival 21.00hrs Last departure 10.00hrs ✂️
A very large holiday complex with plenty of entertainment and access to beach, river, estuary, lake and main A47. The touring pitches are laid out in four separate areas, each with its own amenity block, and all arranged around the main entertainment. A 40-acre site with 220 touring pitches and 421 statics.
Childrens pool, Sauna, Solarium, Fitness centre.
Leisure: 🌊♠️🎢🎱 **Facilities:** 🛖⊙❄️🔌🛒
Services: 🔌🔲🍴💧🔲🔲✕🛒🚬➡️⊙▶️🔨🔌🛢️🍴
🔲🔲🔲🔲🔲

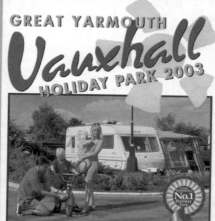

HUNSTANTON   Map 09 TF64

70% Searles of Hunstanton (TF671400)
South Beach PE36 5BB
☎ 01485 534211 & 532342 ext 100
🖷 01485 533815
e-mail: bookings@searles.co.uk
website: www.searles.co.uk
Dir: A149 from King's Lynn to Hunstanton. At rdbt follow signs for South Beach. Straight on at 2nd rdbt. Searles on left
★ 🚐 £11-£27 🚐 £11-£27 ⅄ £9-£22

Open Etr/Mar-Nov (rs Mar-May & Oct-Nov outdoor pool closed) Booking advisable bank hols & Jul-Aug Last arrival 20.45hrs
Last departure 11.00hrs
A large seaside holiday complex with well-managed facilities, adjacent to sea and beach.
contd.

The tourers have their own areas, including two excellent toilet blocks, and pitches are individually lined with small maturing shrubs for privacy. A 50-acre site with 350 touring pitches, 100 hardstandings and 450 statics.
Stables, entertainment programme & hire shop.
Leisure: ⧈ ⧈ ⧈ ⧈ ⛰ Facilities: ➡ ♠ ⊙ ⧈ ✳ ⅄ ⧈ ⧈
⧈ ♬ ⛩ Services: ⧈ ⧈ ⧈ ⧈ ⧈ ⧈ ⧈ ⛳ ✕ ⧈ → ∪ ⧈ ⧈ ⧈ ⅄
♥ ♬ Notes: No single sex groups, minimum booking age 25yrs ⧈ ⧈ ⧈ ⧈ ⧈

KING'S LYNN   See **Stanhoe**

MUNDESLEY   Map 09 TG33

▶ ▶ 58% *Links Caravan Site (TG305365)*
Links Rd NR11 8AE ☎ 01263 720665
Dir: From B1159 at Mundesley turn into Church Road
🚐 🚐 ⅄
Open Etr-1st wk Oct Booking advisable bank hols & peak season Last arrival 22.00hrs Last departure noon
A pleasant site on a south-facing slope with level pitches, with distant rural views. The site is popular with those who enjoy peace and simplicity, and there is a golf course adjacent. A 2-acre site with 55 touring pitches.
Leisure: ⛰ Facilities: ♠ ⊙ ✳
Services: ⧈ → ∪ ⧈ ⧈ ♬ ⧈ ⧈

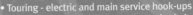

NORTH WALSHAM — Map 09 TG23

▶ ▶ ▶ ▶ **78% Two Mills Touring Park (TG291286)**
Yarmouth Rd NR28 9NA
☎ 01692 405829 📠 01692 405829
e-mail: enquiries@twomills.co.uk
website: www.twomills.co.uk
Dir: 1m S of North Walsham on Old Yarmouth rd past police station & hospital on left
★ 🚐 £10-£14.50 🚐 £10-£14.50 ▲ £10-£14.50
Open Mar-3 Jan Booking advisable Jul & Aug Last arrival 20.30hrs Last departure noon
Situated in superb countryside, in an ideally peaceful spot which is also convenient for touring. Some fully serviced pitches have panoramic views over the site, and the layout of pitches and facilities is excellent. The very friendly and helpful owners keep the park in immaculate condition. This park does not accept children. A 5-acre site with 50 touring pitches.
Tourist information room & library
Leisure: 🖵 Facilities: ℝ⊙ℚ❄ዼᏋৎ◟Åⵟ
Services: 🖭🖩ⁱ◢🖹🖹 → ♪ Notes: No children, 2 dogs max per pitch 💳 💳 💳 💳 🔟

NORWICH — Map 05 TG20

▶ ▶ **64% Camping & Caravanning Club Site (TG237063)**
Martineau Ln NR1 2HX ☎ 01603 620060
website: www.campingandcaravanningclub.co.uk
Dir: From A47 join A146 towards City Centre. Left at lights to next lights, under low bridge to Cock pub, turn left. Site 150yds on right
★ 🚐 £12.30-£15.50 🚐 £12.30-£15.50 ▲ £12.30-£15.50
Open Mar-Oct Booking advisable bank hols & Jul-Aug Last arrival 21.00hrs Last departure noon
A very pretty small site on the outskirts of the city, close to the River Yare. The park is built on two levels, with the lower meadow enjoying good rural views, and there is plenty of screening from nearby houses. The older-style toilet block is kept immaculately clean. Please see the advertisement on page 10 for details of Club Members' benefits. A 2.5-acre site with 50 touring pitches.
Fishing
Facilities: ℝ⊙ℚ❄◟Åⵟ
Services: 🖭ⁱ◢🖹→▶Å⌖🐾◢🔟 💳 💳 💳 💳 🔟

SADDLE BOW — Map 09 TF61

▶ ▶ ▶ **70% Bank Farm Caravan Park (TF593157)**
Fallow Pipe Rd PE34 3AS ☎ 01553 617305
📠 01553 617648
Dir: Leave A47 at signs for Saddlebow. In village cross river bridge. After 1m turn right into Fallow Pipe Rd. Farm at end of road
★ 🚐 £7 🚐 £7 ▲ £5
Open Mar-Oct Booking advisable bank holidays Last arrival 23.00hrs Last departure 11.00hrs
A very pleasant, quiet park on a working farm on the banks of the River Ouse. Pitches are well laid out among mature trees, and facilities are housed in converted farm buildings. A 1.5-acre site with 15 touring pitches.
contd.

Putting green, snooker table
Leisure: 🔍 Facilities: ℝ⊙ℚ❄◟Åⴱ
Services: 🖭🖩ⁱ◢🖹 → ♪
Notes: No ball games, dogs must be on leads

ST JOHN'S FEN END — Map 09 TF51

▶ ▶ **64% Virginia Lake Caravan Park (TF538113)**
Sneeth Rd, Marshland PE14 8JF
☎ 01945 430332 & 430676 📠 01945 430128
Dir: From A47 E of Wisbech follow tourist board signs to Terrington St John. Park on left
★ 🚐 £10 🚐 £10 ▲ £6-£10
Open all year Booking advisable Last arrival 23.30hrs Last departure noon
A well-established park beside a 2-acre fishing lake with good facilities for both anglers and tourers. A clubhouse serves a selection of meals and offers weekend entertainment. A good base for touring West Norfolk. A 5-acre site with 50 touring pitches and 4 statics.
Fishing
Leisure: ⚠ Facilities: ℝ⊙ℚ❄◟Åৎ⌂ⴱ
Services: 🖭🖩ⁱ◢🖹✕🖐→∪▶◉🐾♪

SANDRINGHAM — Map 09 TF62

▶ ▶ ▶ ▶ **74% Camping & Caravanning Club Site (TF683274)**
The Sandringham Estate, Double Lodges PE35 6EA
☎ 01485 542555
website: www.campingandcaravanningclub.co.uk
Dir: From A148 turn left onto B1440 signed West Newton. Follow signs to site. Or take A149 turning left & following signs to site
★ 🚐 £14.50-£17.50 🚐 £14.50-£17.50 ▲ £14.50-£17.50
Open Feb-Nov Booking advisable bank hols & high season Last arrival 21.00hrs Last departure noon
A prestige park, very well landscaped and laid out in mature woodland, with toilets and other buildings blending in with the scenery. There are plenty of walks from the site, and this is a good touring base for the rest of Norfolk. Please see the advertisement on page 10 for details of Club Members' benefits. A 28-acre site with 275 touring pitches, 2 hardstandings.
Leisure: ⚠ Facilities: ℝ⊙ℚ❄◟Åⴱ
Services: 🖭🖩ⁱ◢🖹→∪▶◉♨◢ 💳 💳 💳 💳 🔟

SCOLE — Map 05 TM17

▶ ▶ ▶ **60% Willows Camping & Caravan Park (TM146789)**
Diss Rd IP21 4DH ☎ 01379 740271 📠 01379 740271
Dir: At Scole rdbt on A140 turn onto A1066, site 150yds on left
★ 🚐 £8-£10 🚐 £8-£10 ▲ £7-£8
Open Etr-Oct Booking advisable Spring bank hol & school hols Last arrival 23.00hrs Last departure noon
A quiet garden site on the banks of the River Waveney, bordered by willow trees. The park is well placed on the Norfolk/Suffolk border, and ideal for touring both counties. A 4-acre site with 32 touring pitches.
contd.

Leisure: 🏊 Indoor swimming pool 🏊 Outdoor swimming pool ◔ Tennis court 🔍 Games room ⚠ Children's playground ∪ Stables ▶ 9/18 hole golf course ⛵ Boats for hire 🎦 Cinema ◢ Fishing ◉ Mini golf ⚠ Watersports 🖵 Separate TV room

Willows Camping & Caravan Park

Washing-up sinks.

Leisure: /↑\ **Facilities:** ↑ ⊙ ✳
Services: ♀ ♠ ⬚ ⬚ ⬚ → ↑ ♪ ⬚ ⬚

SCRATBY   **Map 09 TG51**

► ► ► 65% **Scratby Hall Caravan Park** (TG501155)
NR29 3PH ☎ 01493 730283
Dir: Signed off B1159
★ ♣ £5.25-£11.50 ♣ £5.25-£11.50 ▲ £5.25-£11.50

Open Spring bank hol-mid Sep (rs Etr-Spring bank
hol & mid Sep-Oct reduced hours & shop closed)
Booking advisable Spring Bank hol wk & Jul-Aug
Last arrival 22.00hrs Last departure noon
*A neatly-maintained site with a popular children's
play area, well-equipped shop and outdoor
swimming pool with sun terrace. The toilets are
kept spotlessly clean, and the beach and the Norfolk
Broads are close by. A 5-acre site with 108 touring
pitches.*
Washing-up & food preparation room.

Leisure: ◆ /↑\ **Facilities:** ↑ ⊙ ⛱ ✳ ⬚ ⬚ ⬚
Services: ♀ ⬚ ♠ ⬚ ⬚ ⬚ → ∪ ↑ ↳ ♪

STANHOE   **Map 09 TF83**

► ► ► 69% **The Rickels Caravan & Camping Park**
(TF794355)
Bircham Rd PE31 8PU ☎ 01485 518671
▤ 01485 518969
*Dir: From King's Lynn take A148 to Hillington, then
B1153 to Great Bircham. Then B1155 to x-roads, straight
over, site 100yds on left*
♣ ♣ ▲
Open Mar-Oct Booking advisable Bank hols Last
arrival 21.00hrs Last departure 11.00hrs
*Set in three acres of grassland, with good open
views and a pleasant, relaxing atmosphere. The
land is slightly sloping with some level areas and*

contd.

---

*sheltering for tents. Children using the play
equipment can be safely watched from all pitches.
A 3-acre site with 30 touring pitches.*

The Rickels Caravan & Camping Park

Leisure: /↑\ ⬚ **Facilities:** ↑ ⊙ ✳ ⬚ ↑
Services: ♀ ♠ ⬚ ⬚ → ♪ **Notes:** Dogs must be on
leads, no ground sheets

SWAFFHAM   **Map 05 TF80**

► ► ► 70% **Breckland Meadows Touring Park**
(TF809094)
Lynn Rd PE37 7PT ☎ 01760 721246
e-mail: info@brecklandmeadows.co.uk
website: www.brecklandmeadows.co.uk
Dir: 0.5m W of Swaffham on the old A47
★ ♣ £8-£10 ♣ £8-£10 ▲ £6-£8
Open all year (rs Nov-Feb strictly bookings only)
Booking advisable Nov-Feb & BH's Last arrival
21.00hrs Last departure 12.00hrs
*Enthusiastic owners have completely redeveloped
this small, well-landscaped park on the edge of
Swaffham. The impressive toilet block has been
refurbished, and there are hardstandings and full
electricity. Plenty of planting will eventually result in
mature screening. A 2.5-acre site with 45 touring
pitches, 10 hardstandings.*
Tourist info centre

Leisure: /↑\ **Facilities:** ↑ ⊙ ✳ ⬚ ⬚ ⬚ ↑
Services: ♀ ♠ ⬚ ⬚ → ∪ ↑ ♪ ⬚ ⬚ ⬚ ⬚ ⬚ ⬚ ⬚

SYDERSTONE   **Map 09 TF83**

► ► ► 69% **The Garden Caravan Site**
(TF812337)
Barmer Hall Farm PE31 8SR ☎ 01485 578220
▤ 01485 578178
e-mail: nigel@mason96fsnet.co.uk
website: www.gardencaravansite.co.uk
*Dir: Signed off B1454 at Barmer between A148 and
Docking, 1m W of Syderstone*
★ ♣ fr £10 ♣ fr £10 ▲ fr £10
Open Mar-Nov Booking advisable Last departure
noon
*In the tranquil setting of a former walled garden
beside a large farmhouse, with mature trees and
shrubs, and surrounded by woodland, a secluded
site. A 3.5-acre site with 30 touring pitches.*

Facilities: ↑ ⊙ ⛱ ✳ ⬚ ⬚ ⬚ ⬚ ↑
Services: ♀ ♠ ⬚ → ∪ ↑ ⬚

England

TRIMINGHAM
Map 09 TG23

► ► ► 58% *Woodlands Leisure Park (TG274388)*
NR11 8AL ☎ 01263 579208 🖷 01263 833071
e-mail: info@woodland-park.co.uk
website: www.woodland-park.co.uk
Dir: 4m SE on B1159 coast road
🚐 🚐

Open Mar-Oct Booking advisable public hols & Jul-Aug Last arrival 23.00hrs Last departure noon
A pleasant woodland site close to the sea but well sheltered from winds. Pitches in open areas among the trees, and good clubhouse with bowling green. A 10-acre site with 85 touring pitches and 220 statics.
Leisure: 🏊 🎣 🎠 Facilities: 🌳⊙🧺☀️🚻👶🏠🛒🎪
Services: 🍴🍺🛒🚿❌🚮→ʊ▶♨️🟦💷

WEST RUNTON
Map 09 TG14

► ► ► 69% Camping & Caravanning Club Site (TG189419)
Holgate Ln NR27 9NW ☎ 01263 837544
website: www.campingandcaravanningclub.co.uk
Dir: From King's Lynn on A148 towards West Runton turn left at Roman Camp Inn. Site track on right at crest of hill, 0.5m to site
★ 🚐 £14.50-£17.50 🚐 £14.50-£17.50 🅰 £14.50-£17.50
Open Mar-Nov Booking advisable bank hols & peak periods Last arrival 21.00hrs Last departure noon
A lovely, well-kept site with some gently sloping pitches on pleasantly undulating ground. This peaceful park is surrounded on three sides by woodland, with the fourth side open to fields and the coast beyond. Please see the advertisement on page 10 for details of Club Members' benefits. A 15-acre site with 225 touring pitches.
Leisure: 🎠 Facilities: 🌳⊙🧺☀️🚻👶📞🐕🎪
Services: 🍴🛒👶🚮→ʊ▶♨️🟦💷

WORTWELL
Map 05 TM28

► ► ► ► 74% Little Lakeland Caravan Park (TM279849)
IP20 0EL ☎ 01986 788646 🖷 01986 788646
e-mail: information@littlelakeland.co.uk
website: www.littlelakeland.co.uk
Dir: From W leave A143 at sign for Wortwell. In village turn right 300yds past garage. From E on A143, left onto B1062, then right. After 0.25m turn left
🚐 £8.50-£10.60 🚐 £8.50-£10.60 🅰 £8.50-£10.60
Open 15 Mar-Oct (rs Mar-Etr restricted laundry facilities) Booking advisable bank hols & peak periods Last arrival 22.00hrs Last departure noon

contd.

A well-kept and pretty site built round a fishing lake, and accessed by a lake-lined drive. The individual pitches are sited in hedged enclosures for complete privacy, and the purpose-built toilet facilities are excellent. A 4.5-acre site with 40 touring pitches and 20 statics.
Library & fishing on site.
Leisure: 🎠 Facilities: 🌳⊙🧺☀️👶🛒
Services: 🍴👶🚮🟦🚮→ʊ▶♨️🚮

NORTHAMPTONSHIRE

THRAPSTON
Map 04 SP97

► ► 63% Mill Marina (SP994781)
Midland Rd NN14 4JR ☎ 01832 732850
website: www.mill-marina.co.uk
Dir: Take Thrapston exit from A14 or A605. Site signed
★ 🚐 £10.40-£11.40 🚐 £9.40-£10.30 🅰 £8.40-£9.20
Open Apr-Dec (rs Jan-Mar maintenance access for stored caravans) Booking advisable public hols & summer wknds Last arrival 21.00hrs Last departure 18.00hrs
A pretty site between the River Nene and the old mill race, with mature willows and other trees, and clean but dated toilet facilities. There are moorings and a slipway for boat owners, and a licensed bar with picnic tables outside, where the attractive views can be enjoyed. An 8-acre site with 45 touring pitches and 6 statics.
Slipway for boats & canoes, coarse fishing on site
Facilities: 🌳⊙🧺☀️📞🏠🐕
Services: 🍴🛒👶🚮🟦🚮→ʊ♨️🚮🛒
Notes: Twin-axled units by arrangement only

NORTHUMBERLAND

BAMBURGH
Map 12 NU13

► ► ► ► 69% Waren Caravan Park (NU155343)
Waren Mill NE70 7EE ☎ 01668 214366
🖷 01668 214224
e-mail: enquiries@warencp.demon.co.uk
website: www.meadowhead.co.uk
Dir: 2m E of town on B1342. From A1 turn onto B1342 signed Bamburgh and take unclass road past Waren Mill, signed Budle
★ 🚐 £8.75-£14.45 🚐 £8.75-£14.45 🅰 £8.75-£14.45
Open Apr-Oct Booking advisable Spring bank hol & Jul-Aug Last arrival 20.00hrs Last departure noon
Attractive seaside site with footpath access to the beach, surrounded by a slightly sloping grassy embankment giving shelter to caravans. The park offers excellent facilities including several family bathrooms. A 4-acre site with 120 touring pitches, 11 hardstandings and 300 statics.
100 acres of private heathland.
Leisure: 🏊 🎣 🎠 Facilities: 🚿🌳⊙🧺☀️🚻👶🛒🏠🐕
Services: 🍴🛒👶🚮🟦🚮❌🚿→ʊ▶⊙🚮
Notes: No single sex groups 💷🟦🟥

Facilities: 🚿 Bath 🌳 Shower ⊙ Electric Shaver 🧺 Hairdryer ☀️ Ice Pack Facility ♿ Disabled Facilities 📞 Public Telephone 🛒 Shop on Site or within 200yds 📱 Mobile Shop (calls at least 5 days a week) 🏠 BBQ Area 🌲 Picnic Area 🐕 Dog Exercise Area

►►► 64% Glororum Caravan Park (NU166334)
Glororum Farm NE69 7AW ☎ 01668 214457
🖹 01688 214622
e-mail: info@glororum-caravanpark.co.uk
website: www.glororum-caravanpark.co.uk
*Dir: Leave A1 at junct B1341 (Purdy's Lodge), in 3.5m
turn left onto unclass rd. Site 300yds on left*
★ 🚐 £9-£11 🚐 £9-£11 Å £9-£10
Open Apr-Oct Booking advisable school hols, BH's
Last arrival 22.00hrs Last departure 11.00hrs
*A pleasantly situated site where tourers have their
own well-established facilities. The open
countryside setting affords good views of
Bamburgh Castle and surrounding farmland. A
6-acre site with 100 touring pitches and 150 statics.*
Leisure: ⚠ Facilities: 🝕⊙🝑☀✆🝞🝓🝝
Services: 🔌🝓🝃⊿🝆→∪🝟◉◬🝣⊿

BEADNELL   **Map 12 NU22**

**►► 63% Camping & Caravanning Club Site
(NU231291)**
NE67 5BX ☎ 01665 720586
website: www.campingandcaravanningclub.co.uk
*Dir: Leave A1 & follow B1430 signed Seahouses. At
Beadnell ignore signs for Beadnell village. Site on left
after village, just after left bend*
★ 🚐 £11.10-£14.50 Å £11.10-£14.50
Open May-Sep Booking advisable bank hols & Jul-
Aug Last arrival 21.00hrs Last departure noon
*A level grassy site in a coastal area just across the
road from the sea and sandy beach. Popular with
divers, anglers, surfboarders and canoeists, and
ideal for visiting many tourist attractions.
Motorvans and tents only. Please see page 10 for
details of Club members' benefits. A 6-acre site with
150 touring pitches.*
Facilities: 🝕⊙🝑☀✆🝞🝝
Services: 🝃🝆⊿→∪🝟◬🝣⊿🝡🝒🝨🝩🝪

BELLINGHAM   **Map 12 NY88**

**►►►► 69% Brown Rigg Caravan & Camping
Park (NY835826)**
NE48 2HR ☎ 01434 220175 🖹 01434 220175
e-mail:
enquiries@northumberlandcaravanparks.com
website: www.northumberlandcaravanparks.com
Dir: On B6320, 0.5m S of Bellingham
🚐🚐Å

Open wk before Etr-Oct Booking advisable bank &
school hols Last arrival 20.30hrs Last departure
noon   *contd.*

---

*Set in a pleasant rural location, this quiet park is
surrounded by trees on one side and extensive
views on the other. The camping area is flat and
grassy, with marked pitches for caravans. Sanitary
facilities are modern and first class, with spacious
showers and toilets. The park is handy for the
various attractions of Northumberland. A 5.5-acre
site with 60 touring pitches, 9 hardstandings.*
Tea room, small garden centre
Leisure: ♦ ⚠🝓🝃⌀☀✆🝞🝚🝝
Services: 🔌🝓🝃⌀🝐🝋🝭→🝟⊿
Notes: Dogs must be kept on leads at all times

BERWICK-UPON-TWEED   **Map 12 NT95**

**72% Haggerston Castle
(NU041435)**
Beal TD15 2PA
GOLD
☎ 01289 381333 & 381200 🖹 01289 381337
*Dir: On A1, 5.5m S of Berwick-upon-Tweed and
signed*
🚐🚐
Open Mar-Oct Booking advisable Last arrival
21.00hrs Last departure 10.00hrs
*A large holiday centre with a very well equipped
touring park, offering comprehensive holiday
activities. The entertainment complex contains
amusements for the whole family, and there are
several bars, an adventure playground, boating
on the lake, a children's club, a 9-hole golf
course, tennis courts, and various eating outlets.
A 7-acre site with 156 touring pitches and 1200
statics.*
Leisure: 🝡 🝢🝣◉⚠🝒 Facilities: 🝕⊙🝑☀✆🝞🝚
🝓🝝 Services: 🔌🝓🝏🝐🝋🝭🝭→∪🝟◉◬🝣
🝡🝒🝨🝩🝪

**►►►►► 76% Ord House
Country Park (NT982515)**
East Ord TD15 2NS
GOLD
☎ 01289 305288 🖹 01289 330832
e-mail: enquiries@ordhouse.co.uk
website: www.ordhouse.co.uk
*Dir: On A1, Berwick bypass, turn off at 2nd rdbt at
East Ord, follow 'Caravan' signs*
★ 🚐 £8-£13.95 🚐 £8-£13.95 Å £5-£13.95
Open all year Booking advisable bank hols &
Jul-Aug Last arrival 23.00hrs Last departure
noon
*A very well run park set in the pleasant grounds
of an 18th-century country house. Touring
pitches are marked and well spaced, some of
them fully-serviced. The very modern toilet
facilities include family bath and shower suites,
and first class disabled rooms. There is a six-
hole golf course and an outdoor leisure shop
with a good range of camping and caravanning
spares, as well as clothing and equipment. A
42-acre site with 79 touring pitches, 46
hardstandings and 200 statics.*
Crazy golf, table tennis & 6 hole pitch & putt.
Leisure: ⚠ Facilities: 🝭🝕⊙🝑☀✆🝞🝚🝓🝝
Services: 🔌🝓🝏🝐🝋⌀🝭🝭→🝟◉◬🝲🝣
Notes: No single sex groups 🝡🝒🝨🝩🝪

⊔ Old Mill Caravan Site (NU055401)
West Kyloe Farm, Beal TD15 2PG ☎ 01289 381279
🖹 01289 381279
e-mail: treasamalley@westkyloe.demon.co.uk
website: www.westkyloe.co.uk
Dir: Take B6353 off A1, 9m S of Berwick-Upon-Tweed.
Road signposted to Lowick. West Kyloe farm 1m up
road
★ 🚐 £7-£12 🚐 £5-£10 ▲ £5-£10
At the time of going to press the pennant
classification for this site was not confirmed.
Open Etr-Oct Booking advisable at all times Last
arrival 19.00hrs Last departure 11.00hrs
A 2-acre site with 10 touring pitches.
Facilities: ⋒⊙♿ **Services:** 🔌→🛒
Notes: Dogs must be kept on lead when on site

CRASTER   Map 12 NU21

▶ ▶ ▶ 69% **Camping & Caravanning Club Site**
(NU236214)
Dunstan Hill, Alnwick NE66 3TQ ☎ 01665 576310
website: www.campingandcaravanningclub.co.uk
Dir: From A1 take B1340 signed Seahouses. Right at T-
junct at Christon Bank. Next right signed Embleton.
Right at x-roads then 1st left signed Craster
★ 🚐 £12.30-£15.50 🚐 £12.30-£15.50 ▲ £12.30-£15.50
Open Mar-Oct Booking advisable BH's & Jul-Aug
Last arrival 21.00hrs Last departure noon
An immaculately maintained site with pleasant
landscaping, close to the beach and Craster
harbour. The historic town of Alnwick is nearby, as
is the ruined Dunstanburgh Castle. Please see the
advertisement on page 10 for details of Club
Members' benefits. A 14-acre site with 150 touring
pitches, 5 hardstandings.
Facilities: ⋒⊙🍳❄♿ᄂ✝
Services: 🔌🖥🛢⌀🔜→∪▲🍴🧺🛒 🍴🔌🔵🔶

HALTWHISTLE   Map 12 NY76

▶ ▶ ▶ 64% **Camping & Caravanning Club Site**
(NY685621)
Burnfoot, Park Village NE49 0JP ☎ 01434 320106
website: www.campingandcaravanningclub.co.uk
Dir: From A69 Haltwhistle bypass (do not go into town)
take Alston Rd S signed A689, then turn right signed
Kellan
★ 🚐 £10.20-£12.90 🚐 £10.20-£12.90 ▲ £10.20-£12.90
Open Mar-Oct Booking advisable bank hols & high
season Last arrival 21.00hrs Last departure noon
An attractive site on the banks of the River South
Tyne amidst mature trees, on the Bellister Castle
estate. This peaceful, relaxing site is a good cross
country transit stop in excellent walking country.
Please see the advertisement on page 10 for details
of Club Members' benefits. A 3.5-acre site with 50
touring pitches, 17 hardstandings.
Fishing
Facilities: ⋒⊙🍳❄♿ᄂ✝
Services: 🔌🖥🛢⌀→▲🧺🛒 🍴🔌🔵🔶

HEXHAM   Map 12 NY96

▶ ▶ ▶ 64% **Causey Hill Caravan Park (NY925625)**
Causey Hill NE46 2JN ☎ 01434 602834
🖹 01434 602834
e-mail: causeyhillcp@aol.com
Dir: take B6306 from Hexham Town Centre to Whittey
Chapel. Right for Hexham Racecourse, right again for
caravan park
★ 🚐 £9.50-£13.50 🚐 £9.50-£13.50 ▲ £8-£10
Open Mar-Oct Booking advisable public hols &
May-Sep Last arrival 22.00hrs Last departure noon
A well-maintained site on very sloping ground with
some level pitches. Attractively screened by trees. A
6-acre site with 35 touring pitches, 20 hardstandings
and 105 statics.
Off Licence.
Leisure: ⚑ **Facilities:** ⋒⊙❄ᄂ🛒✝
Services: 🔌🖥🛢⌀→∪▸🧺🛒⌀

▶ ▶ ▶ 60% **Hexham Racecourse Caravan Site**
(NY919623)
Hexham Racecourse NE46 3NN ☎ 01434 606847 &
606881 🖹 01434 605814
e-mail: hexhrace@aol.com
Dir: From Hexham take B6305 signed Allendale/Alston,
turn left in 3m signed to racecourse. Site 1.5m on right
🚐🚐▲
Open May-Sep Booking advisable wknds & bank
hols for electric hook-up Last arrival 20.00hrs Last
departure noon
A part-level and part-sloping grassy site on
racecourse overlooking Hexhamshire Moors.
The facilities are functional and well-maintained.
A 4-acre site with 40 touring pitches.
Leisure: ♠⚑ **Facilities:** ⋒⊙🍳❄ᄂᄀ✝
Services: 🔌🖥🛢⌀🔜→∪▸🧺🛒⌀🔌

ROTHBURY   Map 12 NU00

▶ ▶ ▶ 65% **Coquetdale Caravan Park (NU055007)**
Whitton NE65 7RU ☎ 01669 620549 🖹 01669 620559
e-mail: enquiries@coquetdalecaravanpark.co.uk
website: www.coquetdalecaravanpark.co.uk
Dir: 0.5m SW of Rothbury on road to Newtown
★ 🚐 £8-£14 🚐 £8-£14 ▲ £6-£11
Open mid Mar/Etr-Oct Booking advisable bank hol
wknds Last arrival anytime Last departure evening
A very pleasant mainly static site in a lovely
location beside the River Coquet, with good open
views of moorland and the Simonside Hills. Tourers
are on the site's upper area with their own purpose-
built toilet facilities. An ideal place for relaxing and
touring. A 13-acre site with 50 touring pitches and
160 statics.
Adventure playground for Older Children/Adults
Leisure: ⚑ **Facilities:** ⋒⊙❄ᄂ🛒ᄀ✝
Services: 🔌🛢⌀→∪▸⌀🛒 **Notes:** Families &
couples only, no single sex groups

Leisure: 🐟 Indoor swimming pool   🐟 Outdoor swimming pool   ❄ Tennis court   ♠ Games room   ⚑ Children's playground   ∪ Stables
▸ 9/18 hole golf course   🔜 Boats for hire   🎬 Cinema   ⌀ Fishing   ◎ Mini golf   🌊 Watersports   📺 Separate TV room

NOTTINGHAMSHIRE

CLUMBER PARK   Map 08 SK67

▶ ▶ **60% Camping & Caravanning Club Site** (SK626748)

The Walled Garden S80 3BD ☎ 01909 482303
website: www.campingandcaravanningclub.co.uk
Dir: From A1 onto A614 southbound, take 1st entrance into Clumber Park, follow signs
★ ⊕ £10.20-£12.90 ▲ £10.20-£12.90
Open Mar-Oct Booking advisable bank hols & Jul-Aug Last arrival 21.00hrs Last departure noon
Pleasant and peaceful site, well-maintained and situated in the splendid wooded surroundings of Clumber Park. Members' caravans only. Please see the advertisement on page 10 for details of Club Members' benefits. A 2.5-acre site with 55 touring pitches.

Facilities: ⋔ ⊙ ⏶ ⚘ ❋ ⚄ ⛾ ⊁
Services: ⊟ ⓘ ⌀ ⊞ → ∪ ⥤ ∕ ⦿ ▦ ◗ ◪ ⑨

MANSFIELD WOODHOUSE   Map 08 SK56

▶ ▶ **70% Redbrick House Hotel (SK568654)**
Peafield Ln NG20 0EW ☎ 01623 846499
Dir: Off A6075, 1m NE of Mansfield Woodhouse
⊡ ⊡
Open all year
Set in the grounds at the rear of a hotel, this adults only site is a peaceful base from which to tour the Sherwood Forest area. A gently-sloping site with good hard stands, plenty of trees, and a new lake nearing completion. A 5-acre site with 30 touring pitches.

NEWARK   See **Southwell & Wellow**

RADCLIFFE ON TRENT   Map 08 SK63

▶ ▶ ▶ **Thornton's Holt Camping Park (SK638377)**
Stragglethorpe Rd, Stragglethorpe NG12 2JZ
☎ 0115 933 2125 & 933 4204 ▤ 0115 933 3318
e-mail: camping@thorntons-holt.co.uk
website: www.thorntons-holt.co.uk
Dir: Take A52, 3m E of Nottingham. Turn S at lights towards Cropwell Bishop. Park 0.5m on left. Or A46 SE of Nottingham. N at lights. Park 2.5m on right
★ ⊕ £8-£9 ⊕ £8-£9 ▲ £8-£9
Open all year (rs 2 Nov-Mar No pool, laundry or washing up facilities) Booking advisable bank hols & wknds mid May-Oct Last arrival 21.00hrs Last departure 13.00hrs
A well-run site in former meadowland among young trees and bushes which lend a rural atmosphere and outlook. The toilets are housed in converted farm buildings, and there is an indoor swimming pool. A 13-acre site with 84 touring pitches, 27 hardstandings.
Washing-up facilities.

Leisure: ⚲ ⚘ ⋔ ▱ **Facilities:** ⋔ ⊙ ⏶ ❋ ⚄ ⚘ ⛾ ⊁
Services: ⊟ ⓘ ⓘ ⌀ ⊞ ⏁ ✕ → ∪ ⥤ ⚐ ⚄ ⚘ ∕

SOUTHWELL   Map 08 SK65

▶ ▶ **65% Robin Hood View Caravan Park** (SK668593)

Middle Plantation Farm, Belle Eau Park, Kirklington NG22 8TY ☎ 01623 870361 ▤ 01623 870361
Dir: From A617/A614 rdbt, E for 1.5m, follow tourist signs to site
⊡ ⊡ ▲
Open 31 Mar-14 Nov Booking advisable Peak season & bank hols Last arrival 20.00hrs Last departure 14.00hrs
A pleasant family-run site in a peaceful rural location, with many mature trees and shrubs, and good views over open country. Now an adult-only site, with excellent security. A 5-acre site with 30 touring pitches and 1 static.

Leisure: ⚲ **Facilities:** ⊙ ❋ ⊁
Services: ⊟ → ∪ ⥤ ⦿ ⚘ ∕ ◪ ⚄

TEVERSAL   Map 08 SK46

▶ ▶ ▶ ▶ **75% Shardaroba Caravan Park** (SK472615)

Silverhill Ln NG17 3JJ ☎ 01623 551838 & 0771 259 0158 ▤ 01623 551838
e-mail: stay@shardaroba.co.uk
website: www.shardaroba.co.uk
Dir: M1 junct 28 onto A38 towards Mansfield. At 1st traffic lights left onto B6027. At top of hill, straight over x-rds. After 200yds at next x-rds left at Peacock Hotel. After 1.4m at T-junct right onto B6014 signed Stanton Hill at Carnarvon Arms turn left onto Silverhill Ln, site 300yds on left
★ ⊕ £8-£13 ⊕ £8-£13 ▲ £8-£13

Open all year Booking advisable Peak season Last arrival 22.30hrs Last departure 12.00hrs
A well developed site with excellent purpose-built facilities, set in a rural area. Each pitch is spacious, and there are views and access to the surrounding countryside and nearby Silverhill Country Park. A 6-acre site with 100 touring pitches.
Tourist info & book lending room

Leisure: ⚲ **Facilities:** ⋔ ⊙ ⏶ ❋ ⚄ ⚘ ⛾ ⚄ ⊡ ⊁
Services: ⊟ ⓘ ⓘ ⊞ ⏁ → ∪ ⥤ ⚐ ∕ ⦿ ▦ ◪ ⑨

See advertisement on opposite page

TUXFORD
Map 08 SK77

► ► ► 70% *Orchard Park Touring Caravan & Camping Park* (SK754708)
Marnham Rd NG22 0PY ☎ 01777 870228 & 870320
🖷 01777 870320
e-mail: info@orchardcaravanpark.co.uk
website: www.caravanparksnottinghamshire.com
Dir: Turn off A1 at Tuxford via slip road onto A6075. After 0.5m turn right into Marnham Road & site is 0.75m on right
🚐🚐🛆
Open mid Mar-Oct Booking advisable bank hols & Jul-Aug Last arrival mdnt
This rural site retains many of the features of the fruit orchard in which it is set. The marked pitches are spacious, and most have water and electricity. The park's position in the midst of Sherwood Forest makes it an excellent touring base. A 7-acre site with 60 touring pitches.
Family shower room.

Leisure: ⚑ Facilities: 🌾☉❋&C🐾🛅🛧
Services: 🖳🛢⌀🖸🕾→Ü🜲🍽🚧🔲🛒🖾

WELLOW
Map 08 SK66

► ► ► 66% **The Shannon Caravan & Camping Park** (SK665666)
Wellow Rd NG22 9AP ☎ 01623 869002 & 07979 018565 🖷 01623 869002
Dir: From Ollerton follow A616 towards Newark, park 1.5m left just after Ollerton House Hotel.
★ 🚐 £8-£10 🚐 £8-£10 🛆 £8-£10
Open all year Last arrival anytime Last departure flexible
A well-equipped site with a new toilet block and good facilities throughout. There is a separate tenting area, and the park is 0.5m from Ollerton on the edge of the village of Wellow, which is famous for its maypole celebrations and local hostelries. A 4-acre site with 37 touring pitches, 37 hardstandings.
caravan storage

Leisure: ⚑ Facilities: 🌾☉❋🐾🛧
Services: 🖳→Ü🍽🛒🖾🛅

OXFORDSHIRE

BANBURY
Map 04 SP44

► ► ► ► 74% **Barnstones Caravan & Camping Site** (SP455454)
Great Bourton OX17 1QU ☎ 01295 750289
Dir: 3m N of M40 junct 11. Take A423 from Banbury signed Southam. After 3m turn right signed Gt Bourton/Cropredy, site 100yds on right
★ 🚐 £6-£9.50 🚐 £6-£9.50 🛆 £6
Open all year Booking advisable public hols
Popular, neatly laid-out site with plenty of hardstandings, some fully serviced pitches, and a smart, newly-refurbished toilet block. Well run by personable owner. A 3-acre site with 49 touring pitches, 44 hardstandings.

Leisure: ⚑ Facilities: 🌾☉❋&C🏧🛧
Services: 🖳🗄🛢⌀🖸🛗→Ü🜲☉△🜲🚻🍽🛅

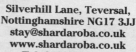

► ► ► ► 72% **Bo Peep Farm Caravan Park** (SP481348)
Bo Peep Farm, Aynho Rd, Adderbury OX17 3NP
☎ 01295 810605 🖷 01295 810605
e-mail: warden@bo.peep.co.uk
website: www.bo.peep.co.uk
Dir: 1m E of Adderbury & A4260, on B4100 Aynho Road
🚐🚐🛆
Open Apr-Oct Booking advisable Bank hols, British Grand Prix Last arrival 20.00hrs Last departure noon
A delightful park with good views. Four well laid out camping areas, including a paddock with hardstandings, that are all planted with maturing shrubs and trees. The facility buildings are made from attractive Cotswold stone, and include spotless toilets. A 13-acre site with 114 touring pitches.

Facilities: 🌾☉❑❋C🛅🏧🛧
Services: 🖳🛢⌀🖸🛗→🜲🍽

► ► ► 68% *Anita's Touring Caravan Park* (SP443477)
The Yews, Mollington OX17 1AZ
☎ 01295 750731 & 07966 171959 🖷 01295 750731
Dir: M40 junct 11 onto A422 signed Banbury. A423 signed Southam, site 3.5m on left. Do not go into village, site on main road just past village entrance
🚐🚐🛆
Open all year Booking advisable banks hols Last arrival 22.00hrs

contd.

Facilities: 🛁 Bath 🌾 Shower ☉ Electric Shaver 🗨 Hairdryer ❋ Ice Pack Facility & Disabled Facilities C Public Telephone 🛅 Shop on Site or within 200yds 🖾 Mobile Shop (calls at least 5 days a week) 🏧 BBQ Area 🪧 Picnic Area 🛧 Dog Exercise Area

England

Anita's Touring Caravan Park
A neat, well-run small farm site with brick-built toilet facilities. On the edge of the village, adjacent to A423. A 2-acre site with 24 touring pitches. Field play area.
Facilities: ⊙✻🔥 **Services:** 🔌→∪◎🔧

BLETCHINGDON Map 04 SP51

▶ ▶ ▶ 70% **Diamond Farm Caravan & Camping Park (SP513170)**
Islip Rd OX5 3DR ☎ 01869 350909 ☐ 01869 350059
e-mail: warden@diamondpark.co.uk
website: www.diamondpark.co.uk
Dir: From M40 junct 9 onto A34 S for 3m, then B4027 to Bletchingdon. Site 1m on left
★ ⊟ £7-£10 ⊟ £7-£10 ▲ £7-£10

Open Mar-Nov Booking advisable bank hols & Jul-Sep Last arrival 22.00hrs Last departure noon
A well-run, quiet rural site in good level surroundings, and ideal for touring the Cotswolds. Situated 7m N of Oxford in the heart of the Thames Valley. This popular park is well planted, and offers a heated outdoor swimming pool and a games room for children. A 3-acre site with 37 touring pitches, 13 hardstandings.
Leisure: ⌇♨⚲ **Facilities:** ⇥⊙✻☀🔥
Services: 🔌🚿♀🔧⊟⊤→🔧

CHARLBURY Map 04 SP31

▶ ▶ ▶ ▶ 70% **Cotswold View Touring Park (SP365210)**
Enstone Rd OX7 3JH ☎ 01608 810314
☐ 01608 811891
e-mail: bookings@gfwiddows.f9.co.uk
website: www.cotswoldview.co.uk
Dir: Signed from A44 on to B4022
★ ⊟ £8-£11 ⊟ £8-£11 ▲ £8-£11

Cotswold View Touring Park
Open Etr or Apr-Oct Booking advisable bank hols
Last arrival 21.00hrs Last departure noon
A good Cotswold site, well screened and with attractive views across the countryside. The toilet facilities include fully-equipped family rooms and bathrooms, and there are spacious, sheltered pitches, some with hardstandings. Breakfast and take-away food available from the shop. A 10-acre site with 125 touring pitches.
Off-licence, cycle hire, skittle alley.
Leisure: ♨♦⚲ **Facilities:** ⇥⊙✻☀🔥
Services: 🔌⊟🚿⊘⊟⊤⇥→🔧🍴☕⊞🗲

CHIPPING NORTON Map 04 SP32

▶ ▶ ▶ 65% **Camping & Caravanning Club Site (SP315244)**
Chipping Norton Rd, Chadlington OX7 3PE
☎ 01608 641993
website: www.campingandcaravanningclub.co.uk
Dir: Take A44 to Chipping Norton. Then A361 Burford road. In 1.5m bear left at fork signed Chadlington
★ ⊟ £12.30-£15.50 ⊟ £12.30-£15.50 ▲ £12.30-£15.50
Open Mar-Oct Booking advisable bank hols & Jul-Aug Last arrival 21.00hrs Last departure noon
A hilltop site surrounded by trees but close to a busy main road. Toilets very clean. Please see the advertisement on page 10 for details of Club Members' benefits. A 4-acre site with 105 touring pitches.
Leisure: ⚲ **Facilities:** ⊙✻☀🔥
Services: 🔌⊟🚿⊘⊟→∪🍴☕🔧🍴⊞🗲

▶ ▶ 56% *Churchill Heath Touring Caravan & Camp Site*
Kingham OX7 6UJ ☎ 01608 658317 ☐ 01608 659231
Dir: On B4450 between Churchill & Kingham, 3m SW of Chipping Norton
⊟ ⊟ ▲
Open all year Booking advisable bank hols & school hols Last arrival 22.00hrs Last departure noon
A peaceful little site on the Cotswold Way, with good views and sheltered pitches in a woodland setting. A 7.5-acre site with 50 touring pitches.
Leisure: ⚲ **Facilities:** ⊙✻☀🔥
Services: 🔌⊟🚿⊘⊟→∪🍴🔧

contd.

HENLEY-ON-THAMES   Map 04 SU78

▶ ▶ ▶ 58% **Swiss Farm International Camping**
(SU759837)
Marlow Rd RG9 2HY ☎ 01491 573419
▤ 01491 579934
e-mail: enquiries@swissfarmcamping.co.uk
website: www.swissfarmcamping.co.uk
*Dir: On A4155, N of Henley, next left after rugby club,
towards Marlow.*
★ ⊞ £10-£12 ⊞ £10-£12 ▲ £9-£12

Open Mar-Oct Booking advisable bank hols Last
arrival 21.00hrs Last departure 16.00hrs
*A pleasantly-screened rural site within a few
minutes walk of Henley. Visitors are invited to fish
in the park's well-stocked lake, which is set in a
secluded wooded area. A 6-acre site with 165
touring pitches, 12 hardstandings and 6 statics.
Football pitch & fishing lake.*
Leisure: ⚓ ⚓ ⚓ Facilities: ⚓ ⚓ ⚓ ⚓ ⚓ ⚓ ⚓ ⚓ ⚓ ⚓
Services: ⚓ ⚓ ⚓ ⚓ ⚓ → ∪ ▶ ⚓ ⚓ ⚓ ⚓ ⚓ ⚓ ⚓

OXFORD   Map 04 SP50

▶ ▶ ▶ 64% **Camping & Caravanning Club Site**
(SP518041)
426 Abingdon Rd OX1 4XN ☎ 01865 244088
website: www.campingandcaravanningclub.co.uk
*Dir: From M40 leave A34 at A423 for Oxford. Turn 1st
left into Abingdon Road & site on left behind
Touchwood Sports*
★ ⊞ £12.30-£15.50 ⊞ £12.30-£15.50 ▲ £12.30-£15.50
Open all year Booking advisable bank hols & Jul-
Aug Last arrival 21.00hrs Last departure noon
*A very busy town site with handy park-and-ride into
Oxford. All pitches are on grass, and most offer
electric hook-ups. See advertisement on page 10
for details of Club Members' benefits. A 5-acre
site with 84 touring pitches.*
Facilities: ⚓ ⚓ ⚓ ⚓ ⚓ ⚓
Services: ⚓ ⚓ ⚓ ⚓ ⚓ → ⚓ ⚓ ⚓ ⚓ ⚓ ⚓ ⚓ ⚓ ⚓ ⚓

STANDLAKE   Map 04 SP30

PREMIER PARK

▶ ▶ ▶ ▶ ▶ 78% **Lincoln Farm Park**
(SP395028)
High St OX29 7RH ☎ 01865 300239
▤ 01865 300127
*Dir: In village off A415 between Abingdon & Witney,
5m SE of Witney,*
★ ⊞ £6.95-£13.95 ⊞ £6.95-£13.95 ▲ £6.95-£13.95
contd.

Lincoln Farm Park
Open Feb-Nov Booking advisable bank hols,
Jul-Aug & most wknds Last arrival 21.00hrs
Last departure noon
*An attractively landscaped park in a quiet village
setting, with superb facilities and a high
standard of maintenance. Family rooms, fully-
serviced pitches, two indoor swimming pools
and a fully-equipped gym are part of the
comprehensive amenities. Winner of Best
Campsite of the Year, and Best Campsite for
England 2002. A 9-acre site with 90 touring
pitches, 42 hardstandings and 19 statics.
Indoor leisure centre, putting green.*
Leisure: ⚓ ⚓ Facilities: ⚓ ⚓ ⚓ ⚓ ⚓ ⚓ ⚓ ⚓ ⚓
Services: ⚓ ⚓ ⚓ ⚓ ⚓ ⚓ → ∪ ▶ ⚓ ⚓ ⚓ ⚓ ⚓ ⚓

WESTON-ON-THE-GREEN   Map 04 SP51

▶ ▶ 65% **NEW Godwin's Caravan Park** (SP534185)
Manor Farm OX25 3QL ☎ 01869 351647 & 350354
e-mail: neil@westononthegreen.freeserve.co.uk
★ ⊞ £8-£10 ⊞ £8-£10 ▲ £5-£7
Open Mar-Oct Booking advisable Last arrival
20.00hrs Last departure noon
*A developing caravan park on a working dairy farm
which makes its own ice cream and sells it in a café
bar. The open farmland setting is ideal for nature
lovers, walkers and cyclists. A 2-acre site with 60
touring pitches.*
Ice cream parlour, coffee shop & restaurant daily
Facilities: ⚓ ⚓ ⚓ ⚓ Services: ⚓ → ∪ ▶ ⚓

RUTLAND

GREETHAM   Map 08 SK91

▶ ▶ 68% **NEW Rutland Caravan & Camping**
(SK925148)
LE15 7NX ☎ 01572 813520 ▤ 01572 812616
e-mail: info@rutlandcaravanandcamping.co.uk
website: www.rutlandcaravanandcamping.co.uk
*Dir: From A1 N or S, turn off onto B668 to Greetham.
Before Greetham turn right at x-rds, then 2nd left to site*
★ ⊞ £8-£10 ⊞ £8-£10 ▲ £8-£10
Open all year Booking advisable BH's
*A brand new caravan park built to a high
specification, and surrounded by newly-planted
banks which will provide good screening. The
spacious grassy site is close to the Viking Way and*
contd.

Leisure: ⚓ Indoor swimming pool ⚓ Outdoor swimming pool ⚓ Tennis court ⚓ Games room ⚓ Children's playground ∪ Stables
▶ 9/18 hole golf course ⚓ Boats for hire ⚓ Cinema ⚓ Fishing ⊙ Mini golf ⚓ Watersports ⚓ Separate TV room

England

other footpath networks, and well sited for visiting Rutland Water and the many picturesque villages in the area. A 3-acre site with 30 touring pitches, 3 hardstandings.

Leisure: ⚕ **Facilities:** ⬚⊙⚑✳⬚☖⌕☂
Services: ⬚⬚⬚⬚⬚⬚→∪❘⊙⬚⬚⬚⬚⬚

SHROPSHIRE

BRIDGNORTH   Map 07 SO79

▶ ▶ ▶ ▶ **74% Stanmore Hall Touring Park (SO742923)**
Stourbridge Rd WV15 6DT ☎ 01746 761761
▤ 01746 768069
e-mail: stanmore@morris-leisure
Dir: 2m E of Bridgnorth on A458
★ ⬚ £12-£17.50 ⬚ £12-£17.50 ▲ fr £12

Open all year Booking advisable school hols, bank hols & Jul-Aug Last arrival 20.00hrs Last departure noon
An excellent park in peaceful surroundings offering outstanding facilities. The pitches, many of them fully-serviced, are arranged around the lake in Stanmore Hall, home of the Midland Motor Museum. A 12.5-acre site with 131 touring pitches, 44 hardstandings.

Leisure: ⚕ **Facilities:** ⬚⊙⚑✳⬚☖⬚⌕☂
Services: ⬚⬚⬚⬚⬚⬚⬚→❘⬚⬚⬚⬚⬚⬚⬚

BROOME   Map 07 SO48

▶ ▶ ▶ **61% Engine & Tender Inn (SO399812)**
SY7 0NT ☎ 01588 660275
Dir: W from Craven Arms on B4368, fork left to B4367, site in village, 2m on right
⬚⬚▲
Open all year Booking advisable bank hols Last departure 14.00hrs
A pleasant country pub site with gently sloping ground, in a rural setting with very clean facilities. A 2-acre site with 30 touring pitches and 2 statics.

Leisure: ⚓ **Facilities:** ⬚⊙✳⬚⬚
Services: ⬚⬚⬚✕⬚→∪❘⬚⬚⬚⬚⬚⬚⬚

ELLESMERE   See Lyneal

HAUGHTON   Map 07 SJ51

▶ **75% Camping & Caravanning Club Site (SJ546164)**
Ebury Hill, Ring Bank TF6 6BU ☎ 01743 709334
website: www.campingandcaravanningclub.co.uk
Dir: 2.5m through Shrewsbury on A53. Turn left signed Haughton & Upton Magna. Continue 1.5m site on right
★ ⬚ £9-£10 ⬚ £9-£10 ▲ £9-£10
Open Mar-Oct Booking advisable bank hols & high season Last arrival 21.00hrs Last departure noon
A wooded hill fort with a central lake overlooking the Shropshire countryside. Well-screened by very mature trees. Own sanitary facilities essential. Please see the advertisement on page 10 for details of Club Members' benefits. An 18-acre site with 104 touring pitches, 21 hardstandings.
Fishing.

Leisure: ⚕ **Facilities:** ✳⬚⌕
Services: ⬚⬚⬚⬚⬚→❘⬚⬚⬚⬚⬚⬚⬚

HUGHLEY   Map 07 SO59

▶ ▶ ▶ **64% Mill Farm Holiday Park (SO564979)**
SY5 6NT ☎ 01746 785208 & 785255
▤ 01746 785208
Dir: On unclass road off B4371, 3m SW of Much Wenlock, 11m NE of Church Stretton
⬚⬚▲
Open Mar-Jan Booking advisable peak periods Last arrival 20.00hrs Last departure noon
A well-established farm site set in meadowland adjacent to river, with mature trees and bushes providing screening, situated below Wenlock Edge. A 20-acre site with 55 touring pitches and 90 statics. Fishing & horse riding.

Facilities: ⬚⊙⚑✳⬚⬚⌕☂
Services: ⬚⬚⬚⬚⬚→∪❙

LYNEAL (NEAR ELLESMERE)   Map 07 SJ43

▶ ▶ ▶ ▶ **71% Fernwood Caravan Park (SJ445346)**
SY12 0QF ☎ 01948 710221 ▤ 01948 710324
e-mail: fernwood@caravanpark37.fsnet.co.uk
website: www.ranch.co.uk
Dir: From A495 in Welshampton take B5063, over canal bridge, turn right as signed
★ ⬚ £11-£15 ⬚ £11-£15
Open Mar-Nov Booking advisable bank hols Last arrival 21.00hrs Last departure 17.00hrs
A peaceful park set in wooded countryside, with a screened, tree-lined touring area and fishing lake. The approach is past flower beds, and the static area which is tastefully arranged around an attractive children's playing area. There is a small child-free touring area for those wanting complete relaxation, and the park has 20 acres of woodland walks. A 26-acre site with 60 touring pitches and 165 statics.
Lake for coarse fishing on site.

Leisure: ⚕ **Facilities:** ⬚⊙⚑✳⬚☖⬚⌕☂
Services: ⬚⬚⬚⬚⬚→✳⬚⬚⬚⬚⬚⬚⬚

MINSTERLEY
Map 07 SJ30

► ► 77% **The Old School Caravan Park**
SO322977)
Shelve SY5 0JQ ☎ 01588 650410 &
1797 4135659
📠 01588 650410
Dir: 5m SW of Minsterley on A488
★ 🚐 £8 🚐 £8 ▲ £8

Open 21 Mar-Nov Booking advisable bank hols Last
arrival 21.00hrs Last departure 10.30hrs
*A very well designed park in a beautiful setting,
with impressive facilities housed in an attractive
brick and stone building. Self-contained cubicles
with shower, wash basin and toilet are an added
bonus of this small park, and the grounds are
immaculate. A 1-acre site with 18 touring pitches.
Dish washing with hot water. CCTV over park.*
Facilities: 🦺⊙☀🛁🚿 **Services:** 🔌🗑️→∪🚗🚽

SHREWSBURY
Map 07 SJ41

PREMIER PARK

► ► ► ► ► 74% **Beaconsfield Farm Caravan
Park** (SJ522189)
Battlefield SY4 4AA ☎ 01939 210370 & 210399
📠 01939 210349
e-mail: mail@beaconsfield-farm.co.uk
website: www.beaconsfield-farm.co.uk
*Dir: At Hadnall, 2.5m NE Shrewsbury, follow sign for
Astley off A53 or A49*
★ 🚐 £8.50-£10.50 🚐 £8.50-£10.50 ▲ £8.50-£10.50
Open all year Booking advisable bank hols &
Aug Last arrival 19.00hrs Last departure
12.00hrs
*A purpose-built family-run park on a farmland in
open countryside. This pleasant park offers
quality in every area, including superior toilets,
heated indoor swimming pool, and attractive
landscaping. Fly and coarse fishing are available
from the park's own fishing lake. Only adults
over 21 years are accepted. A 16-acre site with
50 touring pitches, 35 hardstandings and
35 statics.*
Fly fishing, coarse fishing, bowling green.
Leisure: ⚓ **Facilities:** 🛁🦺⊙☀🛁🚿
Services: 🔌🗑️✗→🛒🍽️🚗🚽
Notes: Adults only (over 21yrs)

► ► ► ► 73% **Oxon Hall Touring Park** (SJ455138)
Welshpool Rd SY3 5FB ☎ 01743 340868
📠 01743 340869
e-mail: oxon@morris-leisure.co.uk
website: www.morris-leisure.co.uk
*Dir: Leave A5 ring road at junct with A458. Park shares
entrance with 'Oxon Park & Ride'*
★ 🚐 £12.60-£15.60 🚐 £12.60-£15.60 ▲ £9.60-£12.60

Open all year Booking advisable high season Last
arrival 21.00hrs
*An excellent new park with quality facilities,
offering grass and fully serviced pitches. A small
adult-only area has proved very popular with those
wanting a peaceful holiday, and a restful patio area
overlooks a small lake, next to the reception and
shop. Ideally located for Shrewsbury and the
surrounding countryside. A 15-acre site with 124
touring pitches, 60 hardstandings and 42 statics.*
Leisure: ⚓ **Facilities:** 🦺⊙🛁🚿
Services: 🔌🗑️🛒→🛒🍽️🚗🚽

TELFORD
Map 07 SJ60

► ► ► 73% **Severn Gorge Park** (SJ705051)
Bridgnorth Rd, Tweedale TF7 4JB ☎ 01952 684789
📠 01952 684789
e-mail: info@severngorgepark.co.uk
website: www.severngorgepark.co.uk
Dir: Signed off A442, 1m S of Telford
★ 🚐 fr £9.10 🚐 fr £9.10 ▲ fr £9.10

Open all year Booking advisable bank hols & wknds
summer months Last arrival 23.00hrs Last
departure 12.00hrs
*A very pleasant wooded site in the heart of Telford,
well-screened and maintained. The sanitary
facilities are fresh and immaculate, and landscaping
of the grounds is carefully managed. A 6-acre site
with 50 touring pitches, 50 hardstandings.*

contd.

Facilities: 🛁 Bath 🚿 Shower ⊙ Electric Shaver 🌀 Hairdryer ❄ Ice Pack Facility ♿ Disabled Facilities 📞 Public Telephone
🛒 Shop on Site or within 200yds 🚐 Mobile Shop (calls at least 5 days a week) 🔥 BBQ Area 🍽 Picnic Area 🐕 Dog Exercise Area

Leisure: ⚑ Facilities: ♜⊙☜✳⚲❅⚒⊞⊼☂
Services: 🔌🔋💧∅⊞⊤➜∪▶⊙♨⚑🍴
💳🚗🔀🔲

WEM   Map 07 SJ52

▶ ▶ ▶ 65% **Lower Lacon Caravan Park (SJ534304)**
SY4 5RP ☎ 01939 232376 🖹 01939 233606
e-mail: info@llcp.co.uk
website: www.lowerlacon.co.uk
Dir: Take A49 to B5065. Site 3m on the right
★ ⚑ £11-£16.50 ⛺ £11-£16.50 ▲ £11-£16.50

Open all year (rs Nov-Mar club wknds only, toilets
closed if frost) Booking advisable public hols & Jul-
Aug Last arrival 20.00hrs Last departure 18.00hrs
*A large, spacious park with lively club facilities and
an entertainments barn, set safely away from the
main road. The park is particularly suitable for
families, with an outdoor swimming pool and
livestock. A 48-acre site with 270 touring pitches, 30
hardstandings and 50 statics.*
Crazy golf.
Leisure: ⚲ ◕ ⚑ ▢ Facilities: ➡♜⊙☜✳⚕⚲☜☂
Services: 🔌🔋♀💧∅⊞⊤✗♨➜▶🍴 💳🚗🔀🔲

WENTNOR   Map 07 SO39

▶ ▶ ▶ 65% **The Green Caravan Park (S0380932)**
SY9 5EF ☎ 01588 650605 🖹 01588 650605
e-mail: info@greencaravanpark.co.uk
website: www.greencaravanpark.co.uk
*Dir: 1m NE of Bishop's Castle to Lydham Heath on
A489. Turn right & site signed*
★ ⚑ fr £7 ⛺ fr £7 ▲ fr £7
Open Etr-Oct Booking advisable bank hols Last
arrival 21.00hrs Last departure 15.00hrs
*A very pleasant spot with many recent
improvements and more planned. Mostly level,
grassy pitches. A 15-acre site with 140 touring
pitches and 20 statics.*
Leisure: ⚑ Facilities: ♜⊙☜✳⚲❅☂
Services: 🔌🔋♀💧∅⊞⊤✗➜∪🍴
Notes: Dogs must be kept on leads at all times
💳🚗🔀🔲

SOMERSET

BATH   Map 03 ST76

▶ ▶ ▶ *Bath Marina & Caravan Park (ST719655)*
Brassmill Ln BA1 3JT ☎ 01225 424301
🖹 01225 424301
*Dir: From Bath centre head for suburb of Newbridge.
Site signed off A4 1.5m W towards Bristol/Wells*
⚑ ⛺
Open all year Booking advisable bank hols & Jun-
Sep Last departure noon
*A pleasant site on the edge of Bath in park-like
grounds among maturing trees and shrubs. A
footpath to the nearby Park and Ride gives good
access to the city, and there is also a riverside walk
into the centre. A 4-acre site with 88 touring pitches.*
Leisure: ⚑ Facilities: ♜⊙☜✳⚕⚲☜☂ Services:
🔌🔋♀💧∅⊞⊤➜∪▶⊙♨♨🍴 💳🚗🔀🔲

▶ ▶ ▶ 66% **Newton Mill Caravan and Camping Park (ST715649)**
Newton Rd BA2 9JF ☎ 01225 333909
🖹 01225 461556
e-mail: newtonmill@hotmail.com
website: www.campinginbath.co.uk
*Dir: From Bath travel W on A4 to A39 rdbt, take
immediate left and site 1m on left*
★ ⚑ £10.95-£13.95 ⛺ £10.95-£14.95 ▲ £9.95-£11.95

Open all year Booking advisable public hols & Jul-
Aug Last arrival 21.00hrs Last departure noon
*An attractive park set in a sheltered valley and
surrounded by woodland, with a stream running
through. The city is easily accessible by bus and the
site is beside the level traffic free Bath/Bristol
cyclepath. A 42-acre site with 195 touring pitches,
85 hardstandings.*
Fishing & Satellite TV hook ups.
Leisure: ◕ ⚑ Facilities: ♜⊙☜✳⚕⚲☜☂
Services: 🔌🔋♀💧∅⊞⊤✗♨➜∪▶♨🍴
💳🚗🔀🔲

BAWDRIP   Map 03 ST33

▶ ▶ ▶ 60% **Fairways International Touring Caravan & Camp (ST349402)**
Woolavington Corner, Bath Rd TA7 8PP
☎ 01278 685569 🖹 01278 685569
e-mail: fairwaysint@btinternet.com
Dir: 3.5m E of Bridgwater, 100yds off A39 on B3141
★ ⚑ £8-£10 ⛺ £8-£10 ▲ £8-£10   *contd.*

Services: ⊤ Toilet Fluid ✗ Café/ Restaurant ⚑ Fast Food/Takeaway ♨ Baby Care 🔌 Electric Hook Up
🔲 Launderette ♀ Licensed Bar 🔋 Calor Gaz ∅ Camping Gaz ⊞ Battery Charging

Fairways International Touring Caravan & Camp
Open Mar-15 Nov Booking advisable Spring BH &
Jul-Aug Last departure noon
*A quiet, family-orientated park which makes a good
base for touring the north Somerset coast,
Glastonbury and the Quantocks. A 5.5-acre site with
200 touring pitches.*
Off-licence.

Leisure: ◣ ⚠ ☐ **Facilities:** ⋔ ⊙ ♋ ✳ ᵶ ℂ ቜ ⊞ ⊼ ꝏ
Services: 凰 ⬓ ⓘ ⊘ ⊞ ⊤ → ∪ ♢ ✦ ꝏ ⅃

BLUE ANCHOR   **Map 03 ST04**

► ► ► 68% **Hoburne Blue Anchor Park**
(ST025434)
TA24 6JT ☎ 01643 821360 ▤ 01643 821572
e-mail: enquiries@hoburne.com
website: www.hoburne.com
Dir: 0.25m E of West Somerset Railway Station on B3191
★ ⊞ £8-£16 ꝏ
Open Mar-Oct (rs Mar & Oct shop & swimming pool
limited) Booking advisable bank hols & Jul-Aug Last
arrival 22.00hrs Last departure 10.00hrs ⅏
*Large coastal site, partly wooded on level ground
overlooking bay with individual areas screened. A
29-acre site with 103 touring pitches and 331 statics.*
Crazy golf.

Leisure: ⋩ ⚠ **Facilities:** ⋔ ⊙ ♋ ✳ ᵶ ℂ ቜ
Services: 凰 ⬓ ⓘ ⊘ ⊞ ✕ ⬥ → ∪ ⅂ ⊙ ⅃ ⬤ ▦ ▨ ⌑ ⬙

BREAN   **Map 03 ST25**

68% **NEW** **Warren Farm Holiday Park**
(ST297564)
Brean Sands TA8 2RP
☎ 01278 781036
e-mail: enquiries@warren-farm.co.uk
website: www.warren-farm.co.uk
*Dir: M5 junct 22 and follow B3140 past Burnham on
Sea to Berrow and Brean. Park 1.5m past Brean
Leisure Park*
★ ⊞ £5.50-£10.50 ꝏ £5.50-£10.50 ▲ £5.50-£10.50
Open Apr-mid Oct Booking advisable BH's &
school hols Last arrival 20.00hrs Last dep 12.00hrs
*A large family-run holiday park close to the
beach, divided into several fields each with its
own designated facilities. Pitches are spacious
and level, and enjoy panoramic views of the
Mendip Hills and Brean Down. A bar and
restaurant are part of the complex, and provide
entertainment for all the family, and there is
also separate entertainment for children.*
                                        contd.

Bath Road, Bawdrip, Bridgwater, Somerset TA7 8PP.
Tel: (01278) 685569   Fax: (01278) 685569
E-mail: fairwaysint@btinternet.com
Web: http//www.fairwaysint.btinternet.co.uk
Situated on the Polden hills in rural Somerset. Level
5½ acres purpose built site with excellent facilities
including disabled. Free showers and vanity
cubicles. Laundry. Dishwasher room. Children's
play area with TV and games room. Baby changing
facilities. 1½ miles junction 23 M5. Junction of A39
and B3141. Easy reach for seaside and places of
historical interest. Good pubs and food nearby.
Fishing within ½ mile. Rallies welcome. Dogs are
welcome on leads. Special – 7 nights for 6.
"Loo of the Year Award Winner 1994 – 2002"

Warren Farm Holiday Park
*A 100-acre site with 575 touring pitches and
800 statics.*

Leisure: ◣ ⚠ ☐ **Facilities:** ⇥ ✳ ᵶ ℂ ቜ ⊼ ꝏ
Services: ♋ ⓘ ⊘ ⊞ ⊤ ✕ ⬥ → ∪ ⅂ **Notes:** No single
sex groups, no commerical vehicles ⬤ ▦ ▨ ⬙
See advertisement on page 188

► ► ► 74% **Northam Farm Caravan & Touring
Park (ST299556)**
TA8 2SE ☎ 01278 751244 & 751222 ▤ 01278 751150
e-mail: enquiries@northamfarm.demon.co.uk
website: www.northamfarm.co.uk
*Dir: From M5 junct 22 follow signs to Burnham-on-Sea.
In Brean, site on right 0.5m past leisure park*
★ ⊞ £4.25-£10.75 ꝏ £4.25-£10.75 ▲ £4.25-£10.75
Open Apr-Oct (rs Oct shop & takeaway closed, no
dog areas) Booking advisable bank & school hols
Last arrival 21.00hrs Last departure 10.30hrs
                                        contd.

Leisure: ⋩ Indoor swimming pool ⋨ Outdoor swimming pool ♋ Tennis court ◣ Games room ⚠ Children's playground ∪ Stables
► 9/18 hole golf course ✦ Boats for hire ᵒᵒ Cinema ⅃ Fishing ◎ Mini golf ◬ Watersports ☐ Separate TV room

England

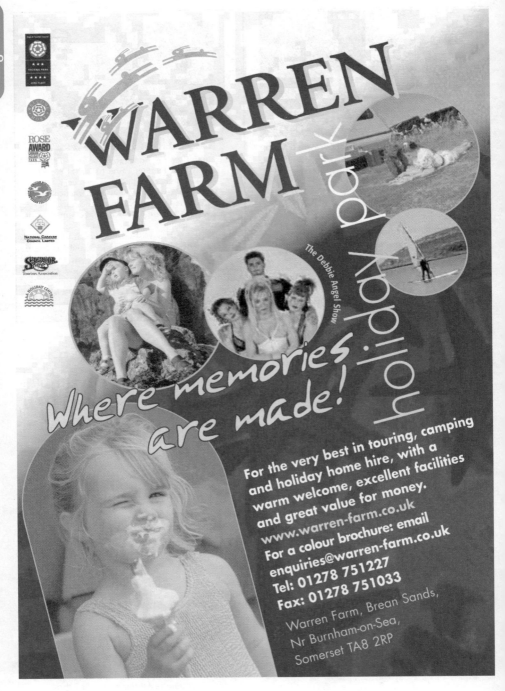

WARREN FARM holiday park

The Debbie Angel Show

Where memories are made!

For the very best in touring, camping
and holiday home hire, with a
warm welcome, excellent facilities
and great value for money.
www.warren-farm.co.uk
For a colour brochure: email
enquiries@warren-farm.co.uk
Tel: 01278 751227
Fax: 01278 751033

Warren Farm, Brean Sands,
Nr Burnham-on-Sea,
Somerset TA8 2RP

Northam Farm Caravan & Touring Park
*An attractive site a short walk from the sea with
game, coarse and sea fishing close by. This good
quality park also has lots of children's play areas,
and is near a long sandy beach. A 30-acre site with
350 touring pitches, 137 hardstandings and 112
statics.*
Fishing lake

Leisure: 🅐 **Facilities:** ➡ ☊ ⊙ ☖ ✳ ⅏ ⚹ 🔋
🎍 ⊼ **Services:** 🔲 🗓 🗓 ⊘ 🔲 🔟 ✕ 🚠 ➔ ∪ ▶ ⊙ ◢
Notes: Families & couples only, no motorcycles
💳 💳 💳 📶 🈁

BRIDGETOWN   Map 03 SS93

▶ ▶ ▶ 65% *Exe Valley Caravan Site (SS921332)*
TA22 9JR ☎ 01643 851432
Dir: On A396 between Dunster and Dulverton
🚐 🚐 🛆
Open Mar-Oct Booking advisable Last arrival
22.30hrs
*Set in Exmoor National Park, this delightful site lies
alongside the River Exe close to the water mill and
its stream, and offers fly fishing and good walks.
This adult-only park has the benefit of an inn just
across the road. A 2.5-acre site with 30 touring
pitches.*
Facilities: ☊ ⊙ ☖ ✳ ⅏ ⚹ 🔋 🏬 ⊼
Services: 🔲 🗓 ⊘ 🔲 **Notes:** No children under 18

BRIDGWATER   Map 03 ST23

▶ ▶ ▶ ▶ 69% *Mill Farm Caravan & Camping Park
(ST219410)*
Fiddington TA5 1JQ ☎ 01278 732286
*Dir: From Bridgwater take A39 W, turn left at
Cannington rdbt for 2m, then right just beyond Apple
Inn towards Fiddington and follow camping signs*
🚐 🚐 🛆

Mill Farm Caravan & Camping Park
contd.

Facilities: ➡ Bath ☊ Shower ⊙ Electric Shaver ☖ Hairdryer ✳ Ice Pack Facility ⅏ Disabled Facilities ⚹ Public Telephone
🔋 Shop on Site or within 200yds 🔲 Mobile Shop (calls at least 5 days a week) 🏬 BBQ Area 🎍 Picnic Area ⊼ Dog Exercise Area

Open all year Booking advisable peak periods Last arrival 23.00hrs Last departure 10.00hrs
An established, mature site with plenty of interest all the family, and helpful owners. A waterfall, stream and safe boating pool are popular features, and there are heated indoor and outdoor swimming pools, a 50 metre waterslide, a games room, and pony and horse riding school. The park is divided into three caravan areas and a large space for tents, each with its own facilities and play equipment. A 6-acre site with 125 touring pitches.
Canoes for hire, pool table, trampolines.
Leisure: ⌇ ⚓ ⚠ ▢ **Facilities:** ➡ ♐ ⊙ ☍ ✳ ⟓ ♨ ⚲ ♈
Services: ⊡ 🖵 ⛾ 🛈 ⌀ 🅴 🆃 🖩 → ▸ ◎ ♩

Ⓤ **Somerset View Caravan Park (ST295335)**
A38 Taunton Rd, North Petherton TA6 6NW
☎ 01278 661294
Dir: S of North Petherton, L at layby, by rugby club
Open 2 Feb-29 Dec
As we went to press the pennant rating for this site was not confirmed

---

► ► **62% Batcombe Vale Caravan & Camping Park (ST681379)**
Batcombe Vale BA4 6BW ☎ 01749 830246
e-mail: donaldsage@compuserve.com
website: www.batcombevale.co.uk
Dir: follow signs from Evercreech & Bruton
★ ♐ fr £10 ♐ fr £10 ▲ fr £10
Open May-Sep Booking advisable bank hols & Jul-Aug Last arrival 22.00hrs Last departure noon
A very attractive site approached down a steep hill into a secluded valley, with three lakes which offer coarse fishing. This lovely remote location offers superb views and a peaceful environment, a very special place with rustic facilities. A 4-acre site with 30 touring pitches.
Coarse fishing, free boats for use.
Leisure: ⚠ **Facilities:** ♐ ⊙ ✳ ⚲ ♐ ♈
Services: ⊡ 🛈 ⌀ 🅴 → ∪ ⌂ ✛ ♩ ⚞
Notes: No single sex or motorcycle groups

 69% **NEW** Burnham-on-Sea Holiday Village (ST305485)
Marine Dr TA8 1LA
☎ 01278 783391
website: www.british-holidays.co.uk
★ ♐ £12-£45 ♐ £12-£45 ▲ £12-£45
Open Mar-Oct Booking advisable Last arrival 22.00hrs Last departure 12.00hrs ♒
A large family-orientated holiday village complex with a separate touring park with 43 super pitches. There is a wide range of activities including excellent indoor and outdoor pools, plus bars, restaurants and entertainment for all the family. The coarse fishing lake is very popular, and the seafront is only 0.5m away. A 76-acre site with 75 touring pitches.
Leisure: ⌇ ⌇ ⚓ ⚠ ▢ **Facilities:** ⚲
Services: ⊡ ⛾ 🛈 ✗ 🖩 ⚟ 🖾 ⓪ 🈺 🈹 ⑨

► 60% **Ye Olde Burtle Inn and Restaurant (ST397434)**
Catcott Rd TA7 8NG ☎ 01278 722269 & 722123
🖷 01278 722269
e-mail: chris@burtleinn.fsnet.co.uk
website: www.burtleinn.fsnet.co.uk
Dir: From M5 junct 23 onto A39, approx 4m, left onto unclass road to Burtle, site by pub in village centre
★ ▲ £4.95-£5.95
Open all year Booking advisable Jul-Aug Last arrival anytime
A cider apple orchard at the rear of a lovely old inn and restaurant in the depths of the Somerset Levels. Cycle hire available at the inn. No caravans allowed. A 0.75-acre site with 30 touring pitches.
Leisure: ⚓ ⚠ **Facilities:** ⊙ ✳ ⚲ ♐ ♈
Services: ⛾ ⊡ ✗ 🖩 → ∪ ♩ 🍺 🖾 ⓪ 🈺 🈹 ⑨

► ► ► **66% Alpine Grove Touring Park (SY342071)**
Forton TA20 4HD ☎ 01460 63479
e-mail: stay@alpinegrovetouringpark.com
website: www.alpinegrovetouringpark.com
Dir: Turn off A30 between Chard & Crewkerne towards Cricket St Thomas, follow signs. Park 2m on right
★ ♐ £8-£10 ♐ £8-£10 ▲ £8-£10
Open Apr-1 Oct Booking advisable bank hols & Jul-Aug Last arrival 23.00hrs Last departure 14.00hrs
An attractive, quiet wooded park with both hardstandings and grass pitches, close to Cricket St Thomas wildlife park, in a rural location. A 7.5-acre site with 40 touring pitches and 1 static.
Leisure: ⌇ ⚠ **Facilities:** ♐ ⊙ ✳ ⚲ ♨ ♐ ♈
Services: ⊡ 🛈 ⌀ 🅣 → ∪ ▸ ♩
Notes: Dogs must be kept on leads, no littering

► ► ► **62%** *South Somerset Holiday Park (ST279098)*
Howley TA20 3EA ☎ 01460 62221 & 66036
🖷 01460 66246
Dir: 3m W of Chard on A30 in Exeter direction
♐ ♐ ▲
Open all year Booking advisable bank hols & High Season Last arrival 23.00hrs Last departure noon
Set in a lightly wooded rural location overlooking the Blackdown hills, this family-run park offers both hardstandings and grass pitches on a spacious plot. A 7-acre site with 110 touring pitches and 42 statics.
Leisure: ⚠ **Facilities:** ♐ ⊙ ✳ ⚫ ⚲ ♨ ♈
Services: ⊡ 🛈 ⌀ 🖩 → ♩

PREMIER PARK

► ► ► ► ► **65% Broadway House Holiday Caravan & Camping Park (ST448547)**
Axbridge Rd BS27 3DB ☎ 01934 742610
🖷 01934 744950
e-mail: enquiries@broadwayhouse.uk.com
Dir: From M5 junct 22 follow signs to Cheddar Gorge & Caves (8m). Park midway between Cheddar & Axbridge on A371
★ ♐ £7-£14.50 ♐ £7-£11 ▲ £7-£14.50

Open Mar-mid Nov (rs Mar-end May & Oct-Nov No bar or pool open, limited shop hours) Booking advisable bank hols & end Jul-Aug Last arrival 23.00hrs Last departure noon *A well-equipped family park on the slopes of the Mendips with an exceptional range of activities for all ages. This is a busy and lively park in the main holiday periods, but can be quiet and peaceful off-peak. Broadway has its own activity centre based on the site, providing archery, shooting, climbing, caving, ballooning and much more. The slightly-terraced pitches face south, and are backed by the Mendips. A 30-acre site with 200 touring pitches, 35 hardstandings and 37 statics.* Sunbed, table tennis, crazy golf

Leisure: ➤ ◣ ⚏ ◻ **Facilities:** ➡ ◖ ⊙ ◨ ✳ ◭ ◗ ◧ ◰
◲ ◱ **Services:** ▣ ⬚ ◙ ⬚ ◨ ⬚ ✕ ◗ → ∪ ▶ ◎ ◢
⬤ ⬛ ◍ ⬛ ⬛ ⑤

▶ ▶ ▶ 67% **NEW** Cheddar Touring Caravan &
Camping Park (ST460528)
Gas House Ln, off Draycott Rd BS27 3RL
☎ 01934 740207 ◈ 01934 740207
e-mail: Jocelyn@jocelyn114fsnet.co.uk
website: www.caravancampingsites.co.uk/
somerset/cheddar.htm
Dir: M5 junct 22 towards Cheddar. Continue through Cheddar on Wells Rd, campsite on left next to football field
★ ◛ £9.50-£12 ◛ £9.50-£12 ▲ £7.50-£9
Open Mar-Oct Booking advisable Last arrival 22.00hrs
An attractively-developing site on the edge of Cheddar village with easy access to the famous Gorge and caves. Facilities are good, and the park provides an ideal base for visiting the many local attractions of the Mendip area. A 3.75-acre site with 80 touring pitches.

Leisure: ⚏ **Facilities:** ◖ ⊙ ✳ ◭ ◰ ◱
Services: ▣ ⬚ ◗ → ◭ ◙ **Notes:** Children not
allowed to play in or around amenities block

▶ ▶ ▶ 60% Froglands Farm Caravan & Camping
Park (ST462529)
BS27 3RH ☎ 01934 742058 & 743304
e-mail: froglands@aol.com
website: www.froglandsfarm.co.uk
Dir: On A371, 150yds S of Cheddar church
◛ ◛ ▲
Open Etr or Apr-30 Oct Booking advisable Whitsun,
Jul-Aug & school hols Last arrival 22.00hrs Last
departure 12.00hrs
A farmland site set in undulating countryside, with level pitches located in two paddocks, and mature trees and shrubs for shelter. Located on the outskirts of Cheddar, close to the famous caves and gorge. A 3-acre site with 68 touring pitches.

Facilities: ◖ ⊙ ✳ ◙ ◱ **Services:** ▣ ⬚ ◙ ◨ ◨
→ ∪ ▶ ◎ ◢ **Notes:** No single sex groups,
motor bikes by arrangement

CROWCOMBE   **Map 03 ST13**

▶ ▶ ▶ ▶ 76% Quantock Orchard Caravan Park
(ST138357)
TA4 4AW ☎ 01984 618618 ◈ 01984 618618
e-mail: qocp@flaxpool.freeserve.co.uk
website: www.flaxpool.freeserve.co.uk
Dir: Site set back from A358
★ ◛ £10.95-£15.95 ◛ £10.95-£15.95 ▲ £7.95-£12.95
Open all year Booking advisable bank hols & Jul-
Aug Last arrival 22.00hrs Last departure noon
An attractive, quiet site with wonderful views, sitting at the western foot of the Quantocks midway between Taunton and Minehead. The park is laid out in an old orchard with plenty of colourful flower beds, and the quality facilities are very well maintained. A fitness complex next to the swimming pool offers jacuzzi, sauna and exercise machines. Ideal for visiting Exmoor National Park, and the nearby West Somerset Steam Railway. A 3.5-acre site with 75 touring pitches.
Gym & leisure suite, off-licence on site

Leisure: ➤ ◣ ⚏ ◻ **Facilities:** ➡ ◖ ⊙ ◨ ✳ ◭ ◗ ◧ ◰
Services: ▣ ⬚ ◙ ⬚ ◨ ◨ → ∪ ▶ ◢ ⬤ ⬛ ◍ ⬛ ⬛ ⑤

Leisure: ➤ Indoor swimming pool ➤ Outdoor swimming pool ◔ Tennis court ◣ Games room ⚏ Children's playground ∪ Stables
▶ 9/18 hole golf course ⌇ Boats for hire ◨ Cinema ◢ Fishing ◎ Mini golf ◭ Watersports ◻ Separate TV room

DULVERTON   Map 03 SS92
See also **East Anstey, Devon**

▶ ▶ ▶ 64% **Wimbleball Lake** (SS960300)
TA22 9NU ☎ 01398 371257
*Dir: From A396 Tiverton-Minehead road take B3222
signed Dulverton Services, follow signs to Wimbleball
Lake. Ignore 1st entry (fishing) and take 2nd entry for
watersports & camping*
★ 🚐 fr £7.50 ▲ fr £7.50
Open 1 Apr-1 Nov Booking advisable high season
Last departure 14.00hrs
*A grassy site overlooking Wimbleball Lake, set high
up on Exmoor National Park. The camping area is in
its own paddock with modern toilet facilities, and
surrounded by farmland in a quiet setting. The lake
is nationally renowned for its trout fishing, and
boats can be hired with advance notice. 6 touring
pitches, 4 hardstandings.*

Leisure: ⚑ **Facilities:** ↾⊙♨⛗
Services: ✕→∪♨⊁♩🛒
Notes: Dogs must be kept on leads 🍴 💳 🍽 📷 🔲

EMBOROUGH   Map 03 ST65

▶ ▶ ▶ 68% **Old Down Touring Park** (ST628513)
Old Down House BA3 4SA ☎ 01761 232355
🖷 01761 232355
e-mail: olddown@talk21.com
website: www.ukparks.co.uk/olddown
*Dir: On A37 from Farrington Gurney through Ston
Easton. After 2m left onto B3139 to Radstock. Site
opposite Old Down Inn on right*
★ 🚐 £9-£11 🚐 £9-£11 ▲ £7
Open Mar-Nov Booking advisable Bank hols & Jul-
Aug Last arrival 22.00hrs Last departure 11.00hrs
*A small family-run site set in open parkland, with an
ancient oak tree at the centre of the reception area.
The toilet facilities are excellent, and well
maintained along with every other aspect of the
park. Children are welcome, but the park is mainly
used by retired caravanners. A 4-acre site with 30
touring pitches, 15 hardstandings and 1 static.*

Facilities: ↾⊙♨✳⛗🛒🏠
Services: ⚡🛢🚰🚾→∪▶♩🔲
Notes: Dogs must be kept on leads at all times

EXFORD   Map 03 SS83

▶ ▶ 64% **Westermill Farm**
(SS825398)
TA24 7NJ ☎ 01643 831238 & 831216
🖷 01643 831660
e-mail: holidays@westermill-exmoor.co.uk
website: www.exmoorcamping.co.uk
*Dir: Leave Exford on Porlock road. After 0.25m fork left,
pass another campsite until 'Westermill' sign on tree.
Take left fork*
🚐 £9 ▲ £9

contd.

Westermill Farm

Open all year (rs Nov-May larger toilet block & shop
closed) Booking advisable Spring bank hol & Jul-
Aug
*An idyllic site for peace and quiet, in a sheltered
valley in the heart of Exmoor, which has won
awards for conservation. Four waymarked walks
over 500 acre working farm. Approach not suitable
for caravans. A 6-acre site with 60 touring pitches.
Shallow river for fishing/bathing Marked walks*
Facilities: ↾⊙♨✳✫🛒🏇 **Services:** 🛢🛢∅→∪♩

FROME   Map 03 ST74

▶ ▶ ▶ 66% **Seven Acres Caravan &
Camping Site** (ST777444)
Seven Acres, West Woodlands BA11 5EQ
☎ 01373 464222
*Dir: On B3092 approx 0.75m from rdbt with A361,
Frome bypass*
★ 🚐 £7.50-£10 🚐 £7.50-£10 ▲ £6.50-£8
Open Mar-Nov Booking advisable
*A level meadowland site beside the shallow River
Frome, with a bridge across to an adjacent field,
and plenty of scope for families. Set on the edge of
the Longleat Estate with its stately home, wildlife
safari park, and many other attractions. A 3-acre site
with 22 touring pitches, 22 hardstandings.*
Leisure: ⚑ **Facilities:** ↾⊙♨✳⛗🏠🏇 **Services:** ⚡
→∪▶🍴♩🔲🛒 **Notes:** Dogs must be kept on leads

GLASTONBURY   Map 03 ST53

PREMIER PARK

▶ ▶ ▶ ▶ ▶ 71% **Old Oaks
Touring Park** (ST521394)
Wick Farm, Wick BA6 8JS
☎ 01458 831437 🖷 01458 833238
e-mail: info@theoldoaks.co.uk
website: www.theoldoaks.co.uk
*Dir: From A361 towards Shepton Mallet in
1.75m turn left at sign Wick, site on left in 1m*
★ 🚐 £8-£11 🚐 £8-£11 ▲ £8-£11
Open Apr-Oct (rs Oct shop hours) Booking
advisable bank hols & main season Last arrival
21.00hrs Last departure noon
*An idyllic park on a working farm with
panoramic views towards the Mendip Hills.
Old Oaks offers sophisticated services whilst
retaining a farming atmosphere, and there are
some super pitches as well as en suite toilet*

contd.

The Old Oaks Touring Park facilities. Glastonbury's two famous 1,000-year-old oak trees, Gog and Magog, are on site. This is an adult-only park. A 10-acre site with 80 touring pitches, 18 hardstandings. Fishing & off-licence on site.

Facilities: ➜ ⛺ ⊙ ⚲ ✳ ♿ ☎ ▨ ★ **Services:** ▣ ▨ ⓘ ∅
⊞ ⊺ → ✔ **Notes:** No children, group or block bookings (at owners' discretion) ◉ ▭ ▱ ▨ ▨

▶ ▶ ▶ ▶ 73% *Isle of Avalon Touring Caravan Park* (ST494397)
Godney Rd BA6 9AF ☎ 01458 833618
▤ 01458 833618
Dir: M5 junct 23, A39 to outskirts of Glastonbury, 2nd exit signed Wells at B & Q rdbt, straight over next rdbt, 1st exit at 3rd rdbt (B3151), 200yds right
▣ ▨ Å

Open all year Booking advisable mid Jul-mid Aug
Last arrival 21.00hrs Last departure 11.00hrs
An excellent site of a very high standard set below this historic town, and an ideal touring centre. The level park offers a quiet and restful environment in which to unwind, and a warm welcome to visitors. An 8-acre site with 120 touring pitches.
Cycle hire.

Leisure: ⚠ **Facilities:** ⛺ ⊙ ⚲ ✳ ♿ ☎ ▨
Services: ▣ ▨ ⓘ ∅ ⊞ ⊺ → ∪ ▨ ✔ ◉ ▭ ▱ ▨ ▨

HIGHBRIDGE	Map 03 ST34

▶ ▶ ▶ 67% *New House Touring Farm Caravan & Camping Park* (ST338469)
Walrow TA9 4RA ☎ 01278 782218 & 783277
Dir: From M5 junct 22 onto A38 towards Highbridge. At rdbt signed Isleport Business Park turn left onto B3139, cross motorway bridge, park on right
▣ ▨ Å

contd.

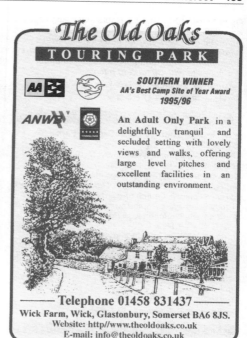

Facilities: ➜ Bath ⛺ Shower ⊙ Electric Shaver ⚲ Hairdryer ✳ Ice Pack Facility ♿ Disabled Facilities ☎ Public Telephone
▨ Shop on Site or within 200yds ▨ Mobile Shop (calls at least 5 days a week) ▦ BBQ Area ⌐ Picnic Area ★ Dog Exercise Area

Open Mar-Oct Booking advisable Jul & Aug Last arrival 23.30hrs Last departure 18.30hrs
An expanding park surrounded by trees, with hardstandings next to grass for awnings. The park hosts many rallies, and is very close to the M5. A 4-acre site with 30 touring pitches.

Leisure: ♨ **Facilities:** ⋒⊙✕⅏⊓
Services: ⊟⊡❶⊞→Ʊ▶△⬝⬝⬝

LANGPORT — Map 03 ST42

▶ ▶ ▶ 69% **Thorney Lakes Caravan Park** (ST430237)
Thorney West Farm, Muchelney TA10 0DW
☎ 01458 250811
website: www.thorneylakes.co.uk
Dir: From A303 at Podimore rdbt take A372 to Langport. At Huish Episcopi Church turn left for Muchelney, then in 100yds left again (signed Muchelney & Crewkerne). Site 300yds after John Leach Pottery
★ ⊞ fr £8 ⊞ fr £8 ▲ fr £8
Open 16 Mar-Oct Booking advisable
A small, basic but very attractive park set in a cider apple orchard, with coarse fishing in the three well-stocked on-site lakes. The famous John Leach pottery shop is nearby. A 6-acre site with 16 touring pitches.
Coarse fishing on site.
Facilities: ⋒⊙ **Services:** ⊟→▶⬝⬝

MARTOCK — Map 03 ST41

▶ ▶ ▶ ▶ 69% **Southfork Caravan Park** (ST448188)
Parrett Works TA12 6AE ☎ 01935 825661
▤ 01935 825122
e-mail: southfork.caravans@virgin.net
website: www.uk.parks.co.uk/southfork
Dir: 8m NW of Yeovil, 2m off A303. From E take exit after Cartgate rdbt. From W 1st exit off rdbt signed South Petherton, follow camping signs.
★ ⊞ £7-£10 ⊞ £7-£10 ▲ £7-£10
Open all year Booking advisable bank hols & Jul-Aug Last arrival 23.00hrs Last departure noon
A neat grass park in a quiet rural area, offering spotless facilities to those who enjoy the countryside. Located on the outskirts of a pretty village, with good amenities. A 2-acre site with 30 touring pitches and 3 statics.
Caravan service/repair centre & accessories shop.
Leisure: ♨ **Facilities:** ⋒⊙❄✕⬝⬝⊓
Services: ⊟⊡❶⬝⊞⊓→▶⬝⬝⬝⬝⬝

MINEHEAD — Map 03 SS94

▶ ▶ ▶ 66% **Camping & Caravanning Club Site** (SS958471)
Hill Rd, North Hill TA24 5LB ☎ 01643 704138
website: www.campingandcaravanningclub.co.uk
Dir: From A39 towards town centre. At T-junct turn right onto dual carriageway & take 1st left into Blenheim Rd. Next left into Marlet Rd, keep left at church, follow narrow rd for 1m to site on right
★ ⊞ £10.20-£12.90 ▲ £10.20-£12.90
Open 16 May-23 Sep Booking advisable bank hols & Jul-Aug Last arrival 21.00hrs Last departure noon

contd.

A secluded site on a hilltop with glorious views of the Bristol Channel and the Quantocks. Good clean facilities plus a laundry and information room make this a popular choice for those seeking an isolated holiday. Please see advertisement on page 10 for details of Club Members' benefits. A 3.75-acre site with 60 touring pitches, 10 hardstandings.
Facilities: ⋒⊙❄✕⬝⬝
Services: ⊟⊡❶⬝⊞→Ʊ▶△⬝⬝ ⬝⬝⬝⬝⬝

▶ ▶ ▶ 57% **Minehead & Exmoor Caravan Site** (SS950457)
Minehead & Exmoor Caravan Park, Porlock Rd
TA24 8SW ☎ 01643 703074
Dir: 1m W of Minehead, close to A39
★ ⊞ fr £10 ⊞ fr £10 ▲ fr £10
Open Mar-22 Oct Booking advisable bank hols & Jul-Aug Last arrival 22.00hrs Last departure noon
A small terraced park on the edge of Exmoor, spread over four paddocks and surrounded by mature trees for screening. The level pitches provide a comfortable space for each unit on this family-run park. A 2.5-acre site with 50 touring pitches.
Leisure: ♨ **Facilities:** ⋒⊙❄⬝⬝
Services: ⊟⊡❶⬝⊞⊓→Ʊ▶△⬝⬝⬝⬝

NORTH WOOTTON — Map 03 ST54

▶ ▶ 70% **Greenacres Camping** (ST553416)
Barrow Ln BA4 4HL ☎ 01749 890497
e-mail: harvie.greenacres@talk21.com
Dir: A361 to Glastonbury. Turn at Steanbow Farm, from A39 turn at Browns Garden Centre. Follow signs
★ ⊞ £9.80 ▲ £9.80
Open Apr-Oct Booking advisable school hols Last arrival 21.00hrs Last departure noon ⌘
An immaculately maintained site peacefully set within sight of Glastonbury Tor. Mainly family orientated with many thoughtful extra facilities provided. A 4.5-acre site with 30 touring pitches. Free use of fridges & freezers
Leisure: ♨ **Facilities:** ⋒⊙❄✕ **Services:** ⊟❶⬝⊞ →Ʊ▶△⬝⬝⬝⊡⬝ **Notes:** No caravans

PORLOCK — Map 03 SS84

▶ ▶ ▶ 68% **Burrowhayes Farm Caravan & Camping Site** (SS897460)
West Luccombe TA24 8HT ☎ 01643 862463
e-mail: info@burrowhayes.co.uk
website: www.burrowhayes.co.uk
Dir: Follow A39 from Minehead towards Porlock for 5m. Take left turn signed Horner & West Lucombe, site 0.25m on right, immediately before humpback bridge
★ ⊞ £6-£8.50 ⊞ £6-£8.50 ▲ £6-£8.50
Open 15 Mar-Oct shop closed until Sat before Etr Booking advisable Etr, Spring bank hol & Jul-Aug Last arrival 22.00hrs Last departure noon
A delightful site on the edge of Exmoor, sloping gently down to Horner Water in glorious surroundings. The farm buildings have been converted into riding stables which offer escorted rides on the moors, and the well-kept facilities are

contd.

Burrowhayes Farm Caravan & Camping Park *housed in timber-clad buildings. An ideal site for exploring the surrounding area, with many walks directly into the countryside. An 8-acre site with 120 touring pitches, 3 hardstandings and 20 statics. Pony-trekking available, riding stables*

Facilities: ⚑⊙✳✆❧❦

Services: ▯▯✦⊡↯↣▸➤◗⚏▦⎏

▶ ▶ ▶ 63% **Porlock Caravan Park** (SS882469)
TA24 8ND ☎ 01643 862269 ▤ 01643 862239
e-mail: info@porlockcaravanpark.co.uk
website: www.porlockcaravanpark.co.uk
Dir: Through village fork right signed Porlock Weir, site on right
★ ⌂ fr £9 ⌂ fr £8 ▲ fr £9
Open 15 Mar-Oct Booking advisable Etr, Whitsun & Jul-Aug Last arrival 23.00hrs Last departure noon
Located close to the town centre and with the seaside town of Minehead just 6m away, this sheltered touring park offers a quiet resting place in the centre of lovely countryside. Exmoor is right on the doorstep. A 3-acre site with 40 touring pitches and 56 statics.

Facilities: ⚑⊙✳✆❧❦

Services: ▯▯✦⊡↯↣▸➤⚏

PRIDDY Map 03 ST55

▶ ▶ ▶ 65% **Mendip Heights Camping & Caravan Park** (ST522519)
Townsend BA5 3BP ☎ 01749 870241
▤ 01749 870368
e-mail: enquiries@mendipheights.co.uk
website: www.mendipheights.co.uk
Dir: Take A39 N from Wells. After 3m turn left at lights onto B3135 to Cheddar. After 4.5m turn left. Site 200yds on right
★ ⌂ £6.60-£9.90 ⌂ £6.60-£9.90 ▲ £6.60-£9.90
Open Mar-15 Nov Booking advisable bank & school hols Last arrival 22.00hrs
Quiet family park on the Mendip Hills above Cheddar Gorge. The enthusiastic owners organise walks, and badger and deer watches. A 4.5-acre site with 90 touring pitches, 9 hardstandings and 2 statics.
Archery, canoeing, abseiling, caving, table tennis.

Leisure: ⛰ **Facilities:** ⚑⊙✳✆❧❦
Services: ▯▯✦⊡↯↣➤⚏▦⎏

PORLOCK CARAVAN PARK

Select family run site in the beautiful Exmoor National Park close to the sea, only 2 minutes walk from the quaint old village of Porlock. Situated in a vale at the foot of Porlock Hill. The site offers magnificent views all around. We have new modern well equipped caravans for hire all with mains, electricity, gas cooker/heating, colour T.V., W.C., fridges, hot water, and showers.
Dogs allowed in some letting units.
Facilities include: shower block, launderette, and public telephone. Tourers, dormobiles and tents welcome. Full facilities including electric hook-up.
10 acre rally field available for exempt organisations.
▶▶▶
Porlock, Nr. Minehead, Somerset, TA24 8ND.
Tel: (01643) 862269 Fax: (01643) 862239
E-mail: info@porlockcaravanpark.co.uk
www.porlockcaravanpark.co.uk
Proprietors: Tony & Denise Hardick
Last caravan park before Porlock Hill
Phone or Write for free colour brochure.

REDHILL Map 03 ST46

▶ ▶ ▶ 60% **Brook Lodge Farm Camping & Caravan Park** (ST486620)
Cowslip Green BS40 5RD ☎ 01934 862311
▤ 01934 862311
e-mail: brooklodgefarm@aol.com
Dir: M5 junct 18 follow signs for Bristol Airport. Park 3m on left of A38 at bottom of hill after passing Darlington Arms
★ ⌂ £12.50-£17.50 ⌂ £10-£15 ▲ £10.50-£16.50

Open Mar-Oct Booking advisable 22 May-4 Sep Last arrival 22.30hrs Last departure 12.00hrs
A naturally sheltered country touring park nestling in a valley of the Mendip Hills, surrounded by trees and a historic walled garden. Country walks can be enjoyed from the park, and there is trout fishing nearby. A 3.5-acre site with 29 touring pitches, 3 hardstandings.

contd.

Bicycle hire & walking maps provided

Leisure: ⚑ **Facilities:** 🖍⊙🕾☀🧇🗺🛱

Services: 🔌🛈🖉⊟→ ∪ ▶🖋 **Notes:** Small dogs only & must be on lead 💳💳💳🔲 🗐

RODNEY STOKE   Map 03 ST44

▶ ▶ ▶ ▶ 65% **Bucklegrove Caravan & Camping Park** (ST487502)
Wells Rd BS27 3UZ ☎ 01749 870261
🖷 01749 870101
e-mail: info@bucklegrove.co.uk
website: www.bucklegrove.co.uk
Dir: On A371 midway between Cheddar & Wells
★ 🚐 £5-£12.50 🚐 £5-£12.50 ▲ £5-£12.50
Open early Mar-early Jan (rs Mar-Etr & Oct-Jan
Pool closed) Booking advisable bank hols & peak
periods Last arrival 21.00hrs Last departure noon ⌧
*A well-sheltered site on the southern slopes of the
Mendip Hills providing superb views of Somerset.
This popular park offers good facilities and
amenities including an indoor swimming pool and a
new bar/restaurant. An ideal touring base, and a
pleasant suntrap. A 7.5-acre site with 125 touring
pitches, 17 hardstandings and 35 statics.
Separate tourist information room.*

Leisure: 🕈 ◕⚑🖵 **Facilities:** ➡🖍⊙🕾☀🧇🕽
🗺🎋 **Services:** 🔌🖥🛈🍴🖉⊟🕕✕🖐→∪▶⊙🎪🖋
💳💳💳🔲 🗐

SPARKFORD   Map 03 ST62

▶ ▶ ▶ 66% **Long Hazel International
Caravan/Camping Park** (ST602262)
High St BA22 7JH ☎ 01963 440002 🖷 01963 440002
e-mail: longhazelpark@hotmail.com
website: www.sparkford.f9.co.uk/lhi.htm
*Dir: Turn off A303 at Hazelgrove rdbt follow signs for
Sparkford. Site next to Sparkford Inn in the High Street*
★ 🚐 £8-£10 🚐 £8-£10 ▲ £8-£10
Open Mar-Dec Booking advisable Last arrival
22.30hrs Last departure 11.30hrs
*A very neat, smart site next to the Sparkford Inn in
the village high street. This attractive park is run by
a friendly owner to a good standard. A 3.5-acre site
with 75 touring pitches, 30 hardstandings and 3
statics.*
Badminton, Bowls, 9 Hole Putting Green

Leisure: ⚑ **Facilities:** 🖍⊙🕾☀🧇🗺🎋🖐🛱🎋
Services: 🔌🛈🖉⊟→∪▶🖋

TAUNTON   Map 03 ST22

▶ ▶ ▶ 67% **Ashe Farm Camping & Caravan Site**
(ST279229)
Thornfalcon TA3 5NW ☎ 01823 442567
🖷 01823 443372
e-mail: camping@ashe-farm.fsnet.co.uk
*Dir: From M5 junct 25 take A358 E for 2.5m. Turn right
at Nags Head pub. Site 0.25m on right*
★ 🚐 £8-£10 🚐 £8-£10 ▲ £8
Open Apr-Oct Booking advisable Jul-Aug

contd.

Ashe Farm Camping & Caravan Site
*A well-screened site surrounded by mature trees
and shrubs, with two large touring fields. A new
facilities block includes smart toilets and a separate
laundry room, while the old portaloos remain very
clean and well-maintained. Not far from the
bustling market town of Taunton, and handy for
both coasts. A 7-acre site with 30 touring pitches,
8 hardstandings and 3 statics.*

Leisure: 🔍◕⚑ **Facilities:** 🖍⊙🕾☀🧇🛱🎋
Services: 🔌🖥🛈🖉⊟🕕➡→∪▶🎪🖋🗺

▶ ▶ ▶ 65% **Holly Bush Park** (ST220162)
Culmhead TA3 7EA ☎ 01823 421515
🖷 01823 421885
e-mail: beaumont@hollybushpark.ndo.co.uk
website: www.hollybushpark.co.uk
*Dir: M5 junct 25 towards Taunton. At 1st traffic lights
turn left signed Corfe/Taunton Racecourse. 3.5m past
Corfe on B3170 turn right at x-rds at top of hill on
unclass road towards Wellington. Right at next junct,
site 150yds on left*
★ 🚐 £6.50-£8.50 🚐 £6.50-£8.50 ▲ £6.50-£8.50
Open all year Booking advisable bank hols & high
season Last arrival 22.00hrs Last departure noon
*An immaculate small park set in an orchard in
attractive countryside with easy access to
Wellington and Taunton. A 2-acre site with 40
touring pitches.*

Facilities: 🖍⊙☀🧇🗺🖧🎋
Services: 🔌🖥🛈🖉⊟🕕→∪▶🖋

WATCHET   Map 03 ST04

 67% **Doniford Bay Holiday Park**
(ST095433)
TA23 OTJ ☎ 01984 632423
🖷 01984 633649
*Dir: Follow A39 towards Minehead. At West
Quantoxhead fork right after St Audries Garage,
site on right of B3191 in 1.5m*
🚐
Open Etr-end Oct Booking advisable Jul-Aug &
Whitsun Last arrival 20.00hrs Last departure
10.00hrs
*A fun-packed park in rolling Somerset
countryside overlooking the sea, with a wide
range of leisure facilities and entertainment for
all the family. The level touring area is away
from the entertainment complex in its own well-
appointed paddock. A 3-acre site with 46 touring
pitches and 200 statics.*

contd.

Free evening entertainment, amusements, Go-karts.
Leisure: ⚑ ⚑ ⚘ ⚑ ⚑ /M **Facilities:** ⚑⊙⚑⚑⚑⚑⚑⚑
Services: ⚑⚑⚑⚑✕⚑→ ⚑ **Notes:** No single sex groups, max 2 dogs per pitch ⚑ ⚑ ⚑ ⚑ ⚑

► ► ► **72% Home Farm Holiday Centre (ST106432)**
St Audries Bay TA4 4DP ☎ 01984 632487
▤ 01984 634687
e-mail: dib@homefarmholidaycentre.co.uk
website: www.homefarmholidaycentre.co.uk
Dir: Follow A39 towards Minehead, fork right onto B3191 at West Quantoxhead after St Audries garage, then right after 0.25m
★ ⚑ £8-£12 ⚑ £8-£12 ⚑ £8-£12
Open all year Booking advisable all year Last arrival dusk Last departure 12.00hrs
In a hidden valley beneath the Quantock Hills, this park overlooks its own private beach. The atmosphere is friendly and quiet, and there are lovely sea views from the level pitches. Flower beds, woodland walks, and a koi carp pond all enhance this very attractive site, along with a lovely indoor swimming pool and a beer garden. A 35-acre site with 40 touring pitches, 35 hardstandings and 230 statics.
Leisure: ⚑ /M **Facilities:** ⚑⊙⚑⚑⚑⚑⚑⚑⚑
Services: ⚑⚑⚑⚑⚑⚑→ ⚑ ⚑ ⚑ ⚑ ⚑
Notes: No cars by caravans or tents

WELLINGTON   **Map 03 ST12**

► ► ► **62% Gamlins Farm Caravan Park (ST083195)**
Gamlins Farm, Greenham TA21 0LZ
☎ 01823 672596 ▤ 01823 672324
Dir: From M5 junct 26 turn left on A38 towards Tiverton, after 4m turn right to Greenham, site on right
★ ⚑ £6.50-£7.50 ⚑ £6.50-£7.50 ⚑ £5.50-£7.50
Open Etr-Sep Booking advisable bank hols Last arrival 20.00hrs Last departure noon
A well-planned site in a secluded position with panoramic views. The friendly owners keep the toilet facilities to a good standard of cleanliness. A 3-acre site with 25 touring pitches.
Leisure: ⚑ **Facilities:** ⚑⊙⚑⚑⚑⚑
Services: ⚑⚑→ ⚑ ⚑ ⚑ ⚑

WELLS   **Map 03 ST54**
See also **Priddy**

► ► ► **63% Homestead Park (ST532474)**
Wookey Hole BA5 1BW ☎ 01749 673022
▤ 01749 673022
e-mail: homestead.park@virgin.net
Dir: 0.5m NW off A371 Wells to Cheddar road
★ ⚑ £8-£11 ⚑ £8-£11 ⚑ £8-£11
Open Etr-Oct Booking advisable Bank holidays Last arrival 20.00hrs Last departure noon
Attractive small, adults only site by a stream, with mature trees. Set in hilly woods and meadowland
contd.

with access to the river and Wookey Hole. A 2-acre site with 50 touring pitches and 28 statics.
Facilities: ⚑⊙⚑⚑⚑⚑⚑ **Services:** ⚑⚑⚑⚑
→ ⚑ ⚑ ⚑ ⚑ ⚑ **Notes:** Adults only

WESTON-SUPER-MARE   **Map 03 ST36**

► ► ► **63% Country View Caravan Park (ST335647)**
Sand Rd, Sand Bay BS22 9UJ ☎ 01934 627595
▤ 01934 627595
Dir: From M5 junct 21 take A370 towards Weston-super-Mare. Immediately take left lane & follow signs for Kewstoke/Sand Bay. Turn right at Homebase, straight over 3 rdbts onto Norton Ln. At Sand Bay right into Sand Ln, site on right
⚑ ⚑ ⚑
Open Mar-Oct Booking advisable bank hols & peak periods Last arrival 21.00hrs Last departure noon
A pleasant open site in a country area a few hundred metres from Sand Bay beach. There are plenty of amenities for all the family, and the park is well placed for energetic walks along the coast at either end of the beach. An 8-acre site with 120 touring pitches and 65 statics.
Leisure: ⚑ ⚑ /M **Facilities:** ⚑⊙⚑⚑⚑⚑⚑⚑
Services: ⚑⚑⚑⚑⚑⚑→ ⚑ ⚑ ⚑ ⚑ ⚑ ⚑

► ► ► **64% Purn Holiday Park (ST332568)**
Bridgwater Rd, Bleadon BS24 0AN ☎ 01934 812342
▤ 01934 812342
Dir: From Weston-super-Mare take A370 towards Burnham-on-Sea, site on right by Anchor Inn, about 1m from hospital rdbt
⚑ ⚑ ⚑
Open Mar-Oct (rs Mar-Apr & Oct Club only open at weekends) Booking advisable Jul & Aug Last arrival mdnt Last departure 10.30hrs
A tree-lined park in a handy position for touring the Somerset coast. The town centre and beaches are only 2 miles away, and the park is well geared towards the family. An 11-acre site with 168 touring pitches and 120 statics.
River with fishing.
Leisure: ⚑ ⚑ /M **Facilities:** ⚑⊙⚑⚑⚑⚑⚑⚑⚑
Services: ⚑⚑⚑⚑⚑⚑→ ⚑ ⚑ ⚑ ⚑ ⚑ ⚑

► ► ► **70% West End Farm Caravan & Camping Park (ST354600)**
Locking BS24 8RH ☎ 01934 822529 ▤ 01934 822529
Dir: From M5 junct 21 onto A370. Follow signs for International Helicopter Museum. Turn right at rdbt, follow signs to site
⚑ ⚑ ⚑
Open all year Booking advisable peak periods Last arrival 22.00hrs Last departure noon
A flat, hedge-bordered site by helicopter museum with good landscaping and clean facilities. Good access to Weston-super-Mare and the Mendips. A 10-acre site with 75 touring pitches and 20 statics.
Leisure: ⚑ /M **Facilities:** ⚑⊙⚑⚑⚑⚑⚑⚑
Services: ⚑⚑⚑⚑⚑⚑→ ⚑ ⚑ ⚑ ⚑ ⚑ ⚑
⚑ ⚑ ⚑ ⚑ ⚑

▶ ▶ ▶ 59% **Weston Gateway Caravan Site**
(ST370621)
West Wick BS24 7TF ☎ 01934 510344
Dir: From M5 J21, take A370 towards Weston-super-Mare, then immediately take left lane, then 1st left signed Banwell & Westwick, site on left
🚗🚐⚠
Open Apr-Oct Booking advisable Jul-Aug Last arrival 23.00hrs Last departure noon
A pleasant site set amongst trees and shrubs, with quite simple toilet facilities. Site security is very tight, and there is some entertainment. A 15-acre site with 175 touring pitches.
Leisure: ◕ ⚙ **Facilities:** ⌂⊙☖✻⚑& ⚘☎
Services: 🚰🅿️🛁🔌⊿🔧→U ▸☏ ᛃ **Notes:** Families only, no singles, no commercial vehicles

▶ ▶ 71% *Rose Tree Caravan Park (ST348639)*
Lower Norton Ln, Kewstoke BS22 9YR
☎ 01934 620351 & 07747 692167
Dir: From Weston-super-Mare take A370 E to rdbt at West Wick. Turn left onto unclass road, straight on at 3 rdbts. Site on right in Lower Norton Ln
🚗🚐⚠
Open Apr-Sep (rs Mar & Oct Park closed if weather conditions bad) Booking advisable Last arrival 23.00hrs Last departure noon
An attractive little park with very well-maintained and equipped facilities, located just 2 miles from a sandy bay. A stream along one side of the park is mostly fenced off. Due to site refurbishments, it is advisable to contact the site before arrival. A 5-acre site with 20 touring pitches.
Facilities: ⌂⊙✻☎ **Services:** 🚰⊡→▸☏ᛃ🛒
Notes: No single sex groups, families max 5

WINSFORD   **Map 03 SS93**

▶ ▶ ▶ 68% **Halse Farm Caravan &**
Camping Park (SS894344)
TA24 7JL ☎ 01643 851259
🖨 01643 851592
e-mail: enquiries@halsefarm.co.uk
website: www.halsefarm.co.uk
Dir: From Minehead take A396, turn right just before Bridgetown towards Winsford, then left by pub up narrow winding lane to top. Entrance over cattle grid
★ 🚐 £7-£9 🚐 £7-£9 ⚠ £7-£9

Open 22 Mar-Oct Booking advisable bank hols & mid Jul-Aug Last arrival 22.00hrs Last dep noon
A peaceful little site on Exmoor overlooking a wooded valley with glorious views. This moorland
contd.

site is quite remote, but it provides good modern toilet facilities which are kept immaculately clean by the enthusiastic owner. A 3-acre site with 44 touring pitches, 11 hardstandings.
Leisure: ⚙ **Facilities:** ⌂⊙☖✻&☎
Services: 🚰🅿️🛁🔌🔧→U⊿🛒 🍴🚂🛢🚿🎯🦮

WIVELISCOMBE   **Map 03 ST02**

▶ ▶ ▶ 73% **Waterrow Touring**
Park (ST053251)
TA4 2AZ ☎ 01984 623464 🖨 01984 624280
e-mail: taylor@waterrowpark.u-net.com
website: www.waterrowpark.u-net.com
Dir: From M5 junct 25 take A358 (signed Minehead) around Taunton, then B3227 through Wiveliscombe. Site 3m at Waterrow, 0.25m past Rock Inn
★ 🚐 £8-£11 🚐 £8-£11 ⚠ £8-£11
Open all year Booking advisable Bank holidays, summer Last arrival 20.30hrs Last dep 11.30hrs
A pretty park for adults only with individual pitches and plenty of hardstandings. The River Tone runs along a valley beneath the park, accessed by steps to a nature area created by the owners, where fly fishing is permitted. Painting and photographic workshops are available, and the local pub is a short walk away. A 6-acre site with 45 touring pitches, 27 hardstandings and 1 static.
Facilities: ⌂⊙☖✻☎🏮☶☎ **Services:** 🚰🅿️🛁☎→🛢
ᛃ🛒 **Notes:** Adults only (over 18yrs) 🍴🚂🚿🎯🦮

STAFFORDSHIRE

CANNOCK CHASE   **Map 07 SJ91**

▶ ▶ ▶ 74% **Camping & Caravanning**
Club Site (SK039145)
Old Youth Hostel, Wandon WS15 1QW
☎ 01889 582166 🖨 024 7669 4886
website: www.campingandcaravanningclub.co.uk
Dir: From Rugeley take A460, turn left past cemetery and right in 1m for site
★ 🚐 £11.10-£14.50 🚐 £11.10-£14.50 ⚠ £11.10-£14.50
Open Mar-Oct Booking advisable bank hols & Jul-Aug Last arrival 21.00hrs Last departure noon
Very popular site in an excellent location in the heart of the Chase with gently sloping ground and timber-built facility blocks. Please see the advertisement on page 10 for details of Club Members' benefits. A 5-acre site with 60 touring pitches, 6 hardstandings.
Parent & child room
Facilities: ⌂⊙☖✻&☎☎
Services: 🚰🅿️🛁🔌⊡→U▸ᛃ🛒 🍴🚂🚿🎯🦮

CHEADLE   **Map 07 SK04**

▶ ▶ ▶ 71% **Quarry Walk Park (SK045405)**
Coppice Ln, Croxden Common, Freehay ST10 1RQ
☎ 01538 723412 🖨 01538 723412
e-mail: quarry@quarrywalkpark.co.uk
website: www.quarrywalkpark.co.uk
Dir: From A522 Uttoxeter-Cheadle road turn at Crown Inn at Mobberley signed Freehay. In 1m at rdbt by Queen pub turn to Great Gate. Site signed on right in 1.25m
contd.

★ ⊞ £9-£10 ⊞ £9-£10 ▲ £8-£9
Open all year Booking advisable bank hols Last
arrival 21.00hrs Last departure noon
*A pleasant park in an old quarry with well-screened
pitches, all with water and electricity. Mature trees
and shrubs enhance the peaceful ambience, and
recently added facilities include a small shop and
information area, and disabled and family toilet
facilities. A 14-acre site with 40 touring pitches,
40 hardstandings.*
Leisure: ⚙ **Facilities:** ⚑⊙⚒⚐⚙⚘⚶⚓⚡
Services: ⚙⚡⚙⚙⚡ → ⚙

Ⓤ **Hales Hall Caravan & Camping Park (SK045435)**
Oakamoor Rd, ST10 4QR ☎ 01538 753305
Dir: On B5417, 0.75m E of Cheadle, signed Oakamoor
⚞ £9.50 ⚞ £9.50 ▲ £9.50
Open mid Mar-Oct
Leisure: ⚓ ⚓ ⚙ **Facilities:** ⚑⊙⚒⚐⚐⚓⚶⚓
Services: ⚙⚡⚙⚙✕

LEEK   **Map 07 SJ95**

▶ ▶ ▶ 72% **Camping & Caravanning Club Site**
(SK008599)
Blackshaw Grange, Blackshaw Moor ST13 8TL
☎ 01538 300285 📠 02476 694886
website: www.campingandcaravanningclub.co.uk
*Dir: 2m from Leek on A53 Leek to Buxton road. Site
200yds past sign for 'Blackshaw Moor' on left*
★ ⚞ £12.30-£15.50 ⚞ £12.30-£15.50 ▲ £12.30-£15.50
Open all year Booking advisable All year, especially
Jul-Aug & BH's Last arrival 21.00hrs Last dep noon
*A beautifully located club site, with well-screened
pitches. The facilities have been completely
refurbished, with an extra new toilet block. Please
see the advertisement on page 10 for details of Club
Members' benefits. A 6-acre site with 75 touring
pitches, 39 hardstandings.*
Facilities: ⚑⊙⚒⚐⚐⚶⚓⚶⚓ **Services:** ⚙⚡⚙⚙⚐⚙
→ ⚐⚙⚙ **Notes:** Club rules apply ⚫⚫⚫⚫⚫

LONGNOR   **Map 07 SK06**

▶ ▶ ▶ ▶ 69% **Longnor Wood Caravan Park**
(SK072640)
SK17 ONG ☎ 01298 83648 & 01298 83648
e-mail: leek@rwedd.fsbusiness.co.uk
website: www.adultstouring.co.uk/longnor
*Dir: From Longnor turn off B5053 signed Leek & Royal
Cottage, 1m left, immediately right*
★ ⚞ £9-£10.50 ⚞ £9-£10.50 ▲ £9
Open Apr-Oct Booking advisable Bank hols, Jul-Aug
Last arrival 22.00hrs Last departure 14.00hrs
*A delightful woodland park in a beautiful Peak
District location, a good walking base and ideal for
visiting Leek and Buxton. This park is for adults
only, and does not accept children. A 5-acre site
with 33 touring pitches and 15 statics.*
Off licence, pitch & putt, boules, skittles, croquet
Facilities: ⚑⊙⚒⚐⚒⚐⚶⚓⚓⚓
Services: ⚙⚡⚙⚙⚐ → ⚙ **Notes:** Adults only

OAKAMOOR   **Map 07 SK04**

▶ ▶ ▶ 63% **Star Caravan & Camping Park**
(SK066456)
Cotton ST10 3BN ☎ 01538 702219
website: www.starcaravanpark.co.uk
Dir: 1.25m N of Oakamoor off B5417, 1.5m S of A52
★ ⚞ £10 ⚞ £10 ▲ £10

Open Mar-Oct Booking advisable anytime Last
arrival 23.30hrs Last departure 13.00hrs
*A well-screened park in an attractive setting, with
good facilities. Alton Towers is just over a mile
away, and the park is very popular with visitors to
this attraction. Disposable barbecues are not
allowed on site. A 20-acre site with 120 touring
pitches and 58 statics.*
Rally fields
Leisure: ⚙ **Facilities:** ⚑⊙⚒⚐⚶⚓ **Services:** ⚙⚡⚙⚐
⚐ → ⚙ ⚐⚙⚙⚶ **Notes:** No single sex groups

SUFFOLK

BECCLES   **Map 05 TM48**

▶ ▶ ▶ 65% **Waveney Lodge Caravan Site**
(TM434937)
Elms Rd, Aldeby NR34 0EJ ☎ 01502 677445
e-mail: waveneylodge25@hotmail.com
*Dir: A143 to Gt Yarmouth off A146, right after 1m,
1st left into Elms Rd, site 0.25m right*
★ ⚞ £8 ⚞ £8 ▲ £8
Open May-Oct Booking advisable Bank hols, Jul &
Aug Last arrival 22.00hrs Last departure 11.00hrs
*A lovingly developed little site adjacent to a small
lake and the owner's house, with two hedged areas
for caravans and tents, and wood-clad portacabin
toilet facilities. This peaceful park is well placed for
the Norfolk Broads and the Suffolk Heritage coast.
A 2-acre site with 15 touring pitches.*
Leisure: ⚙ **Facilities:** ⚑⊙⚒
Services: ⚙ → ⚐⚶⚙⚶

▶ ▶ 68% **Beulah Hall Caravan Park (TM478892)**
Dairy Ln, Mutford NR34 7QJ ☎ 01502 476609
📠 01502 476453
e-mail: carol.stuckey@fsmail.net
*Dir: 0.5m from A146, mid-way between Beccles and
Lowestoft*
★ ⚞ £7-£9 ⚞ £7-£9 ▲ £7-£9
Open Apr-Oct Booking advisable Jul-Aug Last
arrival 22.00hrs Last departure 12.00hrs   *contd.*

England

The Dell Touring Park

Beyton Road, Thurston, Bury St. Edmunds, Suffolk IP31 3RB   Tel/Fax: 01359 270121

Central for Bury St. Edmunds, Newmarket Races and Stowmarket, short distance from A14. Ideal base to tour East Anglia, Cambridge, Norwich and Ipswich, all within easy reach of this well run family site and yet less than 1 hour from the Suffolk coast. Prices include free showers, hot water, clean toilets and disabled facilities, Electric hook-ups, quiet site with lots of mature trees, good pubs and leisure facilities within easy reach. Holiday caravans to rent.

Small secluded site in well kept grounds with mature trees and hedging. The neat pitches and pleasant tent area are beneath large trees opposite the swimming pool and there are clean and well maintained portaloo toilets. A peaceful spot for those wishing to visit the Broads and the Suffolk coast. A 2.5-acre site with 30 touring pitches.
Facilities: ⁿ⊙❋ℍ
Services: ⊡ℹ⌀⊞→▶⌂⅄⌁⊡⅋

BUNGAY   Map 05 TM38

▶ ▶ ▶ 58% **Outney Meadow Caravan Park (TM333905)**
Outney Meadow NR35 1HG ☎ 01986 892338
🖥 01986 896627
Dir: At Bungay park signed from rdbt junction of A143 & A144
★ 🚐 £9-£14 🚐 £9-£14 ▲ £9-£14

contd.

Open Mar-Oct Booking advisable public hols Last arrival 21.00hrs Last departure 17.00hrs
Three pleasant grassy areas beside the River Waveney, with screened pitches. The toilets are dated but quite functional. A 6-acre site with 45 touring pitches, 5 hardstandings and 30 statics. Fishing, boat, canoe and bike hire.
Facilities: ⁿ⊙❋※ℙℍ **Services:** ⊡ℹℹ⌀⊞⊡
→⊍▶⌂⅄⌁ **Notes:** Dogs must be kept on leads

BURY ST EDMUNDS   Map 05 TL86

▶ ▶ ▶ 66% **The Dell Touring & Caravan Park (TL928640)**
Beyton Rd, Thurston IP31 3RB ☎ 01359 270121
🖥 01359 270121
e-mail: thedellcaravanpark@btinternet.com
Dir: Signed off A14 at Beyton/Thurston, 4m E of Bury St Edmunds. Also signed off A143 at Barton/Thurston
★ 🚐 £8.50 🚐 £8.50 ▲ £6-£10.50

Open all year Booking advisable bank hols Last arrival anytime Last departure anytime
A small site with enthusiastic owners which is being developed to a high specification. Set in a quiet spot with lots of mature trees, the quality purpose-built toilet facilities include family rooms, dishwashing and laundry. An ideal base for exploring this picturesque area. A 6-acre site with 60 touring pitches.
Leisure: △ **Facilities:** ➡ⁿ⊙❋※⅋ℙℍ
Services: ⊡ℹℹ⌀⊞⊡→▶⌁

BUTLEY   Map 05 TM35

▶ ▶ ▶ 64% **Forest Camping (TM355485)**
Rendlesham Forest IP12 3NF ☎ 01394 450707
e-mail: admin@forestcamping.co.uk
website: www.forestcamping.co.uk
Dir: From junct of A12 with A1152, follow tourist signs to Rendlesham Forest Centre on B1084
★ 🚐 £10-£12.50 🚐 £10-£12.50 ▲ £10-£12.50

contd.

Open Apr-10 Jan Booking advisable bank & school hols Last arrival 22.00hrs Last departure noon
Set off the beaten track deep in Rendlesham Forest, this peaceful park is in an open grassy area surrounded by pine trees. The facilities are good, and there are plans to upgrade in the near future. A 7-acre site with 90 touring pitches.
Washing-up sinks.

Leisure: 🄰 **Facilities:** ⌐⊙ℛ☀🗙🛁
Services: 🖃🗑🛢🖊🗄🆃 → ∪ ▶ **Notes:** No fires, dogs must be kept on leads 💳 📧 💳 📧 🗓

DUNWICH
Map 05 TM47

▶ ▶ ▶ 64% **Cliff House Holiday Park** (TM475692)
Minsmere Rd IP17 3DQ ☎ 01728 648282
🗎 01728 648996
e-mail: info@cliffhouseholidays.co.uk
website: www.cliffhouseholidays.co.uk
Dir: From A12, turn off at Yoxford to Westleton, to Dunwich Heath. Right at Dunwich Heath, park 0.75m on left
★ 🚐 £12-£20 🚐 £12-£20 ⚠ £12-£20
Open Etr or Apr-Oct Booking advisable all year
Last arrival 21.00hrs Last departure 11.00hrs
A delightful woodland park on the cliffs near Minsmere Bird Reserve. At its centre is a large house with a walled garden. A 30-acre site with 100 touring pitches, 15 hardstandings and 93 statics.
Campers, wash room, pool

Leisure: ♠ 🄰 **Facilities:** ⌐⊙ℛ☀🗙🛁🏇
Services: 🖃🗑🛢🖊🗄🆃🗙 → 🗘

Notes: Dogs must be kept on leads 💳 📧 💳 📧 🗓

🅄 **Haw-wood Caravan Park** (TM420700)
Hinton, Darsham IP17 3QT ☎ 01986 784248
Dir: On A12 turn past Little Chef, site 0.5m on R
🚐 £8-£11 🚐 £8-£11 ⚠ £8-£11
Open Apr-Oct
As we went to press the pennant rating for this site was not confirmed.

Facilities: ⌐⊙ℛ☀🏇 **Services:** 🖃 → ♈▶🗙🗘

EAST BERGHOLT
Map 05 TM03

PREMIER PARK

▶ ▶ ▶ ▶ ▶ 69% *Grange Country Park* (TM098353)
The Grange CO7 6UX ☎ 01206 298567 & 298912
🗎 01206 298770
Dir: 3m off A12 between Colchester and Ipswich
🚐🚐⚠
Open 31 Mar-Oct (rs Oct-Mar) Booking advisable for stays of 1 wk or more Last arrival 22.00hrs Last departure 18.00hrs
Set in gently rolling countryside close to Flatford Mill in the heart of Constable country, a first class park sheltered by mature trees and bushes. The well-laid out grassy site offers plenty of screened super pitches, and the toilet facilities are of a superb standard. An attractive poolside area with a café is a new addition. An 8-acre site with 120 touring pitches and 55 statics.

Leisure: ⌇♠🄰🖵 **Facilities:** ⌐⊙ℛ☀🛆🗙🛁🛒🏇
Services: 🖃🗑♈🖊🗄🆃🗙🛒 → ∪🛆🗘

FELIXSTOWE
Map 05 TM33

▶ ▶ ▶ 63% **Peewit Caravan Park** (TM290338)
Walton Av IP11 2HB ☎ 01394 284511
🗎 01473 659824
e-mail: peewitpark@aol.com
website: www.peewitcaravanpark.co.uk
Dir: Signed from A14 in Felixstowe, 100mtrs past dock gate
🚐 £8.50-£13 🚐 £8.50-£13 ⚠ £8-£10
Open Apr or Etr-Oct Booking advisable school & bank hols Last arrival 21.00hrs Last departure 11.00hrs
A grass touring area fringed by trees, with well-maintained grounds and a colourful floral display. This handy urban site is not overlooked by houses, and the toilet facilities are clean and well cared for. A new function room contains a TV and library. The beach is a few minutes away by car. A 3-acre site with 65 touring pitches and 200 statics.
Boules area, bowling green, washing up sink.

Leisure: 🄰 **Facilities:** ⌐⊙ℛ☀🛆🛁🏇
Services: 🖃🗑🛢🆃 → ▶ ◎🛆☀🛒🗘🛁

IPSWICH
Map 05 TM14

▶ ▶ ▶ ▶ 73% **Priory Park** (TM198409)
IP10 0JT ☎ 01473 727393 & 726373 🗎 01473 278372
e-mail: jwl@priory-park.com
website: www.priory-park.com
Dir: Leave A14 at Ipswich southern bypass towards town centre. After 300mtrs left towards Priory Park. Follow single carriageway into park
★ 🚐 £15-£17 🚐 £15-£17 ⚠ £15-£17

Open Apr-Oct (rs Apr-Jun & Sep-Oct limited number of sites, club/pool closed) Booking advisable bank & school hols Last arrival 20.00hrs Last departure noon
A well-screened and very peaceful south-facing park set close to the banks of the tidal River Orwell, and with panoramic views out over the water. The park is attractively landscaped, and offers superb new toilet facilities with smartly-tiled fully-serviced cubicles. A 100-acre site with 75 touring pitches, 59 hardstandings and 260 statics.
9 hole golf, small boat launching, table tennis.

Leisure: ⌇♉🄰 **Facilities:** ➡⌐⊙ℛ☀🛁🛒🖵🏇
Services: 🖃🗑♈🖊🗄🗙 → ∪ ▶🛆🛒🗘🛁 **Notes:** No commercial vehicles, pup tents or group bookings
See advertisement on page 202

Leisure: ⌇ Indoor swimming pool ⌇ Outdoor swimming pool ♉ Tennis court ♠ Games room 🄰 Children's playground ∪ Stables ▶ 9/18 hole golf course 🛒 Boats for hire 🍴 Cinema 🗘 Fishing ◎ Mini golf 🛆 Watersports 🖵 Separate TV room

► ► ► **68% Low House Touring Caravan Centre** (TM227425)

Bucklesham Rd, Foxhall IP10 0AU

☎ 01473 659437 & 07710 378029 ▤ 01473 659880

e-mail: john.e.booth@talk21.com

Dir: From A14 take A1156 signed East Ipswich. Right in 1m, right again in 0.5m. Site on left

★ ⊞ fr £7.50 ⊞ fr £7.50 ▲ fr £7.50

Open all year Booking advisable

An appealing, secluded site with immaculate facilities and a very caring owner. A beautifully kept garden contains ornamental trees and plants, and there are unusual breeds of rabbits, bantams and guinea fowl. Tents accepted only if room available. A 3.5-acre site with 30 touring pitches.

Leisure: ⚙ **Facilities:** ⬤⊙⬤※⬤⊓

Services: ⬤⬤⬤⊞→∪⬤⊚⬤⬤⬤

Notes: Dogs must be kept on leads

KESSINGLAND	Map 05 TM58

► ► ► ► **69% Camping & Caravanning Club Site** (TM520860)

Suffolk Wildlife Park, Whites Ln NR33 7SL

☎ 01502 742040 ▤ 01203 694886

website: www.campingandcaravanningclub.co.uk

Dir: On A12 from Lowestoft at Kessingland rdbt, follow Wildlife Park signs, turn right through park entrance

★ ⊞ £12.30-£15.50 ⊞ £12.30-£15.50 ▲ £12.30-£15.50

Open Mar-Oct Booking advisable bank hols & Jul-Aug Last arrival 21.00hrs Last departure noon

contd.

A well-screened site next to Suffolk Wildlife Park, where concessions are available for visitors. Superb facilities, including three new family rooms, a disabled unit, and smart new reception. A well-equipped laundry and covered dishwashing sinks add to the quality amenities. Please see advertisement on page 10 for details of Club Members' benefits. A 5-acre site with 90 touring pitches.

Leisure: ⚙ **Facilities:** ⬤⊙⬤※⬤⬤⬤

Services: ⬤⬤⬤⊞→⬤⬤⬤⬤⬤⬤⬤⬤⬤

► ► ► ► **74% Heathland Beach Caravan Park** (TM533877)

London Rd NR33 7PJ ☎ 01502 740337

▤ 01502 742355

e-mail: heathlandbeach@btinternet.com

website: www.heathlandbeach.co.uk

Dir: 1m N of Kessingland off A12 onto B1437

★ ⊞ £15-£18 ⊞ £15-£18 ▲ £7.50-£18

Open Apr-Oct Booking advisable peak periods Last arrival 21.00hrs Last departure 11.00hrs

A well-run and maintained park offering superb toilet facilities. The park is set in meadowland, with level grass pitches, and mature trees and bushes. There is direct access to the sea and beach, and good provisions for families on site with a heated swimming pool and three play areas. An 11-acre site with 106 touring pitches and 200 statics. Freshwater/sea fishing.

contd.

Abbreviations: BH/bank hols-bank holidays　Etr-Easter　Whit-Whitsun　dep-departure　fr-from　hrs-hours　m-mile　mdnt-midnight
rdbt-roundabout　rs-restricted service　wk-week　wknd-weekend　⚉-no dogs

Leisure: ⚲ ⚲ ⋀ **Facilities:** ⋔ ⊙ ⚲ ✳ ⚹
⚑ ⛲ 📷 ⋔ **Services:** 🔌 🅿 ⛽ ⌀ Ⓣ ✕ ✈ → ∪ ⮞ ⚠ ⚑ ⚒ ⚲
Notes: 1 dog only per unit 🐕 ⚏ ⚏ ⚏ 🄪

LEISTON ──────── Map 05 TM46

► ► ► **66% Cakes & Ale (TM432637)**
Abbey Ln, Theberton IP16 4TE ☎ 01728 831655 &
01473 736650 📠 01473 736270
e-mail: moonsix@dircon.co.uk
*Dir: From Saxmundham E on B1119, after 3m follow
minor rd over level crossing, turn right, after 0.5m
straight on at x-roads, entrance 0.5m on left*
★ ⚑ £12-£20 ⚑ £12-£20 ▲ £12-£20
Open Apr-Oct (rs low season shop, shop/reception
open limited hours) Booking advisable public &
school hols Last arrival 20.00hrs Last departure
13.00hrs
*A large, well spread out site with many trees and
bushes on a former Second World War airfield.
The spacious touring area includes plenty of
hardstandings and super pitches, and there is a
good bar and a well-maintained toilet block.
A 5-acre site with 50 touring pitches,
50 hardstandings and 200 statics.*
Tennis, 5 acre recreation ground,
Driving Range & Net

Leisure: ⚲ ⋀ **Facilities:** ⇥ ⋔ ⊙ ⚲ ✳ ⚹ ⚑ ⚓ ⋔
Services: 🔌 ⛲ 🅿 ⌀ → ∪ ⚒ ⚲ 🐕 ⚏

LOWESTOFT ──────── See **Kessingland**

POLSTEAD ──────── Map 05 TL93

► ► ► **72% Polstead Touring Park (TL986480)**
Holt Rd CO6 5BZ ☎ 01787 211969 📠 01787 211969
*Dir: 150yds off A1071 between Boxford & Hadleigh, opp
Brewers Arms Inn*
★ ⚑ £8-£9.50 ⚑ £8-£9.50 ▲ £5-£9

Open Mar-Oct (rs Feb & Nov) Booking advisable Jul
& Aug Last arrival 22.30hrs Last departure noon
*A gradually maturing and immaculately maintained
new site in the heart of unspoilt Suffolk countryside
close to Lavenham and Sudbury. A well-equipped
purpose-built toilet block provides very spacious
showers, and the sheltered pitches are attractively
laid out. A 2.5-acre site with 30 touring pitches, 24
hardstandings.*
Rally field

Leisure: ⋀ **Facilities:** ⋔ ⊙ ⚲ ✳ ⚹ ⚑ ⚓ 📷 ⋔
Services: 🔌 ⛲ 🅿 ⌀ ⊞ → ∪ ⮞ ⚲

SAXMUNDHAM ──────── Map 05 TM36

► ► ► **65% Whitearch Touring Caravan Park
(TM379610)**
Main Rd, Benhall IP17 1NA
☎ 01728 604646 & 603773
Dir: At junct of A12 & B1121
⚑ ⚑ ▲
Open Apr-Oct Booking advisable bank hols Last
arrival 20.45hrs no cars by caravans
*A small, maturing park set around an attractive
coarse-fishing lake, with decent toilet facilities and
secluded pitches tucked away among trees and
shrubs. The park is popular with anglers; there is
some traffic noise from the adjacent A12. A 14.5-
acre site with 40 touring pitches.*
Fishing lake, tennis courts

Leisure: ⚲ ⋀ **Facilities:** ⋔ ⊙ ✳ ⚹ ⚑ ⚓ 📷 ⋔
Services: 🔌 ⛲ ⌀ → ⚲

► ► **61% Carlton Park Caravan Park (TM383632)**
Carlton Park IP17 1AT ☎ 01728 604413
*Dir: Turn off A12 at sign for Carlton Park Ind Est, park is
adjacent*
★ ⚑ fr £9.50 ⚑ fr £9.50 ▲ fr £9.50

Open Etr or Apr-Oct Booking advisable
*Set in the grounds of a sports club on the edge of
Saxmundham, and sharing the club's toilet
facilities. The gently-sloping touring field is well
trimmed and tidy. A 4-acre site with 45 touring
pitches.*

Leisure: ⚲ ⋀ **Facilities:** ⋔

► ► **64% Marsh Farm Caravan Site (TM385608)**
Sternfield IP171HW ☎ 01728 602168
*Dir: From A12 take A1094 Aldeburgh road, at Snape x-
roads turn left signed Sternfield, follow signs to farm*
★ ⚑ fr £10 ⚑ fr £10 ▲ fr £8
Open all year Booking advisable Jun-Aug Last
arrival 21.00hrs Last departure 17.00hrs
*A very pretty site overlooking reed-fringed lakes
which offer excellent coarse fishing. The facilities
are very well maintained, and the park is a truly
peaceful haven. A 30-acre site with 45 touring
pitches.*

Facilities: ⋔ ✳ ⚑ ⚓ 📷 ⋔ **Services:** 🔌 ⊞
→ ∪ ⮞ ⚒ ⚲ 🄪 **Notes:** Dogs must be kept on leads

Facilities: ⇥ Bath ⋔ Shower ⊙ Electric Shaver ⚲ Hairdryer ✳ Ice Pack Facility ⚹ Disabled Facilities ⚘ Public Telephone
⚑ Shop on Site or within 200yds ⊞ Mobile Shop (calls at least 5 days a week) 📷 BBQ Area ⚓ Picnic Area ⋔ Dog Exercise Area

SHOTTISHAM — Map 05 TM34

▶ **59% St Margaret's House** (TM323447)
Hollesley Rd IP12 3HD ☎ 01394 411247
e-mail: ken.norton@virgin.net
Dir: Turn off B1083 at village. Site in 150yds on left past
Sorrel House pub
🚐 £7-£9.50 🚐 £7-£9.50 ▲ £7-£8.50
Open Apr or Etr-Oct Booking advisable bank hols &
Jul-Aug Last arrival 22.00hrs Last departure noon
A pleasant little family-run site in an attractive
village setting beside the church. This lovely
peaceful site is in an ideal position for touring the
Suffolk coast. A 3-acre site with 30 touring pitches.
Milk & newspapers to order.
Facilities: ⋔ ⊙ ⚒ **Services:** 🖦 🗓 ⌀ 🖽 Ⓣ → ∪ ▶ 🏪 ◢ 🖾 🖴

STONHAM ASPAL — Map 05 TM15

▶ ▶ ▶ **66% Stonham Barns Caravan &**
Camping Park (TM145592)
Pettaugh Rd IP14 6AT ☎ 01449 711901
🖨 01473 890036
Dir: From A140 follow A1120 into Stoneham Aspal,
caravan park at Stonham Barns centre.
🚐 🚐 ▲
Open all year Booking advisable Last departure
12.00 hrs
A brand new touring park set beside Stonham
Barns leisure and craft shopping complex east of
Stowmarket. The park is very well equipped, and
pitches are screened in three hedged areas. The
contd.

Stonham Barns Caravan & Camping Park
portacabin toilets are of a good quality with spacious
facilities. A 7.25-acre site with 60 touring pitches.
Facilities: ⋔ ⊙ ⚎ ⚒ ⅁ 🖽 🛆 ⴲ ✿ **Services:** 🖦 🗓 ⌀ 🖽
Ⓣ → ∪ ▶ ◎ ◢ **Notes:** Dogs must be kept on leads
at all times 🍴 🚆 ⬛ 🚆 ⑤

SUDBURY — Map 05 TL84

▶ ▶ ▶ **67% Willowmere Caravan Park** (TL886388)
Bures Rd, Little Cornard CO10 0NN ☎ 01787 375559
Dir: 1.5m S of Sudbury on B1508 Bures road
★ 🚐 £9-£10
Open Etr-Sep Booking advisable Bank holidays Last
arrival any Last departure 12.00hrs
A pleasant little site in a quiet location tucked away
beyond a tiny residential static area, offering
spotless facilities. A 3-acre site with 40 touring
pitches and 9 statics.
fishing
Facilities: ⋔ ⚒ **Services:** ▮ → ∪ ▶ ◎ ⚒ ◢ 🖾

Services: Ⓣ Toilet Fluid ✗ Café/ Restaurant ⴲ Fast Food/Takeaway 🛒 Baby Care 🔌 Electric Hook Up

WOODBRIDGE Map 05 TM24

PREMIER PARK

▶ ▶ ▶ ▶ ▶ 78% **Moon & Sixpence** (TM263454)
Newbourn Rd, Waldringfield IP12 4PP
☎ 01473 736650 ▤ 01473 736270
e-mail: moonsix@dircon.co.uk
website: www.moonsix.dircon.co.uk
*Dir: Follow caravan & Moon & Sixpence signs from
A12 Ipswich (E bypass). Turn left at x-roads 1.5m
from A12*
★ ⊞ £12-£22 ⊞ £12-£22 ▲ £12-£22

Open Apr-Oct (rs low season
club/shop/reception open limited hours)
Booking advisable school & bank hols
Last arrival 20.00hrs Last departure noon
*A well-planned site, with tourers occupying a
sheltered valley position around an attractive
boating lake with a sandy beach. Toilet facilities
are housed in a smart Norwegian cabin, and
there is a laundry and dishwashing area. Leisure
facilities include two tennis courts, a bowling
green, fishing, boating and a games room.
There is an adult-only area, and a strict no
groups, and no noise after 9pm policy. A 5-acre
site with 65 touring pitches and 200 statics.
Lake, Woodland cycle trail,10 acre Sports &
Rec area*

Leisure: ⊙ ◆ ⁄Λ **Facilities:** ⇥ ⋔ ⊙ ⊙ ※ ⌧ ᘐ ᕊ
Services: ⊠ ⊡ ⊻ ᵢ ⌀ ᓂ ✕ → ▶ ▲ ᗑ ᕀ
Notes: No group bookings or commercial
vehicles. Quiet 9pm-8am ⊜ ⊟
See advertisement on opposite page

▶ ▶ 71% **NEW** **Moat Barn Touring Caravan Park**
(TM269530)
Dallinghoo Rd, Bredfield IP13 6BD ☎ 01473 737520
website: www.moat-barn.co.uk
*Dir: Turn off A12 at Bredfield, take 1st right at village
pump through village for 1m campsite on left*
★ ⊞ fr £12 ⊞ fr £12 ▲ fr £12
Open Apr/Etr-Oct Booking advisable Last arrival
22.00hrs Last departure 12.00hrs
*An attractive small park set in idyllic Suffolk
countryside, ideally located for touring the heritage
coastline and Sutton Hoo. The modern toilet block
is well equipped and maintained. Bed and breakfast
and cycle hire are available. A 2-acre site with 25
touring pitches.*

Facilities: ⋔ ⊙ ⊙ ᘐ **Services:** ⊠ → ∪ ▶ ᕀ ⊡
Notes: No ball games, breathable groundsheets
only, dogs on leads

SURREY

CHERTSEY Map 04 TQ06

▶ ▶ ▶ 64% **Camping & Caravanning Club Site**
(TQ052667)
Bridge Rd KT16 8JX ☎ 01932 562405
▤ 01203 694886
website: www.campingandcaravanningclub.co.uk
*Dir: M25 junct 11, follow A317 to Chertsey. At rdbt take
1st exit to lights. Straight over at next lights. Turn right
400yds turn left into site*
★ ⊞ £14.50-£15.50 ⊞ £15.50 ▲ £15.50
Open all year Booking advisable Jul-Aug & bank
hols Last arrival 21.00hrs Last departure noon
*A pretty Thames-side site set amongst trees and
shrubs in well-tended grounds, ideally placed for
the M3/M25 and for visiting London. Some
attractive riverside pitches are very popular, and
boating is allowed from the site on the river. Please
see the advertisement on page 10 for details of Club
Members' benefits. An 8-acre site with 200 touring
pitches, 32 hardstandings.*
Table tennis & fishing.

Leisure: ◆ ⁄Λ **Facilities:** ⋔ ⊙ ⊙ ※ ⌧ ᘐ ᕊ ᕀ
Services: ⊠ ⊡ ᵢ ⌀ ᓂ → ▶ ▲ ᗑ ᕀ ᗘ ⊜ ⊟ ᗕ ⊠ ⊡

EAST HORSLEY Map 04 TQ05

▶ ▶ ▶ ▶ 68% **Camping & Caravanning Club
Site** (TQ083552)
Ockham Rd North KT24 6PE ☎ 01483 283273
▤ 01203 694886
website: www.campingandcaravanningclub.co.uk
*Dir: M25 junct 10 take A3 S. Turn right onto B2039 and
site is 2.25m on right (slow for concealed entrance)*
★ ⊞ £12.30-£15.50 ⊞ £12.30-£15.50 ▲ £12.30-£15.50
Open Mar-Oct Booking advisable bank hols & Jul-
Aug Last arrival 21.00hrs Last departure noon
*A beautiful lakeside site with plenty of trees and
shrubs and separate camping fields, providing a
tranquil base within easy reach of London. Toilet
facilities are well maintained and clean. Please see
the advertisement on page 10 for details of Club
Members' benefits. A 9.5-acre site with 130 touring
pitches.*
Table tennis & fishing

Leisure: ⁄Λ **Facilities:** ⋔ ⊙ ⊙ ※ ⌧ ᘐ ᕊ ᕀ
Services: ⊠ ⊡ ᵢ ⌀ ᓂ → ∪ ▶ ▲ ᗑ ⊜ ⊟ ᗕ ⊠ ⊡

SUSSEX, EAST

BATTLE Map 05 TQ71

▶ ▶ ▶ 62% **Brakes Coppice Park** (TQ765134)
Forewood Ln TN33 9AB ☎ 01424 830322
e-mail: brakesco@btinternet.com
website: www.brakescoppicepark.co.uk
*Dir: From Battle on A2100 towards Hastings. After 2m
turn right for Crowhurst. Site 1m on left*
⊞ £8-£10 ⊞ £8-£10 ▲ £8-£10
Open Mar-Oct Booking advisable public hols &
Jul-Aug Last arrival 21.30hrs Last departure noon
contd.

Brakes Coppice Park

Secluded farm site in meadow surrounded by woodland with small stream and fishing lake. Pitches are neatly laid out on a terrace, and tents are pitched on grass edged by woodland. A 3-acre site with 30 touring pitches, 10 hardstandings. Fishing

Leisure: ⚑ **Facilities:** ♠⊙ℚ☀╚⚑⛺☵ ✽
Services: ♨️🔲🛢🚿🚮⊞Ⓣ→∪▶✈⚡ 💳🔲⚙

▶ ▶ ▶ **66% Crazy Lane Touring Park (TQ782169)**
Whydown Farm, Crazy Ln, Sedlescombe TN33 0QT
☎ 01424 870147 📠 01424 870147
e-mail: info@crazylane.co.uk
website: www.crazylane.co.uk
Dir: 100yds past B2244, off A21 travelling S, opposite Black Brooks Garden Centre
★ ⚐ £12-£14 ⚐ £12-£14 ▲ £10-£12
Open Mar-Oct Booking advisable bank hols Last departure 14.00hrs
Set in a scenic part of this cider-producing area, a very pretty park overlooking orchards. The touring pitches are terraced and provide water and electricity, while tents are located on an upper paddock; all enjoy good views. There is some traffic noise during the day from the A21. A 3.5-acre site with 36 touring pitches, 4 hardstandings.
Facilities: ♠⊙ℚ☀╚⚑╚
Services: ♨️🔲🛢🚿🚮⊞Ⓣ→∪▶✈

▶ ▶ **58% Senlac Park Caravan & Camping Site (TQ722153)**
Main Rd, Catsfield TN33 9DU
☎ 01424 773969 & 752590 📠 01424 752146
Dir: From Battle take A271, then left on B2204 signed Bexhill
⚐ ⚐ ▲
Open Mar-Oct Booking advisable bank hols Last arrival 20.30hrs Last departure noon
A pretty woodland site with many secluded bays, well landscaped and attractively laid out. The functional toilet facilities are clean, and the site is ideal for anyone looking for seclusion and shade. A 5-acre site with 32 touring pitches.
Facilities: ♠⊙☀╚✽
Services: ♨️🛢⊞Ⓣ→∪▶✈⚡💳🔲

CROWBOROUGH   Map 05 TQ53

▶ ▶ ▶ ▶ **68% Camping & Caravanning Club Site (TQ520315)**
Goldsmith Recreation Ground TN6 2TN
☎ 01892 664827
website: www.campingandcaravanningclub.co.uk
Dir: From N turn right & from S left off A26 into entrance to Goldsmiths Ground, signed Leisure Centre. At top of road right onto site lane
★ ⚐ £12.30-£15.50 ⚐ £12.30-£15.50 ▲ £12.30-£15.50
Open Mar-16 Dec Booking advisable bank hols & peak periods Last arrival 21.00hrs Last departure noon
A spacious terraced site with stunning views across the Weald to the North Downs in Kent. This good quality site has clean, modern toilets, a new kitchen and eating area for campers, and good provision of hardstandings. An excellent leisure centre is adjacent to the park. Please see the advertisement on page 10 for details of Club Members' benefits. A 13-acre site with 90 touring pitches, 26 hardstandings.
Leisure: ♠ ⚑ **Facilities:** ♠⊙ℚ☀╚╚
Services: ♨️🔲🛢🚮⊞→∪▶△✈⚡💳🔲🔳⚙

FURNER'S GREEN   Map 05 TQ42

▶ ▶ **66% Heaven Farm (TQ403264)**
TN22 3RG ☎ 01825 790226 📠 01825 790881
e-mail: butlerenterprises@farmline.com
website: www.heavenfarm.co.uk
Dir: On A275 between Lewes and East Grinstead, 1m N of Sheffield Park Gardens
★ ⚐ £9-£10 ⚐ £9-£10 ▲ £9-£10
Open Apr-Oct (rs Nov-Mar) Booking advisable Last arrival 21.00hrs Last departure noon
Delightful small rural site on a popular farm complex incorporating a farm museum, craft shop, tea room and nature trail. Good clean facilities in well-converted outbuildings. A 1.5-acre site with 25 touring pitches.
Facilities: ♠⊙☀╚╚⚑☵✽ **Services:** ♨️✖→∪▶✈

HASTINGS & ST LEONARDS   Map 05 TQ80

▶ ▶ ▶ **65% Shearbarn Holiday Park (TQ842112)**
Barley Ln TN35 5DX ☎ 01424 423583 & 716474
📠 01424 718740
e-mail: shearbarn@pavilion.co.uk
website: www.shearbarn.co.uk
Dir: From A259 to Rye-Folkstone, right at Stables Theatre into Harrow Rd, right into Gurth Rd, left at end into Barley Lane. Site signed
⚐ ⚐ ▲
Open Mar-15 Jan (rs Mar-Etr, early May & mid Sep-15 Jan facilities may be closed (shop, bar etc))
Booking advisable bank hols & Jul-Aug Last arrival 22.00hrs Last departure 10.00hrs
A large touring area set away from the statics and clubhouse on a high hill above Hastings with good sea views. Pitches are spacious, and good planting provides shade and shelter. A 16-acre site with 450 touring pitches and 180 statics.
Entertainment & amusements on site.
Leisure: ♠ ⚑ **Facilities:** ♠⊙☀╚╚╚ **Services:** ♨️🔲
♈🛢🚮⊞Ⓣ✖♨→∪▶♨✈⚡💳🔲🔳🔲🔳⚙

HEATHFIELD   Map 05 TQ52

▶ ▶ **63% Greenviews Caravan Park (TQ605223)**
Burwash Rd, Broad Oak TN21 8RT ☎ 01435 863531
🖥 01435 863531
Dir: Through Heathfield on A265 for 1m. Site on left after Broad Oak sign
★ 🚐 fr £6.50 🚐 fr £6.50 ▲ £3-£6
Open Apr-Oct (rs Mar-Apr & Oct-Dec bookings only, subject to weather) Booking advisable Jul-Aug Last arrival 22.00hrs Last departure 10.30hrs ⊗
A small touring area adjoining a residential park, with older-style facilities and a smart clubhouse. The owners always offer a friendly welcome, and they take pride in the lovely flower beds which adorn the park. A 3-acre site with 10 touring pitches and 51 statics.
Facilities: ℕ ☺ ⚡ ❄ ❤ **Services:** ⚙ 🗑 🏕 ⓐ ⌀

HORAM   Map 05 TQ51

▶ ▶ ▶ **67% Horam Manor Touring Park (TQ579170)**
TN21 0YD ☎ 01435 813662
e-mail: camp@horam-manor.co.uk
website: www.horam-manor.co.uk
Dir: On A267, 3m S of Heathfield and 10m N of Eastbourne
★ 🚐 £12.50 🚐 £12.50 ▲ £12.50

Open Mar-Oct Booking advisable peak periods Last arrival 22.00hrs Last departure 18.00hrs
A well landscaped park in a peaceful location on former estate land, set in gently-sloping grassland surrounded by woods, nature trails and fishing lakes. A 7-acre site with 90 touring pitches.
Parent and toddler room
Leisure: ⚡ **Facilities:** ℕ ☺ ❄ ⚙ ❤ ⚡ 🛒 ☰ ✝
Services: ⚙ 🗑 🏕 ⓐ ⓣ → ∪ ▶ ⌀

PEVENSEY   Map 05 TQ60

▶ ▶ ▶ **68% Camping & Caravanning Club Site (TQ682055)**
Norman's Bay BN24 6PR ☎ 01323 761190
website: www.campingandcaravanningclub.co.uk
Dir: From rdbt at junct of A27/A259 follow A259 signed Eastbourne. In Pevensey Bay village 1st left signed Beachlands only. After 1.25m site on left
★ 🚐 £12.30-£17.50 🚐 £12.30-£17.50 ▲ £12.30-£17.50
Open Mar-Nov Booking advisable bank hols & peak periods Last arrival 21.00hrs Last departure noon
A well-kept site with immaculate toilet block, right beside the sea. This popular family park enjoys

contd.

good rural views towards Rye and Pevensey. Please see the advertisement on page 10 for details of Club Members' benefits. A 3-acre site with 200 touring pitches.*
Recreation hall
Leisure: ⚡ ❤ ⚠ **Facilities:** ℕ ☺ ⚡ ❄ ⚙ ❤ ⚡ ✝
Services: ⚙ 🗑 🏕 ⓐ ⓣ → ⚠ ⌀ → 💷 ━━ 🚫 ⌀

PEVENSEY BAY   Map 05 TQ60

▶ ▶ ▶ **70% Bay View Caravan and Camping Park (TQ648028)**
Old Martello Rd BN24 6DX ☎ 01323 768688
🖥 01323 769637
e-mail: holidays@bay-view.co.uk
website: www.bay-view.co.uk
Dir: Signed from A259. On sea side of A259 along private road towards beach
🚐 £9.85-£13.45 🚐 £9.85-£13.45 ▲ £9.20-£11.55
Open 4 Apr-6 Oct Booking advisable bank & school hols Last arrival 22.00hrs Last departure noon
A pleasant well-run site just yards from the beach, in an area east of the town centre known as 'The Crumbles'. The level grassy site is very well maintained. A 3.5-acre site with 49 touring pitches, 9 hardstandings and 5 statics.
Leisure: ⚠ **Facilities:** ℕ ☺ ⚡ ❄ ⚙ ❤ ⚡ 🛒 **Services:** ⚙ 🗑 🏕 ⓐ ⓣ → ▶ ◉ ⚠ ☰ ⌀ **Notes:** Couples & families only, no commercial vehicles

SEAFORD   Map 05 TV49

▶ ▶ ▶ **64% Buckle Caravan & Camping Park (TV469960)**
Marine Pde BN25 2QR ☎ 01323 897801
🖥 01323 873767
e-mail: holiday@buckle-park.freeserve.co.uk
website: www.buckle-camping.ukti.co.uk
Dir: Signed off A259 on W side of Seaford towards Newhaven
★ 🚐 £8-£12 🚐 £8-£12 ▲ £8-£10
Open Mar-2 Jan Booking advisable bank hols & Jul-Aug Last arrival 21.00hrs Last departure noon
A friendly, well-maintained site set alongside the sea wall. The main area is for adults only, with grassy pitches, low fencing and selective planting, while a second area with relaxed pitches is for families. A 9-acre site with 110 touring pitches, 6 hardstandings.
Mother & baby room in toilets
Leisure: ⚠ **Facilities:** ℕ ☺ ⚡ ❄ ⚙ ❤ ⚡ 🛒 ✝
Services: ⚙ 🏕 ⓐ ⓣ ⓣ → ▶ ◉ ⚠ ⌀ 🗑

SUSSEX, WEST

BOGNOR REGIS   Map 04 SZ99

▶ ▶ **65% Lillies Nursery & Caravan Park (SU964040)**
Yapton Rd, Barnham PO22 0AY ☎ 01243 552081
🖥 01243 552081
e-mail: thelillies@hotmail.com
website: www.lilliescaravanpark.co.uk
Dir: On B2233 in Barnham, 2m off A27 & 6m from Bognor Regis
🚐 £10-£14 🚐 £10-£14 ▲ £10-£14

contd.

Lillies Nursery & Caravan Park
Open all year (rs Nov-Feb touring pitches only)
Booking advisable Jul-Sep Last arrival 22.00hrs
Last departure 11.00hrs
*A friendly little site tucked behind the owner's
nursery, with gradually improving facilities in
secluded peaceful countryside. A 3-acre site with
36 touring pitches, 4 hardstandings and 9 statics.
Play area for ball games.*

Facilities: ⌐⊙❣✻⅋ℂ✇⅏

Services: ⛽◫🏧⌕⊞🅃→∪▶✛☎⌗●═🔋⛴

CHICHESTER — Map 04 SU80

▶ ▶ ▶ **66% Ellscott Park (SU829995)**
Sidlesham Ln, Birdham PO20 7QL ☎ 01243 512003
📠 01243 512003
e-mail: angieparks@lineone.net
website: www.idms.co.uk/ellscottpark
*Dir: Take A286 Chichester/Wittering road for approx 4m,
left at Butterfly Farm sign, site 500yds right*
★ 🚐 £7-£10 🚐 £7-£10 ▲ £7-£10
Open Mar-Oct Booking advisable Bank holidays
& Aug
*A developing park set in two fields behind the
owners' nursery and van storage area. The park
attracts a peace-loving clientele, and is handy for
the beach and other local attractions. A 2.5-acre site
with 50 touring pitches.*

Leisure: ⚠ **Facilities:** ⌐⊙✻⅋⅏⅏
Services: ⛽◫⌕⊞🅃→∪▶⚙✛⌗⅋

DIAL POST — Map 04 TQ11

▶ ▶ ▶ ▶ **70% Honeybridge Park
(TQ152183)**
Honeybridge Ln RH13 8NX ☎ 01403 710923
📠 01403 710923
e-mail: enquiries@honeybridgepark.co.uk
website: www.honeybridgepark.co.uk
*Dir: 10m S of Horsham on A24. Turn left 1m past Dial
Post sign at Old Barn Nurseries, continue for 300yds
park on right*
★ 🚐 £13-£17 🚐 £13-£17 ▲ £11-£13
Open all year Booking advisable bank hols & high
season Last arrival 22.00hrs Last departure 20.00hrs
*Gently sloping and part level site surrounded by
hedgerows and mature trees. The hardworking and*
contd.

Honeybridge Park
*enthusiastic young owners keep the sanitary
facilities immaculate, and there are plenty of
hardstandings and electric hook-ups. An excellent
children's play area includes an aerial runway and
adventure equipment. A 15-acre site with 100
touring pitches, 50 hardstandings.*

Leisure: ⚓⚠ **Facilities:** ⌐⊙❣✻⅋ℂ✇⅏⅏
Services: ⛽◫🏧⌕⊞🅃→∪▶⚙⌕
Notes: No groups of under 18s ●═🔋⛴
See advertisement on opposite page

FORD — Map 04 SU90

▶ ▶ **61% Ship & Anchor Marina (TQ002040)**
Station Rd BN18 0BJ ☎ 01243 551262
*Dir: From A27 at Arundel take road S, signed Ford. Site
is 2m from Arundel on left after level crossing*
★ 🚐 £10-£11.50 🚐 £10-£11.50 ▲ £10-£11.50
Open Mar-Oct Last departure 12.00hrs
*A neat and tidy site in a pleasant position beside the
Ship & Anchor pub and the tidal River Arun. There
are good walks from the site both to Arundel and to
the coast. A 12-acre site with 160 touring pitches.
River fishing from site*

Leisure: ⚠ **Facilities:** ⌐⊙❣✻⅋ℂ✇
Services: ⛽⚙🏧⌕⊞🅃✗

GOODWOOD — Map 04 SU81

▶ ▶ ▶ **60% Goodwood Racecourse Caravan Park
(SU885111)**
Goodwood Racecourse PO18 0PS
☎ 01243 755033 & 755022 📠 01243 755025
e-mail: racing@goodwood.co.uk
*Dir: Off A285, Petworth/Chicester road or A286
Midhurst/Chichester road*
🚐 🚐 ▲
Open Etr-Sep (rs during race meetings site is
closed) Booking advisable public hols & Jul-Aug
Last arrival 20.00hrs Last departure noon
*A neat and clean site high up on Goodwood
Racecourse, with lovely South Downs views.
The site is closed during race meetings and at other
times, and it is advisable to telephone for opening
times.
A 3-acre site with 59 touring pitches.*

Leisure: ⚠ **Facilities:** ⌐⊙⅋ℂ⅏
Services: ⛽🏧🅃→∪▶●═🔋⛴

Services: 🅃 Toilet Fluid ✗ Café/ Restaurant ⅏ Fast Food/Takeaway ⚙ Baby Care 🔌 Electric Hook Up

GRAFFHAM
Map 04 SU91

▶ ▶ ▶ **69% Camping & Caravanning Club Site**
(SU941187)
Great Bury GU28 0QJ ☎ 01798 867476
website: www.campingandcaravanningclub.co.uk
Dir: From Petworth on A285 pass Badgers pub on left &
BP garage on right. Take next right signed Selham
Graffham. Follow camping sign to site
★ ⊞ £12.30-£15.50 ⊞ £12.30-£15.50 ▲ £12.30-£15.50
Open Mar-Oct Booking advisable BH's & Jul-Aug
Last arrival 21.00hrs Last departure 21.00hrs
*A superb woodland site, with each pitch occupying
its own private, well-screened area. A peaceful
retreat or base for exploring the South Downs,
Chichester and the south coast. Please see
advertisement on page 10 for details of Club
Members' benefits. A 20-acre site with 90 touring
pitches.*
Facilities: ⬡⊙🔧⚒❄⚓💧🅿🏧♨
Services: 🔌🗑🔷🚰🗑→∪🍴💳📠🎫📶⌫

HENFIELD
Map 04 TQ21

▶ ▶ **68% Downsview Caravan Park** (TQ239139)
Bramlands Ln, Woodmancote BN5 9TG
☎ 01273 492801 🖥 01273 495214
e-mail: phr.peter@lineone.net
Dir: 1.5m SE of Henfield. At Woodmancote turn off
A281 into Bramlands Lane (campsite signed)
150yds left, camp site 1m on left
⊞ £9-£11 ⊞ £9-£11 ▲ £9-£11
Open Etr or Apr-Oct Booking advisable Jul & Aug
Last arrival 21.00hrs Last departure 12.00hrs
*A pleasant, quiet park set amongst trees and fields
in the depths of the countryside, yet only 15
minutes drive from Brighton and the coast. The
South Downs Way is handily close for walkers, and
this park is particularly suitable for adults, with no
facilities for children. A 3.5-acre site with 36 touring
pitches, 12 hardstandings and 28 statics.*
Washing up sinks
Facilities: ⬡⊙🔧⚒❄⚓💧
Services: 🔌🔷🗑→∪🍴🗑💳📠📶⌫

HORSHAM
See Dial Post

LITTLEHAMPTON
Map 04 TQ00

▶ ▶ ▶ **68% White Rose Touring Park** (TQ029039)
Mill Ln, Wick BN17 7PH ☎ 01903 716176
🖥 01903 732671
e-mail: snowdondavid@hotmail.com
website: www.whiterosetouringpark.co.uk
Dir: From A27 take A284 turn left into Mill Lane
★ ⊞ £12-£16 ⊞ £12-£16 ▲ £12
Open 15 Mar-14 Jan Booking advisable bank hols &
Jul-Aug Last arrival 22.00hrs Last departure noon
*A well-maintained family run site providing level,
well-drained ground surrounded by farmland.
Located close to Arundel and Littlehampton which
provide good local facilities. A 7-acre site with 127
touring pitches and 14 statics.*
Leisure: ⚠ **Facilities:** ⬡⊙🔧⚒❄⚓💧🅿♨
Services: 🔌🗑🔷🗑🎫→∪🍴◎⚡💧🗑
💳📠📶⌫

SELSEY
Map 04 SZ89

66% Warner Farm Touring Park
(SZ845939)
Warner Ln, Selsey PO20 9EL
☎ 01243 604121 & 604499 🖥 01243 604499
e-mail: warner.farm@btinternet.com
Dir: Turn right onto School Lane & follow signs
⊞ ⊞ ▲

Open Mar-Oct Booking advisable 4 wks prior
to arrival Last arrival 20.00hrs Last departure
10.00hrs
*A well-screened touring site adjoining three
static sites under same ownership. A courtesy
bus runs around the complex to entertainment
and supermarkets. The park backs onto open
grassland, but the new leisure facilities with bar,
amusements and bowling alley, and the*

contd.

England

Touring holiday fun for all the family

BUNN leisure

Unbeatable family fun at prices you'll like

Warner Farm really does offer great value for money holidays

✔ Excellent facilities for all our visitors including modern showers and toilets, BBQ's, dog walking and children's play areas.
✔ A choice of standard, electric and super pitches.
✔ Take full advantage of all the daytime activities and our comprehensive evening entertainment programme that is second to none.
✔ Located in Selsey, West Sussex, we're positioned near to the beach with views of the South Downs. Bunn Leisure is just what you're looking for.

✔ Free swimming pools   ✔ Free washing facilities
✔ Free live entertainment ✔ Free Bunni Club

For a FREE brochure or to make a booking telephone 01243 604499
Visit our web site www.bunnleisure.co.uk

swimming pool/sauna complex are also accessible. A 10-acre site with 250 touring pitches and 1500 statics.
Leisure: 🏊 🎿 🎱 ♨ 🎠 ⛏ **Facilities:** 🛁 ⊙ 🦺 ※ ⚓ ➂ 🚐
🏪 🎣 🐾 **Services:** 🔌 🗜 ♀ 🐕 💧 ⊞ 🕕 ✕ 🧺 → ∪ ▶ ◎ ♨ 🗡
💳 💳 💳 💳 🅿

SLINDON   Map 04 SU90
▶ ▶ 65% **Camping & Caravanning Club Site** (SU958084)
Slindon Park BN18 0RG ☎ 01243 814387
📠 024 7669 4886
website: www.campingandcaravanningclub.co.uk
Dir: From A27 Fontwell to Chichester turn right at sign for Brittons Lane & 2nd right to Slindon. Site on this road
★ 🚐 £9-£10 🚐 £9-£10 ▲ £9-£10
Open Mar-Sep Booking advisable bank hols & peak periods Last arrival 21.00hrs Last departure noon
A beautiful former orchard, completely screened by National Trust trees, and very quiet. Ideal for the self-contained camper, and own sanitary facilities are essential. Please see the advertisement on page 10 for details of Club members' benefits. A 2-acre site with 40 touring pitches.
Facilities: ※ ⚓ 🐾 🎣
Services: 🔌 🗜 ⚙ ⊞ → ▶ 🗡 💳 💳 💳 🅿

SOUTHBOURNE   Map 04 SU70
▶ ▶ ▶ 74% **Camping & Caravanning Club Site** (SU774056)
343 Main Rd PO10 8JH ☎ 01243 373202
website: www.campingandcaravanningclub.co.uk
Dir: From Chichester take A259 to Southampton, site on right past Inlands Rd
★ 🚐 £14.50-£17.50 🚐 £14.50-£17.50 ▲ £14.50-£17.50
Open Feb-Nov Booking advisable bank hols, wknds & mid Jun-mid Sep Last arrival 22.00hrs Last departure 12.00hrs
Situated in open meadow and orchard, a very pleasant, popular site with well looked after, clean facilities. Well placed for Chichester, South Downs and the ferry ports. Please see the advertisement on page 10 for details of Club Members' benefits. A 3-acre site with 57 touring pitches, 41 hardstandings.
Facilities: 🛁 ⊙ 🦺 ※ ⚓ 🐾 🚐
Services: 🔌 🗜 ⚙ ⊞ 🕕 → ∪ ▶ ♨ 🗡 💳 💳 💳 🅿

WEST WITTERING   Map 04 SZ79
▶ ▶ ▶ 68% **Wicks Farm Holiday Park** (SZ796995)
Redlands Ln PO20 8QD ☎ 01243 513116
📠 01243 511296
website: www.wicksfarm.co.uk
Dir: From Chichester take A286/B2179 to West Wittering. Follow road for 6m, then 2nd right after Lamb Inn.
★ 🚐 £11-£12.50 ▲ £11-£12.50
Open 14 Mar-Oct Booking advisable peak periods Last arrival 21.00hrs Last departure noon
A pleasant rural site, well screened by trees and with good clean toilet facilities. The park has a spacious recreation field, and good local walks, with the beach just 2m away. A 14-acre site with 40 touring pitches.
Bicycle hire.
Leisure: 🎱 ♨ **Facilities:** 🛁 ⊙ 🦺 ※ 🐾 🚐 🎣
Services: 🔌 🗜 ⚙ 🕕 → ▶ ◎ ♨ 🗡
Notes: No touring caravans 💳 💳 💳 🅿

TYNE & WEAR

SOUTH SHIELDS   Map 12 NZ36
▶ ▶ ▶ 59% **Lizard Lane Caravan & Camping Site** (NZ399648)
Lizard Ln NE34 7AB ☎ 0191 454 4982 &
0191 455 7411 📠 0191 427 0469
Dir: 2m S of town centre on A183 Sunderland road
🚐 🚐 ▲
Open Mar-Oct Booking advisable for complete wks Jul-5 Sep Last arrival anytime Last departure 11.00hrs
A well-kept site on sloping ground near the beach, not far from the city of Sunderland with its many attractions. A 2-acre site with 45 touring pitches and 70 statics.
9 hole Putting Green
Leisure: ♨ **Facilities:** 🛁 ⊙ 🦺 ※ 🐾 🚐 🎣
Services: 🔌 🗜 ⚙ ⊞ → ∪ ▶ ♨ ✚ 🧺 🗡 🅿 💳

▶ ▶ ▶ **59% Sandhaven Caravan & Camping Park (NZ376672)**
Bents Park Rd NE33 2NL ☎ 0191 454 5594 & 0191 455 7411 🖥 0191 455 7411
Dir: On A183, 0.5m from town centre with entrance on Bents Park Rd
🚐 🚙 ⛺
Open Mar-Oct Booking advisable for complete wks Jul-5 Sep Last arrival anytime Last departure 11.00hrs
A delightful park setting with flowerbeds and trees, close to a beach and boating lake which make this an ideal holiday base. Tents have their own hedged area amongst cherry trees, and the good portakabin facilities are clean and well located. Plenty of attractions locally include the Catherine Cookson festival, the Souter lighthouse, and an Anglo-Saxon farm. A 3.5-acre site with 75 touring pitches and 50 statics.
Facilities: 📶 ⊙ 🍴 ✳ 🚻 ♿ 🛒 🍖 🏕
Services: 🚑 🏪 🖉 → U ▶ 🔫 💈 🚗 🅾

WARWICKSHIRE

▶ ▶ ▶ **69% Island Meadow Caravan Park (SP137596)**
The Mill House B95 6JP ☎ 01789 488273 🖥 01789 488273
e-mail: holiday@islandmeadowcaravanpark.co.uk
website: www.islandmeadowcaravanpark.co.uk
Dir: From A46 or A3400 for Aston Cantlow. Park 0.25m W off Mill Ln
★ 🚐 £11.50 🚙 £11.50 ⛺ £10
Open Mar-Oct Booking advisable peak periods Last arrival 21.00hrs Last departure noon
A small well-kept site bordered by the River Alne on one side and its mill stream on the other. Mature willows line the banks, and this is a very pleasant place to relax and unwind. A 7-acre site with 34 touring pitches and 56 statics. Free fishing for guests.
Facilities: 📶 ⊙ 🍴 ✳ 🚻 ♿ 🛒 🍖 🏕
Services: 🚑 🏪 🖉 🖥 → U ▶ 🔫

▶ ▶ ▶ **61% Camping & Caravanning Club Site (SP202968)**
Kingsbury Water Park, Bodymoor, Heath Ln
B76 0DY ☎ 01827 874101
website: www.campingandcaravanningclub.co.uk
Dir: From M42 junct 9 take A4097 Kingsbury road. Left at rdbt, past main entrance to water park, over motorway, next right, 0.5m to site
★ 🚐 £10.20-£12.90 🚙 £10.20-£12.90 ⛺ £10.20-£12.90
Open Mar-Oct Booking advisable bank hols & Jul-Aug Last arrival 21.00hrs Last departure noon
A former gravel pit, now reclaimed and landscaped, the site is part of a level complex of lakes, canals, woods and marshland with good access roads.

contd.

Please see the advertisement on page 10 for details of Club Members' benefits. An 18-acre site with 120 touring pitches.
Area for ball games
Facilities: 📶 ⊙ 🍴 ✳ ♿ 🛒 🏕
Services: 🚑 🅿 🏪 🖉 🖥 → ▶ ⛴ 💈 🔫 💈 🚗 🚗 🚗 🅾

▶ **60% Tame View Caravan Site (SP209979)**
Cliff B78 2DR ☎ 01827 873853
Dir: 400yds off A51 Tamworth-Kingsbury road, 1m N of Kingsbury opposite pub. Signed 'No through road'
🚐 🚙 ⛺
Open all year Booking advisable 1 month in advance Last arrival 23.00hrs Last departure 23.00hrs
A secluded spot overlooking the Tame Valley and river, sheltered by high hedges. Sanitary facilities are minimal, but the site is popular with many return visitors. A 5-acre site with 55 touring pitches. Fishing.
Facilities: ✳ 🛒 🍖 🏕 **Services:** 🖥 → U ▶ ⊙ 🔺 🔫 💈 🔫 🅾

▶ ▶ **62% Lodge Farm Campsite (SP476748)**
Bilton Ln, Long Lawford CV23 9DU
☎ 01788 560193 🖥 01788 550603
e-mail: alec@lodgefarm.com
website: www.lodgefarm.com
Dir: From Rugby take A428 Lawford Road 1.5m towards Coventry. At Sheaf & Sickle PH left into Bilton Lane, site in 500yds
★ 🚐 £8 🚙 £8 ⛺ £5
Open Etr-Nov Booking advisable Bank Holidays Last arrival 22.00hrs
A small, simple farm site set behind the friendly owner's home and self-catering cottages, with converted stables housing the clean, well-maintained toilet facilities. Rugby is only a short drive away, and the site is tucked well away from the main road. A 2.5-acre site with 35 touring pitches, 3 hardstandings and 35 statics.
Facilities: 📶 ✳ ♿ 🍖 🏕 **Services:** 🚑 🏪 🖥
→ U ▶ ⊙ 🔺 🔫 💈 🔫 🅾 💈 🚗 🚗 🚗 🅾

▶ ▶ ▶ **59% Wolvey Villa Farm Caravan & Camping Site (SP428869)**
LE10 3HF ☎ 01455 220493 & 220630
Dir: From M6 junct 2 take B4065 follow Wolvey signs. Or M69 junct 1 & follow Wolvey signs
★ 🚐 £6.40-£6.70 🚙 £6.40-£6.70 ⛺ £6.20-£6.50

contd.

Booking advisable Spring bank hol-mid Aug Last arrival 22.00hrs Last departure noon
A level grass site surrounded by trees and shrubs, on the borders of Warwickshire and Leicestershire. A 7-acre site with 110 touring pitches. Fishing, putting green & off licence.
Leisure: ⚐ Facilities: ↖⊙⚑✳ 冬 ℄ ⬛ ⊀
Services: ⚙ ▣ ✦ ⊘ ⊞ ⊤ → ∪ ▶ ◢

WIGHT, ISLE OF

BEMBRIDGE	See **Whitecliff Bay**

FRESHWATER	Map 04 SZ38

▶ ▶ ▶ **71% Heathfield Farm Camping** (SZ335879)
Heathfield Rd PO40 9SH ☎ 01983 756756
▤ 01983 756756
website: www.ukparks.co.uk/heathfieldfarm
Dir: 2m W from Yarmouth ferry port on A3054, left to Heathfield Rd, entrance 200yds on right.
★ ⊟ £7-£10 ⊟ £7-£10 Å £7-£10

Open May-Sep Booking advisable bank hols & Jul-Aug Last arrival 22.00hrs Last departure 22.00hrs
A good quality park with friendly owners and lovely views across the Solent to Hurst Castle. The toilet facilities which include a family room are immaculate, and this park is constantly improving to meet the needs of campers and caravanners. A 10-acre site with 60 touring pitches. Separate playing field for ball games etc.
Facilities: ↖⊙⚑✳ 冬 ℄ ⬛ 冉 ⊀
Services: ⚙ ▣ ✦ ⊘ → ∪ ▶ ◉ ⚑ ✚ ◢ ⬛
Notes: Family camping only, no single sex groups.

NEWBRIDGE	Map 04 SZ48
PREMIER PARK	

▶ ▶ ▶ ▶ ▶ **75% Orchards Holiday Caravan Park** (SZ411881)
PO41 0TS ☎ 01983 531331
& 531350 ▤ 01983 531666
e-mail: info@orchards-holidays-park.co.uk
website: www.orchards-holiday-park.co.uk
Dir: 4m E of Yarmouth and 6m W of Newport on B3401.
★ ⊟ £8.30-£12.10 ⊟ £8.30-£12.10 Å £8.30-£12.10
contd.

Orchards Holiday Caravan Park
Open 14 Feb-3 Jan (rs Nov-Jan & Feb-mid Mar shop/takeaway closed, pool closed Sep-May) Booking advisable Etr, Spring BH, Jun-Aug, Oct half term Last arrival 23.00hrs Last departure 11.00hrs
An excellent, well-managed park set in a peaceful village location amid downs and meadowland, with glorious downland views. Pitches are terraced, and offer a good provision of hardstandings, including super pitches. The toilet facilities are immaculate, and the park has indoor and outdoor swimming pools. There is excellent provision for families, and disabled access to all facilities on site, plus disabled toilets. An 8-acre site with 175 touring pitches, 62 hardstandings and 65 statics. Coarse fishing, petanque.
Leisure: ⚵ ⚶ ◣ ⚘ ⚐ Facilities: ↣ ↖⊙⚑✳ 冬 ℄ ⬛ ⊀ Services: ⚙ ▣ ✦ ⊘ ⊞ ⊤ ✕ ⬛ → ∪ ◢
⬤ ▦ VISA ▦ ▦ ◼ ◢
See advertisement opposite

NEWCHURCH	Map 04 SZ58
PREMIER PARK	

▶ ▶ ▶ ▶ ▶ **77% Southland Camping Park** (SZ557847)
PO36 0LZ ☎ 01983 865385
▤ 01983 867663
e-mail: info@southland.co.uk
website: www.southland.co.uk
Dir: Take A3056 to Sandown. Take 2nd road on left after Fighting Cocks pub towards Newchurch. Site 1m on left
★ ⊟ £9.50-£13.60 ⊟ £9.50-£13.60 Å £9.50-£13.60

Open Etr-Sep Booking advisable Jun, Jul-Aug Last arrival 21.30hrs Last departure 11.00hrs
contd.

Beautifully maintained site, peacefully located and impressively laid out, on the outskirts of the village in the Arreton Valley. Spotless, newly extended sanitary facilities, including spacious family rooms, enhance the park. Pitches are well screened by lovely trees and shrubs, and everything is under the personal supervision of the hard-working owners. A 9-acre site with 120 touring pitches.
12 volt transformers available.
Leisure: /A **Facilities:** ⬅🦶☺🛇⚒🛆🔌⚑🏪🚿 🏕 🐾
Services: 🖳🗄🐕⌀🖽🎫🚾⬅→∪🅿⊙🛆🌡 ⚐
⬅ 🚋 🅱 🔲 🟢

PONDWELL   Map 04 SZ69
▶ ▶ ▶ **62% Pondwell Camp Site (SZ622911)**
PO34 5AQ ☎ 01983 612330 📠 01983 613511
Dir: From Ryde take A3055 turning left along B3350 to Seaview. Site is next to Wishing Well pub
★ 🚐 £6-£8 🚐 £6-£8 🅰 £6-£8
Open May-26 Sep Booking advisable Aug Last arrival 23.00hrs Last departure 11.00hrs 🐾
A secluded site in quiet rural surroundings close to the sea, on slightly sloping ground with some level areas. The village is within easy walking distance. A 9-acre site with 250 touring pitches.
Leisure: 🔸 /A 🔲 **Facilities:** ⬅🦶☺🛇⚒🔌🏪🚿
Services: 🖳🗄🐕⌀🖽→🅿⊙🌡🌡⚐📠 ⬅🚋 🟢

SANDOWN   Map 04 SZ58
PREMIER PARK
▶ ▶ ▶ ▶ ▶ **75% Camping & Caravanning Club Site (SZ590855)**
Lower Adgestone Rd PO36 OHL ☎ 01983 403432
website:
www.campingandcaravanningclub.co.uk
Dir: Take A3055 between Sandown & Shanklin, turn at Old Manor House pub, along The Fairway, follow signs.
★ 🚐 £14.60-£18 🚐 £14.60-£18 🅰 £14.60-£18
Open Mar-Oct Booking advisable high season Last arrival 21.00hrs Last departure 12.00hrs
A popular, well-managed park in a quiet, rural location not far from Sandown. The level pitches are imaginatively laid out, and surrounded by beautiful flower beds and trees set close to a small river. This planting offers good screening as well as enhancing the appearance of the park. Spotless sanitary facilities include two family rooms, and there is excellent provision for families in general. Please see advertisement on page 10 for details of Club Members' benefits. A 22-acre site with 250 touring pitches.
River fishing
Leisure: 🐾 🔸 /A **Facilities:** 🦶☺🛇⚒🔌⚑🏪🚿
🐾 **Services:** 🖳🗄🐕⌀🖽🎫🍴⬅→∪🅿⊙🛆🌡🐾⚐
⬅ 🚋 🅱 🔲 🟢

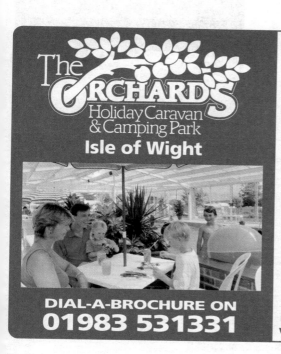

The ORCHARDS
Holiday Caravan & Camping Park
Isle of Wight

DIAL-A-BROCHURE ON
01983 531331

Leisure: 🐾 Indoor swimming pool 🐾 Outdoor swimming pool 🐾 Tennis court 🔸 Games room /A Children's playground ∪ Stables ▶ 9/18 hole golf course 🐾 Boats for hire 🐾 Cinema 🐾 Fishing ⊙ Mini golf 🛆 Watersports 🔲 Separate TV room

England

▶ ▶ ▶ ▶ **70% Old Barn Touring Park** (SZ573833)
Cheverton Farm, Newport Rd, Apse Heath
PO36 9PJ ☎ 01983 866414 📧 01983 865988
e-mail: oldbarn@weltinet.com
website: www.oldbarntouring.co.uk
Dir: On A3056 from Newport, site on left after Apse Heath
★ 🚐 £7.20-£10.50 🚐 £7.20-£10.50 ▲ £7.20-£10.50

Open Etr-Sep Booking advisable bank hols & peak periods Last arrival 21.00hrs Last departure noon
A terraced site with good quality facilities, bordering on open farmland. The spacious pitches are secluded and fully serviced, and there is a decent modern toilet block. A 5-acre site with 60 touring pitches, 9 hardstandings.
Leisure: 🌊 ☐ **Facilities:** 🛁⊙🍳✳🕿🛍 **Services:** 🔌📶🛢🖊🔥🗓️📅➡🚶⊙◐♨🕙🗑🔌 💳 💳 💳 🔲 🔲

▶ ▶ **63% Cheverton Copse Holiday Park** (SZ570833)
Scotchells Brook Ln PO36 0JP
☎ 01983 403161 📧 01983 402861
e-mail: berriesdandm@aol.com
website: www.cheverton-copse.co.uk
Dir: 400yds from A3056 towards Newport, 1m from Lake
★ 🚐 £6-£9 🚐 £6-£9 ▲ £6-£9
Open Apr-Sep (rs Jun-20 Jul & 7-30 Sep Clubhouse closed or no entertainment) Booking advisable 20 Jul-1 Sep Last arrival 21.00hrs Last departure noon
⊘ no cars by caravans
A small park on the edge of open farmland close to the resort attractions of Sandown and Shanklin. The smart, newly-refurbished toilets offer excellent sanitary facilities, and many of the pitches are set on cut-away terraces in the slightly-sloping land. A 1-acre site with 14 touring pitches and 57 statics.
Leisure: 🌊 ⚲ **Facilities:** 🛁⊙🍳✳🕿🛍 **Services:** 🔌📶
♨➡🚶⊙◐♨🕙🗑 **Notes:** No dogs 💳 💳 💳 🔲 🔲

▶ **60% Queen Bower Dairy Caravan Park** (SZ567846)
Alverstone Rd, Queen Bower PO36 0NZ
☎ 01983 403840 & 407392 📧 01983 409671
e-mail: qbdcaravanpark@aol.com
website: www.queenbowerdairy.co.uk
Dir: 3m N of Sandown off A3056 turn right towards Alverstone, site 1m on left
★ 🚐 £4-£6 🚐 £4-£6 ▲ £4-£6

contd.

Open May-Oct Booking advisable Jul & Aug Last arrival anytime Last departure anytime
A small site with basic amenities that will appeal to campers keen to escape the crowds and the busy larger sites. The enthusiastic owners keeps the facilities clean. A 2.5-acre site with 20 touring pitches.
✳ **Services:** 🔌🗓️➡🚶⊙♨🕙🗑🔌 **Notes:** Dogs must be kept on leads & exercised off site

SHANKLIN **Map 04 SZ58**

▶ ▶ ▶ **67% Landguard Camping Park** (SZ577825)
Landguard Manor Rd PO37 7PH
☎ 01983 867028 📧 01983 865988
e-mail: landguard@fsbdial.co.uk
website: www.landguard-camping.co.uk
Dir: Take A3056 to Sandown turn right after passing Safeways at Lake into Whitecross Lane. Follow signs to site
★ 🚐 £7.60-£11.50 🚐 £7.60-£11.50 ▲ £7.60-£11.50
Open Etr-Sep Booking advisable school hols Last arrival 22.00hrs Last departure noon ⊘
Surrounded by trees in a rural setting, this peaceful and secluded touring park is within walking distance of Shanklin. Facilities are clean and tidy, and the park benefits from a very good outdoor pool. A 7-acre site with 150 touring pitches, 6 hardstandings.
Horse riding.

Leisure: 🏊 ⚲ 🎾 **Facilities:** 🛁⊙🍳✳🕿🛍 **Services:** 🔌📶🍳🛢🖊🗓️📅✖🔥➡🚶⊙♨🕙🗑 **Notes:** Families only 💳 💳 💳 🔲 🔲

▶ ▶ ▶ **65% Ninham Country Holidays** (SZ573825)
Ninham Farm PO37 7PL ☎ 01983 864243 & 866040
📧 01983 868881
e-mail: office@ninham-holidays.co.uk
Dir: Signposted off A3056 Newport to Sandown road
★ 🚐 £7-£12 🚐 £7-£12 ▲ £7-£12
Open Etr-Sep Booking advisable Jun-Sep
Enjoying a lofty rural position with fine country views, this delightful, spacious park occupies two separate well-maintained areas in a country park setting near the sea and beach. An 8-acre site with 88 touring pitches.
Coarse fishing.
Leisure: ⚲ 🎾 **Facilities:** 🛁⊙🍳✳🕿🛍🗄🎋🕿 **Services:** 🔌📶🛢🗓️📅✖🔥➡🚶⊙♨🕙🐾🗑 💳 💳 🔲 🔲

TOTLAND BAY Map 04 SZ38

► ► **65% Stoats Farm Camping** (SZ324620)
PO39 0HE ☎ 01983 755258 & 753461
e-mail: david@stoats-farm.co.uk
website: www.stoats-farm.co.uk
Dir: On Alum Bay road, 1.5m from Freshwater &
0.75m from Totland
★ 🚐 £8-£10 🚐 £8-£10 ▲ £7.50-£8.50

Open Mar-Oct Booking advisable Aug
A friendly, personally run site in a quiet country
setting close to Alum Bay, Tennyson Down and The
Needles. It has good laundry and shower facilities,
and the shop, though small, is well stocked. Popular
with families, walkers and cyclists. A 10-acre site
with 100 touring pitches.
Facilities: 🅁⊙☀️🔥🐕
Services: 🔌🔋🎛️→∪▶♣♨🔧🔋🍴💳🚬📠🛒

WHITECLIFF BAY Map 04 SZ68

63% Whitecliff Bay Holiday
Park (SZ637862)
Hillway Rd, Bembridge
PO35 5PL ☎ 01983 872671 ▤ 01983 872941 SILVER
e-mail: holiday@whitecliff-bay.com
website: www.whitecliff-bay.com
Dir: 1m S of Bembridge, signed off B3395 in village
★ 🚐 £7.20-£12.60 🚐 £7.20-£12.60 ▲ £7.20-£12.60

Open May-Oct (rs Mar-Apr limited
entertainments) Booking advisable Jul-Aug Last
departure 10.30hrs
A large seaside complex on two sites, with
tourers and tents on one, and tourers and statics
on the other. There is plenty of traditional on-
site entertainment, and easy access to the
beach. A 49-acre site with 400 touring pitches
and 227 statics.
Leisure centre with fun pool, spa bath & sauna.
contd.

Leisure: 🎣🏹⚓🎢 **Facilities:** 🚿🐕⊙🅁☀️🔥🔋
🐕 **Services:** 🔌🔋🎮💈🎛️📺✖️🚿→∪▶♣🔧
💳🚬📠🛒

See advertisement in preliminary section

WOOTTON BRIDGE Map 04 SZ59

► ► ► **64% Kite Hill Farm Caravan Park**
(SZ549206)
Firestone Copse Rd PO33 4LE
☎ 01983 882543 & 883261
e-mail: barry@kitehillfarm.freeserve.co.uk
Dir: Signposted off A3054 at Wootton Bridge, between
Ryde and Newport
★ 🚐 £7-£8

Open all year Booking advisable Jun-Aug
The park, on a gently sloping field, is tucked away
behind the owners' farm, just a short walk from the
contd.

England

village and attractive river estuary. Facilities are well maintained and the atmosphere pleasantly relaxing. A 12.5-acre site with 50 touring pitches, 10 hardstandings.

Leisure: ⚠ Facilities: ⬤⊙✲⬤⅄

Services: ⬤⬤⬤⬤⬤→∪⬤⬤⬤⬤⬤

WROXALL
Map 04 SZ57

► ► ► 62% **Appuldurcombe Gardens Caravan & Camping Park** (SZ546804)
Appuldurcombe Rd PO38 3EP ☎ 01983 852597
🖹 01983 856225
e-mail: appuldurcombe@freeuk.com
website: www.appuldurcombe.freeuk.com
Dir: From Newport take A3020, turning off towards Shanklin. Proceed through Rookley & Godshill. Turn right at Whiteley Bank rdbt towards Wroxall
★ ⬤ £9-£16 ⬤ £9-£16 Å £9-£16

contd.

Appuldurcombe Gardens
Caravan & Camping Park

We are surrounded by open countryside with beautiful panoramic views and are just a few miles by car from the lovely beaches of Shanklin, Sandown and Ventnor. We are an ideal base for families and are within easy reach of local attractions. There is a bar and family room with entertainment during high season. We also have a heated swimming pool, cafe, shop and laundrette on the park

Isle of Wight PO38 3EP
Tel: 01983 852597
www.appuldurcombe.freeuk.com

Open 30 Mar-Oct (rs Mar-Spring bank hol & Aug bank hol-Oct) Booking advisable Jul-Aug Last arrival 23.00hrs Last departure noon
An attractive secluded site close to the ruins of Appuldurcombe House, with a stream running through it. There is a good swimming pool, and a shop. A 12-acre site with 110 touring pitches and 42 statics.
Crazy golf & putting.

Leisure: ⭐⚠ Facilities: ⬤⊙⬤✲⬤⬤⬤

Services: ⬤⬤⬤⬤⬤⬤⬤→∪⬤⊙⬤⬤⬤

Notes: Family groups only, no cars by caravans
⬤⬤⬤⬤

YARMOUTH
See Newbridge

WILTSHIRE

CALNE
Map 03 ST97

► ► ► 71% **Blackland Lakes Holiday & Leisure Centre** (ST973687)
Stockley Ln SN11 0NQ ☎ 01249 813672
🖹 01249 811346
e-mail: info@blacklandlakes.co.uk
website: www.blacklandlakes.co.uk
Dir: From Calne take A4 E for 1.5m, turn right at camp sign & site on left in 1m
★ ⬤ £8.45-£10.40 ⬤ £8.45-£10.40 Å £8.45-£10.40

Open all year (rs Nov-mid Mar bookings only) Booking advisable all year Last arrival 23.00hrs Last departure noon
A well-kept site in a rural area surrounded by the North and West Downs. The park is divided into several paddocks separated by hedges, trees and fences, and there are two well-stocked carp fisheries for the angling enthusiast. Some excellent walks close by, and the interesting market town of Devizes is a few miles away. A 17-acre site with 180 touring pitches, 25 hardstandings.
Wildfowl sanctuary, fishing facilities, bike trail

Leisure: ⚠ Facilities: ⬤⊙⬤✲⬤⬤⬤⬤⬤⅄

Services: ⬤⬤⬤⬤⬤⬤⬤⬤→∪⬤⬤

Notes: No groups of all males ⬤⬤⬤⬤

See advertisement on opposite page

DEVIZES   Map 03 SU06

▶ ▶ ▶ ▶ **77% Camping & Caravanning Club Site**
(ST950621)
Scout Ln, Seend, Melksham SN12 6RN
☎ 01380 828839
website: www.campingandcaravanningclub.co.uk
*Dir: From Devizes on A361 turn right onto A365, over
canal, next left down lane beside 3 Magpies pub.
Site on right*
★ ⊞ £14.50-£15.50 ⊞ £14.50-£15.50 ▲ £14.50-£15.50
Open all year Booking advisable All year Last arrival
22.30hrs Last departure 12.00hrs
*An excellent club site with well-designed, quality
facilities and a high level of staff commitment. This
popular park is set beside the Kennet and Avon
Canal, with a gate to the towpath for walking and
cycling, and with fishing available in the canal. Well
situated for exploring Salisbury Plain and the
Marlborough Downs. Please see advertisement on
page 10 for details of Club Members' benefits. 90
touring pitches, 50 hardstandings.*

Leisure: ⚲ Facilities: ⏏ ⊙ ⚏ ✳ ⚳ ⛱ ⛟
Services: 🔌 🗄 🛁 🖉 🖽 ➶ → ∪ ▶ ❄ ⟋ 🛒 ⟋ 🛒 ☎ ▭ ▦ ▦ ▦

LACOCK   Map 03 ST96

▶ ▶ ▶ **73% Piccadilly Caravan Site (ST913683)**
Folly Ln West SN15 2LP ☎ 01249 730260
🖹 01249 730260
e-mail: piccadillylacock@aol.com
*Dir: 4m S of Chippenham. From Melksham on A350
towards Lacock for 3m. Turn left at sign marked
Gastard & site is 200yds on the left*
⊞ £9.50-£11.50 ⊞ £9.50-£11.50 ▲ £9.50-£11.50

Open Apr-Oct Booking advisable school & bank
hols Last arrival 22.00hrs Last departure noon
*A peaceful, pleasant site, well established and
beautifully laid out, close to the village of Lacock.
Facilities and grounds are immaculately kept, and
there is very good screening. A 2.5-acre site with
41 touring pitches.*

Leisure: ⚲ Facilities: ⏏ ⊙ ⚏ ✳ ⚳ ⛱
Services: 🔌 🗄 🛁 🖉 🖽 → ∪ ▶ 🛒 ⟋ 🛒

LANDFORD   Map 04 SU21

▶ ▶ ▶ **62% Greenhill Farm Camping & Caravan
Park (SU266183)**
Greenhill Farm, New Rd SP5 2AZ
☎ 01794 324117 & 02380 811506
Dir: M27 junct 2, A36 towards Salisbury, approx 3m
                                              contd.

BLACKLAND LEISURE LTD
Holiday & Leisure Centre
BLACKLAND LAKES
Stockley Lane, Calne,
Wiltshire, England SN11 0NQ
Tel: 01249 813672 or
Fax: 01249 811346
Visit us on: www.blacklandlakes.co.uk
E-mail: info@blacklandlakes.co.uk

Blackland Lakes, Calne in Wiltshire, is a premier
camping and caravan site. Adjacent to the
Marlborough Downs, ideal for walking and cycling
etc. Nature lovers will enjoy the natural beauty of
the tree-lined paddocks and trail. Fishing Lakes
and a Wildfowl Lake add to the interest of this
peaceful, tranquil country site. Children and dogs
welcome. Adults only paddock.

Greenhill Farm Camping & Caravan Park
*after Hants/Wilts border, (Shoe Inn pub on right, BP
garage on left) take next left into New Rd, signed
Nomansland, 2nd site on left*
★ ⊞ £7.50-£10 ⊞ £7.50-£10 ▲ £8
Open all year Booking advisable bank hols
Last arrival 21.30hrs Last departure 13.00hrs
*A tranquil, well-landscaped park hidden away in
unspoilt countryside on the edge of the New Forest.
Pitches overlooking the fishing lakes include
hardstandings and an 'adults-only' area. Toilet
facilities are housed in clean portaloos. A 13-acre
site with 80 touring pitches, 30 hardstandings.
Fishing*

Facilities: ⏏ ⊙ ✳ ⛱ Services: 🔌 🗄 🖽 → ∪ ▶ ◎
⚠ ❄ ⟋ 🛒 **Notes:** Mainly adults, children by
arrangement only , dogs must be on leads

Leisure: ⚲ Indoor swimming pool ⚲ Outdoor swimming pool ⚲ Tennis court ⚫ Games room ⚲ Children's playground ∪ Stables
▶ 9/18 hole golf course ❄ Boats for hire ⚏ Cinema ⟋ Fishing ◎ Mini golf ⚠ Watersports ▭ Separate TV room

MARSTON MEYSEY   Map 04 SU19

▶▶ 67% **Second Chance Touring Park (SU140960)**
SN6 6SZ ☎ 01285 810675 & 810939
Dir: Take A419 from Cirencester towards Swindon, at
junct with Cotswold Water Park turn left to Down
Ampney & turn right through village. Turn left at next
junct & follow signs to site
★ 🏕 £8 🚐 £8 ▲ £8
Open Mar-Nov (rs Dec-Feb short stay) Booking
advisable peak periods Last arrival 21.00hrs Last
departure 13.30hrs �
An attractive, quiet site located near the source of
the Thames, and well-positioned for those wishing
to visit the nearby Cotswold Water Park. A 1.75-acre
site with 22 touring pitches, 10 hardstandings and
4 statics.
Fishing on site
Facilities: ⋒⊙❋🗚 **Services:** 🖭🛈→⌐△⤴🗑🚾

Notes: No loud music or parties

SALISBURY   Map 04 SU12

▶▶▶▶ 70% **Coombe Touring Park (SU099282)**
Race Plain, Netherhampton SP2 8PN
☎ 01722 328451 🖨 01722 328451
Dir: 2m SW off A3094, adjacent to Salisbury racecourse
🏕 £8-£10 🚐 £8-£10 ▲ £8-£10

Open all year (rs Sep-Etr gas only, shop) Booking
advisable bank hols (by letter only) Last arrival
21.00hrs Last departure noon
A very neat and attractive site adjacent to the
racecourse with views over the downs, and
outstanding flower beds. The park is well
landscaped with shrubs and maturing trees, and the
very colourful beds are stocked from the owner's
greenhouse. A comfortable park with a superb
luxury toilet block. A 3-acre site with 50 touring
pitches.
Childrens bathroom & dishwashing sinks no charge
Leisure: ⚠ **Facilities:** ⋒⊙🔍❋🕽
Services: 🖭🗄🛈🖋🍴🖭🔟→∪▶🚾

> Practise setting up your tent at
> home before you take it on
> holiday, and check that all guy
> ropes, pegs and poles are present
> and intact

▶▶▶ 67% *Alderbury Caravan & Camping Park*
(SU197259)
Southampton Rd, Whaddon SP5 3HB
☎ 01722 710125 e-mail: alderbury@aol.com
Dir: Off A36, 3m from Salisbury, opp Three Crowns
🚐🏕▲
Open all year Booking advisable anytime Last
arrival 22.00hrs Last departure 13.00hrs

A pleasant, attractive park set in the village of
Whaddon not far from Salisbury. The small site is
well maintained by friendly owners. A 1.5-acre site
with 39 touring pitches.
Washing-up room.
Leisure: ⚠ **Facilities:** ⋒⊙❋🕭🕽🚾
Services: 🖭🛈🔍🔟→∪▶🍴🚾🗑🖭

▶▶▶ 74% **Camping & Caravanning Club Site**
(SU140320)
Hudsons Field, Castle Rd SP1 3RR ☎ 01722 320713
website: www.campingandcaravanningclub.co.uk
Dir: 1.5m from Salisbury on A345. (Large open field
next to Old Sarum)
★ 🏕 £12.30-£15.50 🚐 £12.30-£15.50 ▲ £12.30-£15.50
Open Mar-28 Oct Booking advisable bank hols &
peak periods Last arrival 21.00hrs Last dep noon
Well placed within walking distance of Salisbury,
this tidy site has friendly and helpful wardens, and
immaculate toilet facilities with cubicled wash
basins. Please see the advertisement on page 10 for
details of Club Members' benefits. A 4.5-acre site
with 150 touring pitches, 16 hardstandings.
Facilities: ⋒⊙🔍❋🕭
Services: 🖭🗄🛈🔍→∪▶🚾🍴🖭🚾🖭

SHREWTON   Map 04 SU04

▶▶▶ 64% **Stonehenge Touring Park (SU061456)**
Orcheston SP3 4SH ☎ 01980 620304 620902
🖨 01980 621121
e-mail: julieyoung@vizzavi.net
website: www.orcheston.freeserve.co.uk
Dir: Turn right off A360
★ 🏕 £6.50-£11 🚐 £6.50-£11 ▲ £6.50-£11
Open all year Booking advisable bank hols & Jul-
Aug Last arrival 21.00hrs Last departure 11.00hrs
A quiet site adjacent to the small village of
Orcheston near the centre of Salisbury Plain and 4m
from Stonehenge. A 2-acre site with 30 touring
pitches, 12 hardstandings and 5 statics.
Leisure: ⚠ **Facilities:** ⋒⊙🔍❋🕭🕽🚾🖭🕭
Services: 🖭🗄🖤🛈🔍🔟✕🖭🖭🚾🚾🖭

England

TROWBRIDGE   Map 03 ST85

▶ 64% **Stowford Manor Farm** (ST810577)
Stowford, Wingfield BA14 9LH ☎ 01225 752253
e-mail: stowford1@supanet.com
website: www.stowfordmanorfarm.co.uk
*Dir: From Trowbridge take A366 W towards Radstock.
Site is on left hand side 3m out of town*
★ ♛ £6-£7.50 ♛ £6-£7.50 ▲ £4-£6
Open Etr-Oct Booking advisable School & Bank Hols
*A very simple farm site set on the banks of the River
Frome behind the farm courtyard. The owners are
friendly and relaxed, and the park enjoys a similarly
comfortable ambience. A 1.5-acre site with 15
touring pitches.*
Riverside site, fishing, boating, swimming
Facilities: ↑⊙☆↑
Services: ♨⊞✕→∪▶△✦✔☺⊿

WESTBURY   Map 03 ST85

▶ ▶ ▶ 68% **Brokerswood Country Park**
(ST836523)
Brokerswood BA13 4EH ☎ 01373 822238
▤ 01373 858474
e-mail: woodland.park@virgin.net
website: www.brokerswoodcountrypark.com
*Dir: From M4 travel S on A350. Right at Yarnbrook to
Rising Sun pub at North Bradley, then left & follow lane
for 1m to site on right. Other approaches difficult for
caravans*
★ ♛ £8-£15 ♛ £8-£15 ▲ £8-£15
Open all year Booking advisable Peak season Last
arrival 21.00hrs Last departure 11.00hrs
*A pleasant, newly-established site on the edge of an
80-acre woodland park with nature trails and fishing
lakes. An adventure playground offers plenty of fun
for all ages, and there is an indoor play centre and a
miniature railway of one-third of a mile. A 6-acre
site with 69 touring pitches, 21 hardstandings.*
Country park with playgrounds, fishing lakes
Leisure: ⁄Ⱥ **Facilities:** ↑⊙℥☆氐ぐ氙⊞冊☂↑
Services: ♨🛢⌀⊞✕➡→∪⊿☺🚐⚑

WORCESTERSHIRE

BROADWAY   Map 04 SP03

▶ ▶ ▶ 70% **Leedon's Park** (SP080384)
Childswickham Rd WR12 7HB ☎ 01386 852423
▤ 01386 853665
*Dir: From A44 Evesham-Oxford take B4632 6m SE of
Evesham*
♛ ♛ ▲
Open all year Booking advisable peak periods &
BH's Last arrival 20.00hrs Last departure 11.00hrs
*A large site on the edge of the Vale of Evesham,
1m from the historical village of Broadway; an ideal
base from which to tour the Cotswolds. The park
enjoys 40 acres of lawns and gardens, with
duckponds proving popular with children. Pet and
pet-free areas cater to all needs, and there is a large
play fort complex. A 16-acre site with 450 touring
pitches and 86 statics.*
contd.

Leedons Park
Leisure: ⊰℥◕⁄Ⱥ▯ **Facilities:** ➡↑⊙☆氐ぐ氙↑
Services: ♨🛢🍴⌀⊞⊤✕♨→∪▶☺🚐⚏⚑🟦
See advertisement on page 147

CLENT HILLS   See **Romsley**

HANLEY SWAN   Map 03 SO84

▶ ▶ ▶ 72% **Camping & Caravanning Club Site**
(SO812440)
Blackmore Camp Site No 2 WR8 0EE
☎ 01684 310280 ▤ 024 7669 4886
website: www.campingandcaravanningclub.co.uk
*Dir: A38 to Upton on Severn. Turn N over River Bridge.
Take 2nd left, then 1st left signed Hanley Swan. Site is
on right after 1m*
★ ♛ £14.50-£15.50 ♛ £14.50-£15.50 ▲ £14.50-£15.50
Open all year Booking advisable Jan-Mar Last
arrival 21.00hrs Last departure noon
*Blackmore is a well-established wooded park,
ideally located for exploring the Malvern Hills and
Worcester. The excellent toilet facilities are
spotlessly maintained. Please see the advertisement
on page 10 for details of Club Members' benefits.
A 17-acre site with 200 touring pitches, 27
hardstandings.*
Pool table, table tennis & recreation hall
Leisure: ◕⁄Ⱥ **Facilities:** ↑⊙℥☆氐ぐ↑
Services: ♨🛢⌀⊞→∪△✦⊿🍴☺🚐⚏⚑🟦

HONEYBOURNE   Map 04 SP14

▶ ▶ ▶ ▶ 71% **Ranch Caravan Park**
(SP113444)
Station Rd WR11 7PR ☎ 01386 830744
▤ 01386 833503
e-mail: enquiries@ranch.co.uk
website: www.ranch.co.uk
*Dir: Through village x-rds towards Bidford, entrance
400mtrs on left*
★ ♛ £11-£16 ♛ £11-£16
Open Mar-Nov (rs Mar-May & Sep-Nov swimming
pool closed, shorter club hours) Booking advisable
school hols Last arrival 20.00hrs Last departure
noon
*An attractive and well-run park set amidst farmland
in the Vale of Evesham and landscaped with trees
and bushes. Tourers (but not tents) have their own
excellent facilities in two locations, and the use of
an outdoor heated swimming pool in peak season.
There is also a licensed club serving meals. Tents*
contd.

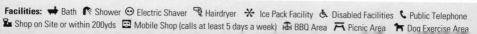

Facilities: ➡ Bath ↑ Shower ⊙ Electric Shaver ℥ Hairdryer ☆ Ice Pack Facility 氐 Disabled Facilities ぐ Public Telephone
氙 Shop on Site or within 200yds ⊞ Mobile Shop (calls at least 5 days a week) 冊 BBQ Area ☂ Picnic Area ↑ Dog Exercise Area

Established family-run park
Located in the vale of Evesham
Tourers welcome
Electric hook-ups available
multi-service hook-ups
Licensed club serving meals
Heated outdoor swimming pool
Shop
Laundry

HONEYBOURNE
EVESHAM
WORCS
WR11 7PR

AA

Tel: Evesham (01386) 830744

Ranch Caravan Park

not accepted. A 12-acre site with 120 touring pitches, 30 hardstandings and 180 statics.
Leisure: ↝ ⚓ ⚠ ☐ **Facilities:** ⋒ ⊙ ⊕ ✳ ⅀ 🐾 ☂
Services: 🖳 🖿 ♀ ⅋ ⊘ ⊞ ☰ ✕ ⚒ → ∪ ✦ **Notes:** No unaccompanied minors, no single sex groups, no tents 🖭 🖭 🖭 📶

MALVERN
Map 03 SO74

▶ ▶ ▶ **62% Riverside Caravan Park (SO833463)**
Little Clevelode WR13 6PE ☎ 01684 310475
🖹 01684 310475
Dir: From A449 signed onto B4424
★ 🚐 fr £7 🚐 fr £7 ▲ fr £7
Open Mar-Dec Booking advisable bank hols & end May-end Aug Last arrival 20.00hrs Last departure noon ⊘
An open grassy field with mostly level pitches, with fishing in the River Severn which runs past the
contd.

---

lower part of the park. Close to the Malvern Hills. A 25-acre site with 70 touring pitches and 130 statics. Fishing on river.
Leisure: ↝ ⚓ ⚠ ☐ **Facilities:** ⋒ ⊙ ✳ 🐾 ☂
Services: 🖳 🖿 ♀ ⅋ ⊘ ⊞ → ∪ ✦ ⊹ ✦ **Notes:** No bicycles & skateboards, dogs only allowed in statics

ROMSLEY
Map 07 SO98

▶ ▶ ▶ ▶ **67% Camping & Caravanning Club Site (SO955795)**
Clent Hills, Fieldhouse Ln B62 0NH ☎ 01562 710015
website: www.campingandcaravanningclub.co.uk
Dir: From M5 junct 3, take A456 then left on B4551 to Romsley, right past Sun Hotel, take 5th left & next left for site at Clent Hill
★ 🚐 £12.30-£15.50 🚐 £12.30-£15.50 ▲ £12.30-£15.50
Open Mar-Oct Booking advisable bank hols & peak periods Last arrival 21.00hrs Last departure noon
A very pretty, well tended park surrounded by wooded hills. The site offers excellent facilities, including new hard stands to provide flat pitches for motorhomes. Lovely views of the Clent Hills can be enjoyed from this park, and there are plenty of local scenic walks. Please see the advertisement on page 10 for details of Club Members' benefits. A 7.5-acre site with 115 touring pitches, 18 hardstandings.
Leisure: ⚠ **Facilities:** ⋒ ⊙ ⊕ ✳ ⅀ 🐾 ☂
Services: 🖳 🖿 ⅋ ⊘ ⊞ → ∪ ⊘ ✦ 🖭 🖭 🖭 🖭 📶

WOLVERLEY
Map 07 SO87

▶ ▶ ▶ **65% Camping & Caravanning Club Site (SO833792)**
Brown Westhead Park DY10 3PX ☎ 01562 850909
website: www.campingandcaravanningclub.co.uk
Dir: From Kidderminster A449 to Wolverhampton, turn left at lights onto B4189 signed Wolverley. Follow brown camping signs, turn right. Site on left
★ 🚐 £11.10-£15 🚐 £11.10-£15 ▲ £11.10-£15
Open Mar-Nov Booking advisable bank hols & Jul-Aug Last arrival 21.00hrs Last departure noon
A very pleasant grassy site on the edge of the village, with the canal lock and towpath close to the entrance, and a pub overlooking the water. The site has good access to and from nearby motorways. Please see advertisement on page 10 for details of Club Members' benefits. A 12-acre site with 120 touring pitches.
Table tennis & darts.
Leisure: ⚓ ⚠ ☐ **Facilities:** ⋒ ⊙ ⅀ ✳ ⅀ 🐾 ☂
Services: 🖳 🖿 ⊘ ⊞ → ∪ ⊘ ⊹ ✦ 🖭 🖭 🖭 🖭 📶

YORKSHIRE, EAST RIDING OF

BRANDESBURTON
Map 08 TA14

▶ ▶ ▶ **66% Dacre Lakeside Park (TA118468)**
YO25 8RT ☎ 01964 543704 & 542372
🖹 01964 543851
e-mail: dacresurf@aol.com
website: www.dacrepark.co.uk
Dir: Off A165 bypass, between Beverley and Hornsea
★ 🚐 £8-£8.50 🚐 £8-£8.50 ▲ £8-£8.50
contd.

England

Dacre Lakeside Park

Open Mar-Oct Booking advisable bank hols Last
arrival 21.00hrs Last departure noon
*A large lake popular with watersports enthusiasts is
the focal point of this level grassy site. The
clubhouse offers plenty of indoor amenities, while
the lake is used for windsurfing, sailing and
canoeing. An 8-acre site with 120 touring pitches.
Windsurfing, fishing, canoeing, tennis & bowling.*

Leisure: ⚊ ⚊ **Facilities:** ⚊⚊⚊⚊⚊⚊⚊⚊
Services: ⚊⚊⚊⚊⚊⚊⚊→⚊⚊⚊⚊⚊

BRIDLINGTON   Map 08 TA16
See also **Rudston**

► ► ► **72% Fir Tree Caravan Park (TA195702)**
Jewison Ln, Sewerby YO16 6YG ☎ 01262 676442
🖹 01262 676442
e-mail: info@flowerofmay.com
website: www.flowerofmay.com
*Dir: 1.5m from centre of Bridlington. Turn left off B1255
at Marton Corner & site is 600yds on left*
★ ⚊ £11-£15.50 ⚊ £11-£15.50
Open Apr-Oct (rs Etr & late season) Booking
advisable Jul-Aug & bank hols Last arrival 21.00hrs
*A well-equipped site in a pleasant rural setting, with
touring pitches kept separate from the very large
static area. A large swimming pool complex is a
popular recent addition, and there is a small shop
on site. A 22-acre site with 50 touring pitches and
400 statics.*

Leisure: ⚊ ⚊ ⚊ **Facilities:** ⚊⚊⚊⚊⚊⚊⚊⚊
Services: ⚊⚊⚊⚊⚊→⚊⚊⚊⚊⚊⚊⚊⚊

FANGFOSS   Map 08 SE75

► ► ► **62% Fangfoss Old Station Caravan Park
(SE747527)**
Old Station House YO41 5QB ☎ 01759 380491
e-mail: fangfoss@pi2000.co.uk
website: www.ukparks.com/fangfoss
*Dir: Turn off A1079 at Wilberfoss, follow sign in centre
of Wilberfoss, 1.5m towards Fangfoss*
★ ⚊ £7.50-£10.50 ⚊ £9-£10 ▲ £6-£12.50
Open Mar-Oct Booking advisable bank hols Last
arrival 19.30hrs Last departure noon
*A well-maintained site in a pleasant rural area.
The track and sidings of the old railway station are
grassed over and provide excellent hardstanding
with a level landscaped field adjacent. A 4.5-acre
site with 75 touring pitches.*

Leisure: ⚊ **Facilities:** ⚊⚊⚊⚊⚊⚊⚊⚊⚊⚊
Services: ⚊⚊⚊⚊⚊⚊→⚊⚊⚊⚊⚊

HULL   See **Sproatley**

RUDSTON   Map 08 TA06

► ► ► **68% Thorpe Hall Caravan
& Camping Site (TA108677)**
Thorpe Hall YO25 4JE
☎ 01262 420393 & 420574 🖹 01262 420588
e-mail: caravansite@thorpehall.co.uk
Dir: 5m from Bridlington on B1253
⚊ ⚊ ▲

Open Mar-Oct reception & shop limited opening
hours Booking advisable bank hols & peak periods
Last arrival 22.00hrs Last departure noon
*A very attractive and well-ordered site in the walled
garden of a large estate on the edge of the village.
A 4.5-acre site with 90 touring pitches.
Covered outside washing up sinks with hot water.*

Leisure: ⚊ ⚊ ⚊ **Facilities:** ⚊⚊⚊⚊⚊⚊⚊⚊⚊⚊
Services: ⚊⚊⚊⚊⚊⚊→⚊⚊

See advertisement on page 222

Leisure: ⚊ Indoor swimming pool   ⚊ Outdoor swimming pool   ⚊ Tennis court   ⚊ Games room   ⚊ Children's playground   ⚊ Stables
⚊ 9/18 hole golf course   ⚊ Boats for hire   ⚊ Cinema   ⚊ Fishing   ◎ Mini golf   ⚊ Watersports   ⚊ Separate TV room

EAST YORKSHIRE'S QUALITY SITE

Quiet, sheltered within kitchen garden walls. Centrally heated toilet block. Toilet and bathroom for disabled persons. Dogs welcome. Own Coarse Fishery.

Thorpe Hall Caravan and Camping Site, Rudston, Driffield, East Yorkshire YO25 4JE
Tel: 01262 420393 Fax: 01262 420588
Manager Mrs Jayne Chatterton
Residence: 01262 420574
E-mail: caravansite@thorpehall.co.uk

SKIPSEA   **Map 08 TA15**

75% **Low Skirlington Leisure Park (TA188528)**
YO25 8SY
☎ 01262 468213 & 468466 🖷 01262 468105
e-mail: info@skirlington.com
Dir: *From M62 towards Beverley then Hornsea. Follow tourist signs onto B1242 to Skirlington*

Open Mar-Oct Booking advisable Jul-Aug

A large seaside park on partly sloping grass with young trees and shrubs, set in meadowland close by the beach. The site has five toilet blocks, and a new supermarket and amusement arcade. The wide range of family amenities include an indoor heated swimming pool complex with sauna, jacuzzi and sunbeds. Outdoors there is a well-stocked fishing lake, pitch and putt, and a large new children's play area. A 24-acre site with 285 touring pitches and 450 statics.

Sauna, sunbed, jacuzzi.

Leisure: 🕏 ◣ 灬 ▭   **Facilities:** ➤ ↰⊙◥✳⟐ 🗏
🞓 ⛫   **Services:** 🖵🖳⛻❍⟐⊞✕🖙➙∪↑⊚⟐↵ ↲
💳 ⬛ ▤ ⓢ

For a relaxing break or a great day out on the beautiful East Yorkshire coast

Situated in over 70 acres of park land adjoining open countryside and the sea, we have a choice of 2 or 3 bedroom luxury holiday homes which are available to rent or buy, as well as a large number of pitches for touring caravans and tents.

Whether you're looking for a holiday break or just visting for the day you are welcome to enjoy our extensive facilities...

- BAR, RESTAURANT & REGULAR ENTERTAINMENT PROGRAMME
- SHOPPING CENTRE & AMUSEMENT ARCADE
- TAKE-AWAY FOOD OUTLET
- LEISURE CENTRE WITH INDOOR SWIMMING POOL, JACUZZI & SUNBED
- ALL-WEATHER PLAY AREA & MULTI-SPORT BALL COURT
- FRESHWATER FISHING LAKE
- ADJACENT GOLF COURSE & CROWN GREEN BOWLING
- DIRECT BEACH ACCESS
- VINTAGE MACHINERY MUSEUM
- SUNDAY MARKET

There's something for all the family... We hope to see you soon!

Some attractions are only available during the season. If in doubt, please enquire before visiting.

Skirlington Leisure Park Skipsea Driffield East Yorkshire YO25 8SY
Tel: 01262 468213 Fax: 01262 468105 E-mail: info@skirlington.com

www.skirlington.com

► 67% **NEW** **Mill Farm Country Park (TA168554)**
Mill Ln YO25 8SS ☎ 01262 468211
*Dir: A165 Hull/Bridlington. At Beeford take the B1249 to
Skipsea. At x-rds turn right then 1st left up Cross Street,
which leads on to Mill Lane. Booking office at Mill Farm
on right*
★ ⌺ £7.50-£9.50 ⌺ £7.50-£9.50 ▲ £7.50-£9.50
Open Mar-5 Oct Booking advisable all times
*A meadow site on an arable farm, well run by
competent, friendly owners. The toilet facilities are
maintained to a high standard, and there is a large
area for ball games, plus good walks around the
farm. A 3-acre site with 56 touring pitches, 7
hardstandings.*
Childrens playfield, Farm walk
Facilities: 🅡⊙💺🐕 Services: 🅚→🅟⌂🅙🖩🛒

SPROATLEY	Map 08 TA13

► ► ► 75% **Burton Constable Country Park**
(TA186357)
Old Lodges HU11 4LN ☎ 01964 562508 & 562316
🖨 01964 563420
e-mail: bchall@dircon.co.uk
website: www.bchall.dircon.co.uk
*Dir: Off A165 onto B1238 to Sproatley.
Follow signs to park*
★ ⌺ £8.50-£10 ⌺ ▲ £7.50-£12.50
Open Mar-Oct Booking advisable bank hols Last
arrival 23.00hrs Last departure 16.00hrs
*A beautiful site close to boating and fishing lakes in
the grounds of Burton Constable Hall, with a brand-
new toilet block and all-electric touring pitches.
A 30-acre site with 200 touring pitches, 6
hardstandings and 200 statics.*
Two 10 acre fishing lakes
Leisure: ⛰ Facilities: 🅡⊙💺❄💺🐕
Services: 🅚🖩🅨🅙🖨🖩🅣→∪🅟🅙
Notes: Dogs must be kept on leads

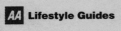

YORKSHIRE, NORTH

ACASTER MALBIS	Map 08 SE54

► ► ► 74% *Chestnut Farm Caravan Park
(SE589456)*
YO2 1UQ ☎ 01904 704676 🖨 01904 704676
*Dir: Leave A64 at Copmanthorpe, turning S signed
Acaster Malbis. Site on unclass road in 2m*
🅚⌺▲
Open Apr-Oct Booking advisable public hols &
Jul-Aug Last arrival 23.00hrs Last departure noon
*Plenty of trees and shrubs provide shelter and
privacy at this grass park sitting alongside a river.
The pleasant owners maintain a friendly
atmosphere. A 5-acre site with 25 touring pitches
and 56 statics.*
Facilities: ➡🅡⊙💺❄💺🐕🛒
Services: 🅚🖩🅨🖨🅣→∪🅟🅙🖩🅙

► ► 64% **Moor End Farm (SE589457)**
YO23 2UQ ☎ 01904 706727 & 0860 405872
🖨 01904 706727
e-mail: moorendfarm@acaster99.fsnet.co.uk
website: www.ukparks.co.uk/moorend
*Dir: Follow signs to Acaster Malbis from A64/A1237
junct at Copmanthorpe*
★ ⌺ £10-£12 ⌺ £10-£12 ▲ £9-£12
Open Etr or Apr-Oct Booking advisable bank hols &
end Jul-Aug Last arrival 22.00hrs Last departure
14.00hrs
*A very pleasant, quiet farm site with clean,
modernised toilet facilities. The friendly owners
keep the grass well trimmed, and all pitches have
electric hook-ups. A 1-acre site with 10 touring
pitches and 6 statics.*
Use of fridge/freezer & microwave, washing up sink
Leisure: ⛰ Facilities: 🅡⊙💺❄🛒
Services: 🅚🖩→🅟🅙🖩🅙

ALLERSTON	Map 08 SE88

► ► ► ► 73% **Vale of Pickering
Caravan Park (SE879808)**
Carr House Farm YO18 7PQ
☎ 01723 859280 🖨 01723 850060
e-mail: tony@valeofpickering.co.uk
website: www.valeofpickering.co.uk
*Dir: On B1415, 1.75m off A170, Pickering-Scarborough
road*
★ ⌺ £6.75-£11.25 ⌺ £6.75-£11.25 ▲ £6.75-£11.25
Open Mar-10 Jan (rs Mar) Booking advisable all
BH's Last arrival 21.00hrs Last departure noon
*An attractively maintained park with high quality
facilities, and surrounded by mature hedges with
lots of colourful landscaping. Set in open
countryside within the North Yorkshire Moors
National Park. An 8-acre site with 120 touring
pitches, 80 hardstandings.*
Leisure: ⛰ Facilities: ➡🅡⊙💺❄💺🐕
Services: 🅚🖩🅨🖨🅣➡→∪🅟🅙🖩

Facilities: ➡ Bath 🅡 Shower ⊙ Electric Shaver 💺 Hairdryer ❄ Ice Pack Facility 💺 Disabled Facilities 🅙 Public Telephone
🛒 Shop on Site or within 200yds 🖩 Mobile Shop (calls at least 5 days a week) 🖩 BBQ Area 🅣 Picnic Area 🐕 Dog Exercise Area

ALLERTON PARK Map 08 SE45

► ► ► 59% **Allerton Park Caravan Site (SE417576)**
Allerton Mauleverer HG5 0SE
☎ 01423 330569 & 01759 371377
01759 371377
website: www.yorkshireholidayparks.co.uk
Dir: *Off A59, 400yds E of junct with A1(M)*
★ £9-£11 £9-£11 ▲ £9-£11
Open Feb-3 Jan Booking advisable bank hols Last arrival 21.00hrs Last departure 17.00hrs
A well placed stopover site for those travelling to and from Scotland and the North, or well-positioned for touring the Dales, and York. Several modern cubicle suites in the sanitary block contain various combinations of toilet/washbasins/showers or baths. A 12-acre site with 30 touring pitches and 90 statics.
Leisure: **Facilities:**
Services:

ALNE Map 08 SE46

► ► ► ► 70% **Alders Caravan Park (SE497654)**
Home Farm YO61 1RY ☎ 01347 838722
Dir: *From A19 turn off at signs to Alne, in 1.5m turn left at T-junct, 0.5m Alders on left in village centre in Monk Green left off Main St.*
★ £7-£10 £7-£10 ▲ fr £6.50

Open Mar-Oct Booking advisable Bank holidays Last arrival 21.00hrs Last departure 14.00hrs
A tastefully developed park on a working farm with pitches laid out in horseshoe-shaped areas, and individually screened by trees and shrubs. This well designed park offers excellent toilet facilities including bathroom and fully-serviced washing and toilet cubicles which offer total privacy. A newly planted woodland and a water meadow are pleasant places to walk and enjoy the local fauna and flora. This park has no laundry. A 6-acre site with 40 touring pitches.
Summer house, herb garden
Facilities:
Services:

ARNCLIFFE Map 07 SD97

► ► ► ► 69% **Hawkswick Cote Caravan Park (SD947703)**
BD23 5PX ☎ 01756 770226 01756 770327
Dir: *From B6160 1m N of Kilnsey, take unclass road signed Arncliffe. Site 1.5m on left*
★ £10-£14 £10-£14 ▲ £10-£12
Open Mar-14 Nov Booking advisable bank hols & Jul-Aug Last arrival 22.00hrs Last departure noon
A spacious site in the Dales, with mature landscaping and views of the surrounding fells. Various camping areas are divided by traditional dry stone walling, which complement the stone park buildings, some of which have been converted from farm buildings. The park blends in with the towering fells on both sides of Littondale, and there are pleasant views in all directions. Also convenient for Skipton and surrounding area. A 3-acre site with 50 touring pitches, 19 hardstandings and 90 statics.
Leisure: **Facilities:**
Services:

AYSGARTH Map 07 SE08

► ► ► ► 72% **Westholme Caravan & Camping Park (SE016882)**
DL8 3SP ☎ 01969 663268
Dir: *1m E of Aysgarth off A684*
★ £7.50-£10 £7.50-£10 ▲ £7.50-£10

Open Mar-Oct Booking advisable Bank hols & Jul-Aug Last arrival 22.00hrs Last departure noon
A beckside site with level grassy pitches in various paddocks set into the hillside. The modern sanitary facilities and other amenities are maintained to a consistently high standard. There is a well-equipped children's playground, a well-stocked shop, and a licensed bar and club room where meals are served every weekend throughout the season, and daily during the peak months. The famous Aysgarth Falls are nearby. A 22-acre site with 70 touring pitches and 44 statics.
Fishing free on site.
Leisure: **Facilities:**
Services:

BISHOP MONKTON   Map 08 SE36

► ► **68% Church Farm Caravan Park (SE328660)**
Knaresborough Rd HG3 3QQ ☎ 01765 677668
Dir: From A61, 3m S of Ripon, take unclass rd to Bishop Monkton. In 1m at x-rds turn right towards Knaresborough, site 500mtrs on right

Open Apr-Oct Booking advisable peak periods
A meadowland park set in a delightfully secluded rural environment, with good sanitary facilities. A 5-acre site with 30 touring pitches and 3 statics.

Facilities: ⬚⊙✳⬚⬚⬚⬚
Services: ⬚⬚⬚⬚→∪▶⬚⬚

BOROUGHBRIDGE   Map 08 SE36

► ► ► ► **72% Camping & Caravanning Club Site (SE384662)**
Bar Ln, Roecliffe YO51 9LS ☎ 01423 322683
website: www.campingandcaravanningclub.co.uk
Dir: From A1(M) junct 48 follow signs for Bar Lane Ind Est & Roecliffe. Site 0.25m from rdbt
★ ⬚£14.50-£15.50 ⬚ £14.50-£15.50 ⋀ £14.50-£15.50
Open all year Booking advisable bank hols & Jul & Aug Last arrival 21.00hrs Last departure noon
A quiet, riverside site completely upgraded recently and offering very upmarket facilities. There is direct access onto the River Ure, with fishing and boating available. The natural features of the park are complemented by landscaping and planting to provide a pleasant, relaxing rural environment. Close to the dales and the market town of Boroughbridge. Please see the advertisement on page 10 for details of Club Members' benefits. A 5-acre site with 90 touring pitches, 17 hardstandings. Fishing.

Leisure: ⬚ ⬚ **Facilities:** ⬚⊙⬚✳⬚⬚⬚⬚
Services: ⬚⬚⬚⬚→⬚⬚⬚⬚⬚⬚⬚⬚⬚

CAWOOD   Map 08 SE53

► ► ► ► **66% Cawood Holiday Park (SE563385)**
Ryther Rd YO8 3TT ☎ 01757 268450
⬚ 01757 268537
e-mail: william.archer13@btopenworld.com
website: www.ukparks.co.uk/cawood
Dir: A1 take B1222, turn at Cawood lights signed Tadcaster onto B1223 for 1m, park is on left
★ ⬚£12-£16 ⬚£12-£16 ⋀ £12-£16

Open all year Booking advisable bank hols & Jul-Aug Last arrival 21.00hrs Last departure 11.00hrs
contd.

CAWOOD HOLIDAY PARK

Caravan and Camping Centre, Ryther Road, Cawood, Selby, North Yorkshire, YO8 3TT.
Tel: 01757 268450 Fax: 01757 268537
Web: http:www.ukparks.co.uk/cawood
E-mail: william.archer13@btopenworld.com

Twixt York and Selby, an idyllic Country Park for the discerning, in a quiet rural setting in an environment which keeps it's natural simplicity to provide a trouble free holiday. Bungalows with views over our Fishing Lake, Caravans, Touring/Tent Pitches, Bar/Bar meals-Indoor Swimming Pool. Adults only, no under 18's.
A1 9 miles, York 10 miles, Selby 5 miles. From A1 or York take B1222, turn at Cawood lights on B1223 signed Tadcaster for 1 mile.

A peaceful park in a rural area with its own fishing lake, which the camping area overlooks. The 10-acre site is bordered by hedges and mature trees, and is well away from the road. Amenities are modern and consistently maintained to a high standard. The club house with a comfortable bar is sited on one side of the lake, and there is occasional entertainment here. Coarse fishing is available. An 8-acre site with 60 touring pitches, 3 hardstandings and 10 statics.
Coarse fishing.

Leisure: ⬚ ⬚⬚ **Facilities:** ⬚⊙⬚✳⬚⬚⬚
⬚⬚⬚ **Services:** ⬚⬚⬚⬚⬚⬚⬚⬚✗⬚→∪▶⬚⬚
Notes: Adults only ⬚⬚⬚⬚⬚⬚⬚

CONEYSTHORPE (NEAR MALTON) Map 08 SE77

► ► ► **70% Castle Howard Caravan & Camping Site (SE705710)**
YO60 7DD ☎ 01653 648316 ⬚ 01653 648529
e-mail: caravan@castlehoward.co.uk
Dir: Well signposted from A64 & B1257. Caravans prohibited on A170 at Sutton Bank between Thirsk and Helmsley.

Open Mar-Oct Booking advisable public hols Last arrival 21.00hrs Last departure 14.00hrs
A sheltered, peaceful park adjacent to the great lake of Castle Howard, which is well stocked with record catches. A total redevelopment of the site during 2002 has created quality toilet and other facilities,
contd.

and the magnificent castle offers much to see and do. A 13-acre site with 70 touring pitches and 120 statics.

Facilities: ⬤⊙◵♒⚬❤️💆🛁🏤🏕️

Services: 🅿️🔲🛢️💧⬛→Ü🔧

CONSTABLE BURTON — Map 07 SE19

▶ ▶ ▶ **70% Constable Burton Hall Caravan Park (SE158907)**
DL8 5LJ ☎ 01677 450428
Dir: Off A684, but screened behind old deer park wall
★ 🚐 £7.50-£10 🚙 £7.50-£10 ▲ £7.50-£10
Open Apr-Oct Booking advisable public hols Last arrival 22.00hrs Last departure noon
A pretty site in the former deer park of the adjoining Constable Burton Hall, screened from the road by the deer park walls and surrounded by mature trees in a quiet rural location. The large campable area is spacious and comfortable, and most park buildings are made from natural stone in the local style. The laundry, however, is housed in a converted 18th-century deer barn. A 10-acre site with 120 touring pitches and 80 statics.

Facilities: ⬤⊙◵♒⚬❤️🏕️ **Services:** 🅿️🛢️💧⬛🔲❌→Ü
▶💆🔧💆 **Notes:** No ball games, dogs on leads, no commercial vehicles

EASINGWOLD — Map 08 SE56

▶ ▶ ▶ **69% Hollybrook Caravan Park (SE533686)**
Pennycarr Ln, Off Stillington Rd YO61 3EU
☎ 01347 821906
e-mail: enquiries@hollybrookpark.co.uk
Dir: From rdbt on A19 S of Easingwold take unclass road signed Easingwold. In 1m turn right signed Stillington, then right in 0.25m into signed lane
★ 🚐 £8 🚙 £8 ▲ £8
Open Mar-Dec Booking advisable Jun-Sep Last arrival 22.00hrs Last departure 13.00hrs
A level grass site with spacious numbered pitches, in a quiet rural location 0.5m from the village. This site is for adults only. A 2-acre site with 30 touring pitches, 7 hardstandings.
Fridge, freezer, microwave, library

Facilities: ⬤⊙◵♒⚬❤️ **Services:** 🅿️🛢️💧⬛→▶🔧💆

Notes: Adults only

FILEY — Map 08 TA18

67% NEW Blue Dolphin Holiday Park (TA095829)
Gristhorpe Bay YO14 9PU
☎ 01723 515155
website: www.havenholidays.co.uk
Dir: Gristhorpe Bay 2m NW off A165
★ 🚐 £9-£30
Open all year Booking advisable at all times Last arrival 22.00hrs Last departure 12.00hrs
There are great clifftop views to be enjoyed from this fun-filled holiday centre with an extensive and separate touring area. The emphasis is on non-stop entertainment, with organised sports and clubs, all-weather leisure facilities, heated swimming pools and plenty of well-planned amusements. Pitches are mainly on level or gently-sloping grass plus some fully-serviced hardstandings, and the beach is just 2 miles away. There is also an interesting nature trail. An 80-acre site with 352 touring pitches.

Leisure: 🏊♨️⛵🎢🏓 **Facilities:** 💆
Services: 🔲🍴🛢️❌🚿

74% Flower of May Holiday Park (TA085835)
Lebberston Cliff YO11 3NU
☎ 01723 584311 📠 01723 581361
e-mail: info@flowerofmay.com
website: www.flowerofmay.com
Dir: Signed off A165 on Scarborough side of Filey
★ 🚐 £11-£15.50 🚙 £11-£15.50 ▲ £8.50-£13

Open Etr-Oct (rs early & late season) Booking advisable Spring BH wk, Jul-Aug & BH's Last arrival 21.00hrs Last departure noon
A delightful family site with level grassy pitches and excellent facilities. This large landscaped park offers a full range of recreational activities, with plenty to occupy everyone. Grass or hard pitches are available, all on level ground. A 13-acre site with 270 touring pitches, 100 hardstandings and 193 statics.
Squash, bowling, 9-hole golf & basketball court

Leisure: 🏊⛵🎢🏓 **Facilities:** ⬤⊙◵♒⚬❤️💆🛁🏤
🏕️ **Services:** 🅿️🔲🍴🛢️💧⬛🔲❌🚿→Ü▶🔷💆💦🔧💆
🍬🎫🔲🔳🔲

See advertisement on page 235

England

64% NEW Reighton Sands Holiday Park (TA142769)
Reighton Gap YO14 9SJ
☎ 01723 890476
website: www.havenholidays.com
★ 🏕 £8-£30
Open Mar-Oct Booking advisable Last arrival 22.00hrs Last departure 12.00hrs
A large, lively holiday centre with a wide range of entertainment and all-weather leisure facilities, located just 10 minutes walk from a long sandy beach. Each of the three touring areas has its own facilities block, and the site is particularly geared towards families with young children. An 84-acre site with 303 touring pitches.

Leisure: 🏊 ♦ ◬ ▢ Facilities: 🛒
Services: 🔌♀✕💧🍺🎫⊙🏧💷🖥️🌱

► ► ► ► 76% Lebberston Touring Caravan Park (TA077824)
Filey Rd YO11 3PE ☎ 01723 585723
e-mail: lebberstontouring@hotmail.com
Dir: Off A165 Filey to Scarborough road. Site signed from road
★ 🏕 £8-£12.50 🏕 £8-£12.50

Open Mar-Oct Booking advisable bank hols & school holidays Last arrival 21.00hrs Last departure 12.00hrs
A peaceful family park in a gently-sloping rural area. The quality facilities are maintained to a high standard of cleanliness. The keen owners are friendly and helpful, and create a relaxing atmosphere. A 7.5-acre site with 125 touring pitches, 25 hardstandings.
Washing up sinks.
Facilities: ➡️🛁📻⊙♀✕❄️🚿⚗️🪑🛒🐾 Services: 🔌🍺🛒🚽
→⊙🍴⊙🔥🌱🧺🚮🚿 🌱 Notes: No tents 💳🎫🖥️🌱

> Remember that prices and opening times are liable to change within the currency of this guide. It is always best to telephone in advance

► ► ► 58% Centenary Way Camping & Caravan Park (TA115798)
Muston Grange YO14 0HU ☎ 01723 516415 & 512313
Dir: Just off A1039 near junct with A165 on Bridlington side of Filey
★ 🏕 £5.50-£8.50 🏕 £5.50-£8.50 ▲ £3.50-£8.50
Open Mar-Oct Booking advisable bank hols & Jul-Aug Last arrival 21.00hrs Last departure noon
A family-owned park, mainly for tents, with footpath access to nearby beach. Close to the seaside resort of Filey. A 3-acre site with 100 touring pitches.

Leisure: ◬ Facilities: 📻⊙❄️🛒🐾
Services: 🔌🛒🍴→⊙🍴⊙🔥🌱🚽

► ► ► 65% *Crows Nest Caravan Park (TA094826)*
Gristhorpe YO14 9PS ☎ 01723 582206
🖨 01723 582206
Dir: On seaward side of A165, signed off rdbt
🏕🏕▲
Open Mar-Oct Booking advisable Last departure noon
A beautifully-situated park on the coast between Scarborough and Filey, with excellent panoramic views. This large and mainly static park offers lively entertainment, and two bars. The family owners continually improve the facilities. A 2-acre site with 49 touring pitches and 217 statics.
Leisure: 🏊 ♦ ◬ Facilities: 📻⊙❄️🛒🐾
Services: 🔌🗑️♀🍴⚗️🎫🛒→⊙🍴⊙🔥🚽

► ► ► 63% Filey Brigg Touring Caravan & Country Park (TA115812)
North Cliff YO14 9ET ☎ 01723 513852
Dir: 0.5m from Filey town centre on coast road from Scarborough, A165
★ 🏕 £6-£11 🏕 £6-£11 ▲ £3.50-£11
Open Etr/Apr-Oct Booking advisable bank hols & Jul-Aug Last arrival 18.00hrs Last departure noon
A municipal park overlooking Filey Brigg with splendid views along the coast, and set in a country park. The beach is just a short walk away, as is the resort of Filey. A 9-acre site with 158 touring pitches.
Leisure: ◬ Facilities: 📻⊙❄️⚗️🪑🛒🎍🐾
Services: 🔌🗑️🎫✕💧→⊙🍴⊙🔥🌱🚮 🌱💳🎫🖥️🌱

Facilities: ➡️ Bath 📻 Shower ⊙ Electric Shaver 📻 Hairdryer ❄️ Ice Pack Facility ⚗️ Disabled Facilities 🪑 Public Telephone
🛒 Shop on Site or within 200yds 💳 Mobile Shop (calls at least 5 days a week) 🎍 BBQ Area 🌲 Picnic Area 🐾 Dog Exercise Area

Ripley Caravan Park

where the country and enjoyment comes naturally ...

This luxury touring caravan park in the beautiful North Yorkshire countryside, is within easy reach of Ripley Castle and village, and only ten minutes north of Harrogate. First class facilities include indoor heated swimming pool, sauna, games room, nursery playroom, childrens playground and play area. There is a shop, laundry, telephone, electric hook-up points and amenities for the disabled.

For further information:
Peter & Valerie House, Ripley Caravan Park,
Ripley, Harrogate, HG3 3AU.
Tel: (01423) 770050

David Bellamy Silver Award   AA

GRASSINGTON   See **Threshfield**

GUISBOROUGH   Map 08 NZ61

▶ ▶ ▶ 63% *Tockett's Mill Caravan Park (NZ626182)*
Skelton Rd TS14 6QA ☎ 01287 610182
🖥 01287 610182
Dir: 1.5m NE of Guisborough on A173
🚐 🚐
Open Mar-Oct Booking advisable bank hols & high season Last arrival 21.00hrs Last departure noon
Situated in a private wooded valley alongside a stream, the site is centred around a preserved watermill. A 7-acre site with 30 touring pitches and 75 statics.
Leisure: ⚞ **Facilities:** 🛉⊙🔲👌🐾
Services: 🚱🗑️♈🛎️→🔌🔋

HARROGATE   Map 08 SE35

▶ ▶ ▶ ▶ ▶ 70% **Ripley Caravan Park**
(SE289610)
Knaresborough Rd, Ripley HG3 3AU
☎ 01423 770050 🖥 01423 770050
Dir: 3m N of Harrogate on A61. Turn right at rdbt onto B6165 signposted Knaresborough. Park 300yds left
★ 🚐 £6.95-£8.50 🚐 £6.95-£8.50 ▲ £5-£8.50
Open Etr-Oct Booking advisable bank hols Last arrival 21.00hrs Last departure noon

contd.

Ripley Caravan Park

A superb, well-run rural site in attractive meadowland which has been landscaped with mature tree plantings. The resident owners lovingly maintain their high-quality facilities, and there is a heated swimming pool and sauna, a games room, and a covered play room for small children. An 18-acre site with 100 touring pitches and 30 statics.
Nursery playroom, sauna, football.

Leisure: ⚞ ⚑ ⚙ **Facilities:** 🛉⊙🔲☀👌🐾
Services: 🚱🗑️♈🔲🔲→🔌🛎️♨🛒
Notes: Family camping only, dogs on leads, BBQs must be off the ground

---

▶ ▶ ▶ ▶ ▶ 74% **Rudding Holiday Park (SE333531)**
Follifoot HG3 1JH ☎ 01423 870439
🖥 01423 870859
e-mail: holiday-park@ruddingpark.com
website: www.ruddingpark.com
Dir: From A1 take A59 to A658, turn S signed Bradford. Continue for 4.5m then right and follow signs
🚐 £10.50-£23 🚐 £10.50-£23 ▲ £7.50-£10.50

GOLD

Open Apr-Oct (rs 1-21 Mar no hot water no shop) Booking advisable bank hols Last arrival 22.30hrs Last departure 14.00hrs
A spacious park set in the stunning 200-acres of mature parkland and walled gardens of Rudding Park. The setting has been tastefully enhanced with terraced pitches and dry-stone walls. A separate area houses super pitches where all services are supplied including a picnic table and TV connection. The toilet blocks are first class. There is an 18-hole golf course, and a

contd.

---

heated outdoor swimming pool, plus the Deer
House bar and restaurant, and a children's play
area. Winner of the Best Campsite of the Year
2001, and best Campsite for England. A 55-acre
site with 141 touring pitches and 95 statics.
Golf course (18 hole), driving range

Leisure: ₹ ♠ ⚠ **Facilities:** ➡ ♠ ⊙ ⚛ ※ ⚿ ⚹ ⚑ ⚲ ♜
Services: ⚙ ⚎ ⚑ ⚿ ⊘ ⚏ ⚒ ✕ ⚐ → ∪ ▶ ⚒ ⚇ ✈
Notes: No single sex groups, min age
unaccompanied - 18yrs ⚇ ⚏ ⚉ ⚐ ⚐ ⚐

▶ ▶ ▶ ▶ 65% **High Moor Farm Park** (SE242560)
kipton Rd HG3 2LT ☎ 01423 563637 & 564955
01423 529449
ir: On A59 Harrogate-Skipton road
⚑ £12.50-£17 ⚑ £12.50-£17 ▲ £12.50-£17
pen Apr-Oct Booking advisable public hols Last
rrival 23.30hrs Last departure 15.00hrs
n excellent site with first class facilities, set beside
small wood and surrounded by thorn hedges. The
umerous touring pitches are located in
eadowland fields, each area with its own toilet
lock. A large heated indoor swimming pool and a
ames room are very popular, and there is a large
shing lake, a golf course, and a full-sized crown
owling green. A 15-acre site with 320 touring
itches, 51 hardstandings and 159 statics.
ourse fishing, 9 hole golf course, bowling green

eisure: ₹ ♠ ⚠ **Facilities:** ➡ ♠ ⊙ ⚛ ※ ⚿ ⚹ ⚐ ♜
ervices: ⚙ ⚎ ⚑ ⚿ ⊘ ⚏ ⚒ ✕ ⚐ → ∪ ▶ ⚒ ✈
lotes: no single sex groups ⚇ ⚏ ⚉ ⚐ ⚐

▶ ▶ 57% **Shaws Trailer Park** (SE325557)
naresborough Rd HG2 7NE ☎ 01423 884432
01423 883622
ebsite: www.shawstrailerpark.co.uk
*ir: On A59 1m from town centre. 0.5m SW of Starbeck
ailway crossing, by Johnsons Dry Cleaners*
⚑ fr £10 ⚑ fr £10 ▲ fr £8.50
pen all year Booking advisable public hols Last
rrival 21.00hrs Last departure noon
very long-established site with mature trees
round the grassy pitches. Facilities are well worn
ut clean. An 11-acre site with 60 touring pitches
nd 146 statics.

acilities: ➡ ♠ ⊙ ⚐ **Services:** ⚙ ⚎ ⚑ → ∪ ▶ ⚒ ✈

HAWES   **Map 07 SD88**

▶ 64% **Bainbridge Ings Caravan &
amping Site** (SD879895)
L8 3NU ☎ 01969 667354
-mail: janet@bainbridge-ings.co.uk
ebsite: www.bainbridge-ings.co.uk
*ir: Approaching Hawes from Bainbridge on A684, turn
ft at signpost marked Gayle, 300yds on left*
⚑ £8.50 ⚑ £8 ▲ £8
pen Apr-Oct Booking advisable school hols Last
rrival 22.00hrs Last departure 12.00hrs
quiet, well-organised site in open countryside
lose to Hawes in the heart of Upper Wensleydale.
itches are sited around the perimeter of several
elds, each bounded by traditional stone walls.

contd.

RUDDING
HOLIDAY PARK

Relax at Britain's
AA Campsite of
the Year - 2001

• Deer House family pub
• Children's adventure playground • Pets welcome
• Heated outdoor swimming pool and paddling pool
• 18 hole pay & play golf course plus floodlit driving range
• Games room • Launderette • Free showers
• Park lighting • Shop

FOLLIFOOT, HARROGATE, NORTH YORKSHIRE HG3 1JH
TEL: 01423 870439 • FAX: 01423 870859
email - holiday-park@ruddingpark.com

A 5-acre site with 70 touring pitches,
4 hardstandings and 15 statics.
Facilities: ♠ ⊙ ⚐ ※ **Services:** ⚙ ⚎ ⚑ ⊘ ⚏ → ✈ ⚑

HELMSLEY   **Map 08 SE68**

▶ ▶ ▶ ▶ 74% **Golden Square Touring
Caravan Park** (SE604797)
Oswaldkirk YO62 5YQ ☎ 01439 788269
⚏ 01439 788236
e-mail: barbara@goldensquarecaravanpark.com
website: www.goldensquarecaravanpark.com
*Dir: 1m from Ampleporth towards Helmsley on caravan
route*
★ ⚑ £7-£11.50 ⚑ £7-£11.50 ▲ £7-£11.50

Open Mar-Oct Booking advisable bank hols
Last arrival 21.00hrs Last departure noon
An all-round excellent site with manicured grounds
and first class toilets. This friendly park is set in a
quiet rural situation with lovely views over the

contd.

FOXHOLME ▶▶▶
CARAVAN PARK

Campsite of the Year North Region Winner 1986
60 Touring Vans, Motor Caravans & Tents

English
Tourist Council
✓✓✓✓✓

Ryedale, North Yorkshire, (4 miles from Helmsley and the North York
Moors National Park). A quiet site suitable for exploring North
Yorkshire.
60 pitches set in individual clearings in the woodland. Luxury toilet
blocks, AA graded Excellent for environment, wc's, hot water,
showers, wash basins in cubicles and shaver points.
Reception, late arrival park, shop and mains hook-up points.
Some pitches for tents.
Caravan Club approved. Camping Club listed.
For brochure, please send stamp to:

FOXHOLME CARAVAN PARK
(AA), Harome, Helmsley, York YO62 5JG
Tel. (01439) 771241 Fax: (01439) 771744

*N Yorks Moors. The park is terraced on three levels
surrounded by trees, and caters particularly for
families. Country walks and mountain bike trails
start here, and the market town of Helmsley is just
2.5 miles away. Caravans are banned from the
A170 at Sutton Bank between Thirsk and Helmsley.
A 12-acre site with 129 touring pitches.*
Microwave oven.

Leisure: ♦ /Ⅲ **Facilities:** ⊶ 🅙 ⊙ ⌇ ※ ⅙ 🛇 🐾 🛱 ⭢
Services: ⊞ 🗑 🔑 ⌀ 🎬 🎞 ⊶ ⭢ ∪ ▶ ⊚ ⊿

▶ ▶ ▶ **68% Foxholme Caravan Park (SE658828)**
Harome YO62 5JG ☎ 01439 770416 & 771241
▤ 01439 771744
Dir: Follow A170 from Helmsley towards Scarborough,
turn right signed Harome, turn left at church, through
village & follow caravan signs
🚐 £12.50 🚘 £12.50 Å £12.50
Open Etr-Oct Booking advisable bank & school hols
Last arrival 23.00hrs Last departure noon

contd.

---

*A quiet park set in secluded wooded countryside,
with pitches in individual clearings divided by
mature trees. The facilities are well maintained, and
the site is ideal as a touring base or a place to relax.
Caravans are prohibited on the A170 at Sutton Bank
between Thirsk and Helmsley. A 6-acre site with 60
touring pitches.*
Facilities: 🅙 ⊙ ⌇ ※ ⅙ 🛇 🐾 🐾 **Services:** ⊞ 🗑 🔑 ⌀ 🎞 🎞
⭢ ∪ ▶ ⊿

▶ ▶ ▶ **57% Wrens of Ryedale Touring Park
(SE656840)**
Gale Ln, Nawton YO62 7SD ☎ 01439 771260
▤ 01439 771260
e-mail: dave@wrensofryedale.fsnet.co.uk
website: www.wrensofryedale.fsnet.co.uk
Dir: On A170 3m E of Helmsley, turn right in villages of
Nawton/Beadlam into Gale Lane. Park 400mtrs on right
★ 🚐 £6.25-£7.75 🚘 £6.25-£7.75 Å £6.25-£7.75
Open Apr-16 Oct Booking advisable bank & school
hols Last arrival 22.00hrs Last departure noon
*A small family-owned park divided into three areas
by mature trees and shrubs. The sheltered grass
pitches are ideal for those seeking a quiet and
relaxing holiday. Caravans are prohibited on the
A170 at Sutton Bank between Thirsk and Helmsley.
A 2.5-acre site with 45 touring pitches.*
Bike hire.
Leisure: /Ⅲ **Facilities:** 🅙 ⊙ ⌇ ※ ⅙ 🛇 🐾 🛁
Services: ⊞ 🗑 🔑 ⌀ 🎞 🎞 ⭢ ∪ ▶ ⊿

HIGH BENTHAM   Map 07 SD66

▶ ▶ ▶ **62% Riverside Caravan Park (SD665688)**
LA2 7HS ☎ 01524 261272 & 262163 ▤ 01524 262163
e-mail: info@riversidecaravanpark.co.uk
website: www.riversidecaravanpark.co.uk
Dir: Off B6480, signed from town centre
★ 🚐 fr £8.50 🚘 fr £8.50 Å fr £7
Open Mar-Oct Booking advisable bank hols Last
arrival 20.00hrs Last departure 13.00hrs
*This site is set on the banks of the River Wenning,
in delightful countryside and screened by trees. A
12-acre site with 30 touring pitches and 170 statics.*
Free fishing.
Leisure: ♦ /Ⅲ **Facilities:** 🅙 ⊙ ⌇ ※ ⅙ 🛇 🐾 🛱 🐾
Services: ⊞ 🗑 🔑 ⌀ 🎞 🎞 ⭢ ▶ ⊿

HUNMANBY   Map 08 TA07

▶ ▶ ▶ **67% Orchard Farm Holiday Village
(TA105779)**
Stonegate YO14 0PU ☎ 01723 891582
▤ 01723 891582
Dir: Signed from A1039
★ 🚐 £9-£12 🚘 £9-£12 Å £9-£12
Open all year (rs Nov-Mar not all facilities) Booking
advisable bank hols & peak season Last arrival
23.00hrs Last departure 11.00hrs
*A level grassy site with pitches ranged around a
large coarse fishing lake, and with its own small
gauge miniature railway. This all-round high quality
park is run by keen and friendly owners, and offers
a wide range of amenities including an indoor
heated swimming pool and two licensed bars.*

contd.

England

Orchard Farm Holiday Village

A 14-acre site with 91 touring pitches, 34 hardstandings and 46 statics.
Veg prep area, boating lake, fishing.

Leisure: ⚑ ◕ ⩗ ▢   Facilities: ⋔⊙ℚ✳️⚏🐾 🏋️ 📆🏛📠

⋔ Services: 🔌🎛♨️⛽🗑🖲⛺💧→∪ 🍴◉⚠️⤳ ♬

KNARESBOROUGH   Map 08 SE35

▶ ▶ ▶ 62% **Kingfisher Caravan Park** (SE343603)

Low Moor Ln, Farnham HG5 9DQ ☎ 01423 869411
🖥 01423 869411

Dir: *From Knaresborough take A6055. After 1m turn left towards Farnham & left again in village signed Scotton. Site 1m on left*

★ 🚐 £7-£8.50 🚐 £7-£8.50 ▲ £7-£8.50

Open mid Mar/Etr-Oct Booking advisable bank hols & 15 Jul-1 Sep Last arrival 23.00hrs Last departure 16.00hrs

A large grassy site with open spaces set in a wooded area in rural countryside. There is plenty to see and do locally and Harrogate, Fountains Abbey and York are within easy reach. A 4-acre site with 35 touring pitches and 30 statics.

Leisure: ⩗   Facilities: ⋔⊙ℚ✳️⚏🐾🏛📠⋔

Services: 🔌🎛♨️🗑🖲→∪⚠️⤳♬

MARKINGTON   Map 08 SE26

▶ ▶ ▶ 63% **Yorkshire Hussar Inn Caravan Park** (SE288650)

High St HG3 3NR ☎ 01765 677327
e-mail: yorkshirehussar@yahoo.
website: http://yorkshirehussar.topcities.com

Dir: *Between Harrogate & Ripon (A61) turn W at Wormald Green, 1m into Markington*

★ 🚐 £10-£12 🚐 £9-£12 ▲ £6-£12

Open Apr-Oct Booking advisable Bank holidays Last arrival 22.00hrs Last departure Noon

A terraced site behind the village inn with well-kept grass and nicely refurbished toilet blocks. This pleasant site offers spacious pitches with some hardstandings and electricity. A 5-acre site with 20 touring pitches, 2 hardstandings and 73 statics. Pub

Leisure: ⩗   Facilities: ⋔⊙ℚ✳️🏋️   Services: 🔌🎛♨️⛽
🗑→∪ **Notes:** Dogs must be kept on leads

MASHAM   Map 08 SE28

▶ ▶ 63% **NEW** **Black Swan Holiday Park** (SE192808)

Fearby HG4 4NF ☎ 01765 689477
e-mail: blackswanholidaypark@fsmail.net

Dir: *Turn left off A6108 0.25m NW of Masham onto Fearby Road, site 2m on left at rear Black Swan Hotel*

🚐 £9 🚐 £9 ▲ £9

Open Mar-Oct

A sloping site at the rear of the Black Swan Inn, with central toilet facilities, and good open views over a wooded hillside. A 4-acre site with 47 touring pitches and 3 statics.

Facilities: ✳️⋔♨️⋔🏋️ Services: 🔌🎛♨️⛽ℚ✖️
💳 💳 💳 🚫 🔀 🔌

NABURN   Map 08 SE54

▶ ▶ ▶ 59% **Naburn Lock Caravan & Camping Park** (SE596446)

YO19 4RU ☎ 01904 728697 🖥 01904 728697
e-mail: nablock@easynet.co.uk
website: www.scoot.co.uk/naburn_lock_caravan

Dir: *From A64 take on A19 N, turn left signed Naburn, site on right 0.5m past village*

★ 🚐 fr £11 🚐 fr £11 ▲ fr £9

Open Mar-6 Nov Booking advisable anytime Last arrival 22.00hrs

A meadowland site close to river in a rural area south of York. Mainly level pitches divided by

contd.

Facilities: 🚿 Bath   ⋔ Shower   ⊙ Electric Shaver   ℚ Hairdryer   ✳️ Ice Pack Facility   ⚏ Disabled Facilities   📞 Public Telephone
🏋️ Shop on Site or within 200yds   📆 Mobile Shop (calls at least 5 days a week)   🏛 BBQ Area   📠 Picnic Area   ⋔ Dog Exercise Area

Naburn Lock Caravan & Camping Park
mature hedges. A 7-acre site with 100 touring pitches.
Fishing
Facilities: ╭⊙☖✳க℄⅏呙★ **Services:** ☺⊡🔓∅⊞
⊤→∪▸▲↳♨⅃🍴🚬⊙🔜🎣

NORTH STAINLEY   Map 08 SE27

► ► ► 69% **Sleningford Water Mill Caravan Camping Park (SE280783)**
HG4 3HQ ☎ 01765 635201
website: www.ukparks.co.uk/sleningford
Dir: Adjacent to A6108. 4m N of Ripon
★ ☖ £6-£10.50 ☖ £6-£10.50 Å £6-£10.50
Open Etr & Apr-Oct Booking advisable bank hols & school holidays Last arrival 22.00hrs Last departure 12.30hrs
The old watermill and the River Ure make an attractive setting for this touring park which is laid out in two areas. Pitches are placed in meadowland and close to mature woodland, and the park is carefully maintained. A 14-acre site with 80 touring pitches.
Off-licence, canoe access, fly fishing.
Leisure: ◣ ⅏ **Facilities:** ╭⊙✳க℄⅏呙★
Services: ☺⊡🔓∅⊞⊤→▸▲♨
Notes: Youth groups by prior arrangment only

OSMOTHERLEY   Map 08 SE49

► ► ► 67% **Cote Ghyll Caravan & Camping Park (SE459979)**
DL6 3AH ☎ 01609 883425 🖺 01609 883425
e-mail: hills@coteghyll.com
website: www.coteghyll.com
Dir: Exit A19 at A684. Follow signs to Osmotherly. Left in village site 0.5m on right
★ ☖ £7.50-£10 ☖ £7.50-£10 Å £7.50-£10

contd.

Open Mar-Oct Booking advisable bank hols Last arrival 23.00hrs Last departure noon
Quiet, peaceful site in a pleasant valley on the edge of moors, close to village. Major improvements made by new owners have resulted in excellent toilet facilities in one of two blocks. A 7-acre site with 77 touring pitches, 3 hardstandings and 18 statics.
Tourist info, packed lunch service
Leisure: ⅏ **Facilities:** ╭⊙☖✳℄⅏⊞呙★
Services: ☺⊡🔓∅⊞⊤→∪♨ **Notes:** Family park, dogs on lead at all times

PICKERING   Map 08 SE78

► ► ► 72% **Upper Carr Touring Park (SE804816)**
Upper Carr Ln, Malton Rd YO18 7JP
☎ 01751 473115 🖺 01751 473115
e-mail: harker@demon.co.uk
website: www.uppercarr.demon.co.uk
Dir: Off A169 Malton-Pickering road, approx 1.5m from Pickering; signed opposite Black Bull pub
★ ☖ £8-£10.50 ☖ £8-£10.50 Å £8-£10.50
Open Mar-Oct Booking advisable Last dep 12.00hrs
Attractive and well-maintained rural touring park set amongst mature trees and hedges, with an animal corner and adjacent 9-hole golf course.
A nature trail leads to the quaint village of Thornton-le-Dale, which has streams running through the centre. A 6-acre site with 80 touring pitches.
Off-licence, rare hens & owls
Leisure: ⅏ **Facilities:** ╭⊙☖✳க℄⅏★
Services: ☺⊡🔓∅⊞→▸♨♨ **Notes:** No single sex groups 💳🚬⊙🔜🎣

► ► ► 70% **Wayside Caravan Park (SE764859)**
Wrelton YO18 8PG ☎ 01751 472608 🖺 01751 472608
e-mail: waysideparks@freenet.co.uk
website: www.waysideparks.co.uk
Dir: 2.5m W of Pickering on A170, follow signs at Wrelton
★ ☖ fr £11 ☖ fr £11 Å fr £8

Open Etr-early Oct Booking advisable Etr, Spring bank hol & Jul-Aug Last arrival 23.00hrs Last departure noon
Located in the village of Wrelton, this well-maintained park is divided into small paddocks by mature hedging. Caravans are prohibited from

contd

using the A170 at Sutton Bank between Thirsk and Helmsley. A 10-acre site with 75 touring pitches and 80 statics.

Facilities: ⚋⊙⚏⋇⚘⚬⚑⚓ **Services:** ⚍⚎⚏⚐⚑⚒⚓ →∪▶⚏⚒⚐⚑⚓⚔⚕

RICHMOND   Map 07 NZ10

▶ ▶ ▶ ▶ **68% Brompton-on-Swale Caravan & Camping Park (NZ199002)**
Brompton-on-Swale DL10 7EZ ☎ 01748 824629
📠 01748 826383
e-mail: brompton.caravanpark@btinternet.com
website: www.bromptoncaravanpark.co.uk
Dir: Take B6271 off A1 signed Richmond, site 1m on left
★ 🚐 £9-£11.50 🚚 £9-£11.50 ▲ £4-£9
Open Etr or Mar-Oct Booking advisable school & bank hols Last arrival 20.00hrs Last departure 12.00hrs
A peaceful riverside park on former meadowland with mature trees and other natural features. Fishing is available on the River Swale which flows through the park, and there is a good children's playground. A 14.5-acre site with 77 touring pitches and 22 statics.
Fishing on site

Leisure: /M **Facilities:** ⚋⊙⚏⋇⚘⚬⚑⚒⚓ **Services:** ⚍⚎⚏⚐⚑⚒⚓→∪▶⚏⚒⚐⚑⚓⚔⚕

▶ **56% Swale View Caravan Site (NZ134013)**
Reeth Rd DL10 4SF ☎ 01748 823106
e-mail: swaleview@teesdaleonline.co.uk
Dir: 3m W of Richmond on A6108
🚐🚚▲
Open Mar-Oct Booking advisable bank hols & summer hols Last arrival 21.00hrs Last dep noon
A grassy site shaded by trees, lying on the banks of the River Swale in picturesque countryside. Toilet facilities are very basic. A 13-acre site with 60 touring pitches and 100 statics.

Leisure: ⚭ /M **Facilities:** ⚋⊙⋇⚬⚑⚒⚓⚔⚓ **Services:** ⚍⚎⚏⚐⚑⚒⚓→▶⚒⚐⚑⚓⚕

RIPON   Map 08 SE37
See also **Bishop Monkton, North Stainley & Winksley**

▶ ▶ ▶ **72% Riverside Meadows Country Caravan Park (SE317726)**
Ure Bank Top HG4 1JD ☎ 01765 602964
📠 01765 604045
e-mail: info@flowerofmay.com
website: www.flowerofmay.com
Dir: On A61 at N end of new bridge out of Ripon, then W along riverside. Site 400yds, clearly signed
★ 🚐 £11-£15.50 🚚 £11-£15.50 ▲ £8.50-£13
Open Etr-Oct (rs Mar-Apr bar open wknds only) Booking advisable bank hols & high season Last arrival 21.00hrs Last departure noon
This pleasant, well-maintained site stands on high ground overlooking the River Ure, 1m from the town centre. Major improvements have resulted in a new laundry and reception and a new bar complex. There is no access to the river from the

contd.

site. A 28-acre site with 131 touring pitches and 269 statics.

Leisure: ⚭ /M ▢ **Facilities:** ⚋⊙⋇⚘⚬⚑⚒⚓ **Services:** ⚍⚎⚏⚐⚒⚑⚓⚔→∪▶⚏⚔⚕⚒⚐⚑⚓

ROBIN HOOD'S BAY   Map 08 NZ90
See also **Whitby**

▶ ▶ ▶ **67% Grouse Hill Caravan Park (NZ928002)**
Flask Bungalow Farm, Fylingdales YO22 4QH
☎ 01947 880543 & 880560 📠 01947 880543
Dir: Off A171 accessed via loop road, at Flask Inn
🚐🚚▲

Open Spring bank hol-Sep (rs Etr-May shop & reception restricted) Booking advisable public hols Last arrival 22.00hrs Last departure noon
Set in the midst of spectacular scenery in North Yorkshire Moors National Park, this family-run park is surrounded by rugged moorland and woodland, an ideal base for walking and touring. A 14-acre site with 175 touring pitches.

Leisure: ⚭ /M **Facilities:** ⚋⊙⋇⚘⚬⚑⚒⚓
Services: ⚍⚎⚏⚐⚑⚒⚓→∪▶ **Notes:** No singles groups, no motor cycles

---

▶ ▶ ▶ **73% Middlewood Farm Holiday Park (NZ945045)**
Middlewood Ln, Fylingthorpe YO22 4UF
☎ 01947 880414 📠 01947 880871
e-mail: info@middlewoodfarm.com
website: www.middlewoodfarm.com
Dir: Leave A171 towards Robin Hood's Bay, into Fylingthorpe, turn into Middlewood Lane
🚐 £6.50-£11.50 🚚 £6.50-£11.50 ▲ £6.50-£12.50

Open Mar-4 Jan Booking advisable Bank & School Holidays Last arrival 22.00hrs Last departure noon
A peaceful, friendly family park enjoying panoramic views of Robin Hood's Bay in a picturesque fishing

contd.

England

Middlewood Farm Holiday Park

Robin Hood's Bay, Whitby, N. Yorkshire YO22 4UF
Tel: 01947 880414   www.middlewoodfarm.com
E-mail: info@middlewoodfarm.com

Small, peaceful family park. Walkers, artists and wildlife paradise. Magnificent panoramic views of the sea, moors and "Heartbeat Country".
- SUPERIOR LUXURY HOLIDAY HOMES for HIRE
- TOURERS/TENTS/MOTOR HOMES welcome
- Electric Hook-ups
- SUPERB heated facilities
- FREE HOT SHOWERS/Dishwashing
- Children's Adventure Play Area
- Village PUB – 5 minutes walk
- BEACH – 10 minutes walk
- OPEN: 1st March to 4th January

We're waiting to make you Welcome!

AROSA
Caravan and Camping Park

Ratten Row, Seamer, Scarborough, North Yorkshire YO12 4QB

Tel & Fax: 01723 862166

This is a small but friendly family-owned park with excellent facilities for Touring Caravans & Tents. We are only a short drive from beaches and entertainment and it makes an ideal base for surrounding attractions. Our park has an excellent reputation for friendliness and cleanliness.

---

village. The toilet facilities are excellent, and the park is very well maintained. A 7-acre site with 100 touring pitches, 9 hardstandings and 30 statics.
Leisure: ⚲ **Facilities:** ⚏⊙⚒✳✆⚞ **Services:** ⚿⚎⚐
⚎⚏➜⚙∪▶✕⚒⚙⚑ **Notes:** Dogs must be kept on lead at all times, dangerous breeds not accepted, no radios/noise after 10pm ⚌ ⚍ ⚎ ⚏ ⚑

ROSEDALE ABBEY   Map 08 SE79

▶ ▶ ▶ 59% **Rosedale Caravan & Camping Park** (SE725958)
YO18 8SA ☎ 01751 417272
e-mail: info@flowerofmay.com
website: www.flowerofmay.com
Dir: From Pickering turn left onto A170 for 2.25m. Turn right at Wrelton for Cropton & Rosedale on unclass road for 7m. Park on left in village
★ ⚑ £11-£15.50 ⚑ £11-£15.50 ⚑ £4.50-£13
Open Mar-Oct Booking advisable BH's & High season Last arrival 21.00hrs Last departure noon
Set in a sheltered valley in the centre of the North Yorkshire Moors National Park, and divided into separate areas for tents, tourers and statics. A very popular park, with well-tended grounds, and close to the pretty village of Rosedale Abbey. A 10-acre site with 100 touring pitches and 37 statics.
Leisure: ⚲ ⚲ **Facilities:** ⚏⊙⚒✳⚞⚐⚎⚍⚑
Services: ⚿⚎⚐⚏⚎⚍∪▶⚒⚑

SCARBOROUGH   Map 08 TA08
See also **Filey**

▶ ▶ ▶ ▶ 71% **Jacobs Mount Caravan Park**
(TA021868) Jacobs Mount, Stepney Rd YO12 5NL
☎ 01723 361178 ⬛ 01723 361178
e-mail: jacobsmount@yahoo.co.uk
website: www.jacobsmount.co.uk
Dir: Direct access from A170
★ ⚑ £8-£12 ⚑ £8-£12 ⚑ £8-£12

Open Mar-Oct (rs Mar-May & Oct limited hours at shop/bar) Booking advisable bank hols & late Jun-early Sep Last arrival 21.00hrs Last departure noon
A sheltered family-run site surrounded by woodland and open countryside on the edge of Forge Valley National Park area. There are many all-weather full-facility touring pitches in a separate area, and the park is only two miles from Scarborough. An 18-acre site with 156 touring pitches, 131 hardstandings and 60 statics.
Dish wash & food preparation area.
Leisure: ⚲⚲⚏ **Facilities:** ⚎⚏⊙⚒✳⚞⚐⚎⚍
Services: ⚿⚎⚐⚲⚎⚍⚎∪▶⊙⚎✕⚒⚑
⚌⚍⚑

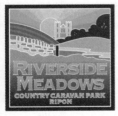

Facilities: 🛁 Bath 🚿 Shower ☺ Electric Shaver 💈 Hairdryer ✳ Ice Pack Facility ♿ Disabled Facilities 📞 Public Telephone
🛒 Shop on Site or within 200yds 🚐 Mobile Shop (calls at least 5 days a week) 🍖 BBQ Area 🪑 Picnic Area 🐕 Dog Exercise Area

The Gateway to the Yorkshire Coast...

Our family run park has been beautifully landscaped around a springwater stream, winding through the beer garden and boardwalk.

Family friendly facilities reflect what you expect of a perfect well deserved holiday. **FREE MODERN HEATED POOL** with luxurious heated toilet and shower rooms including Sauna, solarium, we have got it all here for you.

Always wanted to see the world, well...

Step into our New Mexican themed bar, conservatory and entertainment complex and you will never want to go home again.

For even more fun:

Theme Weekends during off-peak periods are our speciality.

Let your children join **SHARKY'S CLUB** (high season) for a funfilled carefree time.

Sounds good ... it is.

SPRING WILLOWS

TOURING CARAVAN & CAMPING PARK [AA DELUXE]

For more information, please send a s.a.e. to
SPRING WILLOWS TOURING PARK, MAIN ROAD, STAXTON, Nr SCARBOROUGH, YO12 4SB *or ring 01723 891505*

► ► ► ► 71% **Spring Willows Touring Caravan Park** (TA026794)
Main Rd, Staxton Roundabout YO12 4SB
☎ 01723 891505 🖷 01723 891505
e-mail: fun4all@springwillows.fsnet.co.uk
website: www.springwillows.co.uk
For full entry see STAXTON

► ► ► 63% **Arosa Caravan & Camping Park** (TA011830)
Ratten Row, Seamer YO12 4QB ☎ 01723 862166
🖷 01723 862166
e-mail: neilcherry@arosacaravanpark.co.uk
Dir: 4m from Scarborough. From junct with unclass road & A64 S of Seamer, N into village. Site 250yds along Ratten Row
★ 🚐 £12.50-£15.50 🚙 £10.50-£12.50 ▲ £8.50-£12.50

Open Mar-4 Jan Booking advisable bank hols & Aug
Last arrival 24.00hrs Last departure 24.00hrs
A very well laid out site with screening from mature trees. Emphasis at this family-owned park is placed on the friendly clubhouse which offers occasional entertainment. A 3.5-acre site with 105 touring pitches.

Leisure: ♠ ⚂ Facilities: ℞ ⊙ ⚙ ✻ ₺ ⚑ 🛒 ⛽
🟊 Services: 🖵 ⚲ 🛢 ⊘ ⊞ 🔲 ⬦ → ∪ ► △ ✚ ⚌ ⚊
💳 💳 💳 ⚏ ⚏ 🔵

See advertisement on page 234

► ► ► 65% **Killerby Old Hall** (TA063829)
Killerby YO11 3TW ☎ 01723 583799 🖷 01723 583799
Dir: Direct access via B1261 at Killerby, near Cayton
★ 🚐 £7.50-£10.50 🚙 £7.50-£10.50
Open Etr-Oct Booking advisable BH's Last dep noon
A small secluded park, well sheltered by mature trees and shrubs, located at the rear of the old hall. The park has expanded recently, and now has additional toilet facilities. A 2-acre site with 20 touring pitches, 20 hardstandings.

Leisure: ♦ ♠ ⚂ Facilities: ℞ ⊙ ⚂ 🛒 ⛽ 🟊
Services: 🖵 🛢 ⊞ → ∪ ► ⊙ △ ⚌ ₺ 💳 ⚏ 🔵

► ► ► 68% **Scalby Close Park** (TA020925)
Burniston Rd YO13 0DA ☎ 01723 365908
e-mail: admin@scalbyclose.co.uk
website: www.scalbyclose.co.uk
Dir: 2m N of Scarborough on A615, 1m from junct with A171
★ 🚐 £6-£11 🚙 £6-£11 ▲ £6-£11
Open Mar-Oct Booking advisable bank hols & high season Last arrival 22.00hrs Last departure noon
An attractive small park with upgraded facilities and enthusiastic owners. Located only 2m from Scarborough, and handy for exploring both coast and countryside. A 3-acre site with 42 touring pitches, 40 hardstandings and 5 statics.

Facilities: ℞ ⊙ ✻ ₺ 🛒 Services: 🖵 🛢 ⚲ ⊘ ⊞ 🔲
→ ∪ ► ✚ ⚌ ⚊ 💳 ⚏

► ► 70% **Scalby Manor Caravan & Camping ark (TA025911)**
ield Ln, Scalby YO13 0DA ☎ 01723 366212
ir: 2m N of Scarborough town centre on A165 to /hitby
₩ £6-£11 ₩ £6-£11 ▲ £3.50-£11

pen Etr-Oct Booking advisable bank hols Jul & ug Last arrival 18.00hrs Last departure noon *lightly undulating, grassy site in rural urroundings. This large park has plenty of trategically placed facilities, and the grass is well rimmed. A 22-acre site with 300 touring pitches.*
eisure: ⚠ Facilities: ⬤⊙&⌂⊞☰☂ Services: ⊕
🛢⬛📻→∪▶✖☕♨⬛⬛📱🔌📶🔵

SCOTCH CORNER   **Map 08 NZ20**

► ► 64% **Scotch Corner Caravan Park NZ210054)**
L10 6NS ☎ 01748 822530 & 826272
01748 826272
ir: From Scotch Corner junct of A1 & A66 take A6108 wards Richmond. Proceed 250mtrs then cross central eservation and return 200mtrs to site entrance
₩ £10-£12.50 ₩ £10-£12.50 ▲ £10-£12.50

pen Etr-Oct Booking advisable public hols & Jul-ug Last arrival 22.30hrs Last departure noon *well-maintained site with good facilities, ideally ituated as a stopover, and an equally good location or touring. A 7-acre site with 96 touring pitches, hardstandings. Recreation area for children*
acilities: ⬤⊙✖&⊾☕☂ Services: ⊕📻♨🛢⬛⊞⊡
→∪▶♨⬛⬛📱🔵

SHERIFF HUTTON   **Map 08 SE66**

► ► ► 67% **Camping & Caravanning Club Site (SE638652)**
Bracken Hill YO60 6QG ☎ 01347 878660
website: www.campingandcaravanningclub.co.uk
Dir: From York follow 'Earswick/Strensall' signs. Keep left at filling station & Ship Inn. Site 2nd on right
★ ₩ £12.30-£15.50 ₩ £12.30-£15.50 ▲ £12.30-£15.50
Open Mar-Oct Booking advisable bank hols & peak periods Last arrival 21.00hrs Last departure noon *A quiet rural site in open meadowland within easy reach of York. This well established park is friendly and welcoming. Please see the advertisement on page 10 for details of Club Members' benefits. A 10-acre site with 90 touring pitches, 7 hardstandings.*
Leisure: ⚠ Facilities: ⬤⊙☕✖&⊾☂
Services: ⊕⬛🛢⬛⊞→∪▶♨☕♨⬛⬛📱🔵

SKIPTON   **Map 07 SD95**

► ► ► 71% **NEW** Howgill Lodge **(SD065593)**
Barden BD23 6DJ ☎ 01756 720655
e-mail: info@howgill-lodge.co.uk
website: www.howgill-lodge.co.uk
Dir: B6160 from Bolton Abbey signed to Burnsall, 3m. At Barden Tower right signed Appletreewick. 1.5m phone box, right to Howgill
★ ₩ fr £9.50 ₩ fr £9.50 ▲ fr £9.50
Open mid Mar-Oct Booking advisable
A beautifully-maintained and secluded site offering panoramic views of Wharfedale. The spacious

contd.

---

hardstanding pitches are mainly terraced, and there is a separate tenting area with numerous picnic tables. Three immaculate toilet blocks provide good showers and laundry facilities, and there is a well-stocked shop and an excellent café. A 4-acre site with 40 touring pitches, 20 hardstandings.

Facilities:

Services:

SLINGSBY — Map 08 SE67

▶ ▶ ▶ 76% **Camping & Caravanning Club Site (SE699755)**

Railway St YO62 4AA ☎ 01653 628335
website: www.campingandcaravanningclub.co.uk
Dir: *0.25m N of Slingsby village. Signed also from Helmsley/Malton on B1257*
★ £12.30-£15.50 £12.30-£15.50 ▲ £12.30-£15.50
Open Mar-Oct Booking advisable bank hols & peak periods Last arrival 21.00hrs Last departure noon
A well cared for park in a traditional North Yorkshire village with a maypole on the village green. Pitches are a mixture of grass and hardstanding, and the very modern toilet block is clean and bright. Caravans are prohibited on the A170 at Sutton Bank between Thirsk and Helmsley. Please see advertisement on page 10 for details of Club Members' benefits. A 3-acre site with 59 touring pitches, 7 hardstandings.

Facilities:

Services:

▶ ▶ ▶ 67% **Robin Hood Caravan & Camping Park (SE701748)**

Green Dyke Ln YO62 4AP ☎ 01653 628391
01653 628391
e-mail: info@robinhoodcaravanpark.co.uk
website: www.robinhoodcaravanpark.co.uk
Dir: *On edge of Slingsby with access off B1257 Malton-Helmsley Rd*
★ £9-£15 £9-£15 ▲ £9-£11
Open Mar-Oct Booking advisable bank hols & 15 Jul-1 Sep Last arrival 18.00hrs Last departure noon
A pleasant, well-maintained grassy park, in a good position for touring the Yorkshire Dales. A redeveloped park with hardstandings and electric hook-ups to all pitches. A 2-acre site with 32 touring pitches, 22 hardstandings and 30 statics.
Caravan hire, washing up area. Off-licence.

Leisure: **Facilities:**

Services:

SNAINTON — Map 08 SE98

▶ ▶ ▶ 70% **Jasmine Caravan Park (SE928813)**

Cross Ln YO13 9BE ☎ 01723 859240
01723 859240
e-mail: info@jasminepark.co.uk
website: www.jasminepark.co.uk
Dir: *Turn S off A170 in Snainton village, then follow signs*
★ £7.50-£11 £7.50-£11 ▲ £7.50-£11
Open Mar-Dec Booking advisable 3 wks in advance for bank hols Last arrival 22.00hrs Last dep noon

contd.

A well-screened rural site on edge of this peaceful village, sheltered by high hedges. Midway between Pickering and Scarborough, on the edge of the North Yorkshire Moors National Park. A 5-acre site with 94 touring pitches and 11 statics.
Baby changing unit

Facilities: **Services:** **Notes:** No dogs in hire fleet, dogs must be on leads

STAINFORTH — Map 07 SD86

▶ ▶ ▶ 60% **Knight Stainforth Hall Caravan & Campsite (SD816672)**

BD24 0DP ☎ 01729 822200 01729 823387
e-mail: info@knightstainforth.co.uk
Dir: *From W on A65 take B6480 for Settle, turn left before leisure centre signed Little Stainforth. From E continue through Settle on B6480, over bridge to leisure centre, then turn right*
★ fr £10 ▲

Open May-Oct Booking advisable bank hols & Jul-Aug Last arrival 22.00hrs Last departure noon
Located near the River Ribble in the Yorkshire Dales National Park, this well-maintained site is sheltered by mature woodland. It is an ideal base for walking or touring in the beautiful surrounding areas. A 6-acre site with 100 touring pitches and 60 statics.
Fishing on site.

Leisure: **Facilities:**

Services:

Notes: No groups of young people.

STAXTON — Map 08 TA07

▶ ▶ ▶ ▶ 71% **Spring Willows Touring Caravan Park (TA026794)**

Main Rd, Staxton Roundabout YO12 4SB
☎ 01723 891505 01723 891505
e-mail: fun4all@springwillows.fsnet.co.uk
website: www.springwillows.co.uk
Dir: *A64 to Scarborough, then take A1039 to Filey. Entrance on right*
▲
Open Mar-Nov (rs Mar & Oct bar, pool, take-away, restaurant restricted) Booking advisable bank hols, Etr, Jul & Aug Last arrival 18.00hrs Last dep 11.00hrs
A lively park offering a full evening entertainment programme, and a restaurant serving food throughout the day and evening. Other amenities include a Mexican themed bar, and a popular

contd

Spring Willows Touring Caravan Park
*children's club. The pitches are divided by shrubs
and bushes, and sheltered by high sand dunes, with
a natural spring running through the park. A 26-acre
site with 184 touring pitches.*
Washing-up facilities, sauna, solarium, coffee
lounge

Leisure: ⚑ ⚓ ⚙ 🖵 **Facilities:** 🖍 ⊙ ⚲ ✳ ⚓ ⚫ 🗪 🌤 🎠 🐾 🛉
Services: 🖳 🖩 🗜 🖰 ⌀ 🖵 🗓 ✕ 🖦 ⇢ ∪ ▶ 🖛 🌐 📠 🗑 🗒

See advertisement on page 236

STILLINGFLEET   **Map 08 SE54**

▶ ▶ ▶ 65% **Home Farm Caravan & Camping
(SE595427)**
Moreby YO19 6HN ☎ 01904 728263 🗎 01904 720059
Dir: 6m from York on B1222, 1.5m N of Stillingfleet
★ 🚐 fr £8 🚗 fr £8 ▲ fr £6
Open Feb-Dec Booking advisable bank hols Last
arrival 22.30hrs
*A meadowland site on a working farm bordered by
parkland on one side and the River Ouse on
another. Facilities are in converted farm buildings,
and the family owners extend a friendly welcome to
tourers. A 5-acre site with 25 touring pitches.*
Facilities: 🖍 ⊙ ⚲ ✳ ⚓ 🛉 **Services:** 🖳 🖰 ⌀ 🖵 🗓 ⇢ ∪ 🗒

SUTTON-ON-THE-FOREST   **Map 08 SE56**

▶ ▶ ▶ ▶ 72% **Goosewood Caravan
Park (SE595636)**
YO61 1ET ☎ 01347 810829 🗎 01347 811498
e-mail: edward@goosewood.fsbusiness.co.uk
website: www.ukparks.co.uk/goosewood
*Dir: From A1237 take B1363. After 5m turn right. Take
right turn after 0.5m & site on right*
★ 🚐 £7.50-£15 🚗 £7.50-£15

[Best of British logo]

Open Feb-14 Jan Booking advisable BH's, Jul & Aug
Last arrival 20.00hrs Last departure noon
An immaculately maintained park with its own lake
                                           contd.

---

*and seasonal fishing, set in attractive woodland
within the Vale of York. The park offers
hardstandings and patios for all pitches, and the
first-class toilets include plenty of en suite facilities
plus six new bathrooms. In addition to the usual
children's play equipment there is a woodland
assault course. A 20-acre site with 75 touring
pitches, 75 hardstandings and 35 statics.
Fishing lake.*

Leisure: ⚙ **Facilities:** ⇥ 🖍 ⊙ ⚲ ✳ ⚓ 🗪 🎠 🛉
Services: 🖳 🖩 🖰 ⌀ 🖵 🗓 🖦 ⇢ ∪ ▶ 🖛 🗒 🌐 📠 🗑

THIRSK   **Map 08 SE48**

▶ ▶ ▶ 53% **Sowerby Caravan Park (SE437801)**
Sowerby YO7 3AG ☎ 01845 522753 🗎 01845 574520
Dir: 0.5m S of Sowerby on unclass road to Dalton
★ 🚐 £6.75-£7.50 🚗 £6.75-£7.50
Open Mar-Oct Booking advisable bank hols
Last arrival 22.00hrs
*A level grassy site beside a tree-lined river bank.
The park is mainly for statics, and tourers are
tucked away at the bottom of the site. A 1-acre site
with 25 touring pitches, 5 hardstandings and 85
statics.*

Leisure: ⚓ ⚙ **Facilities:** 🖍 ⊙ ✳ ⚓ ⚫ 🗪
Services: 🖳 🖩 🖰 ⌀ 🖵 🗓 ⇢ ∪ 🗒 🗑

▶ ▶ 65% **NEW** **Thirkleby Hall Caravan Park
(SE472794)**
Thirkleby YO7 3AR ☎ 01845 501360 &
07799 641815 🗎 01347 838313
e-mail: greenwood.parks@virgin.net
website: www.greenwoodparks.com
*Dir: Follow A19 from York to Thirsk. After 13m turn
right, through arched gateway to park. From N follow
signs to Northallerton on A168 to Thirsk, then A19 to
York, 3m from Thirsk turn right through arched gateway*
★ 🚐 £11-£12 🚗 £11-£12 ▲ £11-£12

Open Mar-Oct Booking advisable BH's & Aug wknds
Last arrival 22.30hrs Last departure 16.30hrs
*A long-established site in the grounds of the old
hall, with statics in wooded areas around a fishing
lake and tourers based on level grassy pitches. The
well-screened park has superb views of the
Hambledon Hills. A 53-acre site with 50 touring
pitches and 185 statics.*
Fishing lake

Leisure: ⚓ ⚙ 🖵 **Facilities:** 🖍 ⊙ ✳ ⚫ 🎠 🛉
Services: 🖳 🗜 🖰 🗓 ⇢ 🗒 🗑 ⚫ **Notes:** No single sex
teenage groups, dogs must be kept on lead

England

THRESHFIELD   Map 07 SD96

▶ ▶ ▶ ▶ **67% Wood Nook Caravan Park**
(SD974641)
Skirethorns BD23 5NU ☎ 01756 752412
📠 01756 752412
e-mail: bookings@woodnook.net
website: www.woodnook.net
*Dir: From Skipton take B6265 to Threshfield, then B6160
for 50yds. Turn left into Skirethorns Ln, follow signs to
park*
★ 🚐 fr £9.60 🚐 fr £9.60 ▲ fr £9.60
Open Mar-Oct Booking advisable bank hols & peak
periods Last arrival 22.00hrs Last departure noon
*Gently-sloping site in a rural setting, completely
hidden by natural features of surrounding hills and
woodland. Toilet facilities are housed in converted
farm buildings within the farmhouse courtyard, and
pitches are all on firm, well-drained ground or
hardstandings. A separate tenting field also
accommodates non-electric caravans. A 2-acre site
with 48 touring pitches and 11 statics.*
Leisure: 🛝 Facilities: 🍴⊙��✳🕻🥤🕇 Services: 🔌
🔋🛢🗑🚻🕧→∪🍴 Notes: No groups 💳🚩🚩🚩🚩🔵

UGTHORPE   Map 08 NZ71

▶ ▶ ▶ **63% Burnt House Holiday Park (NZ784112)**
YO21 2BG ☎ 01947 840448
*Dir: 9m W of Whitby off A171 Teeside road. Signed onto
unclass rd to Ugthorpe.*
★ 🚐 fr £10 🚐 fr £10 ▲ fr £10
Open Mar-Oct Booking advisable bank hols & Jul-
Aug Last arrival 21.00hrs Last departure noon
*A sheltered park with mature trees and bushes, set
in moorland as part of the North Yorkshire Moors
National Park. There is a long sandy beach at the
pretty seaside village of Sandsend, 4.5m away. A
7.5-acre site with 99 touring pitches and 41 statics.*
Leisure: 🔍🛝 Facilities: 🍴⊙🖊✳🗂
Services: 🔌🔋🛢🗑🕧→🕨🔺🍴

WHITBY   Map 08 NZ81
See also **Robin Hood's Bay & Ugthorpe**

▶ ▶ ▶ ▶ **70% Northcliffe Holiday
Park (NZ930076)**
YO22 4LL ☎ 01947 880477
📠 01947 880972
e-mail: enquiries@northcliffe-seaview.com
website: www.northcliffe-seaview.com
*Dir: 3m S of Whitby on A171, turn left onto B1447
signed High Hawsker & Robin Hood's Bay. Park signed
on left through Hawsker*
★ 🚐 £8-£12 🚐 £8-£12 ▲ £8-£12
Open Etr or end Mar-Oct Booking advisable school
& bank hols & Jul-Aug Last arrival 21.00hrs Last
departure 11.00hrs ♒
*A lovely park in a peaceful position on the outskirts
of Whitby, with clifftop views and country walks.
There are excellent all-round facilities and
amenities, and everything is maintained to a very
high standard. The Cleveland Way footpath, and
the Trailway cycle route both pass beside this park.
A 2-acre site with 30 touring pitches,
30 hardstandings and 171 statics.*
Off-licence.   *contd.*

Leisure: 🔍🛝 Facilities: 🍴⊙🖊✳🕻🥤🕇
Services: 🔌🔋🛢🗑🚻🕧🗙🛒⊕→◎🔺🍴💳🚩🚩🚩🚩🔵

▶ ▶ ▶ **68% Ladycross Plantation Caravan
Park (NZ821080)**
Egton YO21 1UA ☎ 01947 895502
e-mail: enquiries@ladycrossplantation.co.uk
website: www.ladycrossplantation.co.uk
*Dir: On unclass road (signed) off A171 Whitby-Teeside
road, 6m from Whitby centre*
★ 🚐 £8.60-£11.30 🚐 £8.60-£11.30 ▲ £8.60-£11.30

Open Etr-Oct Booking advisable Bank hols & Aug
Last arrival 20.30hrs Last departure noon
*A sheltered and screened woodland park set on
high ground with level, mainly grassy pitches with
some hardstandings set out in bays giving a degree
of privacy. At the end of the North Yorkshire Moors
railway line to Pickering, in Eskdale about 3m from
Grosmont. A 12-acre site with 100 touring pitches,
18 hardstandings.*
Facilities: 🍴⊙🖊✳🕻🥤🕇
Services: 🔌🔋🛢🗑🚻🕧→🍴💳🚩🚩🚩🚩🔵

▶ ▶ ▶ **68% Rigg Farm Caravan Park (NZ915061)**
Stainsacre YO22 4LP ☎ 01947 880430
📠 01947 880430
*Dir: From A171 Scarborough road left onto B1416
signed Ruswarp. Right in 3.25m onto unclass road
signed Hawsker. Left in 1.25m. Site in 0.5m*
★ 🚐 £7.50-£8.50 🚐 £7.50-£8.50 ▲ £7.50-£8.50
Open Mar-Oct Booking advisable bank hols & Jul-
Aug Last arrival 22.00hrs Last departure noon
*A neat rural site with distant views of the coast and
Whitby Abbey, set in peaceful surroundings. The
former farm buildings are used to house reception
and a shop, and the toilet facilities have been
completely refurbished. A 3-acre site with 14
touring pitches, 14 hardstandings and 15 statics.*
Leisure: 🔍🛝 Facilities: 🍴⊙✳🕻🥤🚿🗂 Services:
🔌🔋🛢🗑🚻🕧→∪🕨◎🔺🚼🍴💳🚩🚩🚩🚩🔵

▶ ▶ ▶ **60% York House Caravan Park
(NZ926071)**
YO22 4LW ☎ 01947 880354
Dir: 3.5m S of Whitby, off A171 at Hawsker
★ 🚐 £8-£9 🚐 £8-£9 ▲ £8-£9
Open Mar-Oct Booking advisable Spring bank hol &
mid Jul-Aug Last arrival 22.00hrs Last departure
noon
*On the edge of the North Yorkshire Moors National
Park this is a very well-kept site in an undulating
*   *contd.*

Services: 🕂 Toilet Fluid ✗ Café/ Restaurant 🍴 Fast Food/Takeaway 🍼 Baby Care 🔌 Electric Hook Up
🔋 Launderette ♀ Licensed Bar 🛢 Calor Gaz 🛢 Camping Gaz 🔋 Battery Charging

position located south of Whitby. Ideal for touring coast or moors. A 4-acre site with 59 touring pitches and 41 statics.
Open area for games.

Leisure: 🏔 **Facilities:** ⬤☉🏧⚒⚑✕🚻🛒🎄🏠🐕

Services: 🖳🗑🍴💧✉🛢🚻🖱→∪▶☉⚒🍴🚿♨🥂 **Notes:** No smoking in toilet block, dogs must be on leads

---

WINKSLEY
Map 08 SE25

▶ ▶ ▶ **68% Woodhouse Farm & Country Park** (SE241715)
HG4 3PG ☎ 01765 658309
e-mail: woodhouse.farm@talk21.com
website: www.woodhousewinksley.com
Dir: 6m W of Ripon off B6265 Pateley Bridge road, 2.5m from Fountains Abbey, signed Grantley
★ 🚐 £9-£16 🚐 £9-£16 ▲ £8.50-£12
Open Mar-Oct Booking advisable bank hols & mid Jul-Aug Last arrival 21.00hrs Last departure noon
An attractive rural site on a former working farm, with pitches screened by hedges, and surrounded by meadowland and mature woods. A new toilet complex has been completed, and the owners are friendly and knowledgeable. A 16-acre site with 140 touring pitches and 62 statics.
Coarse fishing lake.

Leisure: 🎣🏔🖵 **Facilities:** ⬤☉🏧⚒⚑🛒🎄🏠🐕

Services: 🖳🗑🍴💧✉🛢🚻✕→∪🍴💳☰☶📷

WYKEHAM
Map 08 SE98

▶ ▶ ▶ ▶ **75% St Helens Caravan Park** (SE967836)
St Helens in the Park YO13 9QD ☎ 01723 862771
🖷 01723 866613
e-mail: caravans@wykeham.co.uk
website: www.wykeham.co.uk
Dir: On A170 in village, 150yds on left beyond Downe Arms Hotel towards Scarborough
★ 🚐 £8.50-£10.60 🚐 £8.50-£10.60 ▲ £6-£10.60
Open Feb-Jan (rs Nov-Jan shop/laundry closed)
Booking advisable bank hols & Jul-Aug Last arrival 22.00hrs Last departure 17.00hrs
Set on the edge of the North York Moors National Park this delightfully landscaped park is extremely well-maintained and thoughtfully laid out with top quality facilities. The site is divided into terraces with tree-screening creating smaller areas, including an adults' zone. A cycle route leads through the surrounding Wykeham estate, and there is a short pathway to the adjoining Downe Arms country pub. A 25-acre site with 250 touring pitches, 2 hardstandings.
Caravan storage.

Leisure: 🎣🏔 **Facilities:** 🖱⬤☉🏧⚒⚑🛒🎄🏠🐕

Services: 🖳🗑🍴💧✉🛢🚻✕🖱🖷→∪▶☉⚒🍴
💳☰☶📷🚚📷

See advertisement on Page 237

> **Fewer than 50 parks have been awarded the coveted 5-pennant rating. For a full list see page 18**

YORK
Map 08 SE65
See also **Acaster Malbis**

▶ ▶ ▶ **63% Riverside Caravan & Camping Park** (SE598477)
Ferry Ln, Bishopthorpe YO2 1SB
☎ 01904 705812 & 704442 🖷 01904 705824
e-mail: info@yorkmarine.co.uk
website: www.yorkmarine.co.uk
Dir: From A64 take A1036. Right at lights signed Bishopthorpe, left into main street at T-junct. At end of road right into Ancaster Ln, left in 150yds
Open Apr-Oct Booking advisable Jul-Sep Last arrival 22.00hrs Last departure noon
A small level grassy park in a hedged field on the banks of the River Ouse, in a village setting on the outskirts of York. A 1-acre site with 25 touring pitches.

Leisure: 🏔 **Facilities:** 🖱⬤☉🏧⚒⚑🛒🎄🏠🐕

Services: 🖳🗑🍴💧✉🛢🚻✕→∪▶☉⚒🍴🖱☶📷

Notes: Dogs must be on leads ☰☶📷

YORKSHIRE, SOUTH

HATFIELD
Map 08 SE60

▶ ▶ ▶ **67% Hatfield Waterpark** (SE670098)
Old Thorne Rd DN7 6EQ ☎ 01302 841572 & 737343
🖷 01302 846368
Dir: Signposted from Hatfield off A18
★ 🚐 fr £7.20 🚐 fr £7.20 ▲ £4.85-£7.20
Open all year (rs Nov-Mar Reduced visitor centre opening Nov-Mar) Booking advisable bank hols Last arrival 17.30hrs Last departure noon
A clean, well run site with fishing and good supervised marine facilities, including windsurfing, sailing and canoeing with equipment for hire. There is also bunkhouse accommodation for 36, handy for tenters in very wet weather. A 10-acre site with 75 touring pitches.
Canoeing, rowing, sailing, windsurfing & fishing.

Leisure: 🏔 **Facilities:** 🖱⬤☉🏧⚒⚑🛒🎄🏠🐕

Services: 🖳🖷→∪▶☉⚒🍴🖱☶📷💳☰

WORSBROUGH
Map 08 SE30

▶ ▶ ▶ **65% Greensprings Touring Park** (SE330020)
Rockley Abbey Farm, Rockley Ln S75 3DS
☎ 01226 288298 🖷 01226 288298
Dir: From M1 junct 36 take A61 to Barnsley. Turn left after 0.25m onto road signed to Pilley. Site entrance 1m at bottom of hill
★ 🚐 fr £7.50 🚐 fr £7.50 ▲ fr £4.50
Open Apr-Oct Booking advisable when hook up is required Last arrival 21.00hrs Last departure noon
A pleasant farm site set within woods and meadowland, with access to the river and several good local walks. Two touring areas, one gently sloping, each with their own toilet block. A 4-acre site with 65 touring pitches, 5 hardstandings.
Cycle hire. TV hook up.

Facilities: 🖱⬤☉🏧⚒⚑🎄

Services: 🖳🗑🍴💧→∪▶🚻🍴🖱☶📷

Leisure: 🏊 Indoor swimming pool 🏊 Outdoor swimming pool ⚭ Tennis court 🎣 Games room 🏔 Children's playground ∪ Stables
▶ 9/18 hole golf course ⚒ Boats for hire 🎦 Cinema 🍴 Fishing ◎ Mini golf ⚠ Watersports 🖵 Separate TV room

YORKSHIRE, WEST

BARDSEY — Map 08 SE34

► ► ► 73% **Glenfield Caravan Park (SE351421)**
Blackmoor Ln LS17 9DZ ☎ 01937 574657
🖹 01937 574242
e-mail: glenfieldcp@aol.com
website: www.ukparks.co.uk/glenfieldcp
Dir: From A58 at Bardsey turn into Church Lane, past church, up hill. Continue 0.5m, site on right
🚐 £9-£12 🚐 £9-£12 ▲ £9-£12

Open all year Booking advisable Last arrival 23.00hrs
A quiet family-owned rural site in a well-screened, tree-lined meadow. The site has an excellent brand new toilet block complete with family en suite room. A convenient touring base. A 4-acre site with 30 touring pitches, 30 hardstandings and 1 static.
Facilities: ↺⊙⬤☀⬤⬤⬤⬤
Services: ⬤⬤⬤⬤⬤→∪▶⬤⬤⬤

► ► ► 64% **Moor Lodge Park (SE352423)**
Blackmoor Ln LS17 9DZ ☎ 01937 572424
🖹 01937 572424
e-mail: moorlodgecp@aol.com
website: www.ukparks.co.uk/moorlodge
Dir: Turn right after Bracken Fox pub (Ling Lane) then right at x-rds, site 0.5m on right
★ 🚐 £8 🚐 £8
Open all year Booking advisable BH's Last arrival 23.00hrs Last departure 23.00hrs
A neat, well-kept site in a peaceful and pleasant rural location convenient to surrounding areas of interest. The touring area is for adults only. A 7-acre site with 12 touring pitches and 60 statics.
Leisure: ⬤ Facilities: ↺⊙⬤☀⬤⬤⬤
Services: ⬤⬤⬤⬤⬤→∪▶⊙⬤⬤
Notes: Adults only ⬤⬤⬤⬤⬤

LEEDS — Map 08 SE23
See also **Bardsey**

► ► 64% **Roundhay Park Site (SE339376)**
Roundhay Park, Elmete Ln, Wetherby Rd LS8 2LG
☎ 0113 265 2354 (in season) & 266 1850
🖹 0113 237 0077
Dir: 6m N of Leeds city centre, off A58 Wetherby rd at Oakwood. Site is signed
🚐 £9-£9.50 🚐 £9-£9.50 ▲ £4.60-£5
Open 16 Mar-Oct Booking advisable Spring bank hol & Jul-Aug Last arrival 21.00hrs *contd.*

Last departure noon
A very tidy municipal site convenient for the ring road and city centre. On a gentle, south-facing slope next to Roundhay Park. An 8-acre site with 60 touring pitches, 15 hardstandings.
Facilities: ↺⊙⬤☀⬤⬤⬤⬤ Services: ⬤⬤⬤
→▶⬤⬤⬤ Notes: Under 18yrs must be accompanied by an adult ⬤⬤⬤⬤⬤⬤

SILSDEN — Map 07 SE04

► ► 59% *Dales Bank Holiday Park (SE036483)*
Low Ln BD20 9JH ☎ 01535 653321 & 656523
Dir: From A6034 in town centre turn N, take left then left again then right into Bradley Road. After 1m turn right. Site in 500yds
🚐 🚐 ▲
Open Apr-Oct (rs Mar) Booking advisable public hols Last arrival 22.00hrs Last departure 16.00hrs
A pleasant farm site in open countryside of typical Dales scenery. The toilet facilities are all cubicles, and kept very clean. A 5-acre site with 40 touring pitches and 12 statics.
Crown green bowling
Leisure: ⬤⬤ Facilities: ↺⊙⬤☀⬤⬤
Services: ⬤⬤⬤⬤⬤⬤✕→∪▶⬤⬤⬤⬤⬤⬤

CHANNEL ISLANDS

GUERNSEY

CATEL (CASTEL) — Map 16

► ► ► 71% **Fauxquets Valley Farm**
GY5 7QA ☎ 01481 255460 🖹 01481 251797
e-mail: info@fauxquets.co.uk
website: www.fauxquets.co.uk
Dir: Off pier. 2nd exit off rdbt. Top of hill left onto Queens Rd. Continue for 2m. Turn right onto Candie Rd. Opposite sign for German Occupation Museum
★ ▲ £9.40-£10.80
Open mid Jun-Aug (rs May-mid Jun & 1-15 Sep Haybarn restaurant and Bar closed) Booking advisable last 2 wks Jul-1st 3 wks Aug
A beautiful, quiet farm site in a hidden valley close to the sea. Friendly helpful owners who understand campers' needs offer good quality facilities and amenities, including an outdoor swimming pool, bar/restaurant, nature trail and sports areas. A 3-acre site with 100 touring pitches.
Nature trail & bird watching.
Leisure: ⬤⬤⬤⬤ Facilities: ↺⊙⬤☀⬤⬤⬤
Services: ⬤⬤⬤⬤⬤⬤✕⬤→∪▶⊙⬤⬤⬤⬤⬤

ST SAMPSON — Map 16

► ► ► 66% **Le Vaugrat Camp Site**
Route de Vaugrat GY2 4TA ☎ 01481 257468
🖹 01481 251841
website: www.users.globalnet.co.uk/~adgould
Dir: From main coast road on NW of island, site is signed at Port Grat Bay into Route de Vaugrat, near Peninsula Hotel
★ ▲ fr £6.80 *contd.*

Le Vaugrat Campsite

Open May-mid Sep Booking advisable all year ⚘
Overlooking the sea and set within the grounds of a
lovely 17th-century house, this level grassy park is
backed by woodland, and close to lovely sandy
beaches. A 6-acre site with 150 touring pitches.
Leisure: ♦ ⚂ ⌂ **Facilities:** ♠ ⚑ ⚹ ⚺ ⚻ ⚼ ⚽ 禾
Services: ⛽ ⚗ ⊞ → ∪ ▶ ⚓ ⚖ ⚍ ☰ ⚎ ⛿

VALE   Map 16

► ► ► **68% La Bailloterie Camping & Leisure**
Bailloterie Ln GY3 5HA ☎ 01481 243636 &
07781 103420 🖷 01481 243225
e-mail: labailloterie@hotmail.com
website: www.guernsey.net.classified/bailloterie
*Dir: 3m N of St Peter Port, take Vale road to Crossways,
turn right into Rue du Braye. Site 1st left at sign*
★ Å £8.80-£10.50
Open 15 May-15 Sep Booking advisable All times
Last arrival 23.00hrs
*Pretty little site with one large touring field and a
few small, well-screened paddocks. This delightful
site has been in the same family ownership for over
30 years, and is continually improving. An 8-acre
site with 100 touring pitches.*
Volleyball net & boules pitch.
Leisure: ♦ ⚂ ⌂ **Facilities:** ♠ ⊙ ⚑ ⚹ ⚺ ⚻ ⚼ 禾 ⚿
Services: ⚙ ⊟ ⚗ ⚗ ⊞ ✕ ⚒ ⚍ → ∪ ▶ ◉ ⚠ ⚷ ⚸ ⚹

HERM

HERM   Map 16

► ► ► **65% Seagull Campsite**
GY1 3HR ☎ 01481 722377 🖷 01481 700334
e-mail: camping@herm-island.com
website: www.herm-island.com
Å

contd.

Open May-Sep Last arrival 17.00hrs Last departure
17.30hrs ⚘
*An away-from-it-all location on the tiny island of
Herm. The grassy site is well maintained,
and all pitches are level, some in individually
terraced bays. Herm is traffic-free, so parking must
be arranged at St Peter Port. Contact Travel Trident
on 01481 721379 or ask when booking at the park.
50 touring pitches.*
Facilities: ⚹ ⚑ → ⚓ ⊟ ⚭ ☰ ⚎ ⛿

JERSEY

ST MARTIN   Map 16

PREMIER PARK

► ► ► ► ► **67% Beuvelande Camp Site**
Beuvelande JE3 6EZ ☎ 01534 853575 & 852223
🖷 01534 857788
*Dir: Take A6 from St Helier to St Martin & follow
signs to campsite before St Martins church.*
Å

Open May-15 Sep Booking advisable Last arrival
anytime
*A well established site with excellent toilet
facilities, in peaceful countryside close to St
Martin. An attractive bar/restaurant is the focal
point of the park especially in the evenings, and
there is a small swimming pool and playground.
A 6-acre site with 150 touring pitches.*
Leisure: ⚐ ♦ ⚂ ⌂ **Facilities:** ♠ ⊙ ⚹ ⚺ ⚻ ⚑
Services: ⚙ ⊟ ⚑ ⚗ ⊞ ✕ → ∪ ▶ ⚸ ⚓
⚭ ☰ ⚎ ⛿

► ► ► **73% Rozel Camping Park**
Summerville Farm JE3 6AX
☎ 01534 856797 & 851656 🖷 01534 856127
e-mail: rozelcamping@jerseyhols.com
website: www.jerseyhols.com/rozel
*Dir: From St Helier follow A6 Bagatelle Road or A7
Saviour's Road then B38*
★ Å £10.40-£15
Open May-mid Sep Booking advisable Jul-Aug Last
departure noon ⚘
*An attractive and well-maintained secluded holiday
site offering excellent amenities in a lovely farm
location. Last arrival time: as soon as possible after
car ferry docks. A 4-acre site with 100 touring
pitches and 20 statics.*
Leisure: ⚐ ♦ ⚂ ⌂ **Facilities:** ♠ ⊙ ⚑ ⚹ ⚺ ⚻ ⚼
Services: ⚙ ⊟ ⚑ ⚗ ⊞ ⊤ → ∪ ▶ ⚠ ⚹ **Notes:** No single
sex groups mid Jul-mid Aug ⚭ ☰ ⚎ ⛿

SARK

SARK   Map 16

► ► **70%** *Pomme de Chien Campsite*
GY9 0SB ☎ 01481 832316 🖹 01481 832316
Dir: Tractor from ferry to top of Harbour Hill, then on foot to x-rds. Left at Nat West bank, then 1st lane on right to site. 0.3m
⚑
Open all year Booking advisable ✍
Sheltered level grassy park in centre of island, close to shops and beaches, in peaceful countryside. Sark is traffic free so parking must be arranged at St. Peter Port. Contact Trident Travel on 01481 721379 or ask when booking at the park. A 1-acre site with 50 touring pitches and 8 statics.
Facilities: ⋔ ❋

► ► **61%** *La Valette*
GY9 0SE ☎ 01481 832066 & 832202 🖹 01481 832636
website: www.sercq.com
Dir: Tractor from ferry to top of Harbour Hill, then on foot, right at Nat West bank. 1st right past Aladdin's Cave shop, at end of lane left, then 1st right down hill. Farm at bottom left.
Open all year Booking advisable
On an elevated position with panoramic views towards Jersey and French coast, this park is on a working farm with direct access to coastal path near the lighthouse. Sark is traffic free so parking must be arranged at St. Peter Port. 50 touring pitches.
Facilities: ⋔ ☉ ❋ → ⤳ ⬛

ISLE OF MAN

GREEBA   Map 06 SC38

► ► **57%** Cronk-Dhoo Farm (SC303810)
IM4 2DX ☎ 01624 851327 & 0762 445 4416
🖹 01624 851327
e-mail: cronkdhoo@talk21.com
Dir: A1 road from Douglas to Peel. 6m from Douglas, 3m from Peel. Private drive 100yds on right from Douglas
★ ⚑ £7-£7.90 ⚑ fr £4 ⚑ £7.90

Open Apr-Nov Booking advisable Last arrival 22.00hrs Last departure 22.00hrs

contd.

Set on a 50-acre farm with good facilities in converted farm buildings which include dog-kennels if needed. This is an ideal TT site, with direct access to the course. A 14-acre site with 120 touring pitches, 4 hardstandings.
Dog kennel service
Leisure: 🅰 ▢ **Facilities:** ⋔ ☉ ⚊ ❋ ⤳ ⬛ ⋔
Services: ⚡ ⊞ ① ⬆ → ∪ ▶ ⤳ ⬛ ⬛
Notes: No fire in fields, on sides only

KIRK MICHAEL   Map 06 SC39

► ► ► **65%** *Glen Wyllin Campsite* (SC302901)
IM6 1AL ☎ 01624 878231 & 878836 🖹 01624 878836
Dir: From Douglas take A1 to Ballacraine, right at lights & follow A3 to Kirk Michael. Left onto A4 signed Peel. Site entrance 100yds on right
⚑ ⚑
Open early May-mid Sep Booking advisable end May-mid Jun Last departure noon
This tree-lined glen is divided by a tarmac road leading down to the beach. One side is for touring and the other offers tents for rental. A 9-acre site with 90 touring pitches.
Sweet shop
Leisure: 🅰 ▢ **Facilities:** ⋔ ☉ ⚊ ❋ ⬛ ⬛ ⬛ ⬛
Services: ⚡ ⊞ ⬛ ⬛ ⊞ → ∪ ▶ ⬛ ⤳ **Notes:** No excess noise after midnight. No dogs in hire tents.

► ► **61%** Cronk Aashen Farm (SC321880)
Barregarroo IM6 1HQ ☎ 01624 878305
🖹 01624 877917
Dir: 1.5m S of Kirk Michael on B10 Sartfield road
⚑ ⚑
Open all year Booking advisable
A pleasant, small family-run site with good facilities in converted farm buildings and with its own wooded glen. Good views of the sea and convenient base for walking. A 3-acre site with 25 touring pitches.
Facilities: ⋔ ☉ ❋ ⚊ ⋔ **Services:** ⚡ ⊞ → ∪ ⤳ ⬛

LAXEY   Map 06 SC48

► ► **59%** *Laxey Commissioners Campsite* (SC438841)
Quarry Rd, Minorca Hill IM7 4BG ☎ 01624 861241
🖹 01624 862623
Dir: Off main road at Fairy Cottage filling station. Down Old Laxey Hill, over bridge, up Minorca hill and left before tram bridge, past school.
⚑
Open May-Sep (rs Etr wknds open only Fri-Mon incl) Booking advisable Apr-May Last arrival anytime Last departure anytime
A level grass park with open views over Laxey Glen, with easy foot access to the village and trams to Douglas and Ramsey. A 2-acre site with 20 touring pitches.
Facilities: ⋔ ☉ ⬛ → ⤴ ⤳ ⬛ **Notes:** No children under 16yrs without responsible adult.

PEEL   **Map 06 SC28**

▶ ▶ **62% Peel Camping Park (SC252839)**
Derby Rd IM5 1RG ☎ 01624 842341 & 843667
▤ 01624 844010
e-mail: ptc@mcb.net
Dir: On A20, 0.25m from Peel, past Clothmaker's School
★ ⛺ fr £11 ⛺ fr £7

Open mid Apr-end Sep Booking advisable 1st & 2nd
week Jun ⚜
A pleasant grass site on the edge of town
surrounded by hedges, with good toilet facilities
and handy for beach and town. A 4-acre site with
112 touring pitches.

Leisure: ▢ **Facilities:** ⬔⊙⬚✳⬩⬩⬩冄
Services: ⬔→∪▶⬩⬩⬩⬩⬩⬩

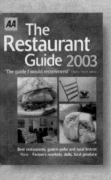

Leisure: ⬔ Indoor swimming pool ⬔ Outdoor swimming pool ⬔ Tennis court ⬔ Games room ⬔ Children's playground ∪ Stables
▶ 9/18 hole golf course ⬔ Boats for hire ⬔ Cinema ⬔ Fishing ◎ Mini golf ⬔ Watersports ▢ Separate TV room

Scotland

SCOTLAND

ABERDEENSHIRE

ABOYNE   Map 15 NO59

▶ ▶ ▶ 56% **Aboyne Loch Caravan Park (NO538998)**
AB34 5BR ☎ 013398 86244 & 01330 811351
📠 01330 811669
GOLD
Dir: On A93, 1m E of Aboyne
★ 🚐 fr £10 🚐 fr £10 ▲ fr £7
Open 31 Mar-Oct Booking advisable Jul-Aug Last arrival 20.00hrs Last departure 11.00hrs
Attractively-sited caravan park set amidst woodland on the shores of the lovely Aboyne Loch in scenic Deeside. The facilities are modern and immaculately maintained, and amenities include boat-launching, boating and fishing. An ideally-situated park for touring Royal Deeside and the Aberdeenshire uplands. A 6-acre site with 55 touring pitches and 40 statics.
Coarse fishing.
Leisure: ♦ ⚑ Facilities: 🅿️⊙ॴ♿🕻🚮🐾⛟
Services: 🖸🖥🛉◪⊤→∪▶♨⚡🗡

FORDOUN   Map 15 NO77

▶ ▶ ▶ 65% **Brownmuir Caravan Park (NO740772)**
AB30 1SJ ☎ 01561 320786 📠 01561 320786
website: www.brownmuircaravanpark.co.uk
Dir: From N on A90 take B966 signed Fettercain & site 1.5m on left. From S take unclass road signed Fordoun, site 1 mile right.
★ 🚐 fr £8 🚐 fr £8 ▲ £6-£8

Open Apr-Oct Booking advisable Last arrival 23.00hrs Last departure noon
A mainly static site set in a rural location with level pitches and good touring facilities. A 7-acre site with 9 touring pitches and 51 statics.
Leisure: ⚑ Facilities: 🅿️⊙✳🕻🚮🐾
Services: 🖸🖥🛉→▶♨⚡

KINTORE   Map 15 NJ71

▶ ▶ ▶ 66% **Hillhead Caravan Park (NJ777163)**
AB51 OYX ☎ 01467 632809 📠 01467 633173
e-mail: enquiries@hillheadcaravan.co.uk
website: www.hillheadcaravan.co.uk
Dir: 1m from village & A96 Aberdeen to Inverness road. From A96 follow caravan signs to park on B994 & taking unclass road to site
🚐🚐▲

contd.

Open all year Booking advisable at all times Last arrival 22.00hrs Last departure 13.00hrs
A peaceful site in the River Don Valley, with pitches well screened by shrubs and bushes, and laid out around a small central area containing a children's play space. The toilet facilities have been greatly improved by new owners, and further redevelopment is already taking place. A 1.5-acre site with 24 touring pitches, 3 hardstandings and 5 statics.
Caravan storage
Leisure: ⚑ Facilities: 🅿️⊙ॴ✳🕻🚮🐾⛟
Services: 🖸🖥🛉◪⊡⊤→▶♨⚡🗡

MACDUFF   Map 15 NJ76

▶ ▶ 59% **Wester Bonnyton Farm Site (NJ741638)**
Gamrie AB45 3EP ☎ 01261 832470 📠 01261 832470
e-mail: taylor@westerbonnyton.freeserve.co.uk
Dir: From A98 1m S of Macduff take B9031 signed Rosehearty. Site 1.25m on right
★ 🚐 £7-£8 🚐 £7-£8 ▲ £5-£7
Open Mar-Oct Booking advisable
A spacious farm site in a screened meadow, with level touring pitches enjoying views across Moray Firth. The site is continually improving, and offers some electric hook-ups and a laundry. A 2-acre site with 10 touring pitches, 3 hardstandings and 26 statics.
Leisure: ⚑ Facilities: 🅿️⊙ॴ🕻🚮🐾⛟
Services: 🖸🖥ॴ⊡⊤→▶♨⚡🗡

NORTH WATER BRIDGE   Map 15 NO66

▶ ▶ ▶ 67% **Dovecot Caravan Park (NO648663)**
AB30 1QL ☎ 01674 840630 📠 01674 840630
e-mail: dovecotcaravanpark@tinyworld.co.uk
website: www.dovecotcaravanpark.com
Dir: Take A90, 5m S of Laurencekirk. At RAF Edzell sign turn left. Site 500yds on left
★ 🚐 £7-£8 🚐 £7-£8 ▲ £6.75-£7.75
Open Apr-Oct Booking advisable Jul & Aug for hook up Last arrival 20.00hrs Last departure noon
A level grassy site in a country area close to the A90, with mature trees screening one side and the River North Esk on the other. A handy overnight stop in a good touring area. A 6-acre site with 25 touring pitches and 44 statics.
Leisure: ♦ ⚑ ⊡ Facilities: 🅿️⊙ॴ✳🕻🚮🐾
Services: 🖸🛉⊡

ST CYRUS   Map 15 NO76

▶ ▶ ▶ ▶ 76% **East Bowstrips Caravan Park (NO745654)**
DD10 0DE ☎ 01674 850328 📠 01674 850328
e-mail: tully@bowstrips.freeserve.co.uk
Dir: From S on A92 coast rd into St Cyrus. Pass hotel on left. Take 1st left then 2nd right. Site signed
★ 🚐 £7.50-£8.50 🚐 £7.50-£8.50 ▲ £7-£8.50
Open Etr or Apr-Oct Booking advisable Jun-Aug Last arrival 22.00hrs Last departure noon
A quiet, rural site close to seaside village, with thoughtfully modernised facilities and a particular welcome for the disabled. The park is surrounded by farmland on the edge of a village, and there are

contd.

Scotland (vertical text)

Scotland

extensive views to be enjoyed. Touring pitches are sited on rising ground amongst attractive landscaping with ornamental trees and shrubs, and flowers. A 4-acre site with 33 touring pitches, 21 hardstandings and 18 statics.
Separate garden with boule pitch

Leisure: ⚴ ♨ Facilities: ♚ ⊙ ☜ ✳ ⑁ ↻ ☎ 戸 ★

Services: ⚑ ▤ ⓘ ⊺ → ∪ ♪ Notes: If camping - no dogs allowed, if touring - dogs must be kept on lead at all times

---

TARLAND   Map 15 NJ40

▶ ▶ ▶ 67% Camping & Caravanning Club Site (NJ477044)
AB34 4UP ☎ 013398 81388
website: www.campingandcaravanningclub.co.uk
Dir: From Aberdeen on A93 turn right in Aboyne at Struan Hotel onto B9094. After 6m take next right & then fork left before bridge, continue for 600yds
★ ⚑ £11.10-£14.50 ⚑ £11.10-£14.50 ▲ £11.10-£14.50
Open 22 Mar-Oct Booking advisable Jul-Aug Last arrival 23.00hrs Last departure noon
A pretty park on the edge of the village, laid out on two levels. The upper area has hardstandings and electric hook-ups, and views over hills and moorland, while the lower level is well screened with mature trees and grassy. Please see advertisement on page 10 for details of Club Members' benefits. An 8-acre site with 90 touring pitches, 20 hardstandings.

Leisure: ♠ ⚴ Facilities: ♚ ⊙ ☜ ✳ ↻ ☎ 戸 ★

Services: ⚑ ⓘ ⌀ ⊡ → ▶ ☜ ☲ ☷ ⑤

ANGUS

EDZELL   Map 15 NO66

▶ ▶ ▶ 69% Glenesk Caravan Park (NO602717)
DD9 7YP ☎ 01356 648565 & 648523
Dir: On unclass road to Glen Esk, 1m N of B966
⚑ ⚑ ▲
Open Apr-Oct Booking advisable public hols & mid Jun-Aug Last arrival 22.00hrs Last dep 16.00hrs
A carefully-maintained woodland site with caravans spread amongst the trees around a fishing lake, and tents located in a separate area. The pleasant owner and warden create a friendly atmosphere. An 8-acre site with 45 touring pitches and 10 statics.

Leisure: ♠ ⚴ ▢ Facilities: ♚ ⊙ ☜ ✳ ↻ ☎ 戸

Services: ⚑ ▤ ⓘ ⌀ ⊡ ⊺ → ∪ ▶ ☞ ♪ ☲

KIRRIEMUIR   Map 15 NO35

▶ ▶ ▶ ▶ 70% Drumshademuir Caravan Park (NO381509)
Roundyhill DD8 1QT ☎ 01575 573284
e-mail: easson@uku.co.uk
Dir: 2.5m S of Kirriemuir on A928
★ ⚑ £9-£10.50 ⚑ £9-£10.50 ▲ £6.50-£7.50
Open all year Booking advisable public hols & Jun-Aug Last arrival 23.00hrs Last departure 16.00hrs
Set amidst farmland with lovely views across the Strathmore Valley. The park offers first class toilet

contd.

---

facilities, and heating in winter ensures visitors' comfort. All pitches have wheel runs or hardstandings so that caravans are always level on the slightly sloping site. Some larger pitches are also available, fenced off from the rest. There is a very good children's play area and a small bar and restaurant. A 15-acre site with 80 touring pitches, 12 hardstandings and 47 statics.
Bar food, putting, woodland walk & caravan storage

Leisure: ⚴ Facilities: ♚ ⊙ ☜ ✳ ⑁ ↻ ☎ 戸 ★

Services: ⚑ ▤ ⓘ ⌀ ⊡ ⊺ ✕ ⓰ → ∪ ▶ ♨ ♪ ☲ ☷ ☲ ☷ ⑤

MONIFIETH   Map 12 NO43

▶ ▶ ▶ ▶ 69% Riverview Caravan Park (NO502322)
Marine Rd DD5 4NN ☎ 01382 535471
▨ 01382 535375
e-mail: riverviewcaravan@btinternet.com
website: www.ukparks.co.uk/riverview
Dir: Signed in both directions from A930 in centre of Monifieth
★ ⚑ £10-£12 ⚑ £10-£12 ▲ £10-£12
Open Apr-Oct Booking advisable Jul-Aug Last arrival 22.00hrs Last departure 12.30hrs
A well-landscaped seaside site with individual hedged pitches, and direct access to the beach. The modernised toilet block has first class facilities which are immaculately maintained. Amenities include a multi-gym, sauna and steam rooms. An 8-acre site with 60 touring pitches, 40 hardstandings and 25 statics.
Multi-gym, sauna, steam bath

Leisure: ♠ ⚴ Facilities: ♚ ⊙ ☜ ✳ ⑁ ↻ ☎ 戸 ★

Services: ⚑ ▤ ⓘ ⊡ ⓰ → ∪ ▶ ♨ ♨ ♪ ☲ ☲ ☷ ☷ ⓓ ☲ ☷ ⑤

ARGYLL & BUTE

BARCALDINE   Map 10 NM94

▶ ▶ ▶ 62% Camping & Caravanning Club Site (NM966420)
PA37 1SG ☎ 01631 720348 ▨ 01203 694886
website: www.campingandcaravanningclub.co.uk
Dir: N on A828, 7m from Connel Bridge turn into site at Camping Club sign on right
★ ⚑ £11.10-£14.50 ⚑ £11.10-£14.50 ▲ £11.10-£14.50
Open Mar-Oct Booking advisable bank hols & Jul-Aug Last arrival 21.00hrs Last departure noon
A sheltered site within a walled garden, bordered by Barcaldine Forest, close to Loch Creran. Tourers are arranged against the old garden walls, with some located outside in quiet grassed areas. There are pleasant woodland walks from the park, including the Sutherland memorial woods close by. Please see the advertisement on page 10 for details of Club Members' benefits. A 4.5-acre site with 75 touring pitches, 28 hardstandings.

Leisure: ♠ ⚴ ▢ Facilities: ♚ ⊙ ☜ ✳ ⑁ ↻ ☎ ★

Services: ⚑ ▤ ⓘ ⌀ ⊡ ✕ → ▶ ♨ ♧ ♪ ☲ ☲ ☷ ☷ ⑤

CARRADALE — Map 10 NR83

▶ ▶ ▶ 66% **Carradale Bay Caravan Park (NR815385)**
PA28 6QG ☎ 01583 431665
e-mail: enquiries@carradalebay.abelgratis.com
website: www.carradalebay.com
Dir: *From Tarbert, take A83 towards Campbeltown, left onto B842, then right onto B879 site is 0.5m*
★ ⊞ £8-£14 ⊞ £8-£14 ▲ £8-£14
Open Apr-Sep Booking advisable bank hols & Jul-Aug Last arrival 22.00hrs Last departure noon
A beautiful, natural site on the sea's edge with superb views over Kilbrannan Sound to the Isle of Arran. Pitches are landscaped into small bays broken up by shrubs and bushes, and backed by dunes close to the long sandy beach. An 8-acre site with 75 touring pitches and 12 statics.
Canoes
Facilities: ⧖⊙☜✻⛯⛱⊟ **Services:** ⬚⬚
➔ ∪ ▶ △ ⅄ ♪

DUNOON — Map 10 NS17

▶ ▶ ▶ 65% **Stratheck Country Park (NS143865)**
PA23 8SG ☎ 01369 840472
Dir: *On A815, 7m N of Dunoon and 12m from Strachur, site on right at end of Loch Eck*
★ ⊞ £12-£15 ⊞ £12-£15 ▲ £7-£9
Open Mar-Oct (rs Mar-Jun & Nov-Dec restricted shop & bar opening hours) Booking advisable Jul & Aug Last arrival 11.00hrs Last departure 16.00hrs
Set in a beautiful valley within tree-lined hills and lying alongside the River Eachaig, this park is undergoing a major refurbishment programme. Nearby Loch Eck is an ideal centre for fishing and boating, and the spectacular countryside attracts walkers, climbers and cyclists. 60 touring pitches, 20 hardstandings and 85 statics.
Leisure: ⬤ ⋔ **Facilities:** ⧖⊙☜✻⛯⛱⛱⛱
Services: ⬚�⛾⊘⊟➔∪⅄♪

GLENDARUEL — Map 10 NR98

▶ ▶ ▶ 68% **Glendaruel Caravan Park (NR005580)**
PA22 3AB ☎ 01369 820267 🖷 01369 820367
e-mail: mail@glendaruelcaravanpark.co.uk
website: www.glendaruelcaravanpark.co.uk
Dir: *From A83 take A815 to Strachur, then 13m to park on A886. By ferry from Gourock to Dunoon then B836, then A886 approx 4m S. (This route is not recommended for towing vehicles as there is a 1:5 uphill gradient on B836)*
★ ⊞ £8.50-£13 ⊞ £8.50-£13 ▲ £8.50-£11
Open Apr-Oct Booking advisable Spring bank hol & mid Jul-Aug Last arrival 22.00hrs Last dep noon
A very pleasant, well-established site in the beautiful Victorian gardens of Glendaruel House. The level grass and hardstanding pitches are set in 23 acres of wooded parkland in a valley surrounded by mountains, with many rare specimen trees. Facilities are immaculately maintained, and the owners are hospitable and friendly. A 3-acre site
contd.

with 45 touring pitches, 34 hardstandings and 30 statics.
Sea trout & salmon fishing.
Leisure: ⬤ ⋔ **Facilities:** ⧖⊙☜✻⛯⛱⛱⊟⛱
Services: ⬚⬚⛾⊘⊟⊟➔ ♪ **Notes:** Dogs must be kept on lead at all times ⊜ ⊞ ⊘

INVERARAY — Map 10 NN00

▶ ▶ ▶ 65% *Argyll Caravan Park (NN075055)*
PA32 8XT ☎ 01499 302285 🖷 01499 302421
Dir: *2.5m S of Inveraray on A83*
⊞ ▲
Open Apr-Oct Last arrival anytime Last departure noon
An attractive touring park on the shores of Loch Fyne, part of a large site with vans on hardstandings with fully-serviced pitches, and two large grass areas for other tourers and tents. There are ample on-site facilities including a large indoor sports hall. A 6-acre site with 100 touring pitches and 187 statics.
Indoor sports hall
Leisure: ⬤ ⋔ **Facilities:** ⧖⊙☜✻⛯⛯⛱⛱
Services: ⬚�⛾⊘⊟⛾✕⬛➔∪▶△⅄♪⊜⊞⊘

INVERUGLAS — Map 10 NN30

▶ ▶ ▶ ▶ 65% **Loch Lomond Holiday Park (NN320092)**
G83 7DW ☎ 01301 704224 🖷 01301 704206
e-mail: enquiries@lochlomond-caravans.co.uk
website: www.lochlomond-lodges.co.uk
Dir: *On A82 3.5m N of Tarbet*
★ ⊞ £11-£15 ⊞ £11-£15
Open Mar-Oct (rs Dec-Jan main amenity building restricted hours) Booking advisable May-Aug Last arrival 21.00hrs Last departure 11.45hrs
A lovely setting on the shores of Loch Lomond with views of forests and mountains, and boat hire available. The small touring area is beautifully situated overlooking the loch, and handily placed for the toilets and clubhouse. A 6-acre site with 18 touring pitches and 72 statics.
Satellite TV, pool tables, boat hire.
Leisure: ⬤ ⋔ ⊡ **Facilities:** ⧖⊙☜✻⛯⛯⛱⛱⊟⛱
Services: ⬚⬚⛾⊘⊟➔∪△⅄♪⊜⊞⊠⊘

LOCHGILPHEAD — Map 10 NR88

▶ ▶ ▶ 68% **Lochgilphead Caravan Site (NR859881)**
PA31 8NX ☎ 01546 602003 🖷 01546 603699
Dir: *Beside A83*
⊞ ⊞ ▲
Open Apr-Oct Booking advisable Jul-Aug
Mainly level, grassy site close to the shore of Loch Gilp, an inlet of Loch Fyne. Convenient to the town centre facilities and with fishing and sailing available on the loch. A 7-acre site with 70 touring pitches and 30 statics.
Mountain bike hire.
Leisure: ⬤ ⋔ **Facilities:** ⧖⊙☜✻⛯⛱⛱⛱
Services: ⬚⬚⛾⊘⊟⊟➔∪▶♪⊜⊞⊘

Scotland

LUSS   Map 10 NS39

▶ ▶ ▶ ▶ 70% **Camping & Caravanning Club Site**
(NS360936)
G83 8NT ☎ 01436 860658 📠 01203 694886
website: www.campingandcaravanningclub.co.uk
Dir: From Erkside bridge take A82 N towards Tarbet.
Turn right at Lodge of Loch Lomond & International
Camping sign. Heading S from Tarbet, take 1st left after
site sign and lodge of Loch Lomond sign. Camp site
approx 200yds
★ ⊞ £12.30-£15.50 ⊞ £12.30-£15.50 ▲ £12.30-£15.50
Open Mar-Oct Booking advisable bank hols & Jul-
Aug Last arrival 21.00hrs Last departure noon
A lovely tenting site on the grassy western shore of
Loch Lomond. The site has two superbly-equipped
toilet blocks, including a parent and child facility,
and a good laundry. Club members' caravans and
motorvans only permitted. Please see
advertisement on page 10 for details of Club
Members' benefits. A 12-acre site with 90 touring
pitches, 29 hardstandings.
Fishing , watersports & area for ball games
Leisure: ∧ Facilities: ⋔ ⊙ ⍵ ⋇ ᕼ ᕼ ⋔
Services: ⌨ ⊡ ⊘ → ∪ ᕒ ▲ ᕼ ⊜ ⊞ ⊞ ⊠ 🔋

MACHRIHANISH   Map 10 NR62

▶ ▶ ▶ 66% **Camping & Caravanning Club Site**
(NR647208)
East Trodigal PA28 6PT ☎ 01586 810366
website: www.campingandcaravanningclub.co.uk
Dir: On A83 from Inveraray take B843 to Machrihanish,
site entrance on right, 200yds past chimney
★ ⊞ £10.20-£12.90 ⊞ £10.20-£12.90 ▲ £10.20-£12.90
Open 9 Apr-23 Sep Booking advisable bank hols &
high season Last arrival 21.00hrs Last departure noon
A very open site with superb sea views, situated
adjacent to the golf course. The pitches are mainly
firm, level grass with a few hardstandings. Please
see the advertisement on page 10 for details of Club
Members' benefits. An 8-acre site with 105 touring
pitches, 5 hardstandings.
Facilities: ⋔ ⊙ ⋇ ᕼ ᕼ ⋔ Services: ⌨ ⊡ ⊘ ⊞
→ ᕒ ▲ ᕼ ⊜ ⊞ ⊞ ⊠ 🔋

OBAN   Map 10 NM82

See also **Barcaldine**

▶ ▶ ▶ 66% **Oban Caravan & Camping Park**
(NM831277)
Gallanachmore Farm, Gallanach Rd PA34 4QH
☎ 01631 562425 📠 01631 566624
e-mail: obancp@aol.com
website: www.obancaravanpark.co.uk
Dir: From Oban follow signs for Mull Ferry, take turn
past terminal signed Gallanach, 2m to site
★ ⊞ £9-£10 ⊞ £9-£10 ▲ £9-£10
Open Etr/Apr-Oct Booking advisable Last arrival
23.00hrs Last departure noon
A well-equipped tourist park in an attractive
location close to sea and ferries. This family park is
an ideal boating centre, and offers two large rally
areas in addition to the touring pitches. A 15-acre
site with 150 touring pitches, 35 hardstandings and
11 statics. *contd.*

Oban Caravan & Camping Park
Indoor kitchen for tent campers
Leisure: ⋐ ∧ Facilities: ⋔ ⊙ ⍵ ⋇ ᕼ ᕼ ⊞ ᕼ Services:
⌨ ⊡ ⊘ ⊞ ⊡ → ∪ ᕒ ▲ ⋇ ᕼ ᕼ ⊜ ⊞ ⊞ ⊠ 🔋

CITY OF EDINBURGH

EDINBURGH   Map 11 NT27

▶ ▶ ▶ 69% **Mortonhall Caravan Park (NT265680)**
38 Mortonhall Gate, Frogston Rd East EH16 6TJ
☎ 0131 664 1533 📠 0131 664 5387
e-mail: mortonhall@meadowhead.co.uk
website: www.meadowhead.co.uk/mortonhall
Dir: Take city by-pass to junct with A702 & follow signs
to Mortonhall
★ ⊞ £9.50-£14 ⊞ £9.50-£14 ▲ £9.50-£14
Open mid Mar-7 Jan (rs Nov-Jan shop closed)
Booking advisable Jul-Aug Last arrival 22.00hrs
Last departure noon   *contd.*

This park is set in the 200-acre Mortonhall country estate to the south of Edinburgh, and provides a spacious camping area with grass-based and hard pitches, some with full service, bordered by mature trees. The excellent facilities are kept spotlessly cleaned and well cared for. A 22-acre site with 250 touring pitches, 22 hardstandings and 19 statics.

Leisure: ◣ ⚲ ▢ **Facilities:** ⋔⊙◖☀⟊ᐸ ᒪ ⍩
Services: ▣⛟♈⌕⍾⊟⛛✕→∪▸♨◉▤▦ ◪

DUMFRIES & GALLOWAY

ANNAN   Map 11 NY16

▶ ▶ 57% **Galabank Caravan & Camping Site**
(NY192676) North St DG12 5BQ ☎ 01556 503806
▤ 01556 503806
Dir: Access site via North Street
★ ⛟ £6.60-£7 ⛟ £6.60-£7 ▲ £6.60-£7
Open May-early Sep Last departure noon
A tidy, well-maintained grassy little park close to the centre of town but with pleasant rural views, and skirted by River Annan. A 1-acre site with 30 touring pitches.
Facilities: ⋔◖ᒪ **Services:** ▣→▸♨↲
Notes: Dogs must be on leads

BALMINNOCH   Map 10 NX26

▶ ▶ ▶ 70% **Three Lochs Holiday Park**
(NX272655)
DG8 OEP ☎ 01671 830304 ▤ 01671 830335
e-mail: info@3lochs.junglelink.co.uk
website: www.3lochs.co.uk
Dir: Follow A75 W towards Stranraer. 10km from Newton Stewart rdbt turn right at small x-roads, follow signs to site, 4m on right.
★ ⛟ £10 ⛟ £10 ▲ £6-£9
Open Mar-Oct Booking advisable bank hols & Jul-Aug Last arrival 22.00hrs Last departure 11.00hrs
A remote and very peaceful park set in beautiful moorland on the banks of Loch Heron, with further lochs and woodland nearby. This spacious grass park offers some fully-serviced pitches in a stunning location, and as well as being an ideal holiday centre for walkers and anglers, it provides a heated indoor swimming pool and well-equipped games room. A 22.5-acre site with 45 touring pitches, 20 hardstandings and 90 statics.
Leisure: ⧘ ◣⚲ **Facilities:** ⋔⊙◖☀ᐸᒪ▦冂
Services: ▣⛟⍾⊟⍉→✕↲

BRIGHOUSE BAY   Map 11 NX64

PREMIER PARK

▶ ▶ ▶ ▶ ▶ 76% **Brighouse**
Bay Holiday Park (NX628453)
DG6 4TS ☎ 01557 870267
▤ 01557 870319
e-mail: aa@brighouse-bay.co.uk
website: www.gillespie-leisure.co.uk
Dir: 2m S of Kirkcudbright turn left off B727 at sign to Brighouse Bay on unclass road

contd.

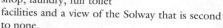

Brighouse Bay Holiday Park
★ ⛟ £9.80-£13.15 ⛟ £9.80-£13.15 ▲ £9.80-£13.15
Open all year Booking advisable Etr, Spring bank hol & Jul-Aug Last arrival 21.30hrs Last departure 11.30hrs
This grassy site enjoys a marvellous coastal setting adjacent to the beach and with superb sea views. Pitches have been imaginatively sculpted into the meadowland, with stone walls and hedges blending in with the site's mature trees. These features together with the large range of leisure activities make this an excellent holiday centre. Winner of AA Best Scottish Campsite for 2003. A 30-acre site with 190 touring pitches and 120 statics.
Mini and 18-hole golf, riding, fishing, quad bikes.
Leisure: ⧘ ◣⚲ **Facilities:** ➤⋔⊙◖☀ᐸᒪ冂
⍩ **Services:** ▣⛟♈⍾⊟⍉✕➤➤◉▤▦ ◪

See advertisement on page 252

Facilities: ➤ Bath ⋔ Shower ⊙ Electric Shaver ◖ Hairdryer ☀ Ice Pack Facility ᐸ Disabled Facilities ᒪ Public Telephone
ᒪ Shop on Site or within 200yds ⊟ Mobile Shop (calls at least 5 days a week) ▦ BBQ Area 冂 Picnic Area ⍩ Dog Exercise Area

CAIRNRYAN
Map 10 NX06

▶ ▶ ▶ 63% **Cairnryan Caravan & Chalet Park (NX075673)**
DG9 8QX ☎ 01581 200231 ▤ 01581 200207
Dir: 5m N of Stranraer on A77
★ ⊞ £9 ⊞ £9 ▲ £5

Open Etr/Mar-Oct (rs Apr-May & Sep-Nov restricted pub hrs Fri & Sat evening) Booking advisable Jul-Aug Last arrival 23.00hrs Last departure noon
A well run park with keen family owners in a lovely location overlooking Loch Ryan. Opposite ferry terminal for Northern Ireland (Larne), 4m from Stranraer. A 7.5-acre site with 10 touring pitches and 83 statics.
Snooker & pool tables.
Leisure: ♦ /Λ **Facilities:** ୮ ⊙ ॰ ☀
Services: ▨ ◈ ♀ ☎ ⊞ Ⓣ → ∪ ▶ ▮ ☎ ☻ ☰ ▨ ▨ ☺

CASTLE DOUGLAS
Map 11 NX76

▶ ▶ ▶ 64% **Lochside Caravan & Camping Site (NX766618)**
Lochside Park DG7 1EZ ☎ 01556 502949 & 503806 ▤ 01556 503806
Dir: Off A75 towards Castle Douglas by Carlingwark Loch
★ ⊞ £8.45-£10.15 ⊞ £8.45-£10.15 ▲ £8.45-£10.15
Open Etr-mid Oct Last departure noon
Municipal touring site incorporating park with recreational facilities, on southern edge of town in attractive setting adjacent to Carlingwark Loch. A 5.5-acre site with 161 touring pitches.
Putting & rowing boats (wknds & high season)
Leisure: ⚲ /Λ **Facilities:** ୮ ⊙ ॰ & ☜ ☎ ⊟ **Services:** ▨ ▣ → ▶ ⚱ ✈ **Notes:** Dogs must be kept on leads

CREETOWN
Map 11 NX45

PREMIER PARK

▶ ▶ ▶ ▶ ▶ 76% **Castle Cary Holiday Park (NX475576)**
DG8 7DQ ☎ 01671 820264 ▤ 01671 820670
Dir: Signed with direct access off A75, 0.5m S of village
★ ⊞ £10.80-£13.50 ⊞ £10.80-£13.50 ▲ £10.80-£13.50

contd.

Castle Cary Holiday Park
Open all year (rs Oct-Mar reception/shop, no heated outdoor pool) Booking advisable BH's & Jul-Aug Last arrival anytime Last dep noon
This attractive site in the grounds of Cassencarie House is sheltered by woodlands, and faces south towards Wigtown Bay. The park is in a secluded location with beautiful landscaping and excellent facilities. The bar/restaurant is housed in part of an old castle, and enjoys extensive views over the River Cree estuary. A 6-acre site with 50 touring pitches, 50 hardstandings and 26 statics.
Mountain bike hire, crazy golf, coarse fishing
Leisure: ⚑ ⚐ ⚫ ⚙ ☐ **Facilities:** ➦ ⚐ ⊙ ⚑ ✳ ☾ ⚫
☎ ☷ ⚑ ⚐ **Services:** ⚑ ⚐ ⚑ ⚐ ⚑ ⚐ ⚑ ✕ ⚑ ➦ →⚐ ⊙ ⚑
Notes: Dogs must be kept on leads at all times
⚑ ⚑ ⚑

See advertisement under Preliminary Section

▶ ▶ ▶ **71% Creetown Caravan Park (NX474586)**
Silver St DG8 7HU ☎ 01671 820377 🖨 01671 820377
e-mail: beatrice.mcneill@btinternet.com
website: www.creetown-caravans.co.uk
Dir: Off A75 into Creetown, turn between clock tower & hotel, then left along Silver Street
★ 🚐 £9.50-£11.50 🚐 £9.50-£11.50 ▲ £9.50-£11.50
Open Mar-Oct Booking advisable Jul & Aug Last arrival 22.30hrs Last departure 14.00hrs
Neat and well-maintained park set in village centre with views across the estuary. In an attractive setting beside the Moneypool Burn on the River Cree. A 3-acre site with 20 touring pitches and 50 statics.
Games room
Leisure: ⚐ ⚫ ⚙ **Facilities:** ➦ ⚐ ⊙ ⚑ ✳ ☾
Services: ⚑ ⚐ ⚑ ⚐ → ⚑ ☷ ⚑ ⚑ ⚑ ⚑ ⚑ ⚑

CROCKETFORD   **Map 11 NX87**

▶ ▶ ▶ ▶ **74% Park of Brandedleys**
(NX830725)
DG2 8RG ☎ 01556 690250
🖨 01556 690681
e-mail: brandedleys@holgates.com
website: www.holgates.com
Dir: In village on A75, from Dumfries towards Stranraer site on left up minor road, entrance 200yds on right
★ 🚐 £12-£19 🚐 £12-£19 ▲ £12-£19

contd.

Park of Brandedleys
Open all year (rs Nov-Mar bar/restaurant open Fri-Sun afternoon) Booking advisable public hols & Jul-Aug Last arrival 22.00hrs Last departure noon
A well-maintained site in an elevated position off the A75, with fine views of Auchenreoch Loch and beyond. This comfortable park offers a wide range of amenities, including a fine new games room and a tastefully-designed bar with adjoining bistro. Well placed for enjoying walking, fishing, sailing and golf. A 24-acre site with 80 touring pitches, 20 hardstandings and 63 statics.
Badminton court & outdoor draughts.
Leisure: ⚑ ⚐ ⚫ ⚫ ⚙ **Facilities:** ➦ ⚐ ⊙ ⚑ ✳ ☾
☾ ☎ ☷ ⚑ ⚐ **Services:** ⚑ ⚐ ⚑ ⚐ ⚑ ⚐ ⚑ ✕ ⚑ ➦ → ⚑
Notes: Guide lines issued on arrival
⚑ ⚑ ⚑ ⚑

DALBEATTIE — Map 11 NX86

▶ ▶ ▶ ▶ 71% **Glenearly Caravan Park**
(NX838628)
DG5 4NE ☎ 01556 611393 🖹 01556 612058
Dir: From Dumfries take A711 towards Dalbeattie. Park entrance is past Edingham Farm on right, 200yds before boundary sign
★ 🚐 £7.50 🚐 £7.50 ▲ £7.50

Open all year Booking advisable Last arrival 19.00hrs Last departure noon
An excellent small park set in open countryside with panoramic views of Long Fell, Maidenpap and Dalbeattie Forest. The park is located in 84 beautiful acres of farmland which visitors are invited to enjoy. A 10-acre site with 39 touring pitches, 4 hardstandings and 57 statics.
Leisure: ◆ ⚠ Facilities: ⋒ ⊙ ⚘ ↦ & ╰ ⋔
Services: 🎦 📧 ⊞ → ∪ ↦ ↲ ♨

ECCLEFECHAN — Map 11 NY17

PREMIER PARK

▶ ▶ ▶ ▶ ▶ 73% **Hoddom Castle Caravan Park** (NY154729)
Hoddom DG11 1AS ☎ 01576 300251
🖹 01576 300757
e-mail: hoddomcastle@aol.com
website: www.hoddomcastle.co.uk
Dir: From M74 junct 19, follow signs to site. From A75 W of Annan take B723 for 5m to signs
★ 🚐 £6-£11 🚐 £6-£11 ▲ £5-£11

Open Etr or Apr-Oct (rs early season cafeteria closed) Booking advisable bank hols & Jul-Aug Last arrival 21.00hrs Last departure 14.00hrs
The peaceful, well-equipped park can be found on the banks of the River Annan, and offers a good mix of grassy and hard pitches, beautifully landscaped and blending into the surroundings.
contd.

There are signed nature trails, maintained by the park's countryside ranger, a 9-hole golf course, trout and salmon fishing, and plenty of activity ideas for children. A 28-acre site with 200 touring pitches, 150 hardstandings and 29 statics.
Nature trails, visitor centre, 9 hole golf course.
Leisure: ⚘ ◆ ⚠ Facilities: ↦ ⋒ ⊙ ⚘ ↦ & ╰ ⋔ ♨ 🎦 ⋔ Services: 🎦 📧 ⊞ ⊘ ⊞ ⊠ ✗ ♨ → ↦ ⊚ ↲ 🖥 📧 📺 🄳

See advertisement on page 257

▶ ▶ ▶ ▶ 68% **Cressfield Caravan Park**
(NY196744)
Park House DG11 3DR ☎ 01576 300702
🖹 01576 300702
Dir: From A74(M) junct 19 take B7076, 0.5m to S of village. 8m N of Gretna Green, 5m S of Lockerbie
★ 🚐 £7-£9 🚐 £7-£9 ▲ £7-£8
Open all year Booking advisable bank hols Last arrival 23.00hrs Last departure 13.00hrs
An open, spacious park with views to the hills, ideal as a stopover or for touring the area. The park is set in beautiful undulating countryside on the edge of the village, and facilities are always immaculately maintained by the friendly owner. There are level hardstandings, and a separate grass area for tents, while a large sports field caters for many activities. A 12-acre site with 99 touring pitches, 20 hardstandings and 54 statics.
Sports enclosure, putting green, boules
Leisure: ⚠ Facilities: ↦ ⋒ ⊙ ⚘ ↦ & ╰ ⋔ Services: 🎦 📧 → ↦ ⊚ ↲

GATEHOUSE OF FLEET — Map 11 NX55

 71% **Auchenlarie Holiday Park** (NX536522)
DG7 2EX ☎ 01557 840251
🖹 01557 840333
Dir: Direct access off A75, 5m W of Gatehouse of Fleet
★ 🚐 £7-£12 🚐 £7-£12 ▲ £7-£12
Open Mar-Oct Booking advisable all year Last arrival 20.00hrs Last departure noon
A well organised family park set on cliffs overlooking Wigtown Bay, with its own sandy beach. The tenting area, in sloping grass surrounded by mature trees, has its own sanitary facilities, while the marked caravan pitches are in paddocks with open views, and enjoy high quality toilets. The leisure centre includes swimming pool, gym, solarium and sports hall. A 5-acre site with 35 touring pitches, 10 hardstandings and 202 statics.
Baby changing facilities
Leisure: ⚘ ◆ ⚠ Facilities: ⋒ ⊙ ⚘ ↦ & ╰ ⋔ ♨ 🎦 Services: 🎦 📧 ⊞ ⊘ ⊞ ✗ ♨ → ↦ ⊚ ↲ 📧 📺 🄳 📺 📧 🄳

▶ ▶ ▶ **70% Anwoth Caravan Site (NX595563)**
DG7 2JU ☎ 01557 814333 & 840251 📠 01557 814333
Dir: From A75 into Gatehouse-of-Fleet, park on right towards Stranraer. Signed from town centre
★ 🚐 £7-£9.50 🚐 £7-£9.50 ▲ £7-£9.50
Open Mar-Oct Booking advisable Jul-Aug Last arrival 20.00hrs Last departure noon
A peaceful sheltered park within easy walking distance of the village, ideally placed for exploring the scenic hills, valleys and coastline. Guests may use the leisure facilities at the sister park, Auchenlarie Holiday Park. A 2-acre site with 28 touring pitches and 44 statics.
Facilities: ➡ 📢 ⊙ 🔍 ☀ ⚡ 🚻 **Services:** 🖵 🖸 🛢 ➜ ▶ 🗲
⊞ 🔁 🔀 📵 ⑤

▶ ▶ ▶ **67% Mossyard Caravan & Camping Park (NX546518)**
Mossyard DG7 2ET ☎ 01557 840226
📠 01557 840226
e-mail: enquiry@mossyard.co.uk
website: www.mossyard.co.uk
Dir: 0.75m off A75 on private tarmaced farm road, 4.5m W of Gatehouse of Fleet
★ 🚐 £10-£11 🚐 £10-£11 ▲ £7-£9
Open Etr/Apr-Oct Booking advisable Spring BH & Jul-Aug
A grassy park with its own beach, located on a working farm, and offering an air of peace and tranquillity. Stunning sea and coastal views from touring pitches, and the tenting field is almost on the beach. A 6.5-acre site with 35 touring pitches and 15 statics.
Facilities: 📢 ⊙ 🔍 ⚡ **Services:** 🖵 🖸 🛢 ⊞ ➜ 🗲 🚻

▶ ▶ ▶ **70% Sandgreen Caravan Park (NX578523)**
DG7 2DU ☎ 01557 814351 📠 01557 814351
e-mail: info@sandgreencaravanpark.co.uk
Dir: Site signed off A75 at Gatehouse of Fleet, situated at end of 3m unclass cul-de-sac to beach
★ 🚐 £7-£8 🚐 £7-£8 ▲ £7-£8
Open Apr-Oct Booking advisable Jul & Aug
A peaceful natural park in secluded unspoilt countryside close to beach, overlooking the picturesque Fleet Bay, and fenced off from other areas. A 40-acre site with 20 touring pitches and 180 statics.
Facilities: 📢 ⚡ 🚻 **Services:** 🖵 🛢 ⊞ ⊞ ➜ ∪ 🗲
Notes: Dogs must be kept on leads

▶ ▶ ▶ **72% Glenluce Caravan & Camping Park (NX201576)**
DG8 0QR ☎ 01581 300412 📠 0870 1371489
e-mail: peter@glenlucecaravan.co.uk
website: www.glenlucecaravan.co.uk
Dir: Off A75 in Glenluce, opp. Inglenook Bistro
★ 🚐 £8-£9.50 🚐 £8-£9.50 ▲ £5.50-£9
Open Mar-Oct Booking advisable Jul-Aug Last arrival 22.00hrs Last departure noon
A neat, well-maintained site situated beside a small river close to the village centre. The large

contd.

camping area is secluded within a walled garden, and a heated swimming pool is the latest attraction at this personally run park. A 5-acre site with 30 touring pitches and 30 statics.
Dish washing facilities
Leisure: 🏊 ⚘ **Facilities:** 📢 ⊙ 🔍 ☀ ⚡ 🚻 🛒 🍴 🐕
Services: 🖵 🖸 🛢 ⊞ ➜ ∪ ▶ 🗲 ⊞ 🔀 📵 ⑤

▶ ▶ ▶ **66% Whitecairn Farm Caravan Park (NX300434)**
DG8 0NZ ☎ 01581 300267 📠 01581 300434
e-mail: enquiries@whitecairncaravans.co.uk
website: www.whitecairncaravans.co.uk
Dir: Turn off A75 at Glenluce. Park signed from main street onto unclassified road to Glassnock Bridge. Park 1.5m N
★ 🚐 £7.50-£9 🚐 £7.50-£9 ▲ £7.50-£9
Open Mar-Oct Booking advisable Last arrival 22.00hrs Last departure 11.00hrs
A well-maintained farmland site, in open countryside with extensive views of Luce Bay. The park is next to the owner's working farm along a quiet country road. A 3-acre site with 10 touring pitches and 40 statics.
Leisure: ⚘ **Facilities:** 📢 ⊙ 🔍 ☀ ⚡ 🍴 🐕
Services: 🖵 🛢 ⊞ ➜ ∪ ▶ 🗲 🚻

▶ ▶ ▶ **70% Glentrool Holiday Park (NX400790)**
Bargrennan DG8 6RN ☎ 01671 840280
📠 01671 840342
e-mail: enquiries@glentroolholidaypark.co.uk
website: www.glentroolholidaypark.co.uk
Dir: Leave Newton Stewart on A714 towards Girvan, right at Bargrennan towards Glentrool. Park on left before village.
★ 🚐 £8-£9 🚐 £8-£9 ▲ £8-£9
Open Mar-Oct Booking advisable Jul-Aug & BH's Last arrival 21.00hrs Last departure noon
A small family-owned park close to the village of Glen Trool and bordered by the Galloway National Park. An ideal base for walking and cycling. A 7.5-acre site with 14 touring pitches, 12 hardstandings and 26 statics.
Trout pond for fly fishing
Leisure: 🎣 ⚘ **Facilities:** 📢 ⊙ 🔍 ☀ ⚡ 🚻
Services: 🖵 🛢 ⊞ ⊞ ➜ ∪ 🗲 ⊞ 🔀 📵 ⑤

▶ ▶ ▶ **65% *Braids Caravan Park (NY313674)***
Annan Rd DG16 5DQ ☎ 01461 337409
📠 01461 337409
website: www.gretnaweddings.com/thebraidshomepage.html
Dir: On B721, 0.5m on right, towards Annan
🚐 🚐 ▲
Open all year Booking advisable Jul-Sep Last arrival 24.00hrs Last departure noon
A well-maintained grassy site in centre of the village just inside Scotland. A good number of hard pitches further enhance this busy and popular park. A 6-acre site with 70 touring pitches and 5 statics.
Leisure: ⚘ **Facilities:** 📢 ⊙ 🔍 ☀ ⚡ 🚻 🛒 🐕
Services: 🖵 🛢 ⊞ ⊞ ➜ ▶ 🗲

▶ ▶ 58% *The Old Toll Bar Caravan Park (NY325670)*
Sark Bridge Rd DG16 5JD ☎ 01461 337439
📄 01461 337439
Open all year Booking advisable Last arrival 23.00hrs
A grassy park on the England/Scotland border beside the River Sark bridge. This is the first house in Scotland, and the park has its own licensed marriage room. A 2.5-acre site with 40 touring pitches and 1 static.
Facilities: ♦ Services: ♦

ISLE OF WHITHORN   Map 11 NX43

▶ ▶ ▶ 58% Burrowhead Holiday Village (NX450345)
DG8 8JB ☎ 01988 500252 📄 01988 500855
Dir: Leave A75 at Newton Stewart on A714, take A746 to Whithorn, then road to Isle of Whithorn. Turn right in village onto single track road
★ 🚐 £6.50-£9 🚐 £6.50-£9 ▲ £6.50-£9
Open Etr-Oct
An extensive holiday park in 100 acres of undulating ground overlooking the waters of Solway Firth and the Isle of Man. The park is geared around the swimming pool and bar complex. A 100-acre site with 100 touring pitches and 400 statics.
Sauna, jacuzzi, swimjet, spa
Leisure: ♦ Facilities: ♦
Services: ♦

KIPPFORD   Map 11 NX85

▶ ▶ ▶ 71% Kippford Holiday Park (NX844564)
DG5 4LF ☎ 01556 620636 📄 01556 620607
e-mail: info@kippfordholidaypark.co.uk
website: www.kippfordholidaypark.co.uk
Dir: From Dalbeattie S on A710, site 3.5m on right, 300yds past junct for Kippford
★ 🚐 £9-£11 🚐 £9-£11 ▲ £7-£11

Open all year (rs Nov-Feb Booking required, no shop) Booking advisable at all times Last departure noon
Part-level, part-sloping grass site surrounded by trees and bushes, set in hilly country adjacent to Urr Water estuary and stony beach. Kippford is a sailing haven with the tidal estuary running into the Solway Firth. An 18-acre site with 45 touring pitches and 119 statics.

contd.

Adventure playground, cycle hire, golf & fishing
Leisure: ♦ Facilities: ♦
Services: ♦

KIRKCUDBRIGHT   Map 11 NX65

▶ ▶ ▶ ▶ 73% Seaward Caravan Park (NX662494)
Dhoon Bay DG6 4TJ ☎ 01557 870267 & 331079
📄 01557 870319
e-mail: aa@seaward-park.co.uk
website: www.gillespie-leisure.co.uk
Dir: 2m SW off B727 Borgue road
★ 🚐 £8.50-£11.60 🚐 £8.50-£11.60 ▲ £8.50-£11.60
Open Mar-Oct (rs Mar-mid May & mid Sep-Oct swimming pool closed) Booking advisable Spring bank hols & Jul-Aug Last arrival 21.30hrs Last departure 11.30hrs
This very attractive elevated site has outstanding views over Kirkcudbright Bay which forms part of the Dee estuary. Access to a sandy cove with rock pools is just across the road. Facilities are well organised and neatly kept, and the park offers a peaceful location. The leisure facilities of the other Gillespie leisure parks are available to guests. An 8-acre site with 26 touring pitches and 30 statics.
TV aerial hook-up, mini-golf, dishwashing facility
Leisure: ♦ Facilities: ♦
Services: ♦

▶ ▶ ▶ 66% Silvercraigs Caravan & Camping Site (NX686508)
Silvercraigs Rd DG6 4BT ☎ 01557 330123 & 01556 503806 📄 01556 503806
Dir: In Kirkcudbright off Silvercraigs Rd, overlooking town. Access via A711, follow signs to site
★ 🚐 £8.45-£10.15 🚐 £8.45-£10.15 ▲ £8.45-£10.15
Open Etr-mid Oct Last departure noon
A well-maintained municipal park in an elevated position with extensive views overlooking the picturesque, unspoilt town and harbour to the countryside beyond. Toilet facilities are of a very good standard, and the town centre is just a short stroll away. A 6-acre site with 50 touring pitches.
Leisure: ♦ Facilities: ♦ Services: ♦
Notes: Dogs must be on leads

KIRKGUNZEON
Map 11 NX86

▶ ▶ ▶ 63% **Mossband Caravan Park** (NX872665)
DG2 8JP ☎ 01387 760208
Dir: Adjacent to A711 to Dalbeattie, 1.5m E of Kirkgunzeon
★ ⊞ £6-£8 ⊞ £6-£8 ▲ £6-£8
Open Etr-Oct Booking advisable mid Jul-mid Aug
Level park on site of old railway station, set in a peaceful rural location. This family-run park has good views of the countryside, and comfortable facilities. A 3-acre site with 25 touring pitches and 12 statics.

Leisure: ◖ /Ⅲ Facilities: ⋒ ⊙
Services: ▯ ⊘ ⊞ → ∪ ▶ ⅃ ⅃

LANGHOLM
Map 11 NY38

▶ ▶ ▶ 64% **Ewes Water Caravan & Camping Park** (NY365855)
Milntown DG13 0DH ☎ 013873 80386 & 80358
▤ 013783 81670
e-mail: jim.balmer@zoom.co.uk
Dir: Directly off A7 approx 0.5m N of Langholm.
★ ⊞ fr £8 ⊞ fr £8 ▲ £5-£7
Open Apr-Sep Booking advisable Last week in July
Last departure noon
On the banks of the River Esk, this is a very attractive park in a sheltered wooded valley close to an unspoilt Borders town. A 2-acre site with 24 touring pitches.
Large play area

Facilities: ⋒ ⊙ ✳ ⅋ ⅃ ⊞ ⊓ ⾕ Services: ▯ ▯ ⊘ ⊞
→ ▶ ⅃ ⅃

LOCHMABEN
Map 11 NY08

▶ ▶ ▶ 69% **Halleaths Caravan Site** (NY098818)
DG11 1NA ☎ 01387 810630 ▤ 01387 810005
Dir: From M74 take A709 to Dumfries. 3m from Lockerbie turn right. Signposted to site
⊞ ⊞ ▲
Open Mar-Nov Booking advisable bank hols & Jul-Aug Last arrival 23.30hrs Last departure noon
An open, gently sloping site with small trees and shrubs and attractive flower beds. A two-acre wood on one side provides an excellent dog walk, and the whole site is bordered by mature trees. Close to the three lochs around this historic little town, and the River Annan. An 8-acre site with 71 touring pitches and 17 statics.
Fishing (charged). Wide range within 1 mile
Leisure: /Ⅲ Facilities: ⋒ ⊙ ⅋ ✳ ⅋ ⅃ ⊓ ⾕
Services: ▯ ▯ ▯ ⊘ ⊞ → ▶ ⅃ ⅃ ⅃ Notes: Dogs must be kept on leads

▶ ▶ 62% **Kirkloch Caravan & Camping Site** (NY082825)
DG11 1PZ ☎ 01556 503806 ▤ 01556 503806
Dir: In Lochmaben access via Kirkloch Brae
★ ⊞ £6.85-£8.20 ⊞ £6.85-£8.20 ▲ £6.85-£8.20
Open Etr-Sep Last departure noon
A grassy lochside site with superb views and well-maintained facilities. Some hard pitches are available at this municipal park, which is adjacent to
contd.

HODDOM CASTLE CARAVAN PARK
10 minutes drive from A74M and A75

QUALITY FACILITIES AVAILABLE ON OR ADJACENT TO HODDOM CASTLE

GOLF Our own nine hole course
FISHING Exclusive beats for quality game and coarse fishing
WALKING Nature trails, foot paths and ranger guided walks
Quad biking, clay pigeon shooting and three 18 hole golf courses all within 10 miles.

ENQUIRIES
THE WARDEN, HODDOM CASTLE, HODDOM, LOCKERBIE DG11 1BE
TEL: 01576 300251
www.hoddomcastle.co.uk
hoddomcastle@aol.com

AA BEST SCOTTISH CAMPSITE 1996/1997

TOP 100 FAMILY PARKS 2000 · Scottish TOURIST BOARD · Best Park in Britain

a golf club, and close to three lochs. A 1.5-acre site with 30 touring pitches.
Leisure: /Ⅲ Facilities: ⋒ ⊙ ⅋ ⅃ Services: ▯ → ▶ ⅃
Notes: Dogs to be kept on lead

LOCHNAW
Map 10 NW96

▶ ▶ ▶ 79% **Drumlochart Caravan Park** (NW997634)
DG9 0RN ☎ 01776 870232 ▤ 01776 870276
e-mail: office@drumlochart.co.uk
website: www.drumlochart.co.uk
Dir: From Stranraer take A718 to Leswalt, then left onto B7043, park 1.5m on right
⊞ ⊞
Open Mar-Oct Booking advisable bank hols & Jul-Aug Last arrival 22.00hrs Last departure noon
A peaceful rural site in hilly woodland, adjacent to Loch Ryan and Luce Bay, offering coarse fishing. This manicured park with sparkling toilet facilities is a credit to the friendly owners. There are many woodland walks to be enjoyed in an Area of Outstanding Natural Beauty, and a heated swimming pool in a sheltered sunny position is very popular. A 9-acre site with 30 touring pitches and 96 statics.
10 acre Loch for coarse fishing & rowing boats.
Leisure: ⅋ ◖ /Ⅲ Facilities: ⋒ ⊙ ⅋ ⅃ ⅃
Services: ▯ ▯ ▯ ▯ → ∪ ▶ ⅃ ⅃ ⊕ ⊠ ⊠ ⊠

LOCKERBIE
See **Ecclefechan**

Scotland

MOFFAT — Map 11 NT00

▶ ▶ ▶ **74% Camping & Caravanning Club Site**
(NT085050)
Hammerlands Farm DG10 9QL ☎ 01683 220436
🖹 024 7669 4886
website: www.campingandcaravanningclub.co.uk
*Dir: Take Moffat sign from A74. After 1m turn right by
the Bank of Scotland, right again in 200yds. Sign for site
on right follow rd round to site*
★ 🚐 £12.30-£15.50 🚐 £12.30-£15.50 ▲ £12.30-£15.50
Open Mar-Oct Booking advisable Spring bank hol &
peak periods Last arrival 21.00hrs Last departure
noon
*Well-maintained level grass touring site, with
extensive views of the surrounding hilly
countryside from many parts of the park. This busy
stopover site is always well maintained, and looks
bright and cheerful thanks to meticulous wardens.
Please see the advertisement on page 10 for details
of Club Members' benefits. A 10-acre site with 180
touring pitches.*

Leisure: ⚐ Facilities: ➖⊙☍❄☌☖
Services: 🖾🖧🛢🖉🚱➡∪►⚡🕮🍴 ▦ 🖾 📶

NEWTON STEWART — Map 10 NX46

▶ ▶ ▶ **64% Creebridge Caravan Park** (NX415656)
Minnigaff DG8 6AJ ☎ 01671 402324 & 402432
🖹 01671 402324
e-mail: johnsharples@btopenworld.co.uk
website: www.creebridgecaravanpark.com
*Dir: 0.25m E of Newton Stewart at Minnigaff on bypass,
signed off A75*
★ 🚐 fr £8 🚐 fr £8 ▲ fr £8
Open Mar-Nov (rs Mar only one toilet block open)
Booking advisable Jul-Aug Last arrival 20.00hrs Last
departure 10.00hrs
*A level urban site a short walk from the town's
amenities. The site is surrounded by mature trees,
and offers good facilities. A 5.5-acre site with 36
touring pitches, 12 hardstandings and 50 statics.
Security street lighting.*

Leisure: ⚐ ⚐ Facilities: ➖⊙☍❄☌☖➖☖
Services: 🖾🖧🛢🖉🚱➡∪►🕮🖾

PALNACKIE — Map 11 NX85

▶ ▶ ▶ **72% Barlochan Caravan Park** (NX819572)
DG7 1PF ☎ 01556 600256 & 870267 🖹 01557 870319
e-mail: aa@barlochan.co.uk
website: www.gillespie-leisure.co.uk
Dir: On A711 N of Palnackie, signed
★ 🚐 £7.75-£10.55 🚐 £7.75-£10.55 ▲ £7.75-£10.55
Open Apr-Oct (rs Apr-mid May & mid Sep-end Oct
swimming pool) Booking advisable Spring bank hol
& Jul-Aug Last arrival 21.30hrs Last departure
11.30hrs
*A small terraced park with quiet landscaped pitches
in a level area backed by rhododendron bushes.
There are spectacular views over the River Urr
estuary, and the park has its own coarse fishing
loch nearby. A 9-acre site with 20 touring pitches
and 40 statics.*
Fishing, pitch & putt, dishwashing facilities.

contd.

Leisure: ⚐ ⚐ ⚐ Facilities: ➖⊙☍❄☌☖➖☖
Services: 🖾🖧🛢🖉🚱➡►🖾

PARTON — Map 11 NX67

▶ ▶ ▶ **67% Loch Ken Holiday Park**
(NX687702)
DG7 3NE ☎ 01644 470282
🖹 01644 470297
e-mail: office@lochkenholidaypark.freeserve.co.uk
website: www.lochkenholidaypark.freeserve.co.uk
Dir: On A713, N of Parton
🚐 🚐 ▲
Open mid Mar-mid Nov (rs Mar/Apr (ex Etr) & late
Sep-Nov restricted shop hours) Booking advisable
Etr, Spring bank hol & Jun-Aug Last arrival 20.00hrs
Last departure noon
*A busy and popular park with a natural water-borne
emphasis, on the eastern shores of Loch Ken, with
superb views. Family owned and run, it is in a
peaceful and beautiful spot opposite the RSPB
reserve, with direct access to the loch for boat
launching. The park offers a variety of water sports,
as well as farm visits and nature trails. A 7-acre site
with 52 touring pitches and 33 statics.*
Bike, boat & canoe hire, fishing on loch.

Leisure: ⚐ Facilities: ➖⊙☍❄☌☖➖☖
Services: 🖾🖧🛢🖉🚱➡⚡🖾

PENPONT — Map 11 NX89

▶ ▶ ▶ **64% Penpont Caravan and Camping Park**
(NX852947)
DG3 4BH ☎ 01848 330470
e-mail: penpoint.caravan.park@ukgateway.net
*Dir: From Thornhill on A702, site on left 0.5m before
Penpont*
★ 🚐 £8.50-£9.50 🚐 £7.50-£9.50 ▲ £7-£9.50
Open Etr or Apr-Oct Booking advisable Jul-Aug Last
arrival 22.00hrs Last departure 14.00hrs
*A slightly sloping site with good facilities, in a rural
area on the edge of the village with extensive views
across the surrounding countryside. The spacious
camping area connects with a sports and recreation
field beside the Scaur Water. A 1.5-acre site with 20
touring pitches and 20 statics.*

Facilities: ➖⊙❄☌☖ Services: 🖾🖧🛢🖉🚱➡►🖾

PORTPATRICK — Map 10 NW95

▶ ▶ ▶ **60% Galloway Point Holiday Park**
(NX005537)
Portree Farm DG9 9AA ☎ 01776 810561
🖹 01776 810561
website: www.gallowaypointholidaypark.co.uk
*Dir: Take A75 W from Dumfries or A77 S from Glasgow.
1st left after 30mph sign on entering Portpatrick. Park is
0.5m on right opposite The Barn Inn*
★ 🚐 £10-£12 🚐 £8-£12 ▲ £7-£10
Open Etr-Oct (rs Apr & Oct Bar & restaurant
restricted to wknds.) Booking advisable Mar & May-
Oct Last arrival 23.00hrs Last departure 14.00hrs
*Strung out along gorse-clad downland, this holiday
park looks out on the North Channel, 1m South of
the unspoilt coastal village. A peaceful spot in
which to relax. An 18-acre site with 100 touring
pitches, 5 hardstandings and 60 statics.*

contd.

Leisure: △ Facilities: ♠ ⊙ ✳ ✆ ☎ ☛ Services: ⚑ ◳ ♀
⬚ ⬚ ⊞ ⊤ ✕ ♨ → ∪ ♪ ⊙ ↯ ♩

▶ ▶ ▶ **63% Sunnymeade Caravan Park (NX005540)**
DG9 8LN ☎ 01776 810293 ▤ 01776 810293
Dir: From A77 onto 1st unclass road on left after 30mph sign. Caravan park 0.25m on left
★ ⚑ £8-£10 ⚑ £8-£10 ▲ fr £8
Open Etr-Oct Booking advisable
Extensive views of the Irish Sea and coast can be enjoyed from this mainly grassy, family-run park. The picturesque village of Portpatrick with its small beach and busy harbour is just one mile away. An 8-acre site with 15 touring pitches, 4 hardstandings and 75 statics.
Private coarse fishing pond on site.
Facilities: ♠ ⊙ ✳ Services: ⚑ ◳ ⬚ → ♪ ♩ ☎

PORT WILLIAM — Map 10 NX34

▶ ▶ ▶ **61% Kings Green Caravan Site (NX340430)**
South St DG8 9SG ☎ 01988 700880
Dir: Direct access from A747 at junct with B7085, towards Whithorn
★ ⚑ £7-£9 ⚑ £7-£9 ▲ fr £5
Open Etr-Oct
Set beside the unspoilt village with all its amenities and the attractive harbour, this level grassy park is community owned and run. Approached via the coast road, the park has views reaching as far as the Isle of Man. A 3-acre site with 30 touring pitches.
Facilities: ♠ ⊙ ♨ ✆ ☛ Services: ⚑ → ♪ ♢ ☎

POWFOOT — Map 11 NY16

▶ ▶ ▶ **61% Queensberry Bay Caravan Park (NY135653)**
DG12 5PU ☎ 01461 700205 ▤ 01461 700205
Dir: From B724 follow signs to Powfoot, through village past golf club, on single track road on shore edge to site in 0.75m
★ ⚑ £8.50-£10 ⚑ £8.50-£10 ▲ £6-£8.50

Open Etr-Oct Booking advisable BH's Last arrival 20.00hrs Last departure noon
A flat, mainly grassy site in a quiet location on the shores of the Solway Firth with views across the estuary to Cumbrian hills. A 17-acre site with 130 touring pitches, 18 hardstandings. Kitchen facilities
Facilities: ♠ ⊙ ✆ ☎ Services: ⚑ ◳ ⬚ ⬚ ⊞ ⊤ → ♪ ♩
See advertisement on page 251

ROCKCLIFFE — Map 11 NX85

▶ ▶ ▶ **56% Castle Point Caravan Park (NX851539)**
DG5 4QL ☎ 01556 630248
e-mail: kce22@dial.pipex.com
Dir: From Dalbeattie take A710. After approx 5m take road to Rockcliffe. On entering village site is signed
★ ⚑ £8.50-£11 ⚑ £8.50-£11 ▲ £8.50-£11

Open Etr-mid Oct (rs Mar-Etr & late Oct limited supervision) Booking advisable Whit wk & Jul-Aug Last arrival 23.00hrs Last departure 11.00hrs
Set in an Area of Outstanding Natural Beauty, this level grass park is adjacent to a rocky shore, and has stunning views across the estuary and the surrounding hilly countryside. The park is noted for its flora and fauna, and has direct access to coastal walks and the attractive sandy beach. A 5-acre site with 22 touring pitches and 33 statics.
Facilities: ♠ ⊙ ♨ ✳ ✆ ☛ Services: ⚑ ◳ ⬚ ⬚ ⊞ → ∪ ♪ ↯ ♩ ☎

SANDHEAD — Map 10 NX04

▶ ▶ ▶ ▶ **71% Sands of Luce Holiday Park (NX103510)**
Sands of Luce D69 9JR ☎ 01776 830456
▤ 01776 830456
e-mail: sandsofluce@aol.com
website: www.sandsofluce.co.uk
Dir: From S & E - left off A75 onto B7084 signed Drummore. Site signed at junct with A716. From N - A77 through Stranraer towards Portpatrick, 2m & follow A716 signed Drummore, site signed in 5m
⚑ £7.50-£11 ⚑ £7.50-£11 ▲ £7.50-£11
Open Mar-Oct Booking advisable Jul-Aug Last arrival 22.00hrs Last departure noon
A friendly site on the grassy banks on the edge of a beautiful sandy beach, with lovely views across Luce Bay. Facilities are well-maintained and clean, and the area around the park is protected by the Nature Conservancy Council. A 17.5-acre site with 50 touring pitches and 40 statics.
Boat launching.
Leisure: ◣ △ Facilities: ♠ ⊙ ♨ ✳ ✆ ☎
Services: ⚑ ◳ ⬚ ⬚ ⊞ → ♩ ⊟ ⬚

SANDYHILLS — Map 11 NX85

▶ ▶ ▶ **73% Sandyhills Bay Leisure Park (NX892552)**
DG5 4NY ☎ 01557 870267 & 01387 780257
▤ 01557 870319
e-mail: aa@sandyhills-bay.co.uk
website: www.gillespie-leisure.co.uk

contd.

Dir: On A710 coast road, 7m from Dalbeattie, 6.5m from Kirkbean
★ ⚏ £7.75-£11.30 ⚏ £7.75-£11.30 ▲ £7.75-£11.30
Open Apr-Oct Booking advisable Spring bank hol & Jun-Aug Last arrival 21.30hrs Last departure 11.30hrs
A well-maintained park in a superb location beside a blue-flag beach, and close to many attractive villages. The flat, grassy site offers access to south-facing Sandyhills Bay and beach, and is sheltered by woods and hills. A 6-acre site with 26 touring pitches and 34 statics.
Leisure: ⚏ Facilities: ⚏⊙⚏※⚏⚏⚏⚏
Services: ⚏⚏⚏⚏⚏⚏⚏⚏⚏⚏⚏

SHAWHEAD   Map 11 NX87

▶ ▶ ▶ 67% **Barnsoul Farm** (NX876778)
DG2 9SQ ☎ 01387 730249 ▤ 01387 730249
e-mail: barnsouldg@aol.com
website: www.barnsoulfarm.co.uk
Dir: Leave A75 between Dumfries & Crocketford at site sign onto unclass road signed Shawhead at T-junct. Turn right & immediate left. Site 1m on left, follow Barnsoul signs
★ ⚏ £7-£10 ⚏ £7-£10 ▲ £7-£10

Open Apr-Oct (rs Mar & Nov Chalets & bothies only) Booking advisable Jul & Aug Last arrival anytime Last departure noon
A very spacious, peaceful and scenic farm site with views across open countryside in all directions. Set in 250 acres of woodland, parkland and farmland, and an ideal centre for touring the surrounding unspoilt countryside. A 10-acre site with 30 touring pitches, 5 hardstandings and 6 statics.
Leisure: ⚏ Facilities: ⚏⊙⚏※⚏⚏⚏
Services: ⚏⚏⚏→⚏⚏⚏

SOUTHERNESS   Map 11 NX95

 68% **Southerness Holiday Village** (NX976545)
DG2 8AZ ☎ 01387 880256 & 880281
▤ 01387 880429
Dir: From S take A75 from Gretna to Dumfries. From N take A74, exit at A701 to Dumfries. Take A710 coast road. Approx 16m, site easily seen
★ ⚏ £10-£15 ⚏ £10-£15
Open Mar-Oct Booking advisable Jul-Aug & BH's Last arrival 22.00hrs Last dep 16.00hrs
contd.

A continually improving holiday centre with the emphasis on family entertainment. On-site facilities include all-weather pitches, a supermarket, large laundry and a leisure centre. A sandy beach on the Solway Firth is close by. An 8-acre site with 90 touring pitches, 59 hardstandings and 350 statics. Amusement centre, disco, videos & kids' club
Leisure: ⚏ ⚏ ⚏ Facilities: ⚏⊙※⚏⚏⚏⚏
Services: ⚏⚏⚏⚏⚏⚏⚏✕⚏→⚏◎⚏
⚏⚏⚏⚏⚏⚏

STRANRAER   Map 10 NX06

▶ ▶ ▶ ▶ 71% **Aird Donald Caravan Park** (NX075605)
London Rd DG9 8RN ☎ 01776 702025
e-mail: aird@mimmanu-net.com
website: www.aird-donald.co.uk
Dir: Turn left off A75 on entering Stranraer, (signed). Opposite school, site 300yds
★ ⚏ £9-£9.50 ⚏ £9-£9.50 ▲ £4.50-£8.70
Open all year Booking advisable Last departure 16.00hrs
A spacious touring site, mainly grass but with tarmac hard standing area, with pitches large enough to accommodate a car and caravan overnight without unhitching. On the fringe of town screened by mature shrubs and trees. Ideal stopover en route to Northern Irish ferry ports. A 12-acre site with 100 touring pitches.
Leisure: ⚏ Facilities: ⚏⊙⚏※⚏⚏⚏
Services: ⚏⚏⚏⚏→⚏⚏✕⚏⚏⚏⚏

EAST LOTHIAN

DUNBAR   Map 12 NT67
PREMIER PARK

▶ ▶ ▶ ▶ ▶ 76% **Thurston Manor Holiday Home Park** (NT712745)
Innerwick EH42 1SA ☎ 01368 840643 & 840688 ▤ 01368 840261
e-mail: mail@thurstonmanor.co.uk
website: www.thurstonmanor.co.uk
Dir: 4m S of Dunbar, signposted off A1
★ ⚏ £10-£16 ⚏ £10-£16 ▲ £8-£16
Open Mar-8 Jan (rs 1-23 Dec wknds only) Booking advisable Etr, bank hols & high season Last arrival 21.00hrs Last departure noon
A pleasant park set in 250 acres of unspoilt countryside. The touring and static areas of this large park are in separate areas. The main touring area occupies an open, level position, and the toilet facilities are modern and exceptionally well maintained. The park boasts a well-stocked fishing loch, a heated indoor swimming pool, steam room, sauna, jacuzzi, mini-gym and fitness room and seasonal entertainment. A 250-acre site with 100 touring pitches, 18 hardstandings and 400 statics.
contd.

Private lake, pony trekking, fitness room, sauna/steam
Leisure: ⚛ ♠ ⋀ ☐ Facilities: �ↄⓞ☜✳⛱⚘⚐♨
⛺ Services: ▯ⓖ☎ⓘ⌀☐Ⓣ✕⚒⚐→∪↺
⊞▥▨▧⊡

► ► ► 62% **Camping & Caravanning Club Site** (NT723773)
Barns Ness EH42 1QP ☎ 01368 863536
Website: www.campingandcaravanningclub.co.uk
Dir: On A1, 6m S of Dunbar (near power station). Sign for Barns Ness & Skateraw 1m down road. Turn right at site sign towards lighthouse
⛺ ⚐ £10.20-£12.90 ⚐ £10.20-£12.90 ▲ £10.20-£12.90
Open 21 Mar-28 Oct Booking advisable bank hols & high season Last arrival 21.00hrs Last departure noon
A grassy, landscaped site close to the foreshore and lighthouse on a coastline noted for its natural and geological history. Please see the advertisement on page 10 for details of Club Members' benefits. A 10-acre site with 82 touring pitches.
Leisure: ⋀ Facilities: ⓞ☜✳⛱⚘⛺
Services: ▯ⓖ☎⌀☐→∪▶⚒⚐↺ ⊞▥▨▧⊡

LONGNIDDRY   Map 12 NT47

 67% *Seton Sands Holiday Village* (NT420759)
EH32 0QF ☎ 01875 813333 & 0345 508508 ▤ 01875 813531
⚐⚐
Dir: Take A1 to Tranent slip road, then B6371 to Cockenzie & right onto B1348. Park 1m on left
Open Mar-Oct Booking advisable Last arrival 23.00hrs Last departure noon
A large, mainly static park, with reasonable touring facilities on a grassy paddock near the road. A 1.75-acre site with 60 touring pitches and 120 statics.
Leisure: ⚛ ⚒ ♠ ⋀ Facilities: ⓞ☜⛱⚘⊞⛺
Services: ▯ⓖ☎⌀☐Ⓣ✕⚒→∪▶◉⚒⚐ ⊞▥▨▧⊡

MUSSELBURGH   Map 11 NT37

► ► ► ► 73% **Drum Mohr Caravan Park** (NT373734)
Levenhall EH21 8JS ☎ 0131 665 6867 ▤ 0131 653 6859
e-mail: bookings@drummohr.org
website: www.drummohr.org
Dir: Leave A1 at junct with A199 towards Musselburgh, at rdbt turn right onto B1361 signed Prestonpans, take 1st left & site 400yds
⚐ fr £9 ⚐ fr £9 ▲ fr £9
Open Mar-Oct Booking advisable Jul-Aug Last arrival 22.00hrs Last departure noon
This attractive park is sheltered by mature trees on all sides, and carefully landscaped within. The park is divided into separate areas by mature hedging and planting of trees and ornamental shrubs. Pitches are generous in size, and there are a *contd.*

Drum Mohr Caravan Park

number of fully serviced pitches with water, waste, electricity and hardstanding. The first-class amenities are immaculately clean and maintained to a very high standard. A 9-acre site with 120 touring pitches and 5 statics.
Leisure: ⋀ Facilities: ⓞ☜✳⛱⚘⛺
Services: ▯ⓖ☎⌀☐Ⓣ→▶⚒⊞▥▨▧⊡
See advertisement on page 250

NORTH BERWICK   Map 12 NT58

► ► ► ► 70% **Tantallon Caravan Park** (NT570850)
Dunbar Rd EH39 5NJ ☎ 01620 893348 ▤ 01620 895623
Dir: Off A198 Dunbar road
⛺ ⚐ £10-£12 ⚐ £10-£12 ▲ £10-£12
Open Mar-Oct Booking advisable Jul-Aug Last arrival 20.00hrs Last departure noon
A large and well-serviced grassland site with *contd.*

Leisure: ⚛ Indoor swimming pool ⚒ Outdoor swimming pool ⚘ Tennis court ♠ Games room ⋀ Children's playground ∪ Stables ▶ 9/18 hole golf course ⚒ Boats for hire ⚒ Cinema ⚐ Fishing ◉ Mini golf ⚠ Watersports ☐ Separate TV room

outstanding views across the water to the coast of Fife. The site is convenient for the town and Edinburgh, with direct access to the beach and many local attractions. A 10-acre site with 147 touring pitches and 60 statics.

Leisure: ◆ 瓜 ☐ **Facilities:** ⋔ ⊙ ⦿ ☀ ᚠ & ⌫ ᛒ ⍟
Services: ☐ ᛋ ⧫ ⌀ ⊞ → ∪ ⍟ ⊙ ⌀ ☻ ⧟ ⧟ ⍟ 𝄞

FIFE

► ► ► **62% Shell Bay Caravan Park (NO465005)**
Kincraig Hill KY9 1HB ☎ 01333 330283 & 330334
📠 01333 330008
Dir: 1.5m NW of Elie off A917, signed off unclass road
☞ ☞ Å
Open 21 Mar-Oct Booking advisable Jul-Aug Last arrival 21.00hrs Last departure noon
A large holiday site set amidst sand dunes in a quiet bay with rocks and sand on the Fife Coastal Footpath. The touring section is separate from a large static area, and facilities are very well kept. A 5-acre site with 120 touring pitches and 250 statics. Children's club
Leisure: ◆ 瓜 ☐ **Facilities:** ⋔ ⊙ ⦿ ☀ ᚠ & ⌫ ᛒ ⌸ ⍾
Services: ☐ ⧫ ⎍ ⌀ ⊞ ✕ ᚤ → ∪ ⍟ ⊙ ⌀ ⅄ ⌀ ☻ ⧟ 𝄞

► ► ► **70% Woodland Gardens Caravan & Camping Site (NO418031)**
Blindwell Rd KY8 5QG ☎ 01333 360319
e-mail: woodlandgardens@lineone.net
website: www.woodland-gardens.co.uk
Dir: Off A915 coast road at Largo. At E end of Lundin Links, turn N off A915, 0.5m signed
★ ☞ £8-£10 ☞ £8-£10 Å £8-£10
Open Apr-Oct Booking advisable Jul-Aug Last arrival 22.00hrs Last departure noon
A secluded and sheltered 'little jewel' of a site in a small orchard under the hill called Largo Law. This very attractive site is family owned and run to an immaculate standard, and pitches are grouped in twos and threes by low hedging and gorse. A 1-acre site with 20 touring pitches and 5 statics.
Leisure: ◆ ☐ **Facilities:** ⋔ ⊙ ⦿ ☀ ᚠ ⌫ ᛒ ⌸ ⍾
Services: ☐ ⧫ ⌀ ⊞ → ∪ ⍟ ⌀ **Notes:** Over 14yrs only

PREMIER PARK

► ► ► ► ► **78% Craigtoun Meadows Holiday Park (NO482150)**
Mount Melville KY16 8PQ ☎ 01334 475959
📠 01334 476424 e-mail: craigtoun@aol.com
website: www.craigtounmeadows.co.uk
Dir: From M90 junct 8 onto A91 to St Andrews.Then via Argyle St & Hepburn Grdns, bearing left at fork
☞ £14.50-£22 ☞ £14.50-£22 Å £14.50-£22
Open Mar-Oct (rs Mar-Etr & Sep-Oct shops and restaurant open shorter hrs) Booking advisable BH's & Jun-Aug

contd.

Craigtoun Meadows Holiday Park
An attractive site set unobtrusively in mature woodlands, with large fully-serviced pitches in hedged paddocks. Some patio pitches have a summerhouse containing picnic tables and chairs. The modern toilet block provides cubicled en suite facilities as well as spacious showers, baths, disabled facilities and baby changing areas. A licensed restaurant and coffee shop are popular, and there is a takeaway, a launderette and shop, and indoor and outdoor games areas. Located near the sea and sandy beaches. Winner of Best Scottish Campsite for 2002. A 32-acre site with 70 touring pitches, 66 hardstandings and 157 statics.
Leisure: ⦿ ◆ 瓜 **Facilities:** ➔ ⋔ ⊙ ⦿ ☀ ᚠ & ⌫ ᛒ ⌸ ⍾
Services: ☐ ᛋ ⧫ ⌀ ⊞ ⊤ ✕ ᚤ → ∪ ⍟ ᛒ ⌀
Notes: No groups under 18yrs ☻ ⧟ ⧟ 𝄞

▶ ▶ ▶ **57%** *Kinkell Braes Caravan Site*
(NO522156)
KY16 8PX ☎ 01334 474250 ▤ 01334 474583
Dir: On A917 1m S of St Andrews
🚐 🚃
Open 21 Mar-30 Oct Booking advisable Jun-Aug
Last arrival 22.00hrs Last departure noon no cars by
tents
*A mainly static park with two areas for tourers, each
with its own toilet block and use of the site laundry
and entertainment facilities. All pitches have good
sea views, looking out over St Andrews and the
Eden Estuary. A 45-acre site with 100 touring
pitches and 392 statics.*
Leisure: ◀ ⋀ ▢ **Facilities:** ♜ ⊙ ⟋ ↻ ⟋ 🏬 ⋒ **Services:**
🖳 🗇 🝙 ✗ 🖦 → ▶ ⤙ ⛺ ⟍ **Notes:** No ball games/kite
flying, no cars by tents, dogs on leads at all times.
🖭 🚍 🗘

ST MONANS   **Map 12 NO50**

▶ ▶ ▶ **58%** *St Monans Caravan Park (NO529019)*
KY10 2DN ☎ 01333 730778 & 310185
▤ 01333 730466
Dir: On A917, 100yds E of St Monans
🚐 🚃 𝗔
Open 21 Mar-Oct Booking advisable Jul-Aug Last
arrival 22.00hrs Last departure noon
*A very pleasant small touring base, part of a larger
static site but with its own well-kept toilet facilities.
On the edge of a coastal village, and next to the
public park. A 1-acre site with 18 touring pitches
and 112 statics.*
Leisure: ⋀ **Facilities:** ♜ ⊙ ↻ 🏬 🖵 🛒 ⅄
Services: 🖳 🗇 → ∪ ▶ 𝗔 ⤙ ⛺ ⟍

HIGHLAND

APPLECROSS   **Map 13 NG74**

▶ ▶ ▶ **56%** *Applecross Campsite (NG714443)*
IV54 8ND ☎ 01520 744268 & 744284
▤ 01520 744268
Dir: Follow unclass road off A896, 300yds from village
🚐 🚃 𝗔

Open Etr-Oct (rs Apr, May, Sep & Oct only 1 toilet
block open) Last arrival 22.00hrs

contd.

---

*A quiet site in a lovely remote area close to
mountains, moorland and beach. This park has the
benefit of a cafe approached through a flower
tunnel. Caravans should approach via Shieldaig.
A 6-acre site with 60 touring pitches and 4 statics.
Bakery.*
Facilities: ♜ ⊙ ⟋ 🏬 **Services:** 🖳 🝙 ⟋ 🖥 ✗ → ⟍ 🚍

ARISAIG   **Map 13 NM68**

▶ ▶ ▶ ▶ **70%** **Camusdarach Campsite**
(NM664916)
Camusdarach PH39 4NT ☎ 01687 450221
▤ 01687 450221
e-mail: camdarach@aol.com
website: www.road-to-the-isles.org.uk/camusdarach
Dir: On A830, 4m N of Arisaig. Signed from road
★ 🚐 fr £10 🚃 fr £10 𝗔 fr £7

Open 15 Mar-15 Oct Booking advisable Jul-Aug
Last arrival 22.00hrs Last departure 18.00hrs
*A very attractive, quiet and secluded park with
direct access to a silver beach. The striking scenery
and coastal setting are part of the appeal here, and
there is a superbly designed and equipped toilet
block. The site is 4m from the Arisaig ferry, and
6m from the Mallaig ferry to the Isle of Skye.
A 2.75-acre site with 42 touring pitches.*
Facilities: ♜ ⊙ ⟋ ⟋ 🏬 ↻
Services: 🖳 🝙 🖥 → ▶ ⤙ ⟋ 🏬 🖭 🚍 🞍 🗘

▶ ▶ ▶ **64%** **Gorten Sands Caravan Site**
(NM640879)
Gorten Farm PH39 4NS ☎ 01687 450283
Dir: A830 to Point, 2m W of Asisaig. Turn left at sign
'Back of Keppoch'. Continue 0.75m to road across
cattle grid
★ 🚐 fr £11 🚃 £9-£11 𝗔 £8-£11.50
Open Etr-Sep Booking advisable Jul-Aug Last
arrival 23.00hrs Last departure 13.00hrs
*A well-run site with mainly modern facilities,
carefully maintained and peacefully located off the
beaten track. The site has direct access to the beach
and sands, with good views of Skye and islands.
A 6-acre site with 45 touring pitches.*
Facilities: ♜ ⊙ ⟋ ⟋ ↻ 🏬 ⅄
Services: 🖳 🗇 🝙 ⟋ 🖥 → ▶ ⟋ 🏬

Facilities: 🛁 Bath ♜ Shower ⊙ Electric Shaver ⟋ Hairdryer ✳ Ice Pack Facility ⅃ Disabled Facilities ↻ Public Telephone
🏬 Shop on Site or within 200yds 🖵 Mobile Shop (calls at least 5 days a week) 🍴 BBQ Area ⛱ Picnic Area ⅄ Dog Exercise Area

DALRADDY HOLIDAY PARK ▶▶▶
Aviemore, Inverness-shire

Quiet family park in 25 acres of woodland with views of the Cairngorm Mountains, within walking distance of the River Spey. Tents, touring caravans and motor homes welcome, static caravans and log chalets for hire. Licensed craft/farm shop, launderette and play park. Nearby activities include fishing, pony trekking, walking, skiing, quad bike treks. Dogs welcome – short breaks available.

For more information, phone (01479) 810330.
E-mail: dhp@alvie-estate.co.uk
Fax: (01479) 810330

▶ ▶ ▶ **58% Portnadoran Caravan Site (NM651892)**
Bunacaimbe PH39 4NT ☎ 01687 450267
🖹 01687 450267
e-mail: at-macdonald@portnadoran.freeserve.co.uk
Dir: A830 Fort William to Mallaig road, 2m N of Arisaig
🚐 🚐 Å
Open Apr-Oct Booking advisable Jul-Aug Last arrival 23.00hrs Last departure noon
Small, level, grassy site situated close to sandy beach overlooking the Islands of Eigg, Rhum and Skye. Very welcoming. A 2-acre site with 55 touring pitches and 9 statics.
Leisure: ⚠ **Facilities:** ⬧⊙✳🔌🖭🛒🛉
Services: 🖾🗓🗄→▶🍴🔧🛅

AVIEMORE — Map 14 NH81

▶ ▶ ▶ **62% Dalraddy Holiday Park (NH859083)**
PH22 1QB ☎ 01479 810330 🖹 01479 810330
e-mail: dhp@alvie-estates.co.uk
website: www.alvie-estate.co.uk
Dir: 3.5m S of Aviemore. From A9, take Aviemore turn. Turn right onto B9152 towards Kincraig. Park 3m
★ 🚐 £7.50-£9.50 🚐 £7.50-£9.50 Å £3.50-£5.50
Open all year Booking advisable Jul-Aug Last arrival 20.00hrs Last departure noon
A secluded site set amidst heather and young birch trees, with views of The Cairngorms. Staff are very welcoming and helpful, and maintenance work is ongoing. A 25-acre site with 23 touring pitches and 99 statics.
Quad bikes
contd.

Dalraddy Holiday Park

Leisure: ⚠ **Facilities:** ⬧⊙✳🔌⛱🛒🛉🖭🛉
Services: 🖾🗓🗄→🔌🛅🔧✂🍴 **Notes:** Late arrivals should contact office before arriving so arrangements can be made 🖾🚾🚰🔋

BALMACARA — Map 14 NG82

▶ ▶ ▶ **67% Reraig Caravan Site (NG815272)**
IV40 8DH ☎ 01599 566215
website: www.reraig.com
Dir: On A87 3.5m E of Kyle, 2m W of junct with A890
★ 🚐 £8.30 🚐 £8.30 Å £8.30
Open mid Apr-Sep Booking advisable Last arrival 22.00hrs Last departure noon
Set on level, grassy ground surrounded by trees, the site is located on the saltwater Sound of Sleet, and looks south towards Loch Alsh and Skye. Very nicely organised with a high standard of maintenance, and handy for the bridge crossing to the Isle of Skye. A 2-acre site with 45 touring pitches, 12 hardstandings.
Dishwashing sinks
Facilities: ⬧⊙🔌🛒 **Services:** 🖾🗓
Notes: Restrictions on awnings, no large or trailer tents 🖾🚾🚰

BOAT OF GARTEN — Map 14 NH91

▶ ▶ ▶ **66% Campgrounds of Scotland (NH939191)**
PH24 3BN ☎ 01479 831652 & 831450
e-mail: briangillies@totalise.co.uk
website: www.campgroundsofscotland.com
Dir: Off A95
★ 🚐 £10.50-£12.50 🚐 £10.50-£12.50 Å £8.50-£10.50

Open all year Booking advisable 26 Dec-2 Jan & 25 Jul-7 Aug Last arrival 22.00hrs Last dep 11.00hrs
A very attractive site in a beautiful location with outstanding views. Young trees and bushes
contd.

Services: 🅣 Toilet Fluid ✕ Café/ Restaurant 🏪 Fast Food/Takeaway 🍼 Baby Care 🔌 Electric Hook Up
🖸 Launderette 🍷 Licensed Bar 🛢 Calor Gaz ⊘ Camping Gaz 🔋 Battery Charging

enhance the park, which is set in mountainous woodland near the River Spey and Loch Garten. A 3.5-acre site with 37 touring pitches, 20 hardstandings and 60 statics.

Leisure: /◭ Facilities: ⛺⊙❑⚡✳❤⚠☕

Services: ♨⊜⌷❦⌂⊞Ⓣ✗→▶♪

CANNICH   Map 14 NH33

▶ ▶ ▶ 60% **Cannich Caravan and Camping Park** (NH345317)

IV4 7LN ☎ 01456 415364 📠 01456 415364

e-mail: enquiries@highlandcamping.co.uk

website: www.highlandcamping.co.uk

Dir: On A831, 200yds SE of Cannich Bridge

★ ⊞ £5.50-£9 ⊞ £5.50-£9 ▲ £4.50-£8.50

Open Mar-Oct (rs Dec-Feb Winter opening by arrangement) Booking advisable Jul & Aug Last arrival 23.00hrs Last departure noon

Quietly situated in Strath Glass, close to the River Glass and Cannich village. This family-run park has attractive mountain views, and is set in ideal walking and naturalist country. A 6-acre site with 43 touring pitches and 7 statics. Mountain bike hire

Leisure: ◣ /◭ ❑ Facilities: ⛺⊙❑✳❤☕⊞

Services: ♨⊜⌷⊞Ⓣ↩→✦♪☕

Notes: Dogs must be kept on leads ⊛ ▦ ▧ 🅖

CORPACH   Map 14 NN07

PREMIER PARK

▶ ▶ ▶ ▶ ▶ 73% **Linnhe Lochside Holidays** (NN074771)

PH33 7NL ☎ 01397 772376

📠 01397 772007

e-mail: holidays@linnhe.demon.co.uk

website: www.linnhe-lochside-holidays.co.uk

Dir: On A830, 1m W of Corpach, 5m from Fort William

⊞ £12.50-£15.50 ⊞ £12.50-£15.50 ▲ £9.50-£11.50

Open Etr-Oct (rs 15 Dec-Etr shop & main toilet block closed) Booking advisable school hols & peak periods Last arrival 21.00hrs Last dep 11.00hrs

An excellently maintained site in a beautiful setting on the shores of Loch Eil, with Ben Nevis to the east and the mountains and Sunart to the west. The owners have worked in harmony with nature to produce an idyllic environment, where they offer the highest standards of design and maintenance. A 5.5-acre site with 85 touring

contd.

Linnhe Lochside Holidays

pitches, 85 hardstandings and 100 statics. Launching slipway, free fishing.

Leisure: /◭ Facilities: ↩⛺⊙❑✳❤☕⚠⊞☕

Services: ♨⊜⌷⊘⊞Ⓣ→▶◉♪

Notes: No cars by tents ⊛ ▦ ▧ 🅖

See advertisement on page 266

DAVIOT   Map 14 NH73

▶ ▶ ▶ 56% **Auchnahillin Caravan & Camping Centre** (NH742386)

IV2 5XQ ☎ 01463 772286 📠 01463 772282

e-mail: info@auchnahillin.co.uk

website: www.auchnahillin.co.uk

Dir: 4m S of Inverness off A9 on B9154

★ ⊞ £8.20-£10.20 ⊞ £8.20-£10.20 ▲ £7.40-£9.40

Open Etr-Oct Booking advisable Jun-Aug Last arrival 22.00hrs Last departure noon

contd.

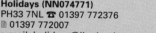

eisure: ↻ Indoor swimming pool   ↺ Outdoor swimming pool   ⚲ Tennis court   ◣ Games room   /◭ Children's playground   ∪ Stables   ▶ 9/18 hole golf course   ↲ Boats for hire   ◉◉ Cinema   ♪ Fishing   ◉ Mini golf   ⬥ Watersports   ⬚ Separate TV room

Tel:
01397
772376

Fax:
01397
772007

Corpach, Fort William, Highlands PH33 7NL
www.linnhe-lochside-holidays.co.uk holidays@linnhe.demon.co.uk

"1999 Best park in Scotland" Award
Almost a botanical garden, Linnhe is recognised as one of the best and most beautiful lochside parks in Britain. Magnificent scenery, wonderful views, peace and tranquility. Hard standings & hook-ups to all pitches. Superb amenities, launderette, private beach and free fishing. Holiday caravans and luxury pine chalets for hire. Pets accepted. Colour brochure sent with pleasure.

Surrounded by hills and forests, this level, grassy site offers clean and spacious facilities. The owner lives in a bungalow on the site. A 10-acre site with 65 touring pitches, 4 hardstandings and 35 statics. Limited facilities for disabled
Leisure: ⅄ Facilities: ⬧☉⬧✳⬧⬧⬧⬧
Services: ⬧⬧⬧⬧⬧⬧⬧⬧✕→∪⬧⬧⬧⬧

DINGWALL — Map 14 NH55

▶ ▶ ▶ ▶ **67% Camping & Caravanning Club Site (NH555588)**
Jubilee Park Rd IV15 9QZ ☎ 01349 862236
🖳 024 7669 4886
website: www.campingandcaravanningclub.co.uk
Dir: Follow A862 to Dingwall, turn right down Hill St, past filling station. Right into High St, 1st left after railway bridge. Site ahead
★ ⬧ £12.30-£15.50 ⬧ £12.30-£15.50 ▲ £12.30-£15.50
Open Mar-Oct Booking advisable bank hols & Jul-Aug Last arrival 21.00hrs Last departure noon
A quiet park with attractive landscaping and very good facilities maintained to a high standard. A convenient touring centre close to the historic market town of Dingwall. Please see the advertisement on page 10 for details of Club Members' benefits. A 6.5-acre site with 85 touring pitches.
Facilities: ⬧☉⬧✳⬧⬧⬧
Services: ⬧⬧⬧⬧⬧⬧⬧→∪▶⬧⬧⬧⬧⬧⬧⬧

DORNOCH — Map 14 NH78

 68% Grannie's Heilan Hame Holiday Park (NH818924)
Embo IV25 3QD ☎ 01862 810383 & 810753 🖳 01862 810368
e-mail: enquiries@parkdean.com
website: www.parkdean.com
Dir: A949 to Dornoch, turn left in square & follow signs for Embo
★ ⬧ £6-£16.50 ⬧ £6-£16.50 ▲ £6-£16.50
Open Mar-Oct Booking advisable Jul-Aug & BH's Last arrival 23.30hrs Last departure 10.00hrs
A holiday centre with a wide range of leisure facilities, including indoor swimming pool with sauna and solarium, separate play areas for under and over fives, putting green, tennis courts and very much more. The sanitary facilities are clean and well maintained, and the park is set on the beach yet handy for the Highlands. A 60-acre site with 300 touring pitches and 148 statics.
Spa bath, sauna, solarium & mini ten-pin bowling.
Leisure: ⬧⬧⬧⅄ Facilities: ⬧☉⬧✳⬧⬧⬧
Services: ⬧⬧⬧⬧⬧⬧⬧✕⬧→▶☉⬧ Notes: No single sex groups under 25yrs ⬧⬧⬧⬧⬧

▶ ▶ ▶ ▶ **64% Pitgrudy Caravan Park (NH795911)**
Poles Rd IV25 3HY ☎ 01862 821253
Dir: On B9168, between A9 and A949
Open May-Sep
An immaculate park in a lovely environment. Many of the pitches are fully serviced, and all have their own water supplies. This very quiet park is close to the historic town of Dornoch in rural surroundings, and convenient for beaches, mountains and lochs. A 3.5-acre site with 50 touring pitches and 38 statics.
Facilities: ⬧☉⬧⬧⬧⅄⬧ Services: ⬧⬧

FORT WILLIAM — Map 14 NN17
See also **Corpach**

▶ ▶ ▶ ▶ **74% Glen Nevis Caravan & Camping Park (NN124722)**
Glen Nevis PH33 6SX
☎ 01397 702191 & 705181
🖳 01397 703904
e-mail: holidays@glen-nevis.co.uk
website: www.glen-nevis.co.uk
Dir: Follow A82 to mini-rdbt on northern outskirts of Fort William. Exit for Glen Nevis. Site 2.5m on right
★ ⬧ £8-£11.50 ⬧ £8-£11.50 ▲ £7.50-£11.50
Open 15 Mar-Oct (rs Mar & mid-end Oct limited shop & restaurant facilities) Booking advisable Jul-Aug Last arrival 22.00hrs Last departure noon
A tasteful site with well-screened enclosures, at the foot of Ben Nevis in the midst of some of the Highlands' most spectacular scenery; an ideal area for walking and touring. The park boasts a restaurant which offers a high standard of cooking

contd

Scotland

Glen Nevis Caravan & Camping Park
*and provides good value for money. A 30-acre site
with 380 touring pitches, 150 hardstandings and 30
statics.*

Leisure: ⚑ **Facilities:** 🛉 ⊙ 🔍 ✻ ♿ ✆ 🛒 🍖 🌲 🐕
Services: 🔧 📶 🛡 🖉 🎲 🖳 ✗ 🚽 → 🏪 🍴 🎵 **Notes:** Closed to
vehicle entry 11pm. Quiet 11pm-8am 📧 💳 🏧 🔲

GAIRLOCH   Map 14 NG87

**▶ ▶ ▶ 66% Gairloch Caravan & Camping Park
(NG798773)**
Strath IV21 2BX ☎ 01445 712373
e-mail: info@gairlochcaravanpark.com
website: www.gairlochcaravanpark.com
Dir: From A832 take B8021 signed Melvaig, towards
Strath. After 0.5m turn right, just after Millcroft Hotel.
Immediately turn, right again
★ 🚐 £8-£10 🚐 £8-£10 ▲ £7-£9
Open Etr-Oct Booking advisable Last arrival
21.30hrs Last departure noon
*A clean, well-maintained site on flat coastal
grassland close to Loch Gairloch. A 6-acre site with
70 touring pitches, 1 hardstanding and 8 statics.
Adjacent cafe, restaurant, activity centre & bar.*
Facilities: 🛉 ⊙ 🔍 ✻ ✆ 🛒 **Services:** 🔧 📶 🛡 🎲 🖳
→ ∪ 🏪 🍴 🎵 **Notes:** Dogs must be kept on
leads at all times 📧 💳

▶ ▶ ▶ 65% Sands Holiday Centre (NG758784)
IV21 2DL ☎ 01445 712152 📠 01445 712518
e-mail: litsands@aol.co.uk
website: www.highlandcaravancamping.co.uk
Dir: 3m W of Gairloch on B8021
★ 🚐 £9.80 🚐 £9.30 ▲ £9.80
Open 20 May-10 Sep (rs Apr 1-19 May & 11 Sep-mid
Oct shop & some toilets closed) Booking advisable
Jul-Aug Last arrival 22.00hrs Last departure noon
*Close to a sandy beach with a panoramic outlook
towards Skye, a well-maintained park with very
good facilities. A large laundry and refitted toilets
make this an ideal family site. A 51-acre site with
360 touring pitches and 20 statics.
Boat slipway.*
Leisure: ◆ ⚑ **Facilities:** 🛉 ⊙ 🔍 ✻ ♿ ✆ 🛒 🍖 🌲 🐕
Services: 🔧 📶 🛡 🖉 🎲 🖳 → ∪ 🏪 🎵 📧 💳 🏧 🔲

GLENCOE   Map 14 NN15

▶ ▶ ▶ ▶ 67% Invercoe Caravan Site (NN098594)
PH49 4HP ☎ 01855 811210 📠 01855 811210
e-mail: invercoe@sol.co.uk
website: www.invercoe.co.uk
*Dir: Turn right off A82 at Glencoe Hotel onto B863
for 0.25m*
🚐 🚐 ▲

Open Dec-Oct Booking advisable Jul-Aug for
electric hook ups Last departure noon
*Level grass site set on the shore of Loch Leven, with
excellent mountain views. The area is ideal for both
walking and climbing, and also offers a choice of
several freshwater and saltwater lochs. Convenient
for the good shopping at Fort William. A 5-acre site
with 60 touring pitches and 5 statics.*
Leisure: ⚑ **Facilities:** 🛉 ⊙ 🔍 ✻ ♿ ✆ 🛒 🐕
Services: 🔧 📶 🛡 🖉 🎲 🖳 → ⅄ 🎵 📧 💳 🔲

Grantown-on-Spey Caravan Park AA ⚑

Grantown-on-Spey, Highland PH26 3JQ
Tel: 01479 872474 Fax: 01479 873696
Web: www.caravanscotland.com
E-mail: team@caravanscotland.com

Quality Park • Close to town • Paradise for dogs
• Water and Waste pitches • Laundry
• Free hot showers

Things to do:
Follow the Whisky Trail • Fishing for salmon on
the River Spey • Popular 18 hole golf course
• Great walking country • Olde Worlde Friendly
atmosphere amidst beautiful surroundings

▶ ▶ ▶ **64% Glencoe Caravan & Campsite**
(NN111578)
PH49 4LA ☎ 01855 811397 & 811278
Dir: 1m SE from Glencoe village on A82
★ ⚑ £8-£11 ⚑ £8-£11 Å £4.50-£11

Open Etr/Apr-Oct Booking advisable Jul-Aug Last
arrival 22.00hrs Last departure 17.00hrs
*A partly sloping site with separate areas of grass
and gravel hard stands. Set in mountainous
woodland 1m from village, and adjacent to the
newly-built visitors' centre. A 25-acre site with 64
touring pitches, 64 hardstandings.*
Facilities: 📶⊙🍴✳️🔥🍺🛱📺
Services: 🔌🛢️🅰️🚰🔳🔲→🔺🔱🚽

GRANTOWN-ON-SPEY   Map 14 NJ02

▶ ▶ ▶ ▶ **74% Grantown on Spey Caravan Park**
(NJ028283)
Seafield Av PH26 3JQ ☎ 01479 872474
🖷 01479 873696
e-mail: team@caravanscotland.com
website: www.caravanscotland.com
*Dir: From town turn N at Bank of Scotland Park,
straight ahead from 0.25m*
★ ⚑ £10-£14 ⚑ £10-£14 Å £6-£14

Open 29 Mar-Oct Booking advisable Etr, May day,
Spring BH & Jul-Aug Last arrival 22.00hrs
*An attractive park in a mature setting near the river,
amidst hills, mountains, moors and woodland. The
park is very well landscaped, and is in a good
location for golf, fishing, mountaineering, walking,
sailing and canoeing. An interesting area for bird
and nature enthusiasts. A 15-acre site with 100
touring pitches, 40 hardstandings and 45 statics.
Football pitch*
Leisure: 🎣🎮 **Facilities:** 📶⊙🍴✳️🔥🍺🛱📺
Services: 🔌🛢️🅰️🔳🔲→🔱🔱🚽🍴🔳🔳🔳🔳

INVERGARRY   Map 14 NH30

▶ ▶ ▶ **68% Faichemard Farm Camping &
Caravan Site** (NH288016)
Faichemard Farm PH35 4HG ☎ 01809 501314
e-mail: dgrant@fsbdial.co.uk
*Dir: 1m W of Invergarry off A87, past Ardgarry Farm
and Faichem campsite.*
★ ⚑ £6-£7 ⚑ £6-£7 Å £6-£7
Open Apr-Oct Booking advisable Jul & Aug Last
arrival 22.00hrs Last departure 11.30hrs
*A beautiful location in mountainous country with
outstanding views. The park has units spread
widely in individual pitches amongst bracken-clad
hills, but all pitches are level. A 10-acre site with 40
touring pitches, 10 hardstandings.*
Every pitch has own picnic table
Facilities: 📶⊙🍴✳️🍺🛱📺
Services: 🔌🛢️🔳→🔺🔱🔱🚽

▶ ▶ ▶ **64% Faichem Park** (NH285023)
Ardgarry Farm, Faichem PH35 4HG
☎ 01809 501226 🖷 01809 501226
e-mail: ardgarry.farm@lineone.net
website: www.campsitesscotland.co.uk
*Dir: Take A87 at Invergarry, 1m. Right at 'Faichem' sign,
up hill.*
★ ⚑ £7-£7.50 ⚑ £7-£7.50 Å £7-£7.50

contd

Open 16 Mar-16 Oct Booking advisable Jul-Aug Last arrival 22.00hrs Last departure 11.00hrs
Small, quiet touring site with good, clean facilities and panoramic views. Customer care is given a high priority here, as is the attention to detail which is meticulous. An ideal location for walking and climbing, and for touring the Highlands. A 2-acre site with 30 touring pitches, 10 hardstandings.
Facilities: **Services:** **Notes:** Dogs must be kept on leads & under control. No smoking or dishwashing in blocks

INVERNESS — Map 14 NH64

PREMIER PARK

75% *Torvean Caravan Park (NH654438)*
Glenurquhart Rd IV3 8JL ☎ 01463 220582
Dir: *1m W of Inverness on A82 at Tomnahuich Canal bridge*
Open Apr-Oct Booking advisable Jun-Aug Last arrival 21.00hrs Last departure 12.00hrs
Located on the Caledonian Canal, this park is quiet and well secluded yet close to Inverness town centre. Every feature of the park has been planned, constructed and maintained to the highest standard. The landscaped grounds are immaculate, and there is a good quality children's play area. A 3-acre site with 50 touring pitches and 10 statics.
Leisure: **Facilities:** **Services:** **Notes:** No single sex groups, no motorcycles, no traders

JOHN O'GROATS — Map 15 ND37

62% John O'Groats Caravan Site (ND382733)
KW1 4YS ☎ 01955 611329 & 077 6233 6359 01955 611329
Dir: *At end of A99*
★ fr £8 fr £8 fr £6
Open Apr-10 Oct Booking advisable Last arrival 22.00hrs Last departure noon
Good clean and attractive site in open position above the seashore and looking out towards the Orkney Islands. Passenger ferry nearby. A 4-acre site with 90 touring pitches, 20 hardstandings.
Facilities: **Services:**

LAIDE — Map 14 NG99

63% *Gruinard Bay Caravan Park (NG903918)*
Laide IV22 2ND ☎ 01445 731225 01445 731225
Dir: *On A832, 300yds N of village*
Open Apr-Oct Booking advisable Jul-Aug Last arrival 22.00hrs Last departure 11.00hrs
Pitches are right next to the water's edge only six feet above the beach at this well-placed site on the outskirts of Laide. Tents are set further back on grass pitches, but enjoy the same views across the

contd.

Gruinard Bay Caravan Park

bay to Gruinard Island. A 3.25-acre site with 43 touring pitches and 14 statics.
Dishwashing sinks/free hot water. Laundry service.
Facilities: **Services:**

LAIRG — Map 14 NC50

65% Dunroamin Caravan Park (NC585062)
Main St IV27 4AR ☎ 01549 402447 01549 402784
e-mail: enquiries@lairgcaravanpark.co.uk
website: www.lairgcaravanpark.co.uk
Dir: *300mtrs from centre of Lairg on S side of A839*
★ £8-£10 £7-£10 £4.50-£10
Open Apr-Oct Booking advisable anytime Last arrival 22.00hrs Last departure noon
An attractive little park with clean and functional facilities, adjacent to a licensed restaurant. The park is close to the lower end of Loch Shin, and a short distance from the town. A 4-acre site with 40 touring pitches, 8 hardstandings and 9 statics.
Facilities: **Services:**

56% Woodend Caravan & Camping Site (NC551127)
Achnairn IV27 4DN ☎ 01549 402248 01549 402248
Dir: *4m N of Lairg off A838, signed at Achnairn*
★ £7-£8 £7-£8 £6-£7
Open Apr-Sep Booking advisable Last arrival 23.00hrs
A clean, fresh site set in hilly moors and woodland with access to Loch Shin. The area is popular with fishing and boating enthusiasts, and there is a choice of golf courses within 30 miles. A spacious campers' kitchen is a useful amenity. A 4-acre site with 55 touring pitches and 5 statics.
Leisure: **Facilities:**
Services:

LOCHALINE — Map 13 NM64

69% *Fiunary Camping & Caravanning Park (NM614467)*
Morvern PA34 5XX ☎ 01967 421225
Dir: *Signed 5m W of Lochaline*
Open May-Oct (rs Apr hot water & showers not available) Booking advisable Last arrival 22.00hrs Last departure noon
A small, carefully maintained site with beautiful loch views, quiet and secluded and in an area of great interest to naturalists. With its beachside

contd.

location it is handy for swimming and boat launching, and ideally placed for trips to Mull, Iona and Staffa. A 3.5-acre site with 25 touring pitches and 2 statics.

Facilities: ⬤⊙✳⬤🎣📷🎔 **Services:** 🔌⊞→🔧🔨📷🔋

NAIRN   Map 14 NH85

▶ ▶ **68% Nairn Lochloy Holiday Park**
(NH895574)
East Beach IV12 4PH
☎ 01667 453764 & 454646 📠 01667 454721
website: www.parkdean.com
Dir: From A96 in Nairn centre turn towards beach down Harbour Road, site signed in 800yds
🔌🚐🅰

Open Mar-Nov Booking advisable Jun-Aug Last arrival 22.00hrs Last departure 10.00hrs
A busy holiday park with good facilities, bordered by the beach, the River Nairn and the golf course. Activities offered include an adventure playground, indoor swimming pool, pool table, lounge bar and fish and chip shop. A 15-acre site with 44 touring pitches and 230 statics.
10% off golf fees, paint balling, quad biking
Leisure: ⌇ ⬤ /🅰 **Facilities:** ⬤⊙🍽✳⬤🛒🎣📷
Services: 🔌📷🍽🛠⊞🛢✕🛒🚮→⬤🍴⊙△🔧🔨
⬤ 💳 💳 💳 🅿 🔋

▶ ▶ ▶ **68% Camping & Caravanning Club Site**
(NH852552)
Delnies Wood IV12 5NX ☎ 01667 455281
website: www.campingandcaravanningclub.co.uk
Dir: Off A96 Inverness to Aberdeen Rd. 2m W of Nairn
★ 🚐 £10.20-£12.90 🚐 £10.20-£12.90 🅰 £10.20-£12.90
Open Mar-Oct Booking advisable Jun-early Aug & BH's Last arrival 21.00hrs Last departure noon
An attractive site amongst pine trees. Facilities have been much improved recently, and the park is close to Nairn with its beaches, shopping, golf and leisure activities. See advertisement on p.10 for details of Club Members' benefits. A 14-acre site with 100 touring pitches, 7 hardstandings.
Pool table & table tennis
Leisure: ⬤ /🅰 **Facilities:** ⬤⊙🍽✳⬤🛒🎣📷🎔
Services: 🔌📷🛢⊞⊞→🍴⬤💳💳💳🅿🔋

POOLEWE   Map 14 NG88

▶ ▶ ▶ **68% Camping & Caravanning Club Site**
(NG862812)
Inverewe Gardens IV22 2LF ☎ 01445 781249
website: www.campingandcaravanningclub.co.uk
Dir: On A832, N of Poolewe village
★ 🚐 £12.30-£15.50 🚐 £12.30-£15.50 🅰 £12.30-£15.50
Open May-Oct Booking advisable bank hols & Jul-Aug Last departure noon
A well run site located on Loch Ewe Bay, not far from Inverewe Gardens. The club has improved this site in the past few years and continues to upgrade the facilities. Please see advertisement on page 10 for details of Club Members' benefits. A 3-acre site with 55 touring pitches, 8 hardstandings.
Facilities: ⬤⊙🍽✳⬤🛒🎔 **Services:** 🔌📷🛢⊞
→🍴⊙🔧🔨📷🔋⬤💳💳🅿🔋

RESIPOLE (LOCH SUNART)   Map 13 NM76

▶ ▶ ▶ ▶ **64% Resipole Farm (NM725639)**
PH36 4HX ☎ 01967 431235 📠 01967 431777
e-mail: info@resipole.co.uk
website: www.resipole.co.uk
Dir: A861 from Corran Ferry. Park 8m W of Strontian
★ 🚐 £9.50-£10.50 🚐 £9-£10 🅰 £7.50-£10
Open Apr-Oct Booking advisable bookings only for elec hook ups Last arrival 22.00hrs Last dep 11.00hrs
A quiet, relaxing park in beautiful surroundings, with deer frequently sighted, and of great interest to naturalists. Situated on the saltwater Loch Sunart in the Ardnamurchan Peninsula, and offering a great deal of space and privacy. Hidden away within the park's woodland is a 9-hole golf course, a restaurant and lounge bar. An 8-acre site with 85 touring pitches, 25 hardstandings and 24 statics. Private slipway, 9-hole golf.
Facilities: ⬤⊙🍽✳⬤🛒🎣📷🎔
Services: 🔌📷🍽🛢🛒⊞⊞✕→🍴🔧🔨📷🔋
Notes: Dogs must be kept on leads ⬤ 💳 💳 🅿 🔋

ROSEMARKIE   Map 14 NH75

▶ ▶ ▶ **68% Camping & Caravanning Club Site**
(NH739569)
Ness Rd East IV10 8SE ☎ 01381 621117
website: www.campingandcaravanningclub.co.uk
Dir: Take A832. A9 at Tore rdbt. Through Avoch, Fortrose then right at Police house. Down Ness Rd. 1st left, small turning signed Golf & Caravan site
★ 🚐 £11.10-£14.50 🚐 £11.10-£14.50 🅰 £11.10-£14.50
Open May-Sep Booking advisable bank hols & Jul-Aug Last arrival 21.00hrs Last departure noon
A very clean and well-maintained site, with pitches close to the road, and along the water's edge. A comprehensive refurbishment has resulted in two excellent toilet blocks, a new reception and disabled room, and a family room with en suite facilities. There are beautiful views over the bay, where resident dolphins swim. Please see the advertisement on page 10 for details of Club Members' benefits. A 4-acre site with 60 touring pitches.
Facilities: ⬤⊙🍽✳⬤🛒🎔
Services: 🔌📷🛢⊞→🍴🔧🔨📷🔋⬤💳💳💳🅿🔋

TAIN   Map 14 NH78

▶ ▶ ▶ **64% Dornoch Firth Caravan Park**
(NH748844)
Meikle Ferry South IV19 1JX ☎ 01862 892292
📠 01862 892292
e-mail: will@dornochfirth.co.uk
website: www.dornochfirth.co.uk
Dir: Just off A9, by island S of Dornoch Firth Bridge
★ 🚐 £8.50-£11.50 🚐 £8.50-£11.50 🅰 £5-£7.50
Open all year Booking advisable Jul-Aug Last arrival 22.00hrs Last departure noon
A pleasant family site with open views of Dornoch Firth and the lovely coastal and country scenery. The immaculately maintained facilities and lovely flower beds make this a delightful base for touring

contd.

the immediate vicinity with its many places of interest. A 2-acre site with 30 touring pitches, 10 hardstandings and 15 statics.

Leisure: ⚙ **Facilities:** ↀ ⊙ ☼ ☀ ✆
Services: ▣ ▤ ⬒ ⬓ → ∪ ▶ ♦ ⬆ ♨ ✉ ▦ ⬙

THURSO   Map 15 ND16

► ► ► 60% *Thurso Caravan & Camping Site (ND111688)*
Smith Ter, Scrabster Rd KW14 7JY ☎ 01847 894631 & 01955 607776 ⬚ 01955 604524
Dir: Signed from A836 W of town
▣ ⬙ Å
Open May-Sep Booking advisable
A large grassy site set high above the coast on the west side of town, with panoramic views out to sea and the Orkney island of Hoy. Convenient for ferries to the islands, and all the town's facilities. A 4.5-acre site with 95 touring pitches and 10 statics.

Leisure: ⚙ ⬒ **Facilities:** ↀ ⊙ & ✆ ⬆ ✿
Services: ▣ ⬙ ✕ ⬆ → ▶ ♦ ✖ ♨

ULLAPOOL   Map 14 NH19

► ► ► 66% **Ardmair Point Camping & Caravan Park (NH108983)**
IV26 2TN ☎ 01854 612054 ⬚ 01854 612757
e-mail: sales@ardmair.com
website: www.ardmair.com
Dir: 3m N of Ullapool on A835, enter by telephone box on beach head at Ardmair
★ ▣ £9.50-£11 ▣ £9-£11 Å £9-£10
Open May-Sep Booking advisable Jul-Aug Last arrival 22.00hrs Last departure noon
An excellent touring site on small peninsula, with superb views of surrounding mountains and sea lochs, and an interesting children's play area. Pitches adjoin and overlook the beaches, and there is a shop and a spacious cafe. A 7-acre site with 60 touring pitches, 14 hardstandings.
Boats, fishing, canoes for hire.

Leisure: ⚙ **Facilities:** ↀ ⊙ ⬒ ☼ & ✆ ⬆ ✿
Services: ▣ ⬙ ▤ ⬓ → ▶ ♦ ✖ ♨ ✉ ▦ ⬙

► ► ► 65% **Broomfield Holiday Park (NH123939)**
West Shore St IV26 2UR ☎ 01854 612020 & 612664
⬚ 01854 613151
e-mail: sross@broomfieldhp.com
website: www.broomfieldhp.com
Dir: Take 2nd right past Harbour
★ ▣ fr £12 ▣ fr £11 Å £10-£12
Open Apr-Oct Booking advisable for group bookings only Last departure noon
Set right on the water's edge of Loch Broom and the open sea, with lovely views of the Summer Isles. The toilets are very well equipped and clean, and the park is close to the harbour and town centre with their restaurants, bars and shops. A 12-acre site with 140 touring pitches.

Leisure: ⚙ **Facilities:** ↀ ⊙ & ⬆ ⬒ ⊞ ⬛
Services: ▣ ⬙ ⬓ → ▶ ⊙ ✖ ♨ ✉ ▦ ⬙

MIDLOTHIAN

DALKEITH   Map 11 NT36

► ► ► 63% **Fordel Caravan and Camping Park (NT359668)**
Lauder Rd EH22 2PH ☎ 0131 663 3046 & 660 3921
⬚ 0131 663 8891
Dir: On A68 1.5m S of Dalkeith
★ ▣ £9-£10.50 ▣ £9-£10.50 Å £7.50-£8.50

Open Apr-Sep Booking advisable Jul-Aug Last departure noon
A small tree-lined park located snugly behind a 24-hour service station, with a well-equipped toilet block. There are electric points to grass and hard pitches, and an adjacent bar/restaurant serves meals. A 3-acre site with 35 touring pitches.

Leisure: ⚙ **Facilities:** ↀ ⊙ ⬒ ☼ ✆ ⬆ ⬒ ⊞ ⌂
Services: ▣ ⬙ ⬔ ⬚ ⬒ ✕ ⬆ → ∪ ▶ ⊙ ♨
✉ ▦ ⬛ ⬙

ROSLIN   Map 11 NT26

► ► ► ► 70% **Slatebarns Caravan Club Site (NT277632)**
EH25 9PU ☎ 0131 440 2192
Dir: From A720 by-pass take A701, signed Penicuik & Peebles. Then S to B7006, turn left signed Roslin Chapel & take unclass road at end of village
★ ▣ £10-£13 ▣ £10-£13 Å £10-£12
Open Etr-Oct Booking advisable Jul & Aug Last arrival 20.00hrs Last departure noon
A good modern site with marked pitches, set in a rural landscape near to Roslin Glen and the historic 15th-century Rosslyn Chapel yet within easy access of Edinburgh. The site offers excellent amenities, and has been planted liberally with trees and shrubs to make for a pleasant and peaceful environment. A 2.5-acre site with 30 touring pitches, 21 hardstandings.

Facilities: ↀ ⊙ ⬒ ☼ & ✆ ⬆ ✿
Services: ▣ ⬙ ⬔ ⬓ → ∪ ▶ ♨ ⬆

All of the campsites in this guide are inspected annually by an experienced team of inspectors

Scotland

MORAY

ALVES   Map 15 NJ16

► ► ► **62% North Alves Caravan Park** (NJ122633)
IV30 8XD ☎ 01343 850223
*Dir: 1m W of A96, halfway between Elgin & Forres.
Site signed on right*
🏕🚐⚑
Open Apr-Oct Booking advisable peak periods Last
arrival 23.00hrs Last departure noon
*A quiet rural site in attractive rolling countryside
within three miles of a good beach. The site was a
farm, and the stone buildings are quite unspoilt. A
10-acre site with 45 touring pitches and 45 statics.*
Leisure: ♦ ⚠ ▢ Facilities: ▣ ⊙ ⚒ ✳ ⚘ ⚄ ⛾ ✗
Services: ▣ ▣ ⬆ ⊘ ⊞ ▢ → ∪ ▶ ✚ ⚞ ⚑

CRAIGELLACHIE   Map 15 NJ24

► ► ► **67% Camping & Caravanning Club Site**
(NJ257449)
Elchies by AB38 9SD ☎ 01340 810414
▤ 024 7669 4886
website: www.campingandcaravanningclub.co.uk
*Dir: From S leave A9 at Carrbridge, follow A95 to
Grantown-on-Spey, leaving Aberlour on A941. Take
next left turn B9102 signed Archiestown. Site 3m on left*
★ 🚐 £12.30-£15.50 🚐 £12.30-£15.50 ▲ £12.30-£15.50
Open Mar-Oct Booking advisable BH's & Jul-Aug
Last arrival 21.00hrs Last departure noon
*A nice rural site with views over meadowland
towards Speyside, and the usual high Club
standards. Hardstandings are well screened on an
upper level, and grass pitches with more open
views are sited lower down. Please see
advertisement on page 10 for Club Members'
benefits. A 7-acre site with 70 touring pitches, 9
hardstandings.*
Leisure: ⚠ Facilities: ▣ ⊙ ⚒ ✳ ⚄ ⚘ ⛾ ✗
Services: ▣ ▣ ⬆ ⊘ ⊞ → ∪ ▶ ⚘ ⚞ ⚄ ⚞ 🍴 ▨▨ ▨ ▣

FOCHABERS   Map 15 NJ35

► ► ► **60% Burnside Caravan Park** (NJ350580)
IV32 7ET ☎ 01343 820511 & 820362 ▤ 01343 821291
Dir: Located 0.5m E of town off A96
★ 🚐 fr £8.50 🚐 fr £8.50 ▲ fr £8.50

Open Apr-Oct Booking advisable Jul-Aug Last
departure noon
*Attractive site in a tree-lined, sheltered valley with a
footpath to the village. Owned by the garden centre*
contd.

on the opposite side of the A96. A 5-acre site with
79 touring pitches, 22 hardstandings and 75 statics.
Jacuzzi & sauna
Leisure: ⚲ ♦ ⚠ ▢ Facilities: ▣ ⊙ ⚒ ⚄ ⛾ ⚞ ✗
Services: ▣ ⬆ ⊘ ▢ → ∪ ▶ ⊙ ⚑

LOSSIEMOUTH   Map 15 NJ27

► ► ► ► **67% Silver Sands Leisure Park**
(NJ205710)
Covesea, West Beach IV31 6SP
☎ 01343 813262 ▤ 01343 815205
e-mail: holidays@silversands.freeserve.co.uk
website: www.travel.to/silversands
Dir: From Lossiemouth follow B9040 2m W to site
★ 🚐 £7.50-£16.25 🚐 £7.50-£16.25 ▲ £6.20-£12.50
Open Apr-Oct (rs Apr, May & Oct shops &
entertainment restricted) Booking advisable Jul-Aug
Last arrival 22.00hrs Last departure noon
*A large holiday park with entertainment for all
during the peak season, set on the links between
the coast road and the shore of the Moray Firth.
Touring campers and caravans are catered for in
three areas: one offers de-luxe facilities including
water, drainage, electricity and hard and grassed
area, while the other areas are either unserviced or
include electric hook-ups and water. A well-stocked
shop sells holiday gear, and there is a clubroom
and bar plus takeaway food outlet. The large
amenity block is modern and well appointed. A 7-
acre site with 140 touring pitches and 200 statics.
Children's entertainment.*
Leisure: ⚲ ♦ ⚠ ▢ Facilities: ✚ ▣ ⊙ ⚒ ✳ ⚄ ⛾ ▥
▤ ✗ Services: ▣ ▣ ⚘ ⬆ ⊘ ⊞ ▢ ✗ ⬆ → ∪ ▶ ⊙ ⚄ ✗ ⚑
Notes: Over 14yrs only in bar 🍴 ▨▨ ▨ ▣

NORTH LANARKSHIRE

MOTHERWELL   Map 11 NS75

► ► ► **66% Strathclyde Country Park**
Caravan Site (NS717585)
366 Hamilton Rd ML1 3ED ☎ 01698 266155
▤ 01698 252925
e-mail: strathclydepark@northlan.gov.uk
Dir: From M74 junct 5, direct access to park
★ 🚐 £8.70 🚐 £8.70 ▲ £3.90-£7.50

Open Apr-Oct Booking advisable Jun-Aug Last
arrival 22.30hrs Last departure noon
*A level grass site situated in a country park amidst
woodland and meadowland with lots of attractions.*
contd

Services: ▢ Toilet Fluid ✗ Café/ Restaurant ▥ Fast Food/Takeaway ⚘ Baby Care ▣ Electric Hook Up
▣ Launderette �‖ Licensed Bar ⬆ Calor Gaz ⊘ Camping Gaz ⊞ Battery Charging

Strathclyde Country Park

North Lanarkshire *welcomes you to*

north lanarkshire **leisure**

One of Scotland's leading Centres for outdoor recreation, with a wide range of activities to choose from, offers...

Something for everyone...

Top class facilities for Land and Water Sports, Countryside Ranger Service, Visitor Centre, Sandy Beaches, Play Areas and Caravan & Camping Site.

Programme of Special Events.

Booking Office, Watersports Centre, Strathclyde Country Park, 336 Hamilton Road, Motherwell, ML1 3ED
Tel: **(01698) 266155** Fax: **(01698) 252925**
E-mail: www.strathclydepark@northlan.gov.uk

A large grass area caters for 150 tents, while 100 well-screened pitches, with electrics and some hardstandings area are also available. 250 touring pitches, 100 hardstandings.

Leisure: ⚊ **Facilities:** 🌳⊙⚒⚑▣▦☰☊
Services: ▣▣▤▦⌀✕▥→∪▶⚑▲❄☎✈
Notes: Site rules available on request by post

PERTH & KINROSS

ABERFELDY
Map 14 NN84

▶ ▶ ▶ **66% Aberfeldy Caravan Park (NN858495)**
Dunkeld Rd PH15 2AQ ☎ 01887 820662 &
01738 475211 ▤ 01738 475210
Dir: Off A827 on E edge of town
★ ⚑ fr £10 ⚑ fr £10 ▲ fr £8.50
Open late Mar-late Oct Booking advisable Jun-Aug Last arrival 20.00hrs Last departure noon
A very well-run and well-maintained site, with good facilities and some landscaping, at the eastern end of the town and lying between main road and banks of the River Tay. Good views from site of surrounding hills. A 5-acre site with 92 touring pitches and 40 statics.
Leisure: ⚊ **Facilities:** 🌳⊙⚒▣▦☰☊
Services: ▣▣▣▦→▶▲✈🌐▦▥

BIRNAM
Map 14 NO04

▶ ▶ ▶ ▶ **69% Erigmore Estate (NO036416)**
PH8 9XX ☎ 01350 727236 & 727677
▤ 01350 728636
e-mail: holidays@erigmore.fsnet.co.uk
website: www.erigmore.fsnet.co.uk
Dir: Situated off A9 on the B898
★ ⚑ £10.35-£17.25 ⚑ £10.35-£17.25
Open Mar-Oct Booking advisable all times Last arrival 22.00hrs Last departure noon
Set in the grounds of 18th-century Erigmore House, with its many unusual trees, and well secluded from the main road. The site is mainly static, but there is a small number of well-appointed touring pitches in two areas. An 18-acre site with 26 touring pitches and 190 statics.
Sauna, solarium & spa bath.
Leisure: ⚄ ⚒ ⚊ **Facilities:** ➦🌳⊙⚑✳⚒⚑▣▦☰
Services: ▣▣▣▦⌀✕▥→▶⚑🌐▦▥▦▥▦

BLAIR ATHOLL
Map 14 NN86

PREMIER PARK

▶ ▶ ▶ ▶ ▶ **69% Blair Castle Caravan Park (NN874656)**
PH18 5SR ☎ 01796 481263 ▤ 01796 481587
e-mail: mail@blaircastlecaravanpark.co.uk
website: www.blaircastlecaravanpark.co.uk
Dir: From A9 junct with B8079 at Aldclune, then NE to Blair Atholl. Site on right after bridge in village
★ ⚑ £9.50-£13.50 ⚑ £9.50-£13.50 ▲ £9.50-£13.50

Open Mar-Nov Booking advisable bank hols & Jul-Aug Last arrival 21.30hrs Last departure noon
Attractive site set in impressive seclusion within the Atholl estate, surrounded by mature woodland and the River Tilt. Although a large park, the various groups of pitches are located throughout the extensive parkland, and each has its own sanitary block with all-cubicled facilities of a very high standard. There is a choice of grass pitches, hard standings, or fully-serviced pitches. This park is particularly suitable for the larger type of motorhome. A 32-acre site with 283 touring pitches and 112 statics.
Internet gallery

contd.

Leisure: ⚄ Indoor swimming pool ⚄ Outdoor swimming pool ⚄ Tennis court ⚄ Games room ⚊ Children's playground ∪ Stables ▶ 9/18 hole golf course ⚓ Boats for hire ⚏ Cinema ⚒ Fishing ◎ Mini golf ⚄ Watersports ⬚ Separate TV room

Scotland

Blair Castle Caravan Park

BLAIR ATHOLL, PERTHSHIRE PH18 5SR
Tel: 01796 481263 Fax: 01796 481587
www.blaircastlecaravanpark.co.uk

- 32 acre Park set amidst spectacular mountain scenery
- Grass and hard-standing mains serviced pitches
- 'Roll-On, Roll-Off' pitches
- Heated amenity blocks
- Spacious park and recreation areas
- Extensive woodland, hill and riverside walks
- Caravan Holiday Homes for hire
- Indoor Games Room with television
- Situated in the grounds of Blair Castle (open to the public)
- Internet Gallery and General Store
- Pony trekking, golf, fishing, bowling, mountain bikes all available from the village of Blair Atholl
- Children's Playground, Putting Green and Miniature Football Pitch

PLEASE WRITE OR TELEPHONE FOR OUR FREE COLOUR BROCHURE

Leisure: ♠ /𝔸 Facilities: ⇥ ⋔ ⊙ ⬘ & ⫓ ⅃ 🐾
Services: ⬢ 🖥 🛢 ⬙ 🅱 🆃 ⇥ → ∪ ⏻ ⫏ 🦴 Notes: No unaccompanied young or single sex groups
● 🚆 ▦ 🕸 🈂

▶ ▶ ▶ ▶ ▶ **70%** *River Tilt Caravan Park (NN875653)*
PH18 5TE ☎ 01796 481467 🖳 01796 481511
Dir: 7m N of Pitlochry on A9, take B8079 to Blair Atholl & site at rear of Tilt Hotel
⚏ ⚎ Å

Booking advisable Jul-Aug Last arrival 21.00hrs Last departure 11.00hrs
An attractive park with magnificent views of the surrounding mountains, idyllically set in hilly
contd.

woodland country on the banks of the River Tilt, next to the golf course. The toilet block is of an extremely high standard, with cubicled en suite facilities for both sexes. Fully-serviced pitches are available, and the park boasts its own bistro and AA 2-rosette Loft Restaurant. There is also a leisure complex with heated indoor swimming pool, sun lounge area, spa pool and gym, all available for an extra charge. Outdoors there is a short tennis court. A 2-acre site with 37 touring pitches and 92 statics.
Multi-gym, sauna & solarium. Steam room, spa pool.
Leisure: ⋺ ⚲ /𝔸 Facilities: ⋔ ⊙ ⬘ ❋ & ⫓ ⬛ ⅃ 🐾
Services: ⬢ 🖥 ⚲ 🛢 ⬙ 🅱 🆃 ✗ → ∪ ⏻ ⊚ 🦴
● 🚆 ⦿ 🕸 🈂

COMRIE   Map 11 NN72

▶ ▶ ▶ **72% Twenty Shilling Wood Caravan Park (NN750218)**
PH6 2JY ☎ 01764 670411 🖳 01764 670411
e-mail: alowe20@aol.com
website: www.ukparks.co.uk/twentyshilling
Dir: 0.5m W of Comrie on A85 opposite 'Farm Food Restaurant'
★ ⚏ £12.50-£13.50 ⚎ £12.50-£13.50
Open 22 Mar-25 Oct Booking advisable bank holidays, Jul & Aug Last arrival 21.00hrs Last departure noon
A secluded and sheltered south-facing park with level, individual pitches all with electric and TV hook-ups. Tents not accepted. A 10.5-acre site with 14 touring pitches, 14 hardstandings and 42 statics.
Leisure: ♠ /𝔸 Facilities: ⋔ ⊙ ⬘ ❋ ∪ 🐾
Services: ⬢ 🖥 🛢 ⬙ 🅱 🆃 → ∪ ⏻ 🦴 ⅄ Notes: Dogs must be kept on leads at all times ● 🚆 ▦ 🕸 🈂

CRIEFF   Map 11 NN82

▶ ▶ ▶ **64%** *Crieff Holiday Village (NN857225)*
Turret Bank PH7 4JN ☎ 01764 653513
🖳 01764 655028
e-mail: katie@turretbank7.freeserve.co.uk
Dir: 1m W of Crieff on A85
⚏ ⚎ Å
Open all year Booking advisable Jul-Aug Last arrival mdnt
A terraced site overlooking the River Turret, within walking distance of the town and three local parks. The level touring area is served by refurbished toilet facilities. A 3-acre site with 30 touring pitches and 50 statics.
Leisure: ♠ /𝔸 ▢ Facilities: ⋔ ⊙ ⬘ ❋ & ⫓ ⬛ 🐾
Services: ⬢ 🖥 🛢 ⬙ 🅱 🆃 → ∪ ⏻ ⊚ ⅄ 🦴 ● 🚆

> Remember to check your tent or caravan thoroughly before leaving home to ensure everything is in good order

Scotland

DUNKELD
Map 14 NO04

See also **Birnam**

► ► ► 64% **Inver Mill Farm Caravan Park (NO015422)**

Inver PH8 0JR ☎ 01350 727477 ▤ 01350 727477

e-mail: invermill@talk21.com

Dir: Turn off A9 onto B822 then immediately right to Inver

★ ⊞ £9-£11

Open Apr-Oct Booking advisable Jul-Aug Last arrival 22.00hrs Last departure 12.00hrs
A peaceful park on level, former farmland, located on the banks of the River Braan and surrounded by mature trees and hills. The active resident owners keep the park in very good condition. A 5-acre site with 65 touring pitches.

Facilities: ⌐ ⊙ ⚲ ✳ ⓗ ⓛ **Services:** ⛽ ▤ ▧ ⌀ ⊞ → ▶ ◢ ⚡

Notes: No single sex groups.

KENMORE
Map 14 NN74

► ► ► ► 66% **Kenmore Caravan & Camping Park (NN772458)**

PH15 2HN ☎ 01887 830226 ▤ 01887 829059

e-mail: info@taymouth.co.uk

website: www.taymouth.co.uk

Dir: A9 to Balliuluig, then W on A827 to Aberfeldy. Then 6m to Kenmore, over bridge park on right.

★ ⊞ £10-£15 ⊞ £10-£15 ▲ £9-£14

Open mid Mar-end Oct Booking advisable mid Jul-mid Aug Last arrival 22.00hrs Last departure 14.00hrs
A pleasant riverside site with an air of spaciousness and a very good licensed bar/restaurant. Set on the banks of the River Tay, it has good views of the surrounding mountains, as well as offering on-site river fishing; fishing in a nearby loch is also available. The modern facilies include a laundry, family bathrooms, and two children's playgrounds. There is a par 70 golf course on the park. A 14-acre site with 160 touring pitches and 60 statics. Cycle hire, fishing & boat hire.

Leisure: ⚲ ⚓ ⚠ ▢ **Facilities:** ⌐ ⊙ ⚲ ✳ ⓖ ⓛ ⚡ ⟊ ♞
Services: ⛽ ▤ ⓨ ⌀ ⊞ ⊡ ✕ ▄ ➦ → ∪ ▶ △ ✦ ◢
Notes: Families and couples only ⬤ ▭

> **Remember sites which take dogs may not accept all breeds**

Faskally
Caravan Park

Pitlochry, Perthshire PH16 5LA
Tel: (01796) 472007 & 473202
Fax: (01796) 473896

This park is situated outside the town and on the banks of the River Garry, which is bordered on one side by the main road. It is on gently sloping grassland dotted with trees and with splendid views. Indoor Leisure Pool with Spa Bath, Sauna and Steam Room. New Chalets introduced in 2002.
Turn off A9 Pitlochry by-pass ½ mile north of town then proceed 1 mile north on B8019.
Bar and Restaurant.

E-mail: ehay@easynet.co.uk
Web: www.faskally.co.uk

KINLOCH RANNOCH
Map 14 NN65

► 59% **Kilvrecht Campsite (NN623567)**

PH8 0JR ☎ 01350 727284 ▤ 01350 727811

Dir: 3m along the S shore of Loch Rannoch. Approach via unclass road along Loch with Forestry Commission signs

⊞ ⊞ ▲

Open Etr-Oct Last arrival 22.00hrs Last departure 10.00hrs
Set in a remote and beautiful spot in a large forest clearing, about 0.75m from Loch Rannoch shore. This small and basic campsite has no hot water, but the few facilities are very well maintained. A 17-acre site with 60 touring pitches.

Facilities: ⓛ ⚲ ♞ **Services:** → ✦ ◢

PERTH
Map 11 NO12

► ► ► 63% **Camping & Caravanning Club Site (NO108274)**

Scone Palace, Scone, Tayside PH2 6BB

☎ 01738 552323

website: www.campingandcaravanningclub.co.uk

Dir: Follow signs for Scone Palace. Once through continue for 2m. Left following site signs. After 1m left into Racecourse Rd. Site entrance from car park

★ ⊞ £11.10-£14.50 ⊞ £11.10-£14.50 ▲ £11.10-£14.50

Open Mar-Oct Booking advisable bank hols & peak periods Last arrival 21.00hrs Last departure noon
A delightful woodland site, sheltered and well screened from the adjacent Scone racecourse. Two very good amenity blocks are built of timber and

contd.

Facilities: ➡ Bath ⌐ Shower ⊙ Electric Shaver ⚲ Hairdryer ✳ Ice Pack Facility ⓖ Disabled Facilities ⓛ Public Telephone ⚡ Shop on Site or within 200yds ⊞ Mobile Shop (calls at least 5 days a week) ⓗ BBQ Area ⚲ Picnic Area ♞ Dog Exercise Area

blend in well with the surroundings of mature trees. Please see advertisement on page 10 for details of Members' benefits. A 16-acre site with 140 touring pitches, 14 hardstandings and 20 statics. Recreation room & table tennis

Leisure: ◕ ⚠ **Facilities:** 🌣⊙ 🔍 ✳ ᴴ 🚻 **Services:** 🔲🔲🔲🔲🔲→U▶🔲🔲🔲🔲🔲🔲🔲🔲

PITLOCHRY   Map 14 NN95

▶ ▶ ▶ ▶ 70% **Faskally Caravan Park (NN916603)**
PH16 5LA ☎ 01796 472007 🖹 01796 473896
e-mail: ehay@easynet.co.uk
website: www.faskally.co.uk
Dir: 1.5m N of Pitlochry on B8019
★ 🚐 £10.30-£11.45 🚐 £9.90-£11 ▲ £9.50-£10.50

Open 15 Mar-Oct Booking advisable Jul-Aug Last arrival 23.00hrs
A large park attractively divided into various sections by mature trees, occupying a rural position in gently sloping meadowland beside the tree lined River Garry. The excellent amenities include a leisure complex with heated indoor swimming pool, sauna and steam room, bar, restaurant and indoor amusements. There are extensive views of the surrounding countryside, and this park is well placed as a centre for touring, being close to but unaffected by the A9. A 27-acre site with 255 touring pitches and 90 statics.
Steam room, spa & sauna

Leisure: ≋ ◕ ⚠ **Facilities:** 🌣⊙🔍✳ᴴ🚻 **Services:** 🔲🔲🔲🔲🔲🔲→U▶🔲🔲🔲🔲🔲🔲🔲
See advertisement on page 275

▶ ▶ ▶ ▶ 69% **Milton of Fonab Caravan Site (NN945573)**
Bridge Rd PH16 5NA ☎ 01796 472882
🖹 01796 474363
e-mail: info@fonab.co.uk
website: www.fonab.co.uk
Dir: 0.5m S of town off A924
🚐 £11-£11.50 🚐 £11-£11.50 ▲ £11-£11.50
Open Apr-Oct Booking advisable Jul-Aug & bank holidays Last arrival 21.00hrs Last departure 13.00hrs
Set on the banks of the River Tummel, this park offers extensive views down the river valley and the surrounding mountains. The flat, mainly grassed park offers level pitches, and is close to the centre of Pitlochry, and adjacent to the Pitlochry Festival Theatre. The sanitary facilities are of an exceptionally high standard, with most contained in
contd.

combined shower/wash basin and toilet cubicles. The owner personally supervises the park, and maintains immaculate conditions throughout. A 15-acre site with 154 touring pitches and 36 statics. Mountain bike hire, free trout fishing.

Facilities: 🚐🌣⊙🔍✳ ᴴ🚻 **Services:** 🔲🔲🔲 →▶⊙✚🔲 **Notes:** Couples & families only, no motor cycles.

TUMMEL BRIDGE   Map 14 NN75

 67% *Tummel Valley Holiday Park (NN764592)*
PH16 5SA ☎ 01882 634221
🖹 01882 634302
Dir: From Perth take A9 N to bypass Pitlochry. 3m after Pitlochry turn onto B8019 signed to Tummel Bridge. Park in 11m on left
🚐 🚐
Open Apr-Oct Booking advisable bank hols & Jun-Aug Last arrival 21.00hrs Last departure 10.00hrs
A well-developed site amongst mature forest in an attractive valley, beside the famous bridge. Play areas and the bar are sited alongside the river, and this is an ideal base in which to relax. A 55-acre site with 37 touring pitches and 153 statics.
Bicycle hire, crazy golf, fishing rod hire.
Leisure: ≋ ◕ ⚠ **Facilities:** 🚐🌣⊙🔍✳ ᴴ🚻🏕 🗻 **Services:** 🔲🔲🔲🔲🔲✕🔲→🔲 **Notes:** No single sex groups. 🔲🔲🔲🔲🔲

SCOTTISH BORDERS

COLDINGHAM   Map 12 NT96

▶ ▶ ▶ ▶ 73% **Scoutscroft Holiday Centre (NT906662)**
St Abbs Rd TD14 5NB ☎ 018907 71338
🖹 018907 71746
e-mail: holidays@scoutscroft.co.uk
website: www.scoutscroft.co.uk
Dir: From A1 take B6438 signed Coldingham & St Abbs & site on edge of Coldingham village
★ 🚐 £9-£18 🚐 £9-£18 ▲ £4.50-£12

Open Mar-Oct Booking advisable bank hols & Jul-Aug Last arrival mdnt Last departure noon
A large family-run site with good facilities and amenities including bars, restaurant, and children's games rooms. Set on the edge of the village and
contd.

close to the sea, with separate areas and toilet blocks for tourers. A 16-acre site with 60 touring pitches, 32 hardstandings and 120 statics. Sub Aqua Centre.

Leisure: ◣ ⚠ ▢ **Facilities:** ➤ ⋔ ☉ ⚲ ✳ ᇰ ⅃ ᆯ ⊞ ⵤ
Services: ▨ ▣ ♀ ⅃ ⊘ ⊞ ⊤ ✕ ♨ → ∪ ▶ △ ♩ ● ⊟ ⊠ ⵤ

ETTRICK VALLEY — Map 11 NT21

▶ ▶ ▶ 61% **Honey Cottage Caravan Park (NT295164)**
Hope House TD7 5HU ☎ 01750 62246 & 01539 531291
website: www.honeycottagecaravanpark.co.uk
Dir: Off B709
★ 🏕 fr £7.50 🚐 ▲ £3.50-£6.50

Open all year Booking advisable
This is a level, riverside site set in the remote and unspoilt Ettrick Valley. The site has modern facilities and is open twelve months a year. The enthusiastic owners are continually improving the facilities. A 7.5-acre site with 22 touring pitches and 40 statics. Fishing

Leisure: ⚠ **Facilities:** ⋔ ☉ ᇰ ᆯ ⊞ ⵤ **Services:** ▨ ▣ ♀
∅ → ♩ **Notes:** Dogs must be kept on leads

JEDBURGH — Map 12 NT62

▶ ▶ ▶ 64% **Camping & Caravanning Club Site (NT658219)**
Elliot Park, Edinburgh Rd TD8 6EF ☎ 01835 863393
website: www.campingandcaravanningclub.co.uk
Dir: Entrance to site lies directly opposite the Edinburgh & Jedburgh Woollen Mills on Northern side of Jedburgh on A68 Newcastle to Edinburgh Rd
★ 🏕 £10.20-£12.90 🚐 £10.20-£12.90 ▲ £10.20-£12.90
Open May-Oct Booking advisable bank hols & Jul-Aug Last arrival 21.00hrs Last departure noon
A touring site on northern edge of town, nestling at foot of cliffs close to Jed Water. New hardstandings are a welcome improvement for caravans. Please see the advertisement on page 10 for details of Club Members' benefits. A 3-acre site with 50 touring pitches, 8 hardstandings.

Facilities: ⋔ ☉ ⚲ ✳ ᇰ ⅃ ⵤ
Services: ▨ ▣ ♀ ∅ ⊞ → ∪ ▶ △ ♩ ᆯ ● ⊟ ⊠ ⵤ

Springwood Caravan Park, Kelso
Tel: 01573 224596
Fax: 01573 224033

Set in 30 acres of wooded parkland, near attractive market town of Kelso only a mile away. The park has short grass and good clean modern facilities. Individual shower/toilet cubicles and spacious disabled facilities. We have long wooded walks along the river Teviot and through the winding paths of Springwood Estate. Winner of "The AA Best Campsite in Scotland 1998/99".

For further information contact:
Springwood Estate, Kelso, Scottish Borders TD5 8LS.
Tel: 01573 224596 Fax: 01573 224033
E-mail: admin@springwood-estate.co.uk
www.springwoodestate.co.uk

▶ ▶ ▶ 66% **Jedwater Caravan Park (NT665160)**
TD8 6PJ ☎ 01835 840219 & 7050 219219
🖨 01835 840219
e-mail: jedwater@clara.co.uk
website: www.jedwater.co.uk
Dir: Located 3.5m S of Jedburgh on A68
★ 🏕 £9-£10 🚐 £9-£10 ▲ £8-£10
Open Etr-Oct Booking advisable high season Last arrival mdnt Last departure noon
A quiet riverside site in a beautiful valley, run by resident owners as a peaceful retreat. The touring area is separate from statics, and this site is an ideal touring base. A 10-acre site with 60 touring pitches and 60 statics.
Bike hire, trampoline, football field.

Leisure: ◣ ⚠ ▢ **Facilities:** ⋔ ☉ ⚲ ✳ ᇰ ⅃ ᆯ ⊞ ⵤ
Services: ▨ ▣ ♀ ∅ ⊞ ⊤ → ∪ ▶ ♩

KELSO — Map 12 NT73

▶ ▶ ▶ ▶ 72% **Springwood Caravan Park (NT720334)**
TD5 8LS ☎ 01573 224596 🖨 01573 224033
e-mail: admin@springwoodestate.co.uk
website: www.springwoodestate.co.uk
Dir: On A699, signed Newton St Boswells
★ 🏕 £14 🚐 £14 ▲ £11
Open end Mar-mid Oct Booking advisable bank hols & Jul-Aug Last arrival 23.00hrs
A very well-maintained site with a pleasant atmosphere, set in a secluded position on the banks of the tree-lined River Teviot about 1m W of town.

contd.

---

eisure: ⚑ Indoor swimming pool ⚑ Outdoor swimming pool ⚘ Tennis court ◣ Games room ⚠ Children's playground ∪ Stables
▶ 9/18 hole golf course � Boats for hire ⚬⚬ Cinema ♩ Fishing ◉ Mini golf

Scotland

Springwood Caravan Park
The well-maintained mature parkland offers a peaceful, spacious landscape in which to relax. The park is under the careful supervision of the owners, and offers a high standard of modern toilet facilities which are mainly contained in fully cubicled units with shower, washbasin and toilet. The park is close to the historic town of Kelso, and Floors Castle. A 4-acre site with 35 touring pitches and 260 statics. Ideal either as a touring base or transit site, it is extremely well maintained.

Leisure: ♦ ⚊ **Facilities:** ↑ ⊙ ⚈ ✳ ⚘ ⚐ ⚊ ⚘
Services: ⚐ ◉ ⚋ → ∪ ↾ ⊙ ⚏ ⤴
Notes: No dogs if camping in tent ⚈ ⚏ ⚏ ⚏ ⚏

LAUDER   Map 12 NT54

▶ ▶ ▶ **70% Camping & Caravanning Club Site (NT508533)**
Carfraemill, Oxton TD2 6RA ☎ 01578 750697
website: www.campingandcaravanningclub.co.uk
Dir: From Lauder, turn right at rdbt onto A697, then left at the Lodge Hotel (signposted). Site is behind Carfraemill Hotel
★ ⚑ £11.10-£14.50 ⚑ £11.10-£14.50 ▲ £11.10-£14.50
Open Mar-Oct Last arrival 21.00hrs Last departure 12.00hrs
A meadowland site with good facilities housed in pine lodge buildings, and pleasant surroundings. Ideal either as a touring base or transit site, it is extremely well maintained. Please see the advertisement on page 10 for details of Club Members' benefits. A 5-acre site with 60 touring pitches, 9 hardstandings.

Leisure: ▭ **Facilities:** ↑ ⚈ ✳ ⚘ ⚐ ⚋ ⚘
Services: ⚐ ◉ ⚋ ⚈ ⚏ → ↾ ⤴ ⚋ ⚈ ⚏ ⚏ ⚏ ⚏

▶ ▶ ▶ **69% Thirlestane Castle Caravan & Camping Site (NT536473)**
Thirlestane Castle TD2 6RU ☎ 01578 722254 & 07976 231032 ⬚ 01578 718749
e-mail: maitland_carew@compuserve.com
Dir: Signed off A68 & A697, just S of Lauder
★ ⚑ fr £8 ⚑ fr £8 ▲ fr £8
Open Apr-1 Oct Booking advisable Jul-Aug Last arrival anytime Last departure anytime
Set in the grounds of the impressive Thirlestane Castle, with mainly level grassy pitches. The enthusiastic manager keeps the park and facilities in sparkling condition. A 5-acre site with 60 touring pitches.

Facilities: ↑ ⊙ ⚋ **Services:** ⚐ ◉ → ↾ ⤴ ⚋

PEEBLES   Map 11 NT24

▶ ▶ ▶ ▶ **68% Crossburn Caravan Park (NT248417)**
The Glades, 95 Edinburgh Rd EH45 8ED
☎ 01721 720501 ⬚ 01721 720501
e-mail: enquiries@crossburncaravans.co.uk
website: www.crossburncaravans.com
Dir: 0.5m N of Peebles on A703
★ ⚑ fr £9 ⚑ fr £8.50 ▲ fr £8

Open Apr-Oct Booking advisable Jul-Aug Last arrival 22.00hrs Last departure 14.00hrs
A level site in a peaceful and relatively quiet location, despite the proximity of the main road which partly borders the site, as does the Eddleston Water. There are lovely views across the Eddleston Valley, and the park is well stocked with trees, flowers and shrubs which give it a particularly rural feel. Facilities are maintained to a high standard, and the site shop, which is comprehensively stocked, also keeps a large supply of caravan spares. Fully-serviced pitches are available, as well as a choice of grass or hard pitches. A 6-acre site with 45 touring pitches, 15 hardstandings and 85 statics.
9-hole putting course, mountain bikes for hire.

Leisure: ♦ ⚊ **Facilities:** ⤴ ↑ ⊙ ⚈ ✳ ⚋ ⚘ ⚊ ⚘
Services: ⚐ ◉ ⚋ ⚈ ⚏ ⬚ → ∪ ↾ ⤴
Notes: Dogs must be kept on leads ⚈ ⚏ ⚏ ⚏

▶ ▶ ▶ **69% Rosetta Caravan & Camping Park (NT245415)**
Rosetta Rd EH45 8PG ☎ 01721 720770
⬚ 01721 720623
Dir: Signposted from all main roads from Peebles.
★ ⚑ fr £11 ⚑ fr £11 ▲ fr £10

contd

ROSETTA CARAVAN PARK
Peebles, Borders – Scotland
Tel: 01721 720770 Fax: 01721 720623

Family owned Park, Georgian Mansion with wooded estate. 45 acres. Lounge Bar in Courtyard, Shop, Childrens Bowling and Putting Green, Play Area, Electric hook-ups, adjacent to Golf Course. Fishing available on River Tweed. Quiet and peaceful Park. Write or phone for colour brochure.

Open Apr-Oct Booking advisable BH's, Jul & Aug Last arrival 23.00hrs Last departure 15.00hrs
A pleasant site set in 40 acres of parkland around a late Georgian mansion and stable block. Some of the stable buildings house the toilet facilities and bar. A 25-acre site with 160 touring pitches and 48 statics.
Bowling & putting greens.
Leisure: ♦ ⁄⁄ ▢ **Facilities:** ➔⊙⊙✳ॖ ᰱॖ ᰯ
Services: ᰯॖ⊙ᰱॖॖ ⊤ → ∪ ▶ ↳ ✦

SELKIRK   Map 12 NT42
▶ ▶ ▶ 66% **Victoria Park Caravan & Camping Park** (NT465287)
Victoria Park, Buccleuch Rd TD7 5DN
☎ 01750 20897 ᰯ 01750 20897
Dir: From A707/A708 N of town, cross river bridge & take 1st left, then left again
⊞ ⊞ ⅄
Open Apr-Oct (rs 10-18 Jun site closed) Booking advisable Jul-Aug Last arrival 21.00hrs Last departure 14.00hrs
A consistently well-maintained site with good basic facilities forming part of public park and swimming pool complex close to River Ettrick. A 3-acre site with 60 touring pitches.
Fitness room & sauna.
Leisure: ᰯ ⁄⁄ **Facilities:** ➔⊙⊙✳ᰱॖ ᰯ
Services: ᰯॖ⊙ᰱ✕ → ∪ ▶ ↳ ᰯ

SOUTH AYRSHIRE
AYR   Map 10 NS32
68% NEW **Craig Tara** (NS300184)
KA7 4LB ☎ 01292 265141
website: www.british-holidays.co.uk
Open Mar-Oct Last arrival 22.00hrs
Last departure 12.00hrs
A large, well-maintained holiday centre with on-site entertainment and sporting facilities to suit all ages. The touring area is set apart from the main complex at the entrance to the park, and campers can use all the facilities, including water world, soft play areas, sports zone, show bars and supermarket with in-house bakery. There is a bus service to Ayr. A 213-acre site.
Facilities: ᰯ **Services:** ᰯ

▶ ▶ ▶ 67% **Heads of Ayr Leisure Park** (NS285180)
Dunure Rd KA7 4LD ☎ 01292 442269
ᰯ 01292 500398
Dir: 5m S of Ayr on A719
★ ⊞ £10-£14 ⊞ £8.50-£12.50 ⅄ £8.50-£12.50
Open Mar-Nov Booking advisable bank hols & Jul-Aug Last arrival 23.30hrs Last departure 15.00hrs
A small family-run site with attractive, well-screened pitches, 0.5m from a beach overlooking the Firth of Clyde. Facilities include a lounge bar, family room and non-smoking restaurant. An 8-acre site with 36 touring pitches and 126 statics.
contd.

HEADS OF AYR LEISURE PARK
Dunure Road, Ayrshire, Scotland KA7 4LD
Tel: 01292 442269
Fax: 01292 500298

This park has been operated by The Semple family for over 30 years and caters for families and small parties. Entertainment to suit all ages. Activities close by include pony trekking, fishing, tennis, bowling, skating and golf. This park is an ideal base for your holiday.

Leisure: ⚠ Facilities: 🌡⊙🔧☀🌡☕🐾 Services: 🔌
🔲🍴🛁🚮🔖🗓✕🛵→∪▶🛒♪ Notes: No youth groups

Leisure: ⚠ Facilities: 🌡⊙🔧☀🌡🐾🐕
Services: 🔌🔲🛁🚮🔖🗓→∪▶♪🌐💳💳🔖🚐🅖

BARRHILL   Map 10 NX28

▶ ▶ ▶ **62% Windsor Holiday Park (NX216835)**
KA26 OPZ ☎ 01465 821355 🖨 01465 821355
e-mail: bookings@windsor-park.freeserve.co.uk
website: www.windsor-park.freeserve.co.uk
*Dir: On A714 between Newton Stewart & Girvan, 1m N
of Barrhill village*
★ 🚐 £8-£9 🚐 £8-£9 ▲ £5-£8.50
Open Mar-Oct (rs Nov-Feb open wknds only)
Booking advisable Jun-Aug Last arrival 22.00hrs
Last departure 16.00hrs
*A small family-run site in a rural location, well-
screened from A714 by mature trees. The site is
terraced and well landscaped with shrubs and
hedging. A 6-acre site with 30 touring pitches, 9
hardstandings and 26 statics.*

Leisure: ⚠ Facilities: 🌡⊙🔧☀🌡☕🔖🗓🅰🐾
Services: 🔌🛁🚮🗓→▶♪🛒🌐🔖🚐

COYLTON   Map 10 NS41

**64% Sundrum Castle Holiday Park
(NS405208)**
KA6 5JH ☎ 01292 570057
🖨 01292 570065
e-mail: sundrum.castle@ecosse.net
website: www.parkdean.com
Dir: Just off A70, 4m E of Ayr near Coylton.
★ 🚐 £8-£21 🚐 £8-£21 ▲ £6-£16.50
Open Mar-Oct Booking advisable all times Last
arrival 21.00hrs Last departure noon
*A large family holiday centre, with plenty of on-
site entertainment, just a 10 minute drive from
the centre of Ayr. A 30-acre site with 40 touring
pitches and 250 statics.*
Amusement arcade.

Leisure: ❄ ⚲ ⚫ ⚠ ⬜ Facilities: 🌡⊙🔧☕🌡
Services: 🔌🔲🍴🛁🚮✕🛵→∪▶🛒♪

Notes: No single sex groups, no under
25 bookings, no cars by tents 💳💳💳🚐🅖

MAYBOLE   Map 10 NS20

▶ ▶ ▶ ▶ **62% Camping & Caravanning Club Site
(NS247103)**
Culzean Castle KA19 8JX ☎ 01655 760627
website: www.campingandcaravanningclub.co.uk
*Dir: From S on A77 turn left onto A719. Site 4m on left.
From N on A77 turn right onto B7023 in Maybole. After
100yds turn left. Site 4m*
★ 🚐 £12.30-£15.50 🚐 £12.30-£15.50 ▲ £12.30-£15.50
Open Mar-Oct Booking advisable bank hols & Jul-
Aug Last arrival 21.00hrs Last departure noon
*A mainly level grass park with some gently sloping
pitches and hard stands along the bed of an old
railway, situated at the entrance to the castle and
country park. The park is surrounded by trees on
three sides and with lovely views over Culzean Bay.
Please see the advertisement on page 10 for details
of Club Members' benefits. A 10-acre site with 90
touring pitches, 25 hardstandings.*

contd.

▶ ▶ ▶ ▶ **73% The Ranch (NS286102)**
Culzean Rd KA19 8DU ☎ 01655 882446
🖨 01655 882446
website: www.theranchscotland.co.uk
Dir: On B7023, 1m S of Maybole towards Culzean
★ 🚐 £9.50-£13.50 🚐 £9.50-£13.50 ▲ £6-£10
Open Mar-Oct & wknds in winter Booking advisable
bank hols & Jul-Sep Last arrival 20.00hrs Last
departure noon
*A very attractive privately-run park with two distinct
areas for statics and tourers, but all sharing the
same excellent leisure facilities, including a heated
indoor swimming pool. Touring pitches are fully
serviced, and screened for privacy by shrubs and
rose bushes. A 9-acre site with 40 touring pitches,
40 hardstandings and 68 statics.*
Mini gym, sauna & sunbed.

Leisure: ❄ ⚲ ⚠ Facilities: 🌡🔧☀🌡🐾🌡
🔖🅰🐕 Services: 🔌🔲🛁🚮🔖🗓→∪▶✕♪

TARBOLTON   Map 10 NS42

▶ ▶ ▶ **64% Middlemuir Park (NS439263)**
KA5 5NR ☎ 01292 541647 🖨 01292 551649
Dir: Off B743, Ayr to Mauchline road
🚐🚐
Open Mar-Oct Booking advisable bank hols & Jul-
Aug Last arrival 22.00hrs Last departure noon
*A rural site in the partly-walled garden where
Montgomerie House used to stand. Set in rolling
farmland. A 17-acre site with 25 touring pitches and
60 statics.*

Leisure: ⚲ ⚠ Facilities: 🌡⊙🔧☀☕🐕
Services: 🔌🔲🛁🚮🔖🗓→∪▶♪ Notes: No tents

SOUTH LANARKSHIRE

KIRKFIELDBANK   Map 11 NS84

▶ ▶ **55% Clyde Valley Caravan Park (NS868441)**
ML11 9TS ☎ 01555 663951 & 01698 357684
🖨 01698 357684
*Dir: From Glasgow on A72, cross river bridge at
Kirkfieldbank & site on left. From Lanark on A72,
right at bottom of steep hill before bridge*
★ 🚐 £8 🚐 £8 ▲ £8
Open Apr-Oct Booking advisable anytime Last
arrival 23.00hrs Last departure noon
*A long-established site with a central grassy touring
area surrounded by trees and shrubs, set in hilly
country with access to the river, and adjacent to the
Clyde Walk. A 5-acre site with 50 touring pitches
and 65 statics.*

Leisure: ⚠ Facilities: 🌡⊙🔧🌡🐾
Services: 🔌🔲🛁🚮🗓→∪▶✕🛒♪

STIRLING

ABERFOYLE
Map 11 NN50

PREMIER PARK

▶ ▶ ▶ ▶ ▶ 70% **Trossachs Holiday Park (NS544976)**
FK8 3SA ☎ 01877 382614
🖷 01877 382732
e-mail: info@trossachsholidays.co.uk
website: www.trossachsholidays.co.uk
*Dir: Access on E side of A81 1m S of junct A821 &
3m S of Aberfoyle*
★ 🚐 £9.50-£12.50 🚐 £9.50-£12.50 ▲ £9.50-£12.50

Open Mar-Oct Booking advisable anytime
Last arrival 21.00hrs Last departure noon
*An imaginatively designed terraced site offering
a high degree of quality all round, with fine
views across Flanders Moss. All touring pitches
are fully serviced with water, waste, electricity
and TV aerial, and customer care is a main
priority. Set in 20 acres of ground within the
Queen Elizabeth Forest Park, with plenty of
opportunities for cycling off-road on mountain
bikes, which can be hired or bought on site.
A 40-acre site with 65 touring pitches,
45 hardstandings and 70 statics.
Cycle hire.*
Leisure: ⚓ ⛰ ▯ **Facilities:** ⌐ ⊙ ⚒ ☀ ⚲ ⛴ ⌺ ⍢
Services: ⊞ ⊡ ⅃ ⌀ ⊞ ⊤ → ⅂ ⅄ ✈ ⊜ ⊟ ⊠ ⊡

AUCHENBOWIE
Map 11 NS78

▶ ▶ ▶ 58% *Auchenbowie Caravan & Camping
Site (NS795880)*
FK7 8HE ☎ 01324 823999 🖷 01324 822950
*Dir: 0.5m S of M9 junct 9. Turn right off A872 for 0.5m,
signposted*
🚐 🚐 ▲

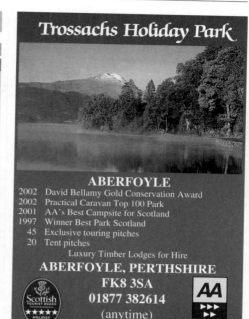

contd.

Leisure: 🏊 Indoor swimming pool 🏊 Outdoor swimming pool 🎾 Tennis court 🎱 Games room 🎠 Children's playground ♘ Stables
▶ 9/18 hole golf course ⏗ Boats for hire 🎦 Cinema 🎣 Fishing ◎ Mini golf △ Watersports ▯ Separate TV

Open Apr-Oct Booking advisable mid Jul-mid Aug
Last departure noon
A pleasant little site in a rural location, with mainly level grassy pitches. The friendly owner and warden create a relaxed atmosphere, and given its position close to the junction of the M9 and M80 motorways, this is a handy stopover spot for tourers. A 3.5-acre site with 60 touring pitches and 7 statics. Paddling pool.
Leisure: ⚙ Facilities: ⬠⊙⛇⌂⊞⼐
Services: ⬛🗑⌀→◷▸⚏⼐🗑⊡⛟🍴🍴

BALMAHA   Map 10 NS49

▶ ▶ ▶ 72% Camping & Caravanning
Club Site (NN407927)
Milarrochy Bay G63 0AL ☎ 01360 870236
website: www.campingandcaravanningclub.co.uk
Dir: A811 Balloch to Stirling Rd, take Drymen turn. In Drymen take B837 for Balmaha. After 5m road turns sharp right up steep hill. Site 1.5m further on
★ 🚐 £12.30-£15.50 🚎 £12.30-£15.50 ▲ £12.30-£15.50
Open Mar-Oct Booking advisable Jul-Aug & BH's
Last arrival 21.00hrs Last departure noon
On the quieter side of Loch Lomond next to the 75,000-acre Queen Elizabeth Forest, this attractive site offers very good facilities. New toilets including disabled and family rooms and is to a high standard, and a welcome addition to this popular park. Please see advertisement on page 10 for details of Club Members' benefits. A 12-acre site with 150 touring pitches, 25 hardstandings.
Boat launching & fishing.
Leisure: ⚙ Facilities: ⬠⊙⛇✳⛊⚾⛐⼐
Services: ⬛⊡🗑⌀⊞→◷▸⌁🍴⊡⛟🍴🍴🗑

CALLANDER   Map 11 NN60

▶ ▶ ▶ 68% Gart Caravan Park (NN643070)
The Gart FK17 8LE ☎ 01877 330002 📄 01877 330002
Dir: 1m E of Callander on A84
★ 🚐 fr £12.50 🚎 fr £12.50
Open Etr or Apr-15 Oct Booking advisable BHs & Jul-Aug Last arrival 22.00hrs Last departure noon
A well-screened caravan park bordered by trees and shrubs, near to the Queen Elizabeth Park amidst ideal walking and climbing country. A feature of the park is the careful attention to detail in the maintenance of facilities, and the owners are very helpful and friendly. A 25-acre site with 122 touring pitches and 66 statics.
Fishing on site.
Leisure: ⚙ Facilities: ⬠⊙✳⛊⚾⼐
Services: ⬛⊡🗑→▸⌁🍴⛟🍴🍴🗑

> **If you are dissatisfied with any aspect of a campsite, discuss the problem at the time with a member of staff**

LUIB   Map 10 NN42

PREMIER PARK

▶ ▶ ▶ ▶ ▶ 65% *Glendochart Caravan Park (NN477278)*
FK20 8QT ☎ 01567 820637 📄 01567 820024
e-mail: info@glendochart-caravanpark.co.uk
website: www.glendochart-caravanpark.co.uk
Dir: 5m E of Crianlarich on A85
🚐🚎▲
Open Etr-Oct Booking advisable Jul & Aug
Last arrival 22.00hrs Last departure noon
A small, well-maintained site with imaginative landscaping, set on hillside in Glendochart with glorious mountain and hill-country views. A new sanitary block has transformed the facilities here. The site is well located for trout and salmon fishing. A 7-acre site with 45 touring pitches and 40 statics.
Leisure: ⚙ Facilities: ⬠⊙⛇✳⛊⚾⛐🖼⼐
Services: ⬛⊡🗑⌀⊞⊡→◷▸⌁⌁🍴⛟🍴🗑

STIRLING   See Auchenbowie

WEST DUNBARTONSHIRE

BALLOCH   Map 10 NS38

▶ ▶ ▶ ▶ 66% Lomond Woods
Holiday Park (NS383816)
Old Luss Rd G83 8QP
☎ 01389 759475 & 01389 755000
📄 01389 755563
e-mail: lomondwoods@holiday-parks.co.uk
website: www.holiday-parks.co.uk
Dir: Turn right off A82, onto A811 Park 0.25m
★ 🚐 £8.50-£13 🚎 £8.50-£13 ▲ £8.50-£13

Open Jan-Oct Booking advisable BH's & Jul-Aug
Last arrival 22.00hrs Last departure noon
A mature park with well-laid out pitches screened by trees and shrubs, surrounded by woodland and hills. The park is within walking distance of 'Loch Lomond Shores', a complex of leisure and retailing experiences. Amenities include an inspiring audio-visual show, open-top bus tours, and loch cruises. A 13-acre site with 120 touring pitches, 80 hardstandings and 35 statics.
Leisure: ♦⚙⌂ Facilities: ➡⬠⊙⛇✳⛊⚾⛐⌂⼐
Services: ⬛⊡🗑⌀⊞⊡➡→◷▸⌁⌁🍴⛟🍴🍴🗑

WEST LOTHIAN

EAST CALDER
Map 11 NT06

► ► ► 72% **Linwater Caravan Park**
(NT104696)
West Clifton EH53 0HT ☎ 0131 333 3326
e-mail: linwater@supanet.com
website: www.ukparks.com/linwater
*Dir: Signposted along B7030 off M9 junct 1 or from
Wilkieston on A71*
🚐 £9-£11 🚐 £9-£11
Open late Mar-late Oct Booking advisable BH's &
Aug Last arrival 21.00hrs Last departure 12.00hrs
*A farmland park in a peaceful rural area within easy
reach of Edinburgh. The very good facilities are
housed in a Scandinavian-style building, and are
well maintained by resident owners. Nearby are
plenty of pleasant woodland walks. A 5-acre site
with 60 touring pitches.*
Leisure: ⚠ Facilities: 🍴⊙🔧☀🏃🛒 🛠
Services: 🔌🅿️🛢🚿📅 → ∪ 🅿️ ✚ 🚮 🍴 🍺 🎳 💱 🛍

SCOTTISH ISLANDS

ISLE OF ARRAN

LOCHRANZA
Map 10 NR95

► ► ► 66% **Lochranza Caravan & Camping Site
(NR942500)**
KA27 8HL ☎ 01770 830273 📄 01770 830600
e-mail: office@lochgolf.demon.co.uk
*Dir: On A84 at N tip of island, beside Kintyre ferry and
14m N of Brodick for ferry to Ardrossan*
★ 🚐 £12-£14 🚐 £10-£12 ▲ £6-£11
Open mid Mar-Oct Booking advisable Whit & Aug
Last arrival 22.00hrs Last departure 13.00hrs
*Attractive park in a beautiful location, run by
friendly family owners. The park is adjacent to an
18-hole golf course, opposite the famous Arran
Distillery, between tree-lined hills on the edge of the
village. Golf and ferry packages can be arranged.
A 2.5-acre site with 60 touring pitches, 10
hardstandings.*
Facilities: 🍴⊙🔧☀🏃🛒🛠
Services: 🔌🅿️🛢🚿📅 → ∪ 🅿️ 🚮 Notes: No fires

ISLE OF MULL

CRAIGNURE
Map 10 NM73

► ► ► 67% **Shieling Holidays (NM724369)**
PA65 6AY ☎ 01680 812496
e-mail: graciemull@aol.com
website: www.shielingholidays.co.uk
*Dir: From ferry, left onto A849 to Iona. After 400mtrs left
at church, follow campsite signs towards sea*
★ 🚐 £11-£12.50 🚐 £11-£12.50 ▲ £11-£12.50
Open Apr-Oct Booking advisable Spring bank hol &

contd.

Jul-Aug Last arrival 22.00hrs Last departure noon
*A lovely site on the water's edge with spectacular
views, and less than 1m from ferry landing. There is
a campers' shelter in a disued byre which is
especially popular in poor weather. Hardstandings
and service points are provided for motorhomes,
and there are astro-turf pitches for tents. The park
now offers bunkhouse accommodation for families.
A 7-acre site with 65 touring pitches, 9
hardstandings and 15 statics.*
Adventure playground
Leisure: 🏊 ⚠ 🏓 Facilities: 🍴⊙🔧☀🏃🛒🛠
Services: 🔌🅿️🛢🚿📅 → 🅿️🚮✚🚮 🍴 🍺 🎳 💱 🛍

ISLE OF SKYE

EDINBANE
Map 13 NG35

► ► ► 66% **Loch Greshornish Caravan Site
(NG343524)**
Borve, Arnisort IV51 9PS ☎ 01470 582230
e-mail: info@greshcamp.freeserve.co.uk
website: www.greshcamp.freeserve.co.uk
*Dir: By loch-shore at Edinbane, approx 12m from
Portree on A850 Dunvegan road*
★ 🚐 £8 🚐 £8 ▲ fr £7.25
Open Apr-Oct Booking advisable Jul-Aug Last
arrival 22.00hrs Last departure noon
*A pleasant open site, mostly level and with a high
standard of maintenance. There is a campers'
shelter in a disused byre which is popular in poor
weather, and a licensed shop. A 5-acre site with 130
touring pitches.*
Bike hire, canoe hire & licensed shop.
Facilities: 🍴⊙🔧☀🏃🛒🛠
Services: 🔌📅 → ∪ 🚮 Notes: Dogs must be
kept under control and exercised off site

STAFFIN
Map 13 NG46

► ► 60% NEW **Staffin Camping & Caravanning
(NG492670)**
IV51 9JX ☎ 01470 562213
Dir: On A855, 16m N of Portree
🚐🚐▲
Open Apr-Oct
*A large sloping grassy site with level hardstandings
for motor homes and caravans, close to the village
of Staffin. The refurbished toilet block is to a very
good standard. A 2-acre site with 50 touring pitches,
18 hardstandings.*
Facilities: 🛒 Services: 🔌

Many sites do not accept groups,
or unaccompanied young people.
Always check with the site
when booking

Scotland

Wales

WALES

ANGLESEY, ISLE OF

BRYNSIENCYN   Map 06 SH46

▶ ▶ ▶ 67% **Fron Caravan & Camping Park**
(SH472669)
LL61 6TX ☎ 01248 430310 📄 01248 430310
e-mail: froncaravanpark@brynsiencyn.fsnet.co.uk
Dir: Off A4080 Llanfair to Newborough road, 1m W of
Brynsiencyn
★ 🚐 fr £9.50 🚐 fr £9.50 ▲ fr £9.50
Open Etr-Sep Booking advisable Spring bank hol &
Jul-Aug Last arrival 23.00hrs Last departure noon
A quiet family site in a pleasant rural area, ideally
situated for touring Anglesey and North Wales. The
farm buildings which house facilities are well
maintained and mainly attractive. A 5.5-acre site
with 60 touring pitches.

Leisure: 🏊 ♣ 🎢 Facilities: 🄼 ⊙ 🦶 ❄ ⅃ 🛁 🌂
Services: 🖵 🅰 📄 🖃 🔁 → ∪ ▶ 🧺

BRYNTEG   Map 06 SH48

▶ ▶ ▶ ▶ 67% *Nant Newydd Caravan Park*
(SH485814)
LL78 8JH ☎ 01248 852842 & 852266
Dir: 1m from Brynteg on B5110 towards Llangefni
🚐 🚐 ▲

Open Mar-Oct (rs May & Sep pool restricted)
Booking advisable Jul-Aug Last arrival mdnt
Last departure 17.00hrs
Gently sloping grass site sheltered by mature trees
and gorse bushes, set in meadowland in a small
valley. The park is well landscaped with flower and
shrub gardens and water features, and aims to cater
for those seeking a quiet, restful holiday in near
natural surroundings. A large heated swimming
pool and small toddler pool are very popular, and
the long sandy beach of Benllech is just three miles
away. A 4-acre site with 30 touring pitches and 83
statics.
Satalite TV & licensed shop.

Leisure: 🏊 ♣ 🎢 🖵 Facilities: 🄼 ⊙ 🦶 ❄ 🔥 🛁 🌂 ⚔ 🎋 🌂
Services: 🖵 🖃 🅰 📄 🖃 🔁 → ∪ ▶ 🔺 🎵 🧺

Small select, family-run country park, with beautiful gardens
and water falls, two and a half miles from Benllech Bay.
Facilities include excellent toilet facilities, free showers,
Disabled toilet, Laundry room, well equipped Licensed shop,
children's play grounds, Games room, T.V. room with
Satellite, Large heated outdoor Swimming pool with paddling
pool and water slide. Tennis court and free aside football
pitch. Luxury fully equipped caravans for hire. Dogs on lead
welcomed. Pitches with hard standing, main water, electricity,
and toilet emptying point on pitch. Pony trekking, Golf, Sub-
aqua diving, Water Skiing, Rambling, Climbing, Fishing, etc.
all within 3 miles of Park. Ring or write for tariff and brochure.
Runners up to Best Park in Wales for two consecutive years.

Nant Newydd Caravan Park
▶▶▶▶ Brynteg, Benllech, Isle of Anglesey.
Tel: Tynygongl (01248) 852842 or 852266
Fax: (01248) 852218
Website: www.nantnewydd.co.uk

▶ ▶ 65% **Ysgubor Fadog Caravan & Camping Site**
(SH497820)
Ysgubor Fadog, Lon Bryn Mair LL78 8QA
☎ 01248 852681
Dir: Turn off A5 onto A5025 for Benllech. After 7m turn
left onto B5108. Outside 30mph limit take 3rd left turn.
Site 400yds on right
★ 🚐 £6.50-£7 🚐 £6.50-£7 ▲ £5-£7
Open Etr-Sep Booking advisable Whitsun & school
hols Last arrival 20.00hrs Last departure 18.00hrs
A peaceful and remote site reached along a narrow
lane where care is needed. The small park has
dated but very clean facilities. A 2-acre site with 15
touring pitches and 1 static.
Facilities: 🄼 ⊙ ❄ 🔥 🌂 Services: 🖵 🖃 → ∪ ▶ 🧺 🖥 🌂

DULAS   Map 06 SH48

PREMIER PARK

▶ ▶ ▶ ▶ ▶ 70% **Tyddyn Isaf Caravan**
Park (SH486873)
Lligwy Bay LL70 9PQ ☎ 01248 410203
📄 01248 410667
e-mail: enquiries@tyddynisaf.demon.co.uk
website: www.tyddynisaf.demon.co.uk
Dir: 0.5m off A5025 between Benllech & Amlwch
★ 🚐 £12.50-£16.50 🚐 £12.50-£16.50 ▲ £8-£13
Open Mar-Oct (rs Mar-Etr & Sep-Oct clubhouse
& shop opening limited) Booking advisable May
bank hol & Jun-Aug Last arrival 22.00hrs
Last departure 11.00hrs
contd.

Wales

► ► ►

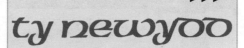

LEISURE PARK

Proprietors: Mike & Cathi

Llanbedrgoch, Isle of Anglesey LL76 8TZ
Tel: 01248 450677 / 07712 676505
Fax: 01248450 711

This small, select, family-run park is ideally situated for Benllech Bay with extensive views of Snowdonia. Facilities include licensed country club and restaurant serving meals for the family, well-equipped shop, excellent toilet facilities, free showers, disabled toilet, baby changing room, laundry room, children's playground and games room, heated outdoor swimming pool, health centre with spa, sauna, pool and gymnasium equipment, electric hook-ups and luxury fully-equipped caravans for hire.

Dogs on leads are welcomed.

Sailing, water skiing, fishing, climbing, walking, golf, pony trekking and safe sandy beaches are available on the island. 9 hole golf course within ½ mile.

Tyddyn Isaf Caravan Park

A beautifully situated family park on gently rising ground adjacent to sandy beach, and with magnificent views overlooking Lligwy Bay. Access to the long sandy beach is by private footpath, or by car. Other footpaths along the coast lead to Dulas Bay and the small harbour village of Moelfre with its lifeboat station and seawatch centre. The park offers a superb toilet block, a well-stocked shop, and a clubhouse serving meals and takeaway food. A 16-acre site with 80 touring pitches, 20 hardstandings and 50 statics.

Leisure: ⚲ ▢ **Facilities:** ⌂ ☺ ⊕ ✳ ⚿ ⚲ 🛒 ☂ ✝
Services: ⊟ 🖩 ⏚ 🗋 ⌀ ⊞ ① ✕ 🚿 → ∪ ▶ ⚡ ⚂
Notes: No groups, families only

► ► ► 67% Ty Newydd Leisure Park (SH508813)
LL76 8TZ ☎ 01248 450677 & 077 1267 6505
🖷 01248 450711
e-mail: tynewyddcc@aol.com
website: www.members.aol.com/tynewyddcc
Dir: A5025 from Brittania Bridge. Through Pentraeth, left at layby. Site 0.75m, on right
★ ⚲ £10-£22 ⚲ £10-£22 ▲ £10-£22

Open Whit-mid Sep (rs Mar-Whit & mid Sep-Oct club/shop wknds only, outdoor pool closed)
Booking advisable Etr, Whit & Jul-Aug Last arrival 23.30hrs Last departure 10.00hrs
A low-density park with many facilities including a heated outdoor pool, a country club with restaurant, and a fitness centre with pool and gym for which an extra charge is made. The toilet block is attractive and very clean, and the whole park is well kept. A 4-acre site with 48 touring pitches and 60 statics. Health centre.

Leisure: ⚲ ⚲ ⚲ ⚲ **Facilities:** ⌂ ☺ ⊕ ✳ ⚿ ⚲ 🛒 ✝
Services: ⊟ 🖩 ⚲ ⏚ ⌀ ⊞ ① ✕ → ∪ ▶ ⚡ ⚂ 🚮 ⊟ 🚙 ⚂

► ► ► ► 79% Home Farm Caravan Park (SH498850)
LL73 8PH ☎ 01248 410614
🖷 01248 410900
e-mail: enq@homefarm-anglesey.co.uk
website: www.homefarm-anglesey.co.uk
Dir: On A5025, 2m N of Benllech, with park entrance 300mtrs beyond church
★ ⚲ £8.50-£14.50 ⚲ £8.50-£14.50 ▲ £8.50-£13
Open Apr-Oct Booking advisable bank hols Last arrival 21.00hrs Last departure noon
A first class park in an elevated and secluded position sheltered by trees. The peaceful rural setting affords views of farmland, the sea, and the mountains of Snowdonia. The modern toilet block has helped to win numerous awards, and there are excellent play facilities for children both indoors and out. The area is blessed with sandy beaches, and local pubs and shops cater for everyday needs. Winner of AA Best Campsite of the Year 2003, and Best Campsite for Wales. A 6-acre site with 61 touring pitches, 21 hardstandings and 72 statics. Indoor adventure playground.

Leisure: ⚲ ⚲ ⚲ ▢ **Facilities:** ⇥ ⌂ ☺ ⊕ ✳ ⚿ ⚲ 🛒 🐾
Services: ⊟ 🖩 ⏚ ⌀ ⊞ ① → ∪ ▶ ⚲ 🚙 ⊟ ⊙ 🚮 ⚂

Wales

PENTRAETH Map 06 SH57

▶ ▶ 65% **Rhos Caravan Park (SH517794)**
Rhos Farm LL75 8DZ ☎ 01248 450214
📠 01248 450214
Dir: Site on A5025, 1m N of Pentraeth
⛺ £8-£11 🚐 fr £7.50 ▲ fr £7.50
Open Etr-Oct (rs Mar shop & showers restricted)
Booking advisable Spring bank hol & Jul-Aug Last
arrival 22.00hrs Last departure 16.00hrs
*A spacious park on level, grassy ground off the
main road to Amlwch. Enthusiastic owners keep the
site tidy and well maintained. A 15-acre site with 98
touring pitches and 60 statics.*
Leisure: △ Facilities: ♀⊙☀✆♨⛺👉
Services: 🚙👁🛢⌀🅱🚽→∪▶✚♨✔

RHOSNEIGR Map 06 SH37

▶ ▶ 57% **Ty Hen (SH323737)**
Station Rd LL64 5QZ ☎ 01407 810331
📠 01407 811261
e-mail: bernardtyhen@hotmail.com
website: www.tyhen.com
*Dir: A55 across Anglesey. At exit 5 follow signs to
Rhosneigr, at clock turn right. Entrance adjacent to
Rhosneigr railway station.*
⛺ £13-£15 🚐 £13-£15 ▲ £7-£13
Open Mar-Oct Booking advisable All year Last
arrival 21.00hrs Last departure Noon
*Attractive seaside position near a large fishing lake
and riding stables, in lovely countryside. Friendly,
considerate owners keep the very basic toilet
facilities in a reasonable condition. A 7.5-acre site
with 38 touring pitches, 3 hardstandings and
7 statics.*
fishing, family room
Leisure: ➹ ♦ △ Facilities: ♀⊙☀✆♨⛺👉
Services: 🚙👁🅱→∪▶✚♨
Notes: 1 motor vehicle per pitch, dogs on leads,
children in tents/tourers by 10pm 💳 💳 💷

CAERPHILLY

CWMCARN Map 03 ST29

▶ ▶ 64% **Cwmcarn Forest Drive Campsite
(ST230935)**
Visitor Centre & Campsite NP11 7FA
☎ 01495 272001 📠 01495 271403
e-mail: cwmcarn-vc@caerphilly.gov.uk
website: www.caerphilly.gov.uk/
visiting/wheretostay
*Dir: From M4 junct 28 follow signs for Risca, 7m on
B467. Site is well signed*
⛺ £7.50-£8.50 🚐 £7.50-£8.50 ▲ £5-£7.50
Open Jan-24 Dec Booking advisable All year Last
arrival 17.00hrs
Last departure 12.00hrs
*Set behind the visitor centre and nestling alongside
the banks of the Nantcarn stream, this small park is
set in a stunningly scenic spot. It can be found at
the start of a seven-mile drive through forest and
rolling hills, with strategic parking spots containing*
contd.

Cwmcarn Forest Campsite
*picnic tables and barbecues. An idyllic spot for
cyclist and walkers. A 2.5-acre site with 40 touring
pitches, 3 hardstandings.*
Orienteering, forest drive, fishing
Facilities: ♀⊙♨✆👉 Services: 🚙👁✖→♨🖴
Notes: No youth groups, no open fires,
dogs must be on leads 💳 💳 💷

CARDIFF

CARDIFF Map 03 ST17

▶ ▶ ▶ 71% **Cardiff Caravan Park (ST171773)**
Pontcanna Fields CF11 9LB ☎ 029 2039 8362 &
2044 5919 📠 029 2045 3636
e-mail: p.owens@cardiff.gov.uk
*Dir: Turn off M4 onto A48 towards Cardiff. Pass Tesco
Extra on left, under footbridge and fork left onto A4119
signed Llandaff & City Centre. Follow signs to Sophia
Gardens and Welsh Institute of Sport, site in park just
past Glamorgan County Cricket ground*
⛺ 🚐 ▲
Open all year Booking advisable All Year Last
departure noon
*A popular municipal park within easy walking
distance of the city centre, Cardiff Castle, and the
Millennium Stadium. This busy park is often full,
and the facilities are well kept by a keen and
friendly warden. A 2-acre site with 95 touring
pitches.*
Facilities: ♀⊙♨☀♨✆♨
Services: 🚙👁🛢🅱→∪▶✚♨✔💳💳Ⓓ💷💷💷

CARMARTHENSHIRE

CROSS HANDS Map 02 SN51

▶ ▶ 62% **NEW** **Black Lion Caravan & Camping
Park (SN572129)**
78 Black Lion Rd, Gorslas SA14 6RU
☎ 01269 845365 📠 01269 831882
e-mail: bazdgorslas.com
website: www.caravansite.com
*Dir: M4 junct 49 onto A48 continue to Cross Hands rdbt,
turn right onto A476 (Llandeilo) in 0.5m at Gorslas
sharp right into Black Lion Rd, site 0.5m on right*
★ ⛺ £8-£12 🚐 £8-£12 ▲ £8-£12
contd.

Facilities: 👉 Bath 🚿 Shower ⊙ Electric Shaver ⊛ Hairdryer ☀ Ice Pack Facility ♿ Disabled Facilities ✆ Public Telephone
🛒 Shop on Site or within 200yds 💳 Mobile Shop (calls at least 5 days a week) 🍖 BBQ Area 🌲 Picnic Area 👉 Dog Exercise Area

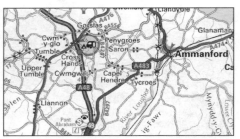

Black Lion Caravan & Camping Park
Open Etr-Oct Booking advisable all times Last
arrival 22.00hrs Last departure 10.00hrs
*Cheerful and friendly owners keep this park clean
and well maintained, and it is a popular overnight
stop for people travelling on the Irish ferry. The
National Botanic Garden of Wales is about 10
minutes' drive away. A 12-acre site with 45 touring
pitches, 10 hardstandings.*

Leisure: 🅰 Facilities: 🅵⊙⚹🅰&🚿🆒🏪🚻
Services: 🆀🅸📁🍴→♨🍴🅾🛒🌮🆋

HARFORD   Map 03 SN64

▶ ▶ ▶ **65% *Springwater Lakes (SN637430)***
SA19 8DT ☎ 01558 650788 🖷 01558 650788
*Dir: 4m E of Lampeter on A482, entrance well signed
on right*
🆅🆒🅰
Open Mar-Oct Booking advisable Jun-Aug Last
arrival 22.00hrs Last departure 11.00hrs
*In a rural setting overlooked by the Cambrian
Mountains, this park is adjoined on each side by
four spring-fed and well-stocked fishing lakes. All
pitches have hardstandings, electricity and TV hook-
ups, and there is a small but very clean toilet block
and a shop. A 20-acre site with 20 touring pitches.
TV hook ups, coarse & fly fishing lakes*

Facilities: 🅵⊙⚹& Services: 🆀→♨🛒🆋
Notes: Dogs must be kept on leads at all times,
children must be supervised around lakes

LAUGHARNE   Map 02 SN31

▶ ▶ ▶ **65% Ants Hill Caravan Park (SN299118)**
SA33 4QN ☎ 01994 427293 & 427355
🖷 01994 427293
e-mail: antshillcaravanpark@tinyworld.co.uk
*Dir: From St Clears on A4066 signed Laugharne and
Pendine. The entrance to the park is a sharp left turn
before Laugharne sign*
★ 🆅 £10-£14 🆅 £10-£14 🅰 £10-£14
Open Etr-Oct Booking advisable Jul-Aug & public
hols Last arrival 23.00hrs Last departure 10.30hrs
*A small, well-run touring site on sloping grass,
located near the village on the Taff estuary. A
clubhouse offers entertainment for all the family,
and the town is famous for Dylan Thomas's
boathouse and a 12th-century castle. A 4-acre site
with 60 touring pitches and 60 statics.*

Leisure: 🎿♦🅰 Facilities: 🅵⊙⚹🍴🆒🚻
Services: 🆀🅾🍷🅸📁🅸🆆→♨🍴🆋

LLANDDEUSANT   Map 03 SN72

▶ ▶ **64% Black Mountain Caravan & Camping Park
(SN773259)**
SA19 9YG ☎ 01550 740217 🖷 01550 740217
e-mail: blackmountain@mapsweet.force9.co.uk
website: www.breconbeacons-holidays.com
*Dir: From A40 turn left at Trecastle (brown caravan site
sign), continue for 10m across moor to Cross Inn, turn
right to site, 30yds on left*
★ 🆅 £7-£9 🆅 £7-£9 🅰 £7-£9
Open all year Booking advisable bank hols Last
departure 12.00hrs
*A very pleasant small park in a secluded position in
the centre of excellent walking country in the
Brecon Beacons National Park. There are plenty of
attractions within easy reach of the park. A 5-acre
site with 25 touring pitches, 3 hardstandings and 2
statics.*

Facilities: 🅵⊙⚹☀🍴&🆒 Services: 🆀♨🅸📁🆋→♨
Notes: Dogs must be kept on leads at all times
🔁🍴🆖🆋

LLANDOVERY   Map 03 SN73

▶ ▶ **61% Erwlon Caravan & Camping Park
(SN776343)**
Brecon Rd SA20 0RD ☎ 01550 720332
e-mail: peter@erwlon.fsnet.co.uk
Dir: 1m E of Llandovery on A40
★ 🆅 £8-£10 🆅 £8-£10 🅰 £8-£10
Open all year (rs Oct-Apr Limited pitches) Booking
advisable bank hols Last arrival anytime Last
departure noon
*Long-established family-run site set beside a brook
in the Brecon Beacons foothills. The town of
Llandovery and the hills overlooking the Towy
Valley are a short walk away. An 8-acre site with 40
touring pitches, 4 hardstandings.*

Leisure: 🅰 Facilities: 🅵⊙⚹☀&🍴🆒🚻🏪🚻
Services: 🆀🅾🅸📁🆋→♨♨🆋

LLANGADOG   Map 03 SN72

▶ ▶ ▶ **66% Abermarlais Caravan Park (SN695298)**
SA19 9NG ☎ 01550 777868 & 777797
website: www.ukparks.co.uk/abermarlais
*Dir: With direct access off A40 on Llandeilo side of
A482, 6m W of Llandovery*
★ 🆅 £8 🆅 £8 🅰 £8
Open 15 Mar-15 Nov (rs Nov, Dec & Mar 1 toilet
block, water point, no hot water) Booking advisable
bank hols & 15 Jul-Aug Last arrival 23.00hrs Last
departure noon
*An attractive, well-run site with a welcoming
atmosphere. This part-level, part-sloping park is in
wooded valley on the edge of the Brecon Beacons
National Park, beside the River Marlais. A 17-acre
site with 88 touring pitches, 2 hardstandings.
Volleyball, badminton court & softball tennis net.*

Leisure: 🅰 Facilities: 🅵⊙⚹🍴🆒🚻
Services: 🆀🅸📁🅸🆋→♨♨
Notes: Dogs must be kept on leads,
no open fires 🔁🍴🅾🆖🆋

Services: 🅣 Toilet Fluid ✖ Café/ Restaurant 🍴 Fast Food/Takeaway 🍼 Baby Care 🆆 Electric Hook Up
🅾 Launderette 🍷 Licensed Bar 🍴 Calor Gaz 🅰 Camping Gaz 🆋 Battery Charging

LLANWRDA See Harford

NEWCASTLE EMLYN Map 02 SN34

PREMIER PARK

► ► ► ► ► 73% **Cenarth Falls Holiday Park (SN265421)**
Cenarth SA38 9JS ☎ 01239 710345
📠 01239 710344
e-mail: enquiries@cenarth-holipark.co.uk
website: www.cenarth-holipark.co.uk
Dir: Off A484 on outskirts of Cenarth village
🚐 £10-£18 🚐 £10-£18 ▲ £10-£18

Open Mar-9 Jan Booking advisable bank hols &
Jul-Aug Last arrival 20.00hrs Last departure
11.00hrs
*A high quality park with excellent facilities,
close to the village of Cenarth where the famous
salmon and sea trout River Teifi cascades
through the Cenarth Falls Gorge. A well-
landscaped park with a new indoor heated
swimming pool and fitness suite, and a
restaurant and bar. A 2-acre site with 30 touring
pitches, 30 hardstandings and 89 statics.
Pool table & health & leisure complex*
Leisure: ⚲ ⚲ ⚲ ⚙ Facilities: 🏪 ⊙ 🍽 ✳ ⚓ ⚭ ⚲ 🐕
Services: 🔌 🚽 ⚲ 🚿 ⚡ 🔲 ⚙ ✕ → ⚭ ⚲ ⚲ ⚲ 🍽 ⚲ 🔲
See advertisement on page 290

► ► ► 64% **Afon Teifi Caravan & Camping Park (SN338405)**
Pentrecagal SA38 9HT ☎ 01559 370532
e-mail: afon.teifi@virgin.net
Dir: Signed off A484, 2m E of Newcastle Emlyn
★ 🚐 £8-£9 🚐 £8-£9 ▲ £8-£9
Open Apr-Oct (rs Nov-Mar when facilities limited,
no toilet block) Booking advisable peak periods Last
arrival 23.00hrs
*Set on the banks of the River Teifi, a famous salmon
and sea trout river, this park is secluded with good
views. Family owned and run, and only 2 miles
from the market town of Newcastle Emlyn. A 6-acre
site with 110 touring pitches and 3 statics.
15 acres of woodland, fields & walks.*
Leisure: ⚲ ⚙ Facilities: ➡ 🏪 ⊙ 🍽 ✳ ⚓ ⚭ ⚲ ⚲ 🎡 ⚲ 🐕
Services: 🔌 🚽 ⚲ 🚿 🔲 ⚡ → ⚭ ⚲ ⚲ 🍽 ⚲

RHANDIRMWYN Map 03 SN74

► ► ► 67% **Camping & Caravanning Club Site (SN779435)**
SA20 0NT ☎ 01550 760257
website: www.campingandcaravanning.co.uk
*Dir: From Llandovery take A483 at level crossing, turn
left in 300yds by fire station signed Rhandirmwyn,
continue 7m to village. Left at pub/post office, down
steep hill past church for 0.5m to site on left before
bridge*
★ 🚐 £12.30-£15.50 🚐 £12.30-£15.50 ▲ £12.30-£15.50
Open 21 Mar-28 Oct Booking advisable bank hols &
peak periods Last arrival 21.00hrs Last dep noon
*On the banks of the Afon Tywi near Towy Forest
and the Llyn Brianne reservoir, this secluded park
has superb views from all pitches. The park is
divided into paddocks by mature hedging, and
facilities and grounds are very well tended. Please
see advertisement on page 10 for details of
Members' benefits. An 11-acre site with 90 touring
pitches, 12 hardstandings.*
Leisure: ⚙ Facilities: 🏪 ⊙ 🍽 ✳ ⚓ ⚲ 🐕
Services: 🔌 🚽 ⚲ 🚿 🔲 → ∪ ⚭ ⚲ ⚙ ⚲ ⚲ ⚲ 🔲

ST CLEARS Map 02 SN21

► ► ► 67% **NEW Afon Lodge Camping Park (SN197273)**
Parciau Bach SA33 4LG
☎ 01994 230647 📠 01994 231717
e-mail: yvonne@afonlodge.f9.co.uk
website: http://fp.afonlodge.f9.co.uk
★ 🚐 £8-£12 🚐 £8-£12 ▲ £5.50-£8
Open Mar-9 Jan Last arrival 22.00hrs Last dep noon
*A small secluded park in a wooded valley just 2
miles from the small market town of St Clears. This
location is ideal for those seeking peace and quiet,
with its fine views and proximity to the
Pembrokeshire Coast National Park. A 7-acre site
with 25 touring pitches, 10 hardstandings.*
Facilities: 🏪 ⊙ 🍽 ✳ ⚓ ⚲ 🔲
Services: 🔌 🚽 ⚲ 🚿 🔲 → ∪ ⚭

CEREDIGION

ABERAERON Map 02 SN46

► ► ► 71% **Aeron Coast Caravan Park (SN462633)**
North Rd SA46 0JF ☎ 01545 570349
e-mail: aeroncoastcaravanpark@
aberaeron.freeserve.co.uk
website:
www.aberaeron.co.uk/aeron_coast/awast2.htm
*Dir: On A487 coastal road on northern edge of
Aberaeron. Filling station at entrance*
🚐 £9-£12.50 🚐 £9-£12.50 ▲ £9-£12.50
Open Mar-Oct Booking advisable bank & school
hols Last arrival 23.00hrs Last departure 11.00hrs
*Set in a spacious 22 acres of coastal parkland, with
direct entry onto the beach and only 200yds from the
attractive small town and harbour. This park has a
wide range of indoor and outdoor activities, and*
contd.

Wales

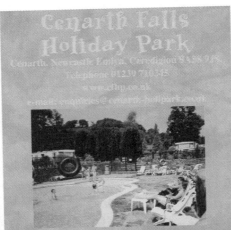

Award winning family-run Park in pretty landscaped gardens. Luxurious 2/3 bedroomed caravan accommodation. All weather touring pitches for year round convenience with excellent facilities. Newly opened "Coracles Health & Country Club" offering swimming pool, spa, sauna/steam rooms, fitness suite, bar and restaurant with weekly live entertainment. An ideal base for touring, walking, golfing, salmon fishing, exploring the stunning coastline with lovely beaches or just simply relaxing

caters well for the whole family. A 22-acre site with 50 touring pitches, 10 hardstandings and 150 statics. Indoor leisure rooms & entertainment hall

Leisure: ⅂ ⅃ ⚡ ⚑ ▢ **Facilities:** ⌦ ⊙ ✻ ⅃ ⛯ ⅃ ⛟
Services: ⊞ ⓔ ⅃ ⅃ ⌖ ⊞ ⓣ ⅃ ⟶ ⊚ ⚠ ⅃
Notes: Families only, no motorcycles, no letting static caravans ⅃ ⅃ ⅃ ⅃ ⅃

ABERYSTWYTH Map 06 SN58

► ► ► 68% **Ocean View Caravan Park** (SN592842)
North Beach, Clarach Bay SY23 3DT
☎ 01970 828425 & 623361 ◨ 01970 820215
e-mail: alan@grover10.freeserve.co.uk
website: www.oceanviewholidays.com
Dir: Turn off A487 in Bow Street. Follow road to x-rds and site straight ahead. 2nd on right
★ ⌑ £7.50-£9.50 ⌑ £7.50-£9.50 ▲ £7-£9.50
Open Apr-Oct (rs Mar Statics only) Booking advisable bank hols Last arrival 22.00hrs Last departure noon
In a sheltered valley on gently sloping ground, with wonderful views of both the sea and the countryside. The beach of Clarach Bay is just 200 yards away, and this welcoming park is ideal for all the family. A 9-acre site with 24 touring pitches, 10 hardstandings and 50 statics.
Leisure: ⋀ **Facilities:** ⌦ ⊙ ⓠ ✻ ⅃ ⅃ ⅏ 禺 ⅃
Services: ⊞ ⓐ ⅃ ⊞ ⟶ ⅃ ⌖ ⊚ ⚠ ⅃ ⅃ ⓸

BETTWS EVAN Map 02 SN34

► ► ► 61% **Pilbach Holiday Park** (SN306476)
SA44 5RT ☎ 01239 851434 ◨ 01239 851969
e-mail: pilbach@fsbdial.co.uk
Dir: S on A487, turn left onto B4333
★ ⌑ £5-£10 ⌑ £5-£10 ▲ £5-£10
Open Mar-Oct (rs Mar-Spring BH & Oct swimming pool closed) Booking advisable Spring BH & Jul-Aug Last arrival 22.00hrs Last departure 10.30hrs
Set in secluded countryside, with two separate paddocks and pitches clearly marked in the grass. This park makes a good base for visiting this very scenic area and nearby seaside resorts. It has a heated outdoor swimming pool, and entertainment in the club in high season. A 15-acre site with 65 touring pitches and 70 statics.
Leisure: ⅂ ⅃ ⚡ ⋀ **Facilities:** ⌦ ⊙ ⓠ ✻ ⅃ ⅏ 禺 ⅃
Services: ⊞ ⓔ ⅃ ⅃ ⌖ ⊞ ⓣ ✕ ⅃ ⟶ ⅃ ⌖ ⚠ ⅃ ⅃
⅃ ⅃ ⅃ ⅃ ⅃

BORTH Map 06 SN69

► ► 66% **NEW** **Mill House Caravan Park**
(SN626881)
Dol-y-Bont SY24 5LX ☎ 01970 871481
website: www.ukparks.co.uk/millhousecp
Dir: From A487 turn W at Rhyd-y-Pennau onto B4353 through Llandie, 1m, under railway bridge by white railings and into Dol-y-Bont, 1st right before hump back bridge
★ ⌑ £10-£11 ⌑ £10-£11 ▲ £10-£11
Open Mar-Oct Booking advisable Last arrival 20.00hrs Last departure 11.00hrs
A delightful sheltered and quiet site beside a trout stream, with spotlessly clean but

contd

---

slightly dated toilet facilities. Fishing is available on site, and the seaside at Borth is just one mile away. A 6-acre site with 25 touring pitches and 15 statics.

Facilities: ☏ ⊙ ⻌

Services: ▮ ⌀ → ∪ ▶ ⌂ ᠕ ⊟ ♨ 🞿 ▱

CROSS INN · Map 02 SN35

▶ ▶ ▶ **67% Camping & Caravanning Club Site (SN383566)**

Llwynhelyg SA44 6LW ☎ 01545 560029
website: www.campingandcaravanningclub.co.uk
Dir: Left from A487 Cardigan-Aberystwyth at Synod Inn. Take A486 signed Newquay. 2m in Cross Inn, left after Penrhiwgaled Arms. Site 0.75m on right
★ ⊞ £11.10-£14.50 ⊞ £11.10-£14.50 ▲ £11.10-£14.50
Open 21 Mar-23 Sep Booking advisable bank hols & peak periods Last arrival 21.00hrs Last dep noon
An excellent, attractive touring site in an elevated rural position with extensive country views. A footpath from the site joins the coastal walk, and the pretty village of New Quay is only a short drive away. Please see advertisement on page 10 for details of Club Members' benefits. A 14-acre site with 90 touring pitches, 6 hardstandings.

Leisure: ⚲ **Facilities:** ☏ ⊙ ⚛ ✳ ᚼ & ⌲ ⻌
Services: 🞿 ⊟ ▮ ⌀ ⊟ 🞿 ⊓ → ∪ ▶ ⌂ ♨ ᠕ 🞿 ▱ ▣ ▱ ▱

LAMPETER · See **Harford (Carmarthenshire)**

LLANARTH · Map 02 SN45

▶ ▶ **70% NEW Llanina Caravan Park (SN421575)**
SA47 0NP ☎ 01545 580947
Dir: On A487(Aberystwyth towards Cardigan) through Llanarth, pass filling station on right, entrance next right
★ ⊞ £7.50-£9.50 ⊞ £7.50-£9.50 ▲ £5-£5.50
Open Etr-2 Nov Booking advisable Jun-Sep Last departure 10.30hrs
Sheltered by mature trees, a completely refurbished park with decent facilities. Close to the park entrance are a garage, shop and village inn serving meals, and the pretty fishing village and harbour of New Quay are a few miles away. A 5-acre site with 45 touring pitches.

Facilities: ☏ ⊙ ✳ ♨ ᚼ ⊟ ⍍ ⻌ **Services:** 🞿 ⊟ → ∪ ▶ ᠕
Notes: Dogs must be kept on leads

LLANDRE · Map 06 SN68

▶ ▶ ▶ **62% Riverside Park (SN634878)**
Lon Glanfred SY24 5BY ☎ 01970 820070
Dir: On A487, 4m N of Aberystwyth, take B4353 & turn right at 2nd turning
⊞ ⊞ ▲
Open Mar-Oct Booking advisable bank & school hols Last arrival 23.30hrs Last departure noon
A quiet site with good quality facilities and easy access to the seaside. Set amongst well-wooded hills and bounded by a stream. A 4-acre site with 24 touring pitches and 76 statics.
River fishing on site.

Leisure: ⚲ **Facilities:** ☏ ⊙ ⚛ ✳ & ⌲ ♨ ⍍ ᚼ ⻌
Services: 🞿 ⊟ ▮ ⌀ ⊟ ⊓ ⤳ → ∪ ▶ ⊙ ⌂ ♨ ᠕

LLANON · Map 02 SN56

▶ ▶ ▶ **63% Woodlands Caravan Park (SN511668)**
SY23 5LX ☎ 01974 202342 & 202454
⊞ 01974 202342
Dir: Through village of Llanon right off A487 at international sign, park 280yds on right.
★ ⊞ £10-£15 ⊞ £10-£15 ▲ £8-£15

Open Apr-Oct (rs Mar toilet block closed) Booking advisable school hols Last arrival 21.30hrs Last departure noon
A level grass site surrounded by mature trees and shrubs near woods and meadowland, adjacent to a stoney beach. A 4-acre site with 80 touring pitches and 60 statics.

Facilities: ☏ ⊙ ⚛ ✳ ♨ ⻌
Services: 🞿 ⊟ ▮ ⌀ ⊟ ⊓ → ∪ ▶ ⊙ ♨ ᠕

LLANRHYSTUD · Map 06 SN56

▶ ▶ **65% Pengarreg Caravan Park (SN539697)**
SY23 5DJ ☎ 01974 202247
Dir: On A487 W of Llanrhystud at S end of village
★ ⊞ £4.50-£7.50 ⊞ £4.50-£7.50 ▲ £4.50-£7.50
Open Mar-Jan Booking advisable Last arrival 24.00hrs Last departure 10.00hrs
Situated right on the water's edge, with spacious pitches in an adjoining field, this gently sloping park has boat-launching facilities and access to cliff walks. A very good bar is well away from touring areas, and is popular with locals. The decent toilet block is well maintained. A 7-acre site with 50 touring pitches and 155 statics.
Slipway to beach for sailing.

Leisure: ⚓ ⚲ **Facilities:** ☏ ⊙ ⚛ ✳ & ⌲ ♨ ⻌
Services: 🞿 ⊟ ♨ ⌀ ⊟ ⊓ ✕ → ▶ ᠕

YSTRAD AERON · Map 02 SN55

▶ ▶ **71% NEW Hafod Brynog (SN525563)**
SA48 8AE ☎ 01570 470084
e-mail: amies@hafodbrynog.fsnet.co.uk
Dir: On A482 Lampeter to Aberaeron road in entrance to Brynog Arms pub
★ ⊞ £7-£8 ⊞ £7-£8 ▲ £6-£8
Open Apr-Oct Booking advisable Bank Hols
A popular park with fine views over the surrounding countryside, located in the centre of a small village.

contd.

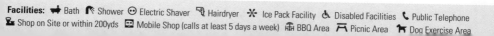
Facilities: ⛁ Bath ☏ Shower ⊙ Electric Shaver ⚛ Hairdryer ✳ Ice Pack Facility & Disabled Facilities ⌲ Public Telephone
♨ Shop on Site or within 200yds 🞿 Mobile Shop (calls at least 5 days a week) ᚼ BBQ Area ⍍ Picnic Area ⻌ Dog Exercise Area

The pleasant owners keep the grounds and facilities to a good standard. Lots of amenities close by include two pubs which offer meals at reasonable prices. A 7-acre site with 25 touring pitches, 2 hardstandings.

Facilities: ⌂ ⊕ ⚲ ⛟ **Services:** 🔌 🗄 🔋 ⌀ → ⚘

CONWY

ABERGELE   See **Betws-Yn-Rhos**

BETWS-YN-RHOS   Map 06 SH97

▶ ▶ ▶ 67% **Hunters Hamlet Caravan Park** (SH928736)
Sirior Goch Farm LL22 8PL
☎ 01745 832237 & 077 2155 2106 🖨 01745 832237
e-mail: huntershamlet@aol.com
website: www.caravancampingsites.co.uk/conwy/huntershamlet.htm
Dir: From A55 westbound, A547 into Abergele. Straight through traffic lights and 1st left onto A548. After 2.75m right at x-rds onto B5381. Site 0.5m on left
★ 🚐 £9-£19 🚎 £8-£11

Open 21 Mar-Oct Booking advisable bank hols & Jul-Aug Last arrival 22.00hrs Last departure noon
A quiet working farm park next to the owners' Georgian farmhouse. Pitches are in two grassy paddocks with pleasant views, and the beach is 3 miles away. A 2-acre site with 23 touring pitches, 23 hardstandings.
Baby bath & changing facilities

Leisure: ⚲ **Facilities:** ➛ ⌂ ⊕ ⚑ ⚹ ⚲ ⛟ 🐾 ⛛
Services: 🔌 🔋 🗄 → ▶ ⚘ ⛟ **Notes:** No tents, dogs must not be left unattended 💳 💳 💳 📶 🔵

CERRIGYDRUDION   Map 06 SH94

▶ ▶ ▶ 68% **Glan Ceirw Caravan Park** (SJ067454)
Ty Nant LL21 0RF ☎ 01490 420346 🖨 01490 420346
e-mail: glanceirwcaravanpark@tinyworld.co.uk
Dir: From A5 Betws-y-Coed onto unclass road 1m after Cerrig-y-Drudion, and park 0.25m on left. From Corwen for 8m, then 2nd left onto unclass road after Country Cooks
★ 🚐 £6-£12 🚎 £6-£12 ▲ £6-£12
Open Mar-Oct Booking advisable bank hols & Jul-Sep Last departure noon no cars by tents
A small riverside site in a rural location, with pleasant owners. Guests can enjoy the use of two

contd.

games rooms, a bar lounge and a jacuzzi. An ideal touring point for Snowdonia and North Wales. A 4.5-acre site with 15 touring pitches, 9 hardstandings and 29 statics.*

Leisure: ⚲ ⚑ ⛛ **Facilities:** ⌂ ⊕ ⚹ ⚲ ⛟ 🐾 ⛛
Services: 🔌 ⚲ 🔋 🗄 → ⚘ ⛟

CONWY   Map 06 SH77

▶ ▶ ▶ 69% **Conwy Touring Park** (SH779757)
Trefriw Rd LL32 8UX ☎ 01492 592856
🖨 01492 580024
website: www.conwytouringpark.com
Dir: 1.5m S on B5106
★ 🚐 £4.85-£11.30 🚎 £4.85-£11.30 ▲ £4.85-£11.30

Open Etr-Sep Booking advisable public hols & Jul-Aug Last arrival 19.00hrs Last departure noon
There are lovely mountain and river views on this informal park set high above the Conwy Valley. Children are well catered for, with an indoor playground and teenage games area, and there is plenty of woodland to provide screening around the park. A 70-acre site with 319 touring pitches, 100 hardstandings.
Indoor playground, storage facilities for caravans

Leisure: ⚲ ⚑ **Facilities:** ⌂ ⊕ ⚹ ⚲ ⛟ 🐾 ⛛
Services: 🔌 🔋 ⚲ ⌀ 🗄 → ∪ ▶ ⚲ ⚘ ⛟ 💳 💳 💳 📶 🔵
See advertisement on opposite page

LLANDDULAS   Map 06 SH97

▶ ▶ ▶ ▶ 74% **Bron Y Wendon Caravan Park** (SH903785)
Wern Rd LL22 8HG ☎ 01492 512903 🖨 01492 512903
e-mail: bron-y-wendon@northwales-holidays.co.uk
website: www.northwales-holidays.co.uk
Dir: Take A55 W. Turn right at sign for Llanddulas A547, then sharp right. Continue 200yds under A55 bridge. Park on left
★ 🚐 £9-£11 🚎 £9-£11
Open 21 Mar-30 Oct Booking advisable bank hols Last arrival anytime Last departure 11.00hrs
A good quality site with sea views from every pitch, and one excellent purpose-built toilet block. Staff are helpful and friendly, and everything from landscaping to maintenance has a stamp of excellence. An 8-acre site with 130 touring pitches, 80 hardstandings.
Tourist information

Leisure: ⚲ ⚑ **Facilities:** ⌂ ⊕ ⚑ ⚹ ⚲ ⛟ 🐾 ⛛
Services: 🔌 🔋 🔋 → ∪ ▶ ⚲ ✕ ⚘ 💳 💳 💳 📶 🔵

LLANRWST   Map 06 SH86

► ► ► **69% Bodnant Caravan Park** (SH805609)
Nebo Rd LL26 0SD ☎ 01492 640248 🗎 01492 640248
e-mail: ermin@bodnant-caravan-park.co.uk
website: www.bodnant-caravan-park.co.uk
*Dir: S in Llanrwst, turn off A470 opposite Birmingham
garage onto B5427 signed Nebo. Site 300yds on right,
opposite leisure centre*
🚐 £9-£10.50 🚘 £9-£10.50 ▲ £9-£10.50
Open Mar-end Oct (rs Mar 1 toilet block open if
weather very bad) Booking advisable Etr, May Day,
Spring bank hol & Jul-Aug Last arrival 22.00hrs Last
departure 11.00hrs
*This stunningly attractive park is filled with flower
beds (many times winner of Wales in Bloom
competition for the best kept touring caravan park),
and the landscape includes shrubberies and trees.
The statics are unobtrusively sited, and the toilet
block is very well kept. A 5-acre site with 54 touring
pitches and 2 statics.*
Two outside dishwashing sinks.
Leisure: ⚊ **Facilities:** ⚫⊙🚰☀⚫🖭🛉
Services: ⚑🐟⊘🗒→🏴🍴⚓🗑🛒
Notes: Main gates locked 11pm-8am

TAL-Y-BONT (NEAR CONWY)   Map 06 SH76

► **75% Tynterfyn Touring Caravan Park** (SH768692)
LL32 8YX ☎ 01492 660525
e-mail: glentynterfyn@tinyworld.co.uk
*Dir: 5m S of Conwy on B5106, road sign Tal-y-Bont, 1st
on left*
🚐 fr £6.50 🚘 fr £6.50 ▲ fr £4.50
Open Mar-Oct Booking advisable bank hols & Jul-
Aug Last arrival 22.00hrs Last departure noon
*A quiet, secluded little park set in the beautiful
Conwy Valley, and run by family owners. The
grounds are tended with care, and the older-style
toilet facilities sparkle. A 2-acre site with 15 touring
pitches, 4 hardstandings.*
Leisure: ⚊ **Facilities:** ⚫⊙🚰☀🛉
Services: ⚑🐟⊘🗒→∪🍴⚓🛒

TOWYN (NEAR ABERGELE)   Map 06 SH97

66% Ty Mawr Holiday Park
(SH965792)
Towyn Rd LL22 9HG
☎ 01745 832079 🗎 01745 827454
e-mail: admin.tymawr@parkresorts.com
website: www.park-resorts.com
Dir: On A548, 0.25m W of town
★ 🚐 £7-£19.50 🚘 £7-£19.50 ▲ £5-£19.50
Open Etr-Oct (rs Apr (excluding Etr)) Booking
advisable at all times Last departure 10.00hrs
*A very large coastal holiday park with extensive
leisure facilities including sports and
recreational amenities, and club and eating
outlets. The touring facilities are rather dated
but clean. An 18-acre site with 300 touring
pitches and 352 statics.*
contd.

Wales

isure: 🏊 Indoor swimming pool   🏊 Outdoor swimming pool   🎾 Tennis court   🎱 Games room   ⚊ Children's playground   ∪ Stables
▶ 9/18 hole golf course   🚤 Boats for hire   🎬 Cinema   🎣 Fishing   ◎ Mini golf   🌊 Watersports   🖵 Separate TV room

Ty Mawr Holiday Park

Free evening entertainment

Leisure: ☜ ☀ ⚅ **Facilities:** ☌⊙☍✳♿☏☎♂
Services: ☎⬚♀☒⬧✕♨→∪▶◎ **Notes:** No single sex groups or groups young people
☺ ☰ ☰ ☰ ☰ ☰

TREFRIW	**Map 06 SH76**

► ► ► **73% Plas Meirion Caravan Park (SH783630)**
Gower Rd LL27 ORZ ☎ 01492 640247
🖨 01492 640247
e-mail: colin_linda@plasmeirion.worldonline.co.uk
website: www.ukparks.co.uk/plasmeirion
Dir: On B5106, turn left opposite Woollen Mill, site 200mtrs on left
★ ⬚ £7.50-£10 ⬚ £7.50-£10
Open Etr-Oct Booking advisable school hols Last arrival 22.00hrs Last departure 10.30hrs ⚘
A small select park in the lovely garden of the owner's house, peacefully set in the Conwy Valley with many attractive trees. The very good toilets have been decorated with cartoon pictures, and attention is paid to all aspects of the park. A 2-acre site with 5 touring pitches and 22 statics.
Facilities: ➡☌⊙☍✳☎☷
Services: ☎⬚⬚→♨✎

DENBIGHSHIRE

CORWEN	**Map 06 SJ04**

See also **Llandrillo**

► ► **65% Llawr-Betws Farm Caravan Park (SJ016424)**
LL21 0HD ☎ 01490 460224 & 460296
website: www.ukparks.co.uk/llawrbetws
Dir: 3m W of Corwen off A494 Bala road
★ ⬚ fr £6 ⬚ fr £6 Å £4-£6
Open Mar-Oct Booking advisable bank hols & Jul-Aug Last arrival 23.00hrs Last departure noon
A quiet grassy park with mature trees and mainly level pitches. The friendly owners keep the facilities in good condition. A 2.5-acre site with 35 touring pitches and 72 statics.
Fishing.
Leisure: ☀⚅ **Facilities:** ☌⊙✳☏☎♂
Services: ☎⬚⬚♨⬚⬚→⬚✎☎

LLANDRILLO	**Map 06 SJ03**

► ► ► **60% Hendwr Caravan Park (SJ035386)**
Tyddyn Hendwr LL21 0SN ☎ 01490 440210
🖨 01490 440730
website: www.hendwrcaravanpark.freeserve.co.uk
Dir: From Corwen (A5), take B4401 for 4m. Right at sign for Hendwr. Site 0.5m down wooded driveway on right
★ ⬚ £10 ⬚ £10 Å £10
Open all year (rs Nov-Mar no toilet facilities during this period) Booking advisable BH's & school hols Last arrival 22.00hrs Last departure 16.00hrs
Level grass site with mature trees near river, hills, woods and moorland. A 10-acre site with 40 touring pitches, 2 hardstandings and 80 statics.
Wet weather camping facilities.
Facilities: ☌⊙☍✳☏☎ **Services:** ☎⬚⬚♨⬚⬚→✎

LLANGOLLEN	**Map 07 SJ24**

► ► ► **65% Ty-Ucha Caravan Park (SJ232415)**
Maesmawr Rd LL20 7PP ☎ 01978 860677
Dir: 1m E of Llangollen. Signed 250yds off A5
⬚ £8 ⬚ £7.50
Open Etr-Oct (rs Mar toilet block closed) Booking advisable BH's Last arrival 22.00hrs Last departure 14.00hrs
A very well-run site in beautiful surroundings, with a small stream on site, conveniently placed close to the A5. Ideal for country and mountain walking. A 4-acre site with 40 touring pitches.
Leisure: ☀ **Facilities:** ☌⊙
Services: ☎⬚♨⬚→∪▶☀✎⬚☎ **Notes:** No tents

PRESTATYN	**Map 06 SJ08**

 65% **NEW** Presthaven Sands (SJ091842)
Gronant LL19 9TT ☎ 01745 856471
website: www.havenholidays.com
★ ⬚ £9-£35 ⬚ £9-£35 Å £9-£35
Open Mar-Nov Booking advisable at all times Last arrival 22.00hrs Last departure 12.00hrs
Set beside two miles of superb sandy beaches and dunes, this large holiday centre offers extensive leisure and sports facilities and lively entertainment for all the family. The park land-train runs between reception and the leisure complex, with its clubs, pools, restaurants, shops, hair salon, launderettes and pub. The tourers have their own good toilet block in a separate area from the statics. A 130-acre site with 220 touring pitches.
Leisure: ☜ ☍�☀⚅☐ **Facilities:** ☎
Services: ☎♀✕♨➡☺☰☰☰☰☰☰

All of the campsites in this guide are inspected annually by an experienced team of inspectors

---

RHUALLT
Map 06 SJ07

▶ ▶ ▶ **70% Penisar Mynydd Caravan Park (SJ093770)**

Caerwys Rd LL17 0TY ☎ 01745 582227

🖥 01745 582227

e-mail: sue@chayo.freeserve.co.uk

Dir: 2m NE of Penisar. From Chester take A55 W beyond Prestatyn exit, take 2nd right turn in 2m. From Llandudno take 1st left at top of Rhuallt Hill

★ 🚐 £10-£12 🚐 £10-£12

Open Apr-Oct Booking advisable bank hols Last arrival 19.00hrs Last departure noon

An attractively laid out park with some fully-serviced pitches, set in two grassy paddocks. Sanitary facilities are dated but spotlessly clean, and maintenance standards throughout the park are high. Close to the seaside resort of Rhyll. A 2-acre site with 36 touring pitches, 36 hardstandings.

Leisure: 🜂 Facilities: ♠⊙✳↺🐕⛺

Services: 🔌🗑🚰🖳→🛒◉🞂

RUABON
Map 07 SJ34

▶ ▶ ▶ **70% James' Caravan Park (SJ300434)**

LL14 6DW ☎ 01978 820148 🖥 01978 820148

e-mail: ray@carastay.demon.co.uk

Dir: Ruabon 0.5m W of A483/A539 junct to Llangollen

★ 🚐 £8-£10 🚐 £8-£10 🛖 £5-£10

Open all year Booking advisable BH's Last arrival 21.00hrs Last departure 11.00hrs

A well-landscaped park on a former farm, with modern heated toilet facilities. Old farm buildings house a collection of restored original farm machinery, and the village shop, four pubs, chippy and launderette are a ten-minute walk away. A 6-acre site with 40 touring pitches.

Facilities: ♠⊙✕✳↺🐕⛺ Services: 🔌🗑🚰🖳→🛒◉🞂

GWYNEDD

ABERSOCH
Map 06 SH32

▶ ▶ ▶ **65% Beach View Caravan Park (SH316262)**

Bwlchtocyn LL53 7BT ☎ 01758 712956

Dir: From Abersoch to Sarn Bach turn left 40yds after end of 30mph speed limit towards Bwlchtocyn and Porthtocyn Hotel. Approximately 100yds past church turn left signed Machroes, hotel & beach, and park in 0.25m

★ 🚐 £10-£12 🚐 £10-£12 🛖 £8-£12

Open mid Mar-mid Oct Booking advisable Jul, Aug & Bank hols Last arrival 21.00hrs Last departure 11.00hrs

A compact family park that has benefited from their enthusiasm already, and many improvements have been made. It has fantastic sea views and is within a six-minute walk of the beach. A 4-acre site with 47 touring pitches.

Facilities: ♠⊙✳🐕⛺

Services: 🔌🗑🚰🖳→↺🛒⚡🞂🛒🚰

▶ ▶ ▶ **65% Trem y Môr (SH305262)**

Sarn Bach LL53 7ET ☎ 01758 712052 & 0796 7050 170 🖥 01758 713243

website: www.tggroup.co.uk/holidays/seaview.htm

Dir: Left at square in Sarn Bach. Site 200yds on right

🚐 £12 🚐 £12 🛖 £8-£12

Open Mar-Oct Booking advisable Last arrival 23.00hrs Last departure noon

A very popular park with boat owners and watersports enthusiasts, in a quiet, elevated point on the Lleyn Peninsula. Some level pitches have been created by terracing the gently-sloping ground, and the decent toilet facilities are well maintained. A 4-acre site with 97 touring pitches, 15 hardstandings.

Facilities: ♠⊙✕✳↺🐕⛺🚰🞂

Services: 🔌🗑🚰🖳→↺🛒◉🞂⚡🚰

BALA
Map 06 SH93

▶ ▶ ▶ ▶ **69% Camping & Caravanning Club Site (SH962391)**

Crynierth Caravan Park, Cefn-Ddwysarn LL23 7LN ☎ 01678 530324

website: www.campingandcaravanningclub.co.uk

Dir: A5 onto A494 to Bala. Through Bethal and Sarnau. Pass Cefn-Ddwysarn sign. Right up lane before red phone box. Site 400yds on left

★ 🚐 £12.30-£15.50 🚐 £12.30-£15.50 🛖 £12.30-£15.50

Open 21 Mar-28 Oct Booking advisable bank hols & peak periods Last arrival 21.00hrs Last dep noon

A quiet pleasant park with interesting views and high class facilities, set back from the main road in a very secluded position. Lake Bala offers great appeal for the water sports enthusiast, as does the nearby River Tryweryn, a leading slalom course in white-water rafting. Please see the advertisement on page 10 for details of Club Members' benefits. A 4-acre site with 50 touring pitches, 8 hardstandings.

Leisure: 🜂 Facilities: ♠⊙✕✳↺🐕⛺

Services: 🔌🗑🚰🖳→↺🛒⚡🞂🚰⚡🚰🛒

▶ ▶ ▶ ▶ **70% Pen Y Bont Touring & Camping Park (SH932350)**

Llangynog Rd LL23 7PH ☎ 01678 520549

🖥 01678 520006

e-mail: information@penybont-bala.co.uk

website: www.penybont-bala.co.uk

Dir: From A494 take B4391. Site 0.75m on right

★ 🚐 £10-£10.90 🚐 £10-£10.30 🛖 £9.90-£10.90

contd.

Wales

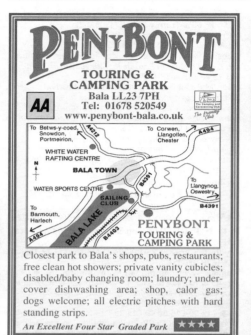

PEN Y BONT
TOURING & CAMPING PARK
Bala LL23 7PH
Tel: 01678 520549
www.penybont-bala.co.uk

AA

Closest park to Bala's shops, pubs, restaurants; free clean hot showers; private vanity cubicles; disabled/baby changing room; laundry; undercover dishwashing area; shop, calor gas; dogs welcome; all electric pitches with hard standing strips.

An Excellent Four Star Graded Park ★★★★

Open Apr-Oct Booking advisable BH's & school hols Last arrival 22.30hrs Last departure 13.00hrs
A very attractively landscaped park in a woodland country setting, very close to the River Dee and Bala Lake. The park offers excellent facilities, and most pitches have water and electricity. Lake Bala is famous for its water sports, with Afon Tryweryn catering for enthusiasts of canoe slalom and white-water rafting. A 7-acre site with 95 touring pitches. Dishwashing & vegetable preparation area.
Facilities: ⊞⊙♥✕🛇🔥🕭🏊🚿🔥💢 **Services:** 🔋🖭🛈🅰
🔋🖭🛒→🍴🌳🎪🥤💳🆑🔟💳🆑💷📶🗑

▶ ▶ ▶ ▶ 65% **Pen-y-Garth Caravan & Camping Park (SH940349)**
LL23 7ES ☎ 01678 520485 & 0780 8198717
📠 01678 520401
e-mail: stay@penygarth.co.uk
website: www.penygarth.co.uk
Dir: Leave A494 in Bala onto B4391. After 1m fork right at sign to Rhosygwaliau. Site 600yds on right
★ 🚐£7.95-£9.50 🚐£7.95-£9.50 ▲£7.50-£8.95
Open Mar-Oct Booking advisable bank hols & Jul-Aug Last arrival 22.00hrs Last departure noon
A good park in an area of great tranquillity, attractively landscaped amongst trees and natural scenery. There are excellent views of Mount Arenag and the Berwyns, and nearby Bala is an ideal centre for water sports, walking and climbing. A 20-acre site with 63 touring pitches and 54 statics.

contd.

Pen-y-Garth Garavan & Camping Site
Table tennis,10 acres recreation, dishwashing room
Leisure: ♦ ⚙ **Facilities:** 🄝⊙♥✕🛇🔥🔥
Services: 🔋🖭🛈🄓🛈→🅄🍴🛆🥤🎪🥤🔟💳🆑🗑

BARMOUTH   **Map 06 SH61**

▶ ▶ ▶ ▶ 74% **Hendre Mynach Touring Caravan & Camping Park (SH605170)**
Llanaber Rd LL42 1YR ☎ 01341 280262
📠 01341 280586
e-mail: mynach@lineone.net
🚐£10-£18 🚐£10-£18 ▲£8-£18

Open Mar-9 Jan (rs Nov-Feb shop closed or restricted opening) Booking advisable bank hols & Jul-Aug Last arrival 22.00hrs Last departure noon
A lovely site with immaculate facilities, situated off the A496 on the northern outskirts of Barmouth and near to railway, with almost direct access to promenade and beach. Caravanners should not be put off by the steep descent, as park staff are always on hand if needed. The toilet facilities are modern and excellent, and pitches have TV and satellite hook-up as well as water and electricity. A small cafe serves light meals and take-aways. A 10-acre site with 205 touring pitches, 50 hardstandings.
TV hook ups.
Leisure: ⚙ **Facilities:** 🄝⊙♥✕🛇🔥🔥
Services: 🔋🖭🛈🄓🛈✕🛆🛒→🅄🥤🔟💳🆑🗑

NEW - AA Quality % Score for each pennant category. See page 7 for a full explanation

---

Services: 🅣 Toilet Fluid ✕ Café/ Restaurant 🛒 Fast Food/Takeaway 🛒 Baby Care 🔋 Electric Hook Up
🄓 Launderette ♀ Licensed Bar 🛈 Calor Gaz ⌀ Camping Gaz 🔋 Battery Charging

▶ ▶ ▶ 73% **Trawsdir Touring & Caravan Park (SH596198)**
Caerddaniel Caravan Park, Llanaber LL42 1RR
☎ 01341 280999 & 280611 01341 280740
e-mail: enquiries@barmouthholidays.co.uk
website: www.barmouthholidays.co.uk
Dir: *3m N of Barmouth on A496*
★ £10-£20 £10-£20 £7-£15
Open Mar-Oct Booking advisable Etr, Whitsun & Jul-Aug Last arrival 21.00hrs Last departure noon
A recently developed park on a working sheep farm with views to sea and hills, and very accessible to motor traffic. The facilities are of a very good standard. 50 touring pitches.
Leisure: **Facilities:** **Services:** **Notes:** Families & couples only

BETWS GARMON — Map 06 SH55

▶ ▶ ▶ ▶ 77% **Bryn Gloch Caravan & Camping Park (SH534574)**
LL54 7YY ☎ 01286 650216 01286 650591
e-mail: eurig@easynet.co.uk
website: www.bryngloch.co.uk
Dir: *On A4085 7m SE of Caernarfon*

Open all year Booking advisable school & bank hols Last arrival 23.00hrs Last departure 17.00hrs
An excellent family-run site with modern toilets, and all level pitches in beautiful surroundings. The park offers the best of two worlds, with its bustling holiday atmosphere and the peaceful natural surroundings. The 25 acres of level fields are separated by mature hedges and trees, guaranteeing sufficient space for families wishing to spread themselves out. There are plenty of walks in the area, and a constant source of interest is the babbling stream, Gwyrfai. A 12-acre site with 160 touring pitches and 14 statics.
Family bathroom & mother & baby room.
Leisure: **Facilities:**
Services:

BRYNCRUG — Map 06 SH60

▶ ▶ ▶ 61% **Woodlands Holiday Park (SH618035)**
LL36 9UH ☎ 01654 710471 01654 710100
Dir: *2m from Tywyn on B4405 road to Tal-y-Llyn*
★ £8.50 £8.50
Open Etr & Apr-Oct Booking advisable Jul-Aug Last arrival 22.00hrs Last departure 11.00hrs

contd.

WOODLANDS
Holiday Park & Country Club

Within the Snowdonia National Park, Club, outdoor swimming pool, launderette, amusements and high-season entertainment. ***Grassed & Hard Standing, full service hook-up points for electric, water, T.V.*** *Three miles from the sandy beaches of Tywyn and surrounded by beautiful countryside.*

Telephone for brochure: 01654 710471 Bryncrug, Tywyn, Gwynedd LL36 9UH

Snowdonia
Award-winning family-run Caravan park

28 acre picturesque park nestled between Snowdonia mountain ranges and on the banks of the river Gwyrfai with breathtaking views. Clean, peaceful site, electric hook-ups, luxury toilet/showers and launderette, mother & baby room, shop and off-licence, games room, spacious play area, fishing, mini-golf and disabled facilities.

- Dragon Award Static Caravans
- Touring Pitches • Tent Pitches
- Modern Self-Catering Acc.

Footpath to Snowdon 2½ miles. 2 pubs & restaurants within 1 mile. Many local attractions close by, plus Watersports, Climbing, Walking, Horseriding & much more.

Bryn Gloch Caravan & Camping Park
AA ★★★★★ TOURING PARK

For brochure call:
01286 650216
www.bryngloch.co.uk
Eurig@easynet.co.uk

Wales

A large holiday park and country club with mainly statics and chalets, and a small, separate touring section. There is a wide range of amenities. A 2-acre site with 20 touring pitches, 10 hardstandings and 122 statics.
Entertainment in high season.
Leisure: ⚑ ⚘ ⚙ 🎱 **Facilities:** 🛁⊙🔥🚿🕭🍴🎣🌲
Services: 🔌🚽🏪🍴✗→🅿🅤🔥⊙△♨🦮🚐🍺🗑

CAERNARFON   Map 06 SH46
See also **Dinas Dinlle & Llandwrog**

▶ ▶ ▶ **62% Cwm Cadnant Valley (SH487628)**
Cwm Cadnant Valley, Llanberis Rd LL55 2DF
☎ 01286 673196 📠 01286 675941
e-mail: aa@cadnantvalley.co.uk
website: www.cadnantvalley.co.uk
Dir: On the outskirts of Caernarfon on A4086 to Llanberis
★ 🚐 £9.50-£12.50 🚐 £9.50-£12.50 ▲ £7.50-£10.50

Open 15 Mar-Oct Booking advisable bank hols & Jul-Aug Last arrival 22.00hrs Last departure 11.00hrs
Set in an attractive wooded valley with a stream is this terraced site with secluded pitches. It is located on the outskirts of Caernarfon, close to the main Caernarfon-Llanberis road. A 4.5-acre site with 69 touring pitches.
Leisure: ⚙ **Facilities:** 🛁⊙🔥✳🚿🕭🍴🎣🌲
Services: 🔌🚽🏪🍴🔥🕭🅣→🅤🔥△♨🦮🚐🍺🗑

▶ ▶ ▶ **65% Glan Gwna Holiday Park (SH502622)**
Caeathro LL55 2SG ☎ 01286 673456 & 676402
📠 01286 672322
e-mail: touring@glangwna.com
website: www.glangwna.com
Dir: Take A4085 signed Beddgelert. 1.5m from Caernarfon
★ 🚐 £10-£17 🚐 £10-£17 ▲ £10-£17
Open Etr-Oct (rs mid Apr-May & mid Sep-Oct some facilities are closed) Booking advisable bank hols & Jul-Aug Last arrival 22.00hrs Last departure noon
Beautifully situated on a bend in the Afon Seiont, and part of a large holiday complex with excellent facilities. A 7-acre site with 90 touring pitches and 130 statics.
Fishing.
Leisure: ⚑ ⚙ **Facilities:** 🛁⊙✳🔥🕭🌲
Services: 🔌🚽🏪🍴✗🚮→🅤🔥🗑
Notes: No single sex groups 🦮🚐🍺🗑

▶ ▶ ▶ **69% Plas Gwyn Caravan Park (SH523632)**
Llanrug LL55 2AQ ☎ 01286 672619
e-mail: info@plasgwyn.co.uk
website: www.plasgwyn.co.uk
Dir: A4086, 3m E of Caernarfon
★ 🚐 £6.50-£8 🚐 £6.50-£8 ▲ £4-£7
Open Mar-Oct Booking advisable BH's
Last arrival 22.00hrs
A secluded park with bright and cheerful toilet facilities, handy for beaches, historic Caernarfon, and walking. The site is set within the grounds of Plas Gwyn House, a Georgian property with colonial additions. A 1.5-acre site with 27 touring pitches, 2 hardstandings and 18 statics.
Facilities: 🛁🕭✳🌲🕭
Services: 🔌🚽🏪🔥🕭🅣→🅤🔥△♨🗑

▶ ▶ ▶ **72% Riverside Camping (SH505630)**
Seiont Nurseries, Pont Rug LL55 2BB
☎ 01286 672524 & 678781 📠 01286 677223
e-mail: brenda@riversidecamping.freeserve.co.uk
Dir: 2m from Caernarfon on right of A4086
★ 🚐 £8-£10 🚐 £8-£10 ▲ £6-£9
Open Etr-end Oct Booking advisable Jul-Aug & BH's
Last arrival anytime Last departure 20.00hrs
A secluded park divided up by shrubs and trees, adjacent to the small River Seiont. A 4.5-acre site with 55 touring pitches.
Family shower room & baby changing facilities
Leisure: ⚙ **Facilities:** 🛁⊙🔥✳🕭🍴🎣🌲
Services: 🔌🚽🍴🚮→🅤🔥⊙△♨🗑🦮 **Notes:** No fires, no loud music. Dogs must be kept on leads

▶ ▶ ▶ **64% Ty'n yr Onnen Mountain Farm Caravan & Camping (SH534588)**
Waunfawr LL55 4AX ☎ 01286 650281
📠 01286 650043
Dir: At Waunfawr on A4085, turn down unclass road opposite church. Site is signposted
★ 🚐 fr £8 🚐 fr £7 ▲ fr £6

Open Spring bank hol-Oct (rs Etr & May Day bank hol open if weather premitting) Booking advisable Spring bank hol & Jul-Aug Last arrival 21.00hrs Last departure 10.00hrs
A gently-sloping site on a 200-acre sheep farm, set in magnificent surroundings with mountain views. This secluded park is well equipped, with quality toilet facilities. Access is down a winding single track with stone walls and overhang, and not suitable for very large units. A 4-acre site with 20 touring pitches and 4 statics. *contd*

Fishing & nature park

Leisure: ◕ ⚖ ▭ **Facilities:** ➡ ✚ ⊙ ⟐ ✳ ᕋ ᕫ ₼
ᕕ ♠ **Services:** ⊞ ▣ ▸ ∅ ⊞ Ⓣ → ∪ ▸ ♢ ✦ ⚌ ⤻ ₽
⬤ ▭ ▭ ▧ ⛟

▶ ▶ **57% Tyn-y-Coed Farm Caravan Park
(SH544629)**

Llanrug LL55 2AQ ☎ 01286 673565 📄 01286 673565
Dir: 3m from Caernarfon, just off A4086 Caernarfon to
Llanberis road, large blue sign at roadside
★ ⊞ £8-£10 ⊞ £8-£10 ▲ £8-£10
Open Mar-Sep (rs Mar & mid-end Sep) Booking
advisable Jul & Aug Last arrival 22.00hrs Last
departure noon
*A secluded wooded park set on farmland, with
attractive views and in an ideal position for walking,
mountaineering and access to beaches. This adults-
only park is geared towards quiet retired couples,
and there are plans to upgrade the simple facilities.
A 0.75-acre site with 20 touring pitches and 40
statics.*
Facilities: ᕋ ⊙ **Services:** ⊞ ▸ → ∪ ▸ ⬡ ♢ ⤻ ▣ ₽
Notes: Dogs must be kept on leads

CRICCIETH | Map 06 SH43

▶ ▶ **65% Llwyn-Bugeilydd Caravan & Camping
Site (SH498398)**
LL52 0PN ☎ 01766 522235
Dir: 1m N of Criccieth on B4411.
Site 1st on right
★ ⊞ fr £9.50 ⊞ fr £9.50 ▲ fr £8.50
Open Etr/Apr-Oct Booking advisable Etr, Whit & Jul-
Aug Last arrival anytime Last departure 11.00hrs
*A quiet rural site with sea and mountain views, and
well-tended grass pitches. The toilets are kept very
clean, and the resident owners are always on hand.
A 6-acre site with 45 touring pitches.*
Facilities: ᕋ ⊙ ⟐ ✳ ᕫ ᕕ ♠
Services: ⊞ ▸ ∅ ⊞ → ∪ ▸ ⬡ ⚌ ⤻ ₽

▶ ▶ **67% Tyddyn Cethin Caravan Park
(SH492404)**
LL52 0NF ☎ 01766 522149
Dir: N from Criccieth on B4411 &
Tyddyn Cethin is 4th site on right
★ ⊞ £7.50-£10 ⊞ £7.50-£10 ▲ £6.50-£7.50
Open Mar-Oct Booking advisable Feb-Mar Last
arrival 22.00hrs Last departure noon
*A very high quality little park in a pretty setting on
the banks of the River Dwyfor. The enthusiastic
owners maintain the grounds and sanitary facilities
to an excellent standard. An 8-acre site with 60
touring pitches and 40 statics.*
Fishing on site.
Facilities: ➡ ᕋ ⊙ ✳ ᕫ ♠
Services: ⊞ ▸ ∅ ⊞ → ∪ ▸ ⬡ ✦ ⚌ ⤻ ₽

Fewer than 50 parks have been
awarded the coveted 5-pennant
rating. For a full list see page 18

▶ **58% Tyddyn Morthwyl (SH488402)**
LL52 0NF ☎ 01766 522115
Dir: 1.5m N of Criccieth on B4411
★ ⊞ fr £7 ⊞ ▲
Open Etr-Oct (rs Mar & Oct) Booking advisable
Spring bank hol & Jul-Aug Last departure 14.00hrs
*A quiet sheltered site with level grass pitches in
three fields. The simple facilities include some
electric hook-ups, and the sea is close by. A 10-acre
site with 60 touring pitches and 22 statics.*
Facilities: ᕋ ⊙ ✳ ᕕ ᕫ **Services:** ⊞ ⊞ → ∪ ▸ ✦ ⤻ ₽
Notes: Dogs must be kept on leads at all times

DINAS DINLLE | Map 06 SH45

▶ ▶ ▶ ▶ **65% Dinlle Caravan Park (SH443568)**
LL54 5TW ☎ 01286 830324 📄 01286 831526
e-mail: enq@tuornleyleisure.co.uk
website: www.tuornleyleisure.co.uk
Dir: Exit A499 at sign for Caernarfon Airport. 2
★ ⊞ £6.50-£15.50 ⊞ £6.50-£15.50 ▲ £6.50-£15.50

Open May-Aug (rs Mar-Apr & Sep-Nov club, shop,
swimming pool restricted hours) Booking advisable
Spring bank hol & Jul-Aug Last arrival 23.00hrs Last
departure noon
*A very accessible, well-kept grassy level site,
adjacent to sandy beach, with good views to
Snowdonia. The park is situated in acres of flat
grassland, with plenty of room for even the largest
groups. A lounge bar and family room are
comfortable places in which to relax, and children
are well provided for with an exciting adventure
playground. The beach road gives access to the golf
club, a nature reserve and to Air World at
Caernarfon Airport. An 11-acre site with 175 touring
pitches and 167 statics.*
Leisure: ᐟ ◕ ⚖ **Facilities:** ᕋ ⊙ ⟐ ✳ ᕫ ⎑
Services: ⊞ ▣ ▸ ⟐ ▸ ∅ ⊞ → ∪ ⤻ ₽ ⬤ ▭ ▭ ▧ ⛟

See advertisement on page 300

DYFFRYN ARDUDWY | Map 06 SH52

▶ ▶ ▶ **69% Murmur-yr-Afon Touring Park
(SH586236)**
LL44 2BE ☎ 01341 247353 📄 01341 247353
e-mail: mills@murmuryrafon25.freeserve.co.uk
Dir: On A496 N of village
★ ⊞ £5.50-£10.75 ⊞ £5.50-£10.75 ▲ £5.50-£10.50
Open Mar-Oct Booking advisable bank hols Last
arrival 23.00hrs Last departure 11.30hrs
*A pleasant family-run park alongside a wooded
stream on the edge of the village, and handy*

contd.

Facilities: ➡ Bath ᕋ Shower ⊙ Electric Shaver ⟐ Hairdryer ✳ Ice Pack Facility ᕫ Disabled Facilities ♠ Public Telephone
₽ Shop on Site or within 200yds ⊞ Mobile Shop (calls at least 5 days a week) ᕫ BBQ Area ᕕ Picnic Area ♠ Dog Exercise Area

COASTAL SNOWDONIA

*A Tourist Board "DRAGON" Award Park
for High Standard of Accommodation*
Only 300 yds. from Long Sandy Beach

★ New luxury 6/8 berth caravans for hire (some 3 Bedrooms).
All with shower, toilet, fridge, colour TV, continental quilts.

★ Licensed Club House
★ Supermarket
★ Launderette
★ Flush Toilets, hot showers
★ Children's Games Room

★ Tourers & Campers on level grassland
★ Electrical Hook-ups available.
★ Razor Points
★ Pets welcome
★ Children's Play Area

★ Outdoor Heated Swimming Pool

Excellent beach for swimming, surfing, canoeing, sailing
and fishing. Riding, climbing, golf and many other
sporting activities nearby.

For brochure write or telephone: **AA** ☰ Dragon Award ⊚

**Dinlle Caravan Park,
Dinas Dinlle, Caernarfon. Tel: 01286 830324**

Murmur-yr-Afon Touring Park
*for large sandy beaches. Expect good, clean
facilities, and lovely views of rolling hills and
mountains.
A 4-acre site with 67 touring pitches.*

Leisure: 🅰 **Facilities:** 🏕☉🍴⚡☀🚿🛁🚻🏪🎠🛒
Services: 🔌🗑🛢→ U 🔩🛒

LLANDWROG　　　　　Map 06 SH45

► ► ► ► 72% **White Tower Caravan Park
(SH453582)**
LL54 5UH ☎ 01286 830649 & 07802 562785
🖨 01286 830649
e-mail: whitetower@supanet.com
website: www.whitetower.supanet.com
*Dir: 1.5m from village along Tai'r Eglwys road. From
Caernarfon take A487 Porthmadog road. Cross over
rdbt, then take 1st right. Park 3m on right*
★ 🚐 £6-£11.50 🚙 £6-£11.50 ⛺ £6-£11.50

contd.

Open Mar-15 Jan (rs Mar-mid May & Sep-Oct bar
wknds only) Booking advisable bank hols & Jul-Aug
Last arrival 23.00hrs Last departure noon
*There are lovely views of Snowdonia from this well
maintained park located just 2 miles from the
nearest beach at Dinas Dinlle. An immaculately
maintained toilet block has key access, and the hard
pitches have water and electricity. Popular
amenities include an outdoor heated swimming
pool, a lounge bar with family room, and a games
and TV room. A 6-acre site with 104 touring pitches,
80 hardstandings and 54 statics.*

Leisure: 🏊♦🅰🖥 **Facilities:** 🏕☉🍴☀🚿🛁🛒 **Services:**
🔌🗑🛢🥫🗑🚽→ U 🔩🛒♨🛢🚽🍴🎠⊛ 🚮 Bottas CONNECT 🚰🔧

LLANYSTUMDWY　　　　Map 06 SH43

► ► ► ► 69% **Camping & Caravanning
Club Site (SH469384)**
Tyddyn Sianel LL52 0LS ☎ 01766 522855
website: www.campingandcaravanningclub.co.uk
*Dir: From Criccieth take A497 W, 2nd right to
Llanystumdwy, site on right*
★ 🚐 £12.30-£15.50 🚙 £12.30-£15.50 ⛺ £12.30-£15.50
Open 21 Mar-28 Oct Booking advisable bank hols &
peak periods Last arrival 21.00hrs Last departure
noon
*An attractive site close to one of many beaches in
the area, and with lovely mountain and sea views.
There is a good range of well-maintained facilities,
and the site is handy for walking in the Snowdonia
National Park or on the local network of quiet
country lanes. Please see the advertisement on
page 10 for details of Club Members' benefits. A
4-acre site with 70 touring pitches, 4 hardstandings.*
Playfield

Facilities: 🏕☉🍴☀🚿🛁🛒🚻🎠
Services: 🔌🗑🛢🥫🗑🚽→ U 🔩🛒♨🛢🍴⊛ 🚮 Bottas CONNECT 🚰🔧

PONTLLYFNI　　　　　Map 06 SH45

► ► ► 69% **St Ives Touring Caravan Park
(SH432524)**
Lon-Y-Wig LL54 5EG ☎ 01286 660347
website: www.stivestouringcaravans.co.uk
*Dir: Off A499 along lane towards beach from village
centre*
★ 🚐 £7.50-£9.50 🚙 £7.50-£9.50 ⛺ £7.50-£9.50
Open Mar-Oct Booking advisable all times Last
arrival 21.00hrs Last departure noon
*An immaculate little site with good facilities, within
easy walking distance of beach. A 1.25-acre site
with 20 touring pitches, 2 hardstandings.*

Facilities: 🏕☉☀🚿🛁🛒🖥🚻 **Services:** 🔌🗑🛢🥫🗑🚽♨
→ U 🔩🛒♨♨🛢 **Notes:** No ball games

► 65% **Llyn-y-Gele Farm & Caravan Park
(SH432523)**
LL54 5EG ☎ 01286 660289 & 660283
*Dir: Off A499, 7m S of Caernarfon. Right in village of
Pontllyfni by shop and garage.*
★ 🚐 £7-£9 🚙 £7 ⛺ £6-£7
Open Etr-Sep Booking advisable Jul-Aug Last
arrival 22.00hrs Last departure 13.00hrs

contd

A quiet, well-kept farm site with its own path to the beach 5-7 minutes' walk away. This small park is in the centre of the village, and is well located for touring the Lleyn Peninsula, Anglesey and Snowdonia. A 4-acre site with 6 touring pitches and 24 statics.

Leisure: 🏸 Facilities: ⚫☉✳️🐾🐕
Services: 🖵🛢️→∪🔧

PONT-RUG   See **Caernarfon**

PORTHMADOG   Map 06 SH53

70% **NEW** **Greenacres (SH560381)**
Black Rock Sands, Morfa Bychan LL49 9YB ☎ 08457 125931
website: www.british-holidays.co.uk
Dir: After Porthmadog high street, turn between Woolworths and the post office towards Black Rock Sands. After 2m, park entrance on left
★ 🚐 £12-£27 🚐 £12-£27
Open 22 Mar-28 Oct Booking advisable at all times Last arrival 18.00hrs Last departure 10.00hrs
A holiday park on level ground just a short walk from Black Rock Sands, and set against a backdrop of Snowdonia National Park. All touring pitches are on hardstandings surrounded by closely-mown grass, and near the entertainment complex. A full programme of entertainment, organised clubs, indoor and outdoor sports and leisure including a high-level 'ropeworks' adventure course, pubs, shows and cabarets all add to a holiday here. A 121-acre site with 58 touring pitches and 370 statics.
Leisure: 🏊 🎾 🎱 🏸 Facilities: ⚫🐾 Services: 🖵♿
✗♨️→∪▶♨️🔧 🍴 Notes: No single sex groups or groups of under 18s 💳 ▨ ▨ ▨ ▨

TALSARNAU   Map 06 SH63

▶ ▶ ▶ ▶ 76% **Barcdy Touring Caravan & Camping Park (SH623368)**
LL47 6YG ☎ 01766 770736
Dir: From Maentwrog take left turn for Harlech, on A496. Barcdy 4m on left
★ 🚐 £8.50-£11 🚐 £8.50-£11 ⛺ £8.50-£11

Open Apr-Oct (rs Etr-Spring bank hol & mid Sep-Oct only two fields open, food shop closed) Booking advisable 🐾

contd.

A quiet picturesque park on the southern edge of the Vale of Ffestiniog near Dwryd estuary. The enthusiastic and hard-working owners maintain the park to very high standards. Two touring areas are available, one a large flat piece of land near the park entrance, and the other with more secluded terraced pitches running along one side of a narrow valley. Footpaths through adjacent woodland lead to small lakes and an established nature trail. A 12-acre site with 68 touring pitches and 30 statics.
Dishwashing sinks
Facilities: ⚫☉🐾✳️⚫🎏
Services: 🖵🛢️🛢️▨🗓️→∪🔧♿💳 ▨ ▨ ▨ ▨ 🔌

TAL-Y-BONT   Map 06 SH52

▶ ▶ 60% *Benar Beach Camping & Touring Park (SH573226)*
LL43 2AR ☎ 01341 247571 & 247001
Dir: 1m from A496, halfway between Harlech & Barmouth
🚐 🚐 ⛺
Open Mar-3 Oct Booking advisable peak periods
Friendly family site consisting of a large, level camping field with much improved facilities. Adjacent to sandy beach with view of mountains. A 5-acre site with 40 touring pitches. Satellite & TV hook-ups.
Facilities: ⚫☉✳️⚫🐕 Services: 🖵→∪🔧♿

TYWYN   Map 06 SH50
See also **Bryncrug**

▶ ▶ ▶ 70% **Ynysymaengwyn Caravan Park (SH602021)**
LL36 9RY ☎ 01654 710684 ▤ 01654 710684
e-mail: rita@ynysy.co.uk
website: www.ynysymaengwyn.co.uk
Dir: On A493, 1m N of Tywyn, towards Dolgellau
★ 🚐 £8-£11 ⛺ £7-£10
Open Etr or Apr-Oct Booking advisable Jul-Aug Last arrival 23.00hrs Last departure noon
A very smart municipal park with a well-designed and clean sanitary block and a pleasant environment. Ideally placed close to the seaside in one direction, and beautiful countryside and hills in the other. A 4-acre site with 80 touring pitches and 115 statics.
Leisure: 🏸 Facilities: ⚫☉✳️♿⚫🐾🖵🎏🐕
Services: 🖵🛢️🛢️▨🗓️→∪▶☉♿♨️🔧
Notes: Dogs must be kept on leads at all times

MONMOUTHSHIRE

CHEPSTOW   Map 03 ST59

▶ ▶ ▶ 67% **St Pierre Camping & Caravan Site (ST509901)**
Portskewett NP26 5TT ☎ 01291 425114
Dir: From Chepstow take A48 towards Newport, turn left at 1st rdbt, then immediate left
★ 🚐 fr £15 🚐 fr £15 ⛺ fr £12
Open all year Booking advisable bank hols Last departure 18.00hrs

contd.

Monmouth Caravan Park
Tel: (01600) 714745 Fax: (01600) 716690

A select touring and camping park situated in the ancient Borough of Monmouth. Easy walking distance from the town centre. Quiet, good access. Ideal for exploring the Wye Valley, Brecon Beacons and Forest of Dean. Family run flat grass touring park. New licensed club room, small shop, toilet and shower facilities and fishing nearby. Voted one of The Top 100 Parks in Britain. Featured on Top 35 Parks Video – Practical Caravan Magazine.

First right past Fire Station on B4233.

Rockfield Road out of Monmouth

Rockfield Road, Monmouth, Monmouthshire NP5 3BA AA

Well established site with immaculately kept facilities and a peaceful atmosphere, overlooking the Severn Estuary. A 4-acre site with 50 touring pitches.
Boule, croquet.
Facilities: ⬤ ☉ ◵ ✴ ⚲ ⛄ ⛺ ⛱ ♞
Services: ⬤ ▣ ⬧ → ∪ ▶ ⚡

DINGESTOW
Map 03 SO41

▶ ▶ ▶ 63% **Bridge Caravan Park & Camping Site (SO459104)**
Bridge Farm NP25 4DY ☎ 01600 740241
Dir: Signposted from Raglan & located off A449
⛟ ⛟ Å
Open Etr-Oct Booking advisable bank hols Last arrival 22.00hrs Last departure 16.00hrs
The River Trothy runs along the edge of this quiet village park, which has been owned by the same family for many years. Pitches are both grass and hardstanding, and there is a backdrop of woodland. A 4-acre site with 94 touring pitches.
Fishing.
Facilities: ⬤ ☉ ◵ ✴ ⚲ ⛄ ⛺ ♞
Services: ⬤ ▣ ⬧ ⊘ ▣ ⊤ → ∪ ▶ ⚴ ⚡ ⚡

MITCHEL TROY
Map 03 SO41

▶ ▶ ▶ 62% **Glen Trothy Caravan & Camping Park (SO496105)**
NP25 4BD ☎ 01600 712295 ▤ 01600 712295
website: www.glentrothy.co.uk
Dir: Approx midway between Monmouth & Raglan, signed off B4293. Site at entrance to village
★ ⛟ fr £7.50 ⛟ fr £7.50 Å fr £6
Open Mar-Oct Booking advisable BH's & high season Last arrival 21.00hrs Last departure noon
A very pretty park in a well-wooded area beside the River Trothy, where free fishing by licence is available. Three large fields are neatly cut, and the friendly owners are currently upgrading the facilities to a good standard. A 6.5-acre site with 84 touring pitches.
Dishwashing room
Leisure: ⚄ Facilities: ⬤ ☉ ◵ ✴ ⚲ ⛄ Services: ⬤ ▣ ⬧
▣ → ▶ ⚄ ⚴ ⚡ ⚴ Notes: No camp fires, BBQs must be purpose built & 18in off ground

---

MONMOUTH
Map 03 SO51

▶ ▶ ▶ 69% **Monmouth Caravan Park (SO498135)**
Rockfield Rd NP5 3BA ☎ 01600 714745
▤ 01600 716690
e-mail: mail@monmouthcaravanpark.co.uk
Dir: From A40 take B4233 S of Monmouth, leading into Rockfield Road & site is opposite fire station
★ ⛟ £10-£12 ⛟ £10-£12 Å £5.50-£12

Open Mar-4 Jan Booking advisable Jun-Sep Last arrival 20.00hrs Last departure 20.00hrs
A neat, attractive park has been upgraded to a good standard, and offers clean and bright toilet facilities. There is a small licensed bar with occasional entertainment, and Offa's Dyke footpath is only a few yards away. The town is within easy walking distance. A 3-acre site with 60 touring pitches, 12 hardstandings.
Facilities: ⬤ ☉ ◵ ✴ ⚲ ⛄ ⛺ ⛱ ♞ Services: ⬤ ▣ ⬧ ⬧
▣ ⊤ ✕ ⬧ → ∪ ▶ ⚄ ⚴ ⚴ ▣ ⊝ ⬛ ⬛ ⬛ ⬛ ⬛

USK
Map 03 SO30

▶ ▶ ▶ ▶ 69% **Pont Kemys Caravan & Camping Park (SO348058)**
Chainbridge NP7 9DS ☎ 01873 880688
▤ 01873 880270
e-mail: info@pontkemys.com
website: www.pontkemys.com
Dir: On B4598, 300yds N of Chainbridge
★ ⛟ £9-£11 ⛟ £9-£11 Å £4.50-£5

contd

Wales

Open Apr-Sep Booking advisable BH's
Last arrival 23.00hrs
A peaceful, newly-developed park next to the River
Usk, offering a very high standard of facilities. The
park is in a rural area with mature trees and country
views, and attracts quiet visitors who enjoy the
many attractions of this area. An 8-acre site with
65 touring pitches.
Mother & baby room, kitchen facilities for groups
Leisure: ❏ Facilities: ✿⊙🥤※⅄⚭🛒⊓🕇
Services: 🗜🗑🛢� BT → ▶ ⅄ ✔
Notes: Dogs must be kept on leads at all times

PEMBROKESHIRE

BROAD HAVEN   Map 02 SM81

▶ ▶ 65% **South Cockett Caravan & Camping Park
(SM879135)**
South Cockett SA62 3TU ☎ 01437 781296 & 781760
🗐 01437 781296
e-mail: wjames01@farming.co.uk
website: www.southcockett.co.uk
*Dir: Park signed and located just through Broadway on
B4341*
★ 🚐 £6-£8.50 🚐 £6-£8.50 ▲ £4.50-£7
Open Etr-Oct Booking advisable Jul-Aug Last arrival
23.30hrs
*A small park on a working farm, with touring areas
divided into neat paddocks by high, well-trimmed
hedges. Good toilet facilities, and in a convenient
location for the lovely beach at nearby Broad
Haven. A 6-acre site with 73 touring pitches and 1
static.*
Facilities: ✿⊙※✆ Services: 🗜🗑🛢🔆BT → ∪⅄✔🛒

FISHGUARD   Map 02 SM93

▶ ▶ 71% **Fishguard Bay Caravan & Camping
Park (SM984383)**
Garn Gelli SA65 9ET ☎ 01348 811415
🗐 01348 811425
e-mail: enquiries@fishguardbay.com
website: www.fishguardbay.com
Dir: 1m N of A487
★ 🚐 £10-£12 🚐 £10-£12 ▲ £9-£11

Open Mar-9 Jan Booking advisable Jul-Aug Last
departure noon
*Set high up on cliffs with outstanding views of
Fishguard Bay, and the Pembrokeshire Coastal Path
running right through the centre. The park is*
contd.

extremely well kept, with three good toilet blocks, a
common room with TV, a lounge/library, decent
laundry, and well-stocked shop. A 5-acre site with
50 touring pitches and 50 statics.
View point.
Leisure: ❦/Ⅱ❏ Facilities: ✿⊙🥤※✆⚭
Services: 🗜🗑🛢🔆BT → ∪⅄😊✔🍴🚮⊡⑩🔌🔩🗐

▶ ▶ ▶ 65% **Gwaun Vale Touring Park (SM977356)**
Llanychaer SA65 9TA ☎ 01348 874698
e-mail: margaret.harries@talk21.com
Dir: From Fishguard take B4313. Site 1.5m on right
★ 🚐 £10-£11.50 🚐 £10-£11.50 ▲ £8.50-£10
Open Apr-Oct Booking advisable Jul-Aug
*Located at the opening of the beautiful Gwaun
Valley, this well-kept park is set on the hillside with
pitches tiered on two levels. There are lovely views
of the surrounding countryside, and good facilities.
A 1.75-acre site with 30 touring pitches.*
Free loan of boules, guide books available
Leisure: /Ⅱ Facilities: ✿⊙🥤※✆⚭🚮⊓🕇
Services: 🗜🛢🔆BT → ∪⅄😊✔🗐
Notes: Dogs must be kept on leads

HASGUARD CROSS   Map 02 SM81

▶ ▶ ▶ 66% **Hasguard Cross Caravan Park
(SM850108)**
SA62 3SL ☎ 01437 781443 🗐 01437 781443
e-mail: hasguard@aol.
website: www.hasguardcaravanpark.pembs.net/
*Dir: Take B4327 from Haverfordwest. After 7m turn right
at x-rds & site is 1st on right*
★ 🚐 £8.50-£10.50 🚐 £8.50-£10.50
Open all year Booking advisable Spring bank hol &
Jun-Aug Last arrival 21.00hrs Last departure
10.00hrs
*A very clean, efficient and well-run site in
Pembrokeshire National Park with views of
surrounding hills. 1.5m from sea and beach at Little
Haven. A 3-acre site with 16 touring pitches and 44
statics.*
Facilities: ✿⊙※✆⚭⊓🕇
Services: 🗜🍴🛢🔆❎🧹 → ∪▶🔼⅄✔🗐⚭

▶ ▶ ▶ 72% NEW Redlands Touring
Caravan & Camping Park (SM853109)
SA62 3SJ ☎ 01437 781300 🗐 01437 781300
e-mail: jenny.flight@virgin.net
website: www.redlandstouring.co.uk
*Dir: From Haverfordwest take B4327 towards Dale.
Redlands 7m on right*
★ 🚐 £7.50-£11.25 🚐 £7.50-£11.25 ▲ £6
Open Mar-1 Jan Booking advisable Jul-Aug, Xmas
& New Year, Spring BH Last arrival 22.00hrs Last
departure noon
*A family owned and run park set in five acres of
level grassland with tree-lined borders, close to
many sandy beaches and the famous coastal
footpath. Ideal for exploring the Pembrokeshire
National Park. A 5-acre site with 64 touring pitches,
6 hardstandings.*
contd.

Wales

Facilities: 🛁 Bath 🛡 Shower ⊙ Electric Shaver 🥤 Hairdryer ※ Ice Pack Facility ⅘ Disabled Facilities ✆ Public Telephone
⚭ Shop on Site or within 200yds ❏ Mobile Shop (calls at least 5 days a week) 🚮 BBQ Area 🎍 Picnic Area 🕇 Dog Exercise Area

Redlands Touring Caravan and Camping Park
Shop during peak season Use of deep freeze
Facilities: ⟡⟨※⟨⟨⟨⟨ **Services:** ⟨⟨⟨⟨→⟨⟨

HAVERFORDWEST   Map 02 SM91

▶ ▶ ▶ **73% Pelcomb Cross Farm Caravan Park
(SM919179)**
Pelcomb Cross SA62 6AB ☎ 01437 710431
e-mail: jameshelen@aol.com
Dir: Take A487 to St David's from Haverfordwest for 2m.
Pass Pelcomb Inn on right and site 100yds on right
★ ⟨⟨ £9-£12 ⟨⟨ £9-£12 ⟨⟨ £3-£9

Open Mar-Oct Booking advisable BH's Last arrival
22.00hrs Last departure 13.00hrs
*A smart terraced park with scenic views of the
Preseli and Plumbstone Hills and surrounding
countryside. The modern facilities include very
clean and bright toilets, new laundry equipment,
and a popular café/tea room serving meals until
8pm in high season. This is an ideal base for
exploring the Pembrokeshire National Park
including both coastal areas and countryside. A 4-
acre site with 30 touring pitches, 10 hardstandings.*
Leisure: ⟨⟨ **Facilities:** ⟨⟨⟨⟨⟨⟨⟨⟨⟨⟨
Services: ⟨⟨⟨⟨⟨⟨→⟨⟨⟨⟨⟨⟨

▶ ▶ **63% Nolton Cross Caravan Park (SM879177)**
Nolton SA62 3NP ☎ 01437 710701 ▤ 01437 710329
e-mail: noltoncross@nolton.fsnet.co.uk
website: www.noltoncross-holidays.co.uk
Dir: 1m off A487 at Simpson Cross.
★ ⟨⟨ £5.50-£7.50 ⟨⟨ £5.50-£7.50
Open Mar-Dec Booking advisable High season Last
arrival 22.00hrs Last departure noon
*High grassy banks surround the touring area of this
park next to the owners' working farm. It is located
on open ground above the sea and St Bride's Bay*
contd.

*which are both 1.5m away, and there is a coarse
fishing lake close by. A 4-acre site with 15 touring
pitches and 30 statics.*
Leisure: ⟨⟨ **Facilities:** ⟨⟨⟨⟨⟨⟨⟨⟨⟨⟨
Services: ⟨⟨⟨⟨⟨⟨⟨→⟨⟨

LANDSHIPPING   Map 02 SN01

▶ ▶ **59% New Park Farm (SN026111)**
SA67 8BG ☎ 01834 891284
Dir: 7m W of Narberth, along unclass road off A4075
★ ⟨⟨ fr £8.50 ⟨⟨ ⟨⟨ fr £6.50
Open May Day wknd-Oct Booking advisable peak
periods Last arrival 20.00hrs Last departure noon
*A nice quiet site on a smallholding with basic but
adequate facilities. The grass pitches are well
trimmed, and separate from the static area.
A 2-acre site with 30 touring pitches and 30 statics.*
Facilities: ⟨⟨⟨⟨⟨⟨⟨
Services: ⟨⟨⟨⟨⟨⟨⟨⟨⟨→⟨⟨⟨⟨⟨⟨

LITTLE HAVEN   See **Hasguard Cross**

LUDCHURCH   Map 02 SN11

▶ ▶ ▶ **66% Woodland Vale Caravan Park
(SN140113)**
SA67 8JE ☎ 01834 831319 ▤ 01834 831319
Dir: N of Ludchurch on unclass road, S of B4314
⟨⟨ ⟨⟨

info@woodlandvale.com

Open Mar-Nov Booking advisable bank hols & Jul-
Aug Last arrival 23.00hrs Last departure 12.00hrs
*Informally sited pitches are set between areas of
water created in an old quarry. The popular lounge
bar serves meals, and opens directly into the
swimming pool complex with occasional
entertainment in high season. A 1.5-acre site with
30 touring pitches and 80 statics.*
Free coarse fishing
Leisure: ⟨⟨⟨⟨ **Facilities:** ⟨⟨⟨⟨⟨⟨⟨⟨⟨⟨
Services: ⟨⟨⟨⟨⟨⟨→⟨⟨⟨⟨

NARBERTH   Map 02 SN11

▶ ▶ ▶ ▶ **70% Noble Court Caravan & Camping
Park (SN111158)**
Redstone Rd SA67 7ES ☎ 01834 861191
▤ 01834 861484
Dir: On B4313 between Narberth & A40. Turn off A40
at brown tourist signs to park
⟨⟨ ⟨⟨ ⟨⟨
contd

Wales

Open Mar-Nov (rs early & late season pool & bar opening times restricted) Booking advisable Jul-Aug Last arrival 23.30hrs Last departure 11.00hrs
A sloping park set in rolling countryside with lovely views from pitches which are set into paddocks and terraced. The park has its own fishing lake and picnic areas, and there is a comfortable bar and a games area. Toilet facilities are of a high standard. A 25-acre site with 92 touring pitches and 60 statics. Walks & picnics, 0.5 acres of course fishing lake

Leisure: ⟑ ◖ ⚠ **Facilities:** ⋔ ☉ ⛱ ✳ ⓖ ⛴ ⛾

⊞ ⛨ **Services:** ⊡ ⛁ ⍿ ⓘ ⍜ ⊞ ✕ ⛟ → ∪ ▶ ⏚ ⛋

Notes: No single sex groups ⊜ ▱ ▦

ST DAVID'S   Map 02 SM72

▶ ▶ ▶ **75% Caerfai Bay Caravan & Tent Park** (SM759244)
Caerfai Bay SA62 6QT ☎ 01437 720274
🖹 01437 720577
e-mail: info@caerfaibay.co.uk
website: www.caerfaibay.co.uk
Dir: At St David's turn off A487 at the Visitor Centre/Grove Hotel. Follow signs for Caerfai Bay. Turn right at end of road
★ 🚐 £7.50-£12.50 🚌 £6-£12.50 ⏶ £6-£7.50

Open Mar-mid Nov Booking advisable school hols Last arrival 20.00hrs Last departure 11.00hrs
Gently sloping meadows with magnificent coastal scenery overlooking St Bride's Bay, with a bathing beach 300yds from the park entrance. A new total block provides an excellent range of facilities, and a farm shop is very close by. A 10-acre site with 117 touring pitches and 33 statics.
Facilities: ⋔ ☉ ⛱ ✳ ⓖ ⛾ ⛋
Services: ⊡ ⛁ ⍿ ⍜ ⊞ → ▶ ⤫ ⛟ ⊜ ▱ ⑨

▶ ▶ ▶ **67% Hendre Eynon Camping & Caravan Site** (SM773280)
SA62 6DB ☎ 01437 720474 🖹 01437 720474
Dir: Take Fishguard road from St David's, fork left at rugby club signed Llanrhian, site on right in 2m (do no take turning to Whitesands)
★ 🚐 £6-£12 🚌 £6-£10 ⏶ £6-£12
Open May-Sep (rs 27 Mar-Apr one toilet block & showers rooms only) Booking advisable school hols Last arrival 21.00hrs Last departure noon

contd.

A peaceful country site on a working farm, with a modern toilet block including family rooms. Within easy reach of many lovely sandy beaches, and 2 miles from the cathedral city of St David's. A 7-acre site with 48 touring pitches and 2 statics.

Hendre Eynon Camping & Caravan Site
Facilities: ⋔ ☉ ✳ ⓖ ⛾ ⛨
Services: ⊡ ⛁ ⍿ ⊞ ⍜ → ▶ ⏶ ⤫ ⛟ ⛋

▶ ▶ **68% Camping & Caravanning Club Site** (SM805305)
Dwr Cwmdig, Berea SA62 6DW ☎ 01348 831376
🖹 01203 694886
website: www.campingandcaravanningclub.co.uk
Dir: S on A487, right at Glyncheryn Farmers Stores in Croesgoch. After 1m right following signs to Abereiddy. At x-roads left. Site 75yds on left
★ 🚐 £11.10-£14.50 🚌 £11.10-£14.50 ⏶ £11.10-£14.50
Open May-Sep Booking advisable bank hols & peak periods Last arrival 21.00hrs Last departure noon
An immaculately kept small site in open country near the Pembrokeshire Coastal Path. The slightly sloping grass has a few hardstandings for motor homes, and plenty of electric hook-ups. Please see advertisement on page 10 for details of Club Members' benefits. A 4-acre site with 40 touring pitches, 4 hardstandings.
Facilities: ⋔ ☉ ⛱ ⛾ **Services:** ⊡ ⍿ ⍜ ⊞ ⓣ ⛟
→ ∪ ▶ ⏶ ⛟ ⛋ ⊜ ▱ ▦ ⑨

▶ ▶ **62% Tretio Caravan & Camping Park** (SM787292)
SA62 6DE ☎ 01437 720270 & 781359
🖹 01437 781359
Dir: On leaving St David's keep left at Rugby Football Club & straight on for 3m
★ 🚐 £6-£9.50 🚌 £6-£8.50 ⏶ £6-£8.50
Open 14 Mar-14 Oct Booking advisable bank hols & mid Jul-Aug Last arrival 23.00hrs Last departure 17.00hrs
An attractive site in a very rural spot with distant country views, and beautiful local beaches. Good facilities include a small shop, and the tiny cathedral city of St David's is only 3 miles away. A 6.5-acre site with 40 touring pitches and 30 statics. Pitch & putt, small animal farm corner.
Leisure: ⚠ **Facilities:** ⋔ ☉ ⛱ ✳ ⓖ ⛾ ⛨
Services: ⊡ ⍿ ⍜ ⊞ ⓣ ⛟ → ▶ ☉ ⏶ ⤫ ⛟ ⛋

Kiln Park
Tenby, South Wales

2 FOR 1 Book 2 nights for the price of 1 night during Summer and Autumn. call for full conditions.

Prices start from
£5
per pitch, per night

*Based on a basic Tourer, Tent or Motor Home pitch per family at Kiln Park between 11 and 24 May 2003. Supplements apply

WE WELCOME: ✓ Motor Homes ✓ Trailer Tents ✓ Touring Vans ✓ Tents

Great Family Facilities including: SplashPools, Bars, Clubs, Kids Clubs, and Family Entertainment

Superb Touring Amenities including: Heated Showers and Toilets, Baby Changing, Launderette, Washing and Ironing Facilities

Visit Our Website at: www.british-holidays.co.uk

Information correct as of date of print

Caravan &Camping

BRITISH HOLIDAYS

To book call the park on:
01834 844121
or see your local travel agent quoting: AA
Kiln Park Holiday Centre, Marsh Road, Tenby, Pembrokeshire. SA70 7RB

TAVERNSPITE — Map 02 SN11

► ► ► 68% **Pantglas Farm Caravan Park (SN175122)**
SA34 0NS ☎ 01834 831618 ▤ 01834 831193
e-mail: steve@pantglasfarm.freeserve.co.uk
website: www.pantglasfarm.com
Dir: On B4328 between Ludchurch & Tavernspite. At village pump take middle turning & site signed on right
🚐 🚐 ▲

Open Etr-15 Oct Booking advisable Spring bank hol & Jul-Aug Last arrival 23.00hrs Last departure 11.00hrs
A quiet family-run site in a rural setting, with a welcoming attitude towards children, and a large play area for them. In rolling countryside with views towards Carmarthen Bay, with a lounge bar that offers occasional entertainment in high season.

contd.

A 7-acre site with 75 touring pitches. Year round caravan weekly storage
Leisure: ◀ ⚠ Facilities: ⇥ ↑ ⊙ ⚑ ✳ ♿ Ꮢ ▢ ᗩ
Services: 🔌 ▤ ♀ ▮ ⊘ ⊟ → ∪ ◢ ᒷ

TENBY — Map 02 SN10

72% **Kiln Park Holiday Centre (SN119002)**
Marsh Rd SA70 7RB
☎ 01834 844121 & 08457 433433
▤ 01834 845159
e-mail: gary.turner@bourneleisuregroup.co.uk
Dir: On A4139
★ 🚐 £12-£30 🚐 £12-£30 ▲ £12-£29
Open Mar-Oct (rs Mar-mid May & Sep-Oct less venues available) Booking advisable all times Etr-Sep Last arrival 22.00hrs Last departure 10.00hrs no cars by caravans
A large holiday complex complete with leisure and sports facilities, and plenty of entertainment for all the family. There are bars and cafes, and plenty of security. This touring, camping and static site is on the outskirts of town, with a short walk through dunes to the sandy beach. The well-equipped toilet block is very clean. A 103-acre site with 240 touring pitches and 620 statics.
Entertainment complex, bowling & putting green
Leisure: ❄ ⚲ ◀ ⚠ Facilities: ⇥ ↑ ⊙ ⚑ ✳ ♿ Ꮢ ᒷ ▢ ᗩ ★ Services: 🔌 ▤ ♀ ▮ ⊘ ▥ ✗ ⊟ → ∪ ▶ ⊙ ⚙ ↯ ᒷ ♨
◢ Notes: No dogs when camping during Jul & Aug 💳 🔲 🔳

► ► ► ► 70% **Trefalun (SN093027)**
Devonshire Dr, St Florence SA70 8RD
☎ 01646 651514 & 0500 655314 ▤ 01646 651746
e-mail: trefalun@aol.com
website: www.trefalunpark.co.uk
Dir: W of St Florence, 3m off B4318
★ 🚐 £8-£15 🚐 £8-£15 ▲ £8-£15
Open Etr-Oct Booking advisable bank hols & Jul-Aug Last arrival 20.00hrs Last departure noon
Set within 12 acres of sheltered, well-kept grounds, this park nestles among some of Pembrokeshire's finest scenery. This quiet country park offers well-maintained level grass pitches separated by bushes and trees, with plenty of space to relax in. Children will enjoy the enclosed play area, and can feed the park's friendly pets. Plenty of activities are available at the nearby Heatherton Country Sports Park, including go-karting, indoor bowls, golf and bumper boating. A 7-acre site with 90 touring pitches, 29 hardstandings and 10 statics.
Leisure: ⚠ Facilities: ↑ ⊙ ⚑ ✳ ♿ Ꮢ ▢ ᗩ ★
Services: 🔌 ▤ ▮ ⊘ ⊟ → ∪ ▶ ⊙ ⚙ ↯ ᒷ ◢ ᒷ
Notes: No single sex groups 💳 🔲 🔳
See advertisement on opposite page

► ► ► 69% **Well Park Caravan & Camping Site (SN128028)**
SA70 8TL ☎ 01834 842179 📠 01834 842179
e-mail: enquiries@wellparkcaravans.co.uk
website: www.wellparkcaravans.co.uk
Dir: off A478 on right approx 1m before Tenby
🚐 £9-£14 🚐 £9-£14 ▲ £9-£14

Open Mar-Oct (rs Mar-mid May & mid Sep-Oct bar, launderette, baby room may be closed) Booking advisable Spring BH & Jul-Aug Last arrival 22.00hrs Last departure 11.00hrs
A very well-run park with good landscaping from trees, ornamental shrubs, and attractive flower borders. The friendly resident owners keep the toilets clean and sparkling, and amenities include a launderette and indoor dishwashing, games room with table tennis, and an enclosed and well-equipped play area. The site is ideally placed between Tenby (1m) and Saundersfoot (1.5m), with a 15-minute walk to Waterwych Bay and the contd.

Pembrokeshire Coastal Footpath. A 10-acre site with 100 touring pitches, 14 hardstandings and 42 statics. TV hookups

Leisure: ◭ ⚀ ▢ **Facilities:** ⋒ ⊙ ⚏ ✳ ੯ ⌤ 戸 ⇞
Services: ◲ ▤ ⬟ ⬠ ⬢ 🠖 → ∪ ▶ ◎ △ ⚲ ⚰ ⤳
Notes: No single sex groups

► ► ► 66% **Wood Park Caravans (SN128025)**
New Hedges SA70 8TL ☎ 01834 843414
e-mail: enquiries@woodparkcaravans.co.uk
website: www.woodparkcaravans.co.uk
Dir: At rdbt 2m N of Tenby follow A478 towards Tenby, then take 2nd right & right again
★ 🚐 £7-£14.50 🚐 £7-£14.50 ▲ £6-£10
Open Spring BH-Sep (rs Etr-Spring BH & Sep-Oct bar & launderette may not open) Booking advisable Spring BH & Jul-Aug Last arrival 22.00hrs Last departure 10.00hrs
Nestling in beautiful countryside between the popular seaside resorts of Tenby and Saundersfoot, and with Waterwynch Bay just a 15-minute walk away. This peaceful site provides a spacious and relaxing atmosphere for holidays. The slightly sloping touring area is partly divided by shrubs into three paddocks. A 10-acre site with 60 touring pitches and 90 statics.
Outside dish/clothes washing area.

Leisure: ◭ ⚀ **Facilities:** ⋒ ⊙ ⚏ ✳ ੯ ⇞ **Services:** ◲ ▤ ⬟ ⬠ ▢ → ∪ ▶ △ ⚲ ⚰ ⤳ **Notes:** No single sex groups, 1 car per unit only, small dogs only accepted, no dogs Jul-Aug

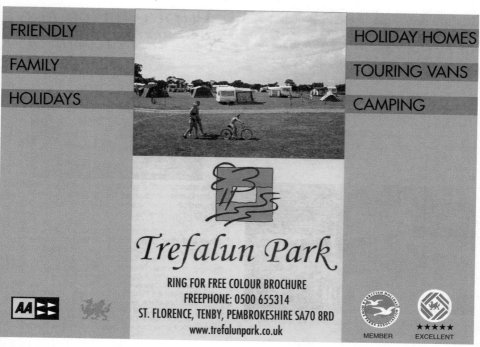
Wales

Facilities: ⇥ Bath 🞖 Shower ⊙ Electric Shaver ⚏ Hairdryer ✳ Ice Pack Facility ௘ Disabled Facilities ✆ Public Telephone
⚓ Shop on Site or within 200yds ▣ Mobile Shop (calls at least 5 days a week) 戸 BBQ Area 戸 Picnic Area 戸 Dog Exercise Area

POWYS

BRECON
Map 03 SO02

► ► ► ► 74% **Brynich Caravan Park (SO069278)**
Brynich LD3 7SH ☎ 01874 623325
🖷 01874 623325
e-mail: brynich@aol.com
website: www.brynich.co.uk
Dir: 2km E of Brecon on A470, 200mtrs from junct with A40
⊞ £8.50-£11 ⊞ £8.50-£11 Å £8.50-£11

Open 31 Mar-2 Nov Booking advisable bank & school hols Last arrival 23.00hrs
A very attractive and well-appointed site with commanding views of the Brecon Beacons. Colourful flower beds create a lovely display in the grounds, and a well-stocked shop is very popular. A 20-minute walk along the canal towpath leads into the charming market town of Brecon. A 20-acre site with 130 touring pitches, 25 hardstandings. Adventure playground, off-licence, dish washing.

Leisure: ⚠ Facilities: ➡ ⋔ ⊙ ℚ ✳ ⅋ & ⌊ ☴ ⍰ ⍐
Services: ▣ ◱ ⌷ ⌧ ⌶ ⌧ ➡ → ∪ ▶ △ ⅄ ⌘ ✔
▱ ▨ ▨ ▨ ⑤

► ► ► ► 78% **Pencelli Castle Caravan & Camping Park (SO096248)**
Pencelli LD3 7LX ☎ 01874 665451
🖷 01874 665452
e-mail: pencelli.castle@virgin.net
website: www.pencelli-castle.co.uk
Dir: Turn off A40 2m E of Brecon onto B4558, follow signs to Pencelli
⊞ £10-£11 ⊞ £10-£11 Å £11

Open all year Booking advisable BH's Last arrival 22.00hrs Last departure Noon ⌽
continued on opposite page

Lying in the heart of the Brecon Beacons National Park, this charming park offers peace, beautiful scenery and high quality facilities. The park is bordered by the Brecon and Monmouth Canal, and there are barge trips from the nearby marina. Attention to detail is superb, and the well-equipped heated toilets with en suite cubicles are matched by a drying room for clothes and boots, full laundry, and shop. Winner of Best Campsite for Wales 2002. A 10-acre site with 80 touring pitches, 32 hardstandings. Bike hire

Leisure: ⚏ Facilities: ⬈☉⚒✳⚘ℂ⚑⊞

Services: ⬚⧉⬚⬚⊟⊞→∪↳↲

Notes: No radios or music ⬤ ▤ ▧ ⬚

▶ ▶ ▶ 66% Bishops Meadow Caravan Park (SO060300)
Bishops Meadow, Hay Rd LD3 9SW
☎ 01874 610000 & 622138 ▤ 01874 614922
e-mail: enquiries@bishops-meadow.co.uk
Dir: From A40 take A470 Hereford road. Turn left onto B4602
★ ⚏ fr £10 ⚏ fr £10 ▲ £6-£10
Open Mar-Oct Booking advisable BH's
A rural park close to the Brecon Beacons and with spectacular views. The family-owned and run park offers a heated outdoor swimming pool, an all-day restaurant, and a lounge bar open in the evenings. Facilities are very well kept, and the town is about one mile away. A 3.5-acre site with 82 touring pitches, 24 hardstandings.

Leisure: ⚲ ⚛ ⚏ Facilities: ⬈☉⚒✳⚘ℂ⚑⚑

Services: ⬚⧉⬚⬚⊟⊞✕⬈→∪↳⚑⚑↲⬚
⬤ ▤ ⟐ ▨ ⬚

▶ ▶ ▶ 68% Anchorage Caravan Park (SO142351)
LD3 0LD ☎ 01874 711246 & 711230 ▤ 01874 711711
Dir: 8m NE of Brecon on A438, in village of Bronllys.
⚏ fr £9 ⚏ fr £9 ▲ fr £9
Open all year (rs Nov-Mar TV room closed)
Booking advisable BH's & Aug Last arrival 23.00hrs Last departure 18.00hrs
A well-maintained site. Touring pitches are on grassy slopes and level ground with good mountain views of the Brecon Beacons National Park. An 8-acre site with 110 touring pitches, 8 hardstandings and 101 statics.
Baby bath room, post office & hairdressers

Leisure: ⚏ ⬚ Facilities: ⬈☉⚒✳⚘ℂ⚑⊞⚑

Services: ⬚⧉⬚⬚⊟⊞→∪↲

Bishop's Meadow Caravan Park,
Hay Road, Brecon, Powys LD3 9SW
Telephone: 01874 610000
Fax: 01874 614922
AA ▶▶▶   ETB ✓✓✓
Conveniently situated on the outskirts of Brecon on the B4602, approximately one mile from the town centre. The park has 80 level pitches with electrical hook-ups and all have excellent views of the Brecon Beacons.
The high standards of the park are reflected in the good facilities offered. The Restaurant is open all day, every day and offers a comprehensive menu for snacks and main meals. The Lounge Bar, open every evening offers a friendly and relaxed atmosphere. A small shop provides many essential items. Heated outdoor swimming pool with patio. Children's play area. Dogs welcome on leads.

▶ ▶ ▶ 66% Fforest Fields Caravan & Camping Park (SO100535)
Hundred House LD1 5RT
☎ 01982 570406 & 570220 ▤ 01982 570444
e-mail: office@fforestfields.co.uk
website: www.fforestfields.co.uk
Dir: From town follow signs to 'New Radnor' on A481, after 4m signed entrance on right
★ ⚏ £7.50 ⚏ £7.50 ▲ £7.50

Open Etr & Apr-Oct (rs Nov-Mar Hardstandings only, toilet/shower closed) Booking advisable BH's & Jul-Aug Last arrival 23.00hrs Last departure 18.00hrs
A sheltered park in a hidden valley with wonderful views and plenty of wildlife. Set in unspoilt

contd.

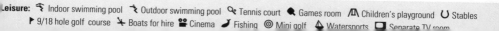

Leisure: ⚲ Indoor swimming pool ⚲ Outdoor swimming pool ⚬ Tennis court ⚛ Games room ⚏ Children's playground ∪ Stables
▶ 9/18 hole golf course ↳ Boats for hire ⚏ Cinema ↲ Fishing ◎ Mini golf ⚛ Watersports ⬚ Separate TV room

Wales

countryside, this is a peaceful park with delightful hill walks beginning on site. The historic town of Builth Wells and the Royal Welsh Showground are only 4 miles away, and there are plenty of outdoor activities in the vicinity, but no clubhouse. A 7-acre site with 40 touring pitches, 10 hardstandings.

Facilities: ⚑⊙ℛ☀️ⓒ☕🐾

Services: ⚑⊡ⓘ⌀⊞→❘🐶♫🧺

CHURCH STOKE · Map 07 SO29

▶ ▶ ▶ ▶ 69% **Daisy Bank Caravan Park (SO303929)**
Snead SY15 6EB ☎ 01588 620471 📠 01588 620471
e-mail: j.spurgeon@tesco.net
website: www.daisy-bank.co.uk
Dir: Off A489 between Craven Arms and Churchstoke
★ ⚘ £13-£15 ⚘ £13-£15 ▲ £9-£11

Open all year Booking advisable at all times
Last departure 12.00hrs
A pleasant park in an idyllic setting amongst the Welsh and Shropshire hills, with glorious views in all directions. The park is for adults only, and offers a peaceful environment in which to relax. The toilet facilities have been upgraded to provide heated en suites of a high quality. A 4-acre site with 55 touring pitches, 35 hardstandings.
Putting green
Facilities: ⚑⊙ℛ☀️&ⓒ☕🐾 **Services:** ⚑ⓘ⌀⊞⊡
→ ♫⊡🧺 **Notes:** Adults only ⊡ ☰ ☰ 🔊

▶ ▶ ▶ 68% **Mellington Hall Caravan Park (SO257920)**
Mellington SY15 6HX ☎ 01588 620011
📠 01588 620853
e-mail: info@mellingtonhallcaravanpark.co.uk
website: www.mellingtonhallcaravanpark.co.uk
Dir: Take A490 out of Welshpool to Montgomery. Follow road for 3m to x-rds at the Blue Bell. Over x-rds, over small bridge and next right into Mellington Hall drive
★ ⚘ fr £12.50 ⚘ fr £12.50 ▲ fr £10
Open all year Booking advisable BH's Last arrival 20.00hrs no cars by caravans no cars by tents
A small touring park set a mile down a wooded private drive in the grounds of Mellington Hall Hotel. The 270 acres of park and farmland guarantee peace and seclusion, and there is plenty of wildlife and thousands of rare trees. Offa's Dyke footpath runs through the grounds, and this park is

contd.

Mellington Hall Caravan Park
ideal for walking and cycling. A 4-acre site with 40 touring pitches, 40 hardstandings and 83 statics. Fishing pool, hiking maps

Leisure: ⚘ **Facilities:** ⚑⊙ℛ&ⓒ☕🐾
Services: ⚑❘☀️✗→∪♫🧺⊡⊡ ☰ 🔊

▶ ▶ 65% **Bacheldre Watermill Touring & Camping Park (SO243928)**
Bacheldre Watermill SY15 6TE ☎ 01588 620489
📠 01588 620105
e-mail: bacheldremill@onetel.net.uk
website: www.bacheldremill.co.uk
Dir: 2m W of Churchstoke on A489.
Site 50yds on right
★ ⚘ fr £10 ⚘ fr £10 ▲ fr £8
Open all year (rs end Oct-Etr) Booking advisable bank hols/summer Last departure noon
A secluded little park in the grounds of an 18th-century working watermill on the border of Wales and Shropshire. Tours of the mill can be arranged. A 2-acre site with 25 touring pitches.
Facilities: ⚑⊙🧺 **Services:** ⚑→♫⊡

CRICKHOWELL · Map 03 SO21

▶ ▶ ▶ 66% **Riverside Caravan & Camping Park (SO215184)**
New Rd NP8 1AY ☎ 01873 810397
Dir: On A4077 & well signed from A40
★ ⚘ fr £8 ⚘ fr £8 ▲ fr £8
Open Mar-Oct Booking advisable for stays over 1 wk Last arrival 22.00hrs
Set in lovely tranquil countryside beside the River Usk, this adults-only site is a short walk from the town of Crickhowell and the pretty village of Llangattock. Facilities are clean and well-kept, and the Brecon Beacons National Park is nearby. A 3.5-acre site with 35 touring pitches and 20 statics.
Facilities: ⚑⊙☀️ⓒ🧺 **Services:** ⚑ⓘ⌀⊞→∪❘♣♫
Notes: Adults only, no hangliders or paragliders

CROSSGATES · Map 03 SO06

▶ ▶ 65% **The Park Motel (SO081651)**
Rhayader Rd LD1 6RF ☎ 01597 851201
📠 01597 851201
e-mail: lisa@theparkmotel.freeserve.co.uk
website: www.theparkmotel.freeserve.co.uk
Dir: 3m N of Llandrindod Wells on A44 on Rhayader Rd
★ ⚘ £8.25-£9 ⚘ £8.25-£9 ▲ £8.25-£9

contd.

Wales

Open Mar-Oct Booking advisable BH's Last arrival
22.30hrs Last departure noon
*This quiet, rural site set in beautiful countryside is
well sheltered by trees, and offers all level pitches.
It makes an ideal touring centre, and has the
advantage of the motel's bar and restaurant.
A 3-acre site with 10 touring pitches and 18 statics.*

Leisure: ♠ ⚠ **Facilities:** ℝ ⊙ ⚘ ⚬ ⅃ ⚘ ⅁
Services: ⚑ ⚧ ⅃ ⚘ ⊡ ✕ ⚘ → ∪ ▶ ⊙ ⚭ ⚋ ⚙ ⅃ ⚙

HAY-ON-WYE   Map 03 SO24

► ► 66% **NEW** Hollybush Inn (SO205406)
HR3 5PS ☎ 01497 847371
Open all year
*An upgraded site on the banks of the River Wye,
ideally situated for canoeists and walkers. The site
is behind a rural inn which serves home cooking,
and only two miles from the famous literary town of
Hay-on-Wye. A 4-acre site with
22 touring pitches.*

Facilities: ℝ ⅃ **Services:** ⚑ ⚧ ✕

LLANBRYMAIR   Map 06 SH80

► ► ► 71% Cringoed Caravan Park (SO887015)
The Birches SY19 7DR ☎ 01650 521237
⋄ 01650 521237
e-mail: cringoedcaravan.park@virgin.net
Dir: *Off A470 onto B4518, park 1.25m on right*
★ ⚘ £9-£12 ⚘ £9-£12 ▲ £7-£10
Open 7 Mar-7 Jan Booking advisable BH's
Last departure noon
*On the banks of the River Twymyn, a family-run
park set amongst beautiful hillside and open
scenery just 30 minutes' drive from the coastal
resort of Aberdovey. An ideal location for touring
the many local attractions, and with bright, clean
toilet facilities. A 20-acre site with 50 touring pitches
and 31 statics.*

Leisure: ♠ ⚠ **Facilities:** ℝ ⚘ ⚘ ⅃ ⚘
Services: ⚑ ⚙ ⚧ ⚘ → ⚬ ⚭ ⅃ ⚙

LLANDRINDOD WELLS   Map 03 SO06

► ► ► 63% Disserth Caravan &
Camping Park (SO035583)
Disserth, Howey LD1 6NL
☎ 01597 860277 ⋄ 01597 860147
e-mail: m.hobbs@virgin.net
website: www.caravanwales.com
Dir: *1m off A483, between Howey & Newbridge on Wye*
⚘ £7.50-£10 ⚘ £7.50-£10 ▲ £5-£10
Open Mar-Oct Booking advisable Last arrival
22.00hrs Last departure noon
*A peaceful site nestling in a beautiful valley on the
banks of the River Ithon, a tributary of the River
Wye. The park is next to a 13th-century church, and
has a small restaurant, tearoom and bar. A 2.5-acre
site with 35 touring pitches and 21 statics.
Private trout fishing.*

Facilities: ℝ ⊙ ⚘ ⚘ ⅃ ⚋ ⅁
Services: ⚑ ⚙ ⚧ ⚘ ⊡ ✕ → ∪ ▶ ⚭ ⚋ ⅃

► ► 64% Dalmore Camping & Caravanning
Park (SO045568)
Howey LD1 5RG ☎ 01597 822483 ⋄ 01597 822483
Dir: *2m S of Llandrindod Wells off A483. 4m N of Builth
Wells*
★ ⚘ £7-£9 ⚘ £7-£9 ▲ £7-£9
Open Mar-Oct Booking advisable Jun-Aug Last
arrival 22.00hrs Last departure noon ⚘
*Wonderful views from this clean and tidy park, with
pitches divided by mature hedges and fencing. The
site is located on the A483, but screened from the
road and traffic noise by a hedgerow. A 3-acre site
with 20 touring pitches and 20 statics.*

Facilities: ℝ ⊙ ⚘ ⅃ ⚘ ⅁
Services: ⚑ ⚧ ⚘ ⊡ → ∪ ▶ ⊙ ⚭ ⚋ ⅃ ⚙ ⚓

LLANGORSE   Map 03 SO12

► ► ► 64% Lakeside Caravan Park
(SO128272)
LD3 7TR ☎ 01874 658226 ⋄ 01874 658430
e-mail: holidays@lakeside.zx3.net
website: www.lakeside-holidays.net
Dir: *Leave A40 at Bwlch onto B4560 towards Talgarth,
site signed towards lake in centre of Llangorse village*
★ ⚘ £7-£9 ⚘ £7-£9 ▲ £7-£9
Open Jun-Sep (rs Mar-May & Oct Pool, clubhouse,
restaurant, shop limited) Booking advisable peak
periods Last arrival 21.30hrs Last departure noon
*Next to Llangorse common and lake, this attractive
park has launching and mooring facilities and is an
ideal centre for water sports enthusiasts. Popular
with families, and offering a clubhouse/bar, with a
well-stocked shop and café/takeaway next door.
Boats and windsurf equipment can be hired on site.
A 2-acre site with 40 touring pitches and 72 statics.
Boat hire & launching, windsurfing & fishing.*

Leisure: ⚘ ⚠ **Facilities:** ℝ ⊙ ⚘ ⚘ ⅃ ⚋ ⅁ ⚘
Services: ⚑ ⚙ ⚧ ⚘ ⊡ ✕ ⚘ → ∪ ⚘ ⚭ ⅃
  ⚘ ⚙

LLANIDLOES   Map 06 SN98

► ► 68% **NEW** Dol-Llys Caravan & Camping
Site (SN963858)
SY18 6JA ☎ 01686 412694
Dir: *A470 off the bypass to rdbt in Llanidloes go over
bridge B4569 past hospital and fork right onto Oakley
Park Rd, site is 1st farm on right*
★ ⚘ £6-£7.50 ⚘ ▲
Open Apr-Oct Dogs on lead Booking advisable
Last arrival 23.00hrs Last departure 14.00hrs
*A small touring park on the lower area of a working
farm with wonderful views, run by friendly farmers
to a very good standard. Part of the toilet facilities
have been upgraded to include quality en suite
rooms. Set on the banks of the River Severn, and
ideal for a fishing or walking holiday. A 3-acre site
with 20 touring pitches.*

Leisure: ⚠ **Facilities:** ℝ ⊙ ⚘ ⅃ ⚘
Services: ⚑ ⊡ → ▶ ⅃ ⚙ ⚓

---

wales

MIDDLETOWN — Map 07 SJ31

▶ ▶ 60% **Bank Farm Caravan Park** (SJ293123)
SY21 8EJ ☎ 01938 570526
e-mail: gill@bankfarmcaravans.fsnet.co.uk
Dir: 13m W of Shrewsbury, 5m E of Welshpool on A458
★ ⊞ fr £9 ⊞ fr £9 Å fr £7
Open May-Oct Booking advisable BH's
Last arrival 20.00hrs
A grass site with two different areas - one gently sloping and the other mainly level. Immediate access to hills, mountains and woodland. A 2-acre site with 20 touring pitches and 33 statics. Coarse fishing pool.
Leisure: ⚓ ⚙ Facilities: ☏ ⊙ ✷ ⚹ 𝄐 ☶ ☰ ♈
Services: ☏ ☎ ⊞ → ▶ ┙ ☎

PRESTEIGNE — Map 03 SO36

▶ ▶ ▶ 67% **Rockbridge Park** (SO294654)
LD8 2NF ☎ 01547 560300 ☏ 01547 560300
e-mail: roy.deakins@lineone.net
Dir: 1m W of Presteigne off B4356
⊞ ⊞ Å
Open Apr-Oct Booking advisable public & school hols Last arrival 21.30hrs Last departure noon ☞
A pretty little park set in meadowland with trees and shrubs along the banks of the River Lugg. A bridge across the stream gives good access to nearby footpaths. Facilities are very well maintained, and the owner is friendly and helpful. A 3-acre site with 35 touring pitches and 30 statics.
Facilities: ☏ ⊙ ✷ ⚹ 𝄐 Services: ☏ ☎ ☐ ⊞ → ▶ ┙ ☎

RHAYADER — Map 03 SN96

▶ ▶ ▶ 67% *Wyeside Caravan & Camping Park* (SO967686)
Llangurig Rd LD6 5LB ☎ 01597 810183
e-mail: info@wyesidecamping.co.uk
website: www.wyesidecamping.cu.uk
Dir: 400mtrs N of Rhayader town centre on A470
⊞ ⊞ Å
Nestling on the banks of the River Wye just 400 metres from the centre of this market town, and next to a recreation park with tennis courts, bowling green and children's playground. There are good riverside walks from the park. 140 touring pitches and 39 statics.
Facilities: ☏ Services: ☐

TALGARTH — Map 03 SO13

▶ ▶ ▶ 68% *Riverside International* (SO148346)
Bronllys LD3 0HL ☎ 01874 711320 & 712064
☏ 01874 712064
e-mail: riversideinternational@
bronllys1.freeserve.co.uk
website: www.wiz.to/riverside/
Dir: On A479 opposite Bronllys Castle
★ ⊞ £9-£10 ⊞ £9-£10 Å £9-£10
Open Etr-Oct Booking advisable BH's & Jul-Aug
Last arrival 22.00hrs Last departure 16.00hrs ☞
A well-appointed touring park in a pretty, elevated position with magnificent views of the Black Mountains and the Brecon Beacons. The leisure

contd.

centre facilities with heated indoor swimming pool, jacuzzi, and well-equipped gym are available to site users at special rates. Trout fishing is available on site, and there are some pitches beside the river. A 9-acre site with 80 touring pitches.
Leisure facilities, sauna, jacuzzi, sunbed & gym.
Leisure: ⚒ ⚓ ⚙ Facilities: ☛ ☏ ⊙ ☜ ✷ ⚹ ☰ ☶ 𝄐
Services: ☏ ☐ ☎ ⓘ ⊘ ⊞ ⊡ ✕ ♒ → ∪ ↺ ┙ ☎ ☷ ⎯ ⚞ ☒

SWANSEA

PONTARDDULAIS — Map 02 SN50

▶ ▶ 64% **River View Touring Park** (SN578086)
The Dingle, Llanedi SA4 1FH ☎ 01269 844876
☏ 01269 832076
e-mail: holiday@riverviewtouringpark.co.uk
website: www.riverviewtouringpark.co.uk
Dir: Exit M4 junct 49, take A483 signed Llandeilo. Take 1st left after layby in 0.5m, follow lane to site
★ ⊞ £8-£10 ⊞ £8-£10 Å £8-£10
Open Mar-Jan Booking advisable Jun-Aug Last arrival 22.00hrs Last departure 12.00hrs
A newly-developed park in a tranquil location with the River Gwili forming a boundary to one side. A small shop and a clean, well-painted toilet block offer good facilities, and the M4 is only half a mile away. Well situated for touring, and for visiting the Gower Peninsula and the Brecon Beacons. A 3-acre site with 30 touring pitches, 8 hardstandings. Outdoor activities organised
Facilities: ☏ ☎ ♈ Services: ☏ → ∪ ▶ ☵ ┙ ☐
Notes: Dogs must be kept on leads

PORT EYNON — Map 02 SS48

▶ ▶ ▶ 68% *Carreglwyd Camping & Caravan Park* (SS465863)
SA3 1NN ☎ 01792 390795 ☏ 01792 390796
Dir: Follow A4118 to Port Eynon, Carreglwyd is adjacent to beach

Set in an unrivalled location alongside the safe sandy beach of Port Eynon on the Gower Peninsula, this popular park is an ideal family holiday spot. Close to an attractive village with pubs and shops, with sea views from most pitches. A 12-acre site with 150 touring pitches.
Facilities: ☏ ⊙ Services: → ☎
Notes: Dogs must be kept on leads at all times

RHOSSILI — Map 02 SS48

▶ ▶ ▶ **63% Pitton Cross Caravan & Camping Park (SS434877)**
SA3 1PH ☎ 01792 390593 ▤ 01792 391010
e-mail: enquiries@pittoncross.co.uk
website: www.pittoncross.co.uk
Dir: 2m W of Scurlage on B4247
★ ⊞ £9-£12.75 ⊞ £8.50-£10.50 ▲ £9-£14

Open Apr-Oct Booking advisable Spring BH & Jul-Aug Last arrival 21.00hrs Last departure noon
Surrounded by farmland close to sandy Menslade Bay, which is within walking distance across the fields. A grassy park divided by hedging into paddocks. Nearby Rhossili Beach is popular with surfers. A 6-acre site with 100 touring pitches, 16 hardstandings.
Motor caravan service bay & baby bath

Leisure: ⋀ **Facilities:** ⋔⊙♋✳⛁⛄⛱⛩ **Services:**
⛽▣🛢⊘🔲�🆃🚮→∪▶✦ **Notes:** Dogs must be kept on leads, quiet at all times. 💳 ▭ ▭ ▨ 🈹

SWANSEA — Map 03 SS69

▶ ▶ ▶ **68% Riverside Caravan Park (SS679991)**
Ynys Forgan Farm, Morriston SA6 6QL
☎ 01792 775587 ▤ 01792 775587
Dir: Leave M4 at junct 45 towards Swansea, and turn left into private road signed to park
⊞ ⊞ ▲
Open all year (rs winter months pool & club closed)
Booking advisable BH's & main school hols Last arrival mdnt Last departure noon
A large park close to the M4 but in a quiet location beside the River Taw. This friendly site has a licensed club and bar with high-season entertainment, and is a good base for touring Mumbles and Gower beaches. A 5-acre site with 90 touring pitches and 256 statics.
Fishing on site by arrangement.

Leisure: ⌇ ◣ ⋀ ☐ **Facilities:** ⋔⊙♋✳⛁⛄⛱⛩
Services: ⛽▣🛢⊘🔲🆃🚮→∪▶♨✦
Notes: Dogs by arrangement only (no aggressive dog breeds permitted) 💳 ▭ ▭ ▨ 🈹

VALE OF GLAMORGAN

LLANTWIT MAJOR — Map 03 SS96

▶ ▶ ▶ **65% Acorn Camping & Caravan Site (SS973678)**
Ham Ln South CF61 1RP ☎ 01446 794024
▤ 01446 794024
e-mail: acorncampsite@aol.com
website: campingandcaravansites.co.uk
Dir: B4265 to Llantwit Major following camping signs. Approach site through Ham Manor residential park
★ ⊞ £6.75-£7.75 ⊞ £6.75-£7.75 ▲ £6.75-£7.75
Open Etr or 1 Feb-8 Dec Booking advisable BH's & Aug Last arrival 22.00hrs Last departure noon
A peaceful country site in level meadowland, with some individual pitches divided by hedges and shrubs. About 1 mile from the beach, which can be approached by a clifftop walk, and the same distance from the historic town of Llantwit Major. A 4.5-acre site with 90 touring pitches, 5 hardstandings and 15 statics.

Leisure: ◣ ⋀ **Facilities:** ⋔⊙♋✳⛁⛄⛱
Services: ⛽🛢⊘🔲🆃🚮→∪✦ 💳 ▭ ▭ 🈹

Leisure: ⌇ Indoor swimming pool ⌇ Outdoor swimming pool ♋ Tennis court ◣ Games room ⋀ Children's playground ∪ Stables ▶ 9/18 hole golf course ⅄ Boats for hire ♨ Cinema ✦ Fishing ◉ Mini golf ⚠ Watersports ☐ Separate TV room

▶ ▶ ▶ **67% Llandow Touring Caravan Park**
(SS956713)
CF7 7PB ☎ 01446 794527 & 792462 📠 01446 792462
e-mail: marcross@farmline.com
Dir: Signed off B4270
★ ⚘ £7.50-£9.50 ⚘ £7.50-£9.50 ▲ £5-£9.50
Open Feb-Nov Booking advisable bank hols & end
Jun-Aug Last arrival 10.00hrs Last departure noon
An open park surrounded by high shrubbed banks
and trees, located midway between the historic
town of Llantwit Major and the quaint market town
of Cowbridge. Glamorgan's Heritage Coast is just
three miles away. A 6-acre site with 100 touring
pitches, 30 hardstandings.
Caravan Storage
Leisure: ⚠ Facilities: 🛭⊙🔾✳🗶🏊🎢🐾
Services: 🖳🗄🛢🖊⊞🔲→🗘♨🖵🍴🍴🆑

WREXHAM

▶ ▶ ▶ **67% Camping & Caravanning Club Site**
(SJ385448)
The Racecourse, Overton Rd LL13 0DA
☎ 01978 781009 📠 01203 694886
website: www.campingandcaravanningclub.co.uk
Dir: From A525 follow racecourse/camping signs
through village, turn left immediately opposite Buck
Hotel, site 1m on right
★ ⚘ £10.20-£12.90 ⚘ £10.20-£12.90 ▲ £10.20-£12.90
Open Mar-Oct Booking advisable bank hols & peak
periods Last arrival 21.00hrs Last dep 12.00hrs
A particularly attractive racecourse park which lies
in a bend of the River Dee. Superb views of the
Clwyd mountain range can be enjoyed from the
mainly level, grassy pitches. Sanitary facilities are
well looked after. Please see advertisement on page
10 for details of Club Members' benefits. A 6-acre
site with 100 touring pitches, 9 hardstandings.
Horse racing
Facilities: 🛭⊙🔾✳🛇🗶🏊🐾
Services: 🖳🗄🛢🖊⊞→🗘🍴🍴🆑

PREMIER PARK

▶ ▶ ▶ ▶ ▶ **77% The Plassey Leisure Park**
(SJ353452)
The Plassey LL13 0SP ☎ 01978 780277
📠 01978 780019
e-mail: enquiries@theplassey.co.uk
website: www.theplassey.co.uk
Dir: Leave A483 at Bangor-on-Dee exit, along B5426
for 2.5m. Follow signs to site
⚘ £13-£16 ⚘ £13-£16 ▲ £13-£16
Open Mar-Oct Booking advisable BH's, wknds &
school hols Last arrival 23.00hrs Last departure
18.00hrs
A lovely park set in 247 acres of quiet farm and
meadowland in the Dee Valley. The superb toilet
facilities include individual cubicles for total
contd.

The Plassey Leisure Park
privacy, while the Edwardian farm buildings
have been converted into a restaurant, coffee
shop, beauty studio, and various craft outlets.
There is plenty to entertain the whole family,
from scenic walks to free fishing, and use of the
9-hole golf course. A 10-acre site with 110
touring pitches, 15 hardstandings.
Sauna, sunbed, badminton, table tennis
Leisure: 🎣♣⚠🏊🖵 Facilities: 🛭⊙🔾✳🛇🗶🐾🎢
🐾 Services: 🖳🗄🚹🖊⊞🔲🗶🖇→🗘▶♨🖊
Notes: No football, bikes, or skateboards.
Dogs must be kept on leads 🍴🍴🆑

Ireland

Ireland

NORTHERN IRELAND
CO ANTRIM

ANTRIM   Map 01 D5

▶ ▶ ▶ 67% **Sixmilewater Caravan Park**
Lough Rd BT41 4DQ ☎ 028 9446 4131
e-mail: abs@antrim.gov.uk
*Dir: 1m from Antrim town centre, follow signs for
Antrim Forum and from Dublin road (A26) take turn for
Lough road*
★ 🚐 £5.50-£7 🚐 £5.50-£7 ▲ £5
Open Etr-Sep Booking advisable All dates Last
departure noon
*A pretty tree-lined site in a large municipal park,
within walking distance of Antrim and the Antrim
Forum leisure complex yet very much in the
countryside. The modern toilet block is well
equipped, and other facilities include a laundry and
electric hook-ups.
A 9.75-acre site with 40 touring pitches,
18 hardstandings.*
Watersport & angling stands
Facilities: 🏪 ⊙ ᕕ ᕽ ⬚ 🗑 **Services:** 🔌 🗑 ✕
→ ▶ ⚐ ✿ ✈ 🌡 **Notes:** Maximum stay 7 nights

BALLYCASTLE   Map 01 D6

▶ ▶ 64% **Silver Cliffs Holiday Village**
21 Clare Rd BT54 6DB ☎ 028 2076 2550
🖹 028 2076 2259
Dir: 0.25m W of Ballycastle, off A2
🚐 🚐 ▲
Open 17 Mar-Oct Booking advisable 11-25 Jul & 22-
25 Aug Last arrival 20.00hrs Last departure 17.00hrs
*A large seaside site with a swimming pool and bar.
Close to the beach and River Glenshesk, A 2-acre
site with 50 touring pitches and 250 statics.
Sun beds, sauna, spa & snooker.*
Leisure: ❦ ◆ ⚠ **Facilities:** 🏪 ⊙ ✳ ᕕ ᕽ ⬚ 🗑
Services: 🔌 🗑 ♈ ⬚ ⬡ 📶 🗑 ✕ 🧹 → ∪ ▶ ⬤ 🌡 🍴 💳 ⬚

BALLYMONEY   Map 01 C6

▶ ▶ ▶ 69% **Drumaheglis Marina &
Caravan Park**
36 Glenstall Rd BT53 7QN ☎ 028 2766 6466 &
2766 2280 🖹 028 2766 7659
e-mail: info@ballymoney.gov.uk
website: www.ballymoney.gov.uk
*Dir: Signed off A26, approx 1.5m outside Ballymoney
towards Coleraine, off B66 S of Ballymoney*
★ 🚐 £10-£13 🚐 £10-£13 ▲ fr £10
Open 31 Mar-1 Oct Booking advisable BH's &
summer months Last arrival 20.00hrs Last
departure 13.00hrs
*Exceptionally well-designed and laid out park
beside the Lower Bann River, with very spacious
pitches and two quality toilet blocks. Ideal base for
touring Antrim or for water sports enthusiasts.
A 16-acre site with 53 touring pitches, 53
hardstandings.*
Ski school, marina berthing, banana boat, table
tennis   *contd.*

Leisure: ⚠ **Facilities:** 🏪 ⊙ ᕕ ✳ ᕕ ᕽ ⬚ 🗑 ᕽ
Services: 🔌 🗑 → ∪ ▶ ⚐ 🌡 ⬚ 🧹
Notes: Dogs must be kept on lead 💳 ⬚

BUSHMILLS   Map 01 C6

▶ ▶ ▶ ▶ 75% **Ballyness Caravan Park**
40 Castlecatt Rd BT57 8TN ☎ 028 2073 2393
🖹 028 2073 2713
e-mail: info@ballynesscaravanpark.com
website: www.ballynesscaravanpark.com
Dir: 0.5m S of Bushmills on B66.
★ 🚐 fr £12 🚐 fr £12 ▲ fr £8
Open 17 Mar-Oct Booking advisable Jun-Aug & Etr
Last arrival 21.00hrs Last departure noon
*A quality park with superb toilet and other facilities,
on farmland beside St Columb's Rill, the stream
that supplies the famous nearby Bushmills
distillery. The friendly owners have built this park
with the discerning camper in mind. There is a
pleasant walk around several ponds, and the park is
peacefully located close to the beautiful north
Antrim coast. A 12-acre site with 36 touring pitches,
30 hardstandings and 30 statics.*
Leisure: ⚠ **Facilities:** 🛒 🏪 ⊙ ᕕ ✳ ᕕ ᕽ ⬚ ᕽ
Services: 🔌 🗑 ⬚ ᕽ ⬚ 🗑 🛒 → ▶ 🌡 💳 ⬚ 🗑 ⬚

CUSHENDALL   Map 01 D6

▶ ▶ 68% **Cushendall Caravan Camp**
62 Coast Rd BT44 0QW ☎ 028 2177 1699
Dir: On A2, 1m S of town
★ 🚐 fr £13 🚐 fr £13 ▲ fr £6
Open mid Mar-mid Oct Booking advisable peak
periods Last arrival 21.00hrs Last departure
14.00hrs
*A pleasant site next to the beach and sailing club on
a spectacular stretch of the North Antrim Coast.
A 1-acre site with 14 touring pitches,
3 hardstandings and 64 statics.*
Facilities: 🏪 ⊙ ᕕ ᕕ ᕽ ⬚ 🗑 **Services:** 🗑 🌡 → ∪
▶ ⬤ ⚐ 🌡 **Notes:** Dogs must be kept on a lead

CUSHENDUN   Map 01 D6

▶ ▶ ▶ 70% **Cushendun Caravan Park**
14 Glendun Rd BT44 0PX ☎ 028 2176 1254
*Dir: From A2 take B92 for 1m towards Glenarm,
clearly signed*
★ 🚐 £13-£15 🚐 £13-£15 ▲ £6-£10
Open Etr-Sep Booking advisable Jul-Aug Last
arrival 22.00hrs Last departure 12.30hrs
*A pretty little grassy park surrounded by trees,
with separate secluded areas offering some privacy,
and static vans discreetly interspersed with tourers.
A 3-acre site with 15 touring pitches and 64 statics.*
Leisure: ◆ ⚠ ⬚ **Facilities:** 🛒 🏪 ⊙ ᕕ ᕕ ᕽ
Services: 🔌 🗑 → ∪ ▶ ⬤ ⚐ 🌡

LARNE   Map 01 D5

▶ ▶ ▶ 65% **Curran Court Caravan Park**
131 Curran Rd BT40 1BD ☎ 028 2827 3797
🖹 028 2826 0096
*Dir: Site on A2, 0.25m from ferry. From town centre
follow signs for Leisure Centre*
★ 🚐 fr £10 🚐 fr £10 ▲ fr £5
                                            contd

Services: 🅣 Toilet Fluid ✕ Café/ Restaurant 🛒 Fast Food/Takeaway ➡ Baby Care 🔌 Electric Hook Up
🗑 Launderette ♈ Licensed Bar 🛢 Calor Gaz ⬛ Camping Gaz ⬚ Battery Charging

Open Apr-Sep Booking advisable main season
A handy site for the ferry, with clean facilities and a helpful warden. When the reception is closed, the owners can be contacted at the Curran Court Hotel across the road. A 3-acre site with 30 touring pitches. Bowling & putting greens

Leisure: /A Facilities: ⚓ ⌧ ⬚ ⬚ ⬚ ⬚ ⬚
Services: ⬚ ⬚ → ⬚ ⬚ ⬚ ⬚ ⬚ ⬚ ⬚ ⬚ ⬚ ⬚ ⬚

CO BELFAST

BELFAST   Map 01 D5

▶ ▶ ▶ 74% **NEW** Dundonald Touring Caravan Park
111 Old Dundonald Rd BT16 1XT
☎ 028 9080 9100 & 9080 9101 ▤ 028 9048 9604
e-mail:
leisure&communityservices@castlereagh.gov.uk
Dir: From City Centre follow M3 & A20 to City airport. Onto A20 to Newtownards, follow signs to Dundonald, Ulster Hospital. Before hospital, right at sign for Ice Bowl. Follow signs, site 0.25m
★ ⬚ £13 ⬚ £13 Å £7
Open Apr-Sep (rs Oct-Mar Open on request)
Booking advisable Jul-Aug Last arrival 23.00hrs
A new purpose-built park located in a quiet corner of Dundonald Leisure Park on the outskirts of Belfast. This peaceful park is ideally placed for touring Co Down, and exploring Belfast. A 1.5-acre site with 22 touring pitches, 22 hardstandings. Discount at ice rink, bowling, indoor play area
Leisure: /A Facilities: ⬚ ⬚ ⬚ ⬚ ⬚ ⬚ ⬚ ⬚ ⬚ ⬚
Services: ⬚ ✕ ⬚ ⬚ → ⬚ ▶ ⬚ ⬚
Notes: Dogs must be kept on a lead ⬚ ⬚ ⬚ ⬚

CO DOWN

CASTLEWELLAN   Map 01 D5

▶ ▶ ▶ 68% *Castlewellan Forest Park*
BT31 9BU ☎ 028 4377 8664 ▤ 028 4377 1762
website: www.forestserviceni.gov.uk
Dir: Off A25, in Castlewellan turn right at Upper Square, turn into Forest Park, signed
⬚ £8-£13.50 ⬚ £8-£13.50 Å £8-£12
Open all year Booking advisable wknds & Jul-Aug
Last arrival 21.00hrs Last departure 15.00hrs
Attractive forest park site, situated down a long drive with views of the castle. The site is broken up into smaller areas by mature trees and shrubs. A 5-acre site with 90 touring pitches.
Lake, arboretum, fishing on site, maze, first aid.
Facilities: ⬚ ⬚ ⬚ ⬚ ⬚ ⬚ ⬚ ⬚
Services: ⬚ ⬚ ✕ → ⬚ ▶ ⬚ ⬚ ⬚ ⬚

KILLYLEAGH   Map 01 D5

▶ ▶ ▶ 73% Camping & Caravanning Club Site
Delamont Country Park, Downpatrick Rd BT30 9TZ
☎ 028 4482 1833
website: www.campingandcaravanningclub.co.uk
Dir: From Belfast take A22. Site 1m S of Killyleagh
★ ⬚ £12.40-£17.50 ⬚ £12.40-£17.50 Å £12.40-£17.50
contd.

Open Mar-Oct Booking advisable Jul-Aug, BH's & wknds Last arrival 21.00hrs Last departure 12.00hrs
A spacious park enjoying superb views and walks, in a lovely and interesting area. The facilities are of a very high order, and include fully-serviced pitches and excellent toilets. The site is close to Strangford Loch Marine Water reserve, a medieval fairy fort, and a blue flag beach. Please see advertisement on page 10 for details of Club Members' benefits. A 4.5-acre site with 64 touring pitches, 64 hardstandings.
Facilities: ⬚ ⬚ ⬚ ⬚ ⬚ ⬚
Services: ⬚ ⬚ ⬚ ⬚ ⬚ → ⬚ ⬚ ⬚ ⬚ ⬚ ⬚

NEWCASTLE   Map 01 D5

▶ ▶ ▶ 64% *Tollymore Forest Park*
BT33 0PW ☎ 028 4372 2428 ▤ 028 4372 2428
website: www.forestserviceni.gov.uk
Dir: From A2 at Newcastle take B180, site signed on right
⬚ £8-£13.50 ⬚ £8-£13.50 Å £8-£12
Open all year Booking advisable Last arrival
21.00hrs Last departure 17.00hrs
Popular site with a family field and a large tent area, set in a beautiful forest park. There are extensive walks to be enjoyed and the coast is a short drive away. A 7.5-acre site with 100 touring pitches.
Facilities: ⬚ ⬚ ⬚ ⬚ ⬚ ⬚ ⬚
Services: ⬚ ⬚ ⬚ → ⬚ ▶ ⬚ ⬚ ⬚ ⬚

CO FERMANAGH

ENNISKILLEN   Map 01 C5

▶ ▶ 66% *Blaney Caravan Park*
BT93 7ER ☎ 028 6864 1634
Dir: On A46, approx 12km from Enniskillen
Open all year
A small park with reasonable facilities set in lovely countryside close to Lough Erne, and only 30 minutes' drive from Donegal and the Atlantic. A 3-acre site with 26 touring pitches and 12 statics.

LISNASKEA   Map 01 C5

▶ ▶ ▶ 68% *Mullynascarty Caravan Park*
BT92 0NZ ☎ 028 6772 1040
Dir: 1.5m from Lisnaskea on Enniskillen side
★ ⬚ fr £12 ⬚ fr £12 Å fr £10
Open Mar-Nov Booking advisable Jul-Aug Last
arrival 21.00hrs Last departure noon
A pretty riverside site set in peaceful countryside with well-kept facilities and friendly owners. A 6-acre site with 43 touring pitches, 43 hardstandings and 8 statics.
Leisure: /A Facilities: ⬚ ⬚ ⬚ ⬚ ⬚ ⬚
Services: ⬚ ⬚ ⬚ → ⬚ ▶ ⬚ ⬚ ⬚ ⬚ ⬚

Ireland

CO LONDONDERRY

CASTLEROCK   Map 01 C6

► ► ► 66% *Castlerock Holiday Park*
24 Sea Rd ☎ 028 7084 8381
*Dir: From A2 to Castlerock turn right before railway
station, site signed*
🏠 🏠 👤
Open Etr-Oct Booking advisable Jul-Aug
Last arrival 19.00hrs Last departure noon
*A mainly static site at the seaside with a tidy touring
area, 2 minutes from the beach. A 12.5-acre site
with 22 touring pitches and 260 statics.*
Basketball court
Leisure: ♦ 🛝 **Facilities:** 🅿️⊙👤♿🛒
Services: 🔌🅱️👤🚰🅱️🕐🧺→∪🅿️✕🔩

COLERAINE   Map 01 C6

► ► 70% NEW Tullans Farm Caravan Park
46 Newmills Rd BT52 2JB ☎ 028 7034 2309
▤ 028 7034 2309
e-mail: tullansfarm@hotmail.com
website: www.tullansfarmcaravanpark.co.uk
*Dir: Turn right on ring road on A29 halfway between
Lodge Rd rdbt and Ballycastle Rd. At rdbt follow sign
for Windyhall*
★ 🏠 £12 🏠 £12 👤 £8-£10
Open Mar-Oct Booking advisable BH's & wknds
Last arrival 21.30hrs Last departure 13.00hrs
*A lovely rural site off the beaten track in quiet
farmland, but only one mile away from Coleraine,
and handy for the beaches at Portrush and
Portstewart. Good clean facilities are maintained by
the friendly family owners. A 4-acre site with 35
touring pitches, 35 hardstandings and 20 statics.*
Leisure: ♦ 🛝 🖵 **Facilities:** 🅿️⊙✳♿🛒🏪🐕
Services: 🔌🅱️👤🚰🅱️🕐→∪🛆🎪🔩🧺
Notes: Dogs must be kept on a lead

CO TYRONE

DUNGANNON   Map 01 C5

► ► ► 72% Dungannon Park
Moy Rd BT71 6DY ☎ 028 8772 7327
▤ 028 8772 9169
e-mail: dungannonpark@utvinternet.com
Dir: 1m from A4 on A29, 1m from Dungannon
🏠 £10 🏠 £10 👤 £7
Open all year Booking advisable Last arrival
20.00hrs Last departure 12.30hrs
*Modern caravan park in a quiet area of a public park
with fishing lake and excellent facilities, especially
for disabled. A 2-acre site with 12 touring pitches,
20 hardstandings.*
Vending machine on site.
Leisure: ⚲ 🛝 🖵 **Facilities:** 🅿️⊙🏳️♿🛒🏪🏓🐕
Services: 🔌🅱️🕐→∪🅿️✕🎪🔩🚚🚜🍴

REPUBLIC OF IRELAND

CO CLARE

KILRUSH   Map 01 B3

► ► ► *Aylevarroo Caravan and
Camping Park*
☎ 065 9051102
e-mail: aylevarroo@njogorman.ie
Dir: 1.5m from Kilrush on N67 near Tarbert car ferry
🏠 🏠 👤
Open 24 May-13 Sep Booking advisable Last arrival
22.00hrs Last departure noon ⌀
*A peaceful park in rolling countryside right on the
edge of the Shannon Estuary. A 7.5-acre site with
36 touring pitches and 10 statics.*
Basketball court.
Leisure: ⚲ ♦ 🛝 🖵 **Facilities:** 🅿️⊙✳🔩
Services: 🔌👤🧺→∪🅿️◎🛆✕🔩📁🧺

CO CORK

BALLINSPITTLE   Map 01 B2

► ► ► ► Garrettstown House Holiday Park
☎ 021 4778156 & 4775286 ▤ 021 4778156
e-mail: reception@garrettstownhouse.com
*Dir: 6m from Kinsale, through Ballinspittle, past school
& football pitch on main road to beach. Beside stone
estate entrance*
🏠 €10-€17.50 🏠 €10-€17.50 👤 €8-€14

Open May-Sep (rs Etr-1 Jun No shop) Booking
advisable 10 Jul-15 Aug Last arrival 22.00hrs Last
departure noon
*Elevated holiday park with tiered camping areas
and superb panoramic views. Plenty of on-site
amenities, and close to beach and forest park.
A 7-acre site with 60 touring pitches and 80 statics.*
Children's club, crazy golf, video shows
Leisure: ⚲ ♦ 🛝 🖵 **Facilities:** 🅿️⊙🏳️✳♿🛒🏪🐕
Services: 🔌🅱️👤🚰🅱️🕐✕🧺→∪🅿️◎🛆✕🔩🚙🚚
See advertisement on opposite page

GARRETTSTOWN HOUSE HOLIDAY PARK ►►►►

Garrettstown, Kinsale, Co Cork
Tel: 00 353 21 4778156/4775286

Top class spacious park in old world setting of Garrettstown estate near beach and forest. Ideally located for touring, scenic, historic and amenity areas of the south. Kinsale, gourmet centre of Ireland is 6 miles. Cork/Ringaskiddy ferryport 25 miles. Numerous facilities and activities on site or within 16 km.
Recommended by all main camping clubs including BFE 4 star

BALLYLICKEY　　　　　　　　　**Map 01 B2**

► ► ► ► Eagle Point Caravan and Camping Park
☎ 027 50630
e-mail: eaglepointcamping@eircom.net
website: www.eaglepointcamping.com
Dir: N71 to Bandon, then R586 to Bantry, then N71 4m to Glengarriff, opp Burham petrol station
🚐 €18-€22 🚐 €18-€22 ▲ €18-€22
Open 25 Apr-Sep Booking advisable Last arrival 22.00hrs Last departure noon ✿
An immaculate park set in an idyllic position overlooking the rugged bays and mountains of West Cork. Boat launching facilities and small pebble beaches, in an Area of Outstanding Natural Beauty. A 20-acre site with 125 touring pitches.
Leisure: ♦ /⋀ 🖵 Facilities: 🏕⊙✳⛄ ⓣ ⚡
Services: 🖵🗄🖭→🅿🗘🎫🅿

BLARNEY　　　　　　　　　　　**Map 01 B2**

► ► ► Blarney Caravan & Camping Park
Stone View ☎ 021 4385167 & 4382051
⌐ 021 4385167
e-mail: conquill@camping-ireland.ie
Dir: N20 from Cork or Limerick, then R617 to Blarney
🚐 🚐 ▲
Open Jan-15 Nov Booking advisable anytime Last arrival 22.00hrs Last departure noon
Attractive, well-kept grassy park in elevated position overlooking countryside and Blarney Castle. Very spacious and quiet, surrounded by hedging, with
　　　　　　　　　　　　　　　　contd.

---

adjacent pub and restaurant run by family. A 3-acre site with 40 touring pitches.
Pitch & putt, 18-hole golf
Leisure: 🖵 Facilities: 🏕⊙🖵✳⛄ⓣ⚡🎄🐕
Services: 🖵🗄🗘⌀✗→🅿🖭©🎫🗄🍴💳🚾

CROOKHAVEN　　　　　　　　　**Map 01 A1**

► ► ► ► Barley Cove Caravan Park
☎ 021 35302 & 021 434 6466 📠 021 430 7230
Dir: From Ballydehob follow signs for Crookhaven on R592, site on right by sandy cove, after Goleen
★ 🚐 €12-€17 🚐 €12-€17 ▲ €12-€17
Open Etr & Jun-1 Sep (rs May & Sep) Booking advisable 7 Jul-17 Aug Last arrival 21.00hrs Last departure noon ✿
Spacious holiday park in seaside location beside two coves and lovely sandy beaches. A very rural spot on the scenic Mizen Head peninsula. A 9-acre site with 90 touring pitches and 50 statics.
Pitch & putt, children's playhouse
Leisure: ♦ ⚡ /⋀ 🖵 Facilities: 🏕⊙🖵✳⚡⚡⚡
Services: 🖵🗄🗘⌀🖭🅣✗🍴⛟→🅿🗘🅿🍴

CO DONEGAL

PORTNOO　　　　　　　　　　　**Map 01 B5**

► ► Boyle's Caravan Park
☎ 074 9545131 & 086 8523131
Dir: Turn off N56 at Ardra onto R261 for 6m. Follow signs for Santaann Drive
★ 🚐 fr €18 🚐 fr €18 ▲ fr €15
Open 18 Mar-Oct Booking advisable All year Last arrival 23.00hrs Last departure 11.00hrs
Set at Banna Beach and close to a huge selection of water activities on a magnificent stretch of the Atlantic. This open park nestles among the sand dunes, and offers well-maintained facilities. A 1.5-acre site with 20 touring pitches and 10 statics.
Facilities: 🏕⊙✳⛄ⓣ⚡🐕
Services: 🖵🗘⌀→🅿🗘🗙🍴🗄

CO DUBLIN

CLONDALKIN　　　　　　　　　**Map 01 D4**

► ► ► ► Camac Valley Tourist Caravan & Camping Park
Naas Rd ☎ 01 4640644 📠 01 4640643
e-mail: camacmorriscastle@eircom.net
Dir: Directly off N7, near Clondalkin, follow signs after Red Cow rdbt on N7
🚐 €15-€18 🚐 €14-€16 ▲ €14-€15
Open all year Booking advisable Jul & Aug Last arrival anytime Last departure noon
A pleasant lightly wooded park with top class layout, facilities and security, within 30 minutes' drive or bus ride of city centre. A 15-acre site with 163 touring pitches, 113 hardstandings.
Leisure: /⋀ 🖵 Facilities: 🏕⊙🖵✳⛄ⓣ⚡🐕
Services: 🖵🗄⌀🖭⛟→🅿🖭©🍴💳🚾

Ireland

SHANKILL   Map 01 D3

▶ ▶ ▶ **Shankill Caravan Park**
☎ 01 2820011 ▤ 01 2820108
e-mail: shankillcaravanpark@eircom.net
website: www.eircom.net/shankillcaravancamping
Dir: From Dublin, 10m S on N11. From Dun Laoghaire, follow signs to N11, at N11 turn left. From Rosslare, turn off M11 at Bray/Shankill sign
⌂ €17-€18 ⌂ €17-€18 ▲ €15-€16
Open all year Last departure noon
Pretty tree-studded park with camping areas divided into smaller plots, and offering generous facilities. A 7-acre site with 82 touring pitches and 9 statics.
Facilities: ↑⊙♥✹€⅃
Services: ⊡▤⌀⊞→∪▶✕⚇⚊↙◙

CO KERRY

ARDFERT   Map 01 A2

▶ ▶ *Sir Roger's Caravan & Camping Park*
Banna Beach ☎ 066 7134730
Dir: 3km from Ardfert, 9km NW of Tralee
⌂
Open May-1 Oct
A well-maintained park next to a famous surfing beach, with hire equipment available, and 'Blue Flag' rating. This modern park is well equipped, and run by friendly owners. A 3.5-acre site with 50 touring pitches and 20 statics.

CAHERDANIEL   Map 01 A2

▶ ▶ ▶ ▶ **Wave Crest Caravan and Camping Park**
☎ 066 9475188 ▤ 066 9475188
e-mail: wavecrest@eircom.net
website: www.wavecrestcamping.com
Dir: From Sneem on N70 (Ring of Kerry road), 1m before Caherdaniel on left
⌂ fr €12 ⌂ fr €12 ▲ fr €11

Open 15 Mar-15 Oct (rs 15 Mar-1 May & Sep-15 Oct Shop closed) Last arrival 22.00hrs Last departure noon
Seaside site, with pitches tucked away in the natural contours of the hillside, and offering plenty of privacy. Very good facilities, and an excellent shop.

contd.

A 5.5-acre site with 120 touring pitches, 65 hardstandings and 2 statics.
Boat anchorage, fishing, pool, foreign exchange
Leisure: ♦⚲▢ **Facilities:** ↑⊙♥✹&€⅃⚊⊞⚏🛉
Services: ⊡▤⌀⊞⊡✕⚇→∪▶♠↙◢
Notes: Dogs must be kept on a lead ▭

KILLARNEY   Map 01 B2

Fossa Caravan Park
Fossa ☎ 064 31497 ▤ 064 34459
e-mail: fossaholidays@eircom.net
website: www.camping-holidaysireland.com
Dir: 2.5m SW on N72W
⌂ €14-€15.50 ⌂ €14-€15.50 ▲ €13.50-€15.50
Open Apr-Sep (rs Sep & Apr-May restaurant & takeaway restricted opening) Booking advisable Jul-Aug Last arrival 23.00hrs Last departure noon
Attractive terraced park, in lightly wooded grounds, with good screening and easy access to main facilities. A 6-acre site with 100 touring pitches and 20 statics.
Campers, kitchens, drying room & bikes for hire.
Leisure: ⚲♦⚲▢ **Facilities:** ↑⊙♥✹&€⅃⚊⊞
Services: ⊡▤⌀✕⚇→∪▶◉♠⚇↙🍴▭

KILLORGLIN   Map 01 A2

▶ ▶ ▶ **West's Caravan Park & Static Hire**
Killarney Rd ☎ 066 9761240 ▤ 066 9761833
e-mail: enquiries@westcaravans.com
Dir: 1m on Killarney road from Killorglin town
★ ⌂ fr €15 ⌂ fr €15 ▲ fr €15
Open May-Oct Booking advisable Last arrival 21.00hrs Last departure noon
Pretty little site on banks of, but safely fenced off, from River Laune, offering trout and salmon fishing, and good facilities for families. A 5-acre site with 20 touring pitches and 40 statics.
Salmon & trout fishing
Leisure: ⚲♦⚲▢ **Facilities:** ↑⊙♥✹€⅃⚊⊞
Services: ⊡▤⊞⚇→∪▶↙⚊ **Notes:** Dogs must be on leads and are charged for ▭▭

LAURAGH   Map 01 A2

▶ ▶ **Creveen Park**
Healy Pass Rd ☎ 064 83131 ▤ 064 83998
e-mail: info@creveenlodge.com
website: www.creveenlodge.com
Dir: 1m SE on R574
★ ⌂ fr €12 ⌂ fr €12 ▲ fr €12
Open Etr-Oct Booking advisable Aug BH Last arrival midnight Last departure noon
Wild and beautiful site on hill farm, with views of sea and mountains. Good facilities including equipped kitchen for tenters. A 2-acre site with 20 touring pitches and 2 statics.
Leisure: ⚲▢ **Facilities:** ↑⊙✹€⅃⚊🛉
Services: ⊡▤⌀⊞✕→♠↙

CO KILKENNY

KILKENNY   Map 01 C3

▶ ▶ ▶ *Tree Grove Caravan & Camping Park*
Danville House ☎ 056 7770302 🗎 056 7721512
email: treecc@iol.ie
*Dir: 1km from Kilkenny on R700 New Ross road, on
right immediately past rdbt*
◀ 🚐 Å

Open Apr-Oct Booking advisable
*A pretty park set in the hills of Kilkenny, with tiered
pitches and plenty of space. Friendly, welcoming
owners and good facilities. A 7-acre site with 30
touring pitches.*
Campers' kitchen & sinks.
Leisure: ◀ ⚠ Facilities: 🖪⊙✳🔦🝙🎍🐾🐕🕊
Services: 🖵🔋🛢🕯🖃→∪▶◉🛆🎪🍺🖃

CO MAYO

KNOCK   Map 01 B4

▶ ▶ *Knock Caravan and Camping Park*
Claremorris Rd ☎ 094 9388100 & 9388223
🗎 094 9388295
email: info@knock-shrine.ie
website: www.knock-shrine.ie/accommodation
*Dir: From rdbt in Knock, take N17 Claremorris road. Park
entrance on left 1km, opposite petrol station*
🛏 €12-€13 🚐 €12-€13 Å €6-€13
Open Mar-Nov Booking advisable Aug
Last arrival 22.00hrs Last departure noon
*A pleasant, very well maintained caravan park
within the grounds of Knock Shrine, offering
spacious terraced pitches and excellent facilities.
A 10-acre site with 88 touring pitches, 88
hardstandings and 17 statics.*
Leisure: ◀ ⚠ 🖵 Facilities: 🖪⊙✳🝙✳🔦🝙🎍🐾🐕🕊
Services: 🖵🔋🛢🛢🖃→∪▶🕯🛆
Notes: Dogs must be kept on leads 🍺

CO ROSCOMMON

BOYLE   Map 01 B4

▶ ▶ ▶ *Lough Key Forest Park*
☎ 071 9662363 & 9662212 🗎 071 9663266
email: seamus.duignan@coillte.ie
*Dir: Follow signs for Lough Key Forest Park, site within
grounds, about 0.5m from entrance. Forest park located
5m E of Boule on N4*
🛏 €12-€14 🚐 €12-€14 Å €6-€12
Open 17 Apr-14 Sep Pre-booking essential Booking
advisable 3 wks before arrival Last arrival 22.00hrs
Last departure noon no cars by tents
*A peaceful and very secluded site within the extensive
grounds of a beautiful forest park. Lough Key offers
boat trips and waterside walks, and there is a
viewing tower. A 15-acre site with 72 touring
pitches, 52 hardstandings.*
Leisure: ⚠🖵 Facilities: 🖪⊙🛆🔦🝙🎍🐕🕊
Services: 🖵🖃→▶🛆🎪🕯

CO SLIGO

ROSSES POINT   Map 01 B5

▶ ▶ ▶ ▶ *Greenlands Caravan &
Camping Park*
☎ 071 9177113
Dir: 5m NW of Sligo beside golf club at Rosses Point
🚐🚐Å
Open Etr-mid Sep Last arrival 20.00hrs
Last departure noon
*On Rosses Point peninsula this beachside park built
on the sand dunes overlooking Sligo Bay, and two
lovely bathing beaches. Spacious open camping
areas, and good central facilities. A 6-acre site with
69 touring pitches.*
Leisure: ◀ 🖵 Facilities: 🖪⊙✳🛆🔦🝙🕊
Services: 🖵→▶◉🛆🕯🖃 🍺🖃

STRANDHILL   Map 01 B5

▶ ▶ ▶ *Strandhill Caravan Park*
☎ 071 9168111
Dir: 5m W of Sligo, site at beach on Airport Road
🚐🚐Å
Open Etr-mid Sep Last arrival 23.00hrs Last
departure noon
*Sand dune site overlooking Sligo Bay, with views of
Knocknarea and Benbulben Mountains, and offering
plenty of seclusion and privacy. A 20-acre site with
72 touring pitches.*
Leisure: ◀ 🖵 Facilities: 🖪⊙🝙✳🔦🝙🕊
Services: 🖵→∪▶🛆🕯🖃 🍺🖃

CO WATERFORD

CLONEA   Map 01 C2

▶ ▶ ▶ *Casey's Caravan Park*
☎ 058 41919
*Dir: Take R675 Dungarvan road, following signs to
Clonea Bay. Site at end of road beside sea*
🚐🚐Å

Open May-6 Sep Booking advisable May-Jun Last
arrival 22.00hrs Last departure noon
*Spacious, well-kept park with excellent toilet
facilities, next to beach. A 4.5-acre site with 108
touring pitches and 170 statics.*
Crazy golf & games room.
Leisure: ◀ ⚠🖵 Facilities: 🖪⊙🝙✳🛆🔦🝙
Services: 🖵🔋🛢🛢→▶🝙🎪🕯

Leisure: 🏊 Indoor swimming pool   🏊 Outdoor swimming pool   🎾 Tennis court   ◀ Games room   ⚠ Children's playground   ∪ Stables
▶ 9/18 hole golf course   ⚓ Boats for hire   🎬 Cinema   🎣 Fishing   ◉ Mini golf   🛆 Watersports   🖵 Separate TV room

CO WEXFORD

KILMUCKRIDGE | Map 01 D3

▶ ▶ ▶ **Morriscastle Strand Caravan Park**
Morriscastle ☎ 053 30124 &
087 2304035 (off-season) ⓘ 053 30365
e-mail: camacmorriscastle@eircom.net
*Dir: From Kilmuckridge follow signs for Morriscastle
Strand*
★ ⚑ €15-€18 ⚑ €15-€18
Open Jul-27 Aug (rs May-Jun & 28 Aug-Sep shop,
reception, games & take-away limited) Booking
advisable Whitsun wknd & mid Jul-mid Aug Last
arrival 22.00hrs Last departure 13.00hrs
*Popular holiday park beside a glorious stretch of
beach, with good facilities on site and in the nearby
town. A 16-acre site with 100 touring pitches, 6
hardstandings and 150 statics.*
Dish washing room, indoor cooking facilities
Leisure: ⚲ ⚫ Facilities: ⋒⊙⚑✳⚫⚫⚫
Services: ⚑⚑⚑⚑⚑⚑→∪▶⊙⚑ ⚑ ⚑

WEXFORD | Map 01 D2

▶ ▶ ▶ **Ferrybank Caravan Park**
Ferrybank ☎ 053 44378 & 43274 ⓘ 053 45947
Dir: Beside bridge, NW of Wexford harbour, off R741
⚑ ⚑ ⚑
Open Apr-Sep (rs Etr & Sep no shop) Booking
advisable Whit wknd & Aug bank hol
Last arrival 22.00hrs Last departure 16.00hrs
*An open site beside the sea and on the
edge of Wexford, with level grassy pitches.
A 4.5-acre site with 130 touring pitches.*
Leisure: ⚲ ⚫ ⚑ ⚑ Facilities: ⋒⊙✳⚫⚫⚫⚑
Services: ⚑⚑✕⚑→∪▶⊙⚑⚑⚑⚑

CO WICKLOW

DONARD | Map 01 D3

▶ ▶ ▶ **Moat Farm Caravan & Camping Park**
☎ 045 404727 ⓘ 045 404727
e-mail: moatfarm@ireland.com
Dir: Off N81 in Donard
★ ⚑ €14 ⚑ €14 ⚑ €14
Open Mar-Sep Booking advisable BH's & Jun-Aug
Last arrival 22.00hrs Last departure noon
*Quiet open parkland on an organic farm in the
foothills of the Wicklow Mountains. Plenty of grassy
space and a good area with hardstandings for vans.
Very attractive facilities. A 2.75-acre site with 40
touring pitches.*
Campers' kitchen
Leisure: ⚑⚑ Facilities: ⋒⊙⚑✳⚫⚫⚫⚑⚑⚑⚑
Services: ⚑⚑⚑⚑⚑→∪▶⚑
Notes: Dogs must be kept on leads at all times

ROUNDWOOD | Map 01 D3

▶ ▶ ▶ ▶ **Roundwood Caravan Park**
☎ 01 2818163 ⓘ 01 2818163
e-mail: dicksonn@indigo.ie
*Dir: From N11 Shankill by-pass take R755 at
Kilmacanogue for Glendalough. Park on left at
entrance to Roundwood*
⚑ ⚑ ⚑
Open Apr-Sep Booking advisable Jun-Aug Last
arrival 11.00hrs Last departure noon
*Attractive touring park in the midst of the Wicklow
Mountains, with well-screened pitches and views of
Vantry Lakes. A 6-acre site with 71 touring pitches.*
Campers' kitchen & dining room
Leisure: ⚫ ⚑⚑ Facilities: ⋒⊙✳⚫⚫⚑
Services: ⚑⚑⚑⚑⚑⚑→∪▶⚑

Ireland

STATIC PARKS

The following is a list of parks which have been awarded an English Rose, a Scottish Thistle, or a Welsh Dragon by the National Tourist Boards for the very high quality of their static holiday accommodation. A page number beside a listing indicates a park which is also classified by the AA's Pennant Scheme.

ENGLAND

CORNWALL

Boswinger
Sea View International (See page 33)
Tel: 01726 843425 Fax: 01726 843358

Callington
Trehorner Farm Holiday Park
Tel: 01579 351122

Crantock
Trevella Park (See page 38)
Tel: 01637 830308 Fax: 01872 571254

Newquay
Hendra Holiday Park (See page 51)
Tel: 01637 875778

Nancolleth Farm Caravan Gardens
Tel: 01872 510236 Fax: 01872 510948

Porth Beach Tourist Park
(See page 55)
Tel: 01637 876531 Fax: 01637 871227

Padstow
Mother Ivey's Bay Caravan Park
Tel: 01841 520990 Fax: 01841 520550

Par
Par Sands Holiday Park
Tel: 01726 812868 Fax: 01726 817899

Pentewan
Sun Valley Holiday Park
(See page 57)
Tel: 01726 843266 Fax: 01726 843266

Relubbus
River Valley Country Park
(See page 64)
Tel: 0845 6012516 Fax: 01736 763398

St Austell
River Valley Holiday Park
(See page 66)
Tel: 01726 73533 Fax: 01726 73533

St Issey
Trewince Farm Holiday Park
(See page 68)
Tel: 01208 812830 Fax: 01208 812835

St Ives
Ayr Holiday Park (See page 69)
Tel: 01736 795855 Fax: 01736 798797

St Merryn
Carnevas Farm Holiday Park
(See page 71)
Tel: 01841 520230 Fax: 01841 520230

Truro
Ringwell Valley Holiday Park
(See page 74)
Tel: 01872 862194 Fax: 01872 864343

CUMBRIA

Silloth
Stanwix Park Holiday Centre
(See page 87)
Tel: 016973 32666 Fax: 016973 32555

Windermere
Fallbarrow Park (See page 90)
Tel: 015394 44422 Fax: 015394 88736

Limefitt Park (See page 90)
Tel: 015394 32300

DEVON

Ashburton
Ashburton Caravan Park
(See page 96)
Tel: 01364 652552 Fax: 01364 652552

Bideford
Beachside Holiday Park
Tel: 0845 6012541 Fax: 01237 472100

Surf Bay Holiday Park
Tel: 0845 60 11 132

Dawlish Warren
Welcome Family Holiday Park
Tel: 01626 862070

Kentisbeare
Forest Glade Holiday Park
(See page 111)
Tel: 01404 841381 Fax: 01404 841593

Paignton
Hoburne Torbay (See page 119)
Tel: 01803 558010 Fax: 01803 663336

Plymouth
Bovisand Lodge Estate
Tel: 01752 403554 Fax: 01752 482646

Sidmouth
Salcombe Regis
Camping & Caravan Park
(See page 122)
Tel: 01395 514303 Fax: 01395 514303

Tavistock
Harford Bridge Holiday Park
(See page 124)
Tel: 01822 810349 Fax: 01822 810028

Woodovis Park (See page 124)
Tel: 01822 832968 Fax: 01822 832948

Woolacombe
Woolacombe Bay Holiday Village
(See page 129)
Tel: 01271 870343 Fax: 01271 87008

DORSET

Bridport
Gorselands
Tel: 01308 897232 Fax: 01308 897239

Highlands End Holiday Park
(See page 131)
Tel: 01308 422139 Fax: 01308 425672

Christchurch
Cobb's Holiday Park
Tel: 01425 273301/275313
Fax: 01425 276090

Swanage
Ulwell Cottage Caravan Park
(See page 139)
Tel: 01929 422823 Fax: 01929 421500

HAMPSHIRE

Fordingbridge
Sandy Balls Holiday Centre
(See page 150)
Tel: 01425 653042 Fax: 01425 653067

Milford-on-Sea
Shorefield Country Park
Tel: 01590 648331 Fax: 01590 645610

New Milton
Naish Holiday Village
Tel: 01425 273586 Fax: 01425 270923

KENT

Canterbury
Yew Tree Caravan Park
(See page 156)
Tel: 01227 700306 Fax: 01227 700306

Ramsgate
The Foxhunter Park
Tel: 01843 821311 Fax: 01843 821458

Stansted
Thriftwood Caravan Park
Tel: 01732 822261 Fax: 01732 824636

LANCASHIRE

Silverdale
Holgate's Caravan Park
(See page 164)
Tel: 01524 701508 Fax: 01524 701580

NORFOLK

East Runton
Woodhill Park
Tel: 01263 512242 Fax: 01263 515326

Great Yarmouth
Vauxhall Holiday Park
(See page 173)
Tel: 01493 857231 Fax: 01493 331122

Holt
Kelling Heath Holiday Park
Tel: 01263 588181 Fax: 01263 588599

Hunstanton
Searles of Hunstanton (See page 174)
Tel: 01485 534211 Fax: 01485 533815

Scratby
Summerfields Holiday Village
Tel: 01493 733733 Fax: 01493 730292

NORTHUMBERLAND

Bamburgh
Waren Caravan Park (See page 177)
Tel: 01668 214366 Fax: 01668 214224

Berwick-upon-Tweed
Ord House Country Park
(See page 178)
Tel: 01289 305288 Fax: 01289 330832

Eyemouth
Eyemouth Holiday Park
Tel: 018907 51050 Fax: 018907 51462

Greenlaw
Greenlaw Caravan Park
Tel: 01361 810341 Fax: 01361 810341

Morpeth
Percy Wood Caravan Park
Tel: 01670 787649 Fax: 01670 787034

Seahouses
Seafield Caravan Park
Tel: 01665 720628 Fax: 01665 720088

SOMERSET

Blue Anchor
Beeches Holiday Park
Tel: 01984 640391 Fax: 01984 640361

Hoburne Blue Anchor Park
(See page 187)
Tel: 01643 821360 Fax: 01643 821572

Brean
Warren Farm Holiday Park
(See page 187)
Tel: 01278 781036

Burnham-on-Sea
Sandyglade Holiday Park
Tel: 01278 751271 Fax: 01278 751036

Watchet
Lorna Doone Caravan Park
Tel: 01984 631206 Fax: 01984 633537

STAFFORDSHIRE

Rugeley
Silver Trees Caravan Park
Tel: 01889 582185 Fax: 01889 582185

SUSSEX, EAST

Battle
Crowhurst Park
Tel: 01424 773344 Fax: 01424 775727

YORKSHIRE, EAST RIDING OF

Hull
Patrington Haven Leisure Park Ltd
Tel: 01964 630071 Fax: 01964 631060

Skipsea
Far Grange Caravan Park
Tel: 01262 468248/468293
Fax: 01262 468648

Skipsea Sands Holiday Park
Tel: 01262 468210 Fax: 01262 468454

Stamford Bridge
Weir Caravan Park
Tel: 01759 371377 Fax: 01759 371377

YORKSHIRE, NORTH

Allerton Park
Allerton Park Caravan Park
(See page 224)
Tel: 01423 330569 Fax: 01759 371377

Filey
Crows Nest Caravan Park
(See page 227)
Tel: 01723 582206 Fax: 01723 582206

Harrogate
Rudding Holiday Park
(See page 228)
Tel: 01423 870439 Fax: 01423 870859

Robin Hood's Bay
Flask Country Holiday Home Park
Tel: 01947 880592 Fax: 01947 880592

Middlewood Farm Holiday Park
(See page 233)
Tel: 01947 880414 Fax: 01947 880414

Scarborough
Jacobs Mount Caravan Park
(See page 234)
Tel: 01723 361178 Fax: 01723 361178

Threshfield
Wood Nook Caravan Park
Tel: 01756 752412 Fax: 01756 752412

Whitby
Northcliffe Holiday Park
(See page 240)
Tel: 01947 880477 Fax: 01947 880972

SCOTLAND

ABERDEENSHIRE

Kintore
Hillhead Caravan Park
(See page 247)
Tel: 01467 632809 Fax: 01467 633173

ARGYLL & BUTE

Glendaruel
Glendaruel Caravan Park
(See page 249)
Tel: 01369 820267 Fax: 01369 820367

Inverbeg
Inverbeg Holiday Park
Tel: 01436 860267 Fax: 01436 860266

Inveruglas
Loch Lomond Holiday Park
(See page 249)
Tel: 01301 704224 Fax: 01301 704206

CITY OF EDINBURGH

Edinburgh
Mortonhall Caravan Park
(See page 250)
Tel: 0131 6641533 Fax: 0131 6645387

DUMFRIES & GALLOWAY

Brighouse
Brighouse Bay Holiday Park
(See page 251)
Tel: 01557 870267 Fax: 01557 870319

Crocketford
Park of Brandedleys (See page 253)
Tel: 01556 690250 Fax: 01556 690681

Glenluce
Glenluce Caravan Park
(See page 255)
Tel: 01581 300412 Fax: 0870 1371489

Kippford
Kippford Holiday Park
(See page 256)
Tel: 01556 620636 Fax: 01556 620607

Kirkcudbright
Seaward Caravan Park
(See page 256)
Tel: 01557 870267 Fax: 01557 870319

Palnackie
Barlochan Caravan Park
(See page 258)
Tel: 01557 870267 Fax: 01557 870319

Parton
Loch Ken Holiday Park
(See page 258)
Tel: 01644 470282 Fax: 01644 470297

Sandyhills
Sandyhills Bay Leisure Park
(See page 259)
Tel: 01557 870267 Fax: 01557 870319

EAST LOTHIAN

Dunbar
Belhaven Bay Caravan Park
Tel: 01368 865956 Fax: 01368 865022

Haddington
The Monks' Muir
Tel: 01620 860340 Fax: 01620 861770

North Berwick
Tantallon Caravan Park
(See page 261)
Tel: 01620 893348 Fax: 01620 895623

FIFE

St Andrews
Craigtoun Meadows Holiday Park
(See page 262)
Tel: 01334 475959 Fax: 01334 476424

HIGHLAND

Aviemore
Rothiemurchus
Camp and Caravan Park
Tel: 01479 812800 Fax: 01479 812800

Dornoch
Grannies' Heilan'
Hame Holiday Park
(See page 266) Tel: 0870 242 2222

Gairloch
Sands Holiday Centre (See page 267)
Tel: 01445 712152 Fax: 01445 712152

Glencoe
Invercoe Caravan & Camping Park
(See page 267)
Tel: 01855 811210 Fax: 01855 811210

Nairn
Nairn Lochloy Holiday Park
(See page 270)
Tel: 0870 242 2222

MORAY

Lossiemouth
Silver Sands Leisure Park
(See page 272)
Tel: 01343 813262 Fax: 01343 815205

PERTH & KINROSS

Aberfoyle
Trossachs Holiday Park
Tel: 01877 382614 Fax: 01877 382732

Birnham
Erigmore House Holiday Park
(See page 273)
Tel: 01350 727236 Fax: 01350 728636

Tummel Bridge
Tummel Valley Holiday Park
(See page 276)
Tel: 0870 242 2222

SCOTTISH BORDERS

Coldingham
Scoutscroft Holiday Centre
(See page 276)
Tel: 018907 71338 Fax: 018907 71746

Jedburgh
Jedwater Caravan Park
(See page 277)
Tel: 01835 840219 Fax: 01835 840219

SOUTH AYRSHIRE

Ayr
Craig Tara Holiday Park
(See page 279)
Tel: 0870 242 2222

Coylton
Sundrum Castle (See page 280)
Tel: 0870 242 2222

STIRLING

Luib
Glendochart Caravan Park
(See page 282)
Tel: 01567 820637 Fax: 01567 820024

WALES

ANGLESEY, ISLE OF

Dulas
Minffordd Caravan Park
Tel: 01248 410678 Fax: 01248 410378

CARMARTHENSHIRE

Abercych
Aberdwylan Holiday Home Park
Tel: 01239 841476 Fax: 01239 841476

Newcastle Emlyn
Cenarth Falls Holiday Park
(See page 289)
Tel: 01239 710345 Fax: 01239 710344

CEREDIGION

Borth
Cambrian Coast Holiday Park
Tel: 0500 11 80 52

Clarach Bay
Glan-y-Mor Leisure Park
Tel: 0500 11 80 52

Llanrhystud
Penrhos Holiday Park
Tel: 01974 202999 Fax: 01974 202100

New Quay
Ocean Heights Leisure Park
Tel: 01545 560309 Fax: 01545 561277

CONWY

Kinmel Bay
Palins Holiday Park
Tel: 01745 342672 Fax: 01745 344110

Penmaenmawr
Craiglwyd Hall Caravan Park
Tel: 01492 623355 Fax: 01492 623921

Towyn
Ty Mawr Holiday Park
(See page 293)
Tel: 0870 242 2222

GWYNEDD

Bala
Pen-y-Garth
Caravan & Camping Park
(See page 296)
Tel: 01678 520485 Fax: 01678 520401

Barmouth
Caerddaniel Caravan Park
Tel: 01341 280611 Fax: 01341 280740

Betws Garmon
Bryn Gloch
Caravan & Camping Park
(See page 297)
Tel: 01286 650216 Fax: 01286 650591

Bryncrug
Woodlands Holiday Park
(See page 297)
Tel: 01654 710471 Fax: 01654 710100

Chwilog
Ocean Heights Caravan Park
Tel: 01766 810519

Dinas Dinlle
Morfa Lodge Caravan Park
Tel: 01286 830205 Fax: 01286 831329

Dinlle Caravan Park (See page 299)
Tel: 01286 830324 Fax: 01286 831526

PEMBROKESHIRE

Amroth
Pendeilo Leisure Park
Tel: 01834 831259 Fax: 01834 831702

Fishguard
Fishguard Bay
Caravan & Camping Park
(See page 303)
Tel: 01348 811415 Fax: 01348 811425

Fishguard Holiday Park
Tel: 01348 872462

Haverfordwest
Scamford Caravan Park
Tel: 01437 710304 Fax: 01437 710304

Ludchurch
Blackmoor Farm
Tel: 01834 831242 Fax: 01834 831242

Saundersfoot
Beachdean Leisure Park
Tel: 08000 195382

Saundersfoot Bay Leisure Park
Tel: 01834 812284 Fax: 01834 813387

Tenby
Lydstep Beach
Tel: 0845 607 8099

Trefalun (See page 306)
Tel: 01646 651514 Fax: 01646 651746

County Maps

The county map shown here will help you identify the counties within each county. You can look up each county in the guide using the county names at the top of each page. To find towns featured in the guide use the atlas and the index.

England

1 Bedfordshire
2 Berkshire
3 Bristol
4 Buckinghamshire
5 Cambridgeshire
6 Greater Manchester
7 Herefordshire
8 Hertfordshire
9 Leicestershire
10 Northamptonshire
11 Nottinghamshire
12 Rutland
13 Staffordshire
14 Warwickshire
15 West Midlands
16 Worcestershire

Scotland

17 City of Glasgow
18 Clackmannanshire
19 East Ayrshire
20 East Dunbartonshire
21 East Renfrewshire
22 Perth & Kinross
23 Renfrewshire
24 South Lanarkshire
25 West Dunbartonshire

Wales

26 Blaenau Gwent
27 Bridgend
28 Caerphilly
29 Denbighshire
30 Flintshire
31 Merthyr Tydfil
32 Monmouthshire
33 Neath Port Talbot
34 Newport
35 Rhondda Cynon Taff
36 Torfaen
37 Vale of Glamorgan
38 Wrexham

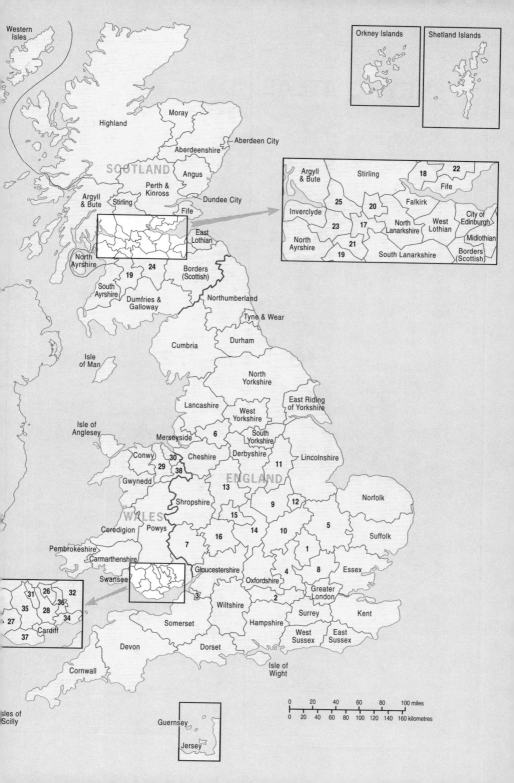

Western
Isles

Orkney Islands   Shetland Islands

Highland

Moray

Aberdeen City

SCOTLAND

Aberdeenshire

Angus

Perth &
Kinross

Argyll
& Bute   Stirling

Dundee City

Fife

North
Ayrshire

East
Lothian

Argyll
& Bute   Stirling   18   22
Fife
25   20   Falkirk
Inverclyde
23   17   North   West   City of
Edinburgh
North   Lanarkshire   Lothian
Ayrshire   21   Midlothian
19   South Lanarkshire   Borders
(Scottish)

24

19

Borders
(Scottish)

South
Ayrshire

Dumfries &
Galloway

Northumberland

Tyne & Wear

Isle
of Man

Cumbria

Durham

North
Yorkshire

Lancashire

East Riding
of Yorkshire

Isle of
Anglesey

West
Yorkshire

Merseyside   6

Conwy

30   Cheshire

South
Yorkshire

Derbyshire   11

Lincolnshire

29

38

Gwynedd

13

ENGLAND

Shropshire

9   12

Norfolk

Ceredigion

Powys

15

16

14

10

5

Suffolk

WALES

7

1

31   26   32
36
35   28   34
27   Cardiff
37

Swansea

Gloucestershire

3

4   8   Essex

Oxfordshire   Greater
London

Pembrokeshire

Carmarthenshire

2   Kent

Wiltshire   Surrey

Somerset   Hampshire   West   East
Sussex   Sussex

Devon   Dorset

Isle of
Wight

Cornwall

sles of
Scilly

Guernsey

Jersey

0   20   40   60   80   100 miles

0   20   40   60   80   100   120   140   160 kilometres

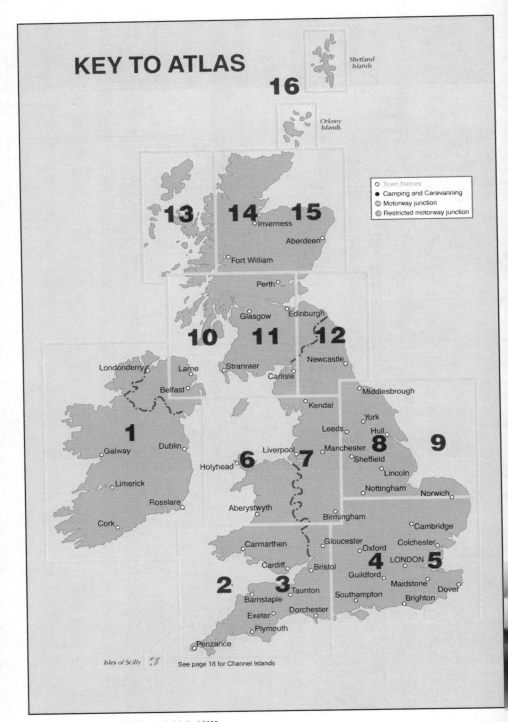

KEY TO ATLAS

Shetland Islands

16

Orkney Islands

- ○ Town Names
- ● Camping and Caravanning
- ⊛ Motorway junction
- ⊛ Restricted motorway junction

13   14   15

Inverness

Aberdeen

Fort William

Perth

Glasgow   Edinburgh

10   11   12

Newcastle

Londonderry   Larne   Stranraer

Belfast   Carlisle

Kendal

Middlesbrough

1   York

Galway   Dublin   Leeds   Hull

Holyhead   Liverpool   Manchester   8   9

6   7   Sheffield

Limerick   Lincoln

Rosslare   Nottingham   Norwich

Cork   Aberystwyth

Birmingham   Cambridge

Carmarthen   Gloucester   Colchester

Cardiff   Oxford

2   3   Bristol   4   LONDON   5

Taunton   Guildford   Maidstone   Dover

Barnstaple   Southampton   Brighton

Exeter   Dorchester

Plymouth

Penzance

Isles of Scilly   See page 16 for Channel Islands

© Automobile Association Developments Limited 2002

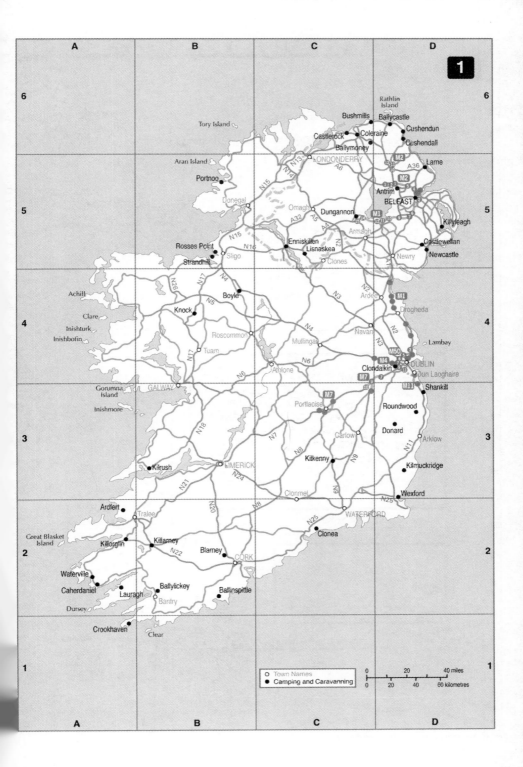

1

	A	B	C	D	

6

Rathlin Island

Tory Island

Bushmills • Ballycastle •
Castlerock • Coleraine • Cushendun •
Ballymoney • Cushendall •

5

Aran Island
LONDONDERRY A6
Portnoo • A36 • Larne
N15 M2
Donegal Omagh A5 Dungannon M2 Antrim
Armagh BELFAST
N14 A32 A4 M1
Rosses Point • N15 Enniskillen Killyleagh •
Strandhill • Sligo N16 Lisnaskea • Castlewellan •
Clones Newry Newcastle •

4

Achill
Clare N26 N17 N4 Boyle • N3 Ardee • M1
Inishturk Knock • N5 Roscommon N4 Navan Drogheda
Inishbofin N17 Mullingar N3 Lambay
Tuam N6 Athlone N6 M50 DUBLIN
Clondalkin M4 Dun Laoghaire
Gorumna M7 7
Island GALWAY Portlaoise M7 M11 • Shankill
Inishmore N18 Roundwood •

3

N7 Carlow Donard •
Kilrush • N8 N11 Arklow
LIMERICK N21 N9 Kilmuckridge •
Kilkenny
N24 N9 Wexford •
Clonmel N25

2

Ardfert • WATERFORD
Tralee A25
Great Blasket Killorglin • Killarney • Clonea •
Island N20 N8 CORK
Waterville • N22 Blarney
Caherdaniel • Lauragh • Ballylickey • Ballinspittle •
Dursey Bantry

1

Crookhaven •
Clear

| ○ Town Names | | 0 | 20 | 40 miles |
| ● Camping and Caravanning | | 0 | 20 | 40 | 60 kilometres |

	A	B	C	D	

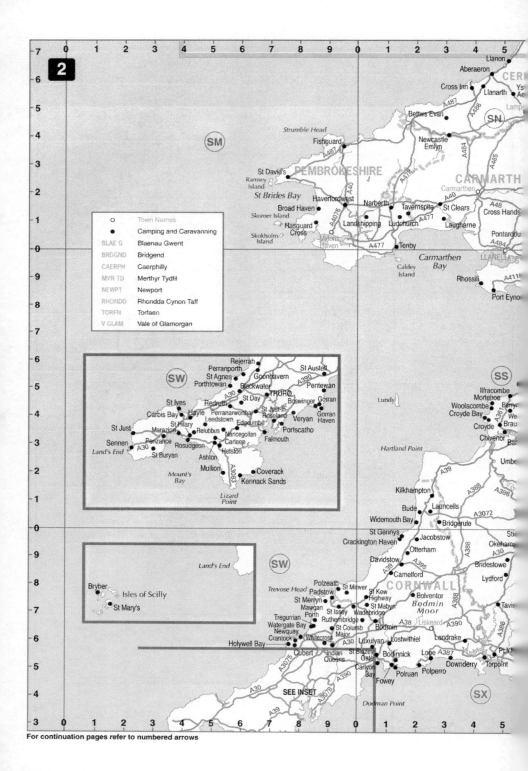

Town Names ○
Camping and Caravanning ●

BLAE G	Blaenau Gwent
BRDGND	Bridgend
CAERPH	Caerphilly
MYR TD	Merthyr Tydfil
NEWPT	Newport
RHONDD	Rhondda Cynon Taff
TORFN	Torfaen
V GLAM	Vale of Glamorgan

PEMBROKESHIRE

CARMARTH

Strumble Head

Fishguard

St David's
Ramsey Island

St Brides Bay
Skomer Island
Skokholm Island

Broad Haven
Hasguard Cross
Milford Haven

Haverfordwest
Landshipping
Ludchurch

Narberth
Tavernspite
Ludchurch

St Clears
Carmarthen

Laugharne

Tenby

Caldey Island

Carmarthen Bay

Rhossili

Port Eyno

Llanon
Aberaeron
Cross Inn
Llanarth
Bettws Evan
Newcastle Emlyn
Cross Hands
Pontardu
LLANELL

SM
SN
SS
SX
SW

St Austell
Rejerrah
Perranporth
St Agnes
Porthtowan
Goonhavern
Blackwater
St Day
TRURO
Pentewan
St Ives
Redruth
Perranarworthal
Boswinger
Gorran
Carbis Bay
Hayle
St Just-in-Roseland
Veryan
Gorran Haven
St Hilary
Leedstown
Edgcumbe
St Just
Marazion
Relubbus
Nancegollan
Portscatho
Penzance
Rosudgeon
Carleen
Falmouth
Sennen
Helston
Land's End
St Buryan
Ashton
Mount's Bay
Mullion
Coverack
Kennack Sands
Lizard Point

Lundy

Hartland Point

Ilfracombe
Mortehoe
Woolacombe
Berry
Croyde Bay
We
Croyde
Brau
Chivenor
Bar
Umbe

Kilkhampton
Bude
Launcells
Widemouth Bay
Bridgerule
St Gennys
Jacobstow
Crackington Haven
Otterham
Davidstow
Camelford
Stie
Okeham
Bridestowe
Lydford
Tavi

A388
A39
A395
A30

Land's End
SW

Bryher
Isles of Scilly
St Mary's

Trevose Head
Polzeath
St Minver
Padstow
St Kew Highway
St Merryn
Bolventor
Mawgan Porth
St Issey
St Mabyn
Wadebridge
Bodmin Moor
Tregurrian
Ruthembridge
Liskeard
Watergate Bay
St Columb Major
Newquay
Bodmin
Landrake
Crantock
Whitecross
Loxulyan
Lostwithiel
Holywell Bay
Indian Queens
St Blazey Gate
Bodinnick
Looe
Downderry
Cubert
Carlyon Bay
Polruan
Polperro
Torpoint
Fowey
PLY

CORNWALL

SEE INSET
Dodman Point

SX

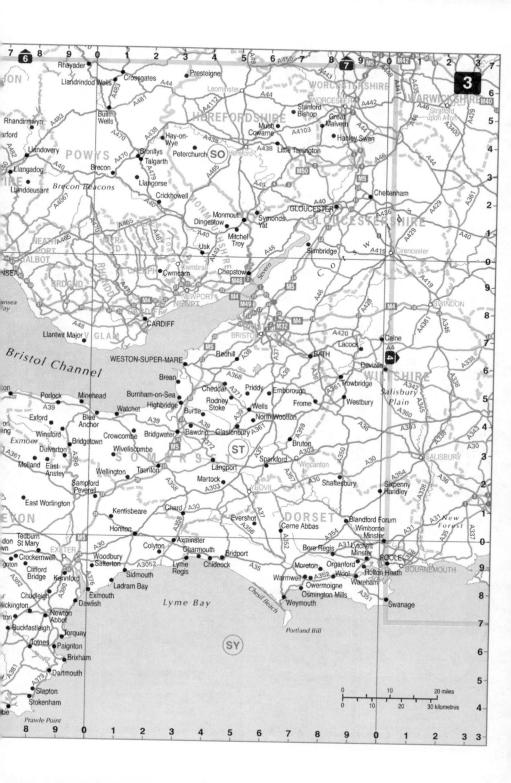

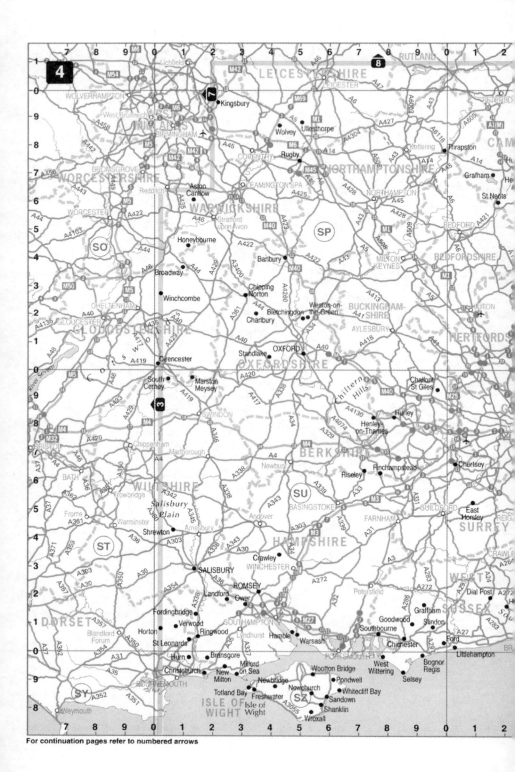

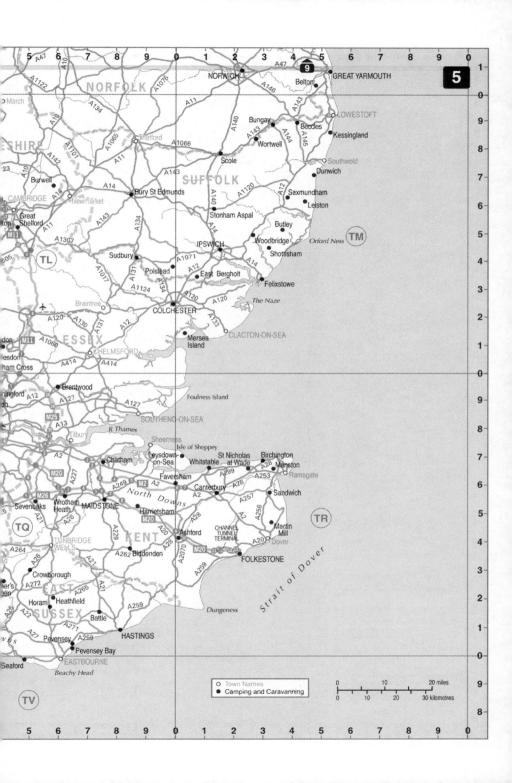

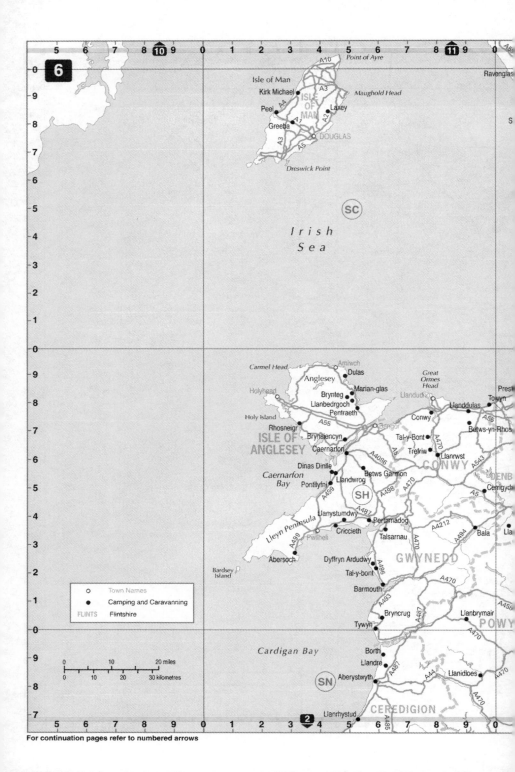

Point of Ayre

Ravenglas

Isle of Man

Kirk Michael

Maughold Head

ISLE OF MAN

Peel

Laxey

Greeba

DOUGLAS

Dreswick Point

Irish Sea

(SC)

Carmel Head

Amlwch

Dulas

Anglesey

Great Ormes Head

Pres

Holyhead

Brynteg

Marian-glas

Llandudno

Llanddulas

Towyn

Llanbedrgoch

Pentraeth

Conwy

A55

Holy Island

Rhosneigr

Betws-yn-Rhos

ISLE OF ANGLESEY

Brynsiencyn

Bangor

Tal-y-Bont

Caernarfon

Trefriw

Llanrwst

CONWY

DENB

Dinas Dinlle

A4086

A5

Cerrigyd

Caernarfon Bay

Llandwrog

Betws Garmon

SH

Pontllyfni

A499

A498

A470

A5

Lleyn Peninsula

Llanystumdwy

A487

Porthmadog

A4212

A494

Bala

Lla

Pwllheli

Criccieth

Talsarnau

A470

GWYNEDD

Abersoch

Dyffryn Ardudwy

A496

Bardsey Island

Tal-y-bont

Barmouth

A470

Borth

A493

A487

Llanbrymair

POWY

Bryncrug

Tywyn

A470

Cardigan Bay

Borth

Llandre

A487

A44

Llanidloes

A470

SN

Aberystwyth

CEREDIGION

A470

Llanrhystud

A485

○	Town Names
●	Camping and Caravanning
FLINTS	Flintshire

0   10   20 miles

0   10   20   30 kilometres

For continuation pages refer to numbered arrows

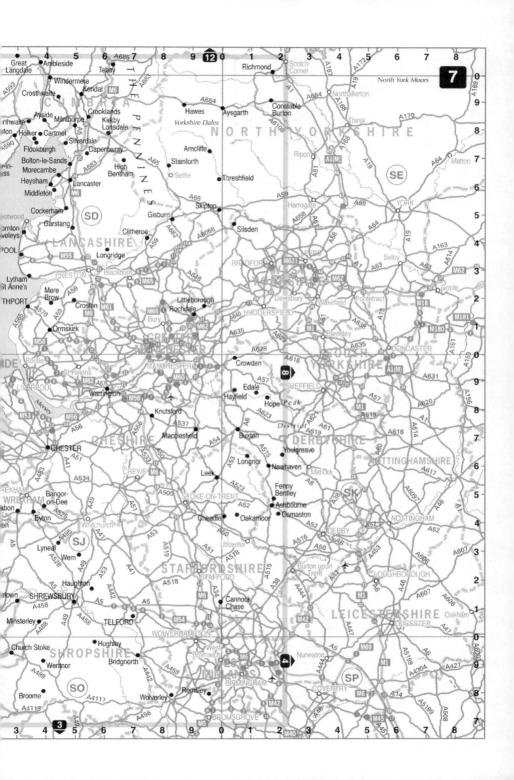

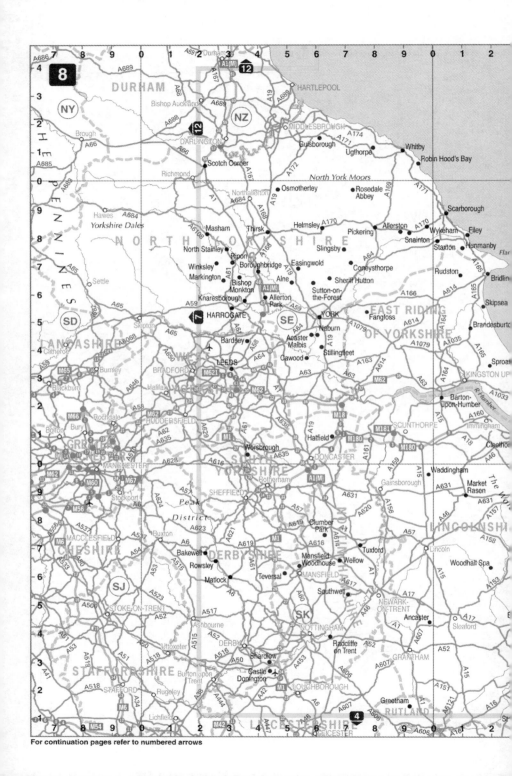

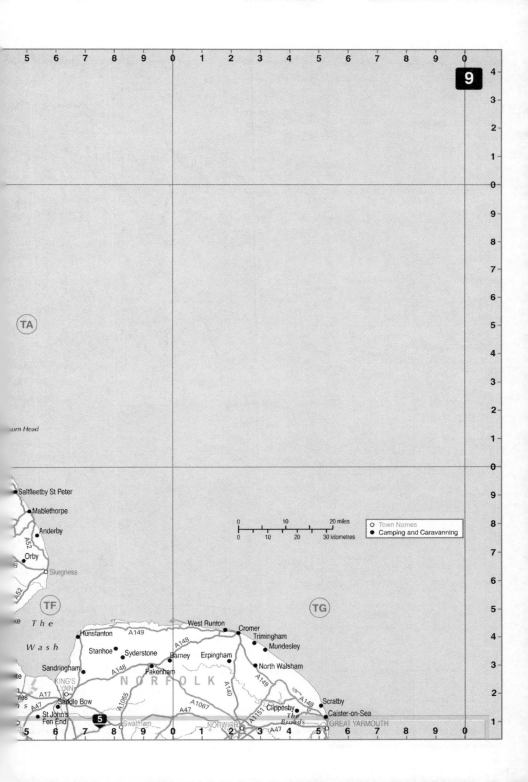

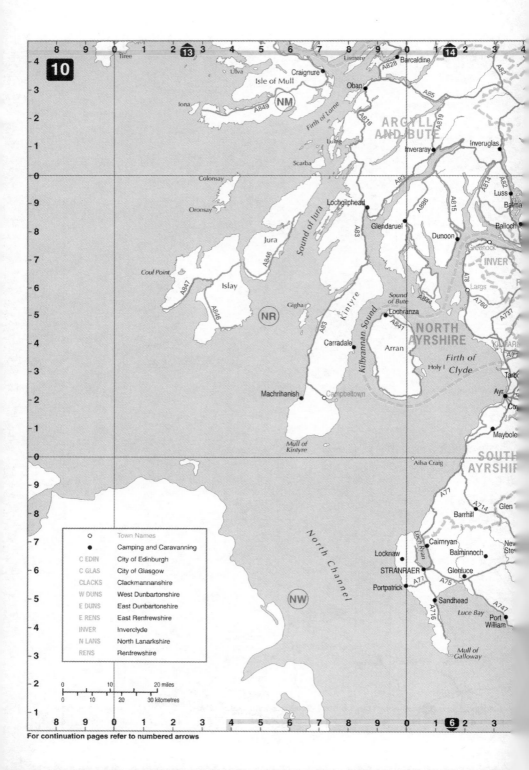

For continuation pages refer to numbered arrows

○	Town Names
●	Camping and Caravanning
C EDIN	City of Edinburgh
C GLAS	City of Glasgow
CLACKS	Clackmannanshire
W DUNS	West Dunbartonshire
E DUNS	East Dunbartonshire
E RENS	East Renfrewshire
INVER	Inverclyde
N LANS	North Lanarkshire
RENS	Renfrewshire

0   10   20 miles
0   10   20   30 kilometres

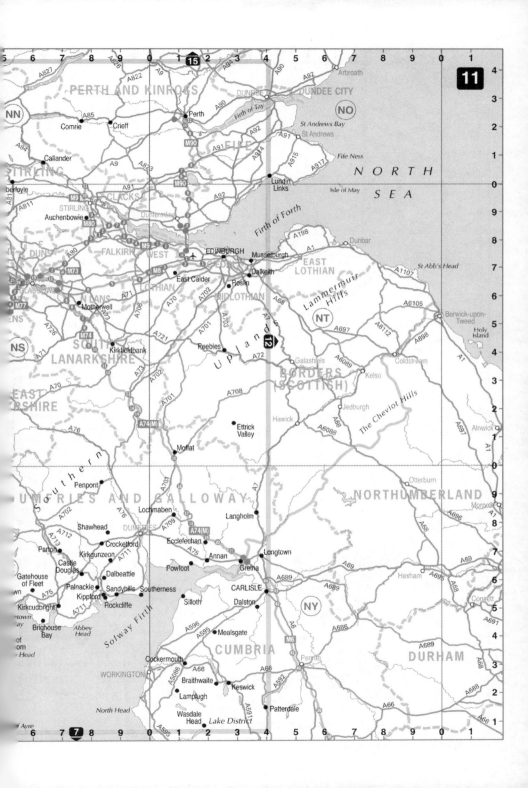

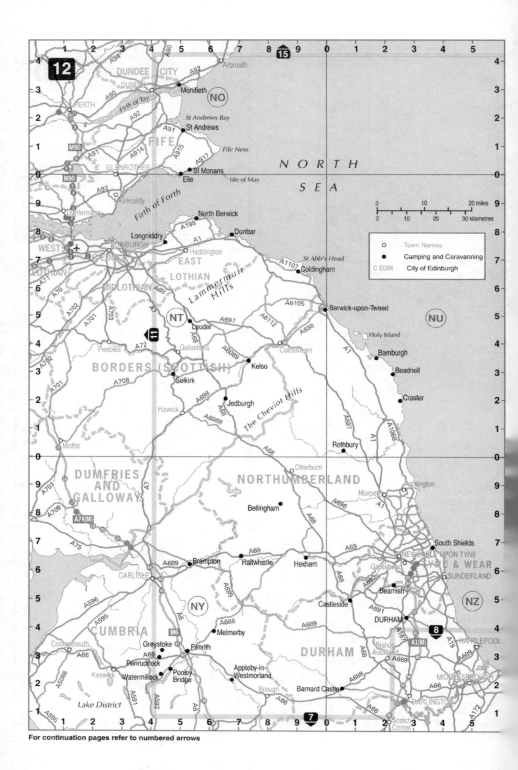

For continuation pages refer to numbered arrows

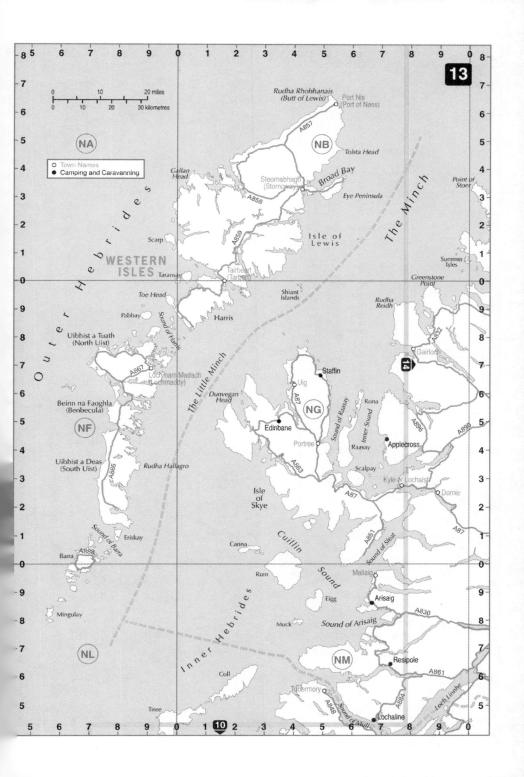

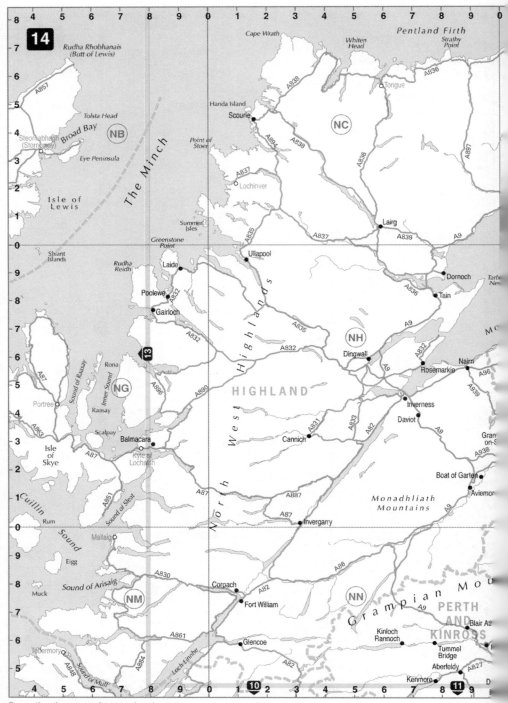

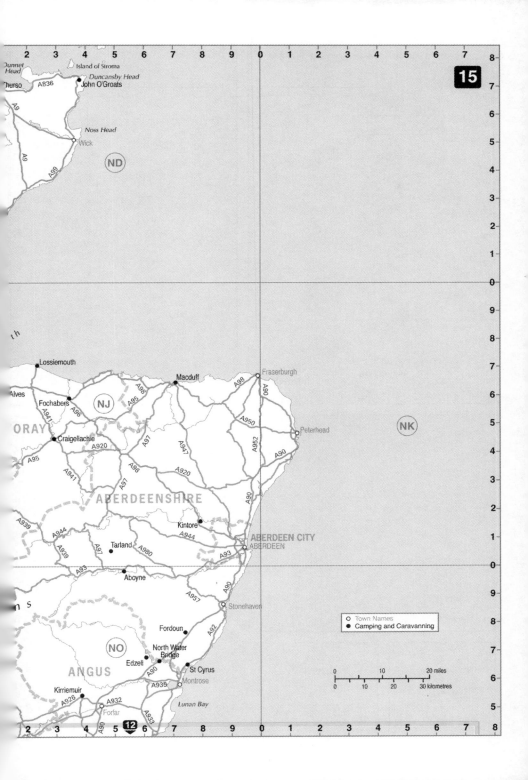

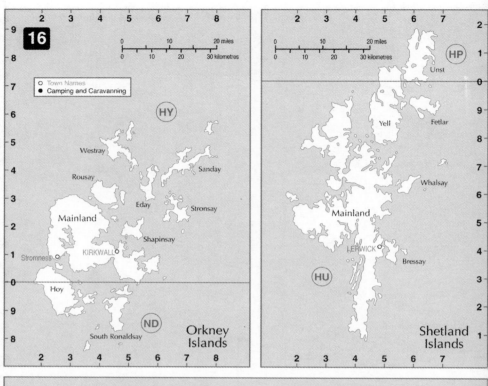

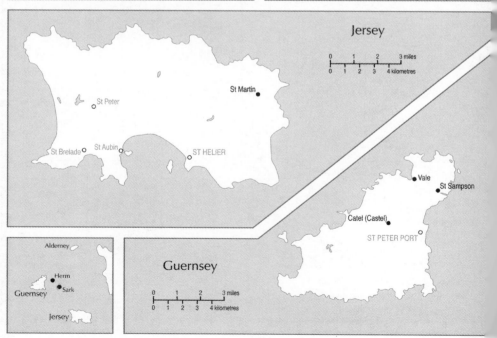

INDEX

Entries are alphabetically arranged by town name, then by campsite name. The following abbreviations have been used: C&C=Caravan & Camping, HP=Holiday Park, CP=Caravan Park, C&C Club=Camping & Caravanning Club Site

347

350

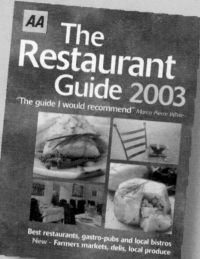

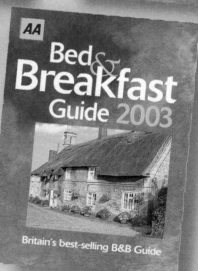

Please send this form to:
    Editor, Caravan & Camping
    Britain & Ireland,
    AA Lifestyle Guides,
    Fanum House,
    Basingstoke RG21 4EA

or fax: 01256 491647
or e-mail: lifestyleguides@theAA.com

Please use this form to recommend any caravan and camping park where you have stayed, whether it is included in the guide or not. You can also help us to improve the guide by completing the short questionnaire on the reverse.

Please note that the AA currently only inspects and rates parks for their touring facilities. Static caravans are not inspected or rated by the AA.

The AA does not undertake to arbitrate between guide readers and campsites, or to obtain compensation or engage in correspondence.

Date:

Your name (block capitals)

Your address (block capitals)

....

....

....

.... e-mail address:

Name of Park:

Comments

....

....

....

....

....

....

....

Readers' Report Form

Readers' Report Form

How often do you visit a caravan park or camp site?

Once a year ☐   Twice a year ☐   3 times a year ☐   More than 3 times ☐

How long do you generally stay at a park or site?

One night ☐   Up to a week ☐   1 week ☐   2 weeks ☐   Over 2 weeks ☐

Do you have a: tent ☐   caravan ☐   motorhome ☐

Which of the following in most important when choosing a site?

☐ Location   ☐ Toilet/Washing facilities   ☐ Awards
☐ Personal Recommendation   ☐ Leisure facilities   ☐ AA Rating
☐ Other

Do you prefer self-contained, cubicled washrooms with WC, shower and washhand basin to open-plan separate facilities?

Yes ☐   No ☐   Don't Mind ☐

Do you buy any other camping guides? If so, which ones?

....

Have you read the introductory pages and features in this guide? ....

Do you use the location atlas in this guide? ....

Which of the following most influences your choice of park from this guide?

Gazetteer entry information and description ☐

Photograph ☐   Advertisement ☐

Do you have any suggestions to improve the guide?

....

....

....

....

....

Thank you for taking the time to complete this form